Procession of the Gods

PROCESSION
OF THE GODS

BY

GAIUS GLENN ATKINS, Litt.D.

Sometime Professor of Homiletics
Auburn Theological Seminary

AND

CHARLES SAMUEL BRADEN, Ph.D.

Professor, History and Literature of Religions
Northwestern University

HARPER & BROTHERS Publishers

New York *London*

CONTENTS

v

the laity—Freedom of the Will in the system—Buddhism converts a great king—The two "vehicles"—The story of one pilgrimage—The temple bells keep ringing.

Contents

PREFACE TO THE SECOND REVISED EDITION

THE first edition of this work had a long preface telling the reader why it came to be written, how the author wrote it and similar items. It was meant for the general reader, and was so received and reviewed. The reviews, of course, criticized, suggested and challenged. There were errata of no great consequence, but pin pricks to an author's pride and a reader's satisfaction, passages needing clearing up and other details to be noted for correction in a second edition. I had no expectation of its being used as a text-book; the work was not written with text-book technique. Its rather wide use in that field was a surprise to me, but after the first three or four years it kept the work going. Having seen the complete exhaustion of the first edition, the question arose what to do next. If the work were to be kept alive it needed correction and some revision. There were new authorities in some fields, and seven years had made a difference even in dead religions.

This revised edition is the result of almost two years' conference and planning. The publisher consented to make new plates and Dr. Braden consented to put his knowledge as a specialist, and his experience as a teacher, at the publisher's service in collaboration with the author. I undertook the textual revision. The narrative has had the "thick places" eliminated and detours have been removed, but taken as a whole it retains its original substance and style. I owe much to Dr. Braden's graciousness in permitting this, even when he would have preferred changes. I told him the first writing was so done and textured that any considerable rewriting would not fit in. And always we have tried to maintain the value of work for the general reader.

Technical matter has generally been put in as foot-notes. The appendix material will, we think, serve both the student and the general reader. I venture to hope that we have succeeded in adapting the work to both uses, that the general reader will not hesitate to take it home because it has text-book features, that the teacher and student will find under Dr. Braden's guidance the factual content. We have been economical with names and dates; they are there

—enough of them—but we have sought to make the long and fascinating story of religion as new and as much alive as we could. It is a vital story.

The authors gratefully acknowledge permission to use translations and quotations from: Underhill, *The Mystic Way* (Dutton); De-Groot, *Religion in China*; Dawson, *Ethics of Confucius*; Naville, *The Old Egyptian Faith* (Putnam); Jastrow, *The Religion of Babylonia and Assyria*; Peters, *The Religion of the Hebrews* (Ginn); Rogers, *The Religion of Babylonia and Assyria* and *Cuneiform Parallels to the Old Testament* (Abingdon); Rogers, *A History of Ancient Persia*; Legge, *The Religions of China* (Scribner); *An Anthology of World Poetry* (Boni); Carter, *Religious Life of Ancient Rome* (Houghton Mifflin); Anderson, *Norse Mythology* (Scott Foresman); Campbell, *Religion in Greek Literature* (Longmans Green); Giles, *Confucianism and Its Rivals* (Williams & Norgate); Moffatt, *The Bible: A New Translation* (Harper & Brothers).

The authors have differed helpfully, of course, mostly about minor matters: the existence or non-existence of a Chinese sage dead almost three thousand years if he ever lived at all, where to put Mohammed, how to spell this or that name, but our collaboration has been a joy to me and each of us has had his way as much as was good for him. There is abundant room for differences of opinion in so vast a field. If the critic does not always agree with either of us we shall not be surprised, or too much cast down. The work is as sound as we have known how to make it. I can not easily say how much labor first and last it really represents. If it continues to help youth and thoughtful readers to become enfranchised citizens of the order of faith and spiritual quest which has been the supreme aspect of our human procession through time we shall be content.

Huntington House
Auburn Theological Seminary
May 20, 1936

GAIUS GLENN ATKINS

THE present edition does not differ greatly from the second edition. One completely new chapter has been added, an altogether too brief treatment of the three principal native religions of America, the Aztec, Maya and Inca. Of these major attention is given to the Aztec, partly because it is so much better known to the average person and partly because there is so much more dependable information concerning it. Also, the relative likeness of the other two to it at many points renders it less necessary to discuss them in great detail.

Questions, topics for report and discussion, and suggested readings for this chapter are added to Appendix A, and a list of books dealing with them appears in the general bibliography in Appendix C.

The major changes have been made in the suggested readings in Appendix A, and in the general bibliography in Appendix C. Many of the books suggested in the earlier editions have been omitted and newer books substituted for them.

The authors have been gratified by the sustained circulation of the book and particularly for its increasing use in American colleges. They will welcome any criticisms or suggestions which might be useful in preparing any future edition of the text. No attempt has been made to revise the main body of the text. In the case of Japan where the status of the old state-religion has been so radically changed by the second World War it has been necessary to add a lengthy section at the end of the chapter on Japanese religion. It is still far too early to assess the total effect of the global war upon religious beliefs and institutions in the various countries—culture levels have been shifted and shattered, temples, shrines and monuments ruined, old ways of use and wont have vanished.

Since religion has always been the conservator of such epochal inheritances, a longer perspective than is now possible will be needed to see fully what the effects of such cataclysmic changes in the world religion has always claimed for its own will be. In a note in connection with the bibliography a further statement is made concerning this matter.

> So fleet the works of men, back to this earth again:
> Ancient and holy things fade like a dream.

G.G.A.
C.S.B.

December 15, 1947

THE perfect text-book on the History of Religions has not yet been written. The writer has used various texts that have appeared in recent years with varying success. One year he decided to use the *Procession of the Gods*. At the end of the semester he asked his class to write a critique of the text. They did so. Their criticisms proved so interesting and suggestive that they were sent on to Dr. Atkins to read. The remarks were for the most part highly laudatory, but there was almost unanimous agreement at one point. The book, delightful as to style and content, was not of the standard text-book type. They found it somewhat lacking in that definiteness of statement which a student, faced with an examination which he fears may call for an array of facts, seems so highly to crave. Nevertheless they recommended almost unanimously the continuance of its use as the text for the course.

Each year the same criticism was received. Each season one thing was noticed. There were almost no second-hand copies of the book to be found in the local text-book exchanges.

Finally it was felt best to try another text, one that was meant specifically to be a text. At the end of the course the customary critique of the book was asked for, and advice sought as to its continued use for the next year. The large majority of the class advised definitely that it be not used again.

What to do then? Meanwhile the author had had occasion to write of text-books and in the course of his article asked which constituted the better text, a book with all the facts, clearly outlined, precise, but not easily read, or a book somewhat lacking in definiteness and factual statement, but with a fine readable style, a comprehensive view of religious development, calculated to leave one with at least a broad sympathetic understanding of the major movements in the world of spiritual questing; a book over which one definitely had to perspire and labor in order to master it, or a book in which specific assignments were often only the beginning of a whole evening or the best part of the night's reading—far ahead of the class.

Dr. Atkins saw the article. He knew it was of his book I was writing. He had, in correspondence, already insisted that he had no thought of its being used as a text-book. "But," he wrote, "would it be possible to make it a good text-book?" I paused and pondered my reply. What should I say? Then I read on, "And if it has possibilities of being made into a text-book, would you be willing to undertake to help do it?"

Here was a challenge indeed. What should I do? At a number of points I, myself, held quite different opinions concerning the development of specific religions. Our points of view and our methods of approach were by no means everywhere alike.

I read and reread certain chapters. I undertook to outline them and discovered that they were for the most part well-planned and executed. I attempted to set down in rather concise form the facts brought out in the chapters, and found that underneath the delightful flow of language which left no rough outline protruding there was an amazing amount of sheer factual matter. I didn't agree always with the writer's conclusions or even his "facts" at every point, but he could invoke very respectable authorities for every position held, and it is well known that finality in this field is impossible.

It seemed to me that with no great amount of labor certain text-book features could be added which would largely offset the oft-cited defect of the book. I would therefore, I agreed, undertake to do so. But, again, we must agree upon certain rather definite principles in the revision.

1. The book must continue to be his and the responsibility his for the particular statements of fact and conclusions, especially where any revision would require extensive rewriting.

2. It must not be revised in such a way as to rob it of what I think of as its chief charm, its graceful literary style, or to break unduly its steady flow of ideas by the introduction of too many mechanical interruptions such as paragraph headings, though a few have been added.

3. The revision must therefore be largely by way of addition either at the end of the chapters or in appendices.

In accordance with these agreements we set to work. I suggested in the case of each chapter matters which ought to be omitted or revised and sent them to Dr. Atkins. In addition, I prepared for each chapter lists of questions, every one of which is answered in greater or less detail within the chapter. I also suggested in each chapter a list of topics for report and discussion, most of which have been tested out in actual practice. Likewise, a list of suggested supplementary readings on various phases of each religion is appended, in most cases readings which have been assigned in my own teaching of the book. Here and there directions have been given for special general assignments that might prove valuable during the whole course, such as directions for making a catalogue of the Gods. In the table of contents a brief analysis of each chapter is given as an aid to the student in getting a clear picture of the developing faith. In the case of the living religions the writer's own book *Modern Tendencies in World Religions* has been suggested as required reading to bring the development of religion down to the present. The bibliography has been revised and enlarged and made to include not only works used by Dr. Atkins in the preparation of the book, but also important books that might contribute helpfully to the further study of students in the field.

With these additions and revisions, I feel that this book is now well adapted to use as a text in college classes. The general reader loses nothing. The student gains much. The revision of the book has been done during the term in which the course is given. All the questions, topics and suggested readings have been placed in the hands of a large class using the book in order to try them out. The result has more than justified our hopes. With these added materials the old criticism has been largely met. The students are agreed in regarding it as an unusually good text. It is the hope of the authors that teachers of the history of religions will find it an adequate guide for use in their classes.

Northwestern University

CHARLES S. BRADEN

TO THE TEACHER

OUT of repeated use of the text come these suggestions to teachers using this book. The time allowed for the course will determine how extensive assignments may be given beyond the text itself. Three hours for one semester suffice to cover the book and *do not a little outside work*. The suggestions are made with this limitation in mind. A whole year would be none too much to give to it. In this case additional material could easily be assigned in the large bibliography at the end of the book.

It has been my own practice, in addition to work done from day to day, to assign either a term paper or a reading option. A list of term paper topics will be found on pp. 552-553. This is only suggestive. Experience has taught that a student works best on a topic of his own choosing, and preferably along the line of his own interest. My own students are required to confer with me personally regarding their topic. A 3500 word length has been suggested as adequate. Not a few bring in 5000 or more. A few have gone beyond 10,000, just because they became interested and wanted to go on.

I have usually allowed upper classmen the option of reading a selected list of books, again on a topic of their own choosing, somewhere within the ample field. A term paper represents usually an intensive study of a relatively limited field. In the reading option, on the other hand, students usually range widely. Of course this is not necessary. A list of books chosen in conference amounting to some 1500 pages is considered as an equivalent of a term paper. Not a few of my own students report from 2000 to 3000 pages read. Instead of writing, the student is required to report his reading in a personal conference of from 30 minutes to an hour. Here also the interest of the student is allowed to guide in the choice of books. A pre-medical student may desire to read in the general field of religion and healing, an art student in the relation of art and religion in various cultures. A political science student may care to trace through the relationship between politics and religion. The possibilities for other papers or reading topics are endless.

In the assignment on a given chapter it has been the writer's custom to allow a reading or writing option, a short written report on some one of the suggested topics or definite reading from among the suggested readings. The reports may be handed in or given orally as the teacher finds most helpful. These extra assignments serve to broaden considerably the students' understanding and appreciation of the religion involved. Experience proves that it is the substance of these readings and reports which the student is most likely to remember. A student of journalism who once put the career of Jeremiah in the form of clippings from a mythical *Jerusalem Gazette* published contemporaneously will never forget Jeremiah. The best of all possible motivations is *interest*. Allowing the student to do the thing within the field which interests him is the best way to get application to the work of the course, and at the same time make some permanent contributions to his store of knowledge and understanding of the world's religions.

The suggested readings will, of course, be supplemented by the teacher. New books are constantly appearing which he will desire to include or to substitute for some already there. Valuable articles in current periodicals can be used to excellent advantage. Students may be asked to clip articles in the newspapers which bear **upon** any of the religions.

Where proximity to a large city permits of personal observation of some of the non-Christian religions actually functioning, a certain amount of "laboratory" work can be required. A visit to a Jewish temple, or a Moslem mosque, or indeed of Protestants to a Catholic church or vice-versa always adds interest to the course. Now and then a living representative of some of the other faiths may be secured for a lecture-and-question period. Where museums are available which contain material bearing upon religion, conducted trips through them are a great asset to the course. One early assignment might well be to list all available resources which it would be worthwhile to use during the term.

Little or nothing has been written concerning the *teaching* of the history of religions. The writer would welcome suggestions from anyone who has used additional methods that have proven of interest and of value.

CHARLES S. BRADEN

Procession of the Gods

CHAPTER I

Faiths of the Dark and the Dawn

THERE have always been two processionals across the field of history; one the succession of cultures and civilizations which constitutes the secular history, the other the succession of faiths and devotions which constitutes the religious history of humanity. They are alike in the antiquity of their origins, their continuously emerging and dissolving forms and their shadowed splendour. It is impossible to separate their movement. Religion has made history. It has been attended by literatures, organizations and authorities. It has mobilized its forces upon bitterly contested battlefields and dictated the policies of emperors. And it has profoundly controlled the conduct and ideals of countless generations.

On the other hand, religion has been rooted in history. It has shared the fortunes of empires. The visions of its prophets have reflected the lights and shadows of their times, their messages have been concerned with politics and diplomacy, its teachers have addressed themselves to the actual conditions of the folk about them. Race and geography have made this or that faith sovereign for a season. The very qualities of the sky, the brilliance of constellations and the revolution of the seasons have combined to enthrone a deity or shape some liturgy of winter death and vernal resurrection. The gods have used earth as well as heaven for their going out and their coming in.

Religion has its setting in such things as these as well as in the need and loneliness of the human spirit. No right account of it can be written without giving them due consideration. But it is possible substantially to detach the forms religion has taken, along with its interests and insights, from the secular processes of history, and consider them all as an august procession of the gods, taking dim shapes in very old and very simple faiths, dissolving in some ruin of the states they ruled, forming again with new races and new civilizations, and yet unbroken and majestic and moving always toward richer visions, a more luminous faith, and finally, to the sovereignty of one

God in whose light the many disappear and the procession comes to an end.

The story of religion is rich in every element of interest and action. It is the story of worship, of temples and altars, lonely seekers and imperial priesthoods. It is seen unfolding through the smoke of sacrifice; some sonorous echo of it is caught in the passion of the prophet; its music is heard in psalms and hymns. It is darkened by shame and cruelty; it is bright with the best of which humanity has been capable. It is always the endeavor of the lonely and perplexed to find a key to the mystery of the world about them, a power not themselves to reach and rest in, and some assurance of what awaits them beyond the gates of death.

The study of religion has within the last fifty or sixty years taken an entirely new direction. A gradual and now massive accumulation of facts has supplied fascinating material. The inscriptions on the tombs of the Pharaohs and the papyrus-leaved books of the Egyptian dead re-create the faith of Egypt. The clay tablets of Nineveh and Babylon have become legible. A Siamese king put the classic Buddhist literature at the service of European scholars. Max Müller organized the English translation of the sacred books of the East. Patient students of folk custom have assembled a wealth of information from every possible source. The very dust of vanished civilizations has been sifted for the potsherd of a fact. Inscriptions have been assembled by the thousands. No word of antiquity is too trivial, no rudely cut sentence too enigmatic to be left unconsidered. The psychologist has added his own valuable contributions. The study of religion now has substance and method.

The interpreter has taken the whole seemingly impossible material in hand. The principle of development, which has furnished the key to every other phase of history, supplied the student of religion his master key. Tylor's epoch-making "Primitive Culture" revolutionized the whole approach to comparative religion. His work has of late been strongly challenged, but he indubitably did establish the fact that religion has grown from dim and remote beginnings through definite stages of advancement.

There was a belief once that religion began with a full knowledge of one true God and that thereafter through human fault and disobedience the light of the first splendid vision was clouded or lost.[1] But this is not the story told by the assembled records. The story of religion is not a recessional. The worship of sticks and stones is not religion fallen into the dark; it is religion rising out of the dark. The procession of the gods has been an advance and not a retreat. The faiths of the dark and the dawn are man's religious awakening and his first suppliant gesture toward the unseen. Why did he make the gesture?

THEORIES OF THE ORIGIN OF RELIGION

Religion, it is held, is an instinct; "man is incurably religious." Religion does seem to be "a constant and universal feature of [man's] mental life."[2] The rude art upon the walls of caves from whose shelter the folk of the Stone Age watched the ice sheet draw near has a religious significance.[3] The graves of the dateless dead testify to their faith. No one denies that religion is as old as any human records, but calling religion instinctive begs too many questions. The religious temper is no one single thing; it is complex. There are doubtless instincts enough in it, though some of them are by no means purely religious. But religion belongs to a higher level than the instinctive reactions with which the dawn-man met the adventure of life.

A small but thoughtful group finds the roots of religion in the subconscious memories of the new-born.[4] Exiles from the shelter of the womb, we live and die seeking some covert from the chill winds of reality. The father and mother symbols are used to make a home for our spirits at the heart of cosmic loneliness. We shape religious symbols out of struggles and reconciliations which are really rooted in the life of the family. We project them into a vaster field to become alienation from God and reconciliation with him, and the peace which we find in the persuasion of his loving care. All this being nothing else than the creation of our wishful thinking, a pathetic make-believe, which in its splendid consummations sent the procession of the gods from zenith to zenith and created temples, creeds, confidences and adoration.

[1] A representative recent statement of this position is *The Origin of Religion*, Samuel M. Zwemer, Nashville.

[2] R. R. Marett, *The Threshold of Religion*, London, 1909, page 32.

[3] Menage, *L'Age Prehistorique*.

[4] Everett Dean Martin, *The Mystery of Religion*, New York, 1924.

Such psychological explanations of religion have an actual value. The general adventure of life does begin with birth and is not altogether to our liking. Job was not the first or the last to wish that he had never been born. The father and mother relations do help "fix" the idealization of all our relations. But primitive man was dealing with something far more concrete than a "mother fixation" or an uncomfortable sense of alienation from the "old man" of a Neanderthal family.[5]

One may gravely doubt whether, if religion were only an unsupported make-believe, it would have commanded the confidence of humanity for so long, or have been able to secure so vast and so seemingly assured a response. The less speculative students of religion do not begin with theories, though they can not wholly escape them; they begin with a patient examination of the facts. They agree that our loneliness and the questing longing of a humanity which has from the first felt itself alien to the order about it have been great stimuli to religion. They agree that fear and helplessness and perplexity have been shaping forces in religion, though not the only forces. They know that the sense of an evil will working to harm him lies darkly in the savage's mind. He believes that the river which drowns his brother does it on purpose. The lightnings search for him, diseases are evil spirits, and, to save himself, he must buy the favor of those who, having him at their mercy, show him so little mercy. Thus propitiation creates its ceremonial of prayer and gift. But there is the longing for good in all religion as well as the fear of evil, the gratitude of praise as well as the obeisance of fear. Religion seeks the finding of greater goods more than the avoidance of the great evils.

One sees through all these dim survivals of what was once alive and gripping, these ghosts of primitive faith, humanity's first adjustment to its world. "Religion was in part," says Frazer, "what passed for wisdom when the world was young. It was the perfect

[5] Martin's approach to religion is much under the influence of Freudian psychology and is peculiar to that school. But the idea that religion comes out of us and is entirely subjective has of late been much enlarged upon. It is held that religion is a shelter humanity has built for itself against loneliness and death and the impersonal vastness of the universe, the enterprise of life being too much for us without its hopes and assurances—which are themselves the creation of our own "wishful thinking." No one, I think, would deny the truth of much of this but it leaves unanswered the crucial question: Is religion anything more than the projection of our hopes against silent and impassive horizons?

pattern after which every man strove to shape his life. Crude and false as that philosophy may seem to us, it would be unjust to deny it the merit of logical consistency."[6] Religion was man's first theory of the force and cause of things, his groping quest for reason and meaning in the world about him and, in its full development, his explanation of why there was a world about him at all and why he, being different from it, was in it.

Finally it was, and is, the resolution of loneliness and longing into a faith in divine beings or Being strong enough to protect, gracious enough to bless, merciful enough to forgive. "Religion is what the individual does with his solitariness."[7] At every point at which religion lays hold of life one finds these ageless things out of which the human spirit is compact; fear and hope and some sense of exile, dim or strong, from its true homeland. And one thing more, the confidence that there is a Power—or powers—to help. This confidence that, beside nature and humanity, there is a "third order," spiritual, personal and sovereign with which a personal relationship is possible, is religion. It has lit the fires on every altar, built every temple, made every creed articulate and supported every prayer. How did that confidence begin?

How Did Man Gain His Sense of a "Spiritual Order"?

It began, says Tylor, in a dream. Through dreams men discovered their own souls and *through their own souls the world soul*. Primitive man was, and is, vividly aware of two things:—sleep and death. He saw his comrades inert around the campfire; an hour before they had drunk and eaten and talked; in the morning they would eat and drink and speak again. But now? He saw them dead in the hunt or on the battlefield—what had happened? Was it only a deeper sleep? He had slept himself, gone hunting, or made some journey in his dreams and waked to find himself still by the campfire with curious friends to assure him he had been there all the while. He had also seen his friends in his dreams—or else they had seen him in theirs.

"Looking at these two groups of phenomena the ancient savage philosophers probably made their first step by the obvious inference

[6] Sir James George Frazer, *The Golden Bough*, New York, 1922, page 263.
[7] Alfred North Whitehead, *Religion in the Making*, New York, 1926, page 47.

that every man has two things belonging to him, namely, a life and a phantom. These two are evidently in close connection with the body, the life as enabling it to feel and think and act, the phantom as being its image or second self; both also are perceived to be things separable from the body, the life as able to go away and leave it insensible or dead; the phantom as appearing to people at a distance from it. The second step would seem also easy for savages to make, seeing how extremely difficult civilized men have found it to unmake. *It is merely to combine the life and the phantom.* As both belong to the body, why should they not also belong to one another and be manifestations of one and the same soul? Let them then be considered as united, and the result is that well-known conception which may be described as an apparitional soul, a ghost-soul."[8]

So the dream-born ghost began his endless wanderings. He has acknowledged no barrier of time or space. He is imponderable yet potent. He can enter the bodies of other men, of animals and things. He possesses the "personal consciousness and volition of his corporal owner." He has haunted all lands and races, sailed the seas in phantom ships, given a motif to song and a theme to literature. He has captured the imagination of the fearsome and the devout, supplied a vocabulary for all discussion of immaterial things, survived the dissolution of death, gone west into land beyond the sunset, descended into the depths of the earth, or mounted to the stars. Did ever so vast an event issue from a dream?—if it did.

Tylor's contribution to the study of religion was epoch-making. He was a pioneer in laying the foundation for such study in the assembling and careful comparison of almost innumerable facts drawn from widely different and distant sources. He was the first to associate religious development with culture levels, and established beyond denial that it has grown from very simple beginnings. He traced its ascending stages, and greatly influenced the thought of his own time. Herbert Spencer used Tylor for the basis of his approach to religion in his massive Synthetic Philosophy and naturally Tylor's work became a storm center of controversy, mostly between the defenders of a "revealed religion" and the advocates of Evolution in religion.

Now Tylor's method is accepted almost without exception by all authorities and the more inclusive ranges of his conclusions. But his

[8] Tylor, *Primitive Religion*, Vol. I, pages 428-9. The italics added.

"dream theory" is not generally accepted. It asks, his critics say, too much of the primitive intellect. The untutored mind of the poor savage is not equal to such abstractions. He is not logical or illogical; he is pre-logical. Marett, therefore, stresses the "feeling" element in primitive religion. It must promise "a mastery over a real life that consists largely of hard knocks." The good that the savage gets from his religion must come either through feeling, thinking or acting, and thinking, he says, has "the weakest claim to be accounted a source of value."[9]

Tylor's theory is, therefore, challenged. Actually there is a general agreement among authorities as to primitive religious conceptions once the first level is passed. They do not agree as to how primitive man got his conception of "the power not himself." According to Tylor, he begins at once with a spirit or phantom-filled world, said spirits or phantoms being much like himself only unseen.

According to Durkheim, primitive man begins with a force-filled world and the sense of this Force everywhere and in everything is the "source of all religiosity." "It embraces all mystery, all secret power, all divinity. . . . It is the principle of all that lives or acts or moves. . . . So also is everything which exhibits power whether in action . . . or passive endurance."[10] The American Indian calls this power "Wakanda."[11] The Polynesian calls it "Mana." If we should take a word from the street and call it "It," we should not be far out of the way. The "Wakanda" of the Sioux is all mystery, all destiny, the earth, the four winds, sun, moon, stars. All life is "Wakanda," and all exhibits of power, whether in action or endurance. If this be true, man first found his own soul through conceiving it as a resting place of this universal force, and found himself through finding something vaster and more universal than himself. Durkheim maintains also that primitive man got his notion of this vaster power from the social group to which he belongs. The sacred principle was only society transfigured and personified. Society was man's first god.

---

[9] *Faith, Hope and Charity in Primitive Religion*. The Macmillan Company, New York, 1932, Chapter I—The Religious Complex. See also Marett's Chapter III for the place of fear in religion. The religious complex, he holds, has or has had Hope, Lust, Cruelty, Faith, Conscience, Curiosity, Admiration and Charity as its factors.

[10] Emile Durkheim, *The Elementary Forms of the Religious Life*, page 193.

[11] Frazer, *op. cit.*, page 216. There are various spellings.

I do not myself accept the social origin of religion.[12] I think the sense of controlling power came from the ways of the world about us and not from the little helpless groups in which society began. The first seekers interpreted that power in terms of what they knew best—themselves. They knew that they could move about and get various things done, create a little and also destroy. They knew, too, that what they did was not without purpose. They assumed something like themselves in action outside themselves. This was the only key they had to the unresting confusion of the world. It seems entirely probable they began to use it.

We still do very much the same thing. The poets sing of the world as if trees and flowers were sentient things, the music of the waters a living voice, and all beauty the revelation of some hidden spirit. Penetrating contemporaneous thought returns by the high road to what the savage found at the end of his low shadowed road. L. P. Jacks believes the universe to be essentially alive. The savage believes much the same thing, though he takes his universe in little broken pieces. He made his religion out of the life-power of his world.[13]

The Earliest Forms of Religion: Totemism

The lowest levels upon which religion has taken definite form are Totemism and Fetishism. To the inquiring Nordic a totem

[12] Durkheim, *op. cit.*, pages 206 et seq. Since the first writing I am ready to qualify the rejection of Durkheim's "Social Theory." I do not accept it for the reasons given, but the shaping power of social environment on religion can not easily be over-estimated.

[13] This relatively short section deals with an extremely important subject about which there are outstanding differences of opinion. It should be "filled in" by the teacher and the class. Religion historically has always assumed a spirit in man, and spirits or a spiritual order or a supreme spirit outside man. The form these conceptions take determines the nature of any religion. The student will want therefore to examine the genesis of so pregnant a conception.

Three terms are used by authorities in this field but they do not agree exactly as to the meaning of the terms. In this book their meaning is as follows:

ANIMISM conceives everything to have its own specific power. The old names for things name them not as objects but as animae—as souls (which may explain the troublesome matter of genders in languages not as unimaginative as our own). SPIRITISM personalizes these vague souls of things. Spirits are like us—which may or may not be a compliment. ANIMATISM, a loose word, conceives of nature as animated by an indwelling and moving power or powers best understood by what we are and do.

pole is only a crudely carved and colored tree trunk. For the Indian who carved it, it was and is, as far as the vigorous and inquiring Nordic has left the Indian either his land or his faith, his coat of arms, his family tree, his confession of faith, and the symbol of group relationships within which he can not marry. The totem pole is only a symbol. The real totem is some species of bird or beast, reptile or fish or else some variety of plant "between which and himself the savage believes a certain intimate relation exists." Totemism is thus a primitive system both of religion and society.

The animals or things which furnish the totem are believed to be related to the group, and one individual totem symbol belongs to one group, as though certain Ojibways had a peculiar right to all the livers of all the bears. Their neighbors must take account of this. The totem is an object of religious regard and is treated as sacred. There is a mystic kinship between each member of the brother-hood and his totem symbol. In wounding the totem he wounds him-self. The Bear-liver group must not eat bear-livers. There is a fence of ceremonial about each totem object. A member of the Bear clan may kill a bear in self-defense but he must apologize to the Bear and appease its resentful spirit. The group members must stand by one another; they must not intermarry, nor violate the chastity of fellow members.

A Swedish scholar, Reuterskiöld,[14] explains totemism in a very simple and suggestive way. Primitive man did not separate himself in thoughts from other living creatures (the evidence of this comes in from all sides). Nor did he think at all in individual terms; he just belonged to his group and his group included the general ani-mal and plant life of his neighborhood. They were all one com-munity needing to live together on as friendly terms as possible. He had bear and wolf neighbors as well as human neighbors. He had a sound respect for animals. They could outrun him, outfly him; they had a practical wisdom which he did not possess, and, barring stones and clubs, could best him in a fair fight. No wonder he called himself and his their people. (Such a sense of kinship with the animal world might be useful now to diminish a little our arrogance toward other forms of life.)

Totemism has been and is a useful way of keeping family records and preventing an inbreeding which would prove injurious to scanty

[14] Hastings, *Encyclopedia of Religion and Ethics*, Vol. XII, page 407.

populations. There is a fairly general association of the whole system with the way of reckoning descent from the mother instead of the father, which makes it very primitive indeed. Members of the same totem group can not intermarry. It was a very serious matter to violate this law, and the savage, being an individual of resources, pricked his totem sign into his skin—since this was about all he was sure to have constantly with him—to warn the maidens of groups having the same totem not to fall in love with him. Nothing proper could come of it. Totemism also went a little way toward creating a comradeship more inclusive than the clan and tribe. There is a kind of totem brotherhood which gives a more kindly quality to the general structure of savage society. It made fighting more humane, since tribal enemies would recognize a totem brother behind a hostile war club. On the other hand, totem rivalry might result in bitter feuds. Totemistic religion was not, in this region, greatly different from many religions since.

Totemism becomes a religion only through some worship of the totem animal and a ritual touched with reverence. But as a window to see the primitive mind through, it is priceless. A world stirred and filled by a nameless power whose resting place may be a man's spirit, or a tree, or a bear, is at least a world in which men may make contacts with "It" through what is nearest to them. A world in which there is but one dimension and men and beasts are on the same level is a world easy to fill with the suggestion of personality. A society in which men are held together by some sense of common descent has at least the beginnings of loyalties and brotherhoods in it. Whatever leads memory back and vision up to some far-off creative source of life, if it be only a cockatoo or a crocodile, creates elemental reverences. There is at least that much religion in totemism.

FETISHISM

Magic and religion meet in fetishism. A fetish is treasured and entreated because it can do something for the possessor. That is magic. It is also treasured and entreated because it is the temporary resting place of the universal power. That is religion. Totemism and fetishism have the same primitive belief behind them, the belief, that is, in a pervasive spiritual force, or, if the word spiritual beg too much, the belief in a pervasive force which can be thought of as alive, even if it make the inanimate its resting place. Fetishism took its own line. The savage shares his totem with his clan, but a fetish is a man's particular possession working its spell for him alone, and he treats it with a strange caprice. He worships it for what it does, he beats it for what it does not do. It does not, however, become a fetish simply because he fancies it; something must be done to it to "make it sacred." Any object can become a fetish if only it has been ritualistically consecrated. Nutshells, antelope horns, brushcat tails, leopard claws and human skull bones acquire a marvelous power to cure a fever, make a warrior invulnerable, or banish a plague of grasshoppers.[15]

Fetishism is the supporting center of the savage's dealings with the supernatural. The system is simple enough but the light and color of primitive life which play about it make it bright with interest. There is a natural relation between the fetish object and the end sought. Some part of a leopard is useful to make a man brave. Some part of an elephant will make him strong, a little admixture of human brains should add wisdom.

"For every human passion or desire . . . for our thousand necessities or wishes a fetish can be made, its operation being limited in power only by the possible existence of some more powerful antagonizing spirit." The entire business of life is thus controlled. There are fetishes to keep a thief out of the garden and evil out of a house, to wing the hunter's arrow and win a lady's smile. From birth to death the fetish and the charm constitute one of the main interests of the primitive negro's life and he has no assurance that some part of him will not become a fetish after he is dead.[16] But he does not worship the thing. He worships the Power which, for the time being, lives in the fetish.

RELIGION TAKES ACCOUNT OF SPIRITS: THE DISCOVERY OF THE "SOUL"

Totemism and fetishism associate the Power with animals and things. "Spiritism" distributes the Power among free, personal and unseen agencies, and lifts religion to a still higher level. Spiritism assumes in its simplest and most elemental forms that the mech-

[15] Robert H. Lowie, *Primitive Religion*, New York, 1924, page 269.
[16] Nassau, *op. cit.*, generally.

anism of nature is worked by spirits, a separate spirit for each operation, just as each machine in a well-equipped modern factory has
its own motor. It is not easy to understand the primitive mind imag-
ining just how spirits can make rain or cause corn to ripen, though
the primitive mind ought not to be blamed too much; the entirely
modern mind has troubles of its own in the same region. The savage
does the best he can, which is not much. The spirits are there, the
processes of nature go on, the spirits control and direct them; the
"how" is beyond his knowledge. Spirits make the fires whose smoke
issues from the craters of volcanoes and throw out red hot stones as
a man would throw a firebrand out of his own hut. Spirits flow in
dangerous rapids to pull down canoes. They put the rocks in rapids
to turn the hunter back; they live and play in all running waters.

Spiritism fairly runs riot when we come to the animal world. The
animal is a person and for the savage is so treated. His good will is
eminently desirable and his anger a thing to be avoided. He has
more to give than his pelt and his meat; he has desirable gifts of
courage, strength and wisdom, which can be appropriated by his
hunters. Eating him, or such parts of him as incarnate his more distinctive or digestible qualities, has generally been considered the
most satisfactory way of appropriating his virtues, but something can
be done by rubbing oneself with his fat. The ceremony of anoint-
ment which began in this literal fashion developed in strange sacrosanct ways to become finally the august ceremony of consecrating
a high priest or crowning a king in Westminster Abbey.

Besides the spirits of all natural things there was the most important spirit of all—a man's own soul. This mystic tenant of man's
mortal frame is the second center of all religion. God and the soul
are the two enduring realities to which faith reduces—

> "The cloud-capp'd towers, the generous palaces,
> The solemn temples, the great globe itself."

These are all that "this insubstantial pageant faded" will leave behind. The possessors of the soul have strained the resources of language to describe it. Primitive folk used the image of the shadow
and a great lore which *The Golden Bough* recites has grown out
of that figure. Later thought has used the wind or breath image.
Whether shadow or breath the soul has exerted its mastery over
literature as well as religion and if the word were lost we should

not know what to do without it. Some doubt of its existence is now abroad. Primitive man entertained no such doubt. He was apt, on the contrary, to overpopulate the body with souls. The Algonquins believed they had two souls; one of them adventured out in dreams while the other lay wrapped up in slumber; one remained with the body after death and needed food; one took the long trail to the land of the dead. Races native to the soil in India believe in four Souls. After death one is restored to God, one becomes the general possession of the tribe and is reborn in some child of the tribe, a third joins the general fellowship of spirits; the fourth, if he chooses, finds a tiger to live in.

Since a man's soul was then—as it is supposed to be now—his most precious possession, he took every care not to lose it. One may nearly lose it in a trance or a fainting fit but it may be brought back by calling after it; in fact, the imperilled one may call after it himself—a proceeding which causes Tylor's usually grave pen to chuckle. The soul escapes, of course, most often through the mouth and nostrils. Some savages, therefore, fasten fish hooks about a sick man's body—they will thus catch his fugitive soul—or else the mouth and nose may be covered over or sealed up to keep the spirit in. One yawns at the peril of one's soul.

THE SOUL AFTER DEATH

But sooner or later the soul gets away. So much primitive man found out. What happens to it then? It joins the invisible fellowship of the discarnate and so adds the spirits of the dead to the spirits of animals and things. It is likely for a season to haunt the spots it knew best—the savage had imagination enough to sense the aching loneliness of a disembodied spirit. The soul is unhappy until its late corporeal dwelling place is properly disposed of. Hence the necessity of some kind of burial and the great importance of proper burial rites. Since the spirits linger on it is far better for them to stay near the resting places of the dead and let the living alone. If they are properly buried, they will keep by their own graves. The fear of graveyards, a wide branched fear casting a long shadow, is rooted just here. Nassau notes its vivid control of the negro imagination. The civilized imagination is not wholly free from it.

Affection as well as fear makes burial a sacred duty. The living can not endure their dead to be homeless and unhappy. Though the Greek knew how to crown the Acropolis with beauty in marble, he knew also that the unburied waited moaning at the gates of Hades and he approved Antigone who went proudly to her own death if only she might lay a handful of consecrating dust upon her brother's body. The souls of those who died a violent death have always been in a perilous state, being vengeful and strangely restless, and it is not so long since the suicide was fastened into his nameless grave by a stake through his body.[17]

There is a widespread belief that there are special foods in shadeland which, once eaten by the spirits of the new-come dead, make them thereafter permanent citizens of that land. They may, like Persephone, return to the light for a little, but their stay is limited. The food furnished the dead by their friends has no such mystic powers; it is meant to support the dead as it supported the living. If they were not so served, they might walk the village by night and eat the leavings of the living. Whatever the living ate the dead could use—maize and rice cakes, milk, water or wine, and flesh. The world's burying grounds have been filled for millenniums with these pathetic witnesses of the dawn of faith.

Affection bade farewell to the departed reluctantly then as always. A single dirge has in it all the pain of unrequited longing, the sad light of the tears of things:

We never scolded you; never wronged you;
Come to us back,
We ever loved and cherished you; and have lived long together under
    the same roof,
Desert us not now!
The rainy nights and the cold blowing days are coming on;
Do not wander here;
Do not stand by the burnt ashes; come to us again;
You can not find shelter under the peepul tree where the rain comes
    down;
The saul will not shelter you from the cold bitter wind,
Come to your home!
It is swept for you and clean; and we are there who loved you ever,
And there is rice put for you; and water;
Come home, come home, come to us again.[18]

[17] In Dante suicides do not share the resurrection of the body.
[18] Tylor, *op. cit.,* Vol. II, page 33.

THE ABODES OF THE DEAD

But they do not come back. Where then do they go? Where do they not go? To rocks and trees, to animals and the new born, to the nether world and the moon and the stars. These homelands of the dead were always lands of mystery. They were the summit of the nearest mountain or beyond "the far horizons' utmost rim." For those who lived near the sea any island, far off and dim, might be the Island of the Blest. As the horizons of mystery have retreated, faith has found it increasingly hard to find a homeland for the dead. Now the telescope denies them even a celestial habitation; they bid fair to become homeless again. More than anything else the dead, in the faith of the dawn, follow the westering sun to a land beyond the purple twilight and the dark. Where should the dead make their last journey more triumphantly than into a region whose gates are so glorious, and pass out of human sight and knowledge comrades of the sun.

The bonds of mutual affection are strained by death but not broken. There is a shadowy borderland here between the natural continuation of old relationships beyond the grave and some slow change in the nature of the dead to make them gods. Those who spread tables for the ancestral shades and sat down thereto themselves could not have been always sure whether they were continuing a happy human relationship with unseen guests or entertaining the lesser divinities. Who can tell what has happened to a remote ancestor in the spirit world? The manes are certainly "exalted ghosts,"[19] and it is well to be kind to them, but the line between an exalted ghost and a lesser divinity is insubstantial.

ANCESTOR-WORSHIP

This gives to ancestor-worship an uncertain character; it may be worship, it may be a family council. But generally speaking the worship of the ancestral dead is a very old and deeply established custom. Earthly ranks and relationships are raised to a higher power; the father still protects his children, the chief guards his tribe. Worship of the dead is a root of religion which has nourished many

[19] E. W. Hopkins, *Origin and Evolution of Religion*, page 154, Yale University Press.

growths. It is shot through with conjectures and confidences as to the state of the dead; it involves burial customs, faiths which have become superstitions and superstitions which persist in western civilization only as time-worn remnants of folk habit so old that the reason for them is forgotten. In some instances the greatest of the dead become recognized divinities.[20] The general idea of father-worship has furnished religion its richest conception of the relation of God to man and found a cherished expression in the most universal and best known of all prayers.

Gifts to the dead have furnished a basis for the whole great system of sacrifice; tables spread for the dead may possibly (though this is not so certain) have supplied the first suggestion of communion with the unseen and truly sacramental meals.[21] Most of all, this persuasion of another order populous with those whom the living remember and revere, has given personal significance to man's whole conception of an unseen world and filled it with living meanings. Fear and wonder have given substance to all the other dim beginnings of religion we have so far considered, but in the worship of the dead love begins to weave its bright web across the two worlds of which man believes himself a citizen.[22]

All this is the ground stuff out of which the great religions have issued—a kind of murky star dust waiting to become constellations. The faiths of the dark and dawn populated the unseen with spirits; they related the believing to powers which may bless or ban. They began a little to establish grades of supernatural powers and to build the thrones from which the greater gods rule. They assume life after death, though not always an endless life, for the shades may grow old again and die a second death. They have established what every religion since has used—the incorporate reality of the soul. They

[20] Spencer went so far as to trace all divinities back to "Hero Ancestors" but his conclusions are not now accepted.

[21] Some element of communion, which religion has since changed and magnified, certainly entered into these meals shared by unseen guests. When the dead ceased to come the gods came, or else the dead came back as gods. Sacraments and sacrifices have begun when gods and men sit at the same table.

[22] There is an enormous literature on the subject of ancestor-worship. (See Hastings, *Encyclopedia of Religion and Ethics*, Vol. I, page 425 et seq.) The practice is or has been practically universal and is always associated with a cult of the dead which leads one into a perfect jungle of tribal customs. Ancestor-worship passes over into Animal-worship and is related to Totemism. But the controlling principles of ancestor-worship are strangely constant.

follow the discarnate into spaces of mystery, lands beyond the sunset. They have begun the awesome adventure of prayer.

THE BEGINNINGS OF WORSHIP

Nature-worship in one form or another is the first entirely clear emergence of a religion which adores.[23] It first called men away from their own shades to vaster and disparate powers. Primitive man lives in an intimacy with nature which civilization has entirely lost. He meets the entire force of it in the open, takes the rain on a half-clothed body, interposes the frailest of roofs between himself and any storm. He has no way to soften its enmities or secure its favor save his poor magic, and only a little strength and less skill to subdue its elemental forces to his needs. The light of his campfires does little more than reveal the darkness which follows the setting sun, the dawn is his reveille. His fortunes change with the changing winds; he takes his blessings or his pains direct from nature's hand and does not know why one is withheld or the other given.

But because there is so thin a roof between him and the stars, he see their lucent majesty undimmed. Because his hut is open to the seasons and his daily round timed to their changes, the states of his own spirit reflect their course. Because he has no way to measure time save by sunrise and sunset, waxing and waning moons, the turn of the sun in midsummer and midwinter, these become his clock and calendar. He takes his food and drink direct from nature's hand; the beneficent forms of nature become his gods, its ways which do him hurt, his demons. He has the child's way of personifying anything in action and adding the play of his own creative fancy to what he sees and shares. He makes poetry and drama out of dawn and sunset, winter and summer, and moving tales to be chanted around his fires and passed on from bard to priest, who has his own way of taking what poets sing and making sober stuff out of it for his followers to believe.

Naturally in nature-worship men began with what they saw first and knew best. Heaven and Earth, Rain, Thunder, Water and Sea,

[23] There are, it is maintained, and always have been, two religious movements: one directed toward nature; the other directed toward spirits. There is a nice debate as to which came first. In general, we shall find, as we get on, that the religion of spiritism becomes the dark religion of the underworld spirits. The other the bright religion of the sky gods.

Fire and Sun and Moon furnished humanity's first pantheon.[24] Their worship spans millenniums and actually girdles the globe. These awesome forces become gods in their rising and administration and begin their long procession. They change their names and their garmenture, but never so entirely lose their primitive nature as to make it impossible to discover Father Sky behind his masquerader's costume or Mother Earth in some strange disguise.

They are attended in the procession by imposing retinues; they grow in majesty and power as they go; they use the souls of men for their imperial roads, conquering armies for the extension of their domain. They began with no temples, few priests and sod for an altar. Their temples became in time the most splendid human creations and only kings could vie with them in wealth. They took time for an inheritance and the great races for their subjects. They followed fair-skinned invaders from the "grassy plain" to India. They made Nineveh and Babylon their capitals; their splendid abodes were mirrored in the Nile; they drank nectar together on Olympus; they ruled from the Seven Hills of Rome, and established their last dominion over the West in the misty north. Yet to begin with, they were only sun and sky and storm, the power and ways of nature—that and the souls of men for whom nature has never been enough.

For every "many-god" religion is built upon some foundation of nature-worship and represents some distinctive development of nature-worship modified by race and circumstance.[25] The five general steps by which religion has reached its most august heights are: Animism, the sense of a general animating power; Spiritism, which vaguely individualizes citizens of the "third order"; Polytheism, which divides the sovereignty of the world between gods and goddesses who are partially, and in some religions entirely, personifications of the more enduring and prevailing nature forces; and Monotheism, which assigns the enduring empire of the universe to one God. Pantheism does not lie in the direct line of this succession. India offers the only example of a vigorous polytheism which was

---

[24] I have capitalized these to give them their worship value. Capitalization in the story of religion is a tricky business.

[25] I say "some" because the theory which makes all religion, even the polytheistic, entirely the development of nature-worship is beginning to break down. At a certain level deities appear which are incarnations of purely personal qualities. We shall come to this again in Greek religion.

dissolved into Pantheism, and that was due to the highly speculative quality of the Indian mind.

WEATHER RELIGIONS

Our race began early to take that natural interest in the weather which their more sophisticated descendants have not lost. Its laws were beyond their knowledge. How could they forecast its operations? No wonder they peopled the skies with capricious divinities who rode abroad on the wings of the winds, darkened the blue with clouds and hurled their weapons at trees or man. They had early dealings with the clouds; they besought the rain-bearers to remember their fields and the hail-bearers to spare them.

The Greeks maintained watchmen at public charge to look out for hail storms. When threatening clouds were noted the farmers and vinedressers sacrificed lambs or fowls or, if they were too poor for that, pricked their fingers and let some drops of their own blood fall upon their barley or vines in the hope of propitiating the cloud gods. If the storm came up notwithstanding, the watchmen were punished for neglect of duty, a procedure likely to have discouraged applicants for the meteorological service of Athens.

Now there is no recognition of Zeus in these archaic rites, though Zeus was the sovereign sky god. The clouds were the deities addressed and sacrificed to, which can only prove that long before clouds and storm and sun and winds were unified in one all inclusive deification of the sky, the simple-minded worshiped them as separate spirits.[26]

The Rain-god has always been sure of worshipers, he means so much to cherished fields. He is worshiped in Africa, Asia and the Pacific Islands. His suppliants tell him that unless he is kind, their fields will be unploughed, their children will die of hunger, the deer will go far away and if he does relent after all that mischief has been done, his rain will fall on a land where there is no living thing or any seed. Then after the manner of all petitioners, having divinity to draw upon, they ask for more rain than would be good for them.

The Finns prayed for rain to Ukko, the Heaven-god.

[26] Frazer, *The Worship of Nature,* page 85 et seq. This book is a scholarly treasury of information and illustration and this section is deeply indebted to it.

> Thou, O Father in the heavens
> Thou who rulest in the cloud lands,
> And the little cloud lambs leadest,
> Send us down the rain from heaven
> Make the clouds to drop with honey,
> Let the drooping corn look upward,
> Let the grain with plenty rustle.[27]

Roman matrons also went out with loosened hair in rain questing processions. In the old Rome of austere habit and pure faith their prayers were always answered and they came home dripping wet. As Rome grew decadent their power began to be lost. Prayers for rain have been a long time being muted. The Thunder-god is as fearsome as the Rain-god is kind, though capricious. His weapons are thunder-bolt stones, in which there is a widespread belief.

The sounds of the Wind-god's going is heard around the world. They furnish a music for old Vedic hymns; they supply the American Indian with a poetry and a faith. The Wind-god is sometimes sovereign of the air, holding all the winds in leash and housing them in caves and on lonely mountain summits. Or else there was a Wind-god for each quarter of the compass; cruel in the north; herald of the dawn in the east; lazy in the south; roystering in the west. Sea-going folk prayed—and pray—especially to the Wind-god, asking according to their need for wind or calm. The imaginative people of old north Europe believed the winds had a mother whose wailing they heard in the rising gales: "Wind's mother wails, who knows what mother shall wail next?"

Sun- and Sky-worship

In such a worship as this nothing is constant. How can anyone disentangle the pageantry of the sky and assign to each god a separate throne and administration? Cloud-god, Rain-god, Thunder-god and Wind-god come up together, fill the zenith with their tumult and disappear. But the sun does not disappear nor the all-containing cerulean firmament. These forces of the upper air thus tend to become the ministers of a vaster, more inclusive divinity; the Sky-god absorbs them all. There is an enormous and fascinating mythology—not all of it seemly—about the relation of Earth and Sky and a wide

[27] Quoted by Tylor, *op. cit.,* page 261.

range of sky-worship, particularly among the Aryan races for whom the sun has never been so sovereign as among southern races. The Sky-god has headed the pantheon from the "grassy plain" to the forests of Northern Europe.

There was a time when Earth and Sky were so near together (so many primitive faiths maintain) that a man could hardly stand erect. This belief is expressed, with unseemly attention to detail, in old Greek myths of the marriage of Earth and Sky, of which union an enormous progeny is the issue.[28] The poets loved and sang to them:

> The Earth doth love the rain, what time the parched ground
> Barren with drought, doth crave a shower,
> The solemn sky too, full of rain, doth love
> To fall upon the Earth, when Aphrodite prompts.
> Then when the two are joined in love's embrace,
> They make all things to grow for us, and feed them too,
> Whereby the race of mortals lives and thrives.
>
> (Euripides, quoted by Frazer, page 41.)

But the worship of the sun is an outstanding aspect of Sky- and Nature-worship. Tylor quotes Sir William Jones as saying that all the gods and goddesses in Rome and Benares alike mean only the powers of nature and, principally, the Sun deified under many names. Frazer maintains the sun-worship is by no means so general as was formerly supposed. It is found "only in very exceptional regions or only in lofty table lands of equatorial latitude" and appears only on the higher levels of race culture.[29] I should think this statement of Frazer open to some qualifications. It is difficult to find any primitive religion without some reflection of a sun-cult. If Plato may be trusted, sun-worship could be found beneath the shadow of the Acropolis.

Helios drove the horses of the chariot of the sun with glorious mastery through the classic lore of Greece. The temple of the sun at Rome housed the spirit from an older temple of the Sun-god at Palmyra. Mithras—the unconquered sun—disputed the rising regnancy of Christianity. Shamash had his temples in Babylon; the sacred city of the strange Egyptian pantheon was, for dynasties,

---

[28] See Hesiod-Theogony for a wealth of detail.
[29] Frazer, *op. cit.,* page 282 et seq.

Heliopolis, the city of the sun. The mingled lights and shadows of sun-worship still fall across India. The Emperor of Japan is a descendant of the sun and white-robed Fujiyama is his shrine and altar. The aviator—comrade of the sun himself—looks down upon the ruins of temples of the sun in the jungles of Peru. The American Indians offered him incense of tobacco smoke. The Mexicans hailed the rising sun with some offering of their own blood or else the more tragic blood of human sacrifice. It is never easy, as has been said, to disentangle an ancient and general heaven-worship and assign to the sun and moon some separate adoration.

The stars have apparently never been so generally worshiped, being too far and faint to assert themselves as gods. But there is always a wealth of solar myth itself seen through mist and cloud drift. The sun and moon have enemies who pursue and swallow them in seasons of eclipse but they always manage to escape. When they are in imminent danger the demons and dragons may be driven away by shouting and making any great noise; so we hear a noise of trumpets and beating of brass or bronze almost the world around to whose hoarse music eclipses have begun, continued and ended. Beneath the transforming touch of time the sun became a hero like Hercules, or, maybe, Samson, of prodigious strength and mighty deeds to be said and sung around a thousand campfires.

The faith, the devotion, the liturgies of many religions associate the Summer solstice, the turn of the sun in the sky in late December and the vernal equinox with festivals for which both racial memory and forgetfulness have supplied a rich supporting detail of incident. Death and rebirth and resurrection are woven through all this marvelous and enduring fabric, till the phases of the sun seem to date the supreme spiritual confidences of humanity. Twentieth-century Christians sing John of Damascus' hymn—

> 'Tis the spring of souls today;
> Christ has burst his prison,
> And from three days' sleep in death
> As a sun has risen:

Such music has a long ancestry; perhaps John himself did not know how much was reborn in Easter or what far-off voices sounded through his lines.

EARTH-WORSHIP

Earth-worship is as old as Sky-worship. While Father Sky was a long way off, Mother Earth was left friendly and near. Her ways were kind and helpful, her gifts were such as nourished life, and, besides, was she not the common mother of us all, taking back into her bosom her weary children when their course was run? "The Earth is my mother and I am the son of the Earth" is a confession of faith and kinship long and indeed truly said. The prayers of the earth-born to Earth are then most natural, "O Mother Earth, kindly set me down upon a well-founded place." And when any son of Earth has lived his life out upon "some well-founded place" he has still another boon to ask of his Earth Mother, or else his friends ask it for him: "Earth, as a Mother, wraps her skirt about her child, so covers him."[30]

The Greeks believe broad-bosomed Earth older than anything save Chaos, the unmated mother of the starry sky whom she later married. Zeus himself belongs to her family line, though his early domestic relationships do the family as a whole no credit. Some of the Greek poets pay poor respect to the earth-goddess, possibly because she supplied them a scant livelihood from a stony soil. Others having fared more fortunately are more grateful—

> . . . happy is he whom thou in heart
> Dost know graciously: he hath all things in plenty
> For him his fruitful land is big with corn, and his meadows
> Abound in cattle and his house is full of good things.
>
> .   .   .   .   .
>
> Hail, Mother of Gods, Spouse of the Starry Sky,
> And graciously for this my song bestow on me
> Substantial enough for heart's ease; so shall I not forget
> To hymn thee in another lay.[31]

Which proves, among other things, the human nature of the poets.

Earth-worship shades off into border regions which tax the learning and interpretative ingenuity of the specialist. There is tree-worship. The primitive belief that trees have souls has created not only

[30] Homeric hymns quoted by Frazer, *op. cit.*, page 320.
[31] Frazer, *op. cit.*, page 320.

a cult of tree-worship but a marvelous growth of mythology, folk-lore and poetry shot through like an ancient forest with mingled light and shadow. The souls of trees protest when trees are wantonly felled; the tree loses its soul or else the soul migrates to another tree. There are certain trees which must not be cut down. This devout feeling for trees reflects an ancient comradeship with nature as though dim ancestral memories woke and whispered like a low wind and leaves talking together. Worship is native to a forest. The depths of ancient forests are haunted with mystery, they possess a power of perpetual renewal, the arched meeting of their branches creates a temple fit to shelter any god. No wonder fear and faith and wonder supplied the god. There were also thousands of years during which trees supplied men their weapons to fight with, their tools to work with, their stuff for walls and roofs, fuel for their hearthstone fires. Tree-worship is not a faith to debase the soul. One might wish that doomed forests might be again invested with their ancient sanctity.

SERPENT-WORSHIP

Strangely enough, tree-worship has been intimately associated with serpent-worship. The serpent leaves a sinuous trail, desperately hard to explain, through widely separated religions. A snake's uncanny mystery, his unlikeness to any other living thing, his way of shedding his skin and coming out reborn, his power to live a long time without eating and his way of dealing death with a stroke all combined to make him feared and worshiped. The widespread belief that the dead came back as serpents had much to do with their worship. The dead are buried in the earth-dark, the serpent comes up out of it. The serpent was, besides, credited with an unearthly wisdom, being the guardian of oracles and the genius of physicians. Does he not still coil about the emblem of the medical staff of the United States Army?[32] In the first chapters of Genesis, he does mankind a tragic mischief. The old wood engravings which show him a twined tempter in the branches of the Tree of Life are repeated in substance in the bas-reliefs of Asian ruins which medieval draughts-men could never have known. The conservative theologian has his

---

[32] This is all taken from Fergusson's *Tree- and Serpent-Worship* without specific reference. The work is mostly concerned with India but is classic and standard.

explanation of the Temptation and Fall story, but those for whom any such account is a dim chapter in the development of faith with still dimmer and older meanings behind it are not so easily satisfied. Something older than the Pentateuch is reflected in its explanation of the shadow which fell across the bright morning of Creation and barred an exiled humanity from the tree of knowledge and life by a flaming sword. Fergusson believes the curse leveled at the serpent really represents the Hebrew prophets' hatred of serpent-worship. For serpent-worship is native to the lands, the times and the races among whom Bible history begins.[33]

Serpent-worship is now naturally most in evidence in snake-infested lands. The shadowed faiths of Africa are full of it. The serpent mounds in America are a witness to a forgotten serpent cult in Mexico and Peru so late as the Spanish Conquest. It is a repulsive worship darkly stained with blood everywhere, for it is widely associated with human sacrifice, and also it is associated with underworld religion which is always somber. There is no room here for an adequate consideration of serpent-worship in India, though the habits of the living and the sculpture remnants of vast temples in regions which the jungle has long since repossessed bear witness to a cult which outlives imperial cities and proud civilizations. The Naga King still rules the East.

The Worship of the Vegetism Spirit

No aspect of nature-worship issued finally in so rich a variety of forms as the worship of the vegetable spirit. It persists in the folk-

[33] Frazer offers another explanation. There were, he thinks, according to the older lore from which the teller of the Genesis story took his narrative, two trees in the garden: one the tree of life, one the tree of death. Man might or might not become immortal, as he ate of one or the other. So the Creator sent the serpent with a message to give man his choice: "Eat not of the tree of death, for in the day you eat thereof ye shall surely die; but eat of the tree of life and live forever." The serpent having a subtle and mischief-making mind changed the message quite about and delivered it to the foolish woman, who believed him and not only ate herself but misled her husband. The result was tragic. Incidentally, the serpent ate of the tree of life himself; hence the immortality with which naïve natural history credited him. There are, curiously enough, some African legends of a changed message to substantially the same effect. In these the Moon sent the message of immortality and the hare changed it. His lip was split for punishment.—*Folk Lore in the Old Testament*, pages 15 et seq. The serpent also made mischief and lost man immortality in a Chaldean epic.

festivals of seed time and harvest. It has furnished subject matter for a wealth of poetry and mythology. The arresting sequences of life and death and life again in the outer world lent themselves to dramatic representation. The more discerning eventually saw in the world of nature impressive parallels to the course of human life. No great discernment was needed for any man to feel within himself the stir of forces which in their general consequences seemed one with quickening life everywhere. Love for the first time begins to claim its own god-head, build its temples and ordain its priests and priestesses—especially its priestesses. The result is one of the most fascinating chapters in the story of religion. It ceases to be religion and becomes a drama of love and loss and quest with a music made by the flutes of Tammuz, the harp of Orpheus and the lovers and devotees of three continents.

It began, I suppose, with Isis and Osiris in Egypt, but it becomes more clearly defined in the story of Ishtar and Tammuz in Babylon. Ishtar is probably the first, and so the oldest, of the goddesses of love and love-begotten life. Tammuz, the husband of her youth, was the "great Asiatic nature-god typifying the changing seasons in their relation to man's needs, desires and passions." He dies—as summer dies—and descends to the underworld. His death left Ishtar and the world desolate. The women of Babylon—and their music found far echoes—sang of that desolation in "The Lament of the Flute for Tammuz."

> Her lament is the lament of the corn
> That grows not in the ear,
>
> .   .   .   .   .
>
> Her lament is for a great river where
> No willows grow,
> Her lament is for a field, where corn
> and herbs grow not.

Therefore Ishtar followed him

.   .   .   .   .

> To the house where dust is their nourishment.
> To the house without light for him who enters therein.[34]

She must pass seven gates to enter "the palace of the land of no

[34] Translation by Jastrow. Other translations vary in detail.

return." She left in succession her jewels, her robes and her girdle with the keepers of these gates and stood at last naked and suppliant in the cold dark asking that Tammuz be dismissed to the upper world.

The detail of the drama varies—Ishtar and Tammuz are too nearly alike to keep their office separate—but the old poems tell with abundant detail how, with Ishtar gone, love ceased in Babylon. The earth-god whose realm was threatened with depopulation sent a messenger to bring her back. She was sprinkled with the water of life,[35] the gatekeeper took her back through the seven gates and re-clothed and readorned her with that of which she had been divested, until, jeweled and crowned, she stood in a light-drenched world. The songs of lovers were heard again in old Babylon. It was spring in Chaldea. She must have brought Tammuz back though she could not keep him—he is always dying and always being recalled to life. But the women of Babylon made a drama of it all and sang their laments yearly over the image of a lovely youth. Ezekiel heard that wailing in Jerusalem and the music filled his Hebrew soul with anger. The worship of youth and love is a hard competitor for the austere worship of the Eternal.

Tammuz and Ishtar, being life and love, could always find wor-shipers. They changed their names but not greatly their natures and went west together. In Syria, this land being always kind to fervent nature-worship in which desire is deified, Tammuz became Adon[36] (lord) and Ishtar became Astarte of Byblus. Ruins of their temples may still be found about Mount Lebanon; the Adonis River still flows seaward; the anemone dyed red with Adon's blood still blooms beneath the cedars. Only the wailing women are heard no more.

DEVELOPMENT OF FERTILITY-WORSHIP MYTHS

Once this cult reached the shores of the Mediterranean the creative and poetic genius of Greece took it over. The myths of Aphrodite and Adonis and Persephone took many changing forms but always there was life and death and love and life again at the heart of them. Cyprus, beloved of Aphrodite, became finally the religious seat of a worship which Babylon created and Syria nourished. There in the

[35] Also in some versions a spring of life from which she drank.
[36] A title of honor of which the Greeks made a proper name.

temple at Paphos the rites proper to such a goddess, drawn from many sources and most of all from old desire, were celebrated. The kind beauty and fruitfulness of the land veiled a little the realities of her cult. Such a worship was easy beneath ardent skies.

The cult of Adonis took another line. He became a harvest god whose festival was celebrated at Athens in midsummer. He died in the ripened grain and lived again in emerald green cornfields. In the end, the joy of his resurrection transformed the tragedy of his death. Spring, whose blossoms seem dyed in blood, became his season. The questing spirit of a seemingly time-doomed humanity found in the rebirth he symbolized an evidence of their own resurrection. Some hope of immortality began to blossom with the anemones of Syria and the hyacinths of Greece. Else why did the women of Phoenicia believe that dead Adonis rose again—and ascended to heaven?

Rome took over another version of the same story in the legend of Attis and Cybele. There the drama of death and resurrection was staged in a frenzied way. The rites of Attis were red and mad. His image was taken from his pine tree and buried with wild lamentation. But the morning saw the sorrow turned to joy. Attis was alive again. It is significant of old forgotten things that the morning of his return to life was, as near as may be, the vernal equinox. But Cybele was not quite Ishtar or Astarte. She was the mother of the gods whose worship Rome adopted during the stress of the wars with Hannibal and much came into Rome with her beside her misshapen stone image. She was akin to Demeter a little and to Mother Earth more.

If we add to this the Egyptian myth and ritual of Isis and Osiris, we have all the elements of the final transformation of vegetation-worship, itself an aspect of nature-worship, into a form of religion which cast its spell across the Roman Empire, and challenged the shadowy sovereignty of the Olympian over Greece.

What was so long maturing did not soon die—it is not dead yet. The Corn Mother guarded the harvest fields of the North under many different names. Christianity itself did not displace what was older than paganism. Something of it lingered on in folklore and folk custom until Adonis or Attis, Demeter or Persephone, came home with the last cart from the harvest field and the faith of a dead world became the dance of youth around a May-pole—or a little basket of flowers on a door knob of a May morning. All this because days shorten and lengthen, anemones bloom again in the spring, fields are resown with the seed of garnered harvests—and man believes that, since all else is reborn, he himself will not die.

The procession of the gods has been lost in the fascinating forms which nature-worship took, but in all we have been considering their august ranks were being mobilized. Sun and Storm, Sky pageantry and Earth-mothered sequence of life and death assume through such ways as these a divine sovereignty. When the mists of time clear away a little, they are enthroned in Egypt and Babylon. Their empire has begun.

We can not, need not, name them yet. All religions save the most advanced have swarmed with nameless spirits. They come and go like motes in the sunlight—or fireflies in the dark. They are as it were the star-dust out of which mature religions shape their ordered, singing systems. The persistent forces in our encompassing world assert their sovereignty over need, devotion and imagination, are named and personalized. The most fortunate become tribal, regional or national deities; then they become historic. We shall meet, but rarely before Greece, divinities of noble bearing who begin to be the personification of ideas instead of forces—a god of war or trade, or a goddess of wisdom. Idealization, of course, and some measure of rationalization along with a vivifying process, a making-the-divinity-really-alive process enters into all religions, even the most primitive.

The basis of that is imagination but it involves insight and, eventually, moral and value judgments. The Greek was the first to make his divinities vividly alive and beautiful. His dramatist brought moral and value judgments to play upon and about them but could not reinstate them upon their dissolving thrones. The Hebrew prophet invested his God with moral and value judgments and saw him as a sovereign power in life and the world. As the august procession passes before us, the personifications of nature and its forces will grow dim and disappear. Ethical and idealistic qualities will begin to appear. Greek thought made the first clear distinction between nature as an order and religion as an aspect of the conduct and content of life. Hebraism made the natural order the revelation of the Creator's power and glory and the vehicle of his moral judgments. Christianity inherited this but invested God with understanding kindness and redeeming love.

The procession ends with the endeavor of contemporaneous Western thought to readjust our knowledge of the outer order to our inherited faith and the needs of our inner lives and secure again in an immensely extended field the synthesis with which in simple and fragmentary ways religion began. *Vexilla Deorum prodeunt*—The banners of the gods advance.

CHAPTER II

The Sphinx-guarded Gods of the Nile

THE CRADLES OF CIVILIZATION AND RELIGION

THREE rivers furnished two great civilizations a soil to root in and gave the gods their first domains. The Valley of the Nile opens upon the Mediterranean; the Valley of the Tigris and Euphrates upon the Persian Gulf; the eastern coast of the Mediterranean with its hinterlands furnishes a road from the mouths of the Nile to the head waters of the Euphrates. These two valleys with the connecting lands between them have come of late to be called the Fertile Crescent, and they deserve the name. The valleys are the home of the date palm; the regions between them nourish the olive; the rich alluvial soils grow wheat and barley. They are ardent, sun-lit lands, guarded by the desert or walled a little by mountains. They are near enough the seas for commerce and because their kings could maintain a diplomatic correspondence or go out to fight one another as they pleased, and because the trader and the traveler could use the roads, they carried on between them for millenniums some commerce of ponderable and imponderable things.

They were mainly administered by a race of great genius, though the strains of their population were mixed. At any rate a happy combination of racial force, climate, soil and strategic position made the Fertile Crescent a stage upon which splendid dramas of history were enacted. There, save perhaps for China, recorded time began and human culture found roothold to ripen into cities whose names once awed their little world, a wisdom which instructed succeeding civilizations, empires which still enthrall the imagination and religions which fascinate the student. If one remembers that little Palestine was a span in the land bridge between the two valleys and that Arabia lies within the arm of the Fertile Crescent, then one may add living religions to the dead. Without the religious bequest of this entire region the story of religion would be unbelievably impoverished. The gods first found their thrones and temples in the

31

valleys which cradled civilization. There their processions became imperially proud. From the uplands of Palestine came the faith to which those of them who were not forgotten bowed. Their first dominance and their final defeat belong to the Fertile Crescent—and Egypt gave them their first great empire.

Egypt still meets a traveler as she met Herodotus—with a low coast line washed by the low tides of the bluest of seas. She meets him also with clamorous porters wearing strange headdresses, a Customs House, motor cars, with slender minarets and narrow streets beneath overhanging latticed windows and some music of the call to prayer. But most of all she meets him with an incalculable wealth of historic association. Memories of Napoleon and Caesar, Antony and Cleopatra, haunt the port which once had one of the Seven Wonders of the World for a lighthouse.[1] Distances are not measured by miles but by ages.

The alfalfa and barley fields have nourished the oldest of cultures, they have watched the passage of almost all the armies that the mutations of empire have released since empire began and the flight of bond servants weary of making bricks without straw. One hears, as one sees through the car windows, the threshing sleds, driven around the threshing floors, the song of the threshers of the New Kingdom:

> Thresh for yourselves, thresh for yourselves, oxen,
> Thresh for yourselves, thresh for yourselves;
> Straw to eat, barley for your masters,
> Give yourselves no rest, it is cool (today).[2]

THE ANTIQUITY AND LURE OF EGYPT

The Nile with its palm-fringed banks is not water; it is what Burns called the Thames—"liquid history." Dominating it all the ghosts of the Pyramids of Gizeh blue and dim break the levels of those haunted fields. An hour later the ghosts become piled stone in the sand and crouching beneath them, scarred, time-worn and inscrutable, the Sphinx becomes Egypt incarnate.

[1] And is now to become the Naval Base of the British Empire in the Eastern Mediterranean.

[2] Adolph Erman, *The Literature of the Ancient Egyptians*, New York, 1929, page 251.

It faces the east, being one of the many forms of the sun-god but it does more than wait for the dawn with immemorial patience. It is the warden of the tombs of the kings who made it; one of them is made to say, "I guard the chapel of thy tomb, I guard thy sepulchral chamber, I ward off the intruding stranger, I cast down thy foes to the ground . . . drive away the wicked one, I destroy thine adversaries in their lurking place."[3] An inscribed tablet on the breast of the Sphinx of Gizeh tells the story of a king's dream—

On one of these days it happened, when the king's son, Thothmes, had arrived on his journey about the time of mid-day, and had stretched himself to rest in the shade of this great god, that sleep overtook him . . . and it seemed to him as though this great god spoke to him, just as a father speaks to his son. "See thou me, my son Thothmes, for I am thy father, and I will grant thee to be King on thy throne . . . wearing the red crown and the white crown, as the Chief of the gods possessing the land in all its length and breadth, the splendour of the lord of all things. . . . Now look at my fate! The sand of the district in which I have my existence has covered me up. See that thou mayest be able to protect my beautiful members. Promise me that thou wilt do what I wish in my heart, then shall I know whether thou art my son. . . . Let me be united to thee."[4]

The whole of Egypt is in that dream—a land in which the king is the son of the gods and the gods are suppliants for the favor of kings, peopled by time-worn monuments of sculptured stone—half-man, half-beast, sun-drenched, Nile-watered, sand-besieged, always being buried, always being resurrected—a land whose tombs were built to make their occupants eternally secure and have instead been plundered for a thousand years. A land with no voice now save from lips of stone, and speaking still in accents of pride and power and mystery—so that the curious are never tired of listening, and never sure of what they hear.

The river which made the land to begin with and has ever since kept it alive rises south of the Equator. It fights its way—cataract by cataract—through Nubian sandstone and a barrier of granite, and thereafter flows from the Tropic of Cancer to the Mediterranean

[3] A. Wiedeman, *Religion of the Ancient Egyptians,* Putnam's, New York, 1897, page 197.

[4] Edouard Naville, *The Old Egyptian Faith,* New York, 1909. Also *Egypt Under the Pharaohs,* Heinrich Brugsch-Bey, London, page 199.

without a tributary. Its sources are dark with savagery; it loses itself
in a sea whose coasts were once bright with classic beauty.

Ancient Egypt thus touched the extremes of culture. It was the one
habitable region in a desert plateau which reached from the Atlantic
seaboard through Northern Africa into the far heart of Asia. The
Nile Valley is really, says Breasted, "a vast canyon cut across the
eastern end of the Sahara to the northern sea," walled on either side
by limestone cliffs, generally a few hundred feet high. The valley
above the Delta is never more than ten miles wide. There are less
than ten thousand square miles of arable land, (about the area of
Maryland). The desert and the blue-green fields meet so sharply that
you may stand with one foot in barley and the other in sand.
Nowhere in the world does wind-swept loneliness frame so rich
and populous a land.

A River-made Land

Aeonian inundations have floored this ribbon valley with an
alluvium of inexhaustible fertility, thirty feet deep and always deepening; the old cities of the Delta have long since been buried. The
swamps of three thousand years ago, through whose reeds the winds
sang softly, are now land holdings where date palms border a web
of irrigating water-ways, the wheels which lift the water to matted
alfalfa fields complain to a sky which has heard so many complaints
and the fellaheen follow the lengthening shadows home as they did
under the Pharaohs.

The Nile now rises fifty feet above low water level at the first
cataract, twenty-five at Cairo. As the land has slowly risen the actual
volume of flood water has decreased. Six thousand years ago the
river, according to rock-hewn records, rose nearly thirty feet higher
than today. The oldest records show dimly a population of hunters,
contending with beasts and their neighbors for the possession of
swampy jungles, living in wicker-work huts in stake-surrounded
villages, beginning to pasture some domestic animals in the marshes.
Wild life now withdrawn into Central Africa, possessed the regions
where kings later built their palaces and their tombs. It would have
been a reptile infested land. Snake ribs have been found to dwarf
any living python. No wonder the serpent has left a trail through all

Egyptian myth and religion, and coils, sculptured, around the head-dresses of goddesses.

EGYPTIAN GEOGRAPHY AND CLIMATE

The land thus slowly made was like a serpent itself; it had length but no breadth. Local differences were naturally strongly marked and persistent; dialects, customs, religions changed as the Nile flowed north. The folk of the Delta would find the language of the First Cataract hard to understand; a god would need to move less than seventy-five miles to leave reverence and worshipers behind him and become an alien divinity in a strange land. The river made Egypt to begin with and has ever since perennially renewed it, but without the sun the gifts of the river would have been sterile. The Egyptian sun is the lord of an always cloudless sky, his fiercest heat endurable because the air is desert dried—a porous water jug will cool its contents on the hottest day through evaporation. Egyptian winters are a kind constancy of crystalline brilliancy. The malarial infections which, it is now believed, sapped the force of ancient Greece, the fevers of the Campagna, are unknown. Egypt has been blessed with every good gift the sun can bestow and never an evil one. No wonder the people made a god of him.

The Egyptians have been agriculturists ever since the jungle was cleared; their most ancient pictures in stone show farmers and stockmen busy at their craft; their kings performed sacred rites at the proper seasons in honor of agriculture; the priests held the plow sacred and, as we shall presently see, believed the dead could find no happier estate than to till another Egypt beyond the sunset. These inexhaustible fields were bordered by a wealth of building materials —limestone of so fine a character as to have made the pyramid of Cheops a white and gleaming marvel before time and vandalism scarred and darkened it; granite whose rose time can never darken; alabaster to furnish vases and bowls for a king's palace.

The cataracts of the Nile were a southern barrier. Waterless wastes of sand fenced the east and west; only the northwestern and northeastern corners were gates for migrant races to come through. While time was measured only by the rise and fall of dynasties, Egypt wrought her destiny alone. If there was another world her kings hardly knew it; her common folk did not know it at all; her priests did not care. The living buried the dead, embalmed against corruption, wrapped in linen, coffined in cedar and stone. The strong made fortresses of their tombs; the rich took their jewels to the grave. Craftsmen wrought lovely things whose remnants are now the treasures of museums, scribes wrote their faith and their lore upon long papyrus strips and made the dead the guardians of their labor. Or else they cut their records on the walls of their temples, or left them upon obelisks and sarcophagi. Cities were built and forgotten, successive dynasties moved their palaces and courts from capital to capital and built grand avenues of guardian figures—half-man, half-beast—leading to massive temples. They began their astronomical year on the morning when Sirius lay level with the eastern horizon at sunrise. They had welcomed him thus for almost four thousand years before history was redated.

Mighty fragments of this civilization remain to testify to the power and pride of it. The tombs which their builders supposed would be eternally inviolate have yielded their secrets. A century and a half of scholarship has read the papyri and translated, though not always with any assuring agreement, the curious hieroglyphics. What does all this tell us of their faith?

THE COMPLEXITY OF EGYPTIAN RELIGION

The primitive Egyptian, probably Ethiopian, lived, as all primitive people live, in a spirit-haunted world. This first phase, however, quickly took on a strongly marked quality of animal-worship due to the variety and vigor of animal life in the prehistoric Nile Valley.[5] The natural surroundings of the early Egyptian worshiper gave a quality to his religion it never escaped. His faith reflected the influence of both his land and his sky. No religion has so many animal or part animal symbols as the Egyptian or in phases of it becomes so completely animal-worship. Erman[6] does not think animal-worship to have been an original part of it but it is difficult to account for it

[5] The animal figures found in graves and tower ruins are: the lion (tail over his back and hooked); bull, hawk, hippopotamus (rarely); frog, serpent (mostly coiled); scorpion and locust. Also (though possibly not worshiped) elephant, stag and hare. The cat, jackal, vulture and crocodile have not yet joined the procession.

[6] *A Handbook of Egyptian Religion*, London, 1907, page 24.

if it were not. It would seem more likely that the later bright sky-worship fused with an older animal-worship and the devout and conservative Egyptian mind met the situation by making the old animal the symbol and incarnation of the new god. The jungle, the swamp and the pasture gave persistent character to Egyptian faith.

Time changed the land and its people. Proud builders endowed Karnak and Luxor with the plunder of provinces, crowned granite columns with papyrus-flowered capitals, floored their temples with silver and paneled their gates with gold—but the jungle lived on. Strange divinities, half-human, half-beast, hawk-headed, ram-headed, jackal-headed, brooded in sculpture over these sanctuaries. They might shelter a bull chosen for his peculiar marks from a thousand unconscious competitors for divinity. The waters of a lake which reflected the creation of master builders contained a sacred crocodile "whose ears and forefeet were ornamented with gold and precious stones," fed from a priest's hand fare too fine for any crocodile—and besides there were the sacred cats.

The sheer number of Egyptian divinities and the tangle of myth and theological lore which time and the priesthood evolved make ancient Egyptian religion most difficult to reduce to order. The book of the dead names five hundred gods and goddesses. Theologians of a later date catalogued twelve hundred—and these twelve hundred take no account of minor local divinities and borderland spirits. A Doctor of Divinity in the nineteenth dynasty would be a learned man if he knew their names. The names themselves are forbidding. Aphrodite and Minerva are singing words, Zeus and Ares have Homeric dignity, but Khnum and Nekhbet, Set and Sebek sound like the staccato of masons' hammers. The names have besides no standardized usage. Horus may be the son of Isis waging an endless feud with Set, or he may be Horus the sun-god; if he is Horus the sun-god, he has one alias in Thebes, another in the Delta.

The myths about them all are fluid as the Nile, changing as they flow through the ages. Here is a religion without system, a thronged pantheon about whose occupants no two specialists are entirely agreed (they do not even agree about the spelling), and all the while the hawk-headed and the jackal-headed weather away amidst desert sands, and embalmed bulls bear testimony to a devotion which made Egypt a temple. Is there any key to a religion like that?

REASONS FOR THIS COMPLEXITY

The key to it all is just Egypt—the serpent strip of green fifteen hundred miles long, a jointed serpent, each joint an old, old province (the Greeks called them Nomes), forty-two joints in all, and each with its local gods older than any memory. The jointed serpent of land slowly became an empire with a reasonable unity of law and administration, though never entirely unified; it was too long. The first long and probably embattled period of consolidation ended with two kingdoms, south and north. This dual structure shows through the later imperial period, the great Pharaohs wore two feathers in their crowns, red for the south, white for the north. When, through any weakness, the state began to fall apart, the ancient divisions reasserted themselves. It has always been hard for kings to join what race and geography have put asunder.

The priests were no more successful in making a unified system of their religion than the Pharaohs in making an indissoluble empire of the land and its folk. Less so in fact for old and deeply rooted religious faith, custom, loyalty are more persistent than law and administration, having something of their own which neither King nor High Priest can reach and change. No essential unity of Egyptian religion was ever secured. The one king who tried it left only a psalm and a dream for all his struggle. The many priests who tried it did no more than group their gods in threes and nines, with no agreement among themselves. The divinities of Thebes and Heliopolis refused to be dethroned, the gods and goddesses of the Nomes lived on.

THE EGYPTIAN MIND

What geography began the essential tenacity of the Egyptian mind continued. The Egyptian was your ideal conservative. He made a net of his faith to catch and hold all that the current of time carried along. He added to his conservatism a quality not often associated with it; he was ideally tolerant. He never surrendered his own gods, but he welcomed with urbane open-mindedness any other divinities who knocked at his temple doors, made room beside his ancestral god for the stranger and worshiped both. It was no great strain on his devotion; the stranger was likely sun or moon or water-god under another name. Sometimes he hyphenated their names and made one god out of two. If Re[7] were his own sun-god and his neighbors had a sun-god, Amon, he built an altar to Amon-Re and went on about his daily ritual unperturbed. The gods did not care—why should he?

Egyptian theology was never from the first to last troubled by higher criticism. If two stories about the same divinity lacked consistency, no matter. The scribe simply wrote them down side by side or dovetailed them in as best he could and left a future of which he never dreamed to puzzle it all out. Erman[8] blames the very early discovery of writing by the Egyptians for the confusion of their religion. Once a thing got written it was sacred and final. A book might get lost or forgotten for a dynasty or two and then be found in some temple housecleaning and become a living influence again. It would be very much as if all the scientific publications for a thousand years were given the same authority. The scribes themselves were careless and in the course of countless recopyings all sorts of blunders crept in. The Egyptian faith grew by a process of accretion shot through with contradictions.

"But the priests," says an acute critic, "did not feel these absurdities as such; they saw profound wisdom in the contradictions and set themselves with an unparalleled ingenuity to disentangle the perplexities of their own creating"—(a not infrequent occupation of theologians). The Doctors of Divinity in Heliopolis acquired a reputation for wisdom, which they may or may not have deserved in the process, but logic meant nothing to them, nor did they ever exercise their wisdom in examining their religious inheritances. They conventionalized the very forms of their divinities. Once Horus became hawk-headed, he remained hawk-headed, and so with all the rest. They must have known the impossibility of it all but it never troubled them. It was all, I suppose, a kind of symbolism to which we have lost the key. They saw behind these curious forms natural forces and, maybe, spiritual reality. The wisest of them saw the idea behind the form; the unthinking worshiped as their fathers' fathers had worshiped and never reasoned at all; the hawk-headed one watched it all.

[7] Or Ra.
[8] *Op. cit.*, page 3.

The World of Egyptian Religion: Its Creation and Creators

Egyptian religion did change for all that. It began and continued as nature-worship but in its nobler aspects it became preeminently a sky and sun religion, the worship of a cloudless sky in which the sun is sovereign. There is no trace of storm gods nor the deified pageantry of the skies under which the Aryan faiths were nurtured. A rainless land vaulted with azure furnished no material for that poetry of nature-worship which is the charm of the old northern religions. The conception of the sky as a celestial sea on which the stars and the sun sail in boats[9] is the most engaging of the Egyptian conceptions.

Others are less poetic. The one significant thing in all these myths is that the Egyptian sky-divinity is feminine and the earth-divinity masculine. Those who claim that primitive religion reflects social organization would probably argue from that that the old Egyptian family was mother-ruled, and the feminine was therefore given the highest place in their religion. Some thought the heaven a great cow with her head in the west, the earth between her fore and hind feet and her underparts studded with stars. Others believed the sky a bending woman who touched the horizons with her hands and feet. She was sister to the earth-god, Seb or Geb.[10] In the beginning the sky lay upon the earth (a very widely held belief) and Shu, the god of space, thrust them apart. The lady thereafter maintained an uncomfortable and responsible position. The ships of the sun and the stars sailed across her body and she needed a god to hold her up.

If the sky were a cow, then the sun was a calf born every morning. If the sky were a woman, the sun was naturally her child. If the sky were a sea, then the sun sailed across it in celestial boats, changing from a morning to an evening boat from which he disembarked on the western horizon well nigh dead with age and needing to be renewed in the dark. The earth was a man lying prone and very patient. In a general way the idea of the sky as a sea was the more persistent. There must then be another waterway by which the boat

---

[9] Erman, *op. cit.*, page 7.

[10] Seb belongs to the oldest strata of Egyptian cosmic theology. Set is quite prehistoric and probably of Asiatic origin. He was eventually associated with the cult of the dead.

of the sun could get back into the east again so they fancied another Nile beneath the earth flowing "through caverns measureless to man." The passage of the sun-god through these dark and spirit-haunted chambers presently developed into a magnificent drama.

Like most primitive peoples, the Egyptians supposed the beginnings of all things to have been in some vast waste of water. In ways about which the Egyptian was somewhat uncertain the sun-god was born of these primeval waters. Some held he was hatched like a waterfowl from an egg, others said he was cradled as a child in a lotus blossom; the main thing is that he did arrive and, taking chaos in hand, finished creation. (These myths have no connection with the belief that the sun was born of the sky mother.) There are two versions of the Egyptian Book of Genesis which differ in detail rather than in substance. They are not altogether seemly in some of their details, but things had to get started somehow. It all comes down from a time which biological impossibilities could not stagger nor improprieties offend.

The Creator God speaks: (I use the second version.) "I was the Creator of what came into being. I came into being in the form of Khepera (the rising sun), coming into being in primeval time . . . I produced myself in primeval matter. My name is Osiris. . . . I have done my will in all in earth this, I have spread abroad in it. I raised up my hand, I was alone; not born were they. . . . I came into being from the primeval matter, coming into being in multitudes of forms from the beginning. Not existed created things any in land this. I made whatsoever was made everything. . . . I made what I made therein by means of a divine soul. . . . Not found I a place whereon I could stand. . . . I worked with the spirit was in my heart, I laid a foundation in my heart, . . . I became from god one gods three, . . . Were raised up Shu and Tefnut from out of the watery abyss . . . vegetation and reptiles came from the tears from me. Cried my eye, came into being mankind."[11] (The story of the generation of other divinities follows.)

Creation began, then, in a void of waters, the creator god issued, self-existent, from that void. No one creative act exhausted his power, creation began without the female principle (which contradicts other myths). But once Khepera had created, in a curious way, the first

[11] E. A. Wallis Budge, *The Gods of the Egyptians,* London, 1903, pages 313 et seq. This account is really a fusion of myths drawn from different sources.

divine pair, they begot divine issue. Men are the tears of the Creator, one of the most haunting conceits of any religion, though the poetry of it is a little clouded by the fact that the eye of Khepera is, plainly enough, the sun. And if man is sun-born, so is the dung beetle which in one way and another plays so large a part in Egyptian lore as symbol both of the sun and immortality.

FAMILIES OF GODS

The Egyptian created, in time, dynasties of gods as they had dynasties of Pharaohs though neither the listed names nor the order of divine succession agree. This was due to the different centers of Egyptian learning, the tangled growth of Egyptian theology and the long course of Egyptian time. The Greeks were fond of finding a resemblance between the gods of Egypt and their own pantheon; but the resemblance is forced. As the system became standardized, the Egyptian divinities fell into groups of three, a convenient family arrangement. One of the three was father, the second mother, the third son. These female divinities are generally forceless and color-less; they exist only to make the family complete. The son was in every respect like his father. When his father grew old and died, for the Egyptians believed that the gods could grow old and die, he took his father's place.

It was only through this natural succession that the gods of Egypt could be called eternal. The son who thus took his divine father's place was for all the practical purposes of Egyptian theology, the father, and, since logic is logic, the father himself is self-begotten since he lives in his son. Curiously enough, nothing is said about the divine mother growing old and passing away. Each great center of worship had its own trinity. There was a further tendency to combine the threes into nines; three was always a perfect number and three threes therefore would be more perfect still. The "nine" of Heliopolis were called "The Ennead," known throughout Egypt as the "Great Ennead."[12] The lesser gods were grouped in another "nine," which

[12] If the reader cares for their names and family tree this, from Adolph Erman, will do.

Sun God

Keb (Seb or Geb)	Tefnut
Shu	Nut
Osiris-Isis	Set-Nephthys

In each case brother marries sister. The Theban historians believed that these gods

gives us the eighteen outstanding divinities. If one stands far enough away from the general system, one sees that these gods are sun and moon, water and air, the reproductive forces of nature, just the unfailing elemental things in whose strength and gifts Egypt and the Egyptians lived. The sun is the greatest of them all. He may change his name but not greatly his nature; he shines through the myth and devotion of forty centuries.

THE SUN-GOD

He is the giver of all desirable gifts. Men and beasts pray to him at his rising and the lesser gods as well. "Glory to thee, thou who risest in the horizon . . . 'Praise to thee,' say the assembled gods. 'Thou beautiful, beloved child.' When he arises mankind live and the people exalt on his account. The gods of Heliopolis and the gods of both the great cities extol him. The baboons laud him, 'Praise to thee,' say all the beasts together. . . . Thou exaltest in thy barks, thy manhood is content and thou rejoicest, lord of the gods, over that which thou hast created. . . . The waters of heaven become blue in thy presence and at thy glance the ocean glistens."[13]

The sun-god changed his name from city to city; he never essentially changed his nature. The names do not matter except for the specialist; Ra, Horus, Aton or Khepri (various spellings) are the most important. They distinguish between the rising and setting sun. The comrades of the sun in the sky become the comrades of the sun-god in granite temples. The moon-god was Thoth, god of wisdom and learning. He gave men the gifts of speech and writing and invented arithmetic; he is the scribe of the gods and the judge in the heavens. All this, the scholars think, because moon phases furnished us our first calendar.

We have seen already how the sky was sometimes believed to be a cow and sometimes a woman in a permanently uncomfortable position. If the sky were a woman, she was the wife of the earth-

---

were the first kings of Egypt ruling in some distant and golden age. Amon-Ra, "the King of the Gods," was the founder of the state followed in order by Mentu, Shu, Seb, Osiris and Horus. (So Brugsch.) All the Pharaohs of the twenty-six dynasties were sons of the gods. The divine sonship of the King is the key to a vast "complex" of Egyptian faith and administration. They made it very concrete by assuming an actual divine generation.

[13] Erman, *op. cit.,* page 9.

god, and bore, to begin with, the unattractive name Nut. She was naturally the chief of the goddesses and, as naturally, worshiped by women; and just as naturally, being both a woman-goddess and a woman's goddess, she both changed her nature and her name, became Hathor, the divinity of pleasure and love. She took, to begin with, the form of the cow goddess but the Egyptians did not take kindly to so bovine a divinity, so they presently made her mostly human, leaving her nothing of her original status except her horns or else a kind of two-horned headdress. In another theological center she was Neith (or Neit), a very joyous divinity. She is sometimes called the mother of the sun. Another goddess who greatly loved dancing and music was represented with a cat's head; the Egyptian theologians could probably explain the connection. Some authorities made different goddesses of these elusive divinities. Breasted thinks them all variants of the sky goddess.[14]

All these are gods and goddesses of the sun-lit earth and sky. There were gods also of the dark and shadowy underworld; one of them, fittingly jackal-headed, superintended the process of embalming. Others were guides to lead the dead through pathless regions and still another was the keeper of the gates which led to the underworld. The gods needed temples and priests, sacrifices to meet their needs or buy their favor, liturgies of praise to satisfy their pride and save them, perhaps, from celestial ennui. Egyptian devotion provided all this. Their primitive temples were very simple, woven wicker-work perhaps, with projecting roof beams and two tall masts in front. The altar was a reed mat. The splendor of the great temples of the great dynasties makes Breasted lyric. Even the ruins of Karnak and Luxor cast such a spell over the imagination as few creations of human pride, power, devotion are capable of creating.

THE GREAT TEMPLES AND THEIR CULTS

These were the domains of the gods. Their massive structures walled out the secular world and secured for the gods an awesome silence in the heart of imperial cities. They were reached by "the road of the god," wide, straight boulevards guarded by statues of rams or lions. The temple enclosure was entered through the pylons, enormous tower flanked gates. A great court surrounded by colon-

[14] James H. Breasted, *A History of Egypt*, New York, 1905, page 9.

nades lay beyond the gates; there the populace gathered for their religious festivals. The temple itself was a long rectangle, two-thirds a noble columned hall. Behind the great hall was a lesser columned space for ritual ceremonies, behind that still, in utter darkness, the holy of holies where the god lived. (His wife and son had little unlighted apartments on either side.) The great hall was rich with color, its walls told in sculptured recitative the glory of the god who lived in the dark, the glory of the king who built the temple—and lived in the light.

Here, while time stood still, the priest performed his daily duties. "At the head of every temple was a high-priest who acted as overseer of all the sacred offices." He was learned in liturgies and the holy books, he administered the temple property and went out to war with the temple lords. He filled the holy of holies with the perfume of incense, he opened the cupboard chapel which curtained the image of the god, chanting ancient hymns of praise, low bent or prostrate. He made the daily toilet of the king of heaven, sprinkling him with water and clothing him with fresh linen. To feed the god he set before him bread, or geese or beef; he offered him wine and water and set his table with flowers. Then he shut up the little chapel in which the image of the god rested and left his divinity to the dark —and a mid-day siesta.[15]

The Place of Death and the Passion for Immortality in Egyptian Religion

By any test, Egyptian religion is a puzzle without a key save as we recognize how the Egyptian passion for immortality not only gave direction to the faiths of the land and strange content to all its customs, but ended finally by making it a land of tombs where the dead were of more concern than the living. We ought not to quarrel with this for the tombs have preserved for us whatever we know of the faith of the living. Other religions have made this present life the threshold of the eternal—Mohammedanism and Christianity, for example, strongly so. Buddhism asked only for those made perfect through the discipline of many incarnations, the bliss of final nothingness.

[15] Substantially from Adolph Erman, *op. cit.,* page 46 et sea. On feast days enormous offerings were made.

But the Egyptian had a passion for life which led him to challenge death with an actual fierceness of attack. He believed, as all primitive peoples, that every man had a double which he called his ka.[16] It is hardly accurate to call this a man's double; it was rather his living self, the force which kept him alive. A man received this ka at his birth as the gift of the sun-god. As long as he possessed it, being the lord of it, he lived, and when it left him, he died. No one ever saw it, least of all the particular lord of it, but it was naturally so exactly like him, the Egyptian believed, that if one could see it and the possessor of it at the same time he could not tell them apart.

The Egyptians were not content with giving a man one soul; they gave him more than one—though all this was the refinement of the general conception upon which the Egyptian doctrine of the future life was established. When a man died his ka left him, or rather, he became his ka. He was still himself but, being without a body, though he had bodily needs, he was at a strange disadvantage. It was necessary, therefore, to keep something to which this discarnate self might attach itself and the most natural thing to keep was the body. The embalmer's art accomplished just this; it was a gruesome art, nothing was left when the embalmer had done his work save bone and flesh and skin, shrunk and dried and asphalt covered. The dry air of the Nile Valley preserved what a gradual decay might otherwise have undone.

Burial Customs

If the Egyptian did not attain the immortality which he desired, he at least secured an uncanny permanence for his dried-up self which makes him a museum piece. The mummy itself was coffined and, if those who buried it were rich enough, it was hidden away at the heart of acres of pyramided stone, at the end of tortuous passages hewn into the living rock, or at the bottom of a shaft a hundred feet deep, filled in clean to the top to make it inaccessible. And all this that a man's soul might not be left bodiless.

It was even supposed that the incorporeal soul might attach itself

[16] May be capitalized. There was also the "Ba"—a bird-like soul, the "ab" used much as we use "heart"—a man would have a kind "ab"—and a "ran," the essence of a name, whatever that means. Used in magic and spell-casting.

to the graven image of a man if it could find no other support. Just at this point Egyptian logic breaks down hopelessly. After taking all this trouble to make a mummy, so to speak, stay put, the Egyptians still believed that a man's double could go back and reanimate his mummy and the two between them lead something of the life they had led before death. This involves some shadow of an older belief that even the mummy had a spirit and could range the world whether it were sealed in stone or not. I suppose there is some dim conception of reincarnation behind it all.

At any rate, in the vast adventures of life after death a man or a woman was going to need everything he or she had had on earth. He would need food and drink—these were provided by his relations, and the jars are still left which held the drink. He would need servants and, at an early time, they too were supplied by burying the servant with the master. This custom was discontinued in the course of time and images were supplied instead. If the image of a servant would be useful in the future life, so would the image of a boat and the general furnishings of house and farm—so these went into the tomb. They are the curiosities of our museums now and seem much like children's toys, though they are useful to teach us how old Egypt baked and brewed and in what state a rich man sailed the Nile.

They had a more serious purpose for those in whose tombs we have found them; they were to furnish them pleasant and opulent ways of life in the land of the dead. There are those who believe that even these furnishings and all the pictured representations of old Egyptian life found on the walls of mortuary chambers do not really represent the actual earthly estate of the buried. They were a sort of happy make-believe, as though these ideal conditions might be secured for the dead merely by painting them upon the wall. Egypt spared no pains to furnish the dead for the life beyond the tomb and gradually created an enormous literature about the under and the future world. The great survivals of Egyptian religious literature fall into two groups distinct enough and yet with a certain relation. The first is the story of the perilous journey of the sun through the underworld; the second, the book of the dead, deals more directly with the final judgment and the issues of the timeless life.

The States of the Dead

There is no more consistency in the vast complexities of the Egyptian conception of the underworld than in any other aspect of their religion. According to the older books, the state of the dead depended entirely upon the favor of the sun-god. They conceived the underworld as dark, spirit-besieged, peril-haunted. Existence there was at the best gray and joyless. Even so late as the Greek kings a woman speaks from the tomb in sculptured lament: "O father, husband, relative, priest, cease not to drink, to eat, to drain the cup of pleasure and of love, and to hold joyous festival; follow thy heart day and night and suffer not sorrow to pierce thy heart through all the years thou shalt spend on earth, for the West is a land of sleep and darkness, an oppressive abode for those who dwell in it. . . . They never wake again to look on their brethren, they know not their father nor their mother, their heart yearns not for their spouses or their children. The living water which earth holds for anyone who inhabits it is for me but a stagnant pool."[17]

There is an echo here of the weary underworld through which the sun fought his way every night. The Egyptians made a drama of it and divided it into twelve parts, each part an hour. The sun-god makes this perilous journey in a boat drawn by the dead themselves—for these regions are windless—through successive serpent-guarded doors, into regions always more remote. He is attended and guarded by lesser divinities, is challenged by hostile spirits, makes his way through darkness lighted only by serpents spitting fire. There is no possible creation of the Egyptian imagination, and no imagination was ever more fertile in the impossible, which does not appear somewhere in the course of this journey. The story of the entire journey is far too long to be told here, though it is illustrated with really consummate art in the papyri which recount it. As far as the dead are concerned, their fortunes are insecure at the best, grimly sad at the worst. They wait at the thresholds of the underworld to take passage in the sun's boat. If they do not secure this they must apparently wait till he comes again.

Certain of them are settled on ghostly lands by the sun-king's

---

[17] *The Old Egyptian Faith, op. cit.,* page 205. Compare Chaldean underworld and Hebrew sheol. Also Dante's Limbo.

favor as though he would supply himself with subjects to support him in his underworld realms. Others of them complete the journey with him and are thereafter free of the regions of light and a happier immortality. Those who are settled in the sad underworld live in darkness save for the one hour the sun passes their holdings. The issue of the soul's adventure after death, according to one school of divinity, depended upon an esoteric wisdom. One must know the proper rites and passwords, capricious and unreal knowledge which only the priests could supply. Since it was beyond any man to carry in his head, it was carved upon his coffin of basalt or diorite or else written down in guide books for the world to come, a kind of underworld Baedeker. These were furnished, doubtless at a fair price and, for the convenience of the dead, buried with them, so that a man might have his saving knowledge near at hand when the occasion came.

Books of the Dead

Our own knowledge of this phase of Egyptian faith we owe to these buried guide books. We can not be even sure that such conceptions of the state of the dead as shine a little through the passage of the sun in the underworld reflect primitive beliefs. The time backgrounds of Egypt are so vast that we are always losing perspective. We see it all as old Egypt, but for the Egyptians themselves, what happened a thousand or two thousand years before would doubtless seem as ancient as what happened in Rome seems to us. Egyptian chronology is a tricky business. There are enormous variations in base-line datings. One authority puts the first Pharaoh on his throne fifty-seven hundred years before Christ, another thirty-six hundred. It is, as Brugsch says, "as if one should hesitate whether to date the accesion of Augustus 200 B.C. or 1872 A.D."

This does not concern us here save as it is one of the keys to the inconsistencies of Egyptian belief about the state of the dead. No religion, even the most logical and authoritatively controlled, has ever managed an entire agreement about that fascinating matter. If in addition to this natural range of belief you add the always changing touch of time, you get a result through which only the wisest can feel their way. The Egyptian did not always house the discarnate in the dark; he dismissed them to sunset lands; all primitive folk have done that. The realms of the dead were called The West, the dead themselves, the dwellers in The West.

They did not, to begin with, draw moral distinctions in the issues of life beyond the grave or the mummy case. The great and the rich, they thought, would naturally fare better than the poor and unconsidered. It would be a gray existence at the best and the character of it was in the hands of the gods.

Or else they supposed that the dead flew up to heaven like birds. "He goes to heaven like the hawks. . . . He rushes at heaven like a crane, he leaps to heaven like the grasshopper. Thus he flies away from you ye men."[18] The heaven to which a man could leap like a grasshopper was not too far away and, since it was star-studded, why should not the dead themselves be the stars? This, too, is an old and almost world-wide belief. The pyramid texts contain almost endless variations of this star-dead motif and once imagination is released in these pathless regions anything is possible. One text describes the deceased as a hunter, who captures the stars themselves and devours the gods. If the dead did not inhabit the dark and fearsome underworld nor shine as stars, then they took boat to the islands of the blessed. Perhaps, as Erman suggests, these islands of the blessed were in the Milky Way which seems sometimes like the quiet wash of celestial waters against shores of illimitable blue.

THE FIELDS OF EARU

There was a natural resemblance between the geography of the beatific islands and Egypt. Their lands yield the departed the food without which even the dead can not continue their immortal course. There is a Tree of Life in the Field of Earu upon which the gods sit, by whose fruit they themselves are nourished and which they share with the blessed dead. The felicities of the delivered are simple enough. "He receives his share of that which is in the granaries of the great god; he is clothed by the immortals; he has unfailing bread and beer. He eats this bread quite alone, no one stands behind him." In general the dead share the food and drink of the god and are beyond the fear of famine.

These fields of the blessed are none too easy to reach; the dead might be carried across the waters by divine birds, or else there were

[18] Erman, *op. cit.,* page 88.

heavenly spirits to ferry them over. Or else, and this echoes another belief, they would get across in the boat of the sun-god himself. The most part, however, believed that there was a ferryman called "He-who-looks-behind" and "Turn-face"—this because he punted his boat across standing with his back toward the celestial fields.[19] (There have doubtless been other pilots to the land of the blessed who have occupied the same inconsistent position.) But he would not take over all claimants; only those who were just, which is the dawn of ethical understanding destined to brighten with the development of the Egyptian faith. The fortunate were welcomed on the other side by divinities who washed and dried them. There is distinct evidence of a belief in a physical resurrection. The scattered members are now in some mysterious way united. Those who believed this took all possible pains to keep the mummy just where it was buried, but we ought not to ask of the Egyptians here a logical consistency beyond our own.

THE MYTHS OF ISIS AND OSIRIS

As the religious faith in Egypt reached its full development, all teaching about the future life was so associated with Osiris as to make it quite necessary now to tell his piteous story. Osiris and Isis were husband and wife and also brother and sister. They were the great-grandchildren of the sun-god. In that ancient time the gods themselves were the kings of Egypt and Osiris ruled over both Egypts, north and south, with a right, therefore, to both the white and the red crowns. He was a good king and kind to all his subjects and "he shone forth on the throne of his fathers as the sun, established truth in Egypt, the fear of him had fallen upon his enemies and he enlarged the boundaries."

He was king of the gods as well, a truly exalted station but not without its perils. Set, his brother, was his sworn enemy and sought in every way to do him harm. For long Isis defended him. "She was his safeguard, warded off his enemies . . . Her word did not fail and she was admirable in command." Set slew Osiris by a trick. He made a chest which just fitted him and persuaded Osiris to try it on whereupon he (Set) locked the chest and threw it into the sea. One sees here clearly enough a dramatic variant of that old struggle

[19] Erman, *op. cit.,* page 93.

between light and darkness which all ancient religion to a degree reflects. Isis set out to find her husband's body. Time made a pathetic legend of it all which grew without ceasing. "She sought him without wearying; full of mourning, she traversed the land and took no rest until she found him." She found him presently and the way of her finding is a long story richly embroidered.[20]

As Plutarch tells the story, the body was again discovered by the enemies of Osiris and torn into fragments but Isis for a little reanimated it and became thereby the mother of Horus. The lament of Isis is thus a comparatively late voicing of an ancient grief and echoes the lament of the women of Babylon over the dead Tammuz, for without any doubt something comes in here from other faiths and Isis herself becomes kin to Astarte and Aphrodite—women who forever seek their dead lovers, the lovers themselves, in all the splendor of their youth, having been to begin with perhaps the vegetation spirit. Osiris was not that to begin with, though when the Greeks and Romans got hold of him he ended as an actor in the age-old drama of the decay and renewal of life.

The sorrow, therefore, which sounds through the lament of Isis is a very old and universal sorrow. "Come to thy house, come to thy house . . . thou who hast no enemies . . . Come to her who loves thee, come to her who is mistress of thy house . . . I call to thee and weep so that it is heard even to heaven but thou dost not hear my voice."[21] This lament according to one variant of the tale moved the gods to pity and through their power the dismembered body of Osiris was restored and Isis became the mother of Horus.

Horus inherited his father's feud against Set and carried on long and indecisive warfare whose tumult is heard incessantly through Egyptian myth. Set became more and more the personification of all evil, the most hated of the gods, so that it was forbidden to pronounce his name but he was never entirely defeated for all that. Why should he have been? He is darkness, the desolation of desert lands, dearth, whatever you please, and though life and light wage a long fight with such as these they are never entirely conquered. Meanwhile, though Osiris could not be again enthroned in Egypt, Isis succeeded in having him enthroned in the halls of the gods. Set challenged his legitimacy even here, but his cause was supported

---

[20] The material for this may be found in any standard study of Egyptian religion.
[21] Erman, *op. cit.,* page 33.

by the supreme court of the Egyptian deities and thereafter he ruled as one dead come to life.

He was, by virtue of all these experiences, preeminently the king of the dead and the guarantor of their immortality. Egyptian faith identified the dead themselves with Osiris, called the dead Osiris, adding their own proper names thereafter as though a man after death should become Osiris John Doe, or Osiris Richard Roe. The resurrection of Osiris, for it was a resurrection, guaranteed the resurrection of all his followers. "Even as Osiris lives, he also will live; even as Osiris is not dead, he also will not die. Even as Osiris is not destroyed, he also will not be destroyed."[22] These great sentences and the faith which lay behind them became the basis of the Osiris mystery and have had an enormous reverberation. There are imaginary speeches of the dead in the Book of the Dead in which Osiris is prefixed to the name of the deceased followed by prayers and hymns of almost every description.

The Hall of Judgment

Egyptian theology finally achieved a dramatic and reasonably unified description of the last judgment. The soul after having won its way to the hall of the Two Truths through many perils and much opposed by evil spirits faces "Osiris the Good Being, the Lord of Life, the King of Eternity." The forty-two judges of the dead surround him, each pronounced judgment in respect to some particular sin. The probationer was received by the goddess of truth and required to repeat the oath of clearing. (It would be interesting to print Job's great oath of clearing in a parallel column.)

> I have not committed fraud and evil against men.
> I have not diverted justice in the judgment hall.
> I have not caused a man to do more than his day's work.
> I have not given way to anxious care.
> I have not been weak.
> I have not been wretched.
> I have not caused a slave to be ill-treated by his overseer.[23]

---

[22] This re-appears in the Graeco-Roman mysteries.
[23] There are many versions of the oath of clearing. See Erman, *op. cit.*, page 103; Naville, *op. cit.*, page 187.

And so the declaration goes on: the one on trial protesting that he
has not brought any to hunger, caused any to weep, committed
murder, been impious or impure, taken milk from the mouths of
children, stolen cattle, diverted irrigation canals, netted the birds of
the gods or defrauded the temples.

These quotations give us the best known record of the moral
standards of Egypt at its best. These texts maintain a noble level
and, if they were lived up to with reasonable consistency, must have
created just and self-mastered character. The dead often plead their
good deeds in epitaphs which are not conspicuous for modesty. "I
did that which is right," says one Egyptian who has been an asbestos-
coated mummy for these thousands of years. "I hated evil, I gave
bread to the hungry and water to the thirsty, clothing to the naked
and succored him who was in need."

Osiris, however, did not accept the mere word of the anxious soul.
The truth of what he said was thereafter tested by balancing his
heart in the scales of judgment. The heart was put into one scale
of the balance and a feather, the symbol of truth, in the other. If
his heart was lighter than the feather the truth was not in him. The
proper gods superintended the weighing with very great care and a
fearsome demon is always near by apparently to tear him to pieces
if the balance went against him. If the soul passed the test, it was
thereafter free of the celestial regions. There is an ancient version of
the verdict of the gods: "The princess is triumphant; she has been
weighed in the balance . . . in presence of the powers of the hall of
justice. No fault has been found in her; her heart is according to
truth, her members are pure . . . the tongue of the balance shows
true . . . Let her go forth victorious to enter into every place she
pleases and be with the spirit of the gods. She will not be repulsed
by the guardians of the gates of the West."[24] Egyptian theology was
not clear as to the fate of the condemned though there seems to be
some intimation of annihilation.

The whole scene is vividly pictured in one of the papyri with all
the actors in their proper places. Curiously enough the sculptured
scenes of the last judgment above the doors of the French cathedrals
repeat the same drama with the soul in the balance, though at Notre
Dame the soul is weighted against a little demon and not against a

---

[24] Naville, *op. cit.*, page 190. For a short study of Ancient Egyptian morality, see
W. M. F. Petrie, *Religion and Conscience in Ancient Egypt,* New York, 1898.

feather. We have already considered the wide variety of Egyptian belief as to the state of the blessed dead. There was a persistent belief that they became the cultivators of the soil in an unfailingly fertile land where the barley grew to an impossible height and no one was ever hungry. One sees through this as through a window that there must have been times in Egypt when a good many people were hungry if heaven were as simple as that.

CONCEPTIONS OF A HAPPY AFTER LIFE

This primitive conception of a purely agricultural heaven did not appeal to luxurious city dwellers; they did not relish the prospect of the manual labor thus involved. Egyptian funeral customs show first and last a good many devices to avoid callousing soft hands in the islands of the blessed. A most convenient and inexpensive device which was later almost universally adopted was to put little toy figures with hoes and baskets in their hands in the tombs. These were by a kind of magic to become servants in the next world. "O thou Ushebti when I am called and when I am required to do any kind of work which is required in the underworld . . . cause the fields to flourish, to irrigate the banks, to convey the sand from the east to the west, thou shalt say: 'Here am I.' "[25] The most characteristic Egyptian conceptions of the life of the blessed in the world to come picture them as living in the prosperous and careless estate of a well-to-do Egyptian citizen.

In such ways as these Egyptian faith placed an enormous emphasis upon the cult of the dead. A variety of funeral custom which would make a book in itself grew out of these beliefs. His proper entombment became the supreme concern of any subject of Pharaoh and Pharaoh himself. The cult of Osiris, the dogma of the underworld the theory of the relation of soul to body made Egypt a land of tombs. These tombs grew from low-walled, flat-roofed shelters containing one or two chambers to terraced pyramids challenging the stars, into whose stone heart one now climbs by long dark passages to find at the center of a million tons of stone only an empty chamber where Cheops once slept with no disturbing dream of a rude invasion. Or else the dead drove their shafts into the cliffs of the valleys of the kings, or committed themselves poor and unconsidered to the

[25] Erman, *op. cit.,* page 140.

sand, but always with the expectation of passing through the judgment hall of Osiris and thereafter to the fields or islands of the blessed.

Since the dead needed food and drink the living supplied that and left endowments for perpetual provision. These endowments suffered, as other pious endowments have suffered, being in the course of time diverted to the uses of those who had more recently died and whose anger was more to be feared. It became the main business of the priests and the guardians of the temples thus to minister to the dead. As the centuries flowed on the real population of the Nile Valley was not the living but the dead.

EGYPTIAN RELIGION AND THE COURSE OF EGYPTIAN HISTORY

The larger aspects of Egyptian religion were bound to be affected by the rise and fall of dynasties and the fortunes of the state. As capital cities were built and deserted, or at least left empty of imperial pomp, gods who had lorded it over centuries and palaces fell back into the shadowy throng of gods and others took their places. Thebes is a name to conjure with in Egyptian history. After the middle kingdom, say 1800 years B.C., Asiatic aliens came in, took by force the throne of the Pharaohs, and dealt harshly with the state. They were rulers of no mean power; they have left their records in Crete, in Palestine, and as far south as the first cataract, but their capital city is so completely perished that even its site is unknown. The Egyptians themselves did everything to efface the records of their rule. They came, they ruled, and they were finally overthrown by a strong prince in Thebes who began a new and glorious period for the delivered land. It is a fascinating story but we are concerned with only the religious aspects of it.

Amon was the hereditary god of Thebes. He was hardly sun-god to begin with, he may have been the reproductive force of nature, but, being just that, it was easy enough for him to become sun-god. In this new incarnation he gained a great following; officials prayed to him for promotion, the oppressed put their piteous estate in his hands, the devout made no promise without adding: "If Amon permits me to live." His really great estate began with the triumph of the Theban Princes who drove out the shepherd kings. Thereafter he ruled in an always crescent splendor. Rā or Re became his associate and as Amon-Rā he ruled a far-flung empire from a grandiose capital.

The great temples of Karnak and Luxor were rebuilt and made splendid in his honor. Hymns sung to other divinities were rephrased to voice his praise. All the powers of the Creator were ascribed to him, "who hath made all, the sole one, with many hands. He commanded and the gods came into being, . . . He it is who makes pasture for the herds and fruit trees for men. . . . He creates what is needed by the mice in their holes and that which feeds the birds upon all trees. He is of kindly heart. When men call for him he delivers the fearful from the insolent. . . . 'Glory to thee,' says every wild creature; 'Praise to thee,' says every desert."[26]

The power of Amon-Rā was challenged by a king of the great line which exalted him. The Pharaohs of this period ruled from the fourth cataract to the Euphrates; their word was law for the princes of Syria-Palestine, the Kings of Babylon and Nineveh besought their favor, "They held the gorgeous East in fee." Amenhotep (Ikhnaton)[27] IV, son of Amenhotep the magnificent, was a dreamer who inherited an empire no dreamer could maintain. He was doubtless influenced by the all-embracing character of his realm and he conceived a divinity sovereign enough for so vast an empire. He claimed to have been the instrument of this new revelation, though he made no attempt to conceal the identity of his new deity with the old sun-god Rā. "It was known in my heart, revealed to my face, I understood."[28]

He broke with the established church and erased the very names of immemorial gods from their monuments. He found an old name for his new divinity and built three new cities for his especial sovereignty. Aton (or Har-Akhte) was really the old sun-god more universally conceived and endowed with new attributes. The hawk-headed figure of the god is gone and instead Aton is symbolized by the disk of the sun itself from which the rays stream out ending as hands extended in gift and benediction, one of them holding the symbol of life.[29]

[26] Erman, *op. cit.,* page 59. Naville, *op. cit.,* page 143.
[27] Also spelled Akhnaton and Akhenaten-Aton or Aten.
[28] Breasted, *op. cit.,* page 360.
[29] There is really a lovely picture of the young king and his wife with their children about them, sitting reached and touched by these sun-ray hands spread palm downwards. I wonder if the ecclesiastic posture of benediction is thus derived. Amenhotep's

The Splendor of the Sun

The parenthetical name for Aton given above, Har-Akhte, means "the splendor, who is in the disk of the sun." It is as though the young king were reaching behind the most splendid symbol he knew for "something far more deeply interfused." He was reaching toward a spiritual interpretation of religion. For the time all that way of thinking of gods in human terms which we call anthropomorphism disappeared. The king sought also to banish superstitions; even the tombs became more bright and human and there are two hymns left which are the distillation of this splendid and ephemeral faith in strophes which will bear comparison with some of the noblest of the Hebrew psalms. Indeed, there is a parallelism between the hymn of the splendor of Aton and the One Hundred and Fourth Psalm absolutely arresting. There are versions enough of this hymn—here are passages from a translation by Breasted:

> Thy dawning is beautiful in the horizon of heaven,
> O living Aton, Beginning of life!
> When thou risest in the eastern horizon of heaven,
> Thou fillest every land with thy beauty;
> For thou art beautiful, great, glittering, high over the earth;
> Thy rays, they encompass the lands, even all thou hast made.
> Thou art Re, and thou hast carried them all away captive;
> Thou bindest them by thy love.
> Though thou art afar, thy rays are on earth;
> Though thou art on high, thy footprints are the day.
> Night
> When thou settest in the western horizon of heaven,
> The world is in darkness like the dead.
> Their heads are wrapt up,
> Their nostrils stopped, and none seeth the other.

.   .   .   .   .

mother was Tiy—a woman of unroyal birth. The more imaginative historians have conjectured that she was Semitic and brought some gleam of Jewish Monotheism to Egypt. No authority for that, says Breasted. His wife was Nofretete, probably of Asiatic birth. He was greatly under the influence of these two women and they may have had some share in what happened. Incidentally there is no standardized way of writing all these names. Each scholar takes his own line—a minor and irritating way of asserting one's authority. The real trouble in all this Egyptian spelling is the lack of vowels in Egyptian written characters.

Every lion cometh forth from his den,
All serpents, they sting.
Darkness reigns (?),
The world is in silence,
He that made them has gone to rest in his horizon.

Day

Bright is the earth,
When thou risest in the horizon,
When thou shinest as Aton by day.
The darkness is banished,
When thou sendest forth thy rays,

. . . . .

How manifold are all thy works!
They are hidden from before us,
O thou sole God, whose powers no other possesseth.
Thou didst create the earth according to thy desire.
While thou wast alone:
How excellent are thy designs, O Lord of Eternity!

. . . . .

By thee man liveth,
And their eyes look upon thy beauty.[30]

The vastness of the Egyptian Empire at its zenith speaks through these great passages but there is something vaster still—the range of spiritual understanding which sees all lands and all living things and beauty and truth and the outgoings and incomings of life as the revelation of a power which considers them all and can establish a temple in the heart of a man. All distinctions of race are swept away and the King of Egypt praises the common father of humanity.

Did Egyptian faith ever attain a loftier range than this? That is a debated question depending upon difficult points in the translation of the texts, conceptions of Egyptian philosophy, and the temperament and the temper of the translator as well. There are passages which seem to support monotheism. "Lord of Heaven, Lord of Earth, Maker of Beings Celestial and Beings Terrestrial, God One." "One alone he made what exists, not is known his growth." There is sufficient authority for and against this point of view. Older scholars believe that Egyptian faith began with monotheism and ended in

[30] *Op. cit.,* page 371.

sadly debased forms. French scholars have maintained this position with eloquence and enthusiasm; but a more hard-bitten scholarship is inclined to doubt it. The idea of a pure monotheistic faith gradually breaking up into polytheism is opposed to the general course of religious development.[31]

Any such study of religion as this is always missing what it meant to the devout through an excessive concern for what it means to the historian. Any religion long vanished leaves only the dead outside things of it behind—such things as time and war and slow decay can not undo. What made it a religion—the devotion of the worshiper, his reverence and adorations, his prayers and the sense of help he took away with him from strange altars are gone.

HYMNS AND PRAYERS

Egypt has kept for us a little of this soul of her religious hymns and ascriptions and now and then a prayer, through which one catches some note of the cares and aspirations which prayer has always voiced: "Come to me, Thoth, . . . Come to me that thou mayest lead me . . . I am a servant of thine house. Let me tell of thy mighty works in whatsoever land I be." Another is more worldly: "O Thoth, place me in Hermopolis, in thy city, where life is pleasant. Thou suppliest what I need in bread and beer, and thou keepest watch over my mouth in speaking."

"Come to me, Ré-Harakti, that thou mayest care for me. . . . My requests are heard and my daily petitions, my praises at night and my prayers, which are perpetually in my mouth—they are heard today." And this which voices a timeless confession: "Punish me not for my many sins, I am one that knoweth not himself. I am a witless man. All day long I follow my mouth like an ox after fodder." There is a prayer for help in a lawsuit and another asking for help in most unseasonable weather: "The winter is same as summer, the months are reversed and the hours are disordered."[32] In such fashion old Egypt prayed.

[31] This whole question is discussed at length in *The Gods of the Egyptians*, E. A. W. Budge, Vol. I, page 131 et seq.

[32] All this from *The Literature of the Ancient Egyptians*, Adolph Erman, New York, 1927, pages 305 et seq.

THE TWILIGHT OF EGYPTIAN RELIGION

The faith of Egypt did not long maintain itself upon the lofty level of the Hymn to Aton. Amon-Ra had too many priests, too many temples, too many vested interests. After the death of King Amen-Hotep IV a family fiercely devoted to Amon came to the throne. They erased the old records, made the old temples still more splendid and rich beyond belief. At the peak of its power the temple of Amon at Thebes "possessed nine hundred twenty-six square miles of land, eighty-one thousand three hundred twenty-two serfs, four hundred twenty-one thousand three hundred sixty-two head of cattle." It is pretty hard to carry through a religious revolution against an endowment like that. Then came the long twilight of Egypt and her gods. After the Rameses nothing vital came into Egyptian religion; there was an increase in the belief in magic, a growth of superstition, an always increasing confusion because, like the Bourbons, the Egyptian theologians of the last thousand years before Christ forgot nothing and learned nothing.

There was a period, no need to date it, when Egypt, having little to ask from the future, turned its eyes to the past and undertook the restoration of old customs, the re-enthronement of old gods. The most dramatic element in this last phase of Egyptian faith is animal-worship. Herodotus saw that in full action and was never done wondering at it. The Sacred Bull Apis was chosen for his markings, stabled in splendid temples, embalmed with oil and wrapped in linen, and after his death coffined in cedar, and to further protect his bovine sacredness, sealed up in a sarcophagus cut from a single block of granite. The cat began to come into her own. Mummified cats were buried in such numbers that their bodies have lately been used to fertilize the land—an unhappy issue for even a feline divinity.

The common people, as always, had their own curious little gods who for all their grotesqueness were near and friendly enough to do those constantly daily services which lowly humanity needs and which the high gods are too much occupied to perform. There was naturally a seepage of other religious faiths into Egypt and just as naturally an extension of Egyptian faith beyond the borders of Egypt. The Greeks were great traders, they were given quarters of their own in Egyptian cities where they had their own temples and their own gods. They were the first accurate observers to see Egyptian civilization before the material splendor of it had begun to grow dim. The strange mystery of it impressed them greatly and they ascribed to the Egyptians a wisdom which probably was exaggerated.

Isis and Osiris Go to Rome

Isis and Osiris crossed the Mediterranean; the other gods and goddesses stayed in the Nile Valley and watched history rewritten. They were so old that there was no record of when they had not been, but they had no power to renew themselves. The old kings became shadows, Persia reached her long arm into the Nile Valley, Alexander took the realm and built his city at the mouth of the Nile. Jews came down from Palestine, new combinations of religion supplanted the gods of the Egyptian pantheon and the lore of the Egyptian priests. Christianity found in the old Egyptian memories, particularly in the legends of Osiris and Isis, something which made it not too strange to the land of the Pharaohs. It suffered, as it has always suffered, some change in winning Egypt, taking into itself something which had been there before it came, but it won Egypt for all that.

As in Rome, there were supporters of the old Egyptian order who distrusted the new and loved the old, and foresaw calamity to the state in the new religion. There is a strange echo of the words of Symmachus, the Roman Senator who fought the last battle of vanishing Roman paganism in front of the altar of Victory, in the last protest of an Egyptian priest who voiced the sadness of a lost cause and a dead faith. As he sees the old religion abandoned and the new one triumphant he cries out:

"O Egypt! Egypt! there will remain to thee nothing of thy religions but vague tales which after ages will not believe; nothing but words graven on stone, telling of thy piety. The Indian, or some other barbarian neighbor, will inhabit Egypt.

.   .   .   .   .

"I address myself to thee, O most holy Stream, and I foretell thy future. Tides of blood, polluting thy divine waves, will overflow thy banks; the number of the dead will exceed that of the living; and if any inhabitants remain, they will be Egyptian only in their speech,

but they will be foreigners in their ways. Dost thou weep, Asclepius?
There will be things sadder still. Egypt herself will fall into apostasy,
the depth of evils. She, in other days the Sacred Land beloved of the
gods for her devotion to their service, will be the perversion of the
holy ones; this school of piety will become the model of every violence. Then, full of the disgust of things, men will no longer have for
the world either admiration or love."[33]

A strange and prescient prophecy! Egyptian Christianity was
always violent. It perished in the blood-bath of Mohammedanism.
The arresting issue of Egyptian religion is its vast sterility. Hebraism
may have been a little influenced thereby. Isis and Osiris found
priests, temples and devotees in Rome. Nothing else ever fed the
living stream of the world's faith. Thebes became a memory, Karnak
and Luxor awesome ruins. The time-scarred Sphinx guards violated
tombs and pathetic memories, gazing in infinite retrospection upon
sun-rises which no longer stir stone Amon to song—and the sons of
an alien race clear the sand from his feet.

CHAPTER APPENDIX: A LIST OF SOME EGYPTIAN DIVINITIES

This chapter has said very little about the 500 (or 1200) major
Egyptian divinities; even the specialists confuse their accounts, do not
agree in their spelling and are often quite vague about the exact
character of the god—or goddess—in question (which is to be expected because, very likely, the Egyptian priests were quite confused
themselves). Flinders Petrie in Hastings (*op. cit.,* Vol. V, pages 244
et seq.) offers a working list and classification.

Sacred Animals: Baboon (emblem of wisdom); lion and lioness;
the cat family (little and big); bull, ram, hippopotamus, jackal (god
of the dead); mongoose and shrew-mouse. The Hawk (important),
vulture, goose, ibis. The crocodile, frog (emblem of crowds, not worshiped), cobra, various fish and the beetle (emblem of immortality).

Animal-headed: Khnumu, ram-headed creator; Sekhmet, lioness
goddess; Bastet, cat-headed; Anubis (important) jackal-headed; Set,
a very old divinity with a checkered career ending as an evil spirit;
Horus, the hawk-god (powerful).

Human gods: Osiris, Isis (see text); Nephthys, sadly neglected
wife of Osiris but loyal to him. Horus again (many myths, ends as

[33] Naville, *op. cit.,* page 318.

son of Isis, influenced Christian art). Amon (see text) Mut, early Theban goddess, protector of kings and queens, occasionally wears vulture headdress. Neit, quite early and presumably domestic.

Cosmic gods: (later periods) Rā, sun-god, important, very likely came in with Semitic invaders, capital city Heliopolis, hyphenated with Amon. Khepera, the rising sun, associated with XIX dynasty creation myths. Aten or Aton, the radiant, energy-giving, life-bestowing sun, reflects Syrian influence, highly praised, almost monotheistic. Nut, goddess of the starry heavens; Seb, earth god, very old, food-giver; symbol, the goose, called the "great cackler." Shu, god of space; symbol, an ostrich feather. Hapi, the Nile god, masculine in form, feminine breasts.

Abstract gods: Ptah, also creator, much fused with other divinities; Min, abstract father-god. Hat-hor, abstract mother-god. Late. Maat, goddess of truth; no temples, no offerings, no personality. Nefertun, attractive young vegetation god, related doubtless to Tammuz and Adonis. Safekht, goddess of writing. The Egyptian loved to write—had papyrus which helped.

There are foreign gods of whom Ashtaroth is an example. That lady always found it easy to get worshipers—anywhere.

The more important of these divinities had their proper feast days which controlled the Egyptian calendar year. Horus had three, Isis three. The feast of the Sorrow of Isis was December 3, as near winter as Egypt could manage.

CHAPTER III

The Gods and Faiths of Babylon and Nineveh

SOMETIME between the early middle ages and the beginning of the nineteenth century a great city was lost. It carried an imperial splendor with it as it melted down into mounds of clay. It once had walls upon which a four-horse chariot could be turned, was entered by a hundred gates of brass and was towered and templed and palaced. It would seem hard to lose a city like that. It carried into dust with it also its gods, its records and all understanding of the characters in which its records were written. Oblivion seemed to have locked its doors and lost the keys, and all its glorious past to have gone as the priests of it believed the dead went:

To the land of no-return

But the past of it has been dug out of the dark, its clay tablets and sculptured slabs have become vocal, its kings have found interpreters for their proud records, its gods have issued from their buried temples. The story of the excavations which have opened streets that Hammurabi used is the romance of archaeology. The barest account of the method and endless labor which have deciphered the combinations of little arrow heads and wedges in which the records of the empires were written is the noblest of testimonies to the power of the human mind.[1] The religions thus recovered are not only of very great interest in themselves but strategically significant through their influence upon other religions, particularly the Hebrew religion. What then is this religion whose recovery has been one of the great achievements of the last one hundred years? The gods of Egypt were stay-at-home gods; their standards never led marauding armies to far conquest, save, perhaps, the winged sun disk. They asked only a darkened holy of holies to keep out sun heat and glare, to be fed and praised and washed and dressed and left to their peace. Their worshipers did not ask too much of them nor they too much of their

[1] For a brief and lucid account of all this see *The Religion of Babylonia and Assyria*, Robert W. Rogers, New York, chapter one. Also *The Civilization of Babylonia and Assyria*, Morris Jastrow, Philadelphia, 1915, chapters one and two.

worshipers. They served the pride of kings, the importance of priests, the speculation of the philosopher, and the need of generations who asked only to pass safely the two Halls of Judgment after death, and live on as before.

The Two Rivers and Their Valleys

Eight hundred miles east everything was changed. Two rivers drain the highlands of Armenia and flow through Mesopotamia as they flow through history. The Euphrates is about eighteen hundred miles long, the Tigris eleven hundred fifty. The two rivers once emptied independently into the Persian Gulf. All the land now south of their junction is made land—made since human history began. Inland towns once were coastal—Eridu, for example. It is now one hundred thirty miles from the Gulf with a proven age of seven thousand years. These rivers, low banked, have created by deposit a soil of marvelous fertility. Wheat and barley seem to have been native to Babylonia—gifts for which an always hungry world should be grateful. Such a land was bound to be a nursery of civilization and to be much fought for by always restless folk whom the parched deserts and the bleak plateaus which border the river valleys could not feed.

Destiny, geography, race and ambition made two states of the valleys of the two rivers. They were not great states territorially. Assyria was a bit smaller than Nebraska, Babylonia about the size of West Virginia. Assyria was mountain-walled. Babylonia looks through shimmering heat across alluvial plains toward the Persian Gulf. Because they had nothing better than brick to build with, time and the elements have reduced their proud cities to mounds, which, for almost a hundred years now, excavators have dug through to recover their records and their monuments. The records thus recovered tell a long and stirring story. It is told on sculptured slabs, on broken clay tiles, or tablets strangely like a hand-grenade, written in a script whose translation is one of the triumphs of scholarship. The scholar has been served by the excavator who has dug from culture to culture and sifted the dust to recover the shards of empire, law and faith. The records themselves reveal a past whose perspective is lost in the morning sky line of history.

The ghosts of vanished Sumeria come to life. Sargon of Akkad goes out to found an empire. Hammurabi decrees that if a man give his son to a nurse and the baby die and the nurse substitute another child without the consent of the parents, her breast shall be cut off. Ashurbanipal defiles the tombs of dead kings, a banking house has its affairs given unexpected publicity, and the women of Babylon weep for Tammuz. If all these vanished folk could read what scholars have made of them, they would wonder twice—once that we know so much and once that knowing so much we can not agree how to spell their names.

Babylonia was always more than Babylon. It was a region of little city states controlling territories as large as half a dozen Nebraska counties. Their fortunes changed with the centuries and there were centuries enough to allow for many changes. Much could happen in a land whose early records can be conservatively dated three thousand years before Christ. For all our knowledge of them they are little more than names and they rise and dissolve like clouds. We know that they were rich, for the golden headdresses of their kings are the treasures of our museums; that they were proud, for they proudly told their conquests to the world; that they were devout, for they have left us the names of their gods and the lore of their priests; we know that they fought, for they have left us their treaties of peace.

Each city state had its god, bore his name. Whether the city was named after the god or the god after the city is a nice point—the god likely gave his name to the city. He possessed no more than the city possessed. His frontiers marched with the frontiers of a rival god and he sat upon a precarious throne, for he shared with his worshipers the fortunes of war. If they conquered a neighboring state he supplanted a defeated deity and established himself in a captured temple; if their army was defeated he himself became captive or subject. This gave Babylonian and Assyrian gods an interest in war and "world politics" which is reflected in prayer and worship. The kings pray their gods for victory and under the circumstances the gods are sure to have done their best. But the kings were just; they acknowledged their indebtedness to their militant deities and built them more splendid temples out of the loot.

THE RACES WHICH PEOPLE THE VALLEYS

The dominant race was Semitic, a race of tenacity, genius and power of adaptation. First and last, the Semitic genius gave its own character to Babylonian-Assyrian religion. But there were the

Sumerians before the Semites. "These were a dark-haired people"—
"black heads," the texts call them . . . "judging by their physical
type they were of the Indo-European stock."[2] They were very likely
hunters and mountain folk before they came down into the valley.
Nimrod the mighty hunter is remembered in Genesis as lord of
Babylon, Uruk and Akkad in the land of Shinar. Sumerian plastic
art remains to show us what they looked like. Jastrow thinks they
conformed to the Mongolian type. You have only to place, as he
has done,[3] the sculptured faces of the Sumerian and Semitic types
side by side to see which was destined to survive in their struggle
for survival. The round-headed placidity of the Sumerian was no
match for the strong-nosed, long-headed, hawk-eyed fierceness of the
Semite.

Actually the matter was not so simple as that. (It is risky business
condensing history into an epigram.) The Sumerian was in the end
supplanted politically, though he reasserted himself vigorously for
one long period. He mixed his racial strain with the Akkadian and
the "Babylonians of history were born." The fusion of races and
cultures made a new race and a new culture, destined to leave
their mark upon history as the seals they used to sign a king's
proclamation, a banker's acceptance or a physician's prescription left
their mark on a clay tablet. Specialists do what they can to assign
the various elements in Babylonian language, script and religion to
their far-off sources and are by no means agreed. A broken clay
tablet is a dusty window through which to see the life and faith of
five thousand years ago.

The Sumerian element in Babylonian religion is certainly the
older and nearer the source of all religion. These round-headed folk
began with spiritism—though possible "animatism" would be nearer
the mark. Everything had life in it—the picture word for life was
a flowering plant. But life was motion, force, energy. It acted in a
sped arrow as well as a date palm—the moving lived, the motion-
less was dead.[4] The moving force in a man was his Zi. It made him
a living personality in this world; it survived death and continued
his existence in the underground world of shades. He was supposed
in the person of his Zi to need, as all primitive folk think their dead

---

[2] They invented cuneiform writing, used principally to hand down religious writings.
[3] *The Civilization of Babylonia and Assyria*, Plate XXII.
[4] Sayce, *The Religions of Ancient Egypt and Babylonia*, page 276.

to need, what he had needed on earth and to love what he had loved
—a child's toys and a woman's beads were buried with them. "A garment to clothe him, and shoes for his feet, a girdle for his loins and
a water-skin for drinking, and food for his journey have I given
him." So the living did their duty to the dead.

A SPIRIT-HAUNTED RELIGION

The gods had their own Zi's as well, for the gods also might grow
old and die. This primitive spiritism faded out, but the idea of dusky
beings, who lived in the underworld or haunted desert places, persisted in the popular religion. One name is as good as another for
such beings; the Sumerians called them "Lil." They were mischief-
making spirits, haunting the dark, coming up in the storm wind
and the dust cloud to torment mankind. It is naturally difficult to
deal logically with ghosts and demons. They are sexless, to begin
with, partly because Sumerian grammar made no distinction in
gender in its word forms. Semitic grammar was more particular; the
name of a demon or a divinity had to be masculine or feminine.
The Lil, therefore, became male and female and, being individual-
ized, were spelled with a capital letter. The ghostly siren of the early
faith who visited men in their dreams to their undoing became Lilith.
Lilith became in Palestine a predecessor of Eve, a woman of no
soul and dangerous allure, supplying a fascinating material for Rabbinic speculation and modern romance.

These beings of the dark and the dust persisted till Babylon was
only a memory. The elemental aspects of any religion may be over-
laid by a richer development, but they never entirely disappear. They
persist in customs whose reasons have been forgotten, in rituals
which take new forms. In Babylonia they were always more real to
the common and unlettered folk than the divinities of the priests.
The actual commerce of the people was with them rather than with
the high-gods.

They were, in Babylonia, the restless spirits of the unburied dead
or else insurgent ghosts who had escaped from the realm of the
dead. They could be summoned from the nether world by black
magic to do mischief to an enemy or answer a question, as Samuel's
ghost was summoned to doom Saul. They might also be supernatural
beings of a low sort and generally malicious. They were highly

specialized. There were demons for consumption, fever, ague, head-ache. They molested women in childbirth and stole new-born children. Their very names betray them: They were "pestilence," "the seizer," "the one lying in wait," "destroyer," "storm." They took terrifying bestial forms masquerading as leopards, dragons and serpents. They are associated in groups of seven—

> Standing on the highway, befouling the street,
> Evil are they, evil are they,
> Seven they are, seven they are,
> Twice seven are they.
>
> . . . . .
>
> No door can shut them out,
> No bolt can turn them back,
> Through the door, like a snake they glide,
>
> . . . . .
>
> Tearing the wife from the embrace of the man
> Snatching the child from the knees of the man.[5]

Babylonian folk-faith was steeped in demonism, and it has carried far. There is sound reason for believing that Hebrew faith got its demonology in part from Babylon and, once between the covers of the Bible, the influence of this darker side of a vanished religion has profoundly influenced western religion.

Were All the Gods Ghosts at First?

Some of these Sumerian ghosts and errant spirits, especially the more important of them, become Semitic gods, though the specialists do not agree as to their characters. More recent scholarship is turning altogether away from the ghost theory which for a long time determined the approaches to Babylonian religion. "In the very earliest Sumerian texts the gods are already present and worshiped."[6] As far as this earlier faith lived on it became a later superstition, creating a popular cult whose object was defense against evil spirits or else the deliverance of those who had fallen into their power.

Some spirits of the old order became the servants and messengers of the gods, charged with errands between the divinities themselves

---

[5] Morris Jastrow, *Religious Beliefs in Babylonia-Assyria*, New York, 1911, page 311.
[6] Rogers, *op. cit.*, page 77.

or between the gods and man. Here, as far as I can make out at least, is the earliest form of that belief in angels which has had so telling an influence upon religion, poetry and art and satisfied so instinctive a need of the devout. There were profound distinctions of character and office among the attendant and messenger spirits of Babylonian faith. Some of them, being in the trains of the gods of light, were angels of light. Others followed and served Tiamat, the mistress of darkness and chaos. There were messengers of darkness and evil, taking on a distinctly demonic character. There are records of great fighting between the two hosts.

The Persian conceived these opposed and always embattled hosts of light and darkness even more clearly and dramatically than the Babylonian—and between them they contributed material for a Christian writer to use in the first century[7] in his expectation of the Last Judgment and for John Milton to unfold in an epic splendor of celestial warfare. The greatest of these spirits of light become archangels. Finally through assimilation with the winged creatures painted on the walls of the temple of Bel, the mightiest of them all become Cherubim and Seraphim, winged presences in constant attendance upon the Most High, bowed in reverence with wing veiled eyes. So Isaiah saw them in his mystic vision. In the last period of mature Chaldean speculation, they become aspects—or perhaps, incarnations of creative power "the successive thoughts of the Creator realizing themselves in the successive acts of creation." Sayce, who makes this suggestion, advances it cautiously. At any rate these wind blown spirits of a faith earlier than history suffered many and strange changes, ending, as so many things in religion do, far and different enough from their beginnings.

The Influence of the Semitic Race on the Religions of Mesopotamia

All authorities are agreed that fully matured Babylonian and Assyrian religion is the creation of the Semitic genius. This gifted race has been the outstanding creator of religions. This is their enduring contribution to the order of the human spirit. They have

[7] "And the angels that kept not their own principality, but left their proper habitation, he hath kept in everlasting bonds under darkness unto the judgment of the great day." Jude, chapter I, verse 6.

had empires neither inconsiderable in extent nor brief in term. A race which dominated western Asia for at least fifteen hundred years and, at intervals, ruled from the Persian Gulf to the Nile has a right to be reckoned among the empire builders. But a strange fatality attended their armed conquest. Their empires dissolved like the brick walls of their old capitals. Their cities are memory and dust. Only gray and weary old Jerusalem of all the cities their kings called their own endures—and Jerusalem is a mandate of the League of Nations.

But in a more imponderable empire, their thrones are secure. Wherever God is clearly conceived, and endowed with wisdom, will and love; wherever he is Creator instead of the vague and formless source of some vast cycle of emanations, there the Semite has been. And the historic value of the religious records of Mesopotamia is that here, for the first time, that genius is seen in full action and we are able to follow its processes across a long millennium. There was, beyond debate, a marked Semitic element in the Egyptian stock, who transformed the marshes of Egypt into ploughed fields and built so strongly that time arrests itself before their creations. But there were other than Semitic strains in Egypt; we can not call Egyptian religion the Semite's pure creation. Allowing for these elements which he took over from the Sumerian, Babylonian religion is his creation. What did he bring to so great a task, how did he carry it through, what did he leave behind him?

He had, to begin with, the courage entirely to personalize his gods. He was not alone in this. As soon as any religion passes from the lower levels to polytheism its gods—or goddesses—are bound to be personalized. But the Semite did a particularly clean cut piece of work. The gods of Egypt never got entirely clear of their brute inheritance. They carried a hawk's head or a ram's head till time beheaded them, but "the deities whose figures are found on the seal cylinders of Babylonia or engraved on the walls of the Assyrian palaces are all alike in 'the likeness of man.'"

The time would come when the Semite Jew would make no image of Jahweh at all nor liken him to any of those creatures from which the gods of Egypt had emerged as from a chrysalis always to carry about some evidence of their metamorphoses—but there was one likeness the viewless Jehovah could not escape—the likeness of man. His ways were higher, but they were not utterly alien. The Semite always gave his gods an ample sovereignty. The gods

of Egypt reign but do not rule; the gods of Babylonia have essential
force. Their names indicate that. Bel means Lord; so does Nin; if
the word were not so strange we should recognize in Bel of Babylon
the Lord of Babylon and sense a kinship with vanished devotees we
do not now feel. These lords were subject to the contingencies of
time and circumstance. They might rise—a few of them—to an imperial sovereignty and go out to conquest with Sargon or Sennacherib; they might themselves be conquered and become exiles in a
strange temple with another god to lord it over them.

Toward the west—in Canaan and Philistia they become lordlings
—or else they were only that to begin with—local gods of fields and
springs, with an association with the goddess of fertility which did
their reputations no good. So they pass out of history diminished
and satirized by the Hebrew prophets. But at the height of their
power they ruled imperially—and too often, mercilessly. As Kipling
says somewhere, the gods who rule with a too high hand are presently forgotten and never regretted.

There was always an intimate relationship between the Babylonian
gods and their worshipers. The god must protect the devout, defend
his own realm, bless the arms of his warriors and give them victory
in battle. The worshiper must honor his god, support his worship
and make his temple splendid. He never entirely refused to recognize
the god-head of other divinities. They were for the most part so like
his own Bel, that he found no great difficulty in acknowledging them
or adding them in some subordinate way to the train of his own
divinities. But he did persist in a very literal way in having no other
gods *above* his own deity, so making him the ruler of the divine
hierarchy. It is the last step but one in the long ascent which leads to
an undivided faith in one God.

GENERAL CHARACTERISTICS OF CHALDEAN AND ASSYRIAN DIVINITIES

Any account of the high-gods and goddesses of Babylonia and
Assyria is in part a study of strange names, in part the story of the
rise and fall of little city-states and, in general, the shifting of the
centers of power from the south to the north. It is a study also in the
Chaldean conception of the universe. All the divinities are personifications of the forces of nature. The great divinities are the great
forces of nature, the sun and moon, the stars, the storm, the all-

containing sky and the void of waters. The same general division of
the visible universe into earth and sky and the underworld which
we find in Egypt and nature religions everywhere holds in Babylonia
with the important addition of the watery void. There is a persistent
tendency in fully developed polytheism toward triads of gods.

On the banks of the Nile the triads are husband and wife and
son, on the banks of the Euphrates they are much the same. Every
city had its own divine family but in the high Babylonian pantheon
family arrangement yielded to cosmic suggestion and the great triad
were the gods of the watery void, the earth and the sky. The ruler
of the underworld was a goddess, though she was later compelled to
share her administration with a masculine deity. Life-begetting and
life-containing forces—especially the vegetation quickening force—
were also deified. These, as Jastrow notes, are the elemental things
upon which nomad races and farming folk depend. Their favor is
food and well-being, their enmity hunger and death. The climate
of Mesopotamia made its valley dwellers keenly conscious of their
dependence upon sun power and sky favor and still more keenly
conscious of their caprice. Irrigation served their need a little, their
canals, whose ruin has gone far to turn the land into malarial
swamps, certainly controlled the overflow of the river. But rain and
drouth counted for far more in Babylonia than Egypt. The winter
rains were kind to the crops, the arid and burning summers unkind.
Even the irrigation canals were dependent upon the water god whose
home was in the two rivers and the Persian Gulf whom the Babylonians named the "Father of Waters."

We shall never know, perhaps they did not know themselves, why
one city chose the sun and another the moon god for its patron
divinity. Given some turn of devotion, some lost association of ideas,
and prayers were said to Shamash, Sin or Enlil in cities through
whose narrow streets the devout sought their temples to ask a
priest to consult the oracles for them, deliver them from misfortune
or supply them some mournful chant to confess their sins. The real
trouble is that we have nothing left but the bare bones—mostly names
—of all these vanished cultures and religions.

If only some worshiper or Enlil could tell us what peace he found
in his prayers or what longing brought him to the temple door,
Enlil and all the rest would begin to live again.

MEANINGS OF THE NAMES

The gods and goddesses are really "Lords" with designations to identify them. There were Lords of the Storm-winds and Lords of the Clouds and a Lady of the High Mountains who should have been a consort of the Lord of the Clouds. They were Lords of now forgotten cities. The Lord of Girsu, for example, as though there should now be a Lord of New York or London. Other names are more general: Lord of that Which is Below; Lord of Strength; The Mighty One of the Great Dwelling-place. (One finds similar ascriptions in the Hebrew psalms.) The Servitor became one of the greatest divinities; another was the Light-furnisher[8]; still another, the Brilliantly Shining One, or else there is simply the title, Lord (Bel). Every Babylonian god whose name begins with Nin is Lord of something or some place. The names suggest greatness and command, they express dependence, reverence and adoration. These are the timeless and creative elements in all religion. Touched with their light any name however strange or remote glows fadelessly. The temples for all their strange names are but the "houses" of the gods. Sometimes they are called after the gods who live in them—did not the Jew call his temple the house of Jehovah?—or else they are named for some forgotten association or distinction. They are literally "the lofty house," "the great house," "the great palace," "the summit house," "the heavenly house," "the house reaching to heaven," "the brilliant house," "the house of the glory of the warrior."[9] They were poets, these builders of vanished temples and they could still teach us something. How much more interesting it must have been to go to "the house of him who gives the scepter of the world" than the "Second Any-Denomination-You-Please-Church"!

The actual course of Babylonian religion was most affected by what is nothing less than the history of the valley of the two rivers. The general course of the empire was northward. The Semite supplanted the Sumerian. The endless fighting between proud little city-states ended, as it always has, in the supremacy of some one of them—and not always the oldest—predestined for empire. Many

[8] Morris Jastrow, *Religion of Babylonia and Assyria*, Boston, 1898, pages 51 et seq. This book is relatively old—some of the interpretations may have been changed.

[9] *Idem*, page 638.

things combine to create an imperial city: Its human stock, capacity for order and administration, the meeting of trade routes, economic hinterlands, and often "the man on horseback."

In such ways as these Babylon became Babylon even to "the man on horseback." After that it planted a colony to the north, warden of the gates of the hills from which the two rivers drew down. The daughter became greater than the mother. For six hundred years Assyrian Nineveh held western Asia in fee—and then was done for almost over night. Patiently waiting Babylon regained her throne, put her crown on again, ruled arrogantly for a hundred years, opened her undefended gates to Cyrus—and being then very old and very tired was content to be only Babylon. Now the gods and goddesses of the race and the region shared all the fortunes of the mighty historic sequence.

THREE OLD TOWNS FURNISH THREE OLD GODS

Three old, old towns finally yielded to Babylon and gave her domain and divinities. Eridu supplied Ea, the god of watery wastes. Nippur gave Enlil, lord of storms (or, maybe, ghosts), Uruk gave Anu, lord of heaven; these three between them ruled the universe. Ea, lord of the watery wastes, should be the oldest of the triad for Babylonian cosmogony began with a landless void of waters. When land was finally created (formed, as one tradition holds, from the body of a great dragon) it was still surrounded by water and supported by water, like an old round Chaldean basket of a boat, bottom side up. There are Babylonian legends enough of creation—to some of which we shall presently return. Eridu, which first worshiped Ea and once faced the Persian Gulf, conceived him as creator of all mankind and everything else. He was the god of the watery world, both of the waters on the earth and the waters beneath the earth. His temple was called "house of the ocean."[10]

He was also the divine potter[11] who made man of clay, clay being the only building material Eridu knew much about anyway and rarely suited to the purpose. Ea was naturally partial to the clay mixed creature he had created. He is always the friend of humanity,

---

[10] Rogers, *op. cit.*, page 81.

[11] A. H. Sayce, *The Religions of Ancient Egypt and Babylonia.* Edinburgh, 1902, page 304.

the teacher instructing men in the arts of life. He teaches them how to farm and how to work in metals and stones, he gives rulers their wisdom and fosters civilization. When the other gods grew impatient of humanity and planned to drown them all, Ea, remembering perhaps that they had once been clay and were slow to escape its earthiness, forewarned a human friend of his and so saved the race. There was a report that Ea had even sought to make man deathless but was defeated in this dubious kindness through man's cautious unwillingness to eat the fruit of the tree of life.

Hammurabi pays such deference to Ea as one king pays another; "the great prince, whose decrees take precedence, the leader of the gods, who knows everything."[12] Something must be allowed for Hammurabi's diplomacy (he flatters all the gods) for, as a matter of fact, Ea though the oldest of the great ones did not head the Babylonian pantheon; which was perhaps just as well for it was a perilous position. He was more honored in being the god of civilization and the friend of mankind. Enlil the god of Nippur was the greatest of the early Babylonian deities. The ancient and sacred associations of his city gave Enlil his prestige.

Nippur was from a staggering antiquity the religious center of the Sumerian settlements and it never lost its primacy. It was the cathedral city of Chaldea. Twenty kings rebuilt or adorned its temple and great conquerors were proud to call themselves Lords of Nippur. When it ceased to be a city of the living, it became through its sanctity a favorite place of burial. Even Jews and Christians used it for a necropolis centuries after the memory of its one-time greatness was lost. All this was very likely because demons would not haunt a soil so sacred. Scholars are not agreed as to Enlil's original nature. Sayce calls him lord of ghosts and discovers in his cult such magic arts as might lay a ghost and protect the living from their malice.

Jastrow began with this explanation and later changed his mind. He makes Enlil "Lord of the Storm" ruling to begin with from mist-hidden, wind-haunted mountain tops and not from the realm of ghosts. He was—so Jastrow believes—a divinity whom the Sumerians brought with them from their native uplands. His worshipers tried to make his temples as much like a mountain as possible—even in the lowlands. They called his house "the mountain house" and built terraced towers at one end of it on the top of which

[12] Code, Harper's translation, page 105.

he had his shrine. The tower of Babel is doubtless a misty memory of such towers. The Mohammedan minarets and the spires of Chartres may alike be remote descendants of these tower shrines built to make a homesick god a little more content.

THE CHANGING FORTUNES OF ENLIL

God Enlil is a very good illustration of the changing fortunes which attended the procession of a storm-god in Babylonia for about two thousand years beginning about 3000 B.C. His cult reflects the rise and fall of city-states, changing conceptions of natural forces, the development of the religious mind, the influence of the theologian, and what time is always doing to any religion. The oldest hymn in his honor exalts his strength and authority.

> O Lord of the lands!
> O Lord of the living command!
> O divine Enlil, father of Sumer!
> O shepherd of the dark-headed people!
>
> .   .   .   .   .
>
> Strong Lord, directing mankind!
> Hero who causes multitudes to repose in peace![13]

He is also addressed as "lord of vegetation," "the great creator and sustainer of life." In an entirely different rôle he is "an onrushing storm none can oppose," destroying crops and homes. In the final formalized adjustment by the Babylonian Doctors of Divinity he was assigned the sovereignty generally of the earth order, its surface, its lower atmosphere and the underworld with some of the glory and responsibility of a sun-god. His worshipers seemed to have felt his storm force before they felt that lordship of the sun which asserts a final sovereignty over every storm. At the peak of his power "he is saluted as Bel, the great lord, the command of whose mouth can not be altered and whose grace is steadfast."[14]

When Babylon had conquered Nippur and Eridu and all the other old cities, it gave to its own local god Marduk the powers and attributes of the conquered deities and, among the rest "the honor and

---

[13] For a slightly different translation see Jastrow, *op. cit.,* page 195.
[14] Rogers, *op. cit.,* page 80.

title of Creator of the World, which had originally belonged to Enlil." Thus he ended in eclipse, but the religious conceptions which he represented persisted in changed forms. He illustrates happily what has always been happening in religion. Enlil had a wife at one time—even the domestic relationships of the gods are unstable—and a son. His consort was the supreme lady and queen of the lower world. She was largely a concession to celestial domesticity but Ninib, the son of Enlil, was a deity of real importance. As far as Enlil was sun-god he was the storm bringing sun. Ninib, his son, was the friendly life-giving sun. For even the empire of the sun-god was divided. There is a sun who blesses his worshipers with verdure and rich crops and a sun which burns the fields and harasses men with pestilence. The theologians finally worked out a fairly consistent solar theology. Ninib was the morning or spring sun.

Nergal, "the mighty one of the great dwelling place," became the noon and mid-summer sun. His association with plague and death gradually darkened his character and, since he sent so many to death, he was properly assigned a lordship over the realm of the dead, a victim to the association of ideas and Babylonian logic. "Great art thou in the realm of the dead, without a rival art thou."

But the sun was, on the whole, more kind than cruel, and Babylon finally fixed upon Shamash as the supreme and beneficent sun-god. His rule was long and unchallenged. He had no especial city of his own, which, perhaps, made him more available for any city. He was strong, friendly and healing. He was asked to give life to the sick and drive darkness from the house. He was "King of Judgment," dispensing justice (the moon-god had that office in Egypt), creator of prosperity and arbiter of fate. As near as there was any god in Babylonia whose judgments were true and righteous altogether— Shamash was that one.

He was praised at sunrise—

> O Lord, illuminator of the darkness . . .
>
> .   .   .   .   .
>
> For thy light the great gods wait,
>
> .   .   .   .   .
>
> The banner for the wide earth art thou,
> All mankind look upon thee with joy.

And at sunset—

> O, Shamash, on thy entrance into the heavens
> May the resplendent hosts of heaven greet thee.

And there was always great concern in Babylon lest he should lose his way across the sky or fail to appear in the morning.

ANU, THE GOD OF THE CELESTIAL EXPANSE

The third of the high gods of old Babylon was Anu. He is in general the god of the heavenly expanse, the whole celestial region of sun and stars and what was above them—in a word, the god of heaven. So relatively abstract a conception as this is slowly reached. It is a theologian's idea. Primitive observation arches earth with a solid firmament and sees in the spaces between only the mystery of dawn and dark, the play of light and cloud and the tumult of warring elements. It needs long observation and some power of abstraction to throne the gods of the heavens in the empyrean. But once his position is established all things combine to do him reverence. He becomes the chief of all the gods, the sun himself is subject to his rule and he directs the celestial order.

In the final recension of Babylonian theology, Anu becomes the father of all the gods and the father of Ishtar as well—is not the fertility of the earth the creation of the brooding sky? Here then is the old Babylonian trinity—Anu, Enlil and Ea—the heavens, earth and the watery void. This Babylonian triad contains everything—the waste and wonder of the shoreless sea, the unresting processes of the earth itself, the entire content of atmosphere and sky, the celestial bodies and life and death. No wonder that the borderlines between the lesser divinities are indefinitely drawn, or that the gods who share this cosmic empire are not always able clearly to delimit their own frontiers. Nor did the great three reign in Babylon unchallenged. They eventually surrendered their power—willingly, as the records of the devout assert—to a deity greater than themselves. The throning and dethroning of these ancient divinities was not entirely a matter of celestial diplomacy or warfare. The gods rose and fell as the center of power shifted from one city to another and possibly from one dynasty to another.

There were two divinities, however, which do not fit easily into any scheme and are still too important to neglect. One of them lay one side the line of historical development, the other was always a goddess to whom the other Babylonian divinities found it difficult to accommodate themselves. The god was the moon, the goddess was love and elemental desire, the creative urge and creative quickening power.

There is sound reason for believing that moon-worship was older than sun-worship in the regions about Babylon. The moon is really more arresting to the primitive mind than the sun. The changing phases of the moon supply the first natural measures of time. There is an old and tenacious association of religious observance with the changing phases of the moon—the times of the new and full moons are most arresting and religiously observed.

Abraham's city, Ur of the Chaldees and Haran were the ancient centers of the worship of the moon-god Sin. The texts and inscriptions exalt him as light-giving and god of wisdom. He is represented on the seal cylinders as an old man with a long beard seated beneath a crescent moon, whom his worshipers reverently approach.[15] The moon-god could punish evildoers with leprosy, he is to be evoked at the founding of a city and he ends in astrology as a guide to action rather than a divinity. If he has any particular interest for us now it is because an old hero of Hebrew faith left the city which worshiped him to seek "a city which hath a foundation, whose builder and maker is God" and because Ur itself has yielded such jeweled treasures to the archaeologist.

The Cult of Ishtar

Ishtar is another story. She had by nature a gift for travel and finally came to Palestine also, where she sadly distracted the sons of Abraham, having changed her name a little and her nature not at all—unless for the worse. She is the one goddess in Babylonian religion with any force. All the other female divinities were only shadows to begin with and finally less than shadows. But Ishtar became *the* goddess, a lady of contradictory qualities but high command. In the Pantheon of Assyria she was a war goddess and the wife of their chief god. She was sometimes almost Diana with her

[15] Jastrow, *op. cit.*, plate LXXVI.

bow, a virgin who demanded the sacrifice of virginity. She may have been the planet Venus to begin with—there are those who think she was—and associated as Venus so often is with the moon-god. But outstandingly she became the goddess of love, divinity of instinct and desire without whose ministrations life would become sterile, worshiped by rites which shocked even Herodotus, and a Greek of Herodotus' time did not blush easily.

But there was more to the sacrifice she asked of womanhood than shame. She is the incarnation of the mystery of generation. Her rites are such as secure the fertility of fields and flocks. Her worship is the worship of life, her rituals are the old, old ways of creative desire, the sacrifice she asked was rendered, as so many sacrifices were rendered, in kind. Herodotus saw the curious shame of it, the sanctity behind the shame he did not see. Her cult, for all you would think no woman would favor it, was a woman's cult. They kept it alive in Babylon perhaps because all the other gods were men's gods, perhaps because they saw in her the deification of the timeless office of womanhood and felt in her worship the consecration of it.[16]

Hammurabi Makes Marduk Supreme

Perhaps if the little states in the lower valley of the two rivers had been left to themselves they and their gods would be forgotten. But about two thousand years b.c. the first of a long succession of empire builders came into action. Hammurabi made Babylon his capital and brought warring city-states to heel. He was a great conqueror, a greater organizer, a law-giver whose code is the first published system of law in the world and, by all the records he has left us, just and kind. He did not destroy, he unified. The Babylonian empire was his creation and thereafter, until Assyria was done for and Cyrus took Babylon without a struggle, the history of the valley of the two rivers is the story of the varying fortunes of the incessant conflict between Babylon and Nineveh. In that long conflict Babylon was once utterly destroyed but it arose from its ruins. Even in the great days of Assyrian supremacy, it remained the capital of religion and learning,

[16] With the addition of Shamash (the Sun), Sin and Ishtar formed a second triad. Adad or Ramman often replaces Ishtar.

a source of influences which are still felt in the development of religion and civilization.

Now the patron divinity of Babylon was Marduk (or Merodach, if one please). The crescent power of Babylon carried him to dizzy heights and Babylonian pride and devotion clothed him with the attributes of vanquished deities. A prayer of Nebuchadrezzar—often quoted—shows in what honor he was eventually held:

> O eternal ruler, lord of all being, grant that the name of the King that thou lovest, whose name thou hast proclaimed, may flourish as seems pleasing to thee. Lead him in the right way. . . . Thou hast created me, and hast intrusted to me dominion over mankind. According to thy mercy, O Lord, . . . may thy supreme rule be merciful. . . . Grant me what seems good to thee, for thou art he that hast fashioned my life.[17]

This shows what a series of royal patrons can do for a god. Marduk was a small-town deity to begin with and a parvenu, for Babylon was a clay-built village, a colony of Eridu perhaps, when Nippur and Eridu were already old. But destiny was with Babylon and Marduk. When Hammurabi had conquered all his enemies and made Babylon the capital of Babylonia, he not only shared his glory with the god of Babylon but gave him credit for his victories and took the land as from his hand He was never done praising him. Marduk was sun-god to begin with but as the supreme deity of a great state he is a magnified king, the protector of the weak, considerate of the imprisoned. Mountains and all waters are subject to his rule. The lesser gods take no action without his advice, life and death are in his hands and he wears a horned crown.

He had few shrines outside Babylon but his temples in that city were called "the lofty house" and "the true house." He permitted the gods of old and proud cities to have shrines within them but their subordination was complete. Theology and tradition conspired to exalt him. He had his poet laureate, his priests contrived explanations of his high estate which would do no dishonor to the great three whom he supplanted. The gods themselves, so the priests said, voluntarily transferred their powers to him in heavenly council and re-

---

[17] Rogers, *op. cit.,* page 163. For a more literal translation see *Cuneiform Parallels to the Old Testament,* R. W. Rogers, New York, 1926, page 369.

turned content to their shadowed shrines if only he might reign in
the light. "They rejoiced, they paid homage, 'Marduk is King!'" He
became all that they had been. Old hymns were edited to praise his
name, old rituals readapted to suit his needs, old prayers redirected
to reach his address.

He became a Hero God. The great Chaldean epic of creation, the
tale of cosmic struggles between chaos and creative order became the
song of the might of Marduk. There are four Chaldean myths of
outstanding importance: The Creation Myth, The Story of Adapa,
The Gilgamesh Epic and the Story of the Deluge and Ishtar's Descent to Hades.[18] Their texts have been recovered from the library of
Ashurbanipal, broken records which a patient scholarship has assembled and translated. Time and war are never kind to baked clay and
there are gaps enough to be filled by conjecture or left unfilled. But
their substance is recovered and between them they reveal to us the
mind of their world and their time about the beginnings of the
world and the first dealings of the gods with one another and with
men.

The Creation Myth

The story begins when the heavens and earth were not named and
no field was formed not even a marsh. Tiamat, the mistress of mis-
rule, chaos itself, lorded it over the formless world and threatened
the very gods. They sent Anu out to fight her and he fled frightened
before her, the story of the titanic fight being vividly told. The other
gods refuse the combat. Marduk volunteers but drives a hard bargain
with the terror-stricken gods.

> When I shall have become your avenger,
> Binding Tiamat and giving life to thee
> My command in place of thine should fix fates
> What I do should be unaltered
> The words of my lips be never changed or annulled.[19]

They accept the conditions having no other choice and Marduk thus
became Lord of fate. He arms himself with the four winds and the

---

[18] Rogers, *Cuneiform Parallels to the Old Testament, op. cit.,* is the most accessible
and best of the English translations.

[19] Jastrow's translation. Also see Rogers, *op. cit.,* page 22.

tempests, a panoply plainly borrowed from Enlil. The gods praise him as he goes on to fight.

> Thy weapons will never be vanquished;
> They will shatter thy enemies.[20]

(I wonder if there is any echo in this of Babylonian bards singing before the chariots of war lords as these went out to battle.)

Armed with the thunderbolt, upright in his chariot, with the seven winds in his train Marduk rides out. There is such boasting on either side as properly introduces an oriental duel and the fight begins. The outcome is decisive. He caught the lady in the net of the winds, directed a wind in her face. Her mouth was unhappily open—probably to have the last word—

> The lord spread out his net and caught her,
> The storm wind, that was behind, he let loose in her face.
> When Tiamat opened her mouth to its widest
> He drove in the evil wind, that she could not close her lips.
> The terrible winds filled her belly,
>
> .   .   .   .   .
>
> He seized the spear . . .
> . . . he pierced her heart.

No more strategic fight was ever won with wind for a weapon.

He seized the tablets of fate from Tiamat's brood and the gods and not chaos are the masters of the universe and destiny. Marduk now proceeds to the work of creation. He splits Tiamat lengthwise— "like an oyster"—

> The one half he fashioned as a covering for the heavens,
> He fixed a bolt, he stationed a watchman
> He commanded them not to let her waters come forth
>
> .   .   .   .   .
>
> He made strong the bolt on the left and on the right,
> In the midst thereof he fixed the zenith.[21]

Here is plainly a conception reflected in the cosmogony of the book of Genesis, with its God-made firmament and division "of the waters which were under the firmament, from the waters above the firmament," and its appointed station for the sun and moon and stars.

[20] See Rogers, *op. cit.,* page 25.
[21] Rogers, *op. cit.,* pages 27-33.

The bolt and the guardian are the Signs of the Zodiac; by such a grandiose belt of constellations the upper waters are kept secure in their place, and the world saved from such a catastrophe as happened, when during forty memorable days the bolt was drawn and the "windows of heaven were opened." Marduk apparently fashioned the earth out of the other half of Tiamat's body, though the poem does not mention it.

Scholars, who are loath to take any epic at its face value, find in all this the sun-god of Spring with his victorious winds driving back the Winter tempest and dark, a glorification of the vernal equinox the issue of whose tumult is warmth and life. The whole gorgeous story was dramatized and acted in Babylon at the vernal equinox. Woven through it all is the result of a relatively mature meditation upon the ways in which earth and heaven came into existence. Marduk is the creator and hero of it all. Did ever a sun-god run so glorious a course?

MARDUK IS CONQUERED BY ASHSHUR

It should not have been far from Marduk to Monotheism.

Hebrew devotion later recast these memories of dawn beginnings, understandings of earth and sky common to the region and the time, poems of creation and cataclysm—in a word material which the priests of Babylonia used—and give it a highly ethical form and an essentially monotheistic spirit. Even the Egyptian psalm to Aton reaches a level of insight and majestic sense of the Divine Spirit to which Marduk was never lifted. Perhaps if Babylon had grown old in undisputed empire and the lesser gods had passed through their twilight to dark, Marduk might have reigned alone. He never reached that aloneness, though there are prayers, psalms, penitences of old Babylon which the purest faith could use. After all the music of any religion is played upon the chords of devotion stretched between the worshiper and his god. Those chords are strangely independent of time and circumstance and one hears some haunting music of them from the clay tablets upon which the prayers and hymns of a vanished faith have been preserved. There is a hymn to Ramman through whose lines one hears the long reverberation of the thunder; a processional hymn to Marduk with very noble lines and many very human prayers. The road from the plains of Babylonia to the Eternal was not barred.

Marduk ran a glorious course, his city ran her glorious course also. Then Assyria seized the reins of empire and ruled the Fertile Crescent from Nineveh. Change of empire and change of gods. Some of them stayed at home; others, being used to moving, went north. There they found Ashshur, Nineveh's patron god. He is strangely colorless, being neither the personification of sun, moon, star nor element, a local deity serving Nineveh's need when the place was only a frontier post. He became the symbol of its might and devotion when the city became an empire—the empire was only the city far flung. He went out with the king to his wars, he had a banner of his own, an old sun-god symbol—a winged disk; perhaps he borrowed that from Egypt, and a figure of a warrior with a bent bow above the disk—the warrior was certainly Assyria's contribution. That banner ranged far and fiercely.

The kings of Assyria, being long victorious, gave Ashshur great praise therefor keeping still sufficient glory for themselves. The creation stories were re-edited to exalt Ashshur. An Assyrian King with a patriotic-theological train of mind, moved the stranding place of the Ark from the mountain of Elam to a mountain of his own. In general Ashshur was everything in Assyria that Marduk had been in Babylon—which is enough. When the great empires of the two rivers passed into history, they had shared between them something like fifteen hundred years of history. So long a period was bound to register so many changes, create an enormous literature and give to religion so continued and enriched a many-sided character.

THE TEMPLES AND PRIESTS

We have noted already how the temples of Babylonia were named; there is abundant testimony to the way in which they were built; in fact, they were always being built and rebuilt. Clay brick to begin with, they were always at the mercy of storm and war. A single rainy season might melt them down but they were always rising from their clay and always rising higher. The most splendid of them were surrounded by great courts, built from level to level of rising terraces, richly ornamented with precious metal and given a semblance of solidity by a veneer of stone slabs upon which the exploits of the gods were sculptured.

The last hidden recess, or the highest level of the many-storied tower, was kept for the god. There he had his holy of holies, his golden altar, his treasures and his priests. The sacred shrines often contained the model of a ship. It must have been first intended to allow the god to take some pleasant excursion on the river; a little later it became his traveling home, and ingenious scholars are inclined to find some connection between this and the Hebrew Ark of the Covenant. When the Chaldean divinities were finally lifted to the skies and made incarnate in the stars, their temple boats became symbols of the celestial craft which carried them across the heavens.

The gods were served by an army of priests, the priests themselves organized in ascending scale with the high-priest, who was the earthly representative of the deity and through whom alone the deity could be approached, at the top. In theory the king should have been high-priest, but having much else to attend to, he assigned this duty to specialists. The king himself later became a god with all the rights and duties appertaining thereto, so that the high-priest was the representative of the divinity of the king as well as his temple gods. This two-fold office of the priest, mediator for the god and representative of the god-head of the king, gave the Babylonian priesthood a many-sided importance. They were responsible first of all for the complicated ritual of worship, sacrifice, care and service of the temple. The great temple would be almost like a town, a kind of sacred skyscraper with living quarters for the priests and their servants, storehouses for food, treasure chambers and the like.

Since the temples were the pride of the kings and their especial care, they were adequately endowed and their wealth increased with the centuries. They were the centers of the intellectual life of the nation. Whatever learning the time had, and it was very considerable, was under the control of the priests. They naturally trained their successors, organizing schools for that purpose. The schools needed libraries and libraries were collected—even a museum of antiquities. Nearly all the remains of Babylonian and Assyrian literature belonged originally to temple collections.

Whether as representative of the god or the king, the priest was the law-giver, the law itself being only the will of the god. When kings like Hammurabi, who was the Justinian of Babylon, turned jurist and codified the laws of the state, they were after all simply re-enacting the will of the gods. The priest in his rôle of law-giver played a double part; as the representative of the gods he revealed their will through the oracles; as representative of the king he proclaimed the state code. He had the power of life and death over the people; he was keeper of the legal archives. The records indicate that this great responsibility was most carefully exercised but the exercise of it magnified the power of the priest.

The temples, being rich both in real and personal property, made it possible for the priests to act as capitalists. They lent money at a rare profit for their divinities, charging as high as 20% interest—religion apparently was not allowed to interfere with business. The affairs of the temple themselves were business enterprises of really vast consequences. It is impossible here to suggest more than this, except to note that the literature of the temple schools has furnished the scholar with his most dependable sources of information about these vanished civilizations.

THE DELUGE POEMS AND THE HEBREW OLD TESTAMENT

Every broken shard of Babylonian myth, theology and devotion has been worked over by scholars, partly because of the fascinating interest of the subject matter, partly because of the relation of much of it to the early books of the Hebrew Old Testament. The parallels are beyond debate and the also undebatable priority of the Chaldean material indicates that it furnished a nebular material which the Hebrew historian later subdued to his own purposes. The Chaldean creation and deluge poems have found their way into the western religious mind through these channels and, in the finer form in which Hebrew devotion recast them, continue to challenge modern science. When the past is invested with sanctity it becomes invulnerable.

We have seen already how Marduk became the creator god and in what fashion he set about the work of creation. In general, the Babylonian never thought of creation as an absolute beginning out of nothing. There were always pre-existent materials, chaotic, void and pregnant. The gods reduced these to order, the sense of order being particularly strong in Babylonian thought. There is some vague conception of evolution in these mother-myths of creation, the conception of the emergence of law and order which, once being established, is not thereafter interrupted. Man is made of clay by the potter god. In one creation cycle dry land is made very much as the arable fields of old Babylonia were won from the marshes, by surrounding a bit of earth by wattles, protecting it from the waters and letting it drain out. According to another legend the land is half the body of Chaos surrounded by water. Man's first home is a land watered by four rivers. An impious city incurs the wrath of the gods and they propose to destroy humanity. The race is saved by the friendship of Ea for one man whom he instructs to build an ark and embark therein with his family and living things.

> O man of Shurippak, son of Ubaratutu,
> Pull down thy house, build a ship,
> Leave thy possessions, take thought for thy life,
>
> . . . . .
>
> Bring living seed of every kind into the ship.

The dimensions of the ark are divinely dictated and the various experiences of the Babylonian Noah are told with great vividness. He builds the ark and goes on:

With all that I had I filled it.
With all the silver I had, I filled it,
With all the gold I had, I filled it,

With all living seed of every kind that I possessed, I filled it.
I brought up into the ship all my family and household,
The cattle of the field, and the beasts of the field, the handicraftsmen
    —all of them I brought in.
A fixed time Shamash had appointed (saying):
"The lord of darkness will at eventide send a heavy rain:
Then go into the ship, and shut thy door."
The appointed season arrived and
The ruler of the darkness sent at eventide a heavy rain,
Of the storm I saw the beginning;
To look upon the storm I was afraid;
I entered into the ship and shut the door.[22]

---

[22] A rather free translation, but they are all pretty much the same.

Even the gods themselves were afraid of the deluge.

> The gods feared the deluge,
> They drew back, they climbed up to the heaven of Anu
> The gods crouched like a dog, they cowered by the walls.[23]

Lady Ishtar cried aloud like a woman in travail as she saw the race of men turned into clay again and the clay dissolved. The ark rode out the flood and stranded on the mountain Nisir (the mountain, as we have seen, could be shifted to suit the pride of a king). The Chaldean Noah sent out a dove, a swallow and a raven. The dove and the swallow found no resting place and came back. The raven waded and croaked about but did not come aboard. Ut-napishtim offered proper sacrifices and the gods gathered like flies in the odorous smoke. There was a widely shared feeling among them that Enlil had gone too far in planning to destroy the whole of humanity for the sin of an upstart city and they submitted the case to Ea who decreed a more equitable administration of divine justice.

> On the sinner visit his sin, and
> On the transgressor visit his transgression
> But hold thy hand, that all be not destroyed.

Thereafter let divine justice go no further than wild beasts, famine, pestilence and stop short of a deluge, which is a somber substitute for the rainbow-edged promise of mercy with which the Hebrew account ends. Enlil finally decided to accept the situation—upon one condition. Since Ut-napishtim had shared the council of the gods, let him be like the gods and live apart:

> They took me and afar off, at the mouth of the rivers they made me to dwell.

This may have saved him from the unhappy incidents which followed Noah's disembarkation.

How Man Missed Immortality

There is another story of a man whom the gods sought to make like themselves. This was Adapa, son of Ea, to whom his father granted large intelligence but not eternal life. (The withheld gift

[23] Rogers, *op. cit.*, page 95.

of eternal life is the motif of a far-flung mythology.) He was priest of the temple of Ea at Eridu and a fisherman. The south wind overturned his fishing boat and he thereupon broke the wing of south wind, who seems to have been—if she bore any family resemblance to the south-west wind—most unattractive. The south wind, being broken winged, ceased to blow, and Anu the sky-god summoned Adapa to the celestial bar of justice. Ea instructed his son how to win the friendship of the heavenly gatekeeper, who might be able to help him. He warned him also against either eating the "meat of death" or drinking the "water of death" which the gods would offer him. Adapa pleaded great provocation, Anu forgave him and then, since he had seen heaven and sat among the gods, decreed that he must be added to that high company.

They brought him, therefore, "the food of life but he ate not" and the "water of life but he drank not." These would have made him immortal but he remembered his father's command and, being suspicious of the celestial hospitality, refused them and thus lost immortality. Hebrew faith modified this also in familiar ways. There is actually a worldwide cycle of stories explaining how man lost immortality through a trick or a stupidity. Behind them all is the suggestion that the gods are jealous of men and wish to keep immortality for themselves though they have not always been successful in this, since the gods also grew old and died. Time alone seems master of gods and men.

THE POPULAR RELIGION

But the actual concern of the Chaldean commonfolk was not with such themes as these which were affairs for the priest and poet, but with the will of the gods for this or that enterprise, protection from evil and deliverance from sickness, loss and pain. Divination thus became the most important and profitable business of the Babylonian priesthood. They read the will of the gods in the liver of animals, in unusual happenings and in the stars. Liver reading particularly created an enormous and most remarkable literature. The liver was long believed to be the principal seat of physical and emotional life. Babylonian poets spoke of the "liver" as poets, recently at least, spoke of the heart. Greek lyricists made the liver and not the heart Eros' target. Even Mohammed, having reason to suspect his favorite wife refers, in tradition, to his "cracking liver" and not his breaking heart. Jastrow in a passage which reveals delightfully the inclusive erudition of a great scholar finds the key to Prometheus' vulture-torn liver in this same old belief.

Babylonian sages added to this the widely shared belief that a god identifies himself with the animal sacrificed to him imparting to certain portions of it a particular sanctity. Where then could the mind of the god be found if not in the liver of the sacrifice? Never was a more futile science more elaborately developed. A study of the basic principles of liver divination reads like a chapter in ancient anatomy embroidered with fantastic imagination. A diseased gall-bladder might portend a king's triumph or defeat. An elaborate "case system" was built up and recorded in "omen" libraries. Coincidence and caprice combined to produce a result like this:

If the gall-bladder is split from left to right, and there is a gallstone at the top of the fissure, thy general will capture the enemy.

Vice versa, the enemy will capture the general. There are thousands of such registered signs bearing upon war, statecraft, life and death though it is impossible that the conduct of great affairs should have been entirely left to such anatomical accidents; Sargon and Sennacherib did not build an empire upon omens. But Babylonian religion was seamed with divination. Sacrifice was more largely for prophecy than propitiation. Any Babylonian going to the Lofty House was likely to be more concerned about some advice about his affairs or a safeguard against fever than the praise of Marduk.

The borderline between religion like that and magic is always narrow and easily crossed. The temples swarmed with exorcisers, specialists in incantations guaranteeing, doubtless for a fee, to lay an evil spirit, drive out a demon, cure the sick who were spirit possessed, purify the unclean. These texts also, burnt into clay, remain to exercise the scholar and open windows into the souls of fearsome folk. They rise sometimes to noble levels of penitence and prayer and fall away again into a showman's patter.

ASTROLOGY

Astrology was developed as elaborately as liver reading and found its subject matter in a nobler region. Man has always recognized

his dependence upon the sun and moon. He has invested the great
solar periods with divine significance, solar and lunar eclipses with
terror and measured the sequence of his days by the phase of the
waxing and waning moon. No wonder he associated the majestic
processes of the skies with his own brief and often troubled state
and sought to read his future in the stars. The elevation of Chaldean
divinities to stellar stations furnished a religious basis for astrology.
The behavior of the stars was the revelation of the divine will. The
Babylonian generally saved the portent of the skies for the fortunes
of the state. Here was something too vast to concern itself with
the fortune of the individual. He would have echoed the words of
the Hebrew psalmist had he known them:

> When I consider the heavens, the work of thy hands,
> What is man that thou art mindful of him?

But kings went out to fight with a favorable conjunction of the
stars and stayed at home, maybe, when the stars in their courses
fought against them. The curious may find the detail of all this in
Jastrow and Sayce or the Encyclopedia. It has had a great influence
upon the western mind through channels never wholly interrupted
and still looks out of curtained windows in sad streets of modern
cities. There was a decline of astrology toward the end of the Assyrian period; astronomy began to displace it. Long and careful vigils
beneath Chaldean skies accumulated a great body of observed facts,
the facts began to be touched with some sense of law-ruled order
with which even the fortunes of an empire had no relation.

The followers of Zoroaster brought to Babylon the sense of a divine sovereignty which left little room for caprice. An exiled Hebrew prophet, to whom the streets of the city were wearily familiar,
chanted the loving goodness of a power who held the stars in leash.
Science did the rest, Jastrow puts it in one vibrant sentence: "The
connecting link between heaven and earth was snapped through the
injection of law in the universe over which even the gods had no
control." The conflict between science and religion began in Babylon.

ETHICS AND ETHICAL SYSTEMS

Divination, the rites of public and private worship, the general
exercise of the many-sided priestly office gave form and color to

Babylonian religion. What of its ethical content? The general standards of morality must, I think, be sought in the legal codes rather
than the teaching of the priests. They never went much further than
the general, and eminently safe, principle that right conduct is agreeable to the gods. There is no strong sense of any relation between
conduct and the estate of the soul after death. There are no halls
of judgment or scales to weigh the soul in the Babylonian underworld. And yet there are gleams of moral insight and even the
shadow of a decalogue through their dusty records. There is a
broken fragment of a tablet in the British Museum not wholly
alien to the Hebrew table of stone which also got broken, though
in another way.

It contains Marduk's admonitions to humanity:

> Toward thy god shalt thou be pure in heart:—
> Early in the morning thou shalt offer to him—
> The fear of god begets mercy.
> Offerings increase life.
> And prayer absolves from sin.

> · · · · ·

> Against friend and neighbor thou shalt not speak evil
> When thou makest a promise . . . give and hold, not break.

The incantation rituals name the possible faults the suppliant may
have committed:

> Has he estranged father and son?

> · · · · ·

> Has he not permitted the prisoner to see the light?

> · · · · ·

> Has he offended a god, neglected a goddess?

> · · · · ·

> For "no" said "yes," for "yes" said "no"?
> Has he removed the limit, mark or boundary?
> Has he shed his neighbor's blood?
> Was his mouth frank, but his heart false?

> · · · · ·

> Has he taught what was impious, instructed in what was not proper?[24]

[24] Jastrow's translations, see also Rogers, *op. cit.*, pages 170 and 171. This should
be compared with the Egyptian Judgment tests and Job, Chapter 31.

These are the fundamental virtues of society: the code builds them into a system of penalty-supported law which goes far to explain the power of Babylon to outlast millenniums.

The spirit of Babylonian religion reaches its finest expression in the penitential psalms. Even these are official rather than personal, meant for kings as the voices of the state and not for conscience-stricken individuals, but they sound a haunting and universal note.

> I, thy servant, says a nameless one to Ishtar
> I, thy servant, full of sins, call upon thee;
> The fervent prayer of him who has sinned do thou accept.
> If thou lookest upon a man, that man lives.
>
> . . . . .
>
> I implore thee to look upon me and hear my sighs.
> Proclaim pacification, and may thy soul be appeased.

and such lines as these "tell of many sorrows in one sigh"

> I seek for help, but no one takes my hand,
> I weep but no one approaches me,
> I call aloud but no one hears me
>
> . . . . .
>
> To the known or unknown God I turn, speaking with sighs
> . . . look upon me, accept my lament
>
> . . . . .
>
> The sin I have committed change to mercy
>
> . . . . .
>
> My god, my sins are seven times seven, forgive me my sins.[25]

LIFE AFTER DEATH

The Babylonian made as much as he could of this world because he had little to look forward to after death. The outstanding difference between Egypt and Babylonia is just here; there is no answering the question why. The imagination of the Egyptian seized upon the future and his vivid sunlit land became only the dim threshold of the eternal. He took more care to build his tomb than his house and coffined himself in basalt and diorite. The Babylonian built himself no many-chambered tomb with painted and sculptured recitation upon their walls, his tombs are simplicity itself—a grave with maybe a mound over it. His coffin was palm wood or a reed mat covered by a clay tub—or else he had a slipper-shaped clay coffin.

Proper burial was necessary to the peace of the soul, otherwise it would wander homeless eating offal in the streets. Assyrian rulers mutilated the bodies of their enemy dead to bring upon them the curse of the unburied. Weapons and ornaments were left on the grave and offerings of food, though not always. Custom never went beyond this. The realm of the dead held neither light nor hope, punishment nor reward. Its pitiful furnishings were dust covered, its inhabitants dismal beyond belief. There was in Babylonian faith one fugitive gleam of the Islands of the Blest—a happier land. A favorite of the gods who escaped the flood was settled there. Otherwise it seems unpopulated.

The first ruler of the underworld was a goddess. She was presently compelled to share her throne with Nergal who, having through pestilence sent so many to Aralû, had rights of his own there. A marriage of convenience was arranged but it made no difference to the dead. The underworld was brightened a little once when Ishtar came down in quest of Tammuz, leaving her garments and her jewels piece by piece with the keepers of the seven gates till she had only the dark for a girdle. But Earth demanded her and she went away with her garmenture mercifully restored. It was Spring again in Chaldea but the love and the light of it never reached the land of No-Return. But there was in the underworld a spring of the water of life with which Ishtar was sprinkled before her return. There was some gleam of hope even in the dark.

BABYLONIAN PHILOSOPHY OF LIFE

The Babylonian consequently made everything of his present life and his colorful world. He feared death and his fear of it—and his love of life—sounds mournfully through the epic of Gilgamesh—even that hero was not exempt from the common fortune.

> Gilgamesh, whither hurriest thou?
> The life that thou seekest thou wilt not find.
> When the gods created man,
> They fixed death for mankind.

.   .   .   .   .   .

> Thou, O Gilgamesh, fill thy belly,
> Day and night dance and be merry!
> Clean be thy clothes,
> Thy head be washed, bathe in water!
> Look joyfully on the child that grasps thy hand
> Be happy with the wife in thine arms.[26]

This song has found many echoes.

What did Babylonia contribute to the general course of religion? The question is half unfair. The values of any religion, being actually for those who held or hold them, are hard to recover from the clay tablets. Imagination is the only key to that lost world, and even imagination may unlock the wrong door. The recovered literature does show the Babylonian and Assyrian to have been personally devout.

Historically Babylonian religion was a higher polytheism with a marked tendency to set one god or a group of gods above all the others. Both theological and political influences contributed to the selection. In no religion, I think, have the mutations of empire affected the gods more dramatically. They went out proudly or turned to names and shadows as the kings who had served them were victorious or defeated. Priestly speculation gave them rank and special office, the inevitable way of humanity invested them with human ways, the course of empire lifted a few of them to lonely supremacy. Faith touched the border of monotheism but never quite attained it.

One name more or less would not seem to matter among so many names; yet there are in the British Museum three fragile tablets upon which a name is scratched, upon which for thirty years an enormous controversy has centered. For they seem to say Ja-u-um-ilu "Jau is God"[27] though some think them only to say "God exists" or "God lives." Now Jau is a very ancient form of Jahweh and though the use of it thirty-five hundred years ago would not prove that Jau's worshipers conceived him as a Hebrew prophet did in Babylon a thousand years later, it does prove that his august name

---

[26] Jastrow, *The Civilizations of Babylon and Assyria*, page 462. This should be compared with Ecclesiastes 9:7-9.

[27] Rogers, see *The Religion of Babylonia and Assyria, op. cit.*, pages 90 et seq., for a brief clear discussion of the points of view.

was not wholly strange to the city. Many evidences combine to show that among the gods of Babylon was one who found no royal patron but who did supply a name which the religious genius of the Hebrew people raised to a Lordship before which the Empire of Bel or Marduk and Ashshur passed as shadows pass when the sun is set.

For the rest Babylon and her gods died together. Her temples melted into clay, the key to her records was lost. Tablets, sculptured slabs, effigies of Marduk and Ashshur lay lost for millenniums in the mounds by mournful rivers. A century of investigation has satisfied our insatiable curiosity about the past, but the vital part of that old faith has perished with the women who mourned for Tammuz and the kings who took Ashshur out to war.

"AND FINALLY ——"

The importance of Babylon as a religious center did not end as abruptly as the last section. The city outlasted her gods. It was the meeting-place for a thousand years of cultures and faiths. There in exile the Hebrew sang some of the saddest of his psalms. He rebuilt Jerusalem, by the permission of Babylonian kings and was profoundly influenced by his unsought sojourn by "the rivers of Babylon." The Persian made it his capital city (it was at least his most important city). The Greek followed Alexander through its gates—(Alexander died there)—but some infiltration of the faith of Babylon reached Greece and finally Rome. One can not understand the religious quests of the Graeco-Roman Empire without Babylon.[28] The debt of Hebrew Genesis to the creation and Deluge myths is a much debated question. Certainly they both use material common to the region and the time. In these and other ways Babylonia left its mark upon Christianity.

From a purely religious approach Babylonia just as certainly attained a warm personal relationship between the gods and their worshipers. There is a rich human element in the old hymns, prayers and liturgies. The perplexed seek assurance, the weary rest and the penitent forgiveness. There are penitential psalms from the library of Ashshur-Banipal which need little change to make them noble

---

[28] See S. Angus, *The Religious Quests of the Graeco-Roman World,* New York, Chas. Scribner's Sons, 1928, Chapter XV.

expressions of those "remedies for calming the heart" which express the brief mystery of life, the mystery of the ways of the gods with men and the inward peace of prayer and worship.

"Prayer was my custom, sacrifice my rule
The day of divine worship was the pleasure of my heart"

The dawn of conscience rises across these broken tablets of clay.

28062

The Aryan Begins His Procession

FOUR thousand years ago—or a little more or less—a procession not of gods but of folk began. The men who walked by their carts drawn by yoked horned cattle were skin-clad, long-haired and masterful, with spears for staffs—yet there was some gleam of mystic quest in their eyes and destiny goaded their oxen. The Aryan had set out upon his migrations. There is now no general agreement about the cradle of Aryanism, even the name itself has not quite the assuring solidity it had thirty years ago. Students of a compromising turn suggest the "grassy plain" extending from North Germany well into Central Asia a most ample nursery for any race.[1] The Aryan named himself, and he was always proud of his color and conscious of his own general superiority. He calls the dark-skinned of North India whose land he took and whose persons he enslaved "riteless, senseless, inhuman, keeping alien laws." There is a familiar sound to this; the Aryan was beginning to take up "the white man's burden."

The household was the social unit out of whose combinations his society was organized. Worship, prosperity, authority and the succession of the family name locked up upon the hearthstone and the divine and friendly flame. An unmarried man was "unfinished"; there was, if he died a bachelor, an old custom of bringing a woman to his grave or funeral pile and marrying her to his shade, which might thus at least go into the land of shades as a householder. Very likely the woman was, in very ancient times, dispatched down the road to shade-land directly after him, but time softened a custom upon which any unmarried woman would look with disfavor. So vital a conception of the family made the marriage bond strong —polygamy was not common—but it made the lot of women hard. The wife was the property of the husband and the family drudge, sons were greatly desired for they supplied warriors to a society

[1] H. D. Griswold, *The Religion of the Rig Veda*, page 18.

bled white by war. The weak and the old were burdens and disposed of as burdens.

He and his dependents lived in huts bedless, chairless, tableless, with skin or mat-spread earthen floors. They fortified their groups of huts, traded a little with their neighbors and fought them quite as much and whole-heartedly. They grew a little barley, but cattle were their wealth, cattle-breeding their vocation, and cattle "lifting" their avocation. They were born wanderers and adventurers, sea-lovers and sea-rovers when they found the sea, mastered by the spell of far horizons and yet with a tenacious power to possess a land and make it rich with immemorial association and vocal with song. Time was to prove them great and socially creative administrators. They have reddened lands enough with blood; they have rarely impoverished them.

.　　.　　.　　.　　.

The House-father was absolute over the living but responsible to the dead. He must furnish them with gear for their discarnate life, hence the gifts left at tomb or fire pile. Hence also food gifts and ritual meals at which the living and the dead sat down together. The family and tribal graves were near some road or at the crossroads—which may account for the long association of ghosts and crossroads or else, because roads then as now were boundary lines of which the shades were guardians. The departed needed at first no remote realm of their own, the little household and clan "ancestor places" served their need. But when such burying grounds were left far behind through migration, the dead having no longer the companionship of the living would need some land of their own. The names for the realms of the shades have long since lost their vivid meaning. Hades was once the "place of the unseen," the Elysian fields were, possibly, "the land of the departed." Such regions naturally grew both dim and distant. They were lighted at the best by the ghost of sunlight, their very peace was pallid—regions they of the silent who cast no shadow.

But the dead still ruled the living from their ghostly thrones. The old worship of the altar-hearthstone centered about them and the House-father was the priest. Long after the affairs of the high gods occupied the official priest the common folk carried on their spiritual commerce with their ancestral spirits. "Honor, Fathers for your comfort, honor for your living sap, honor for your living power, for your gentleness, honor to you, honor." So an East Indian still prays, adding a petition for a man child which his wife dutifully echoes, asking with an unseemly reference to detail to be the mother of a "lotus wreathed boy."

· · · · ·

The second and more creative center of old Aryan-worship was the sky, and all the ways of nature therein contained. Some hold ancestor-worship to have been the earliest form of any "worshiping" religion but one does not discover a road from ancestor- to nature-worship. The gods of the sky, the clouds and the winds are not deified ancestors. They are the creations of wonder, gratitude and a little fear, the achievement of the poet rather than the priest. Even in the later development of the Veda, the heavenly ones are not always clearly personalized; they are likely to have been less so at first. But they were always mysterious and strong, some rush or gleam of a divine power—though I suppose we have no right to read back our ripened use of "divine" into the minds of skin-clad folk who fled before the thunder or met the dawn with quickened spirit. Something was there in the sky to praise and to petition. They have at any rate left us two words which have attended their far-flung migrations. Dyaus Pitar, Zeus Pater and Ju-piter are Sky-Father for Sanscrit, Greek and Roman. The "shining ones" of the Veda are the Dei of Rome and do we not still speak of Deity and the divine.

Egypt and Babylon worshiped the shining ones but always with a difference. It is not wholly true to say it is the difference between poetry and prose. There is a grave music in the psalms to Aton and Anu but the lyric note is missing. The skies of Egypt furnished no veils of mist to be majestically withdrawn, no clouds to furnish a fretted pavement for Aurora's progress. The sky-worship of the northern races has sun love in it and a celestial pageantry, wind-driven clouds, the rising storm, thunder-bolts, life-giving rain and jeweled green when the rain is done. The old Aryan skies were temperate and their divinities mostly kind. But something was due to the sensitive spirits of the worshiper, some more intimate feeling for nature, some power to take it all as kindness and beauty, make a song and a prayer of it. We call it pagan now, the word debases a great inheritance. It was a frank joy in all the sensuous side of life, a sense of human kinship to Mother Earth and Father Sky, a singing joy in light and beauty old as the Vedic hymns to the dawn. Something passed with the passing which we grown old and wise can never recapture. It is the birthright of a child or a faun or Virgil among his bees.

. . . . .

Somewhere behind ancestors and the heavenly ones was, from a very early time, some sense of a vaster power, law, order, finally, necessity or fate. These in their full development have become the most awesome and sovereign conceptions of which the human mind is capable, having had in them from the beginning the roots of science, philosophy, morality and jurisprudence. The seekers who sang their hymns to the dawn and drank Soma with their gods had not got so far as that, but they were feeling for something to give meaning to the puzzle of life, something unchanging in which to rest.

They began with two conceptions; one of a power which made the outer world both orderly and dependable so that one might count on sunrise and so sleep unafraid, find the stars in their familiar stations or plant a crop with the assurance of harvesting it. The other that the course of a man's own life was predetermined from his birth by something beyond his little power to reach and change. The Greek tragedians made fate the motif of their tragedies and bowed the gods themselves to vast, unswerving destinies. The Aryans presently made a god of "right order," but they never got so far as to invest any divinity with omnipotence. Lord Mazda of Zoroaster came as near being thus invested as any but there was always in action against even him a power of evil and darkness— lord of a realm Ahura-Mazda could never entirely win and was not fated to lose.

One must really follow this sense of order in the world and the course of life which shines through the very beginnings of the Aryan religion, along another line to come upon its full unfolding. It has been for the folk of that race something more than the "Fates" of Greek poetry, the "necessity" of the Greek tragedians, the Norns of the misty north. It has been the habit and genius of the northern mind, its impatience with the confused and unexplained, its protest against anarchy in mind or soul or state, its capacity for orderly administration, the drive of its passion for science, the secret of its passion for law.

These then were the religious conceptions common to all the ancestors of the Indo-European races, held 2000 B.C. by long-haired, light-skinned warriors and shepherds in the great grassy plain which reaches from mid-Europe to mid-Asia and especially by an eastern group of them, who began, at least by that time, to take their separate courses to the uplands of Persia and the region of the "Five Rivers" in northwest India. The dates are reasonably important and unreasonably indefinite. Specialists do not agree by a thousand years. 2500 B.C. will do as the earliest separation date, 1500 B.C. as the latest. There are marginal dates, wisely argued, 500 years earlier, 300 years later. Historians deal as freely with time as astronomers with space. We can only be sure that the movement began early, took time and, in Asia, resulted finally in two great religions intimately related and, finally, strongly opposed—the faith of Iran and the faiths of India.

It makes no great difference which stream flowing from such far-off sources one follows first. Since it is most logical to deal with the religions of India in one sequence, one may begin with the Iranian and his prophet Zoroaster. But these hinterlands whose contours we have thus followed have fed the streams of devotion for all the northern races.

CHAPTER IV

Zoroastrianism: The Religion of Embattled Light and Darkness

PERSIAN CIVILIZATION

WHEN these Aryan migrations which have made so much history began, the Iranians took their own line. Their migratory drift may have begun so early as 2500 B.C. It was certainly southernly, probably toward the southwest. They found an open door somewhere between the head waters of the Tigris and Araxes—and Persia was theirs. It was a mountain-guarded table-land. Few of its rivers, such as they are, emptied into any sea; they were—and are—lost in salt marshes, inland lakes and the thirsty soil. Irrigation is so generally needed that it has made a religious duty. But it was a land to breed a hardy race and justify their pride in it. "Persia is beautiful, possessing good horses, possessing good men," said Darius. Its long and fascinating history carries the glamour of great names—Cyrus, Darius, Xerxes, Artaxerxes, Alexander and the glamour of poetry, perfumes, rugs and roses, a peacock throne and oriental splendor. It has furnished architecture a school and our own language alluring words: van, magic, bazaar, shawls and sashes, awning, turquoise, orange, lemon, melon and peach are all Persian. Persian literature has influenced western literature in many ways, but the most far-reaching influences have been religious.

There is a lovely story, still widely known, of wise men from the East, star-led and gift laden, who once sought a King and found him in a strangely unroyal estate. Some gleam of ancient respect for Persian wisdom shines through that story. No religion is more difficult to trace to its sources and definitely characterize than the historic religion of the Persians. Its origins are remote in time and it has in its long course been subject to many contributory influences. All the tides of conquest and empire which have left their mark on Western Asia for 2500 years have affected its development. Its prophet is seen so dimly through the veil of millenniums that his very existence is questioned. Its sacred books are the disorganized fragments of a once very great and always curiously confused religious literature and, as they now exist, are the creation of 1200 years (500 B.C. to 700 A.D.).

There is a tradition that, during Zoroaster's lifetime, they were written in golden letters upon the hides of 12,000 oxen, and another tradition that "evil destined" Alexander burned the sacred books of Persia along with the treasury of the Persian kings. More was lost in the Islamic conquest. A literature which has suffered so sadly through time and circumstance still suffers many things at the hands of its translators; no two translations agree. The "Avesta," the sacred book of the old Persian faith, is a priest's book rather than a Bible—an endless weariness of words to be said once a day or once a month, a weaving together of old tales, old laws, old litanies, old hymns, old prayers. No one could know it all but a school of priests; no one could say it all and do anything else.

And yet it sounds a new note in religion which may bring us as near to Zoroaster as we shall ever come.

> This I ask Thee, tell it to me truly, Lord!
> Who set firmly earth below and kept the sky
> Sure from falling? Who the streams and trees did make?
> Who their swiftness to the winds and clouds hath yoked?
> Who, O Mazda, was the Founder of Good Thought?
>
> This I ask Thee, tell it to me truly, Lord!
> Who, benignant, made the darkness and the light?
> Who, benignant, sleep and waking did create?
> Who the morning, noon and evening did decree
> As reminders, to the wise, of duty's call?[1]
>
> .   .   .   .   .
>
> This and much else do I long, O God, to know.

What is central in the native faith of Persia is all here—a longing to pass behind the old Aryan nature worship to the Creator of the sun and the stars, a quickening sense of some holy order, a listening for the voice of duty, a feeling through the age-old conflict of light and darkness to the power in whose triumph light and goodness would be victorious. Professor Jackson adds a poet's touch to a scholar's erudi-

---

[1] A translation of part of Yasna 44 of the Gathas by A. V. Williams Jackson, quoted from *An Anthology of World Poetry*, Albert and Charles Boni, page 125.

tion in this translation which carries the substance of the standard English texts. The hymns—half invocation—from which it is taken are a curious combination of the childish and the sublime. The prophet asks in one breath whether he is to receive the promised reward of ten mares, a stallion, a camel, and the "future gift of welfare and immortality." But for all that, these old hymns sound a new note in religion.

ZOROASTER

Zoroaster, though we see him dimly enough, I take to have been a real man and rather human, who wanted horses and a camel as well as immortality. His birthplace and his century are alike disputed. If one says that he was born somewhere between the Oxus and the Tigris in the seventh century B.C., one has the high authority of Jackson and the weight of tradition for support.

His own followers believe that he began his ministry two hundred fifty-eight years before Alexander. According to the same tradition, he was thirty years old when he began his public ministry and died at the ripe age of seventy-nine. We have then the accepted time 660-583 B.C. The sacred books call him Zarathustra[2] and there are modern Persian variants enough to make it possible for any scholar to find a name with which few of his fellow specialists agree. The name at any rate includes the old Persian word for camel and might have meant "one whose camels are fierce" or even "camel tormentor." These supposititious translations are probably a better testimony to the scholar's fancy than the prophet's disposition. The name does indicate the occupation of his clan and has no other value save as he gave it distinction.

All his family had the names of farming folk. His father's name means "with gray horses," his mother's one "who has milked the cows," his wife was Hvon, "having fine oxen." "The names suggest a simple pastoral and agricultural environment, and the prophet appears dimly indeed . . . as a man born in humble surroundings and living a simple life."[3] A wealth of legend grew up about him

[2] Zoroaster is the Greek and Roman form of the Prophet's name. Zarathustra is the proper original form and all the scholars use it. We use the more familiar name in this chapter. Some authorities date his birth 1000 B.C.

[3] Rogers, *op. cit.,* page 17.

and among other things supplied him with a fitting ancestry. The genealogies carry his line back to the father of all mankind. No royal house can claim more.

Zoroastrian tradition makes him the third in a family of five. He had four children by his first wife and two by his second. He had no earthly children by his third wife, for whom a higher destiny was reserved. She is now his Celestial Spouse, from whom, in the fulness of time, two prophets and the Messiah will be born.

LEGENDS ABOUT THE PROPHET

The devout always explain their prophets in terms of signs and wonders. Their coming is long prophesied, their birth is gloriously announced. Zoroaster is no exception. Three thousand years before his birth a vision of his ideal image was seen in heaven; three hundred years before his advent an ox foretold, in human speech, the revelation he would bring the world. The Divine Glory, the secret of his inspiration, is imparted to his mother before his birth and touches her with so particular a splendor that her father, persuaded by demons that she had been bewitched, sends her into another country. Demons plot against the conception of the child. Marvelous signs witness the accomplishment, all nature shares the gladness of his birth, a celestial light shone around the house, the child himself came laughing into the world.

But life was no laughing matter for his mother. The demons who saw in his ministry their ultimate defeat were untiring in their efforts to destroy him. A particular demon, in whom all malevolence was incarnate, was the ring-leader. He turned the father against his little son and only a succession of miracles saved him; oxen were turned out to trample him—the lead-ox sheltered him from their drive; wolves would not harm him; an ewe-sheep mothered him in the den. Such stories as these echo from the dim horizons of all religions, invest the birth and infancy of the spiritually elect with wonder. They witness to the persistent feeling that what changes the world should come "trailing clouds of glory." We are strangely slow to learn that the great understandings rise, as the dawn rises, in luminous silence and the dramas of the spirit with their pregnant issues are affairs to which earth and sky give no heed at all.

The only thing one can make of these legends of demoniac opposition is that they project backwards the opposition the prophet met in his reformation of the old faith with its devil worship and murky immoralities. His father, so the traditions say, placed him under wise teachers, but the forces which actually molded the mind of the prophet are unknown. Such men are always deeply rooted in their time and their past but they are more than the creation of their time and their past, otherwise we should never escape the past at all. Something new comes into the world with them, an unknown quantity in the equation of humanity.

The prophet has his own ancestry and his own hidden light. Carlyle says that "it is for him a necessity of nature to live in the very fact of things," which is vague enough but helpful. The prophet does want to get at the reality of things on their moral and religious side. He is not satisfied with religious convention, he feels keenly any divorce between religion and morals. The great prophets have always had the power to overpass the limits of their own times, they have had, above all, some inner illumination upon the veracity of which they risk everything, asking no other authority. They are persuaded that they are the spokesmen of a power not their own; their final and inexplicable formula is: "thus saith the Lord." Zoroaster ended with that; he began by asking for light.

> This I ask Thee, tell it to me truly Lord!
> Who the Sire was, Father first of Holiness?
> Who the pathway for the sun and stars ordained?

Zoroaster, so the legends go, sought an answer to these questions from his fifteenth to his thirtieth year. He left home and wandered through Persia inquiring for those most desirous of righteousness and most considerate of the poor. To such he joined himself and shared their charities. He was sensitive as all prophets have been to any suffering, even a starving dog with puppies tugging at her stirred his compassion. He is said to have kept silent seven years, to have lived upon cheese in desert places for twenty years, or else he lived in a fire-illumined mountain. All prophets have had their periods of wilderness sojourn, long and pregnant times of introspection and assuring communion with the unseen. The revelations which issue from such disciplines can doubtless be explained as the mystic outcome of fasting and wearing brooding. For the prophet they are the voice of God.

Zoroaster's revelations came to him through a period of ten years; the detail is confused and unreliable, but it is safe to conclude that he had the mystic's temperament. The legends magnify his wanderings and his difficulties; they send him through Persia into India and China, and to the nomads of the vast Asian plains, finding no one anywhere to believe in him. A sea he had need to cross divided its waters for him, but those to whom he appealed were less hospitable. Through such accounts we see an itinerant "seeker" and teacher, finding his quest hard enough. The celestial order was more kind than the human; he is granted an entry to the Divine Presence.

The Archangel Good Thought bids him lay aside the garment of his body and, so prepared, guides him to the presence of Ahura-Mazda and his angelic retinue. There he is instructed in heavenly wisdom which, putting on his body again, he begins forthwith to preach. He has for a time no better fortune—a mystic always finds it hard to produce a convincing evidence of his heavenly vision—though he could take comfort in the assurance of Lord Mazda that eternal death awaited those who repulsed him. The trouble was to get them to believe it and to reward the prophet of the Almighty with proper gifts. He found his compensation in renewed visions. He was from his thirtieth to his fortieth year, says Jackson, a citizen of two worlds, the seen and the unseen, a dreamer among the doubting. His dreams took a very practical line; they made a right concern for material things—animals, fire, metals, earth, water and plants a moral responsibility. The faithful must love the land and keep it unpolluted and they must be kind to animals; the voice of the "ox-spirit" is heard in one of the oldest of the hymns, the complaint of the dumb and the unconsidered asking justice, and if there is no justice, pity.

"Unto you" (that is to Ahura-Mazda and his retinue) "wailed the ox-soul. For whom did ye fashion me? Who created me? Violence and rapine hath oppressed me and outrage and might. I have no other herdsman than you; prepare for me then the blessings of the pasture."[4] This is a new note in religion so far as we have come, and all too lacking in the religions to follow. A faith which taught its followers 3000 years ago to respect the ox, be kind to a dog, keep

---

[4] The Gathas' Yasna 29, translated by James Hope Moulton. In later documents this appeal is addressed to Vohu Mano (Right Thought).

water unpolluted and the earth sweet and clean has a high prophetic quality. Its creeds might be kept even now with manifest advantage.

Toward the end of his ten years of vision and novitiate the Powers of evil massed themselves for one final attack upon the prophet. The account of Zoroaster's temptation—what saint has not had his dark night of the soul?—reads much like the account of Christian's set-to with Apollyon in "Pilgrim's Progress." Stones as big as houses fly about but the prophet is unterrified. "I shall not," he says, "renounce the good religion and the worshipers of Mazda, not though life and limb and soul should part asunder."

Here, as in the story of another temptation, the tempter is put to flight by the recitation of the sacred word. Indeed I should think, so long and wearisome is much of the sacred literature of this faith, that a sufficient recital of it would rout any demon. In another account, temptresses more purely human are not wanting but they, too, are unmasked and exorcised. It took Zoroaster ten years to win his first disciple—a cousin—and then everything changed. The prophet converted a king. Visions begin to command respect when a king believes them.

Religious Conditions in Zoroaster's Time

It is difficult to see the actual religious conditions of Zoroaster's time. Herodotus, whom we moderns might envy more than any other traveler and teller of guileless tales, save possibly Marco Polo, gives a classic account of Persian religion two hundred years later. The customs he describes are likely to have absorbed Zoroastrian elements, but they must have also continued old ways and worships. The Persians, he says, have neither images, shrines nor altars. They worship Zeus, from lonely mountain peaks; they sacrifice to sun and moon, earth, fire, water and the winds. Myrtle-crowned they sacrifice, offering the flesh of the victim upon a carpet of tender herbage while a magician chants the sacrificial hymn. They ask no personal favor in their prayers but only for good to befall the whole Persian people. They make much of their birthdays and are not given much to wine; though when they have unwisely drunk too much, they consider again when they are sober what they discussed in their cups. If it then pleases them, they abide by their decisions. They hate lying and debt and teach their youth to ride, to shoot and to be sober. They take care never to pollute water. They still bury in the earth.

Now all this almost idyllic situation would seem to call for little reform. Something is still left of the old Aryan nature worship with a refinement of manners. But the texts tell a different story. Superstition and magic had, by the time of Zoroaster, darkened the childlike simplicity of ancestral faith. Priests were conscienceless and greedy. The fear of demons gave the priests their opportunity and the popular religion had fallen in Persia into the low estate from which, in India, Gautama sought release for himself and others.

Vishtaspa's Conversion

King Vishtaspa's court seems to have been overrun with priests whose demands were extortionate and whose morals were unpleasing. Since there is an old feud between the prophet and the priest in all religions, the king probably found in Zoroaster a welcome ally against the court ecclesiastics. Corrupt church officialdom has often been a great aid to a simpler and, incidentally, a less expensive religion. Devout tradition surrounds Vishtaspa's conversion with signs and wonders. The prophet enters the audience chamber of the King through the roof miraculously opened, holding a cube of fire in his unburnt hand. The court priests resented this intrusion and disputed the prophet's evangel with what reason they had and what disreputable means they could manage.

Zoroaster finally proves the truth of his teaching by curing the King's favorite horse of a lameness which seems to have been sent upon him as a punishment for the prophet's imprisonment. The King accepts the faith and one leg is cured; he dedicates his son to the cause, and another leg comes straight. He grants the prophet the high privilege of converting the Queen and the charger has three sound legs; he reveals the names of those who wickedly plotted against the prophet and the miracle is complete. The credibility of this engaging account is considerably impaired by the fact that the literature which contains it dates from the eleventh century A.D. In the same account the King asks unusual favors as a reward of his conversion. He is compelled to choose one boon out of the four and asks to see the place he will occupy in heaven, which is granted.

There are tales also of assisting archangels. Few conversions have been so marvelously accomplished.

All this is a fog. Little enough is known of the King at the best; even the location of his Kingdom is in dispute. Rogers believes the King to have been Hystaspes father of Darius[5] who owed his conversion, not to the miracle of a lame horse cured, but to the influence of his wife, Hutaosa who accepted the prophet and became intermediary with the King. There are close parallels to this in the early history of Christianity. The residue of fact is that Zoroaster found a royal patron in the crisis of his career, a king fretted by greedy priests and their religion of magic and demon fear.

The new faith was simple, really nobly conceived, favorable to agriculture and settled economic conditions. The King accepted it gladly, gave it the prestige of his name and supported it with his sword. Constantine did the same for Christianity and Asoka for Buddhism. Pure religion and undefiled always finds hard going until the strong set its sign upon their banners; after that it is never quite pure and undefiled. The court circle adopted the King's faith and gave it added prestige. The most distinguished convert after the King himself was his high-spirited son and the faith thus supported made rapid progress.

Religious Wars

The creed of the New Faith was peace and good-will, but peace and good-will then led an embattled existence. Old feuds were rebaptized in religious antagonisms, racial jealousies and royal ambition were aligned, a war of creeds arose and the frontiers of Persia were soon ablaze: The villain of the sacred wars was one Arjasp, a Turk as near as may be learned, who rejected the prophet's appeal and was therefore properly to be damned. He had been in receipt of tribute from Vishtaspa. That monarch witnessed to his conversion by refusing, with the entire approval of Zoroaster, his spiritual director, to pay tax to an infidel. The issue was long and bitterly contested in campaigns whose strategies are on record, in battles where the forces can be reconstructed. The hero of the epic is Isfendir, the King's gallant son. His father at one time turned against him, imprisoned him in a mountain fortress, and suffered

[5] The social conditions the legends suggest do not seem to belong to so late a date.

in consequence crushing defeat. Father and son were reconciled; the Turk beaten, slain, his realm ravished. The son himself is slain in some crusade to make the faith world-wide, and the story ends with the dust of time over it all.

Zoroaster was by this time an old man, due to die. The manner of his death is also disputed. The early Christian fathers who thought him an enemy of their true faith held that he was consumed by a flame from heaven; or else that a star being tired of his magical control of the stars, sent out an angry stream of fire and slew him. His own followers believed that an infidel army invaded Persia, captured the Temple of Fire and slew, in the very presence of the sacred flame, the prophet and ministrant priests who "ceased not to repeat the name of God" until they were slain. The legend of Zoroaster's martyr death is well supported; at least it rightly ends his story.

Zoroaster's Teaching[6]

What did he teach? Next to nothing is left to tell us which has not been recast and reinterpreted. But the old hymns have a consistency which makes them dependable, and now and then a touch of realism which locks them up upon the quests and experiences of a commanding and creative personality. There is in them moreover a depth which bears sounding and the rooting of conceptions

[6] Dr. M. M. Dawson has now in his *The Ethical Religion of Zoroaster* (The Macmillan Co., New York, 1931), given us the best organization in English of the teachings of Zoroastrianism. The literature he quotes makes a strong case for a monotheistic and spiritual conception of God which can not be paralleled outside Hebrew prophecy. The list of divine attributes which, so to speak, constitute the godhead of Ahura-Mazda—called by the Persian theologians the Holy Spirits—reveal a noble insight. There are seven of them (a perfect number). They are also called in the old Persian language the "Amesha Spentas." "They represent," says Dawson, " 'the divine things' men see and know." Dawson opposes the active principle of evil, Ahriman, to Ahura-Mazda from the beginning of the world. Death and winter, pests and plagues, sin and disaster have always been undoing the work of Light and Truth and Goodness.

The ethical system is a balance of rights and duties—wise and inclusive. There are fascinating chapters on the rights of Fellow Men, Ordinary Men, Rights of the Land and the Herd and the Dog. And concerning how to live wisely, die nobly and safely, pass the Sifting Bridge, also there are prayers of tender loveliness for healing after death. Dawson supplies also a thought-provoking list of passages parallel with the Old and New Testaments.

which have had far-reaching influence. The prophet has not been left without witness.

A much quoted inscription of Darius, in which pride and devotion combine, will do to start with:

> To the great god Ahura-Mazda
> Who made this earth,
> Who made yon heaven, Who made man,
> Who made welfare for man, Who set
> Up Darius as King, one King of
> Many, one lord of Many.

We know Darius and something of the pride of kings, but who is Ahura-Mazda? He was more likely than anything else the god of the prophets' clan and a sky-god, since some gleam of his celestial origin now and then shines through the hymns which praise him. In the later phases of the Persian religion, he again clothes himself with light and becomes Mithra, God of the Morning, but this is to anticipate.

Ahura-Mazda means "Wise Lord," more accurately Lord Wise and has a music in it to pray and praise with, but the names of deity do not get their sanctity from their syllables. Faith and wonder make them sacrosanct and the throne of their administration is in the adoring spirit. The rest is a curious arrangement of letters—with a reason behind them. "Ahura-Mazda" is a definition rather than a name of God. I should think it carries some suggestion, which is deeply embedded in Zoroastrianism, of the worship of wisdom as the supreme devotion. Zoroaster actually took an old name, stripped it of the rags and associations of polytheism, gave it new life and filled it with a new power whose influence is not yet spent.[7]

The son of a camel-breeding clan becoming farmers and therefore loving quietness and wanting peace began where his father's faith left off. His long period of quest, lonely meditation, mystic vision issued in one of the epochal creative insights in the history of religion. He lifted Ahura-Mazda by the sheer strength of his persuasion and passion to one-Godness. Dates count here; if Zoroaster was born, by any chance, a century and a half before Amos—and there are scholars to maintain it—he is the first to have conceived

---

[7] Rogers, *op. cit.*, page 21. Carl Clemen, *Religions of the World*, Harcourt, Brace & Co., New York, 1931, Chapter V, thinks Ahura-Mazda akin to the Indian Varuna. He thinks also that the two coeternal spirits, good and bad, were subordinate to him.

and taught an ethical monotheism. If not, he seems to have reached, unguided and uninfluenced by anything save an inner faith, the supreme insight of religion.

THE SUPREMACY OF AHURA-MAZDA

He invested Ahura-Mazda—the Wise Lord—with the ultimate moral and spiritual attributes. Aton of the noble Egyptian psalms is Lord of Life, a light in which the world rejoices, but The Lord of Wisdom "by his wisdom created Right" made "life clothed with body" and "actions and teachings whereby one may exercise choice at one's free will." He created "the ox and waters and plants, Welfare and Immortality, by the Holiest Spirit," "actions and words to have their meed—evil for the evil, a good destiny of the good—through (his) wisdom when creation shall reach its goal." He is best known in Piety and Obedience.[8]

"I strive to recognize by these things thee, O Mazda, creator of all things through the Holy Spirit." Change Mazda to Allah, Jehovah, God and the four great one-God religions could unite in this confession. Hidden thoughts are open to the Wise Lord, he deals to men their portion of Destiny and is himself free from any stain of evil. A really noble reverence breathes through the mingled strains of quest, confession and assurance sounded in these chants, of this old faith. They never reach the highest levels of the Hebrew psalms but there is a music in them to lift the heart.

I said just now that Zoroaster lifted a tribal deity to the level

[8] The quotations here cited from the Gathas are from Dr. James Hope Moulton's translations in the appendix to Early Zoroastrianism, the Hibbert Lectures, 1912. Other translations may be found in the Avesta of Spiegel and Bleeck, London, 1864, and the *Sacred Books of the East*, Vol. III. The standard English translations of all the sacred books of the East are a jungle to work through. The editors in their introductions assume a technical knowledge on the part of their readers *equal* to their own. This whole great literature should really now be taken in hand, judicious selection made of ritual, magic, incantation, prayers, hymns and the utterances of really great spiritual and ethical insight, and the whole put at the service of the interested with plain and untechnical introductions. An anthology of the world's great religious literature is needed. Since this note was so far written (1928), Dr. R. E. Hume's *Treasure House of the Living Religions* (Chas. Scribner's Sons, 1932) has met a real need. It is an admirable anthology of the world's best devotional literature, well organized. *An Anthology of World Poetry,* Mark Van Doren, Boni, New York, 1928, and *An Anthology of World Prose*, Carl Van Doren, Reynal & Hitchcock, New York, 1935, contain valuable selections pertinent to this study. Hume should certainly be used constantly.

of ethical monotheism—but yet not quite—Ahura-Mazda never reigned unopposed. Any doctrine of God involves a doctrine of evil. If any prophet feels the chill of the shadowed side of life, or sees the moral dark of it "stain the white radiance" of creative love and wisdom, he can not finish until he has thought—or felt—through the reconciliation of All-Power with so confusing an exercise of it.

THE PROBLEM OF EVIL

Why should the all-wise and omnipotent have created evil? Or, at least, why permit it? Every great religion has taken its own line here. Hindu pantheism accepts the dark as part of the vast interweaving of the world's scheme and softens all contradictions by wrapping them in the veil of illusion. They would reverse Hamlet's "Seems, Madam, nay it is!" to "Is, seeker, nay, it only seems."

For the Buddhist, life, whether it be light flecked with shadow, or shadow flecked with light, is the weary result of restless desire. Let a man get disentangled from desire, though he be reborn a hundred times in changing form to compass it, and he shall find peace in Nirvana where nothing matters. For the Hebrew prophets evil is moral rebellion against the Divine Will with death and thorn-infested fields the penalty of it. Christianity accepted this and adds thereto the Scheme of Redemption. Zoroaster faced the problem of evil also and though there is a vast difference between those teachings which seem most likely his own and the development of them in Persian religion, the roots which later produced so significant a growth are there.

Zoroaster inherited a belief in evil spirits. That, as we have seen, is old enough, being harassed humanity's first rough and ready way of accounting for the perils and the pains of this earthly pilgrimage. All this involved no moral responsibility on humanity's side. A man might dodge the devil, or trick him, or propitiate him. There were words to be said and curious things to be done, and specialists in magic and incantation to whom the whole difficult business might be handed over for a price. But there was no feeling in primitive faith that a man's own will and desire might become the field on which the issue between good and bad was to be fought out, or that he himself might become the deciding issue in the struggle.

Now something speaks through Zoroaster's doctrine of evil which has no parallel outside Israel, and yet the two faiths do not lie parallel—project them back far enough and they divide. Zoroaster's Wise Lord is supreme and yet not supreme. There was always over against him a spiritual power opposed at every point to his holy purpose and "working havoc with the world," "a Power," to quote Moulton's adaptation of Matthew Arnold's great phrase, "not ourselves making for unrighteousness." There is no hint as to the beginning of it; it was always there. These two backgrounds are older than any dawn. Later theology gave a name to this Lord of lies and evil and darkness and opposed Ahriman (Lord of the dark) to Ormazd (Lord of light) in a dramatic and endless struggle, but Zoroaster did not go as far as that. For him the adversary was always the lie. Bad is as old as Good, Good as old as Bad. His "spirit that denies" is anonymous but he is coeval with Ahura-Mazda.[9]

"Now the two primal spirits, who revealed themselves in vision as Twins, are the Better and the Bad in thought and word and action . . . and when these twain spirits came together in the beginning, they established life and not-life, and that at the last the Worst Existence shall be to the followers of the Lie, but the Best Thought to him that follows Right. Of these twain spirits he that followed the Lie chose doing the worst things; the holiest spirit chose Right, he that clothes him with the massy heavens as a garment." (One hears the echo of another psalm in this—"Thou who coverest thyself with light as with a garment.") In this splendid and daring conception Zoroaster pushes back moral choice to the fountain heads of Divine Being. The good God is good because he chose good; the Lie chose its own essential nature. Zoroaster established moral choice in the foundation of the Eternal. The Good and the Bad have their attendant retinues. "Between these twain the demons also chose not aright, for infatuation came upon them as they took counsel together so that they chose the Worst Thought. Then they rushed together to violence, that they might enfeeble the world of man." But they are not unopposed. Lord Mazda has his arch-angelic captains. Dominion, Good Thought, Right, Piety, Welfare and Immortality.[10]

[9] Carl Clemen supports this statement. "Among the later Persians that evil spirit Zoroaster adopted had developed into a real dualistic principle in opposition to Ahura-Mazda." Authorities, however, differ.

[10] These are the Amesha Spentas, aspects of the Divine as near as may be. Each one of them has his opposite, as, for example, the Evil Spirit opposed to Piety is

We have then two opposed orders between which there can be no truce nor any reconciliation.

I will speak of the spirits Twain at the first beginning of the world, of whom the holier thus spake to the Enemy: "Neither thoughts nor teachings, nor wills, nor beliefs, nor words, nor selves, nor souls of us twain agree." Thus an unbridgeable abyss cleaves the moral order.

We shall presently consider the issues which after ages found for this strife. Zoroaster made it a moral challenge to man. He too had the power to choose, being free to will and intelligent to know. The Lie and the Truth face us all. As we choose, they are victorious or defeated, and the Soul itself is saved or lost.

The practical applications of this system to life are unexpectedly simple; they would need to be to get any hold on the early Persian mind. Since a man does not actually die, there is no suggestion of a resurrection. He resumes after death his interrupted journey but the roads divide. "The paths of Good Thought that are blessed to go in" lead into the House of Song—"Thy House, O Lord." Those who here turned aside with deeds and tongues from the path of Right shall tremble at the "Revelation in the Bridge of the Separator" and trembling fall; or else there is a "red fire" of judgment through which the righteous shall pass unharmed but for the wicked it shall be as molten metal. There is a hint of the annihilation of the wicked here which is not consistently maintained. There is also a saving fear of a "future long age of misery, of darkness, ill food and crying of woe." Ill food certainly suggests a body to loathe it and woe a voice to cry it. This sad destiny is self-determined. "To such an existence, ye liars, shall your own self bring you by your actions, to men of evil creed belongs the place of corruption."[11]

HEAVEN AND HELL

Later Zoroastrianism made much of the "Bridge of the Separator." It spanned the space between earth and heaven with hell directly under the top of its dizzy span. It offered the righteous a safe broad way to the House of Song but it narrowed of itself for

False Pretense. It is all much like the Seven Cardinal Virtues and the Seven Cardinal Sins.

[11] This whole scheme involves a complete personality. Zoroastrianism does not distinguish between a man and his Ka or Zi or take any pains to preserve the body.

the wicked—as though it shrunk from the touch of the feet of the evil—to a razor edge directly over the mouth of hell. It was as automatic as the inner compulsion which according to Dante sends every man to his own place. Paradise is not quite so vividly pictured as hell. It lacks both the dark-eyed women of Mohammed and the golden streets of the New Jerusalem. Sometimes it is the House of Praise, the House of Song; it is more often the House or Kingdom of Good Thought, it is always the House of the Wise-Lord. Zoroaster, says Moulton, knew before Marlowe and Milton that:

> The mind in its own place and in itself
> Can make a heaven of hell, a hell of heaven.

If, then, the outcome of Zoroaster's teaching is an embattled world where Light, Darkness, Right and Wrong are engaged, what issue may a man expect? There have always been watchmen of the Spirit who will not believe that the dark shall last forever. Zoroaster seems to have shared that confidence, but with a kind of wistful doubt. "When, Mazda, shall the sun risings come forth for the world winning of Right?" (The echoes of that question come back from all the horizons of time.) In his braver moments he seems to have expected some immediate triumph of Light and Right and naturally he was disappointed but his vision of a "renovation of the world" persisted. Succeeding centuries greatly changed his teachings; hell became more dreadful—always located, curiously enough, in the north, and heaven richer in felicity. Lengthening experience postponed the millennium. There were finally those who saw no issue at all of the eonian strife. Others believed that

> . . . good shall fall
> At last—far off—at last to all.

And that any man's right life and right deeds would serve the outcome, but they did not know when.

LATER PHASES OF ZOROASTER'S RELIGION

The prophet left his race and state a religion sufficiently rooted to become in time the general religion of Persia. It had been blood-watered and a religion so fertilized has a tremendous tenacity. The sacred texts name "six great upholders of the religion through whom

it was maintained and extended." Zoroastrianism has its own apostolic successor and the priests who tend the sacred fires today in
the fire temple of Bombay claim to represent an unbroken line a
thousand years longer than the successors of St. Peter. Conquering
Alexander ended the first great period of Zoroastrianism and ruined
the Persian realm, burned the sacred books and the treasury of kings,
ended the ancient orders of Asia and dated a new epoch in history.

He did more than that; imponderable but puissant, the mind of
Greece followed the Macedonian phalanx to leaven the western
Asiatic mind and produce strange results. Zoroastrianism became
thereafter half an immemorial faith, half a cloudy philosophy. Persia,
in return, gave to Greece her magic, her astrology. The magic and
astrology were, possibly, a Chaldean contribution native to old Babylon and taken over by the Persian during his long occupation of
Babylonia. At any rate the Greek got them from the Persian and
they did him no good. Astrology particularly took a strong hold on
both the Greek and Roman mind. A great scholar, Cumont, believed
that it long exercised a wider dominion than any religion and created the most elaborate pseudo-science which ever wasted the efforts
of the human mind.[12] It has taken us collectively a long time to
find that

> The fault, dear Brutus, is not in our stars,
> But in our selves that we are underlings.

In a general way the Eastern wisdom greatly impressed the Greek,
possibly because it was so different from his own, and the Persian
sacred writings were translated into Greek, which was an amende
honorable for Alexander's fire.

On the other hand, the later faith of Iran strongly reflects
Greek influence. I should think those names spelled with capital
letters—Right, Good, Thought, Dominion and Piety—which became so prominent in the later faith due in some dim way to
Platonic idealism. More is made of the Soul and the two worlds
corporal and spiritual. A curious doctrine of guardian spirits grew
up; a man's Fravashi is the immortal part of him which existed
in heaven before his terrestrial birth and will survive his death. Dur-

[12] For an exhaustive and fascinating examination of "Astralism" or Religion of
Astrology, see S. Angus, *The Religious Quests of the Graeco-Roman Empire,* Chapters
14, 15, 16.

ing this mortal life it watches over him; after his death it again unites itself to him and lives forever if he has been a good man. What happens to the guardian angel of a bad man is not clear—at any rate it had a thankless task. The guardian spirits of the great and good are particularly remembered. There is a kind of **Te Deum** in their honor—a Who's Who of the saints and heroes of the Avestan faith—which fills half a dozen pages with names of which the most erudite now know nothing.

Becomes a Priestly Cult

Time and the priest naturally took possession of the prophet's teaching and made it a system of law, incantation, magic, prayer and ritual. Something like this always happens to any religion, since time has always more power to add than to subtract and whatever it touches, being hallowed, is allowed to remain until the reformer comes along and starts some fire under it which often burns up too much. The priest also has more power to add or conserve than he has to vitalize; he loves form and it grows beneath his touch into postures, furnishings and words. He loves authority and imposes it in every aspect of life. He loves his religion and magnifies it through creed and ritual. We have nothing left of what happened to Zoroaster's faith during this long process of change, save the literature of the Avesta. Something of it is like Hebrew Leviticus, more of it like nothing else in the world. There are twenty laws for a dog with young and a classic analysis of canine character.

"A dog has the character of eight sorts of people: 'He has the character of a priest, a warrior, a husbandman, a strolling singer, a thief, a wild beast, a courtesan and a child.' " Also a convincing amount of testimony is submitted to prove each point. There are a dozen laws to tell a man what to do with his nail parings, or the clippings of his hair (always, in folk-lore, dangerous matters to dispose of since an evil spirit getting this inconsequential waste of a man in his power may do him great harm). There is at the best a wise weaving of good morals and right habits through these books of law. They maintain in them a wholesome concern for family and cattle.

"O maker of the material world, thou Holy One, who is the fourth that rejoices the earth with greatest joy? He who sows most corn and grass and fruit, . . . who waters ground that is dry or drains ground that is too wet; unhappy is the land that has long lain unsown with the seed of the sower and wants a good husbandman like a well shaped maiden."

The creed of Zoroastrianism generally is hard to formulate, being held in saturation in a diffuse literature—one of the "Collects" of the faith appointed to be said at the commencement of the offering ceremonies would seem to have the essence of the faith in it:

I praise the well-thought, well-spoken, well-performed thoughts, words and works.
I lay hold on all good thoughts, words and works,
I abandon all evil thoughts, words and works,
I bring to you, O Amĕsha-çypĕntas,
Praise and adoration,
With thoughts, words and works, with heavenly mind, the vital strength of my body.

Which sounds very much like New Thought. In addition the devout are to offer all goods to Ahura-Mazda, save cattle from theft and robbery, do no harm to the clans of the faithful, renounce the evil ones and all their works, confess themselves followers of Ahura-Mazda and praise and support his law.

The Bequest of Persian Religion

The embattled gleam and gloom of Zoroastrianism cast a long shadow—or light—over religion. It is easy to accept dualism as the solution of the problem of evil, most religions have taken that line. Man was conscious of his entanglement in an embattled order long before Zoroaster. Primitive man began with good and evil spirits and the general sense of the moral order as an empire divided between God and Satan has persisted. But I doubt if we should ever have had the mature religious form of this belief without the prophet of Iran. His successors made a great drama of it. Light and Darkness, Ormazd and Ahriman became the divine protagonists of the drama and their contending armies filled the earth and the sky. A man's due part, as we have seen, was to cast all his force on the side of Light and Right. Thus only could they conquer.[13]

[13] Yasna XII and Yasna XIII, Avesta, Spiegel, Bleek, *op. cit.*, page 62.

There is an essential nobility in this to challenge our humanity and the challenge carried far; early Greek philosophy reflects it dimly. Stoicism carries elements of it. St. Paul may have heard it discussed in the streets of Tarsus. There are faint echoes of it—with other beliefs common to his time—in his Epistles. Hebraism was certainly affected by it after the exile and Christianity has never escaped it. In its most extreme form (Manichæism) the whole material order was surrendered to hopeless and irremediable evil. That dualism went to the bottom of the moral order and left sense and stuff to the lordship of evil.

The soul belonged to another order. Some sought to escape this entanglement through an asceticism which branded every impulse of sense and every contact with the world as wrong; others found a more curious deliverance. Nothing they said which the body did could hurt the soul; they gave the body a loose rein for all its passions and held the pure part of them still undefiled. Early Christianity found this whole conception hard to deal with; it was at once so alluring and so opposed to the Christian faith. This is the belief Augustine found it soul racking to escape.

The belief in the inherent evil of matter lies at the root of a most curious system (Gnosticism) of cloud built speculation to which the intelligentsia of the second century A.D. gave themselves wholeheartedly. If matter is evil and God is good, how could he have ever created it? Their conclusion was that he did not but employed subordinates to do it. The Christian Church had a stiff bout about this also with doctrinal consequences which do not concern us here. And even this is not the end of the influence of Iranian faith upon the West.

ENTER MITHRA

There is no mention of Mithra in the earliest literature of the faith. There is a hymn to him in the Rig Veda as one who watches the "tillers of the soil with unblinking eye," which is about what the sun does. He is also associated in those old Aryan hymns with Varuna who seems to have been the deity of the celestial vault with its "thousand eyes" of stars with Mithra. These were very old divinities of the ancestors of both Indian and Iranian. After the family separation Varuna possibly became Ahura-Mazda and Mithra slipped into the shadows for a while.[14]

In the later Avestan hymns he comes back as Mithra "Lord of wide pastures . . . truth speaking . . . the sleepless and vigilant," guardian of compacts, avenger of the wronged. He in time became Sun-god again, the warrior of light, truth, right. Something of his influence touched Greece—though not much. The Greeks had no mind to borrow a god from the Persians—Syria took to him more kindly and made a Baal of him, but there was something in this shining god, lord of order and soldier of justice and truth which captured the imagination and devotion of the Roman soldier.

His priests evolved an awe-inspiring ritual performed in caves or underground temples, of which many still remain. His devotees shared sacred meals together, submitted to a bath of blood to cleanse them from their sins and found peace and power in their worship. The Roman eagles and the faith of Mithra crossed the English Channel, guarded Hadrian's wall and penetrated the aisles of the German forests. For a while, it seemed that Mithraism might become the dominant religion of the empire. His worship was chaste, purged of Astarte and all her works, the cult demanded a severe morality. It was a man's religion and a soldier's.

Kipling who has made so many dead things deathlessly alive, has a hymn through whose lines we hear the bronze trumpets of Rome and the faith of men who guarded the longest front in history.

Mithras, God of the Morning, our trumpets waken the wall!
Rome is above the nations, but thou art over all!
Now as the names are answered, and the guards are marched away,
Mithras, also a soldier, give us strength for the day!

Cumant quotes "an oft-quoted sentence of Renan's": "If Christianity had been checked in its growth by some deadly disease, the world would have become Mithraic." I should doubt it. The growing intelligence of Europe would never have been satisfied with a sun-god, nor submitted permanently to a bath of bull's blood in the

[14] Carl Clemen thinks Mithra (or Mithro) to have belonged to an old strata of Iranian religion. He is mentioned under a polysyllabic name (Miidraashshiil) in an ancient document—very likely a tribal deity. He was first and foremost the god of loyalty (Mithra means a treaty). If the Romans thus knew him it would account in part for his place in the devotion of Roman soldiers. He helps soldiers in battle. "The lance from the hand of Mithra's enemy is borne away by the wind." He was also the giver of prosperity. He came to Rome with captives brought back by Pompey.

dark. Christianity supplanted Mithra in the West though, as in other conquests, the victor was not uninfluenced by the vanquished. Also the last stand of the old Roman faith was not in the Taurobolium but around the altar of victory in Mother Rome.

MODERN FIRE-WORSHIPERS

The faith of Zoroaster still lives. In Persia the sacred fires are nearly out—only about 10,000 followers of the prophet are left[15]—but there are about 100,000 Parsees in India mostly in Bombay. These are the descendants of the faithful who fled from Persia after the Mohammedan invasions. They have kept their faith and racial strain pure at great cost in an alien civilization. They are folk of unusual intelligence, business shrewdness and great generosity. They are, at present, divided into "modernist" and "fundamentalist" groups. The modernists want converts from outside the Parsee groups, the fundamentalists would admit no one of alien caste. So keen an observer as Moulton holds that without new blood from the outside "there will be no Parsees to divide the charities in the course of a few generations. Then the sacred fires will be extinguished forever." The sacred fire has become the final symbol of Zoroaster's faith. It is light and pure; no alien is allowed to see its flame. It is housed in a fire-temple, nursed in an urn, fed with sandalwood and served by a zealous priesthood.

When a new fire is to be kindled, it is compounded of sixteen different fires, all purified after a long and complicated ritual. Fire is kindled from fire ninety-one times before the flame is pure enough and one of the contributory fires must have been kindled by lightning. This distillation of flame from flame is one of the most curious rituals in all religion, but there is a poetry in it to appeal to the imagination. "The Tower of Silence" is always the complement of the fire-temple, the Temple for the living, the Tower for the dead. Since fire and earth and water are all sacred the dead can neither be burned, buried nor committed to stream or sea. The towers are round, high and built on a hill if possible and the vultures brood over them perpetually. The dead are carried there by corpse bearers —an unhappy caste doomed to perpetual ceremonial uncleanness—

[15] Known as the Gabars. See *Encyclopedia of Religion and Ethics*, Vol. 6, pages 147-156.

and left for the vultures. When the bones are picked clean, they are cast into a central well and crumble away. The guardians about the towers are visited by the living who there remember their dead, repeat their prayer and repent of their sins. Even the Tower of Silence can not break the link between the living and the dead.

But that tower is a far cry from an ancient prophet in a trance in the hilltops of Iran praying:

> This I ask Thee, tell it to me truly, Lord!
> Who the Sire was, Father first of all Holiness?
> Who the pathway for the sun and stars ordained?
> Who, through whom the moon doth wax and wane again?
> This, and much else do I long, O God, to know.

CHAPTER V

The Faith of Old Aryan India

THE LURE OF INDIA

INDIA has had a magic power to enthrall the western imagination. The great captains have always dreamed of adding it to their empires, its coasts have allured the sea-faring, its jewels are a tradition, its templed cities a wonder of pride and devotion, its rich variety of race and caste and custom a challenge to the scholar. Above all, India is religion incarnate, immemorial religion still alive. If one adds Christianity and Mohammedanism to the religions native to India, there is not a form religion has taken in its entire development which does not now exist there. Ancient animisms are possibly modified, but they exist among the most primitive.

"Hinduism," says Sir Charles Eliot,[1] "has not been made but has grown. It is a jungle, not a building . . . Any attempt to describe Hinduism as one whole leads to startling contrasts. The same religion enjoins self-mortification and orgies: commands human sacrifices and yet counts it a sin to eat meat or crush an insect; has more priests, rites and images than ancient Egypt or medieval Rome and yet outdoes Quakers in rejecting all externals. . . . All who admit the claim [of the Brahman] to direct the thought of India and accord a nominal recognition to the authority of the Veda are within the spacious fold or menagerie, neither the devil-worshiping aborigine nor the atheistic philosopher is excommunicated."

And yet the jungle was once not a jungle, but a nature-worship in which sun and storm, fire and rain-bringing clouds were hymned by priestly bards, worshiped in sacrifices laid on a carpet of grass by warriors who made a virtue of cattle stealing and loved their roan horses. The most learned know little enough of the aboriginal inhabitants of India—dark-skinned folk (Dravidians) who came from none know where, occupied the Peninsula, mixed their blood with the Aryan invaders, colored a nobler religion with their dark

[1] *Hinduism and Buddhism,* Vol. I, page 41 and page xvii.

superstitions and lasted on. The oldest epic of India begins history with the wars of heroes, 3000 B.C. Prose fact knows nothing of that. India did not know how to write till the seventh century B.C. Before that time there is nothing but poetry and memory and the witness of language to old ways of life and old uses of things.

THE ARYAN CONQUEST

We do know that a more vigorous Aryan stock pierced the passes of the mountains which guard the northwestern frontiers of India and settled along the upper reaches of the Ganges and its tributaries. They were blood kin to the stock which settled Persia and yet there were marked differences in religious temper. There is a poetry in their sacred books one does not find in the Persian Bible. They had a gift for vast conjecture and really acute speculation the Iranian never had and, until the heat of India burned the force out of them, they were born warriors. Something of these differences may have turned their backs on their kinsmen and driven them southeast in quest of wealth and adventure. They found plenty of both.

The conquest of a land already occupied was not easy—so much their epics and hymns tell us. There is always the sound of battle mingled with their prayer and praise. The bow and the chariot were their battle furnishings.

> With Bow let us win, with Bow, the battle.
> With Bow be victors in the sharp encounters.
> The Bow does to the foeman what he loves not.
> Bow-weaponed may we subjugate all quarters.

They armed their gods with their own weapons: they heard the chariot wheels of Indra above the storm and prayed the help of celestial charioteers in their charges. As they won the river valleys they built rude forts and carried on forays therefrom. There seem to have been five tribes in the beginning but in time the caste system supplanted the tribes and seamed Indian society with class distinctions, against which time and change have fretted themselves out.

Racial distinctions disappeared; the priest, the king, the subject and the serf remained. The kings were the chief of the nobility, the nobles were the flower of the "twice born" Aryans, distinguished for valor, strength and beauty. Naturally they made their gods in their own image, a heavenly nobility headed by Indra. Priests came into India with the migrants and developed there into a hereditary class, specialists in song, invocation and ritual sacrifice. One does not, in reading the earlier Vedic hymns, get the impression of a highly specialized priestly class. The householder was still his own priest for daily domestic purposes. The accepted authorities think differently, however; they find seven different kinds, of whom the "reciting priest" is most important. Very likely he was, to begin with, both bard and priest, composing the hymns and then offering them as an acceptable sacrifice to the gods—an office in which any poet would delight.

THE RELIGION OF THE VEDAS

The religion of the Rig-Veda is the religion of the old Aryan aristocracy of northwest India before they had seen the copper-colored Indian Ocean or felt the full force of the southern sun. The priesthood and the nobility were mutually dependent; the priest kept his patrons in good standing with the gods; they supplied him with creature comforts.

The material needs of the priesthood are never forgotten in these artless rhapsodies. Many of the Vedic hymns are in praise of a patron's generosity or an adroit poetic appeal for more:

Even him who would not give do thou, O Glorious Pushan, urge to give,
And make the niggard's soul grow soft . . .
And make this hymn of ours produce kine, horses and a store of wealth.

If we can believe the singers, the nobles were often princely in their gifts, though something should be allowed for poetic exaggeration and the desire to excite others to like good works; art for art's sake was never the motto of the Vedic bards.

Nothing remains of all this but the hymns, oldest of the sacred books of India, which the "reciting priests" chanted around the sacrificial fire. Veda means "knowledge" or "wisdom," being blood kin to our English "wit." The Vedas then are the books of knowledge, for all the knowledge India had three thousand years ago was in them. There are four Vedic collections; the Rig-Veda, a book of hymns, the Atharva-Veda, a collection of spells and incantations for all sorts of purposes, some of them by no means seemly; the Yajur-Veda, a priest's ritual and liturgy, and the Sama-Veda, a kind of chant-book with musical notation.

To get these dry details finished, Rig is the name for the poetry of praise—the Rig-Veda is "praise wisdom." It may be more lauda- tory than wise, but it lives up to its name. The four between them are a kind of four gospels of old Aryan-Indian faith—one gospel for the aristocracy, a second for the choir-master, a third for priests and a fourth for common folk who want religion to cure their ills and get them a man-child. The Rig-Veda is the great documentary source for the other three Vedas, very much as the Gospel of Mark is an important source for the Gospels of Matthew and Luke.[2]

The Rig-Veda consists of something over one thousand hymns (1017 or 1028), divided into ten groups, about as much as Homer wrote. Their authorship is ascribed to poetic families—which is as it may be. Their date is disputed. The more daring say the oldest hymns are four thousand years old, the more conservative, three thou- sand. They are at least very old and voice something older still, the customs and the memories which the "fair-skinned" brought with them through the passes of the Hindu-Kush mountains. They were kept alive for centuries only in memory, being passed from genera- tion to generation by word of mouth. Existing manuscripts go back only to the twelfth and fourteenth centuries A.D., and there is not any material thing now left of the world to which they belonged to challenge or support their tradition.

Nothing is left but the hymns themselves—anonymous voices from a dateless past. They were from the first committed to memories so tenacious and exact that the texts have suffered less from being kept in memory and orally transmitted than most written texts have suffered from the copyist. There are even now "living manuscripts" in India, oral reciters whom the scholars consult in editing the great texts and whose accuracy they find infallible. The written texts them- selves are so guarded by curious mnemonic devices as to fix them beyond the possibility of change. We may be sure that we possess now the unchanged words of songs chanted before campfire or altar three thousand years ago.

The art of literary criticism was not yet born, nor was plagiarism a sin for the holy. The sacredness of set phrases being then as now

[2] H. D. Griswold, *The Religion of the Rig-Veda*, Oxford Press, page 57.

a present help in moments of scant inspiration, it was possible most imposingly to expand a matter essentially simple. The Rig-Veda is the old hymns and psalms of a fresh and simple faith, shot through here and there with gleams of insight, and always, always a poet's redaction of the sweep and glory of nature in much praise and a little prayer. The praise and prayer alike are addressed to the personification of the more evident nature forces; Indra, god of the storm clouds; Agni, fire, celestial in the lightning, near and kind on the hearthstone. It is a sun and sky and dawn worship with a place for night. There is a simple wealth of oft repeated imagery and now and then some really noble voicing of the wonder and mystic beauty of the world without, in which faith finds its purest rapture, poetry its noblest inspiration. These priest bards had in their veins the blood and genius of singers who have made literature.

WHAT THE WORSHIPERS SOUGHT

The priest bard would in time become the Brahman, the rajah a jeweled potentate. The religion was to be everything between the grossest of superstitions, and the most subtle of philosophies. But nothing of this had happened when the Indian world was very young. The rajahs rejoiced in a fresh land above which cedar clad hills starred with rhododendron rose to inviolable snows whose melting fed their rivers. The pageantry of the sky above them, the lure of the land about them, the challenge of the foe before them were life enough. The wealth the gods are asked to give is horse and kine and gold and victory. Their altars are earth, their altar cloths were fresh grass and I should think the priests themselves were more concerned about their songs than their sacrifices. They sing out of a life of ample force to lusty and very human gods. The gods are generally kind and ask only to share what their worshipers can give.

There is a very simple sense of sin in the hymns. The gods are by no means faultless and they ask no impossible sanctity of their followers. Such prayers of confession, burdened with the travail of conscience and the futile quest for holiness, as touch Babylonian tablets with pathos and shadow the ritual of the Avestas are not entirely wanting here, but they are rare.

The hymns lie almost entirely within temporal horizons, though

the gods are immortal, and yet there is some dim sense of the eternal
kindness.

> With fond heart thou acceptest even the poor man's prayer,
> When he has brought his gift to gain security
> Thou art called father, caring even for the weak
> And, wisest, to the simple one thou teachest love.

The devout wanted then very much what the devout want now:

> Make long our days of life and wipe out all our sins;
> Ward off our enemies: be with us evermore . . . ,
> Bring us present prosperity with noble offspring,
> Be ye our helpers where men win the booty.

After all a rajah's needs three thousand years ago were comparatively simple. There is a constant and fascinating reference to
weapons, tools and old ways of life. One could reconstruct a chariot,
axle, wheels, lynch-pin, spokes and felly, from the war hymns; the
wheel, especially, being highly praised. Evidently it was still the
craftsman's pride, as a well horsed chariot was the warrior's pride.
In "The Song of the Bow" the archer's equipment is completely
described with a real wealth of poetic imagination:

> Close to his ear, as fain to speak, she presseth,
> Holding her well-loved friend in her embraces;
> Strained on the Bow she whispers like a woman—
> This Bow-string that preserves us in the combat.

The Various and Revealing Character of the Hymns

It is this artless interweaving of old ways and needs of life with
the ways and needs of the gods that gives these hymns their charm
and leads one to linger over them not for the divinities they laud
but for the society they reveal. Some of them are the songs of border-
thieves and cattle raiders, chanted at night amid the camp fires:
"Loud neighed the steeds in frays for kine." They greet the rising
storm with a cheer; one can hear the thunder re-echo the prayer
and praise of devout worshipers. The sun is invoked to help the
traveler and guard him from wolves and robbers.

> Lead us to meadows rich in grass past all pursuers,
> Lead us, fire, smoke bannered spreader of the light.

Kings, chiefs, warriors, come to brief life in the songs that have so long outlived them. Their horses are bay and roan; their cows are black or roan; their women are generally referred to in an honorable way, staid matrons, home makers and home keepers. We see the darkness scattered—there is a fear of the dark behind the Vedic love of light—and the dawn comes up like Guido's Aurora:

> She hath shone brightly like a youthful woman
> Stirring to motion every living creature.

>   .   .   .   .   .

> She hath beamed forth lovely with golden colors,
> Mother of kine, guide of the days she bringeth.

We see the house fire lighted;

> The scattered homes and all life
> The mightly flame of household fire pervadest.

And the day's work begins.

The sky is overcast, the storm clouds come up on the wings of the wind: "The mighty winds break forth, the lightnings flash and fly." The storm is over, the cows come home in the evening and night, elder sister of the dawn, takes man and beast back again to their rest and their fears.

The light and shadow of an older faith than the Vedas lies across these pages. Old Father Sky is there and Mother Earth and a fog of demons and spirits, who may, though I should think it unlikely, have been prehistoric gods fallen from their former estate with little left to do save to oppose the high gods and plague humanity. The enemies of the gods are of great force and the hymns re-echo a celestial warfare in which Indra is always victorious, though the victories are hard won. Soma inflames his courage; he drives his enemies before him, storms and destroys their fortresses, plunders them of their wealth.

Beyond debate there are survivals here of that endless strife which our humanity has discovered and shared in nature. There is, so the primitive believed, a malign force to withhold the rain, the moon is pursued by enemies which now and then possess and darken it—or else the moon itself may be the enemy of the sunlight and darkness. And about these central antagonisms there is a margin of incessant strife. Even the great ones maintain their sovereignty only through vigilance and valor. It is easy for the creative imagination to personify such combatants and make a drama of their deeds, adding detail to detail until myth has become history, clad in garments embroidered of fancy and colored with brave invention.

DEMONS AND PROTECTIVE SPELLS

For all their love of sunlight and their high spirits the men and women who listened to the Vedic chants lived haunted lives. The demons of the Rig-Veda are bad enough, having the gift to take the form of dogs and night birds or even masquerade as a husband or a lover, but they are colorless for terror and evil compared with the evil spirits of later and more fearsome time. These become near kin to the grotesques of mediaeval cathedrals. Their heads or feet are turned backward, they are horned and multi-headed. They haunt weddings and women in childbirth, they cause disease and madness. All the entries to the body must be guarded against them for they love blood as Indra loved Soma. Skulls are their chosen drinking cups.

It needs a fine web of spells to protect a man or woman from such resourceful foes and the priest was always willing to weave the web—at a price. He was likely to use a natural ingenuity in magnifying the dangers of the unprotected. Fear and imagination did the rest, though always somewhere in the background were the natural ills of life, weighted heavy with ignorance.

But there is a brighter side to the religion of the Veda than this. Father Sky, who was to become in time Father Zeus, was never more than a misty vastness of a name—perhaps it needed a steadfast sky brooding over a land more kind to become divine. The pageantry of the sky was pantheon enough for the Vedic bard. Ushas, the dawn, is the daughter of the sky, sister to the night, bride to the sun-god for whom she unveils her bosom. The sun-god himself drives from the horizon in his chariot drawn by red horses accompanied by a divine retinue.

There is no logical consistency in the conceptions of celestial phenomena which lie behind these poems and care has been taken not to burden a narration which is hard enough to keep in hand, with names. The names are distinct enough but the divinities they stand for melt into one another as cloud formations edged with light meet and merge. There are certainly five, perhaps six, sun-gods in the Rig-Veda, properly glorified and opulently described. They were a treasure to the poet since they challenged his invention, but they handicap the student. They really represent different aspects of the sun in his royal progress across the firmament, urging men to action, surveying

> . . . the earth's eight summits lofty
> The three waste lands, the leagues, the seven rivers.

Then the brief twilight becomes a velvet starlit dark:

> The one who weaveth folds her work together,
> The artisan lays down his task half-finished;
>
> . . . . . .
>
> All who have fared abroad yearn for their fireside;
>
> . . . . . .
>
> His nest the egg-born seeks, their stall the cattle,
> Each in his place god Savitar appoints them.

What does it matter whether the god who does all this is Surya, Savitar, Vishnu or Puhan, or whether these are tribal sun-gods or "special-gods" each with his own solar task? This is what the sun does and these old children of the sun praised him for his power, his mercy and his splendor, found in his light—as the devout have always found—the suggestion of a light still more deeply interfused, and prayed to the light behind the light for illumination.

> May we attain that excellent
> Glory of Savitar the god,
> That he may stimulate our thoughts.

Then like another psalmist, seeing themselves in that light, they prayed for pardon:

> If we have done aught 'gainst the gods through thoughtlessness,
> Weakness of will, or insolence, men as we are,
> Whether we've sinned against the gods or mortal man
> Make thou us free from sin and guilt, O Savitar.

INDRA AND OTHER DIVINITIES

Indra is Lord of Lords in the Rig-Veda. He is the entire sky-force friendly to man, the enemy of the enemies of life, "bearer of the bolt," captain of heaven's artillery. He has ruled, changing his name but not his essential nature, from the skies of India, Greece, Rome, Germany and Scandinavia. He passed his thunderbolt to Zeus on Olympus and Jupiter above the Tiber. Thor forged his hammer out of it and went out to fight frost giants. He is nowhere, though, so grandiose, so richly attended, so adorned with murky splendor as in India. He is to Thor what the crashing tumult of an Indian storm is to the leashed thunder of the north.

His bolt is golden, jagged with a hundred—or a thousand—points, his arrows are hundred pointed. He may command a thousand horses with a sheen like peacocks' feathers for his chariot, if he will. He was a Soma drinker from the day of his birth. In one fight-engendered thirst he drank thirty lakes. He had the physical capacity for so mighty a draught; heaven and earth are not big enough to girdle him, he is larger than ten earths. He will eat a hundred buffaloes at a meal. It is hard to furnish a god like that with a proper family tree. His father is naturally an older sky-god. There is a legend that he slew his father to get the Soma (the family relations of the old gods have never been happy). His mother is as nebulous in myth as the mists out of which the storm clouds issue. He asserted his godhead in refusing to be born save through his mother's side.

So lusty a divinity was sure to have had many amours; they are duly on record and do him no credit—though Zeus was as bad or worse. (Thor is the only really respectable thunder-god.) He is always timelessly young and timelessly old. He is kind to man and earth, rain-giver for the pastures and liberator of imprisoned waters. He frees the rain from the clouds and the rivers from mountain prisons. One imaginative scholar believes the serpent demon against which he waged an epic warfare was the glacial ice—or else the ice of the Himalayas. If the first is true, his legends are the stuff of our oldest and dimmest ancestral memories, but there is no proof save allusions which may mean something far more simple and more probable.

Once imagination begins to play about a theme like this, there is no end to it. Indra changes form as cloud forms change. He wears the immensity of the sky as a garment. He is generous as nature is generous, incalculable as nature has always been incalculable to ignorance. He is akin to all those heroes who swagger through legend armed with a club or a lance—dragon-slayers and knights-errant for whom no odds are too great, no task impossible. If they were, to begin with, the all-conquering sun—Sol Invictus—it makes no great difference; humanity has not been without its own heroes and, if they have borrowed some splendor from the sun, they have in turn lent to its light some radiance of the human spirit.

There are no sea-gods in the Rig-Veda; its religion is the faith of an inland folk. But there are water-goddesses, though of no great force or character. They are always young as rivers fed by mountain snows are always young; they cleanse as the rivers cleanse and have gifts of life, wealth and immortality. They are associated with honey in a curious way, perhaps because the river meadows were rich in flowers. Honey is often mentioned in the old hymns—always a delicacy and a most useful figure of speech for all desirable things. Milk was mixed with honey and Soma possibly so sweetened. Some of the divinities who play no great part in the oldest hymns developed later into outstanding gods—Rudra and Vishnu for example. Rudra was doubtless the howling storm to begin with, destructive as wind, beneficent as rain. In the later ritual he is a god both of terror and kindness with so confusing a combination of both attributes as to make his cult a hopeless puzzle. In the earliest hymns, he is attended by the violence of the winds, storm cloud carriers, called Maruts—if the name matters—and much sung about.

The key to all this confusion is simple enough. The general celestial forces are all personalized and then a devout and poetic imagination takes every aspect of day and dawn, wind, storm and cloud and resolves them into divinities who change as the weather changes, to be feared or loved as they are kind or cruel, and to become anything imagination wishes to make them. I do not wonder modern students of a nature religion of wonder, ignorance, awe, naïve imagination and the poet's magic touch, use dusty pages to find a system in it. You might as well give a logician an English March or an Indian rainy season and expect him to make a Critique of Pure Reason out of it.

AGNI AND HIS CULT

Agni, the fire-god, is second only to Indra in the early Indian faith. He is the mediator between earth and heaven, messenger of the gods to man and the porter of the sacrifice to the gods. It is easy enough to see why he is thus empowered. Fire has always been a mystery, a blessing and a fear. It made us masters of the cold and dark; its flame drew the lonely together, its hearthstones became literally the foyer of the family. The gleam of it has marked the path of civilization, the wonder of it kindled the poet's song. No wonder those who first spread cold hands to its warmth believed it the peculiar treasure of the gods, zealously guarded and stolen from them at a tragic price. The fire bringer was humanity's first hero.

Indian mythology has, however, no Prometheus. Agni is the son of earth and sky or else of wood and water. It was a curious conceit to father fire with water, but cloud waters are probably indicated, which would connect Agni with the lightning. The early Aryan kindled his fire with fire sticks and the relation of the two sticks supplied many analogies. Agni lives in earth, air and sky. His form is as fluid as water or flowers, he is one and many. He is the friend of the homes of men, the hearthstone is his altar. Fire kindling and fire keeping created a ritual in which religion and the happy human ways of the Aryan home are beautifully interwoven. The relation of fire to sacrifice is plain as fire light.

When a thing is burnt the gods can get at it. It is Agni's office, then, to offer the gods the grateful gifts of men—melted butter, flesh and Soma, without which their strength would fail. Being both polite and obliging he brings the gods down to the sacrifice and seats them on the strewn grass. He is himself the perfect priest. He makes no mistakes and beneath his touch the grass offerings become fragrant and mystic and rise to ethereal regions—drink and food fit for the divine.

He needs to be fed himself for tasks so demanding and various.

> This is goodness that when kindled in thy house,
> And soma-fed, thou dost awake most merciful,
> Treasure and wealth thou givest to thy worshipper;
> In thine own friendship, Agni, may we live unharmed.

His name gleams through the Rig-Veda as flame through shadows:

> He who at eve and dawn receives
> Praise for his beauty, house by house,
> Whose ordinance is inviolate.

Being so near to human folk, he sees their shameful night-veiled deeds and knows their sin, his flame is judgment for the unrighteous but his warmth is mercy, and, being near to the gods, he also intercedes for the sinful:

> . . . O Agni
> For us appease the gods' fierce indignation,
>
> .   .   .   .   .
>
> As liberal one have mercy, heed our prayers.

He is a guest to be sought and cherished:

> O Agni, holy and divine, with splendor and thy pleasant tongue
> Bring hither and adore the gods.
>
> .   .   .   .   .
>
> Sit with the gods upon the grass.

CONCERNING SOMA

Agni is the agent of sacrifice, flame-robed priest of hearthstone and altar. Soma is the sacrificial drink, dear to gods and men. It would be easy to catalogue, from the Vedic hymns, the effects of this narcotic upon the early Aryan outlook upon life. They seem to explain its allure.

> Ailments have fled away, diseases vanished,
> The powers of darkness have become affrighted.
> With might hath Soma mounted up within us;
> The dawn we've reached, where men renew existence.[3]

Some scholars think it was not alcoholic, because it was freshly prepared three times a day and would hardly have had time to ferment, but the glowing hymns in praise of it could hardly have been sung out of a purely poetic imagination. If it were not fermented, it was herb juice of a most potent character. Unhappily—or happily—the secret of it is lost these thousands of years with the secrets of other ambrosial foods and drinks which men and the gods used together when the world was young; the cup is gone—only the

[3] The Veda is prodigal in praise of Soma. Indra and Agni who have naturally a prodigious thirst loved it. The gods are reported as greatly refreshed by it and were thereby moved to mighty deeds of valor. (These deep-drinking gods loved fighting and horses.) Soma as Haoma appears in Persian religion (see Carl Clemen, *op. cit.*). Zoroaster forbade its use.

song remains. The plant, yellow, with hanging branches, from which it was pressed seems to have grown in the mountains.

A plant so potent was naturally the gift of the gods (an eagle brought it down) and the juice of it was pounded or pressed out in a ritual which became the very soul of this old religion. No priest of a later faith was ever more formal in his movements, more careful of his vessels, more constrained to say the proper words, than the minister of the Soma-pressing rite, with stones and oxhide and strainer for his altar vessels, Mother Earth for his altar and fresh strewn grass for his altar cloth.

This archaic ceremony begun by men who found the Sursum Corda—their uplifted hearts—in some strange and stimulating drink and thought themselves for a season akin to the gods—presently became symbolism. The grossness of it was lost; some finer sense of its spiritual significance remained. A cult which was narcotic stimulation to begin with finishes with a prayer to be made, through purity of life, fit for immortality.

> Where radiance inexhaustible
> Dwells, and the light of heaven is set,
> Place me, clear flowing one, in that
> Imperishable and deathless world.

There are gleams enough of ethical insight in the old Vedic faith but no clear light. For the most part these divinities of light and storm, dawn and cloud-filled sky take their own way half-careless of mankind. They are as dependent upon their worshipers as the devout are dependent upon them. But human fault does not bring drouth, nor repentance rain. A strong caprice drives across the firmament, one sees Dawn bare her breast to her lover the Sun, Indra wield his hundred pointed bolt, the Maruts rush through the jungle. The priest presses the Soma juice; Agni invites the thirsty gods, and they drink on the grass together. Is there nothing finer? No divine power of right and order? Yes, there is.

RITA AND VARUNA

There is the awesome suggestion of a vaster Sovereignty behind the tumult and caprice of the lesser gods. The oldest Aryan faith, as we have seen, was shot through with some sense of an all-encompassing order, Rita,[4] nebulous mother of art and right, law and dignity. Rita is right law for nature, the control out of which the dawn rises and the sun shines; it is right conduct for men. This regnant and unfailing order is associated with divinities older than Indra and Agni; the Adityas, whose name seems to mean the "free" or "unfettered." This profound instinct which associated freedom and law had in it a rare, prophetic quality.

The Adityas are unfettered save by Rita; there is a law to which even the gods are subject and in that they find their freedom. A comparatively late theology made Aditi, the boundless, mother of the highest gods. Take off the "a," which is equivalent to our English "un" in unfettered, and one has "diti" left. The dictionary makers believe that our own great words "time" and "tide" grow from that root. Time and tide are fetters by which all existence and force are bound. Only the gods are the offspring of the unfettered. The theologians of thirty centuries ago believed that the procession of the gods issued out of the infinite: beyond this they could not go.

Varuna "the ethical God" of the old faith is the God of what moral law there was. Sin is the violation of his law:

> Being but men, O Varuna, whatever law
> Of thine we may have broken through thoughtlessness,
> For that transgression do not injure us, O God.

The sacrifices which please him best are a contrite spirit and a humble heart. His are the laws by which the stars are ruled; he appointed a pathway for the sun; he has gifts for all the needs of men.

> The air hath Varuna placed among the tree tops,
> Milk in the cows and strength in the swift horses,
> Wisdom in hearts and fire within the waters,
> In heaven the sun and Soma on the mountains.

. . . . .

If we have sinned against the man who loves us, have ever wronged a brother, friend or comrade,
The neighbor ever with us, or a stranger, O Varuna, remove from us the trespass
If we, as gamesters cheat at play, have cheated, done wrong unwillingly or sinned of purpose,

[4] More accurately Rta.

Cast all these sins away like loosened fetters, and, Varuna, let us be thine own beloved.

And yet in spite of Varuna's mercy the note of moral perplexity is heard, "what count ye truth and what untruth, where is your firm support of law."

There is in general through the Rig-Veda a sense of powers who befriend the five tribes, divine forces in changing forms who meet the great or petty needs of their worshipers, keep their cows from straying, help them in some little long forgotten fray and save them from what is stronger than themselves. If ever the faith of early Aryan India had ripened into an ethical monotheism, Varuna would have been its God. There is sound reason to believe that he belonged to a still older faith, the religion of the folk of the "grassy plain" before they separated to trek into Persia and India, and that Ahura- Mazda of Zoroaster is that same old Law-and-Right-god lifted to his sovereignty by a prophet's genius. But there was never a prophet in India, though there were many teachers and not a few dreamers. There was no force in Varuna to displace Indra and his turbulent following. He rather fades out of the picture and leaves only divini- ties whose capricious grossness the popular mind magnifies and whose divided empire Brahmanism rejected. But that is a story still to be told.

CREATION AND THE FUTURE LIFE

Since no religion is ever content till it has accounted for man and the world, there will be hymns of Genesis in the Rig-Veda. They are wanting in clearness and system and seem to assume the general knowledge of what they sing, as though they voiced a body of myth and tradition familiar to gods and men alike. The gods built the world as a carpenter builds a house—though there is some question as to the source of material. The sun measures the space with his beams for a measuring rod, the sky is the beamless, rafterless roof. This desirable House of the World is furnished with light, rain and air and is ready for man's occupation. So simple a cosmogony was sure to be enriched by later speculators. The Rig-Veda universe ended by becoming heaven, earth and intermediate space. Heaven and earth are two bowls touching at their rims. There may possibly be a firmament above the sky to hold the stars. Primitive folk have always found it difficult to get the setting sun back into the east. The Vedic bards were inclined to think that he stole back to his morning station under cover of darkness. There is little speculation about the creation of man. The rajahs who had taken and held what they wanted of the house of the world with their bows and chariots, were not greatly concerned as to how the first occupants of the house had come into being. Later Indian thought evolved magnificent schemes of creation; the Aryan warrior took himself for granted.

There is, however, a tradition of a father of the human race known as Manu pitar or father Manu. Since Manu is just our word man, the Indian Adam was only Father man, a statement as safe as it is simple. The theologian was, of course, not satisfied with so general a covering statement and presently furnished Father man a god father and, since a mother was also needed, supplied her also, though the detail of the story does the divine father no credit. At this point two creation myths get hopelessly entangled and the result is two ancestors of the human race. Yama is the more important for he becomes a king, dies and sets up another kingdom beyond the grave. This kingdom of Yama is the heaven of the Rig-Veda (though by one more dizzy turn Yama later became Lord of Hell and judge of the wicked).

The dead, then, go to Yama, by ancient pathways worn by ghostly feet—

> Go forth, go forth upon those ancient pathways,
> By which our former fathers have departed,
> Thou shalt behold god Varuna and Yama,
> Both kings, in funeral offerings rejoicing.

There are hymns which describe burial and hymns which describe cremation. Whether burned or buried, the soul, ascending the ancient paths, reaches a world of light. There it finds a heavenly body, unworn, unscarred of battle:

> Leaving behind all blemish homeward hie thee,
> And all-resplendent join thee with a body.

Yama's palace is a pleasant place and eminently desirable, his land is bright and well watered, the dead are reunited and no desire is unsatisfied. That land is kept for the brave, the generous and the pious. The depths of hell are kept for the wicked and impious.

> O Indra, dash the evildoers down
> Into the pit, into the gloom profound and bottomless,
> So that not one of them may ever chance emerge.

Time and devotion naturally evoked an enormous body of comment upon the Rig-Veda. Any edition and the notes which go with it is curiously like a commentary on the Hebrew Psalms. "This hymn," the learned editor begins, "is attributed to Gotama, the Son of Rahugana." (If Gotama was the singer, modesty was not his outstanding quality: "No such hymn was ever known," he says of his own effort, "as this which Gotama sounded for You, O Maruts—." A half dozen pages of notes follow for a half a dozen verses of praise, to justify textual readings, support disputed translations, explain every obscure allusion and finally explain the explanations.

Back of the western editions, translations and commentaries, there are the studies of Indian scholars. Their names carry the same weight of authority as learned Christian commentators carry in the interpretation of the Old and New Testaments. The tireless labor of western scholars for the past fifty years has made possible more advances in the understanding of what Max Müller calls "the dark and helpless utterances of the early poets of India." The East Indian scholars whose erudition—and ingenuity—has sometimes illumined and sometimes obscured the faith and ritual of their fathers' fathers have helped us to recapture a vanished social and religious order.

So much of our knowledge of the past has to be sifted from the dust of buried palaces, tombs and temples. Here is the past brought to us by "winged words," living as only the poet can keep anything alive. Religion, also, grows old and fixed so soon. It is a boon to find it adventurously free, growing beneath each new touch; the very confusions which puzzle the scholar are creative confusions, aspects of the stormy splendor of any great growth of the human spirit, voiced by poets "continually singing out of new powers for worship." But when the commentators east and west have done their best and their worst, the old Vedic hymns remain a sun-and-sky and dawn-worship, with some revelation through their measures of cosmic order, moral law and "unfettered" gods who are in bonds to the integrity of their own natures, whose service is righteousness and peace.

And always beyond are horizons down which Surya—the Sun-God—rides,

Whose goal is distant, speeding onward shining; There is the house of Yama where the "all resplendent" dead are lost in light.

THE DECAY OF VEDIC RELIGION:
THE GROWTH OF RITUALISM AND CHARMS

In spite of the meticulous care with which the old Brahman hymns were preserved, the religion they voice disappeared. That was inevitable. The race whose morning faith they sang had in it an enormous potency of growth and change. The subtle, inquiring speculative mind of Brahmanic India could not rest content with Indra and Agni. That mind began and continued a process of inquiry into the causes, nature and processes of things and personality which finally resulted in a system before which the western mind will always be helpless while acknowledging the range and daring of it.

If India had produced prophets instead of subtle thinkers, men of moral and spiritual vision like Zoroaster and Amos, instead of dreamers contemplating their navels or a Gautama seeking, through the cessation of all desire, an escape from the weariness of life, the whole outcome of religion in India might have been different, and the story of religion robbed of fascinating chapters. But, as Bishop Butler said: "Things are what they are, and the consequences of them will be what they will be"—and it is just now our business to find out what happened instead of guessing at what might have happened.

Dates become important again—if we could only be sure of them. At any rate, there are several centuries, say from 1000 B.C. to about 600 B.C. or 800 to 600, during which, says Sir Charles Eliot,[5] "rites and ceremonies multiplied and absorbed men's minds to a degree unparalleled in the history of the world and literature occupied itself with the description of discussion of this dreary ceremonial." Some of the rituals like the famous horse sacrifice took two years to carry through and needed a prince's wealth to perform them. (There are improbable traditions of sacrificial sessions lasting one hundred years.) The horse must be allowed to wander as he pleased for a year or two before he became the unconscious instrument of the rite. He must be

[5] *Hinduism and Buddhism*, Vol. I, page 53.

guarded in all his straying. If he went into the territory of a neighboring rajah he was likely to have supplied the not unwelcome occasion for a heady little war. When the proper time was come, the altar must be built in the prescribed way. Not a brick could be laid without its appropriate formula, pages and pages of priests' patter which I should think it unlikely the officiating clerics understood themselves. I spent days in the British Museum over this literature till the sheer weariness of it sent me nodding over the pages—to the scorn, I suspect, of real Orientalists and Orientals, learned scholars in their own lands who spent rapt hours over their own sacred books written in strange characters. To go from all that into London streets running full with the tides of western life and washed with the cool watery sunshine of a late August afternoon was a baptism in reality. The reader may find it all in the Yajur Veda—if he can find the Yajur Veda—but I advise against it. There are enough "dusty answers" without parching one's throat with the dust priests raised over killing a horse twenty-five hundred years ago.

The common-folk of India sacrificed no horses; they could not afford to. They did not perform the Soma sacrifice three times a day; they could not get the Soma plant. They could not afford a Hotar (reciting) priest to repeat for them hymns to Indra and Agni. They could and did offer what gods they knew cakes and melted butter poured on the fire from two wooden spoons. But they had cares and needs and humanly diverse longings of their own—some of them distinctly human. They were ignorant and entangled. They wanted a religion to help them through and get them what they wanted. They had also that belief in the magic power of words which is, one suspects, a divine inheritance from the wonder of our kind at the gift and power of language itself. They believed that the proper words said by the proper persons at the proper time would cure, enrich, empower, avenge. There was never so simple a means to ends so desirable; the proper words and formulae grew and multiplied, since there was always demand.

The Atharva-Veda, the book of "popular religion," has a charm, an incantation, a frozen prayer, what you will, for everything. These are mostly four verse hymns, gnomic sentences to be repeated at any rite, to fulfill any desire. One can make a list of all the ills to which flesh was heir in India five hundred years B.C.—sickness of any sort was demon possession—the demon must be prayed or compelled to leave.—

> Release thou him from headache and from cough
> Whatsoever hath entered each joint of him . . .
> Let it attach itself to forest trees and mountains.

There is ritual of magic to go with the words. A fever is cured by heating an axe, dipping it in hot water and making a lotion from the water—like is cured by like! Sometimes the prayers are touching in their simplicity.

> Whoso of you, O Gods, are fathers and sons, do you, accordant, hear this utterance of mine:
> To you all I commit this man. Happy into old age shall you carry him.

Some of them can be quickly said, a kind of pious ejaculation:

> Ye, O Gods, that are in the heaven, that are in the earth, that are in the atmosphere, in the herbs, in the cattle, within the mountains, for long life!

The practice of old Indian medical faculties is curious. In repeating one incantation against disease the patient is doused with prepared water outside the house, a clod of earth and stuff from an ant-hill is bound upon him, he is doused again under an ox-harnessed plough and finally put in an old hole in an empty house. If he lived he was cured. A new born baby could not be properly clothed unless the proper words were said:

> Thee here, of whom we take the garment to be first worn;
> Let all the gods favor; thee here, growing with good growth,
> Let many brothers be born after, as one well born.

Here are the right words to be said in building a home:

> Just here I fix my dwelling, firm may it stand in security,
> Unto thee here, O Dwelling, may we resort with all our heroes . . .
> Stand rich in horses, in kine, in pleasantness, in butter and milk.

The Indian ideal of a wife is evident:

> Do thou come creeping to me, gentle, with fury allayed,
> Entirely mine, pleasant spoken, submissive.

One prayer, as though to the Unknown God, speaks across the centuries:

He who is soul-giving, strength-giving, of whom all, of whom even the gods, wait upon the instruction.

But there is no end to this. One finds an appropriate formula for everything from worms to sin, every kind of disease, bad dreams, enemies, to attach a cow to a calf, to win a woman's love, to strengthen any failing power, for children and the power to beget them, for rain or the lucky face of the dice. There is here that wholly unmoral association of every possible need and deed with some supernatural power which is an outstanding characteristic of Hindu religion. It invests every aspect of Hindu life with religion in a way to perplex and maybe rebuke the western mind, but what religion gains in universality it loses in ethical distinction. Hindu devotion gives religion strange bed-fellows.

In such ways as these the bright dawn of Indo-Aryan faith broadened into a dusty day. The old hymns became rigid word-worshiped texts. Religion became a web of spells and incantations, as though the high powers could be used to make a field or a woman fertile. Religion became, along another line, a weary system of ritual. Along still another line, religion became a tenacious speculative philosophy, the full outcome of which in Brahmanism is still to be considered.

The hot Indian winds took the sap out of a race which needed cold and misty horizons to conserve its strength. The fresh land began to be exhausted, the edge of advancing population pressure began to be felt. India grew tired; the caste system hardened down; the cattle-raiding, fray-loving nobility were sifted out till only kings of provinces were left, shut away from poverty and suffering with their jewels and their women. There was nothing in the old religion to meet a situation like this, nothing but a spell or a priest. The times were ripe for a reformer—or a prophet. India never produced a prophet; she did find a liberator.

The son of a princely house stepped like a shadow out of his father's palace, where the dancing girls slept in shameless abandon, and set out, not to reform an exhausted religion, but to free those who would follow his way from the weariness of all existence. Indian religion had come to the state where the liberator was sure to appear. He came in the fullness of time, the gentlest, strangest prophet in the world, adored still by hundreds of millions of strange, gentle folk. Gautama of the Sakiyas, Siddhartha, Lord Buddha. And with him a new motif came historically into the development of religion. He is the herald of deliverance.[6]

[6] What actually happened is not so simple as these century-spanning paragraphs suggest. The true backgrounds of Buddhism are not in the Vedas nor did Gautama oppose his enlightened wisdom to their poetry or their incantations. He did seek for himself and his followers an escape from the tear-steeped weariness of life, but he opposed his teaching to a vast system of speculation whose roots are in the Vedas but whose full development was the creation of the Indian genius. The chapter on *The Immemorial Faiths of India* is really a rather necessary introduction to the study of Buddhism—at least the first two-thirds of it. Somewhere during the long breakdown of the bright Vedic faith and in ways upon which scholars do not agree, two conceptions emerged which were to color all subsequent Indian thought and life. They were Karma and rebirth or transmigration. Both of these will be considered in the next two chapters. They darkened life with doom and extended the travail of it through an incalculable number of existences, through every phase and form of life from the parasite to the gods. This was the weight of weariness from which Gautama sought escape for himself and those who would follow his way.

CHAPTER VI

Buddhism: Gautama Sits Under the Bo-tree

THERE is an ancient garden in India which reverence tends and nature perennially renews. A great pagoda stands in the center of it and the shadows of a sacred tree fall across the time-worn building. The tree itself is, they say, the descendant of another tree beneath whose considerate and unshifting shadow Gautama sat twenty-five hundred years ago in a travail of mind and soul which issued in his own enlightenment, his assurance that he was at last free from the weary round of birth and rebirth and the beginning of a faith and way of life in which Eastern Asia has for centuries found spiritual peace. They say that Heaven and Earth were shaken by Gautama's enlightenment and the sky rained flowers. Who and what was the man from whom such issues have come?

The plain facts of Siddhartha's life are twice hidden: once by time, once by a wealth of lovely legend. The legends are pictured windows with jeweled settings in which one sees the saint, aureoled by the devotion of the East, through which one sees the man but dimly. Five hundred B.C. is a fairly sound dating for his ministry; a little Indian state brooded over by the Himalayas, one hundred thirty miles north of the city of Benares, was the ancestral home of his people and his own birthplace. The Sakiyas were an Aryan clan, fenced in by the hills to the north, by belligerent neighbors east and west. They kept their holdings and carried on a simple and rather idyllic agricultural life partly because they were a capable folk, partly because their stronger neighbors, jealous of one another, left them alone.

They fought over water-rights as much as anything else, but there was, for a time, a truce between the clans, and rajah Suddhodana married two daughters of a rival chief to make the bond between them doubly strong. Both sisters long remained childless, which was a pity, for a son was much needed to inherit the little principality and secure his father a felicitous immortality by performing the proper ceremonies at his death. There was consequently great rejoicing when the elder sister, forty-five years old, announced a prospective son. There are legendary miracles enough associated with the birth of Gautama; his being born at all at his mother's age is wonder enough.

She set out for her father's house as her time came on, that, in accordance with custom, the child might be born there, but her travail interrupted her journey and the baby—it was a boy—was born literally by the roadside in a pleasant grove of satin trees. The mother died within a week—her age might explain that—and his aunt became a mother to the child. A boy so greatly longed for was sure to be joyously welcomed. He was named Siddhartha, which means "he who has accomplished his aim." Gautama (there is another spelling) was the family name. He might properly be called Siddhartha Gautama, though Gautama is most convenient and accurate. His other names—and there are plenty of them—are not patronymics, they are titles.

GAUTAMA'S EARLY HISTORY

Buddha is a title meaning "The Enlightened One." So is Sakiyamuni (often used) which means the "Sakiya sage." Other much used titles mean "the Happy One," "the Blessed One," "the Omniscient One," "the Highest Crown," "the Perfection of Power" and such other hyphenated attributes as devotion and imagination could conceive between them.

At an early age he married a cousin, daughter of a neighboring rajah, and—if we leave the legends out—lived the pleasant life of his class till his twenty-ninth year. Then he left his family, home and inheritance and devoted himself to the study of religion and philosophy. He seems to have been more than commonly sheltered from all the unpleasant side of life but an arresting sense of sorrow came to him through a growing observation of sickness, old age and death. The legends dramatize all this; what remains is the key to his quest and his ministry.

He was a born seeker. There was a disquiet in his spirit which forbade him to be content with sheltered comfort and happiness in a world across whose human pathways so many shadows fell. He belonged to that select—or elect group—who have here no abiding city, pilgrims of the lonely road through the crowded ways of life.

The circumstance of his own well-being irked him, he envied the hermit free from possession and station.

He rose and left it all. The legends invest his departure with a tender pathos but the bare facts are pathetic enough. The birth of his son had been announced to him while he was considering, in a garden by the clear little snow-fed river, the life of a hermit. He came home with a shouting crowd about him, as though he were the first father in the world. A young cousin, sister of his wife maybe, sang: "Happy the father, happy the mother, happy the wife and son of such a husband." Her thrice repeated "happy" echoed in his thoughts —though he was meditating another kind of happiness—and he gave her a necklace of pearls. She thought he was falling in love with her, but he was considering another mistress.

He saw in his little son only another bond to tie him to what he must forsake. "This," he said, "is a new and strong tie I shall have to break." At midnight, having sent his charioteer for his horse, he stood for a little on the threshold of his wife's chamber and saw the babe asleep in his mother's arms, surrounded by flowers. He would have loved to take his son in his arms, but he could not without awakening his wife. He left with his charioteer. The last tie was broken.

That night he rode far till he reached a territory beyond his mother's people, exchanged his princely garments for a poor man's rags, sent his horse, charioteer and jewels back to his family, shaved his head and his face and became a homeless beggar and the founder of one of the world's great religions. He was about thirty years old, a significant age in the history of prophets and seekers.

Gautama, the Hermit and Ascetic

Being in search of a way to peace, he tried first the way of learning. He studied under two learned Brahmans until he knew all they had to teach him, but he found no peace in philosophy. He next tried the way of asceticism and for six years went to such extremes in fasting and self-discipline that he was wasted to a shadow. "Just like a row of reed-knots my backbone stood out through that lack of sustenance . . . and saying, 'I will touch my backbone,' I seized instead my belly's skin."[1]

[1] *Some Sayings of the Buddha according to the Pali Canon,* translated by F. L. Woodward, Oxford University Press, New York, 1925.

He won thereby fame so great that his name "was like the sound of a great bell hung in the canopy of the skies," but he found no peace in starving himself, nor "any excellence of knowledge and insight surpassing mortal things." At last, after he had fainted from hunger and been left for dead, he began to eat, being persuaded that, at any rate, a dead seeker would find no road. The disciples who had been attracted by his austerities left him saying, "He wavers in his purpose; he has turned back to the life luxurious," and he passed through what the mystics have always called "the dark night of the soul."

Here his experience ran true to the experience of all such seekers. The instant of their spiritual emancipation is always preceded by a period of crushing depression for which the psychologists have their own quite true explanation. Spiritually it is the shadow cast by that complete eclipse of self necessary to the mystic's achievement of victory over self. Gautama was not mystically minded, but he shared the mystic's struggle in his search for inner peace, as all great religious teachers have shared that struggle in one form or another.

The day of his enlightenment is notable in the annals of Buddhism, the circumstance of his victory is magnified till heaven and earth seem to be engaged. He spent the long hours of that day under a tree since known as the Sacred Bo-tree, which is, says Rhys-Davids, to the Buddhist what the cross is to Christians. I should think the olive trees of the Christian Gethsemane a closer parallel, for in that shadow Gautama won peace through renunciation.

THE "GREAT RENUNCIATION"

Rhys-Davids[2] has analyzed what must have taken place in Prince Siddhartha's mind on that epochal day with penetrating insight and made a noble passage of it. It reduces itself to elements of inner struggle with self under many guises of allurement on one side and something, God or duty or peace, in which self must be lost on the other.

The trouble is to put in any single sentence what Gautama of the Sakiyas surrendered to. The saint knows that he has yielded entirely to the will of God; Saul of Tarsus was not disobedient to the heavenly vision; Marcus Aurelius bowed his imperial power to a lonely devotion to duty; the mystic gains the ineffable vision. The simplicity of

[2] *Buddhism,* The Macmillan Co., 1925.

Gautama's peace-bringing insight is almost an anti-climax. "He discovered," says Rhys-Davids, "salvation merely by self-control and love, without any of the rites, any of the ceremonies, any of the charms, any of the priestly powers, any of the gods in which men love to trust."[3] To the devout today this would certainly serve an impoverishment; to the entangled five hundred years B.C. it was an emancipation. Allowing for all the differences in the world there is something strangely parallel here to what Saul of Tarsus found in the Damascene desert. Gautama found freedom in self-control; Saul found it in faith; both of them sensed deeply the futility of rite-encumbered law.

From that time on Gautama spoke with authority and carried on with a kind of selfless self-confidence that nothing could shake. He had, he said, conquered all evil passion, and he meant to share his light with all as a lamp lights a room. He sought certain of his disciples who had left him when he fell from ascetic grace by eating, and to them he preached his first sermon. The document which reports it may very likely carry back his fully developed system to the beginning of his ministry, to invest it all with a perfect authority, but we may be reasonably sure that his message had taken its general form when he began to teach it.

He remained for some time in a park by Benares explaining the "Foundation of the Kingdom of Righteousness" to any who would listen. He had unusual gifts as a teacher and his teaching met the need and temper of his time. He made subtle things plain, he was an artist in illustration, and always there was the man behind his words. Within five months he had won sixty disciples whom he sent out in turn to teach and preach. For the first time in this study, we have found a religion all on fire with missionary zeal and using no force, nothing save conviction and persuasion to win its empire. "Go ye now and preach the most excellent law, expounding every point thereof and unfolding with care and attention in all its bearings and particulars."[4]

GAUTAMA, PREACHER AND TEACHER

Thereafter Gautama became an itinerant preacher of his own gospel. In fair weather he came and went through northwestern

---

[3] *Op. cit.,* page 41.
[4] Bigandet, cited by Rhys-Davids, *op. cit.,* page 55.

Central India for forty-five years, till he must have been as familiar in his yellow robe as John Wesley, "the Lord's Horseman," was in England a hundred and fifty years ago. Buddhist legend sends him still further afield. During the rainy seasons he stayed in one place, giving particular instruction to his converts. Devout Buddhists still go "into retreat" during those months which were the rainy season in Northern India in Gautama's time. He won his first converts from the religiously minded, but afterwards gained a strong following from the mercantile class. In due time he was asked to return home because his father was now an old man and would see his son once more.

His clansmen took no satisfaction in seeing their rajah's son come home a beggar, holy as he was, and gave him no food. He thereupon valiantly set out with his disciples and his bowl to ask alms from house to house, such being the rule of his order, and came as a mendicant to the very door of his father's house. The rajah's protest was immediate and natural:

> Why, master, do you thus put us to shame . . .
> We are descended from an illustrious race of warriors
> And not one of them has ever begged his bread?

"You and your family," his son answered, "may claim descent from kings; my descent is from the Enlightened Ones of old and they, begging their food, have always lived on alms. But, my father, when a man has found a hid treasure, it is his duty first to present his father with the most precious of his jewels." Whereupon he delivered a most edifying discourse to the old man. His father could do no less in turn than ask his son in and fill his bowl.

The stories of his meeting with his wife, who found him, yellow-robed, shaven of head and face, so different from the husband who left her sleeping with their newborn babe in her arms, are beautifully told. Her own love, she said, had never grown cold and, though she could not lie by his side or share his hardships with him, she too had eaten but one meal a day and slept on a mat. He had no answer to a devotion like that except to explain to those who listened how great had been her virtue in a former existence. She afterwards became one of the first Buddhist nuns. His son came to him asking for his inheritance as future head of the clan. Gautama determined to give him a more imperishable wealth and admitted him into the order.

The old rajah was now desolate enough for both his son and his grandson had renounced their station. He asked Gautama therefore to establish the rule that no one should become a Buddhist monk without the consent of his parents. There was sound reason for this request for the movement was sweeping the youth of the land into the current of it. One is reminded of the dangerous power Bernard had to carry the youth of the Middle Ages into monastic seclusion and the protest of grieved parents against that flaming monk.

Piety, tradition and, perhaps, no little invention have made a chronicle of Gautama's life, in which his journeys, his sayings, and his miracles year after year are duly preserved. They are in general much the same. This shaven, humble and masterful recluse had a rare genius for organization. He anticipated the monastic organization of medieval Christianity so closely that Latin Catholic missionaries coming upon Buddhist monasteries for the first time, believed that the devil had been at work there deceiving the heathen with a specious imitation of a holy order.

His converts multiplied and he established rules for their discipline. He had to face division among his followers, the schism being led by his own cousin. (Buddhism has been as fertile in sects as Christianity.) Three years before his death a little up-flaring war destroyed his native town and the Sakiya clan. After all it had made no difference whether his father's son and grandson became monks or not; there was nothing left for them to inherit.

The Gautama chronicles, bare enough for many years after the beginning of his ministry, grow ample as his end draws near. In the forty-fifth year of his enlightenment he had a long, painful illness and foresaw his own death. He gathered his followers together and gave them long and touching instructions. Ananda, the St. John of the Buddhist gospels, was with him to the end. That one had been the most loving and faithful of all his followers but had not himself obtained the inner assurance of endless peace. Gautama lovingly assured him: "For a long time, Ananda, you have been very near to me by kindness in act, and word and thoughtfulness. You have always done well: persevere and you too shall be quite free from this thirst of life, this chain of ignorance. . . . You may perhaps begin to think, 'the word is ended now, our Teacher is gone,' but you must not think so. After I am dead let the Law and the Rules of the order which I have taught, be a teacher to you."

His last words were: "Work out your own salvation with diligence." He died in the forty-fifth year of his public ministry, being, according to the chronicles, eighty years of age. There is a persistent tradition that he died of an illness brought on by eating pork and rice (a more seemly account makes it truffles and rice) though he knew, when he took the dish at a dinner in his honor, that it would be the death of him.

THE JEWELED ROBE OF LEGEND

Now these are the bare facts of Gautama's life as perhaps the most distinguished English scholar in Buddhist literature sifts them out,[5] and even so some elements of doubtful tradition have come through the sieve of his criticism. Buddhist devotion has clothed these essential facts with a jeweled robe. The Far East has revered Buddha while history has been redated. His faith has laid its spell across old Chinese cities which still exist and cities of Siam whose ruins must be sought in the jungle. His monks have told their beads on the roof of the world in Thibet, his disciples have silently held out their begging bowl from low door to low door in Indian villages or turned from the spice-odored winds of Ceylon to seek a peace untouched by any worldly lure. His simple "way" of life soon became an ordered discipline. His philosophy became an unbelievable system of speculation, a little like our latest scientific definition of the universe—limited but without bounds.

Every religion sings with the psalmist—"O magnify the Lord with me," and Buddhism has magnified Gautama of the Sakiyas until the wise teacher has been lost in an ascription of omniscience; the self-contained man who held every desire in leash has become the rotund figure sitting cross-legged in changeless contemplation; the keen eyes which really saw deep into the linked processes of life are closed in mystic sleepiness. His young manhood has been invested with incredible splendors of wealth and power. The heaven of heavens has been bowed over the solitary figure under the Bo-tree. The universe has been shaken by the travail of his soul.

He is invested in Buddhist theology with the mystery of pre-

[5] This account of Gautama's life is substantially condensed from Rhys-Davids, though checked from many standard authorities. Pratt's *The Pilgrimage of Buddha* is a late exhaustive study of historic Buddhism. It is invaluable to any study group. The Macmillan Co., New York, 1928.

existence: "He voluntarily endured, throughout myriads of ages and in numberless births, the most severe deprivations and afflictions, that he might thereby gain the power to free sentient beings from the misery to which they are exposed under every possible form of existence."[6] He could, through the virtue he had attained, have entered into the peace of Nirvana long before his last reincarnation, but he refused. The three worlds were still to be saved. He remembered—so the legends say—the circumstances of their previous existences—there had been twenty-four of them—and he often drew upon the wealth of experience thus secured to illustrate a point or drive home a truth. We have all, according to Buddhist theology, lived in other times in other ways according to our merits, but we forget at birth. Buddha remembered. And he had much to remember. The power to save the three worlds is not lightly won.

When the time came for his last incarnation, the celestial authorities of all the world inquired who should be sent. There was but one in the universe fit for such an office; the heavenly powers begged him to assume it that all the weary and burdened in whatever state might be delivered. He consented and laid aside his heavenly power and glory as a man lays aside a garment, having, first of all, chosen the land, the caste, the family and the parents to be honored by his reincarnation. Then his jewels lost their luster, the flowers which crowned him faded, the shadow of his new earthly life fell darkly across his celestial mansion.

His mother foresaw his conception in a dream and at the moment of its occurrence, the universe bloomed like a garden, the dumb spoke and a heavenly music filled the air. His mother's side became as crystal through which the divine babe could be always seen while all the hosts of heaven guarded her city and her palace. Celestial spirits attended her delivery, the trees of an enchanted garden bent down their branches to shelter her. The child fed himself from the hands of those who held him and a lotus bloomed from the ground his feet first touched. He began to speak at once and proclaimed himself the most excellent being in the world. From birth to death he was attended by wonders. If he sat under a tree the shadow never moved. Gold and jewels were as common in his father's kingdom as stones. His mother being dead, he had sixty-four wet nurses in turn.

[6] Spence Hardy, *A Manual of Buddhism*, page 100.

The fear of losing him to the religious life haunted his father, who was told that he would see four things, old age, sickness, death and a hermit, and become an ascetic. The King built three palaces for the three seasons, in parks of perfect beauty, walled and guarded to keep any sight or sound of sorrow away. But his fate was upon him. He saw one after the other: old age, sickness, death, and the hermit, to whom alone such things as these made no difference. The splendor of his estate became a burden; his forty thousand queens asleep were a sight he could not bear; his new born child had no power to keep him. He fled upon a horse eighteen cubits high, whose hoofs made no sound; a gate a thousand men could not open turned noiselessly on its hinges before him. As the time of his enlightenment drew near all the forces of evil conspired to defeat him, their very weapons were changed into offerings to fall at his feet, six hundred of the most beautiful maidens in the world assailed his virtue in vain. At the moment of his victory he received supreme insight and was clothed with many colored lights.

But there is no end to all this. He takes no step but a legend, like the lotus flower of legend, blossoms behind him. It takes pages to describe the beauty of his person. He had forty teeth; he could touch his forehead with his tongue; his body was shining and golden colored; his voice was eight toned music. He went out to meet death as one whose task is done. Celestial flowers bloomed around his pyre. The fire was kindled by divinities. What was left unburned was like a heap of pearls. Seven relics were left: four teeth, two cheekbones and his skull. These became treasures for kings to desire; they have, since his death, been marvelously multiplied as the relics of the holy always are.

THE LITERATURE

Besides all this maze of legend in which Gautama's life is lost, there is a corresponding wealth of development by which his teaching is obscured. There is an enormous literature of Buddhism,[7] and

---

[7] It is both unwise and impossible to enlarge that simple statement in this book. Besides, only a specialist in the subject could do it with any authority and he would have his troubles. Gautama himself taught by conversation and wrote nothing. All Buddhist doctrine, as we receive it from the past, is simply the general agreement

it is impossible that it should all date back to Gautama. It is very much as if one should take the four Christian Gospels, the writing of the Greek and Latin Church Fathers, the comments of theologians and philosophers, with selections from Christian hymn-books and manuals of devotion and put them all together and call them Christianity. They would be that truly enough, but they would by no means clearly portray the mind of the founder of Christianity. And yet there is, among scholars, a sound confidence that the essentials of primitive Buddhism can be disentangled from this enormous literature. There is also a substantial agreement about these same essentials.

Gautama preached and taught daily for forty-five years. He repeated himself in all human probability; the habit of the Eastern mind is equally certain to have cast his discourses into a set form. He spoke to trained Brahman students who were able "to commit to memory a whole Veda together with subsidiary treatises on ritual, metre, grammar and genealogy.[8] These would count it a small matter to remember a sermon. Their common recollections were compared and sifted not too long after his death. There is a tradition that the first collection of his teachings was made very much as—in another tradition—the Apostles of Jesus are said to have contributed The Apostles' Creed, clause by clause. One disciple chanted the rules of discipline, another the ethical precepts and another still the philosophy of their faith, as far as it then had a philosophy. There is, then, a dependable core of the Master's teaching in the impossibly voluminous Buddhist books.

---

of "Church Councils" in later times as to what was true and ought to be taught. The Buddhist Scriptures claim no divine inspiration. There are three or four principal collections according to the languages in which they are written. The Pali Canon "is accepted by the Buddhists of Ceylon, Burma and Siam." The English translations of Buddhist literature are generally taken from the Pali "Bible." The Sanskrit Canon consists of the Nepalese Scriptures and texts discovered in Central Asia. The Chinese have translations into Chinese of works belonging to all schools, "a gigantic collection made and revised at the command of various emperors." The Buddhist Scriptures are full of repetition due in part, I suspect, to the fact that they were long handed down by oral tradition and the tiresome repetitions were aids to memory. Some one—Rhys-Davids, I think—says that, if all the duplications and repetitions were edited out, the Buddhist Scriptures would be about as long as the Old and New Testaments of the English Bible. Sir Charles Eliot in his *Hinduism and Buddhism*, Vol. I, Chap. XIII, deals in a clear, concise way with this whole great matter.

[8] Eliot, *op. cit.*, Vol. I, page 285.

Keys to His System

There are two keys to the whole Buddhist system. One is, of course, the man himself. The original force and genius of many men diminish as you come close to them. They are finally seen to have been magnified by circumstances, they do no more than reveal in some commanding way the general mind of their time. Gautama was not like that. He stands where the borderlands of philosophy, religion and ethics meet, as one of the commanding figures of all time. Somewhere at the heart of his system, hampered and distorted as it is by a misty range of Oriental speculation, there is the only sound alternative which has ever been offered to the form Western religion has finally taken.

The second key to his system is the faith and practice of his time against which he reacted. He lived and died in the general setting of his time—naturally. No apostle of strange things could turn that world "upside down"—one might as well try to turn a cloud upside down. Except for a challenging opposition from one of his own followers, he lived his life out in peace and gentleness. He would have called himself a reformer, if he had known that word. He had no mind but to correct the abuses and illumine the darknesses about him. His dialogues always begin with some wrong thing in the mind or practice of his world and try to make it right. He had no bitter words—only pity for the misled, only correction for the misled and the misleading, though he laughed at these sometimes, being a man of saving humor.

He compared himself to one who has found in the jungle the site of an ancient city and caused it to be restored. "Just as if, brethren, a man traveling in a forest, . . . should come upon an ancient road . . . and, as he went, should come upon an old time city, a royal city of olden days, laid out with parks and water tanks . . . —a delightful spot." "Then suppose, brethren, that this man should tell of his find to the king or royal minister (and say) . . . 'Sire, restore that city.' . . . Even so, brethren, have I seen an ancient Path . . . traversed by the Perfectly Enlightened Ones of former times. And what is this Path? It is this Ariyan Eightfold Path."[9]

[9] *Some Sayings of the Buddha, op. cit.,* page 63. Ariyan means historically old. But it is surely an echo of the name by which the bards of the old Veda called themselves. Gautama believed his teaching a return to an earlier and simpler faith.

His teaching plays in and out the conditions of his time. Sir Charles Eliot thinks the Sakiyas to have been an independent-thinking folk and Gautama to have shared their spirit; but Gautama did not consciously detach himself from the currents of his time; he sought only to redirect them. The end of the last chapter showed us an Indian world whose gods had lost their characters, never having had much to begin with, whose sacrifices were costly, wearing and often bloody, whose everyday religion was trying to get something—no matter what—by repeating a charm, whose society was seamed by a cruel caste system in which a man's status for time and eternity was determined by his birth. License and extreme asceticism went along hand in hand. The mind of India was beginning to be engaged in boundless and sterile speculations entirely divorced from the practical conduct of life.[10] And across this whole system crossing and recrossing beneath the bright Indian sky, there had fallen the dark shadow of suffering unassuaged and a weariness of life for which there was no relief. Buddhism met all this point by point.

Is Buddhism a Religion?

Gautama himself makes little mention or use of the gods. By the strictest tests Buddhism is not a religion at all but a moral discipline, locked upon self-control, to be rewarded with release from any conscious experience at all. But the gods come back into Buddhism for all that and always with a change for the better. They are no longer nature forces; they are "agents of morality or immorality . . . surrounded with some moral atmosphere." They are, it is true,

---

[10] This sentence needs both qualification and enlargement. All the phases of Indian religion of which the Upanishads are the expression antedate Buddhism. An entirely logical arrangement of the faiths of India would put this chapter and the next between a study of Upanishad Brahmanism and the development of Hinduism. George Foot Moore in his *History of Religions* (Charles Scribner's Sons, New York, 1913) calls Buddhism and the closely related Jainism, "the Great Heresies." They were reactions against the speculative pantheism of the Upanishads and the degenerated Vedic religion. But I do not discover in the teachings of Gautama much direct challenge to any of these systems. One would never know that the Upanishads were in existence save as they do supply—when one reads them and comes back to Gautama—the hidden key to many of his attitudes and particularly his denial of a resident soul in the individual. But when one contrasts attitudes and atmospheres the contrast is challenging. The student might come back to Buddhism after reading two-thirds the chapter on Hinduism. Then he will feel for himself the contrast and correction.

dethroned, because a good Buddhist depends upon himself alone for goodness now and release hereafter. (This is why one may say that Buddhism is the most consistent alternative ever offered to a personal religion.)

Prayer, praise and sacrifice go with their dethronement. Prayer is asking for a help from the outside, when a man ought to rally his own powers; sacrifice is the endeavor to propitiate the gods and escape consequences which, according to Buddhism, a man can not and ought not to escape. He must pay for every fault if it takes a thousand lives to balance the account. Sacrifice disappears also because a Buddhist must shed no blood. The name lingers on but the true Buddhist sacrifices are the alms of kindness, the oblations of love. The caste system disappears also. There is no more room for it in the Buddhist brotherhood than in a medieval monastery. Those who join the fellowship leave family and station behind them. When they have taken the beggar's bowl and put on the yellow robe pieced together of rags, they are reborn as "Sakiyas Sons." Conduct alone determines a man's station and his destiny.

"Not by birth," said Gautama, "does one become an outcast, not by birth does one become a Brahman; by deeds one becomes an outcast, by deeds one becomes a Brahman."

Finally, all speculation as to the beginning or ending of the world order, the creation of men and things, the eternal or temporal character of the universe and its inhabitants disappears. These are futile exercises of a mind which should be occupied with examining its own character and conduct. Buddhism has no Book of Genesis nor any book of Revelation. Perhaps Gautama was not curious, he may have been an Agnostic. We have his own word for it that these things did not matter.

The first of the Dialogues deals with just this. The scene setting of all the Dialogues is much the same. They begin, "Thus have I heard" and go on with the tale. The "Blessed One" is on a journey or else he is stopping in a mango grove or in a king's pavilion. Certain inquirers come to him with a dispute or a question. Whereupon he sits down upon his mat and begins twenty reported pages of edifying discourse—which turn out to be a monologue and not a dialogue—upon some high theme. One can almost hear the monotonous sing-song chant of the monk—for these recitations have been worn smooth with age-old repetition—very much as the old Lama instructed Kim.[11]

In this Dialogue, called The Perfect Net, a young disciple of the Blessed One has been defending the faith against a critic and the Master has overheard the dispute which furnishes him a text. His followers, he says, must never "bear malice or suffer heartburning or feel ill-will" if any speak against the doctrine or the order; that would only stand in the way of his own self-conquest. They must only consider whether their critics are right or not. (Theological discussion has not generally been carried on in the Buddhistic spirit.) The Blessed One then goes on to dispose of futile speculation. This one reveals, incidentally, as many schools of thought about high philosophical themes as one would find now in a joint meeting of the Metaphysical Society and the Society for the Advancement of Science.

"There are recluses and Brahmans, brethren, who reconstruct the ultimate beginnings of things, whose speculations are concerned with the ultimate past, and who on eighteen grounds put forward various assertions regarding it." There are the Extensionists who in four ways set forth the infinity or finiteness of the world, and the Eternalists who maintain the opposite.[12] There are the Eel-Wrigglers—not without lineal descendants—who will take any position and there are the Fortuitous-Originalists who maintain in two ways that the soul and the world arise without a cause.[13]

The Blessed One maintains that these are dusty quests, certain to receive only dusty answers. Even the high gods can not answer them.[14] Those who engage in such speculation are caught in a net

[11] Kipling's *Kim*, which, by the way, comes nearer making a Buddhist alive than most of the learned studies.

[12] See Eddington's *The Nature of the Physical World*, pages 80 et seq., for a modern discussion of the same subject. There is nothing new under the sun.

[13] *The Dialogues of the Buddha*, Rhys-Davids.

[14] Sir Charles Eliot cites a delightful story by which the Blessed One illustrated this point. A monk asked Brahma himself surrounded by a retinue of gods, a highly speculative question. The god replied with an imposing summary of his powers and qualities, very much as if he were giving himself an honorary degree. "But," says the monk, "I did not ask you whether you were indeed all you now say," and repeated his question. Whereupon Brahma took the monk by the arm and led him aside. "These gods," he said confidentially, "think I know and understand everything. Therefore, I give no answer in their presence. But I do not know the answer to your question and you had better go and ask the Buddha." Gautama himself knew the value of a discreet silence. *Hinduism and Buddhism*, Vol. I, page 331.

of theories of their own weaving. Buddhism cuts the net. Such speculations have no final proof, lead to no final freedom, belong to the world of illusion. There is a higher wisdom than that. Buddhism, to begin with, freed the Indian mind from its net of theories and made right conduct the supreme concern.

A SYSTEM OF ESCAPE FROM LIFE-WEARINESS

But when all this was done the weariness of life still remained. How could a man escape that? The answer to this question is the very heart of Buddhism and the explanation of it can not be too hard driven. The fact of suffering is the point of departure for the whole Buddhist system. For Gautama any conscious existence is painfully undesirable; he makes no exceptions nor does he confine himself to our own little world. There is a vast inclusion of other planes of existence in Buddhism, heavens as bright with felicity as Bernard of Cluny's "Jerusalem The Golden" and hells compared with which Dante's Inferno is a desirable residence, but the wheel turns through them all, and all who turn upon it share the same pain —the pain of really existing at all.

A parallel is often drawn between Gautama and Schopenhauer for whom "life swings like a pendulum backward and forward between pain and ennui," and the parallel is justified though there are significant differences. For Schopenhauer the villain in the piece is will; for Gautama it is desire. One doubts if he would have really called himself a pessimist if he had ever heard the word. Life for him was, after all, a rather exciting drama prolonged through many reincarnations in which a man played his own power of self-control against the flawless law of compensation and all the entanglements and illusions of sense, for the final prize of a peace whose very perfection was not being aware of it at all—or aware of anything else.

GAUTAMA'S SENSITIVENESS TO SUFFERING

It is difficult to explain Gautama's distaste for life. As a matter of fact, after the great Renunciation he rather enjoyed being a Buddha. He was much looked up to; his company was sought after; he liked to dine out—or, since he mostly lived "out," to dine "in,"—he could talk to his heart's content and his hearers hung upon his words; he used an acute mind in a congenial way and lived to a ripe old age, dying with the full assurance that all his troubles were over. He was as fortunate as Bernard in leadership and distinction, as happy as John Wesley in occupation and happier in domestic relations, since his wife was a nun and his son his disciple.

Perhaps he felt as few have ever felt that element of strain which is, according to Bergson, the price we pay for being self-conscious. Here, if anywhere, I should find the closest parallel between Gautama's philosophy and some modern philosophies. There is a saving discontent in the very nature and fact of life. High-minded courage finds in just that a stimulus to go as far and as high as we can and so enrich life. Gautama found it a stimulus to end the existence of which it is an inseparable part.

An impossible idealism may also have driven the Blessed One to the denial of the value of any ideals. Sir Charles Eliot[15] finds a certain parallel between aspects of Buddhism and the "fed up" temper of the Hebrew book of Ecclesiastes—"the regretful verdict of one who while sympathizing with the nobler passions—love, ambition, the quest of knowledge—is forced to pronounce them unsatisfactory." Since the human mind wants something it can never really get, it would better stop all wanting, attaining thus a peace beyond all reach of pain and loss. I think Gautama also to have been unusually sensitive to all the suffering in the human world about him.

Finally the doctrine of the transmigration of souls, which Gautama took over without any question from the general faith of his time, must be taken into account. It casts the shadow of an endless weariness over our short years. If the wheel upon which we are bound would stop sometime, we might endure it, but to have it turn forever! One might say as Kent of Lear:

> . . . O, let him pass! he hates him.
> That would upon the rack of this tough world
> Stretch him out longer.

And yet the impermanence of things is one more cause of Gautama's indictment against existence. One wonders if a faith in immortality would have altered his point of view. Probably not; his

---

[15] *Op. cit.,* Vol. I, page 203. "Vanity of Vanities; all is Vanity." Omar Khayyám belonged to the same school.

mind's eye focused upon the essential pain of any quality of being. There is no cure for it but the extinction of self.

The Four Noble Truths

The fact of suffering then is the first of the Four Noble Truths. "Birth is sorrowful, growth is sorrowful, illness is sorrowful and death is sorrowful, and painful is the craving for what can not be attained. . . . Which think you is more—the tears which you have shed as you strayed and wandered on this long journey, grieving and weeping because you were turned to what you hated and separated from what you loved, . . . which are more, these tears or the waters in the four oceans?[16] Gautama answers his own question: "The tears that you shed are more than the four oceans." And no one contradicted him. Given this ugly fact and the general conclusion is unescapable: Stop being born. But the birth control system which Gautama unfolded took a dizzy sweep through time and space.

One must then inquire into the causes of suffering and this is the Second Noble Truth. Since suffering is a shadow to darken all sentient existence, the possibility of escape from it becomes the most insistent human desire, and the extinction of it, if that is possible, the most imperative of duties. Gautama believed that suffering could be ended. That is the Third Noble Truth. Most religions have accepted suffering as an inescapable aspect of this present mortal life and offered the compensation—if it could be merited or won—of immortality. The scientific humanitarianism of our own time seeks the extinction of suffering in many regions through the elimination of its physical and social causes. Stoicism faced it as something to be bravely borne; piety sees in it a purifying discipline.

Gautama took none of these lines, but he did conceive it as something which a man may escape. The path to the extinction of suffering is therefore the Fourth Noble Truth.[17] "We are enclosed in all sides by the rocks of birth, old age, disease and death, and only by considering and practicing the true law can we escape from

[16] See *Some Sayings of the Buddha, op. cit.,* page 183, though this quotation is another translation.

[17] The Four Noble Truths are often compared with the four principles of the Hindu Science of Medicine: Disease, The Cause of Disease, Absence of Disease, Medicine. The Fourth Noble Truth is really amplified into the "Eight-fold Path." (Just about here the class will probably detour into a general discussion of the "Problem of Evil" and why we seek a solution.)

the sorrow-piled mountain." The quest for this narrow and perilous way led Gautama into such an analysis of cause and consequence as no other teacher has ever undertaken and into a consequent analysis of motive and disposition arrestingly acute.

The systems of thought and religion with which we are familiar play fast and loose with the whole problem of evil. They either shift the blame on someone else conveniently distant, as the first parents of mankind, or deny the actual reality of it or piously call it a mystery. Gautama, at least, proceeds with honesty and insight. He eliminates the gods (much that he teaches would be true if he did not). Our destinies are affairs with ourselves. Nothing exists without a cause, but in this long journey, grieving and weeping "because we are bound to what we hate and separated from what we love—we our-selves are cause and effect—neither "Îshvara [A personal god, a deity distinct from and independent of nature] nor the absolute, nor the self, nor causeless chance, is the maker, but our deeds produce results both good and evil. . . . Let us, then, surrender the heresies of wor-shiping Îshvara and praying to him; let us not lose ourselves in vain speculations . . .; let us surrender self and all selfishness, and as all things are fixed by causation, let us practice good that good may result from our actions."

This is the bed-rock of Buddhism; it is a religion (essentially) which contradicts every definition of religion save the very modern ones which say that religion is the attempt to realize right values— and that definition is too spacious to hold faith and worship.

The horizons of Gautama's teachings are always shifting. Some-times he offers his disciples a very tangible—though a very simple— well-being; the peace of the hermit whose bowl is filled by another's toil, care free because he has nothing to care for. "Full of hindrances is the household life, a path for the dust of passion. Free as the air is the life of him who has renounced all worldly passion. How difficult it is for the man who lives at home to live the higher life in all its fullness, in all its purity, in all its bright perfection!"[18] And when the householder has thus emancipated himself, "pure are his means of livelihood, good is his conduct, guarded the door of his senses, mind-

---

[18] Woodward, *op. cit.,* page 116, supplies a more vivid translation: "Oppressive is the household life, a path for the dust of passion; an open air life is the wanderer's; not easy is it for him who dwells in a house to live the holy life . . . in its entire purity, made clean and white."

ful and self-possessed he is altogether happy." Which does not
sound like an "ocean of tears," though something might be said
for his deserted family. Again the horizons fall back and the reward
he offers is the peace of Nirvana. But always what comes to a man
is what a perfect law has assigned him in perfect compensation of
his own deeds.

THE WHEEL OF THE LAW: KARMA

The excellent law is Dharma (or Karma), though "law" is hardly
the equivalent of what Gautama had in mind. Rhys-Davids says
Dharma is "best rendered by truth or righteousness." Carus[19] says
"originally the natural condition of things or beings, the law of their
existence, truth, their religious truth . . . the ethical code of righteousness, the whole body of religious doctrines as a system." One
suspects some underground connection here with awesome Rita,
that vast impersonal order, cosmic in one phase of it, moral in the
other, by which gods and men are contained in the old Aryan faith.
Perhaps it was for Gautama the essential nature of all things, the
reality with which all must reckon; no more to be argued with than
gravitation and yet shot through with even-handed justice essentially
good and the only sure support on which to rest.

This nature of things bears on the individual life through a law
and a process, Karma and the transmigration of souls; these are the
forms in which Buddhism is set and both are older than Gautama.
One might define Karma as moral consequence and escape a deal
of trouble. You may call it the law of cause and effect, if you will
make cause and effect an endless overlapping series in which every
cause is an effect and every effect is a cause—until the chain is broken.
It is retribution and reward; "the results of deeds previously done
and the destiny resulting therefrom," or else Karma is the stream
of existence flowing from pool to pool of some sort of sentient existence in which the last pool in the current is created and colored not
only by the stream but by the character of the next pool above and
nothing can stop the flow, save the purification and final suppression
of desire. It is, says Rhys-Davids, "the doctrine that as soon as a being
(man, animal, or angel) dies, a new being is produced in a more or

[19] Paul Carus, *The Gospel of Buddha,* Chicago, page 147.

less painful and material state of existence, according to the Karma, the desert of merit, of the being who has died."

What one is then is his "Karma"—in the argot of the street— "what was coming to him"—the nature of the old has determined the nature of the new. Karma is akin to the Greek tragedian's fate; it is the inexorable, impersonal necessity to which gods and men alike bow. It is akin to the theologian's predestination, as rigid as though the mold into which our lives are cast were shaped for us before we were born. It is not unrelated to the natural law that out of the embryonic egg, each form will come according to its nature, "the last inheritor and the last result" of all that makes it what it is. Yet fate is not Karma; fate has nothing to do with a man's deserts. Karma is the essential justice of what happens to him. When a Buddhist says "this is my Karma," he means "this is my doing; though I did it in some existence I have forgotten, just and equal is the wheel." The Mohammedan says "Allah is good"; the Hebrew says, "God is just"; the Buddhist says, "Karma is just and inviolate."

It is easy to see what a range of conjecture as to one's past conduct such a doctrine opens. One no longer asks: "Lord, who has sinned, this man or his father, that he was born blind," but rather, what sin did this one commit in a previous life that he was born blind. There is no answer but a guess—and yet the guess is a moral judgment, plumbing the depths of a man's timeless past. Buddhist theology gradually worked out a probable balance of accounts, especially with reference to penalties. The punishments fit the crime with a kind of Dantesque wealth of imagination; a grain thief will be reborn a rat; a back-biter will be reborn in hell with a razor for a tongue.

It needs a long reach of time for this law of compensation to work out; the little span of one mortal life is not enough. The general moral judgments of humanity have always felt that. Death leaves too many open accounts. All religions which assume personal immortality transfer the unbalanced account to the immortal life. There sin is bitterly expiated, there virtue enters upon an endless felicity. The more sensitive have felt that even this was not quite enough. No opportunity is thus allowed the sinful for further repentance or moral endeavor. Transmigration avoids all this; it keeps the moral accounts of existence alive, assumes no desperate estate without a saving hope, no felicity without a possible eclipse.

Transmigration of Souls

The only trouble with the whole system is that the Western mind has never been able to see the slightest proof for it[20] and, though in Buddhism there is continuing existence as though each sequent life were a troubled pool in a stream whose beginnings are unbelievably remote and whose end is to be painfully achieved, there is no continuing recollection. For all practical purposes no matter how the wheel turns we do live time-isolated lives. Buddhism recognizes this, admitting that, with a few exceptions, the individual does not know what his former lives were or what his succeeding lives shall be. Nevertheless one's virtue or one's fault does live on, the virtue to lessen the suffering of all feeling beings, the fault to increase it. Here the social element enters; the individual is responsible for the corporate well-being or ill-being of the future. Something of this the wise are bound to feel; it would be well if it were more strongly felt. In the main, however, Buddhism is a system in which the—

race is run by one and one, and never by two and two.

By oneself evil is done; by oneself one suffers; by oneself evil is left undone; by oneself one is purified.
Purity and impurity belong to oneself; no one can purify another.

The moral order of Buddhism, then, is woven out of the woof of Karma and the web of Transmigration. That faith was old in India when Gautama was born, he took it over and used it without a question. It suited his purpose, his whole scheme would break down without it. The infinite current of existence flows on, though the volume of the river be made of separate threads of water. Each sentient state, whether it be a worm in the dark, a king on his throne, a cross-legged saint under a Bo-tree or an angel with jeweled wings, is the result of the balanced moral accounts of a previous state and will issue in another state heightened or lowered according to desert. This is the endless turning wheel of the law. "You are wheeled about," said Gautama, "in endless eddies of transmigration

---

[20] This statement should be qualified. Plato believed in a previous existence, possibly Origen did. But Plato did not believe that a man might have been a rat and could become a rat again.

. . . we have gone astray so long and wandered in this weary path of transmigration, both you and I, until we have found the truth."

THE LIBERATING TRUTH

And what was this liberating truth? In a sentence, that desire binds us to the wheel and when, in the long discipline of many turnings thereupon, desire is extinguished, we are set free. Actually, it is not so simple as that. Now the subtle speculative mind of Gautama comes into play with its twelve linked chain of causation. Ten of the twelve links are plain enough; two of them are so difficult that the most lucid explanation of the Western mind leaves us like Gautama's perplexed disciple—as if we had a bandage over our eyes.

The first link in the chain, at any rate, is ignorance. Buddhism is primarily salvation through enlightenment. All Gautama's teachings return again and again to the hopeless estate of ignorance. He himself is the "Enlightened One." He called his achievement of peace enlightenment. His instruction was always focused upon the purpose to get his disciples to "see." He assumed that with enlightenment there would come a sufficient drive of motive to lead the illumined to follow the road to its end in Deliverance, no matter what the cost. Perhaps this was the fallacy in his system. The illumined are not always "obedient to the heavenly vision."

Consciousness comes through two difficult links from ignorance, and what we might call individuality comes from consciousness. Sense experience comes from consciousness. After that it is plain going. "From sensation comes craving, from craving comes clinging, from clinging comes existence, from existence comes birth, from birth comes old age and death, pain and lamentation, suffering, sorrow and despair."[21] There are clearly too many links here for one life. The chain, as Eliot says, seems to bring a being into existence twice. The Buddhist theologians explain that. Some of the links, they say, belong to the past and explain the present existence as though one were now reborn because he had been ignorant in some past life and would be reborn and grow old again because of unruly desires here and now.

Actually the Buddhist self-discipline shortcircuits the whole matter.

[21] Any study of Buddhism supplies the "key" quotation; the translations vary in detail.

One suffers the weariness of endless rebirth through ignorance; therefore, seek enlightenment. The enlightened know that sense awakens desire and desire deceives, leading one to cleave existence and so continuing the pain of it.

This, O Hermits, is the noble truth of the cessation of suffering: it ceases with the complete cessation which consists in the absence of every passion—the abandoning of this thirst, with the doing away with it, with the deliverance from it, with the destruction of desire.

He knows that the things men most treasure are a delusion and through self-control he breaks his fetters one by one. When he has worn thin the fetters of Lust, Ill-will and Delusion, he will, after another birth, be delivered from this world; when he is free from sense and any craving he will pass into the formless world; when he has, through searching discipline, reached and broken the last mystic ties, then "he has realized by his own abnormal powers, the taintless heart-release, the wisdom release, and abides therein."

But, Lord, is there a Path, is there a Way leading to the realization of these things?
There is indeed a Path, there is indeed a Way so leading.
What is that Path, Lord? What is that Way so leading?

Verily it is this . . . Eightfold Path, to wit: Right View, Right Aim, Right Speech, Right Action, Right Living, Right Effort, Right Mindfulness, Right Contemplation.
This, Mahale, is the Path, this is the Way leading to the realization of these things.

This Eightfold Path is the essence of the Buddhist "Way."

CREATIVE RENUNCIATION

Here at last Buddhism gets its feet on the ground—all the rest is theology—if you can have a theology without God—a little philosophy, a great deal of psychology and a vast range of speculation. It begins with the fact of suffering; it seeks the cause of suffering and finds its answer in the law of consequence and the tremendous time scale of transmigration. Then it offers a way, to break the many linked chain which binds us to the wheel of existence; that way is the self-directed, moral and spiritual discipline of the eightfold path—the ethics and character-creating force of Buddhism. There is naturally an enormous comment and amplification of the eightfold way.[22] Each quality comes up for examination, illustration and discussion, and since together they offer endless opportunity for such enlargement, the result is something which in range and method corresponds to the Hebrew's examination of his law or the Christian comment upon the teaching of Jesus. But as Gautama enlarged upon his own principles they are both simple and possible.

The ethics of Buddhism are positive but the practical form they take is renunciation. Gautama cut at one stroke clean through the roots of all the ordinary motivations of life when he forbade desire. For desire may be the lawless flame of passion consuming the soul that entertains it, or it may be a steady driving force realizing itself in art, literature and high action and creating as the deposit of its characters of rare beauty and integrity. The master word of Buddhist morality is "Abstain."

Right speech is to abstain from lying and slandering, harsh words and foolish chatter. Right conduct is to abstain from taking any life, from stealing, from immorality. Right livelihood is abandoning wrong occupation: "The pruning of the feelings, the cutting off of every tendril which can cling to the pleasures of sense"[23] is the essence of Gautama's discipline. This apparently negative approach to life is, of course, open to searching criticism and yet such criticism partly misses the mark. It tests Buddhism by a standard it was never meant to be measured by; the passion of the West for action. For it is only yesterday—as one measures time on the dial of history—that hard-driven action became a virtue.

"Neither to Greek philosophy nor to Christianity did it appear that the vocation of man consisted in the rational and scientific control over life and over nature's energies in order to satisfy *human desires*. . . . For the ancient and the medieval worlds, a man's essential vocation was contemplation, the possession in thought or in feeling, of those eternal and absolute perfections which are both the ultimately real and the ultimately valuable."[24] Adams adds that both Greek

[22] S. Tachibana, *The Ethics of Buddhism*, Oxford University Press, 1926, is especially useful here. The first three chapters should be assigned reading if the book is available. They "place" Buddhism in Indian thought, especially in relation to our Chapter VIII better than any other source.

[23] Eliot, *Hinduism and Buddhism*, Vol. I, page 215.

[24] George Plimpton Adams, *Idealism in the Modern Age*, page 8.

philosopher and the medieval saint sought a "good which was one of this world."

Gautama was almost a contemporary of Plato (he died, according to tradition, in the decade in which the philosopher was born) and Thomas Aquinas may never have heard of him, but the three could have got on famously together, being generally agreed as to the essential nature of man's vocation. They would have differed only in their definition of the Good. For Plato, the Good was comradeship with the Ideal; for the Saint, it was a union with God. For Gautama it was the peace of Nirvana. They would have all agreed that our own time, interesting as they would have found it, is under the spell of an illusion and our many-storied splendor a shadow in which we have lost ourselves.

Gautama's ethic and ideal of life will stand, then, the test of standards which have held in wise cultures for ages. He believed "that man's essential vocation was contemplation and the possession in thought or in feeling of the eternal and absolute perfection." There was and is an essential gentleness in his gospel, a range of wide consideration for others, a searching concern for a goodness rooted deep in the hidden places of personality, taught often in phrases of exquisite beauty and insight which invest the yellow-robed ascetic beneath his Bo-tree with a charm no one can escape who lives long and open-mindedly with the records. True the world has driven by and left him under the Bo-tree, but even so he might look up from his meditation and ask: "Where are you driving? Impermanent, alas! are all compounded things. Their nature is to rise and fall, when they have risen,

They cease. . . ."

CHAPTER VII

Buddha Joins the Procession

WHAT IS THE END?

THERE are curious contradictions in Gautama's mind. In every other system death is the end of temporal existence. The devout of most religions have looked beyond death to a permanence of happiness or misery. For Gautama death brought no pause in the endless turning of the wheel unless one had attained Nirvana. It is no light thing to go on forever, settling the unbalanced accounts of a past existence and incurring new debts with a possible range of reincarnation between a rat and a celestial being. This continuing permanence he found unendurable; Gautama promised his disciples the boon of an end to any conscious life. His Nirvana (the particular call it Nibbana) has two aspects. It is, to begin with, something you can enter into here and now sitting under a Bo-tree—elsewhere, if there are no Bo-trees. It is also a state to be entered upon in some final death when all the links binding one to the weary round of rebirth are broken. That final death is actually the only real death, all the other seeming deaths are doors to another phase of fettered life. The Christian says: "The last enemy that shall be destroyed is death." The Buddhist believes there is a death—if only one can win it—where

Beyond these voices there is peace.

But what that peace is has sorely perplexed the Western mind.

The key to the Nirvana of actual experience is found in the general experience of the mystic. There is always in that experience some period of struggle induced by a longing for perfection or the immediate experience of God or salvation. Doubts and fears and reluctances and the tenacious love of what must be given up are mobilized on one side; on the other there is only the longing. The soul is the battlefield and the fight is always hard and sometimes desperate. One can see the dark in which it is carried on and hear the groans (Bunyan abounds in groans) of the hard beset through all the pages of confessional literature. Then in some instantaneous joy-lit moment the victory is won, though always through surrender. Thereafter the victor lives aloof from the struggle though seemingly a part of it. Time ceases to exist for him, only the eternal is real.

Gautama went through a travail like that. He speaks himself of three trances. In the last he saw all his previous existences "evolutions and involutions of aeons . . . conditions of birth and experience in such." All of which is true enough of general mystic experience. The mystic finds in his trance what he was seeking—the vision of God or a communication from another world. Gautama was "twice born" and the fruit of his second birth was a tranquil mind and a sense of timeless security.

His disciples after a due period of self-discipline generally attained the same experience. (Not all of them; it needs the proper temper. Ananda, Gautama's cousin, who was always mindful of his master's needs was long in "getting assurance.") There is a rich reference in Buddhist literature to those who enter into Nirvana; thereafter they are free of "lust, desire, love, craving and fever, possessing naught and cleaving unto naught." The note of tranquillity or joy is constantly sounded. The state of an ascetic with nothing of his own save a single garment of yellow rags and a begging bowl sitting cross-legged and brooding might not seem enviable. Neither was the estate of some of John Wesley's converts—till the convert began to testify to what he had found; fifteen hours a day in a colliery is merely a detail if one is saved.

The practical appeal of Buddhism was just along this line. Gautama freed the ascetic from a futile self-torture, the householder from the cares of this world and the soul-entangled from their doubts and fears. And he gave them all the liberty to think and think without being pulled up by reality—an occupation congenial to the Eastern mind. If their thinking slipped over into formless reverie or they fell asleep, no matter. They lived "estranged from lusts, aloof from evil state in the First Rapture—a state of joy and ease born of detachment, reasoning and investigation going on all the while."

The affairs of the world suffered, of course, from the withdrawal of so many able-bodied men from its entanglements. But there were always the laymen left whose case was not altogether desperate since they had aeons of lives before them—an aeon being possibly the time it would take a man to wear away a solid rock four leagues in height, breadth and length if he should stroke it once a century with a cloth of Benares. A layman might get wisdom a little in each life and so win his freedom. Meanwhile someone must grow the rice for the saint's begging bowl for, though the body be an illusion in great need of discipline, a monk must daily go through the illusion of eating.

Is Nirvana Mere Nothingness?

But all this is not Nirvana; it is only the peace of being certain presently to possess it. If it were as hard to win it as define it, it was well earned. "There is, brethren, a condition wherein there is neither earth, nor water, nor fire, nor air, nor the sphere of infinite space, nor the sphere of infinite consciousness, nor the sphere of the void, . . . nor perception, . . . nor more perception . . . 'no this world' . . . 'no world beyond.' That condition, brethren, do I call neither a coming nor a going, nor a standing still nor a falling away nor a rising up. . . . *That is the end of woe.*"[1]

It would seem to be the end of everything. In another connection, Gautama says the final deliverance is a state of mind in which both sensations and ideas have ceased to be. "Blessed is he who has found the peace of Nirvana. He is at rest in the struggles and tribulations of life; he is above all changes; he is above birth and death; he remains unaffected by the evils of life." He calls it "the ocean of birth"; "the eternal peace," "everlasting bliss." He speaks of the "shore of Nirvana," calls it "life everlasting" and uses phrases practically akin to such expectations of future bliss as the devout have always held.

But he is quite delightfully vague as to what will be left of the blessed to enjoy the bliss. A disputatious Brahman once put the whole matter as clearly as the most acute modern critic can put it. "Thy disciples praise self-extinction as the highest bliss of Nirvana. . . . If I am merely a combination of sensations and ideas and desires, whither can I go at the dissolution of the body? Where is the infinite bliss of which thy followers speak? Is it an empty word and a self-delusion, for nothingness stares me in the face when I consider thy doctrines."

[1] Woodward, *op. cit.*, page 329, a classic quotation.

Gautama did not meet this disconcerting criticism full face. He had come, he said, to teach life and not death. "Where self is, truth can not be; yet when truth comes self will disappear. . . . In the truth thou shalt live forever." Now this is pure mysticism with anticipation of Plato and the Fourth Christian Gospel but it does not answer the Brahman. Rhys-Davids, following Max Müller, holds that Nirvana "is the extinction of that sinful, grasping condition of mind and heart which would otherwise according to the great mystery of Karma be the cause of renewed individual existence."[2] This seems to imply that at the death of any individual so purified the lamp of life finally goes out. It will no longer kindle the flame of another existence, the long day is over and the weary are for the dark.

And yet not quite. The word Nirvana is loosely used in Buddhist literature. It means more often than most students allow a present happy untroubled state as though the mystic should say "I have found God," or the Christian convert say "I have found salvation." But it does not seem entirely to imply extinction after death. Perhaps later Buddhist thought has been influenced by Hindu philosophy and has introduced elements alien to Gautama's practical and on the whole unspeculative mind. But there does seem to be the suggestion, as in the first quotation used, of absorption into the *all*. That means little to the Western mind; the Eastern pantheistic mind does find meaning in it, for to their mind the All is divine.

The numberless succession of individual lives is like the rise and fall of waves. They are the creation of the mobile sea and the restless wind, the struggle of the sea to escape the sea, a form lifted for an instant to dissolve again, flinging jeweled spray into the light— or dark. When it ceases to struggle and sinks back into the deep again, the wave is gone. Yet nothing is lost, neither of the water which rose and broke nor of the wind which impelled it. The wave is at rest in the immensity out of which it came, back to which it has returned.[3] Gautama had, I think, the vision of some final peace, back into which the weary and suffering might face when they were done with struggle and strain. If they lost themselves to find the peace, no matter. They would lose nothing a man should strive to

[2] *Buddhism,* page 111.
[3] This is Sir Charles Eliot's figure.

keep. Had not their struggle to realize and assert themselves been the secret of all their dis-ease?

The key to any definition of Nirvana is generally in the mind of the one who proposes it. If he is able to understand such a definition as this:[4] "Nirvana is a state of ideal spiritual perfection in which the soul, having completely detached itself by the force of its own natural expansion from what is individual, impermanent and phenomenal, embraces and becomes one with the Universal, the Eternal and the Real. . . . The finding of the ideal self . . . through . . . living conscious oneness with the All and the Divine"—well, then this is Nirvana. There is a basis in the literature, especially in what has been influenced by later Indian thought for that kind of definition, though there is in it a disconcerting cloudiness. The Universal, the Eternal and the Real do not become clear through the familiar device of initialing them with capital letters.

Nirvana probably is absorption; before death in the peace of a simple, holy and care-free life; after death in the general sum of all existence. Whether those thus beatified know of this felicity Gautama never said. Who knows?

GAUTAMA'S TEACHING ABOUT THE SOUL

Everything here is complicated by the fact that Gautama denied the existence of the soul. Here is a religion capable of commanding boundless devotion yet without a God and without a human soul. One wonders by what test it is to be called a religion. Yet Gautama is not to be indicted without a plea for the defense. The learned of his time and later did believe in a soul but it was something inside a person which came in and went out. Brahmanic omniscience described it—it was no larger than a thumb—and entered into any amount of detail about its dissolution into the elements of the air after death and its curious course of concentration and return into another incarnation. Also how it got into the body and other such impossibilities. Gautama denied the reality of that kind of soul through an insight far in advance of his time.

He denied soul reality also because he was in search of something unaffected by change or suffering, beyond the reach of mortal error. (He has passages which make one think of Christian Science.) The

[4] Edmund Holmes, *The Creed of Buddha*, page 199.

current conception of the soul entangled it in the web of suffering and delusion. And finally, in a sentence, he substituted personality for soul in all his teaching; which is about what we are just now beginning to do. A very careful student of the various uses of the Greek words in the Christian New Testament (Kremer) supports the conclusion that "psyche" is in substance "the permanent possibility of one's best self." Of course, the soul which Gautama showed the door came in again by the window. The word is inevitable, he could not even argue about it without using it. And besides it does stand for something. Buddha equates soul with personality—a distinctly modern note. He is equally acute in his analysis of personality.

There are three modes of personality he says: the first has form and is compounded of the Buddhist equivalent of chemical elements and is nourished by solid food—being evidently the very material kind of personality which holds a fountain pen. The second is mind, immaterial personality, being evidently the meditative, controlling self whose main effort at this present moment is to get set down on paper something reasonably clear about what the Enlightened One thought the soul to be. The third mode of personality is "made up of consciousness only"—evidently the tied-together sense one has that one, in doing and being all this, really exists, a center of mystery walled off from everything else as the room in which this is written is walled in out of the golden loveliness of an August day.

But these are only "modes" of personality, ways in which one is what he is—and knows it. And now for the knottiest point in Gautama's psychology—and the knottiest point in any psychology. What is the reality behind form and mind and consciousness, the self which passes its little sunlit and shadowed span in saying "I" and living "me," goes "from the great deep to the great deep" and which, if immortality is more than a dream, endures the shock and dissolution of death—and still says "I"? Gautama does not know. The individual is, for him, a "complex," assembled at each new birth in a new way determined by the law and force of consequence (Karma) which undoes a man and makes him a rat because he had been a grain thief, or else lifts a lower "complex" to a higher form and then dissolves it. The attentive listener, seeking light, who sat cross-legged before the Blessed One was only a knot of qualities tied together. Gautama had a name for the bundle—Skandhas (various spellings)—which after all only means "Aggregates." A man is an aggregate of matter, feeling, perceptions, consciences and the power to know. Gautama's analysis divides consciousness into fifty-two elements: sensation, attention, decision, shame, doubt, faith, delusion, pity, envy, worry, flurry, pride and the like. There is a name for them also, they are the Sankharas, if it matters.

"These are all the bodily and mental part and powers of man and neither any one of them or any group of them is permanent. 'The first group, material qualities, are like a mass of foam that gradually forms and then vanishes. The second group, the feelings and sensations, are like a bubble dancing on the face of the water. The third group, the sensations, are like the uncertain mirage that appears in the sunshine . . . and the fourth group, consciousness, is like a spectre or magical illusion.' "[5]

The nearest parallel to this in our own thought is the behavioristic psychology and the parallel is arresting. The only thing, say the teachers of that school, that we can know about personality is that it is a "complex" acting in ways we have decided to call personal. You know the self only from the outside and through its behavior. What tied the knot of self or what happens when it is untied, or whether it ever be untied at all, is not their concern. Nor was it Gautama's. A man's concern is with his disposition, the way he reacts. Dispositions can be changed. "The evil dispositions one has acquired may be put away; the dispositions which tend to purity may increase; and one may continue to see face to face [with truth probably] and by himself come to realize the full perfection and grandeur of wisdom." In the dialogue from which this is quoted the questioner presses home the old, old queries, "Is the soul the same as the body? Is the soul one thing and the body another? Does one who has gained the truth live again after death? Does he not live again after death?"

And to each question the Exalted One made the same reply: "That too is a matter on which I have expressed no opinion." Such questions are irrelevant to a tranquil heart and right conduct. "True wisdom can be acquired by practice only. Practice the truth that thy brother is the same as thou, walk in the noble path of righteousness and thou wilt understand that while there is death in self there is immortality in truth." Which proves that Gautama was among the

---

[5] Rhys-Davids, *Buddhism,* page 93. The quotation cited is from Spence Hardy's *Manual of Buddhism,* page 446 in the edition used.

first to discover that an impressive phrase will generally silence an impertinent question and leave the Enlightened One's reputation for wisdom unimpaired.

The Buddhist Becomes a Monk; Organization

Buddhism, being an exacting discipline of world- and self-renunciation, naturally became the entire occupation of the complete Buddhist. It made him celibate, a recluse and entirely dependent upon charity; the discipline became a vocation and the movement shut out every other interest in life. One can not discover that Gautama ever considered the bearing of the system upon society as a going concern. Naturally a society in which everyone is a monk or a nun will end in one generation and the end will be hastened among Buddhists by the uncomfortable fact that there is no one to fill the begging bowl. A medieval monastery (under Benedict's wise rule) was economically self-supporting providing someone gave the brotherhood endowments of land. In fact, a Clairvaux or Cluny was a more self-sufficient economic group than any other element in twelfth century Europe. But labor was never a rule of a Buddhist community.

Gautama organized his following very simply. The earliest condition of "belonging" was an actual conversion, an experience of ecstasy generally following much travail of soul. Then true "seekers" were admitted upon the simplest confession of faith. Any brother could ordain after the candidate had shaved his head and face, put on the saffron robes properly, saluted the feet of the brethren, squatted down, stretched out his folded palms and repeated the Three Refuges three times:

> To the Buddha I go for refuge,
> To the Law I go for refuge,[6]
> To the Order I go for refuge.

Afterwards even this was modified. Gautama never demanded one set experience, since "brethren are released by emancipation of heart, others by the release of wisdom," each by his own road.

The Dialogues usually end with the request of some questioner who has been properly shown the error of his doctrinal ways to

---

[6] "Law" is also translated "norm."

enter the order. "And I, Sir, betake myself to the Exalted One as my guide, to his Doctrine and to his Order. May the Exalted One accept me as his adherent; as one who from this day forth as long as life endures, has taken him for his guide." The request is always graciously granted and the Dialogue ends with an edifying account of the virtuous life of the new disciple and how, going forth as a homeless wanderer, he became conscious that "after the present life there would be no beyond."

Gautama asked no impossible austerities. He taught the "Middle Way" between a naked asceticism and worldly luxury. His insistent emphasis was upon the discipline of temper and desire, and his disciples were called lax by the thoroughgoing ascetics of his time. He reacted strongly against the excessive asceticism of India:

> Not nakedness, nor matted hair, nor filth,
> Nor fasting long, nor lying on the ground,
> Not dust and dirt, nor squatting on the heels,
> Can cleanse the mortal that is full of doubt.
> But one that lives a calm and tranquil life,
> Though gaily decked,—if tamed, restrained he live,
> Walking in the holy path of righteousness,
> Laying aside all harm to living things,—
> True mendicant, ascetic Brahman he.[7]

The accounts of the first brotherhoods are invested with a really lovely romance. It was all like St. Francis in the first phase of the Franciscans—an idyll of peace. The groves were the first cloisters, there were no hours, the brethren could come and go as they pleased. They were forbidden to destroy life, steal or lie. They must be chaste, use no intoxicants or eat at forbidden times. They must use no garlands, perfumes or ornaments, nor sleep in high beds, nor accept gold or silver. Their robes should properly be pieced together. The novices were attached to masters whose simple needs they served and from whom they received instruction.

The monks in a district must assemble four times a month. A list of offenses was read and the brethren asked three times after each item, "Are you pure in this matter?"[8] Silence indicated a good con-

---

[7] Woodward, *Dhammapada VV*, 141-2, *op. cit.*, page 26. This little book of Woodward's has the whole of real Buddhism in it.

[8] The Buddhist Eight Commandments are: To avoid taking life; taking what is not given; unchastity; intoxicants; lying; unseasonable meals and dancing; music

science. Otherwise the penitent must arise and say, "Transgression, Lord, overcame us: Such was our folly, such was our stupidity, such was our wrongdoing," and the shameful deed is named. Absolution which means only reconciliation with the brethren was granted in a really lovely form. The fault remains to be expiated. A monk was permitted three robes, a girdle, an alms bowl, a razor, a needle and a water strainer, this last to keep him from swallowing life.

The early groups were communities rather than organizations, but a loose monastic organization was inevitable. The laity acquired merit by giving and the monks aided them to that desirable end by accepting cloisters, warmed halls, warm baths and such other illusions as might make the road to Nirvana less wearing. The more sensitive later felt the reproach of this. The "Buddhist year" has already been noted. In the dry season the brethren wandered about, blameless and appealing pilgrims on the road to peace (though the Western mind would have another name for them).

In the wet season they met in the shelters provided by the worldly for self-examination and instruction. A ceremony of mutual pardoning of offenses and the distribution of fresh robes—probably needed —ended the retreat. The whole order was governed by the control of the inner life. No clerical hierarchy ever grew out of the movement save in Thibet. Buddhism substitutes the tests of conduct for the tests of orthodox belief. Its records are undarkened by trials for heresy and unshamed by any story of persecution. Differences of opinion became schools of thought and not organized and embattled sects. Gautama left no regulations for worship or cultus. There is an essential freedom in Buddhism to which it has been historically true. The Blessed One reluctantly permitted women to form an order of their own. He had no burning concern for their release from illusion and thought them a hindrance to the escape of the brethren.

---

and shows. One can get ten, by adding cosmetics and jewels and soft couches. Gautama was an early Puritan.

Woodward's statement concerning the Buddhist commandments is that the *Bhikkus* observe ten, *devotees* eight, and *laymen* five.

The second five are: 1. Against unseasonable meals. 2. Against dancing, song, playing music, and seeing shows. 3. Against the use of flowers, scents, and unguents, wearing ornaments and decorations. 4. Against the use of raised beds, of wide beds. 5. Against accepting gold and silver.

THE PLACE OF WOMEN IN THE ORDERS

Ananda (there are different versions of the story) once asked the Blessed One's advice in a difficult matter:

What conduct toward women do you prescribe for these who have left the world?
Guard against looking on a woman.
But if he sees one inadvertently?
Let it be as though he saw her not.
But if he must speak with her—?
Let it be with a pure heart.
But if she speaks to him—?
Keep awake, Ananda.

Actually in all the traditions women play a considerable part in Gautama's life. He dines with a courtesan, instructs her gravely and accepts her gifts. But he saw clearly through the danger of a mendicant order of women wandering homelessly about. He felt too that woman's place was in the home and said as much, plainly, to the first woman who asked admittance. He had yet to learn that it is easier to win Nirvana than arrest a feminist movement. "Now Maha-Prajapati got her hair cut off, donned saffron robes, and . . . with a number of women of the Sakiyan clan . . . wandering from place to place," found the retreat of the Exalted One "and there she took her stand outside the porch, her feet all swollen and dust begrimed, sad, sorrowful, tearful and wailing."

The venerable Ananda considered this a case in which he might speak to the lady and asked the occasion of her evident distress.

O, my Lord Ananda, it is because the Exalted One permits not that women go forth from the home unto the homeless life under the Law set forth by the Truth-finder.

Ananda pleaded her cause with the Truth-finder.[9]

"Well were it, Lord, if women were permitted so to do," and argued it out. Gautama was just and admitted that a woman was capable of following the Way. Now Maha-Prajapati was Gautama's aunt. Ananda reminded him that "she was nurse, nourisher and

[9] Tathagata.

milk-giver"—the last evidently a figure of speech. Meanwhile the woman kept wailing and weeping. The Exalted One bowed to the inevitable. He laid down eight rules, the substance of which were that the women should live seemly lives, be carefully looked after, hold the brethren in due respect, neither abuse nor censure them and not speak till they were spoken to—if then. But he shook his head sadly and prophesied that, with women admitted, the order would not outlast five hundred years; without them it would have gone a thousand years. The monastic orders of women showed no great force and faded out of the picture. But in general, women had a better status in Buddhism than in any other Oriental religion.

The Place of the Laity

The monks are a society within society, but Gautama gave the laity "a definite and honorable place" in his system. The monk has no such relation to the unordained as the western clergyman. They are not priests or preachers. They will instruct the inquiring but assume no responsibility for their souls nor any authority over them. Also since the door to monkhood opens both ways, a layman can take the bowl and the robe for a season and go back, without reproach, to the world when he wants. Such is still the custom in Siam. A young Buddhist enters the order much as a young Frenchman does his military service. The Siamese, however, sets his own term of monastic retirement and often makes it ridiculously short. No layman can lead a perfect life, but he may secure a happier rebirth and even die in the hope of Nirvana. "There is no distinction," Gautama says, "between a monk who has taken the vows and the man of the world living with his family. There are hermits who fall into perdition and humble householders who rise to the rank of saints."

He laid down five commandments for a layman: to take no life, drink no intoxicants, lie and steal not and observe the chastity of a married life. In addition he is credited with a wealth of really wise advice as to the practical conduct of life in all its relations. No ethical system is richer in humane graces. Gautama kept his followers entirely out of the jungle of sex-deification of which there was plenty in India then and later, with appropriate altar-priests and priestesses.

FREEDOM OF THE WILL IN THE SYSTEM

Making every allowance for what is read back into Gautama, that shaven and saffron-gowned one with no professor's chair save his own crossed legs, could have held his own in his own field with the hooded and gowned of a modern university. Indeed, save for his own assurance that he was free from the wheel, he might be reincarnate in any one of the teachers who now define personality as a mode of behavior. His system should have been darkly fatalistic. If any sentient creature, beast, man or angel, is only an eddy of behavior in the vast and timeless current of existence, as they tell us now that matter is only an eddy in the vast and timeless current of cosmic energy, controlled by a law which does not allow the most fugitive thought to pass unrecorded or unpaid for, then what is man but a series of inevitable consequences?

Gautama never questioned the freedom of the will or the essential moral sovereignty of a person. If some disputatious person had said to the Enlightened One: "Since you teach, Lord, that each man is what the sum of his merits and demerits in other existences have made him, have they not also made him such that what he does whether right or wrong he can not help doing?" He would have answered: "Self is the lord of self; who else should be lord?" and fallen silent. His whole system assumes our power to rule and direct our inner life and he had an acute ethical sense. The Western mind may or may not accept Buddhistic goodness as ideal. It can not, on close acquaintance with it, deny that it is a completely rounded and really richly conceived system.

These are the aspects of Buddhism which have leavened the East for two thousand years. The common folk, householders, far enough from desiring nothing and creating nothing, clung to the wheel but some deep saturation of the temper and ethics of Gautama colored their deeds and their souls. The empires of the East were made and dissolved. Cities were built and the jungle swallowed them up. But always, always outlasting empire and their capitals were the patient folk whose blood the conquerors used to cement their empires, out of whose sweat they built their palaces, kept gentle, honest and kind by the felt influence of a faith whose philosophy they could not understand, whose disciplines demanded what they could not give, but whose assurances promised them an ultimate peace and time enough and lives enough to win it; whose injunctions taught them to be gentle and patient, to shed no blood and to live in their souls.

The whole system tended to focalize character in thought. "All that we are is the result of what we have been through; it is founded in our thoughts, it is made up of our thoughts. If a man speaks or acts with an evil thought, pain follows him, as the wheel follows the foot of him who drives the carriage." Thought must be kind, "for hatred does not cease by hatred at any time; hatred ceases by love, this is an old rule." One must be always on one's guard. "As rain breaks through an ill-thatched house, passion will break through an unreflecting mind." The insights of the Buddhist proverbs are often startling in their quiet wisdom. "An evil deed does not turn suddenly like milk; smouldering it follows the foot like fire covered by ashes." In its moments of clearest insight, Buddhism asserts the supremacy of love with a masterful repetition. "All good works whatsoever are not worth one sixteenth part of love which sets free the heart. Love which sets free the heart comprises them; it shines, gives light and radiance . . . As in the last month of the rains, in the autumn when the sky is clear and cloudless the sun mounts up high and overcomes darkness . . . in the last hour of the night when the dawn is breaking, the morning-star shines and gives light and radiance; even so does love which sets free the soul and comprises all good words, shine and give light and radiance."[10]

BUDDHISM CONVERTS A GREAT KING

Gautama won a considerable following before his death even when the loyally generous statistics of the legends are discounted and the drive of a new and alluring movement carried it strongly for the next two hundred years. It was strongest in northwest India and was already beginning to penetrate northern border regions. Every monk was a missionary, his wandering ways and simple needs demanded no organization to support him.

Then Buddhism found a royal patron—Asoka. He ascended a throne in the northwest about 273 B.C. sixty years after the death of Alexander, and won an empire which he ruled for forty years to

[10] For an exhaustive study of moral standards of Buddhism, see S. Tachibana, *The Ethics of Buddhism*, Oxford University Press, 1926.

its great advantage. By this time the wealth of India was no mere figure of speech. A single king had an army of 80,000 horses, 8,000 chariots, 200,000 men and 6,000 fighting elephants. And so sound a historian as Vincent Smith takes this figure seriously. The court of a king like that was splendidly maintained, rich in gold and gems and brilliant robes; his state was highly organized. The low, timber-built cities which housed so much pride and power are only a memory, but the record of Greek travelers who witness to them remains. Asoka inherited a kingdom like that.

In the thirteenth year of his reign he enlarged it at the expense of a neighbor who had military force enough to make a little war which history does not remember a costly enterprise. Asoka himself records its cost in human life and unhappiness with feelings of "remorse, profound sorrow and regret." Such records of royal grief over victory are rare. He became a confirmed pacifist and declared that "the loss of even the hundredth or the thousandth part of the persons who were there slain, carried away captive or done to death, would now be a matter of deep regret to his majesty," and left his penitence for all the world to read on one of his famous rock inscribed edicts. His singularly sensitive spirit was hospitable to Gautama's "way," his royal power made him a road builder for the Enlightened One and he lifted Buddhism to an imperial station.

He made Buddhism known and acknowledged from Kabul to the Bay of Bengal. He held the passes into Central Asia; it was easy for a monk to slip through. He was the first in India to build with stone buildings so splendid that Chinese pilgrims seven hundred years later saw his palace still standing and judged it spirit built since it was of a grandeur "which no human hands of this world could accomplish." He made noble provision for the monks, built strange cupolas to shelter the relics of the Buddha and wrote his laws upon pillars and rocks. These remain and supply a wealth of information as to a code of humane legislation unparalleled for the time and not too easy to parallel in any period. He planted trees, dug wells, established hospitals for man and beast, had a department of Royal Charity and seems to have found his motivation in the teaching and spirit of Buddhism. A system—call it what you will—which makes a king like that stand well in "the fierce light which beats upon a throne" is not to be disregarded. He was a whole-hearted convert. He has been called the "Constantine of Buddhism" but he was a better man than Constantine ever knew how to be. Armed conquest, he said, is not the chief duty of kings; the only true conquest is effected through the Law of Piety.

He used his full power, and it was very great, to teach and enforce the ethical system of Buddhism. He wrote his golden rules in carven characters upon the living rocks. He made a pilgrimage of piety to all the Holy Places of the faith and left pillars of single stones to mark the stations, as shrines now mark the spots where the body of Queen Eleanor rested on its last pilgrimage. These monuments reach to the foothills of the Himalayas. He stood in the traditional garden where travail came upon Maya and she gave birth to Gautama. "Here," said his guide, "Great King! was the Venerable One born." A pillar inscribed with these words is still there, the inscription uneffaced by twenty centuries.

Ten years before his death, he was fully ordained a monk and sat upon his throne a shaven beggar in his own palace. There is a well based tradition that he called a Buddhist church council to decide what Scriptures were authority and reform abuses. Before Asoka Buddhism had no organized propaganda. Asoka organized the first Foreign Missionary Society and carried it off like a king. His imperial vision included Asia, Africa and Europe. He sent his missionaries to every state under his protection, to "the independent Kingdoms of Southern India, to Ceylon, to the Hellenistic monarchies of Syria, Egypt, Cyrene, Macedonia and Epirus.[11] What memories of the Buddhist gospel may have haunted Syria three hundred years later have supplied a misty basis of conjecture for those who want to put Jesus in debt to Gautama. Beyond debate the lands whose shores are washed by the eastern Mediterranean were the melting pot for religious and philosophic contributions drawn from remote sources during the first three centuries of the Christian Era; something of Gautama's teaching may have contributed a not unworthy element.

Debased forms of Platonic philosophy, the influence of Hebrew Monotheism, the Christian gospels and Zoroaster's age-old strife between light and darkness were all combined in cloud-built systems of speculation and given a forbidding name. There are, Smith thinks, undoubted traces of Buddhist doctrine in Gnosticism. How far orthodox Christianity reflects some leavening of it is an obscure matter,

[11] Vincent A. Smith, *Early History of India,* The Clarendon Press, Oxford, 1908.

not so much debated as it used to be since the critical students of
Christianity have at present a formula for the constitution of it which
does not need that ingredient.

I am persuaded that the general development of religion in the
lands of Zoroaster, Gautama and Jesus for the five hundred years,
say from 300 B.C. to 200 A.D. can not be kept in watertight compartments. Mysterious currents of interchanging influence ebbed and
flowed from the Mediterranean to the Ganges. But I do not see on
the other hand why a creative originality is allowed one teacher and
denied another. The material which the distinctive hopes and faith
of Hebraism supplied and the mind of Jesus recast are sufficient to
account for the Sermon on the Mount without drawing upon the
Sermon under the Bo-tree.

It is as hard to say what Buddhism would have become without
Asoka as to calculate any other vanished alternative of history. Before he lent his imperial force, it was a local Indian sect; the forces
he released made it one of the great religions of the world. But even
an Oriental King can not force an unwelcome faith upon vast regions
and great populations for long. There were profound correspondences
between the dreams and insights of Gautama and the temper of the
lands where Buddhist temple bells are still ringing; in lands where
that temper did not exist it made little or no headway. Egypt would
not surrender Isis and Osiris and the barley fields of its local paradise
for Nirvana. The regions which had acknowledged the spell of the
Greek spirit had no use for the selfless life of a shaven ascetic.

The Two "Vehicles"

The far and southern East accepted the morality and discipline
gladly, clung to it tenaciously—and changed it beyond Gautama's
recognition. Dates are little used here, they are too uncertain and
one must think in centuries; but once Asoka's missionaries had carried Buddhism into lands far beyond the Five Rivers, acute thinkers
with a faculty for speculation which makes Western speculations
restrained and colorless, took it in hand and built upon Gautama's
foundations an immense and cloud-possessed structure. Gautama himself, though he distrusted speculation, was familiar with many systems. He lived in a world already rich in religious faith, speculation
and literature. (Practically the Indian world of half the next chapter.)

He was "highly educated in the learning and philosophy of his day."
He knew the Vedas, some of the thought of the Upanishads[12] and
the heady metaphysical theories of his time. (He mentions sixty-two
philosophic views, each with its ardent expounders and followers.)
He could not in his own teaching despite his realistic, exquisitely
balanced, practical sense, escape some measure of speculation; he left
material for almost boundless future theologies of a cosmic cast.

No religion—not even Christianity[13]—has continued through the
centuries, penetrated cultures and met the always changing human
mind in its sequent phases without itself being very greatly changed.
If it possesses some sovereign principle, it will maintain its identity
and extend its empire of faith and practice. If it have no power to
reassert itself over what it absorbs, it will itself be lost. But it will
never continue as it began. Buddhism through its missionary force
and its power of plastic adaptation to the needs of the long-enduring
East has had a long course. It has given and taken much. (These
sentences are colorless compared with its multi-colored pilgrimage
through a multi-colored world from the Himalayas to spice-scented
isles of southern seas and to the austere shores of the North Pacific.)

The issue, with countless marginal variations, has been two schools
of Buddhist thought. These are sometimes called the Hinayana or
Lesser and the Mahayana or Greater Vehicle. This is a sea-born
figure. (Though it seems to us a mixed metaphor.) The Buddhist
loved to think of his sacred teachings as a vessel in which a man
could safely cross the ocean of manifold existences, itself salt with
tears, and reach his desired haven of Nirvana. The Great Vehicle,
its supporters hold, was a more seaworthy vessel built to carry more
passengers. The Little Vehicle was well enough but, so to speak, of
small tonnage. Hinayana is less widespread and confined to those
territories accessible to the original disciples of Gautama—mostly in
Southern Asia. North and far east Buddhism is generally Mahayana.
Naturally the passengers on the smaller vessel protest that theirs is
not inferior, being soundly built and true to the founder's spirit and
teaching. The followers of Mahayana as naturally defend their vessel.
Gautama, they claim, really adapted his teaching to the needs of his
hearers and kept back inner secrets till the world was ready for them.

---

[12] See next chapter.
[13] See Gardner's *The Growth of Christianity*, A. & C. Black, London, 1907, for an
admirable and suggestive illustration of this.

The difference between the Sermon on the Mount and the great Christian theologies is not a misleading parallel.

Actually, as Pratt makes plain, though there were in the teachings of Gautama "the seeds of many of the doctrines and practices which were to prevail in the North," it was old India—as persistent as her jungles—which took and changed a teaching which was in some ways always alien to her spirit. Her innate religiosity (an awkward but necessary word) never let anything alone till it became a religion. Her genius for spacious speculation was never content until the simple was traced to its source and invested with a trailing garmenture of dreams and clouds and penetrating insight. India—old India—launched the Great Vehicle, China and Japan rebuilt and refitted it;—also and always—some deep human need. Gautama would not have finally recognized it but Mahayana did make Buddhism a religion, added Gautama to the procession of the gods and, by a strange contradiction, became beneath its cloud veils a religion of the heart.

Gautama himself was almost from the first invested with a touch of the supernatural. Faith, love and veneration always do that for their object; it was easy to worship him. Then love provided him a timeless lineage. He had been reincarnate many, many times before he sat under the Bo-tree and won the right to save the world. (He was at first the last of seven Buddhas.) This number was naturally multiplied and provision began to be made for a future supply. Bodhisattvas were added. A Bodhisattva is a Buddha in embryo, so to speak, a future Buddha on his way to enlightenment who will in due time restore the ancient law, by that due time overlain or forgotten, to its ancient authority, and here (says Pratt) something new came into the faith.

This future Buddha, disciplined through many sorrows, is on his way to become not only Enlightener but Savior. His merits can be put to the account of the needy. His suffering and goodness are vicarious. There might be in all this some penetration of Christianity working through lost channels into an alien faith, but that need not be. The conclusion is too vital, too inevitable. Love and goodness must suffer. The conception of suffering Bodhisattvas shifted the center of Buddhist devotion. If the master, then the disciple must suffer for others. Suffering is no longer an evil to be ended in Nirvana. It is a saving force in a shadowed world. Result: A literature of really lovely devotion. "To think that the offender does me a service, this is to conduct oneself in accord with the example of the Perfect Ones." "My own being and my pleasures, all my righteousness . . . I surrender indifferently that all creatures may win to their end." "Make thine own self love its pleasures and bear the sorrow of thy fellows." (See Pratt, *op. cit.,* pages 211 et seq.)

Now there is in all this a tremendous missionary motive and an emotional force early Buddhism lacked. Here the system really becomes a religion evoking devotion and hallowing life. Here also is the beginning of a really great philosophy. Philosophy began as a wisdom-about-life dealing with the meanings and values of daily life. It has always ended with the quest for the Real and the Absolute as though a man could not do his day's work until he had explored his farthest horizons. Out of what Ultimate Reality do we issue? What is its character? Buddhism, beginning with a wise and gentle teacher, by processes as natural in conclusion as they were subtle in process, said: "The real nature of things is the Buddha nature. He is its revelation; he is its *reality*. Here is the true light shining through." So Gautama became Divine.

There are striking parallels here with Christian faith and doctrine and profound differences. Gautama is not a man deified. He is perhaps an emanation. Pratt does not hesitate to use "incarnation." "In the man Sakyamuni . . . the eternal Buddha incarnated himself. The All-One stooped to appear as the son of Maya."[14] "The Infinite Reason became flesh." Naturally this is a doctrine for the elect, but it built temples for Gautama-Buddha, and set him therein, rotund, with half-closed eyes, in endless meditation to be endlessly adored. There little children left, and still leave, a handful of flowers and the troubled prayed for peace. To his worship the temple bells have called across the centuries. The Buddhist saints—and there have been many of them—have sought to reveal his spirit and the Buddhist theologian has seen through the magic the eternally Real.

By 1000 A.D. Buddhism was practically exiled from India, but exile was not death. It blossomed anew in sunny lands, lived amidst Thibetan snows, leavened Confucianism and gave another spirit to the ancestral religion of Japan. There is only one other pilgrimage in the long history of religion to compare with the Pilgrimage of Gautama

[14] Compare Philippians in the New Testament 2:6-9.

from the unmoving shadow of the Bo-tree to Asia's farthest bound. (This section is deeply in debt to Pratt.)

THE STORY OF ONE PILGRIMAGE

The really lovely poetry of the order, impossibly jeweled by an imagination for which anything is possible, is largely the creation of the Buddhists in Ceylon, Burma and Siam. The English translations of Buddhist literature are generally taken from their Canon. There is a tradition that King Tessa asked of King Asoka a branch of the Sacred Bo-tree and his daughter to bring it across. The lady was willing but the King feared to profane the tree. The tree itself detached one of its own branches which planted itself at once in a golden vase made by the goldsmith of the gods and was then, with a retinue of celestial light, music and flowers, carried to Ceylon. A Bo-tree believed to be a perennial growth from the transplanted branch is still there, being to the Buddhist world what the Stone at Mecca and the Holy Sepulchre are to Mohammedans and Christians.

Four hundred years A.D. a young Brahman "seeker" in his pilgrimage for truth crossed to Ceylon and found what he sought there at the feet of an old Buddhist teacher. He has since been called "the voice of Buddha." He had an acute mind and used it tirelessly. He assembled and edited the literature and wrote learned commentaries which modern scholars find useful. One might call him the St. Jerome of Buddhism with a little of Origen thrown in. Any historic religion passes through many minds as astronomers use this or that colored screen to sift the light of the stars. Thereafter it is never the same. The fortunes of Buddhism in Ceylon reflect the fortunes of the state. When the native kings were capable and kind, religion flourished; when they were alien or inhuman it went into eclipse.

One of the greatest native kings—a contemporary of William the Conqueror—gave to his sunlit realm about its last period of legendary splendor. His enemies faded before him "as the glow-worm at the light of the morning." "He consumed all before him as a fire advanced through the forest." He used his power for the glory of the faith and the good of his people, a builder of temples and monasteries, a digger of canals and lakes, a hero Carlyle would have rejoiced in. The history of Ceylonese Buddhism during this long period is strangely like the history of medieval monastic Christianity, too complicated to be dismissed in a silence and best left to the specialist. Our Western way of writing history, as though there were nothing but the West and our way of singing them all out of existence in a single line—

> Where every prospect pleases and only man is vile,

does scant justice to cultures and civilizations which were old when the ancestors of the now Western nations were barbarians and richly human when Western kings were pulling the teeth of Jews to secure contributions for the royal treasury. Then the West reached out to touch the East—and the touch was not kind.

There are now four Buddhist groups in Ceylon. They differ as the teachings of other religions differ, in very little things; one sect leaves the right shoulder bare, another covers both shoulders. In one sect there is a reader and an interpreter, in another one man both reads and interprets; the former are "two-siders," the latter "one-siders"—a matter of pulpit furniture, apparently. There are differences also in theology and social status. Some are puritans and carry only palm leaf umbrellas—others see no sin in silk.[15] The extremists in both groups deny the true church status of one another in a fashion common to other religions. They differ also as to whether the Buddha is still in existence or not. If he is, he must contemplate some of his disciples with a puzzled curiosity.

The monks of Ceylon have ceased to wander about. They live in very little groups—often only a monk and a novice. The orders have a sort of feudal relation to villages, or else own lands now leased as plantations to Europeans. Laymen still acquire merit through offerings. Religious festivals, a little like a "camp meeting," a little like such readings of the Law as the Hebrew Scriptures record and not a little like a great church occasion in Italy, are celebrated, to the evident joy of the populace, at the proper seasons of the year. One may find a low-roofed hut and a cave behind it smelling of bats, burnt incense and camphor with some ancient inscription to say that a king gave it to the community and two or three books brown with age and smoke, or else the Buddhist college at Colombo with its journal "The Buddhist" in English, its scholars and students the last exponents of a time-worn order against a new world and a

---

[15] A friend who knows the country told the writer of seeing one of the silk-sect buy a most expensive umbrella and go off with it proudly and devoutly.

new faith. An echo of a contention in which Buddhism is involved along its whole front—save Thibet—is heard in this tract—

Do Buddhists consider Buddha as one Who by his own virtue can save us from the consequences of our individual sins?
Not at all. No one can be saved by another, he must save himself.
What then was Buddha to us and all other beings?
An all-seeing, all-wise, counselor; one who discovered the safe path and pointed it out; one who shared the cause of and the only cure for human suffering. In pointing to the road, in showing us how to escape dangers, he became our guide. And as one leading a blind man across a narrow bridge over a swift and deep stream saves his life, so in showing us who were blind from ignorance, the way to Salvation, Buddha may well be called our "Saviour."[16]

No modernization of a religion whose essential force is spent has recaptured the wonder of its dawn—the secret of its once high ascendency. It is not likely that the monks of Colombo can turn the shadow on the dial.

THE TEMPLE BELLS KEEP RINGING

I have dwelt thus at length upon Ceylonese Buddhism because it is fairly typical of the course of the faith outside India. It has kept truest to form in the south, having taken in the north a multitude of divergent forms which puzzle the specialist. In China it overlays Confucianism and becomes not so much an order as a modification of the Confucian ethics. (There are universal elements in Gautama's teachings which could be fitted into almost any purely religious system.) Burma is still the stronghold of Buddhism in the Indian Empire. The orders are well organized, the monastic schools are old and effective. The percentage of literates among the men is higher than the proportion in Italy. The many-storied pagodas built to shelter relics and images add color to a native landscape and the temple bells, so Kipling says, are the voice of the East. But the faith itself is deeply saturated with spirit worship. There are pagodas in Siam too—the most considerable in the East. The monasteries are still more highly organized—about 20,000 of them. They are the national centers of culture and education. Western scholarship is

---

[16] Reginald Stephen Copleston, *Buddhism Primitive and Present in Magadha and Ceylon*, New York, 1892, page 476

very deeply in debt to the kings of the present dynasty who have put the Pali texts at the service of Europe and America.

Buddhism has achieved its most imposing ritual, its most mysterious hierarchy on the roof of the world. The barred passes of the Himalayas have shut it in in Thibet and shut the world out. Its Lamas are reincarnations of canonized saints, its Great Lama a reincarnation of some former Buddha, or else a Buddha once removed due for Nirvana after his next reincarnation. A Great Lama really never dies; he simply "goes away." He will return presently, the important thing is to find when and where. A rainbow is a particularly useful sign being sent from the discarnate one to guide his followers. Some interpreter of signs reads the meaning and directs the seekers to the proper place and family. Whereupon they set out and find him often after incredible difficulties. He is often and naturally a baby but in 1888 he was discovered as "three young boys of remarkable intelligence into one of whom beyond a doubt the spirit of the late Lama had passed." Lots were drawn from a golden vase and the children tested before high authorities to prove their distinction.[17]

The monks of Thibet keep matins, nones and vespers with chants and responses and swinging censers of incense. They tell their beads, have their saints' days, exorcise evil spirits and measure out their slow procession to beatification by their own bodies' length on the ground. Sometimes, like the learned in other lands, they think it necessary to their salvation to make their prostrations with a sore burden of books upon their backs. The laity in Thibet are still remarkably devout. They may turn prayer wheels to expedite a mechanical devotion but they are reported as showing their faith, after their light, in sincere and kindly lives. Something lasts in those mountain-guarded fortresses of an ancient faith which a world open to the invasion of changing times and changing minds has lost. I wonder if Thibet is a symbol?

It is impossible in a study like this to follow what Pratt in his great book calls *The Pilgrimage of Buddhism* across the centuries and across all the lands which it has touched and in which it still persists. It has been and is so many things. Like Christianity, it has

---

[17] Sir Monier Monier-Williams quotes this from the *London-Times*, June 15, 1888 (page 288). The late Mr. Edison once chose his successor in much the same way—not quite.

been influenced by every past which it has inherited and every land to which it has come. It is an inclusive form in which it is impossible to incorporate other religions. Both in China and Japan it has allied itself with religions native to the soil. It is continued as Gautama's discipline of life and renunciation of desire. It has become a philosophy and a many storied system of speculation. It would take a specialist to follow through the branchings of it and even then something would be left unnoted. It is still a force to be reckoned with in eastern Asia; it is just now showing itself capable of adapting western methods, it has its own propaganda, its charitable institutions and its systems of education. It has proved itself socially helpful and a leavening influence in a world of action and organization not to be underestimated.[18]

It exemplified and still exemplifies the spiritual strength which grows out of self-renunciation, a vast consideration for the weak and the suffering and the persuasion that this world is only the threshold of something vaster.

It has endured beyond its founder's hopes for it; it has been changed as he never dreamed it would be changed. Perhaps Gautama would not be too greatly concerned about all this if he should return. He did not claim a frontierless future for his order; he pointed what way he could out of the maze of suffering into temporal peace of soul and ultimate release from the strain of existence. The rest he left to time.

"Come now, brethren, I do remind ye: 'Subject to change are all compounded things.' Do ye abide in heedfulness." These were the last words of the Exalted One.

[18] What one may call the modernization of Buddhism under the impact of Western culture and Christianity has gone further in Japan than anywhere else. Dwight Goddard, a former Christian missionary who has lately gone over to Buddhism, suggested a rapprochement of the two religions. The whole program involves an ultra-modern missionary approach. See Pratt, *op. cit.*, pages 746 et seq. Also this book's chapter on Japan.

CHAPTER VIII

Hinduism Regains Mother India

BUDDHISM AN INTERLUDE IN INDIA

BUDDHISM was only an interlude in the religious development of India. Gautama supplied a necessary correction for a popular religion which consisted mostly in repeating incantations. He opposed a real concern for character to a dusty ritualism and a way of life to frontierless speculation, but India really cared for none of these things. She left the Buddhist to his self-examination and took her own line. Many forces contributed to the recession of Buddhism in India; for one thing it was too tolerant. "Now this, I say," so Gautama is reported, "not desiring to win pupils, not wishing to make others fall from their religious vows, not wishing to make others give up their ways of life. . . . Not so!" The general testimony of history is that, though an intolerant religion loses its soul, it often inherits the earth.

Hinduism itself is not intolerant; it is too inclusive. It has been defined as "the collection of rites, worships, beliefs, traditions and mythologies that are sanctioned by the sacred books and ordinances of the Brahmans and are propagated by Brahmanic teaching."[1] A modern Hindu defines a modern Hindu: he "should be born of parents not belonging to some recognized religion other than Hinduism, marry within the same limits, believe in God, respect the cow and cremate the dead." These generous limits would make any heresy trial difficult, but, on the other hand, they give Hinduism a power to wrap itself around another religion and absorb it. "The bottles of Hinduism," says Eliot, using a more classic figure of speech, "have always proved capable of holding all the wine poured in them."

Buddhism faced from the first a force of "inveterate customs and ideas" as old as India, which in time penetrated and undid its structure. No religion has ever entirely escaped what is older than

[1] Lyall, *Religious Systems of the World*, page 114.

any religion; earth-born ancestral fear, ways which will no more be banished from a cathedral than from a pagoda. Converts to a new religion never entirely surrender the old—they can not unless they surrender their general human nature at the same time. They make compromises and adjustments which in time and in the mass tell tremendously, giving continuous solidity to the human enterprise and fretting the souls of impatient reformers.

Buddhism faced from its genesis the proudest and most persistent hereditary priesthood in the world and the tendency of the system was to undo Brahmanism. That was like asking water to flow uphill; the master force of India was against it. Buddhism had no corporate force to stand against this. Buddhism could do without gods; India can not, even though her gods shift like cloud forms. Gautama discouraged speculation; India loves to lose itself in speculation. Gautama challenged the caste system; Brahmanism is tenacious in its pride of race, social station and spiritual authority. Gautama really subordinated religion to Humanism; India has hitherto subordinated all human interests to religion.

It Loses India

In the end Mother India had her way. Buddhism had nothing to oppose to the "boring-in" of Hinduism and the religious lordship of the Brahman. It was loose and open, a state of mind and a discipline of life. "It aimed not at founding a sect but at including all the world as lay believers on easy terms."[2] The frontiers, so to speak, between Buddhism and Hinduism were too open. The invasion came from the Hindu front and even the monasteries; the fortresses of Gautama's system, surrendered to it. The monasteries suffered a much more sanguinary invasion. Beginning with the tenth century A.D. the armies of Islam forced the mountain gates of India; by the beginning of the thirteenth century the Mohammedan was master of Delhi and Benares. Indian Buddhism, being concentrated in the monasteries, suffered greatly. The conquerors could not exterminate a population whose power of passive resistance meets conquest as a sand bank takes a shell, but they could massacre monks.

"Buddhism was concentrated in the great monasteries and when these were destroyed, there remained nothing outside them capable

[2] Sir Charles Eliot, *op. cit.,* Vol. II, page 120.

of withstanding either the violence of the Moslems or the . . . influence of the Brahmans.[3] Indian Buddhism never recovered." However, the bequest of Gautama never entirely disappeared, India absorbed enough of it to influence the whole Indian outlook upon life. Animal sacrifice was largely displaced by a respect for the sanctity of animal life which takes, in excess, extremely inconvenient forms (India could do without cobras). Monasticism lingers on, with perhaps a native gentleness due to the spiritual legacy of the gentlest of teachers.

There has been actually no break in the continuity of Indian religious development. The forces in action before Gautama kept on unchanged and halted only for a little. Not even King Asoka could reach and redirect them. But it is as difficult to find a telling chapter heading for what India is and has been religiously as it is to put the three thousand years of Indian history in a sentence. Hinduism is the covering word but Brahmanism is and has been the really significant contribution of India to religion. During about three creative centuries, say from eight hundred to five hundred B.C., old India carried nature worship over into a poetic, speculative, mystic pantheism which the centuries since have never escaped. Buddhism can be understood, in part at least, only as a reaction against that; Hinduism takes color from it. It lives still in a really noble literature. It is the high road to the heart of Indian faith, even though it leads through the clouds.

Brahma

The gods of the bright Vedic hymns are simple enough; they are sky and sun and storm with their pageantry and retinue. Indra was the most powerful, but no one was essentially supreme. A worshiper could build his highest altar to Indra today and Varuna tomorrow; the gods did not greatly care, or the priests either. But even the gods may fall into disorderly ways without a head and there is a tendency in any religious development either to make one divinity the head of the pantheon or else to seek a Power above them all. The Assyrian settled the rivalries of the gods mostly with the sword; Zoroaster established Ahura-Mazda upon a lonely but not uncontested throne. The Hebrew prophets knew that "the gods of the nations are idols" and consumed polytheism in the fire of their

[3] Sir Charles Eliot, *op. cit.*, page 113.

spiritual passion. The order-loving Greeks who inherited the sky-gods of the grassy plain made them vivid personalities, and set them in timeless beauty of face and form upon Olympus.

Mother India did none of these things. She created Brahma, the most elusive word a dictionary ever tried to define, the earliest anticipation of the most stupendous idea the human mind has ever wrestled with. The sages who conceived Him could not define Him themselves; they could only say "He is"

> Not by speech, not by mind,
> Not by sight can He be apprehended
> How can He be comprehended
> Otherwise than by one's saying "He is"?

Everything is Brahma, "the priest by the altar, the guest in the house." He is the thought and the thinker, the word and the speaker, the deed and the doer, the worshiper and the worshiped, the Pole star and the dust, the order of the universe, the power that pervades and upholds it. He is the timeless flow of all reality and Brahma alone is real; the World-Soul, the essence of the universe, immaterial, uncreated, illimitable, eternal, and all the mighty changing seeming of the universe only phases of His Eternal Being.

THE INDIAN MIND

By what steps did the thinkers, dreamers and poets of Indian States hardly won from the jungle reach a conception like that? One comes now in the East upon gigantic temples, upon which the treasures of kings, the labor of generations and the skill of nameless craftsmen must have been expended, lost in the jungle, "powerful and beautiful and desolate beyond imagination," monuments of vanished empires, carven recitatives of a dead faith. And yet these are no more wonderful than the religious literature of India five hundred years before the Christian Era and the murky splendor of its quest and its conclusions.

And it is not dead. Modern science might borrow some of its passages to voice the conclusions of Eddington and Whitehead. Modern idealistic philosophy turns to it for happy illustrations. Modern religion continues one phase of it in the doctrine of the immanence of God. Scholars like Hume and Deussen trace for us the successive steps in the development of the Brahma conception through the literature it has created. But the real key to it is actually the Indian mind and possibly something older than the Upanishads.

The Western mind has always approached the world from the outside, being quite sure, before Einstein and the very modern science took it in hand, that it was a substantial and satisfactorily going concern, exactly what it looked and sounded and felt like, God created and God directed. The oriental mind approaches reality from the inside and makes of all outward things only dissolving shadows of something vaster and more subtle than themselves. Where the West ends with God, the East ends with soul—not the little souls of our little selves, but a Soul of which the universe is only the garment. A man is only the most inconsequential of inlets into which some tide of the vaster soul flows and for an instant rests, and his true destiny is to be absorbed into the sea of Soul-Being out of which he came.

It is hard to build a bridge of words which will carry any traffic of understanding between the minds of the East and the West and across those abysmal differences which go to the bottom of faith and temperament. But whether words help or not, the concrete differences between the religious life of the West and India are plain enough. They are woven through contrasted writings; they are sculptured in stone upon the façades of Chartres and Amiens and the temples of Benares for all the world to see. They have created different theologies, different philosophies, different disciplines of life and different souls. All religious experience must have some things in common, but for all that

East is East and West is West.

And they will meet at the Judgment Seat before they meet in an utterly clear mutual understanding of one another's religion—which does not argue well for what is to follow. These subtle speculations did not grow in a vacuum. They were, as time goes, a quick and tropical growth, but there must have been roots for them to grow out of. What was there in the early faith of India to supply a point of departure for the speculations of the sages and the pantheistic hymns of nameless poets?

THE SEARCH FOR WORLD-UNITY

Brahma once appeared to the gods, a legend says, and they did not know who it was. So they sent Agni, the God of Fire, to find out. The unknown challenged the Fire-God to burn a straw but he could not. Then the gods sent the Wind-God to inquire. The unknown challenged him to blow the straw away and he could not do it. The gods were facing a Power through whose permission they acted, against whose prohibition they could not act. Now there was in the morning faith of the Aryans of the East a strange suggestion of a power like that. They sensed an authority behind the gods which even the gods could not escape. They called it "Rita" and did no more than suggest their sense of the sweep and power of it, but it was, as nearly as they could say and we can understand, the regnant order of the world, man's duty and nature's master, of which they might have sung, had they known how:

Thou dost preserve the stars from wrong
And the most ancient Heavens, through Thee are fresh and strong.

There are scant references to Rita in the Upanishads; Brahma is once called "the Right," but I do not know what the Sanskrit word so translated is. There is also the suggestion that Brahma is immanent in right conduct—which does not get one far. But the august idea of a controlling unity in the world is expressed in the old Vedic hymns and, though the connection is now impossible to trace, I should think there is an unbroken road from the first dim vision or a timeless and regnant order to Brahma who is the end of all knowledge, the soul of all reality.

SALVATION BY KNOWLEDGE

Given a mind like the Indian mind and such a theme to consider and the result is a literature which contains the dreams, the insight, the poetry of centuries invested with a saving power if only one knew it. Everything else gave way to the passion to know. The saints of old India lived simple and austere lives—if they observed their own precepts—but they did not seek their salvation in action or faith. They were in quest of the supreme knowledge—the word

Brahma seems to have meant a sacred knowledge to begin with.
Truth is their passion, not the little truths of facts and things, but
the vast, mysterious truth hidden behind all veils of appearance.
They were pilgrims and they prayed as they journeyed:

> From the unreal lead me to the real;
> From darkness lead me to light,
> From death lead me to immortality.

For them the unreal was death, the real immortality, the darkness
death, the light immortality. When they knew the real their quest
was over. Brahma was the real, knowledge the road and escape from
the weary round of birth, and death the reward for the student's
toil.

The "way" of Gautama was an alternative to the way of the
Brahman. Both sought escape from an endless and profitless rebirth,
but their roads go entirely different directions. For the Buddhist,
existence is the fruit of desire—purge the self from desire by discipline and the long sequence of deeds and consequences is ended and
the life-weary find Nirvana. For the Brahman existence is a delusion; once a man *knows* that—as a troubled dreamer knows that he
dreams—he is free. Nothing is left to wake to, he is absorbed in the
"All." The "immortality" of the last quotation is not the immortality
of the West. It is the immortality of a drop of water fallen back
into the ocean. Both Buddhism and Brahmanism end in the entire
dissolution of conscious personality.

Knowledge then became the passion of the scholar priests of Old
India. It was "the one object of supreme value, the irresistible means
of obtaining one's end." "He obtains the whole world who knows
this." "This" may be one thing or another and to the Western mind
of little consequence—but one must know the right things. For
the Western mind knowledge is built on a general foundation of
observed fact. The Eastern mind creates knowledge out of its inner
consciousness. What the devout ought, therefore, to know for his
salvation takes a curious range; the proper way to perform a sacrifice, beget a child, attain a great wish, win the three worlds[4] or

---

[4] "Now, there are of a truth three worlds—the World of Men, the World of the
Fathers, and the World of the Gods. The World of Men is to be obtained by a
Son only . . . ; the World of the Fathers by Sacrifice; the World of the Gods by
knowledge. The World of the Gods is verily the best world. Therefore, they praise
knowledge."

become one with God. No sacred literature is so strange a mingling of insight and trivial detail, of what is done in secret and what is proclaimed from the housetop, as the sacred literature of India. It is the creation of acute and subtle minds, entirely free from scientific control, dealing for centuries with the mysteries of life and death, checkered experience, the origin and fate of the universe and the reality which undergirds all reality. It is not a system; it is the mind of India.

What Is the First-cause?

The questions this sacred wisdom undertakes are common to all religion: Zoroaster's—

> This I ask Thee—tell it to me truly, Lord!
> Who the Sire was, Father first of Holiness?

is echoed in India's question—

> What is the cause? Brahma? Whence are we born?
> Whereby do we live? And on what are we established?
> Overruled by whom, in pains and pleasures,
> Do we live our various Conditions, O ye Theologians?[5]

And the Book of Job re-echoes the timeless quest—

Oh, that I knew where I might find Him! That I might come even to His seat!

It is concerned, of course, with creation. The earlier "wisdom" reflects the naïve ideas of child-minded people. The world was just water to begin with, or else all things rose out of space, or else the world, being non-existent, turned into an egg and the egg split asunder. One of the two eggshell parts became silver, one gold.

[5] All the quotations in this section are from Dr. Robert E. Hume's translation of the Thirteen Principal Upanishads. The Upanishads are substantially the philosophy of India from 700 to 300 B.C. (Accurate datings are impossible.) They are the old Scriptures out of which the great line of Indian religion has developed. Dr. Hume's scholarship guarantees their accuracy. It seems an impracticable detail to add citation references. If, for example, one should put Svet. (1.11) after the quotation above it would be like writing a code word with no key (save, for the specialist in the literature). Or, if one should write instead Svetasvatara Upanishad, First Adhyaya, verse one, it would not greatly clarify the matter. This section is greatly in debt to Dr. Hume's introduction for a clear statement of the substance of the Old Indian thought. Also to Professor Paul Deussen's *The Religion and Philosophy of India*. But the basis of what follows is the Upanishads themselves.

"That which was of silver is this earth. That which was of gold is the sky." The outer membranes of the cosmic egg became the mountains, the inner membrane cloud and mist. More acute minds found a flaw in the egg theory: "But verily, my dear," says a father to his son, "how from non-being could being be produced. On the contrary, my dear, in the beginning was just Being, one only without a second." He then proceeds to explain how pure Being became endless variety in a way which suggests Herbert Spencer's famous polysyllabic definition of evolution.

Gradually the quest for a creator faded out of Indian thought. The West has always entertained a lively interest in the creation problem since the West began with the world and sought God through creation. For the East the world is what it is and of no great consequence—a veil of illusion drawn between man and God. God is the only reality. The Indian seeker brushed the veil aside to find that Reality and sought it through his own soul. Indian evolution goes backward. It retreats from the world to what Hume calls the "ultimate world ground." There is a really noble litany of question and answer which carries back and back till that is reached, beyond which question is futile. The world we see and live in is a fabric, but always there is something behind it—veil within veil.

Since all this world is woven, warp and woof on water, on what, pray, is the water woven, warp and woof?

The answer is the wind. "On what then, pray, is the wind woven, warp and woof?" The answers lead from the atmosphere to the sun, from the sun to the stars, from the stars to the gods, from the gods to Indra, from Indra to Prajapati, from Prajapati to Brahma. "On what then, pray, are the worlds of Brahma woven, warp and woof?" "Do not question too much, lest your head fall off. In truth you are questioning too much about a divinity about which further questions can not be asked. . . . Do not ever question."

Another litany of question and answer takes a vaster sweep. "That, which is above the sky, that which is beneath the earth, that which is between these two, sky and earth, that which people call the past and the present and the future—across what is that woven, warp and woof?" "Space." "Across what then, pray, is space woven, warp and woof?" The answer is the Imperishable and, after straining words to define it, the Brahmana[6] goes on: "At the command of that Imperishable the Sun and the Moon stand apart, the Earth and the Sky stand apart, the seasons and the years stand apart. . . . Some rivers flow from the snowy mountains to the east, others to the west. . . . That Imperishable is the unseen Seer, the unheard Hearer, the unthought Thinker . . . Other than that there is naught that sees . . . hears . . . thinks . . . understands." "Across the Imperishable is space woven, warp and woof."

Man Not a Creation but an Emanation

All life then is woven, warp and woof into the Imperishable. Man is not a creation, he has come out of The All, The Imperishable, Brahma. His real self is wrapped in many veils. The body is the outer coarsest one, also a thing of no consequence though it has its uses. I should think one passage in the Maitri Upanishad the most completely condemnatory description of the body ever given. It is unlovely in its origin, unhappy in its history, filled full—among other less quotable contents—"with many diseases like a treasure house with wealth," and a trap for the soul

> Objects of sound and touch and sense
> Are worthless objects in a man,
> Yet the Elemental Soul through attachment to them
> Remembers not the highest place.

Breath is the essential of life and the most sovereign. This is proved by a parable. The faculties, sight, speech, hearing and mind had a dispute as to which was superior. They carried the quarrel to Father Prajapati (the Creator God as near as may be). He told them to try leaving the body and see what happened. Each went off for a year and the body got on though blind, dumb, deaf or a simpleton. But when Breath started to leave "They all came to it and said, 'Sir, remain, you are the most superior of us. Do not go off.'" The soul is the true self. It is only a tenant of the body, having no long lease, or else it is the charioteer and the body is the chariot.

> Know thou the soul as riding in a chariot,
> The body as the chariot,
> Know thou the intellect as the chariot-driver,
> And the mind as the reins.

[6] The 8th.

The senses are naturally the horses and need to be kept in hand. (Plato uses a similar figure.) The poet philosopher who thought of this naturally develops the fancy (being a poet). A man may drive so wisely as finally to escape all the perils of the road or else, being unmindful and impure, he drives only to rebirth. The doctrine of reincarnation is more loosely held in these teachings than in Buddhism, but it is there.

One can easily see through all these pages the backgrounds of current belief against which Gautama protested or which he took and recast. The soul whose existence he denied is the material soul —"A Person of the measure of a thumb . . . ever seated in the heart of creatures," or else the Mystical Soul about which the theologians debated to no practical purpose. He cleared the air of a deal of fog when he exhorted his disciples to stop using words about their souls and consider the far-reaching consequences of their deeds. The sages of the Upanishads not only believe in reincarnation; they have traced the path of the soul in its going and coming. It is a long road. All life is a sacrificial fire in which a person is both conceived and consumed. The funeral pile is at once a pyre and a womb. The burnt dead pass from the flame into the day, from the day into the seasons, from the seasons into the world of the gods, then into the lightning fire, then, if they have driven the horse of the sense with a strong hand and are fit, they pass into the Brahma worlds from which there is no return.

The imperfect get no further than the moon—not so near, for in these scriptures the moon is beyond the sun and the world of space. When their deposit of merit created by good works is exhausted, they are sent as exiles out into space again. After having become space for a season one becomes wind, then smoke, then mist. "After having been mist, he becomes cloud." The rest is simple. "After having become cloud he rains down and is 'born here' as some grain or other." "Thence, verily it is difficult to emerge; for if only some one eats him as food . . . does he develop further"—and not then unless generation is added to digestion. Reincarnation is a chancy business. Gautama's iron law of consequence has not yet hardened down. Present conduct determines one's future state but only in a general way. "Those who are of pleasant conduct here—the prospect is indeed, that they will enter a pleasant womb," preferably the womb of a Brahman or a warrior. "Those who are of a stinking conduct here" are likely to be reborn in a correspondingly malodorous estate becoming dog, swine or outcast.

The soul is the key to Indian thought. Indian thought begins with the one reality of which we are most immediately sure and builds everything around that. This is the really abysmal difference between Eastern and Western thought. We begin with the reality of the world without; we gather and sift the facts of it, organize the facts into systems, deduce the laws of their majestic and unfailing sequence. We pry into every secret of the natural order until we are arrested on the threshold of mystery even as the Indian sage was arrested on the threshold of Brahma. We have no fear that our heads will fall off, and treat ourselves as incidental. We let science legislate for the soul and end, if we do not take care, by reducing ourselves to Behavior Complexes controlled by the ductless glands, with no destiny beyond a chemical reaction. We end, if we do not take care, by making the reports of our laboratories the only reality and ourselves an illusion.

THE SOUL THE ONLY REALITY

Old India, having no laboratories, ended by making the soul the only reality and everything else an illusion. The conceptions of Brahma as the World-Soul is the peak achievement of old Indian thought reached by two lines of approach. The early seekers were sure of only one thing; there is a power which creates and pervades and upholds the Universe. Beyond that they were agnostic. They called it Brahma—Herbert Spencer might have called his "infinite and eternal energy" Brahma if he had wanted. Even the gods did not know. And the sages reproved, as we have seen, the bothersome questioner who wanted to know the impossible; they told him his head would fall off.

In time someone dared to say that Brahma was life. Then a more brave and penetrating insight began to define "It" in terms of personality. It is speech, sight, mind. Finally, in ways which Hume traces with scholarly acumen, the sages endowed Brahma with the quality of the Soul itself. "Verily that great unborn Soul, undecaying, undying, immortal, fearless, is Brahma." The power which creates, pervades, sustains the Universe is Soul—that is the only reality. The individual soul, to begin with, is the familiar self which has a body and a name, eating and sleeping, making love and occupying itself generally in very human ways. It is kept alive by the vital Breaths—a loose way of describing the functions of the body.

But there is another self. It may be scattered to the winds but still something which can neither be undone or lost is blown through the void. This soul may live in space and time served by the senses, or else it may become the citizen of another order, "the person here who is among the senses is made of knowledge . . . he remaining the same, goes along both worlds . . ." This soul is the only true light a person here has. We live in the light of the sun and the moon and the household fire and though these be darkened something is left, for though a man can not travel in the dark nor work in the dark, he can still talk.

But when the Sun has set, Yajñavalkya, and the Moon has set, and the fire has gone out, and speech is hushed, what light does a person here have?

The Soul (Atman), indeed, is his light—for with the Soul as his light one sits, moves around, does his work and returns.[7]

Only the soul endures while the illusions of time and space are created and dissolved.

Is the soul, the self, the Atman something forever shut up in its one little selfhood? Is there another Self than all ourselves? Whence is the soul derived and whither does it tend? What is the final issue of its eonian wanderings? These are the questions a natural human curiosity is always asking. His answers led the Hindu sage to his second creative insight. There is a supreme soul, a "Self which is free from evil, ageless, deathless, sorrowless, hungerless, thirstless . . . He should be searched out, Him one should desire to understand." It is difficult to distinguish between the ideal self which the seeker may attain and the universal Soul, the ocean of infinite being out of which our little tides of personality are drawn and to which they return. They say that God Indra spent one hundred and five years with a god wiser than himself, trying to find the self, "the self by searching out whom one obtains all the worlds and all desires." At the end of the century he professed himself enlightened though I doubt if a

---

[7] Brihad-Aranyaka, 4:3.6. One of the great and often quoted passages of the literature.

mere human would find the matter clear. At any rate modern commentators make hard going of it.

For the answers lead us to Brahma about whom Hindu wisdom says the most contradictory things. He is—

> The being and the beyond,
> Expressible and inexpressible,
> Founded and foundationless,
> Consciousness and unconsciousness,
> Reality and unreality.

It is possible to translate all this and much more into the terms of modern philosophy and mysticism but one may gravely question the parallels. Indian thought did seek and did discover to its own satisfaction, what Dr. Hume calls a "unitary world ground," the All which includes every detail and exists in and through every detail. That also is the quest of the Western scientist; just now he is inclined to offer us the electro-magnetic field as his Brahma and his statements about it sound curiously like this simple little Indian poem. When he says space is "finite but unbounded" he really means the "being and the beyond"; both statements have the same vertiginous quality.

But the Indian "basis for world unity" is soul and not the electro-magnetic field. The finite self is only the gleam of the infinite and eternal self; nor is there any light of sun or star which is not the light of Brahma. The Indian looked beyond his firelit hearth and his star-domed sky to something beyond them all.

> The sun shines not there, nor the moon and stars,
> These lightnings shine not, much less this (earthly) fire!
> And after him as He shines, doth everything shine;
> The whole world is illumined with his light.

And yet Brahma is "nearer than breathing, closer than hands or feet." Like salt dissolved in water, he, "It," is everywhere, the knower and the known, the only reality, sun and fire, wind and water, youth and maiden and the old man tottering on his staff, the seasons and the seas,

> Having no beginning, thou dost abide with immanence
> Wherefrom all beings are born.

The sages strain every resource of language to define Him and always in vain. If He could be defined He would cease to be Brahma—

> There is no likeness of Him
> Whose name is Great Glory.

Since He is defined as the undefinable, they are naturally handicapped. A classic passage names the person to be worshiped in the sun, the moon, lightning, space, wind, fire, shadow of Brahma, and the answer is always the same "Talk not to me about Him." The wise worshiper seeks something beyond them all, and yet something to which he has no key save in himself. "This self is the trace of that All, for by it one knows the All. Just as verily one might find by a footprint, thus . . ."[8]

"THAT ART THOU ——"

A great deal of all this is like fog stabbed by a searchlight. For the most part of the light does no more than make the fog phosphorescent, suffers strange changes in the windblown shifting of it—but from time to time the light comes through in some passage of timeless insight. There are but two alternatives in the interpretation of the awesome order whose tides carry the stars in their courses and the dust at our feet, of which we know ourselves to be so intimately a part, from which we so proudly disengage ourselves. It is either an impersonal machine, though "machine" is a poor enough name for the subtle linking of its processes. Or else it is what L. P. Jacks calls a living Universe, the key to which is what we know first hand in our own minds. Every religion accepts in a degree the second interpretation, every idealistic philosophy is rooted in it. Directly we begin to explain it we lose ourselves in words, naturally.

But so does the mechanistic scientist. It is partly a matter of the kind of words one prefers to lose oneself in. They come strangely to the same thing in the end—the awesome sense of an infinite mystery with which we ourselves are bound up. Any religion finds its gods— or God—by the footprint of the self, personalizing the divine to begin with by some necessity and later supporting its conclusions by argument or authority. A depersonalized God becomes only a "power

[8] What is to be found by the footprint is left to the imagination. The meaning is, says Dr. Hume, "one finds the All by its footprint the Self." *The Thirteen Principal Upanishads*, page 83.

not ourselves" or some such generality, getting a religious value only because the word God itself carries a wealth of old associations and suggestions and, however it is used, brings its old wealth with it. When that is spent, it is very likely that religion will lose its controlling power over life, unless ultimate reality is made personal again. This, incidentally, would seem to be the crisis religion is facing today.

Religion generally has made a one-way road from the self to God. Humanity is the creation of the Divine but not itself the immanent presence of the Divine.[9] Twenty-five hundred years ago Hindu teachers held that the All is found by its footprints, the Self. Man is not the clay image of God: He is the divine footprint in the clay. The actual result is a two-way road; the general traffic of Indian thought moves between the Universal Self and the very human selves of Sages and Warriors with a natural confusion. The same word is used and it is often difficult enough to tell which self is meant, and naturally—they are both the same. The human is held in the general solution of the World Soul, the World Soul is present in each human self. A famous Upanishad puts it thus: A father is instructing his son. There must, he says, have been Being to begin with. "How from non-being could Being be produced?" He wastes a deal of futile wisdom in explaining how Being multiplied and divided itself into the extremely interesting world about them and then goes on to explain how, for all its manifold forms, the one Being is the essence of them all.

"Bring hither a fig from there." "Here it is, Sir." "Divide it." "It is divided, Sir." "What do you see there?" "Nothing at all, Sir." Then he said to him: "Verily, my dear, that finest essence which you do not perceive—verily, my dear, from that finest essence this great tree thus arises. Believe me, my dear, that which is the finest essence—this whole world has that for its soul. That is reality, that is Atman. That art thou, Svetaketu." The father illustrates the same truth from salt dissolved in water, from rivers flowing from ocean to ocean, from honey gathered from a hundred flowers and stored in one comb and always the end is the changed refrain, "That which is the finest essence,—this whole world has that as its soul. That is reality, that is Atman. That art thou, Svetaketu."

[9] Liberal Western theologies are now taking the position that humanity *is* the immanent presence of the Divine.

THE EFFECT OF PANTHEISM ON RELIGION AND MORALS

Certain great conclusions follow from this interweaving of religion and philosophy, which have so influenced Hindu faith that all the rest is a detail.[10] Since everything is only an aspect of Eternal Being, some drop of a shoreless, timeless sea flung into the light, nothing is common or unclean. (This statement is contradicted by the caste system of India but Hinduism is strangely illogical in that. The Buddhist sought to correct it and failed as far as India is concerned.) A father lives again in his son; procreation, then, is an aspect of a divine process, a duty to be invested with a religious significance and performed with a proper ritual.[11]

Women are necessary but passive instruments in the process, a means to an end and not an end in themselves. This has contributed to the unhappy status of women in India. The older Indian teachings exalt chastity, but the whole system leaves an open door for the deification of the creative impulse, its organs and its symbols. Human nature found that door and unlocked it and what came through has carved unseemly symbols on temple fronts and cast a dark shadow across Indian faith. The sharp distinctions which most religions have drawn between spirit and the material world of the senses has generally supplied a strong support for their moral systems. That support is dissolved in Hindu pantheism. It is unfair to blame the great insights of the questing oriental mind for that investiture of lust and violence with the sanctions of religion to which Indian practice has, in some extreme cases, lent itself, but the permission is there.

There is a sense of sin in the Upanishads, more marked in their middle than their early period. It is really an entanglement of the understanding rather than the will. The unhappy sense of powerlessness for good without some divine help which finds an agony of expression in Western confessional literature and even on Babylonian tablets, is generally wanting in the sacred literature of India. Both impurity and unmindfulness bind the soul to rebirth, but un-

---

[10] It is for this reason that so much space is given to the Upanishads; they are the source from which the faith of India has flowed for two and a half millenniums. Buddhism is in many ways a reaction from and correction of this stupendous speculation. The great gods to which we shall soon come and the 30,000 lesser gods are all taken from the inexhaustible storehouse of Being which the Upanishads supply.

[11] Which is supplied with a definiteness of detail commonly left untranslated.

mindfulness is the stronger link in the chain. Apparently the bad-
ness of bad conduct is that it darkens the vision of the truth.

> Not he who has not ceased from bad conduct
> Can obtain Him by intelligence.

The brief prayer supplied for those about to yield the body to ashes
and the breath "to the immortal wind" seeks vision rather than pardon—a single line in a general prayer prays the Fire-God

> Keep far from us crooked going sin.

The absolutions the Upanishads offer are the absolutions of enlightenment, ritual and sacrifice.

The general attitude of Old Indian thought toward sin is strongly
colored by the idea of rebirth. There is no place for pardon in a
linked chain of cause and effect. The soul must win through if it
takes an aeon to do it and win through alone. Evil—whether sin or
sorrow—is an incident in the long sequence of many existences. Life
like running water purifies itself—if the channel is long enough.[12]
Nor is there any room in a system where the Universal Soul is present in every individual soul, for the sin of the Western theologian
for whom sin is an offense against God. How can the tide sin against
the sea?

The Power of Knowledge

The East wants to be delivered chiefly from the unenlightened life.
Knowledge is salvation. Socrates believed this with a difference—he
believed the enlightened man would do right. The sages of India
believed that the enlightened man is right. The very index to Dr.
Robert Hume's translation of the Upanishads is proof enough.
Knowledge supersedes worship and sacrifice, overcomes Karma and
rebirth, frees from evil, leads to immortality, breaks all fetters and
leads to union with Brahma.

Such knowledge is anything from the instructed mind to the self-
induced trance. Some of it is "rune" knowledge, the knowledge of
spell-words, rite-words, the stuff out of which magic is woven, old
as the naïve belief that any word had power and some words an
irresistible power. The very metres of the Vedic hymns were invested
with a sacred meaning. Some of it is the study of the Vedas accom-

[12] It is significant that the consistent modern optimist like Robert Browning—or
the consistent idealist, like Royce—hold much the same views about evil.

panied by proper austerities. Some of it is the give and take of master and pupil discoursing together of high things. Or else it is a secret knowledge shared only by the elect.

In its final religious form it becomes that first-hand knowledge of God which is common to all strongly felt religious experience. Words cease to matter in the peak passages. The Hindu poet says such things of Brahma as the Hebrew poet of Jehovah or the Egyptian king of Aton, save that there is in the Hindu religious poetry a sense of being essentially one with God which the worshipers of a God "out there" never quite attain. But the music is the same: the music of wonder and adoration.[13]

> The one God, hidden in all things,
> All pervading, the Inner Soul of All things,
> The overseer of deeds, in all things abiding
>
> . . . . .
>
> His form is not to be beheld,
> No one soever sees Him with the eye,
> They who thus know Him with heart and mind
> As abiding in the heart, become immortal.
>
> . . . . .
>
> By knowing God one is released from all fetters.

The World of Sense an Illusion

Since there is no reality then but the World Soul out of whose vastness the little selves of space and time ebb and flow, what becomes of the old cities of India, their bazaars and palaces, their merchandise and their passions, the stars in a velvet sky, and all the net of sense and stuff in which the soul is entangled? It is only illusion—Maya. This doctrine in its full form is a late development. The priest-bards of the Vedas had no doubt of the reality of their fresh young world.[14] There are scant passages in the early Upanishads to support the doctrine. But the Hindu mind, taking the line it did, found the same difficulty in accounting for the disconcerting reality of things the modern Idealist does. Dr. Johnson proved the reality of a stone by kicking it and accepting the testimony of his toe. Immanuel Kant cut the knot by holding that we never can know things in themselves.

[13] These quotations are from the Svetasvatara Upanishad, fifth and sixth Adyayās. They sound the finest note of Brahmanic devotion.

[14] Deussen does find hints of Maya in the Vedas.

Practical folk accept the world as a going concern and manage to make weatherproof houses out of brick—whether a brick is an idea or a reality. The Hindu made a fleeting shadow world out of all sense reported things. Brahma is the illusion maker—like Prospero furnishing us with a world of sounds and sweet airs that give delight and hurt not, or else the rougher music of Caliban and, when the revels are ended dissolving it all, cloud-capped towers and gorgeous palaces, like an insubstantial pageant faded and rounding off our little lives in sleep. The Hindu seer said much the same thing,

> Sacred poetry, the sacrifices, the ceremonies, the ordinances,
> The past, the future, and what the Vedas declare—
> This whole world the illusion-maker projects—
> And in it by illusion the other is confined.

Shakespeare might have been reading the Svetasvatara Upanishad.

If one asks why Brahma made this illusion instead of another or why we should be imprisoned in illusion at all there is no answer, but the conclusion is inevitable. If all the pageantry of the world is an illusion of the senses, experience a cheat and the soul itself a tired pilgrim faring from state to state of reincarnation and always with an endurable nostalgia for the World Soul from which it is derived, then the only desirable issue of individual existence is to return into "the All" as a wave sinks into the sea—and there find rest. "From the great deep to the great deep he goes."

The devout of the old Indian faith, the strangest combination of philosopher, mystic and dreamer any faith has produced, had none of that hunger for life which makes the West so tenacious of life here and so concerned about immortality hereafter. One can hardly call this pessimism—it is something deeper being rooted in the very structure of the oriental temperament. The persuasion of a cycle which includes the individual and the universe is outstanding in Indian thought. Brahma is source and Soul. He, the Imperishable, is a spider who spins his threads and draws them in again, a fire whose sparks we are and back into which we fall again, the ocean whose spray we are, back again into which we melt as bubbles.

> In him in whom this universe is interwoven,
> Whatever moves or is motionless,
> In Brahma everything is lost,
> Like bubbles in the ocean.

Steps to the "Bliss of Brahma"

There are many echoes of this solemn and majestic music in the
literature in which humanity considers its destiny. So Alfred Noyes—

But the sins and the creeds and the sorrows that trouble the sea . . .
   they have no stay . . .

.   .   .   .   .

They are all made as one with the deep, they sink and are vanished
   away.

And yet the bubble is not lost in the ocean; it is only absorbed.
Hindu devotion dwells at puzzling length upon this absorption and
strains the resources of language to distinguish it from annihilation.
The Western mind may be forgiven for not always finding the distinction. It is all very like Gautama's Nirvana. There is a sense in
which finding Brahma is like the more familiar phrase "finding
God"; the union with Brahma is like the mystic's union with God,
an ineffable state to be realized before death and by a proper discipline. The simplest discipline is Knowledge, the sage is free, knowing both himself and God, bound by no illusions, a thrall to no fears,
and desiring nothing that he should cling to the body.

> The man who has beheld God
> As his own self face to face;
> The Lord of that which was and is to be,
> He feels no fear, nor hides himself in dread.
> He who beholds the Loftiest and Deepest,
> For him the fetters of the heart break asunder,
> For him all doubts are resolved,
> And all his works become nothingness.[15]

And it would be easy to parallel all this from the rapt speech of
Christian mystics.

The bliss of Brahma, upon which Indian devotional literature
dwells, is a phrase as elusive as the "peace of God." It might mean
the boundless tranquillity of the World Soul, the bliss of absorption
in the World Soul or the bliss of the passionless sage. This too is
much dreamed of by the troubled and much sung of by the poets.
Carlyle composed his spirit beneath the stars finding a strength to

[15] Deussen's translation.

sustain him and a majesty to rebuke him in their far tranquillity.
Tennyson put a deal of fretted longing in a single line—

> To where beyond these voices, there is peace.

A famous passage in the Upanishads seeks the same general effect
in a smother of words. There is no bliss of experience or imagination
to be compared with the "bliss of Brahma." Given an ideal like this
and the temper of the East, mysticism is inevitable. It becomes a
bemused state in which the sense of personal identity is lost and all
the clear lines which make the ordinary man able to say "this is
myself and everything else is not myself" melt into mist. The psychologist can do what he can do with this. We now and then touch it in
reverie or in complete absorption in a demanding task.

India worked out a discipline called Yoga (with which the West
occasionally experiments), whose object was this union. Yoga, being
a quest for a state between sleep and death, is naturally difficult to
define. The steps by which the soul gets unwrapped from its material
veils and back to its source are as ingenuous as they are probably
unreal by any test, save the test of what the Indian mind can do
when it begins to build cloud bridges hung from sky hooks. The
actual discipline is more intelligible. It needs only eight steps to reach

> That which abides in consciousness
> Unknown, beyond conception, wrapped in mystery.

The steps are a searching austerity, self-restraint, sitting in the
proper posture, regulation of the breath, suppression of sense, concentration, meditation, complete union with the object of meditation.[16] There is an edifying instruction as to the detail of each step.
Sitting was to begin with simple enough—erect in some quiet and
sheltered place. Later eighty-four modes of sitting are distinguished.
Breathing is breathing in, holding the breath and breathing out. All
sins may be thus destroyed if the breather meditates on the Hindu
Trinity during the process—. So according to Robert Browning, a
medieval monk drank his pomegranate pulp in three sips.

> I the Trinity illustrate
> Drinking watered orange-pulp—
> In three sips the Arian frustrate;
> While he drains his at one gulp.

[16] Deussen, *The Religion and Philosophy of India*, page 385.

The senses are to be drawn in as a tortoise draws in his limbs. Meditation naturally becomes a science furthered by the soothing repetition of the mystic syllable Om. All the setting for a self-induced hypnotic trance is here. But the seeker thought himself lost in God. It is also easy to lose in any study of this faith so remote, so subtle and so cloud-wrapped, what attends any devout faith and should greatly attend a faith so saturated with the persuasion of the immanence of the World Soul—the sense of a God Who is something beside the worshiper and the All. There are devotion, adoration, reverent wonder in the more rapt utterances of the Upanishads. Like Spinoza, the reciters were God-intoxicated but they had no "control" save the insight, or the audacity of their own speculative rapture.

"To Sleep: Perchance to Dream"

> To that God, Who is lighted by His own intellect
> Do I desirous of liberation, resort as a shelter—
>
> .   .   .   .   .

There is then another union with Brahma than the Yoga trance, or the severity of the sage or the bliss of the mystic. The supreme issue of any transient existence is, after death, to be absorbed in the World Soul. Very likely this faith began in the sense of the general dissolution of death. Then the person goes back again into earth and fire or air as Cleopatra took her departure—

> Give me my robe, put on my crown; I have
> Immortal longings in me—
> I am fire and air; my other elements
> I give to baser life.

But this general fact of return with which the philosophic dignify death becomes something else. It becomes a release from all the fret of life and hampering separatenesses, the comfort the weary find in sleep. Since the soul and the world are only Brahma's dream, the soul finds a bliss in its own dreams.

> Guarding his low nest with his breath[17]
> The Immortal goes forth out of his nest,
> He goes where'er he please—the Immortal,
> The golden person . . .

[17] The breath is the guardian of the body during sleep.

Yet since even dreams are troubled a dreamless sleep is best. The soul then attains its supreme felicity when, as a falcon weary from flying here and yon through space, it folds its wings and is borne down to its nest. "This person hastens to that state when asleep, he desires no desires and sees no dreams." There he is all and nothing, existent and non-existent. This, the Hindu thought, is truly to be lost in Brahma and eminently to be desired. He is never done trying to describe that state. He plods the road by which to gain a state in which, like the slaves in Kipling's "Last Chantey," he should "drouse the long tides idle," but with no awaking trumpet to tear the sea.

There is no one proper name for the system we have just been considering. It is too philosophical to be a religion, and too religious to be a philosophy, too speculative to be science, and too elusive to be a system of morality. And yet it is all of these. It is the plasm out of which all later Indian religion emerged and the one system which has hitherto divided the real empire of believing humanity with the Hebrew Jehovah. Jehovah never faced Brahma directly, though Amos and some of the teachers of the Upanishads may have been contemporaries, but Brahma has controlled the faith of speculative India as long as Hebrew monotheism has controlled the faith of the practical minded West.

The critical Western mind must acknowledge commanding gleams of insight in this old Indian system which shine far into the enveloping mystery of the Universe. It has in it the promise and potency of idealistic philosophy and an anticipation of the Monism—*one*-ism—which has laid hold strongly of some modern minds and offers a possible answer to some of the questions which our most adventurous minds still find unanswerable. It also has in it everything that Indian religion has since become, though it is very likely that the austere sages who envied no king his palace and needed no temple, would be astonished enough at what time and their race have made of their austere speculations.

THE CONTRADICTIONS OF INDIAN RELIGION

For directly you have made everything an emanation of the Divine then you have everything out of which to make a god—or a goddess—including the more elemental instincts of man and beast. A religion shaped out of such substance may be bright with splendor or dark with shame. It may have one God who is no God at all, but a universal all-penetrating, all-supporting, all-receiving World Soul, or three gods, or three million gods; there is nothing to forbid. Any great religion is, on one side, certainly, the reaction of racial temper to the general experience of the particular race. The result is a "complex" whose interwoven fabric can never really be so undone that its threads can be traced one by one, to the looms upon which they were spun and to the spinners.

The strange genius of India, its mingling of racial strains, its history, never a unified and continuous growth but a brilliant mosaic—like the pavements of its temples, made up of elements broken and reassembled in patterns whose confusions are the despair of historians; its climate of fierce growths and withering passions, its iron caste system which for three thousand years has put an impassable gulf between men who might touch hands across it—and never touch; an imagination without bonds, and an art which can build a temple like a bastioned dream and house an image of indescribable and, to the Western mind, obscene ugliness within it; have all combined to make Hinduism the jungle it has been for two thousand years and is today.

India is the most religious land in the world and its religion is everything. Why not? Brahma was and is everything. It is the state religion of an Indian prince, educated at Oxford, playing polo as Kipling says like a "lambent flame,"[18] standing out of the way with all the jeweled decorations of the British Empire across his breast, to keep the blood of a decapitated goat off his whipcord riding breeches. It is an ascetic measuring his length in the dust on a holy pilgrimage, holding a withered arm in the air, his fist clenched so long that his nails have grown through his hand and he could not open it if he would. It is nakedness smeared with cow-dung, crawling with vermin, rotten with disease and the more holy for all that. It is the smoke of burning ghats and a devotion which makes a weary pilgrimage of a thousand miles to die on the banks of a holy river. It is endless prayer, devotion, seamed with sacrifice. It is the refined speculation of the erudite, the pathetic obedience of the devout. It is templed cities and temples vast as cities, forbidden rites which shun the light, and a vast, endless, assured, pathetic outpouring

[18] The phrase is Dryden's.

of the soul of a race and the centuries toward the unseen and eternal. Is there any key to it all?

THE TWO KEYS

No one key at all—two maybe—Brahma and India. The always interrupted and always tenaciously renewed history of India is certainly reflected in its corporate religious life but the transition periods are more or less obscure. They can only be reconstructed through a literature which does shade from form to form but, even so, not clearly. There is a gap between the Vedic period and the Upanishads. Historically Buddhism follows the Upanishad period; Hinduism[19] emerges upon the decay of Indian Buddhism. Now Buddhism was at its peak in India under Asoka (273-232 b.c.) and the revival of Hinduism may be clearly dated from 320 a.d., which leaves five centuries more or less unaccounted for.

Historians fill them in with such names of dynasties and rulers as are left after the sifting of tradition. Foreign influences are hard to trace. Kipling describes craftsmen who told the story of Gautama in stone as "forgotten workmen whose hands were feeling and not unskillfully for the mysteriously transmitted Grecian touch." Eliot says the same thing without Kipling's art. Greece may have taught India, which had no images of its gods to begin with, to make "images" of them in stone. Otherwise the Greek spirit had little influence upon Hinduism. It would have been better if India had not learned so much—or more—from Greece.

If its artists and its priests could have taken over from Greece the austere Grecian spirit of beauty and restraint, their sculptured deities would not have become what they are. Apart from this doubtful contribution from the West, Hinduism is substantially a growth native to India, though Persian influence is a little in evidence and something comes in with invasions from the north and northwest. The sources of Hinduism must really be sought in persistent folk-faith. There was always another religion in the shadow behind Gau-

[19] The term Hinduism is variously used. Many modern scholars call the religion of India as a whole Hinduism, but distinguish historical periods, thus: Vedic Hinduism, Brahmanic or Philosophic Hinduism, Sectarian or Devotional Hinduism, Popular Hinduism, Reformed Hinduism. As used here reference is made to Sectarian or Devotional Hinduism.

tama or dreaming philosophers who sought the World-Soul, a religion of crude concrete divinities seen through old faiths and fears.

The World-Soul is too tenuous and remote for ordinary human nature's daily faith. We have already noted the failure of the early Vedic nature worship to develop into monotheism. (It is, incidentally, an open question whether nature worship ever develops into monotheism without the contribution of a high speculative intelligence or the passionate conviction of the prophet.) With the decay of the vivid Vedic nature worship the variety of Indian gods left the worshiper an ample choice, a pantheistic temper made any candidate eligible. After that influences impossible to follow determined why one, or a few, should become gigantic figures controlling, as Eliot says, "the poetry and passion" of their devotees.

There are fashions in gods as in everything else. The influence of outstanding teachers and leaders has often redirected the currents of faith; Hinduism has had a long succession of religious teachers and leaders but Hinduism is not prophet made. Very likely some strong racial instinct has given character to the gods of a race, as though they were projections of the fears, confidences, desires of a people against the skyline of their faith. Prajapati—"lord of creation"—had the best chance of all the Vedic gods to become the one-god of the speculative Indian mind, but he fades out of the picture. Vishnu, a deity of no special force, dethroned him. Indra was the most vivid and masterful of the Vedic gods but Vishnu gained what Indra lost.

It is all like dealing with cloud forms which mass and dissolve. The substance of them is the pantheistic Indian mind deifying forces and instincts and clothing them with a grandiose mythology. The forces are not the restrained forces of the north temperate zone. The instincts are as tropical as the climate. Everything is "gigantesque." The gods have a hundred arms and enormous bellies and the color-daubed exaggeration of what modesty conceals.[20] They have more wives than an oriental king and children to correspond. Their passions are titanic. They come and go between earth and heaven. They become reincarnate any number of times and each reincarnation changes the god. The Western mind can only use words describing it all. One wonders if the Eastern mind does much better. In a large way, Hindu faith has locked up upon Brahma, Vishnu and Siva as

[20] "—lo membro che l'uom cela," Dante, The Inferno, Canto XXV:116.

the threefold manifestation of the supreme; Brahma the creator, Vishnu the preserver, Siva the destroyer.

There is really little basis in Indian thinking for a creator. Nothing begins and nothing ends. Thought and things are a timeless tide out of the All and back again, endlessly appearing and endlessly dissolving; or else they are the All in timeless action weaving a net of dreams and illusions in which men are caught, themselves a dream to disappear when Brahma wakes. Naturally there is no place for a creator in an order like that. Brahma is only the ghost of a God who might have been if Indian religion had become theistic instead of pantheistic. He has no following and only a temple or two.

Vishnu occupied a respectable place in the Vedas—a Sun-God certainly who crosses the firmanent in three strides. He became incarnate in a dwarf once when the earth was conquered by demons and asked the demon-king to give him as much space as he could cover in three steps. His apparently inconsequential request was carelessly granted whereupon he took on his true form, strode across earth and sky and recovered the world for mankind. Vishnu is a very comfortable god, the god of things as they are, admirably suited to a conservative society. His cult gained a strong following from the eleventh century A.D. on and has been much subject to sectarian division. The finer aspects of Hindu faith seem associated with it.

Vishnu's strong appeal to the common folk in India is through two of his reincarnations as Rama and Krishna. The general character of Indian religious thought makes the incarnation and reincarnation of a god almost incidental; Vishnu is said to have already had nine incarnations and is due for a tenth which has not yet taken place. When he comes next he will come as a Messiah, a warrior, riding down to destroy the wicked and assure the triumph of the pious. Most of these incarnations are mythological fancies but two of them may reflect a hero seen through legend and dim memory as a god.

He—the hero—was born as the son of a king of Oudh and married the princess of another kingdom. She was carried away by the demon tyrant of Ceylon. Rama after a series of adventures captured her with the help of Hanuman, King of the Monkeys, and his monkey army. There is an Indian epic about it all, an endless and (to the Western mind) very wearying recital of valor and prodigious deeds, peril barely escaped and impossible monkey agility. There was, perhaps, somewhere in the dawn of Indian history a masterful Aryan who conquered the world with the help of dark-skinned and mon-keylike aborigines, to supply a historical basis for the epic. As far as Rama worship persists it is wholesome, for Rama is the god of chivalry and his unfortunate bride, Sita, a goddess of chastity. There are none too many Sitas in the Hindu pantheon. In his eighth incar-nation Vishnu became an entirely different sort.

He became Krishna and Krishna is as vivid as India. Sir Charles Eliot brings a great erudition to bear upon this flute-playing god. He believes "that an ancient military hero of the north has been imbued with a deity or perhaps more than one deity." He sees dimly through all the wrappings of legend, sentiment and theology "the figure of some aboriginal hero who, though ultimately conquered, represented a force not in complete harmony with Brahmanic civilization." I venture to believe that the Krishna whom the Indian women love belongs to another line.[21]

[21] Cycles of religious development and a literature only the specialist can master are loosely condensed in pages 264 to 273. Otto Strauss' Chapter (No. 4) in Clemen's *Religions of the World, op. cit.,* should be read in this connection. It is excessively technical but it reveals the range of the literature and the kaleidoscopic character of Hinduism. Vishnu and Siva represent its Aryan and non-Aryan components. Vishnu is as near as may be the God of love and love toward God. Siva represents "the dark, savage elements." Strauss thinks the Vishnu cult "has gathered various other deities around it." Local deities, deified heroes, beings of animal shape and even Buddha have been brought into the vast formless cycle of the Avatars—the descents of Vishnu.

His Krishna incarnation is, to begin with, the creation of the epic poet. He ap-parently began with a godhead of his own, the coalescence of a Rajput hero and a shepherd-god. It was easy in time to make him an incarnation of Vishnu. Krishna's ways with the milkmaids suggested a human kind of love but Indian mysticism has sublimated it into a spiritual passion, BHAKTI, the love of God. Out of this and about it grew a great literature and above all the BHAGAVAD-GITA—the Lay of the Saint or Lord. This is a conversation between a warrior and his charioteer Krishna who is really the Universal God incarnate. Here love and devotion, not knowledge, become the roads to salvation, gentle piety becomes the supreme grace, love of God becomes the master motive—"Only incline thine heart to me, set thy mind on me and thou shalt dwell with me hereafter. Of that there is no doubt."

As nearly as a pantheistic religion can possess an immanent God who is to be worshiped with no thought of reward and upon whom the worshiper may cast all his cares, he is in the Bhagavad-Gita, and here also is one great source—though not the only source—of Hindu mysticism. It was inevitable that such a religious devotion whose language was preeminently the language of love should develop an erotic strain and that in a religion so tolerant as Hinduism this should find an accepted place. This whole strange phase of Hinduism can not be judged by Western standards. The moral sensibility of modern India is making a strong effort to throw off such remnants of it as undoubtedly persist.

He is Tammuz without his descent into the underworld of doubt and darkness, Adonis without his tragedy; no Indian flower has taken a deeper crimson from the blood of Krishna. There is a touch of the sun-god in him—as near Apollo as the East ever comes, he is youth and springtime, never quite the vegetable spirit, but native to the pastures. His flute is heard by the milkmaids, they see in the dawn the nymphs who attend him and his music awakens strange desires. Something older than any aboriginal hero is in action here. It is likely, though there is no proof of this in any documents, that India never made a drama of life and death and vernal resurrection out of this aspect of nature worship, as Syria and Greece did, because the alternation of vegetable life and death in the Indian year is never clean-cut. The parallels between Krishna and Tammuz and Attis and Adonis stop short, but they are there.

Hindu religion is generally wanting in any sense of that human nearness of the divine which supplies an object for affection to lay hold of. Krishna does just that and doubtless the need for a "beloved" in faith has gone far to make him what he is. The affection which surrounds him is strange. He is worshiped as the Butter Thief, a figure of crawling, childish mischief with a handful of curds or butter. Motherhood wants something of the appeal of a little child in any religion—there are other bambinos than this child Krishna. He is worshiped as a graceful young flute player with a thousand mistresses, and not particular in the choice of them, and finally as the mystic object of the soul's desire. There are hymns to Krishna which sound the same note as the ecstasies of the Christian mystic or else the more ardent hymns of Western devotion. There is a borderland in all religious emotion where the great expressions of love and desire carry a double entendre. India has accepted this with a frankness which disconcerts the West—and then magnified it.

SIVA, THE DESTROYER

Siva, "the Destroyer," is an equally complex deity. The name does not mean Destroyer; it is a complimentary title and means the Propitious which by no means represents the true nature of the god. It is very much as if one sought to propitiate a violent man by addressing him as "Gentle Sir." Siva is sung to in the Veda as Rudra, the "roarer." He is the storm and tumult of nature, whence the Destroyer. His early associations were with violent men, haunting mountain and desert places, with a following of ill-formed spirits.

In time, he becomes the vast force of nature. He "dwells in flowing streams and billows and in tranquil waters, . . . in punishments, in property, in the soil, the threshing floor, . . . in sound and in echo, . . . in green things and dry things. . . . Reverence to the leaf and to him who is in the fall of the leaf, the threatener, the slayer, the vexer and the afflictor."[22] The last epithets are tremendously reveal-ing. Siva is the force of things and the force of things in the end destroys what it creates. Sorrow and the withered leaf are on the last harvest of life and growth. The life weariness of India is in that prayer, the key, I think, to what is most characteristic in all Indian faith.

And yet, the Destroyer can not destroy unless he creates; he creates to destroy and destroys to create. The leaf lives to fade, the bud loosens and lets fall the faded leaf. This subtle sense of his two-faced office has given to the worship of Siva a contradictory character. The Destroyer is worshiped through the symbols and relief of procreation. Nowhere does the Western mind trained in austere religions and moralities, find harder going than just here in dealing with Hin-duism. The administrative attitude of the British government is toward a suppression of phases of Hindu worship—which it can reach—as subversive of morality.

On the other hand, the whole matter may be turned into sym-bolism, its basal grossness sublimated into mystic attitudes. This is what the poetic Hindu apologist does. "That, which is so incon-ceivable to a modern mind"—this apologist is speaking of lyrics which sing the love of Krishna for his mistress with a disconcerting frankness—"presents no difficulty to the . . . devotee. To him God is love himself; the sweet flowers, the fresh grass, the gay sounds heard in the woods are direct messages and tokens of love to his soul, bringing to his mind at every instant, that loving God whom he pictures as ever anxious to view the human heart." Hinduism has created a terrible asceticism but its controlling temper is not ascetic. So Tagore sings—

[22] A prayer from the White Yajur Veda, quoted by Sir Charles Eliot, *Hinduism and Buddhism*, Vol. II, pages 141-2.

Deliverance is not for me in renunciation. I feel the embrace of freedom in a thousand bonds of delight.

. . . . . .

No, I will never shut the doors of my senses. The delights of touch and hearing will bear thy delights.

Yes, all my illusions will burn into the illumination of joy, and all my desires reopen into fruits of love.

But it is difficult for a general humanity to keep these thin-aired heights. Sir Charles Eliot deals with the whole difficult subject with restraint and insight, feeling for the really religious element in it and allowing for the nature of the Eastern mind which has never drawn a clean-cut line between the physical and the moral as the Christian West has. "As a philosophy," he says, "Sivaism possesses truth. It recognizes the generative instinct as a creative force to which existence is due—one of the ways of the 'All,' and issuing in the tide of love which ebbs and flows between life and death."[23]

Neither the old philosophic Hinduism nor any revivals of it associate religion with the moral law. Austerity and devotion are urged as religious virtues and a part of the discipline which releases the soul from the weary road of transmigration. Austerity is anything from a terrible asceticism to a temperate life with no concern for possession and honor. The devotee does not conform his conduct to the will of a righteous god; he creates a god to suit the deed. "An immoral occupation need not be irreligious; it simply requires gods of a special character."[24] Hindu morality is a social adjustment; the deposit of very old and very long unlimited ways of living together in a society of an almost impossible complexity.

The laws of such a society are a web of custom, ceremony, rules of diet, sacrifice and oblation, the duties of kings and subjects and the civil, commercial and criminal procedure which the West directs through statutory enactment. And yet almost every conceivable sit-

[23] If worship of Vishnu is frequently directed immediately to some one of his avatars, that of Shiva is often directed to one of his consorts, for he had many—or the one had many names—Kali, Durga, Uma, etc. Shiva, the male principle, had his complementary power or Shakti, the female principle, and it is the Shakti which is the object of worship of a large number of devotees. Kali, the mother, terrible in her outward aspect as depicted in Indian art, but the object of the highest love and devotion of many worshipers, is perhaps the best known of the group. In so-called left-hand Shaktism are to be found the most exaggerated forms of erotic aberration in Hinduism.

[24] Eliot, *op. cit.,* page LXXXIX.

uation is covered. There are, for example, twenty-five divisions in the law of debt. The code of Manu is the great authority and like all great codes it has been commented on endlessly and for one thousand two hundred years. It dates probably from the middle of the third century A.D. The mores of India control all social institutions; women are in utter dependence upon their husbands; family property is held in common under the father's control. The suppression of crime is in the hands of the state "by punishing the wicked and protecting the virtuous he obtains his own absolution." Crime is defined under heads familiar to any well organized society, though punishments were cruel and unusual. A red hot iron spike ten fingers long was to be thrust into the mouth of a low caste person for slandering a Brahman. (Evidently a Brahman wrote that law.) Moral delinquency comes under the jurisdiction of the priest with such penances and expiation as an official church may demand—and enforce.

There is a deposit of really noble precepts in the Laws of Manu. Respect for teachers and parents is urged, truth telling and pledge keeping, the patient endurance of evil. "Let him patiently bear hard words. Let him not insult anybody. Against an angry man let him not in return show anger. Let him bless when he is cursed." There are four stages in the ideal life: a youthful student, a married householder, a retired hermit and a religious mendicant. Twenty years are allowed for each stage and it is not unusual now for a devout Hindu to lay aside his station and his honor like a garment and step out of his world, a devout shadow with no concern save for the peace of his soul.

Hindu Devotion

Hinduism is rich in faith and devotion. Its faith has no such creedal basis as the faith of the West. It is rather trust in and mystic self-dedication to the cherished deity. The devotion is such prayer and praise as faith always evokes touched with a strong emotion. Indian mysticism is a study in itself. "In theory," says Evelyn Underhill,[25] "Hindu religion offers three paths to its disciples: the path of works—that is to say not of the pursuit of virtue, but the accurate fulfillment of ceremonial obligations; the path of knowledge, of philo-

[25] *The Mystic Way*, page 22.

sophic speculation which includes in its higher stages the transcending of illusion, the 'mystical' art of contemplating the Being of God; and the path of devotional love." The fourth and again the twelfth and fourteenth centuries registered a strong mystical movement. The medieval Indian mystics were doubtless influenced by some contact with Christianity or Islam which gave a pure monotheistic quality to their quest for union with God.

A fragment of a hymn to Vishnu (translated by Sir Edwin Arnold) is an arresting example of the power of devotion to take confessedly difficult material and touch it with spirit, which makes all hymns akin.

> Fish! that didst outswim the flood;
> Tortoise! whereon earth hath stood;
> Boar! who with thy tusk heldst high
> The world, that mortals might not die;
> Lion! who hast giants torn;
> Dwarf! who laugh'dst a king to scorn;
> Sole Subduer of the Dreaded!
> Slayer of the many-headed!
> Mighty Ploughman! Teacher tender!
> Of thine own the sure Defender!
> Under all thy ten disguises
> Endless praise to thee arises.[26]

The secret of permanence, the caprice and the fitful splendor of Indian religion is in this "Bhakti"—devotion. There is no element in the long evolution of religion which is not somewhere in India today. Its primitive animism still in action and its philosophic pantheism make a startling combination. God may be worshiped as the "All" or he may be worshiped as the "Any"—a stone or a place. A devout Hindu does both with no sense of inconsistency. Morality is never identified with the will of the deity; the laws of Manu do not run into the temples of Siva. The god is force, desire, the most elemental urgencies and their satisfaction, an eternal spiritual reality or the crudest fact. The worshiper who enters Siva's temple, or the temple of his wife (who has many names), leaves the world of conventional morality—but whatever is done in the temple is still religion.

[26] *An Anthology of World Poetry, op. cit.,* page 79.

THE INFLUENCE OF ISLAM

About 1000 A.D. the followers of Mohammed came, using the pass which the Aryans trod two thousand years and more before them, invaded India and spread throughout the peninsula, where today about one-fifth of the total population are counted as Moslems. It was inevitable that Mohammedanism and Hinduism thus meeting should mutually influence each other. Into the writing of certain Hindu poets there begins to steal a note of monotheism as a result of the invasion of Allah. Finally in the latter part of the fifteenth century this growing note found expression in a dynamic personality, Nanak, who gave organized form to a movement which has since come to be known as the Sikh movement. Like Islam, it is monotheistic and non-idolatrous in its worship, and somewhat akin to it in the militancy which made it for a time a strong contender for the rule of all India. This while growing out of Hinduism differs from it at so many points that by many scholars it is listed as a separate religion.[27]

The modern age of exploration and expansion of Europe took Christianity in its Roman Catholic form into India. The beginnings of the nineteenth century saw a much more vigorous penetration by Protestant Christianity. This meeting of Christianity and Hinduism produced a number of new movements which while considered still to be within Hinduism, nevertheless, bear many characteristics of the imported Christian faith. Most notable of these were the Brahma Samaj founded by Rammohun Roy in 1833 and the Ramakrishna movement which came into being in the latter part of the nineteenth century. A still more numerous and aggressive movement was one of direct reaction to foreign influence, known as the Arya Samaj, which while definitely similar in many respects to Christianity in its social outlook, finds the basis of its modern message in the ancient Vedas of Old India.

For all its contradiction religion controls the Indian mind, more so than in any other country; and yet with an abysmal difference: religion does not control life, life controls religion. A single sentence of Sir Charles Eliot says it all: "In India art, commerce, warfare and

[27] On the Sikh religion, see further, *Encyclopedia of Religion and Ethics,* Vol. II, Art., Sikh.

crime, every human interest and aspiration seek for a manifestation in religion." There is always a deity of some nature to adapt himself to the need of a worshiper. There is a god for the Bandit, a goddess for the Prostitute and the Imperishable of the Sage. The pantheon of India is the projection of the soul of India against the skyline of thirty centuries. The immense religiosity of that soul has subdued everything to its strange devotion. Kipling makes a story of a Lascar who worships a marine engine: every new sentiment, every new power is a manifestation of the "All." If Brahma glows in a Hibiscus blossom and shines in a star, why should he not bring a ship to port?

What the impact of Western civilization and Western religion will do for a land and race like that still remains to be seen. Will the soul of India subdue them to its patient and unmeasured ways—or will that soul be changed?

JAINISM

No study of Indian religion is complete without some notice of the Jains. There are now about thirteen hundred thousand of them and, like the Parsees, they include wealthy and humane merchants. They are industrious and order-loving; their temples are beautiful with richly colored marble and sheltering white and jeweled images. They have temples like cities on mountain tops, cities of shrines and marble courts upon which high spires look down. From sunset to sunrise the only inhabitants of these cities are the sculptured saints of the cult who watch the altar lights, and the flocks of sacred pigeons. During the day devout pilgrims make a round of the shrines, leaving their offerings of flowers, incense and lights, kneeling to sing the praises of their saints. It is a gentle faith. The Jains permit no animal to be slaughtered or sacrificed, the wealthy provide hospitals for old or infirm animals, the ascetics sweep the dust before them to keep from stepping on any living thing, they strain their drinking water and wear a veil over their mouths. The merchants screen their shop lamps to save the moth from the flame.

Jainism is a little older than Buddhism and the two have much in common. It is purely Humanistic, the gods do not enter into its scheme. It is also dualistic. The world is eternal and self-existent, souls are free separate existences whose essence is pure intelligence. It conceals the explanation of how these separate orders are timed

together behind a cloud screen of subtle doctrine. The soul is bound
to the wheel of transmigration going up or down according to merit
or demerit. The wheel turns through boundless periods of time and
through a dizzy radius from the highest heavens to a state where the
soul escapes ceasing to be at all by a margin which only a Jain could
distinguish from annihilation. Theirs is a paradise to be reached by
right faith, right conduct and right works (the three jewels).

Right faith is complete confidence in the founder of the sect and
his teaching; right knowledge is a correct theology—a difficult matter,
one would think, considering the obscure subtlety of the doctrine;
right conduct is not to kill or lie, take nothing that is not given, be
chaste and take no pleasure in the world and the things of the world.
The tests of right conduct include word, thought and deed and are
very searching. Entirely right conduct is possible only for those who
give their lives entirely to the practice of it.

Some accommodation to this present world is permitted through
an inner asceticism of repentance, humility and a weaning of the
soul from desire. But the true seekers are severely ascetic in habit as
well as mind. These rigors may even issue in death by starvation. No
monk is permitted to starve himself to death merely to escape the
wearing discipline of the order, but if he is ripe for Nirvana through
much penance, he may accomplish his final entry into that much
desired estate by ceasing to eat. Many saints have thus freed themselves from the wheel. Jainism has outlived Buddhism in India
largely because it has created and kept a strong body of laymen
who practically form a separate caste.

A chapter like this leaves more untold than it tells. One can not put
the religious development of thirty centuries in thirty pages. Since
Hinduism has no real church control, its sects are always appearing
and dissolving. There is nothing to compare with its sectarian branch-
ing save Protestant Christianity. These variants of the faith are
strangely named; only a specialist could tell what distinguishes them.
They are the creation of honored or forgotten teachers, they reflect
the influence of migration and invasion, subtle speculation and the
long course of time. After the Mohammedan invasion broke the
empire and unity of old India, two religions as remote in nature as
the poles faced one another across the frontiers of little states or met
in the colorful current of Indian life. They were bound to affect one

another, phases of Hindu faith are due just to these contacts—and now there is Christianity.

Meanwhile the worship of Brahma, Vishnu and Siva and countless other gods grows old without ceasing. The devout go on crowded pilgrimages to holy cities counting no difficulty too great and often dying on the way. The temples smell of dead flowers and heavy incense, their pavements are often splashed with sacrificial blood. The priest is honored, the Brahman is aloof, society is caste seamed. The faithful wash their mouths and say a prayer or fill the temples where old rituals are daily repeated. The vivid ways of Indian life touch it all with color, the smoke of the burning ghats darkens the air on the banks of holy rivers, the devout wash their sins away in water stained by many lustrations and the Ganges carries it all, the ashes of the burned, the sin of the contrite and the memories of the ages down to the sea. Brahma dreams on and since all the universe is his dream he has much to dream of. But he has no dream at all like India and the faith which dreams that he dreams.

CHAPTER IX

The Gods Come to Mount Olympus

THE LEGACY OF GREECE

GREECE is not a land at all, but art and beauty, literature and insight all in a magic word, the names of her little states are music, the waters which wash her shores are spread with memories. She nourished a spirit which sings in a single lyric line, is heard, like the rote of the sea, in a single epic verse, broods over the Acropolis and persists in every precious fragment of Hellenic marble. It inspires philosophies and theologies and furnishes an indispensable material for any culture of mind. Greece is the outstanding historic example of what L. P. Jacks calls the civilization of culture as opposed to the civilization of power. There was and is her true seat of empire. She was the clearing house of civilization for almost a thousand years, for she commanded the sea lanes of the ancient world and her islands were stepping stones between Europe and Asia. The cautious galleys which set out from her deeply sheltered harbors maintained a profitable trade but they always took more with them than they ever brought back. In the commerce of the imponderables, art, insight and literature, the balance of trade was always against her and yet, by the laws of that happy commerce, she was never thereby impoverished; in enriching others she grew more rich herself.

The religion of a civilization like that ought to be of supreme significance and yet the very quality of the Greek mind makes it strangely hard to fix. The lovely temples, mellowed by time never entirely contained it. Zeus was there and Apollo and helmeted Athena and laughter-loving Aphrodite, but Greece had a religion which no temple could house. Any line one takes is not enough. There are no sacred books and yet no other literature moves so steadfastly in the realm of the spirit as the Greek. The myths, the cosmologies, the dim memories of the Olympians come down to the windy plains of Troy, the struggles of a doomed house against fate, the high discourse of Socrates and Plato's mind all become literature. The Greek religion can only be recovered as the threads of it are followed through Greek poetry and drama, history and philosophy. One may find Confucianism in the Four Books, Zoroastrianism in the Gathas, Buddhism in the Dialogues and the Discourses, but it needs the entirety of Greek literature to interpret Greek religion.

Certain outstanding aspects of the religions we have so far been studying disappear immediately. Greek travelers and scholars, having a natural curiosity about the ancient divinities of Egypt, found as they believed many of their own gods under alien names in alien temples. Few scholars now believe that Greece borrowed the Olympians from the Nile. There is next to no animal worship in classic Greek religion nor any hawkheaded or dogheaded divinities, though there is some memory of the time when a god might take animal form. Nor is there any such march, as one finds in Mesopotamia, of gods who change their names entirely, and their natures a little, as they move in the train of conquering armies. Greece was too small for that to happen. The High Gods of Greece do change their qualifying titles. Zeus is Zeus-the-Farmer or Zeus-in-the-Earth or Zeus-the-Wealthy, Zeus of the Courtyard, the Piteous or the Loud-Thundering, but he is always Zeus, Lord of Olympus and master of human affairs, though prone to neglect them when otherwise occupied and quite willing to share his administration with the other Olympians.[1]

GREEK RELIGION REFLECTS THE WHOLE GREEK MIND

The Greek shared nothing of that felt weariness of life which cast its long shadow across Buddhism and Hinduism. India piled existence upon existence, so adding to the actual sorrows of any present life the imaginary woes of a thousand lives to come. The normal Greek lived his one life out with a bright and joyous eagerness, which the prospect of death rather intensified than clouded. Except in the Mysteries—and that is a very arresting exception—the classic Greek spirit, feeling itself entirely competent for the general enterprise of life and having no strong sense of moral defeat, sought no deliverance; it wanted rather an added fullness of life. The only salvation it sought was salvation by reason.

The Greek loved the beauty and vigor of his own body too well

[1] Farnell notes seventeen epithets.

to mistreat it and call the result holiness. His gods also loved and required perfection in their worshipers. "The Greeks made life beautiful, not because they were self-pleasers, but because they believed in gods who cared for human perfection—for perfect bodies, perfect minds, perfect works and splendid actions." There is no place for asceticism in a religion like that.

The free and many-sided play of the Greek mind is reflected in his religion. His creative imagination furnished every divinity with an engaging but not always edifying life history. No undue reverence restrained the poet's fancy, he was not above catching Aphrodite and Ares in the net of Hephaestus for all the gods, and all the world, to see and yet with just the touch which makes a Homeric jest a tribute to the immortal loveliness of the goddess. And always the poet, being himself a "maker," adds something of himself to the tale until, as Lewis Campbell says, Homer is sometimes more wise and far-seeing than his Zeus.[2]

The poet, the dramatist and the philosopher, with the lovely ministry of Greek art really shaped the evolution of Greek religion. There is an immense marginal variation but the whole process is always in subjection, till the creative force of the race began to be lost, to the luminous Greek reason which worked unhindered and unafraid. The state supported and regulated an official religion in an orderly way but with a light touch. The trial of Socrates furnished an illustration of how public opinion might act through the state to silence a disturbing teacher and makes his memory immortal, but Greece was not given to heresy trials.[3] Plato does propose a vigorous treatment for three classes of heretics: "The atheist whose offense is the least; the believer in gods who are indifferent to human things and (worst of all) the believers in gods who can be bribed by prayers and incenses to the remission of sins."[4] But he was probably out of patience with the mysteries at the time he wrote the "Laws," besides he was an old man.

The Greek, for all his free thinking, forward-mindedness, never surrendered his past; he mocked it a little even as he venerated it, but he carried some trailing garment of his ancient faith to his loftiest heights of insight. Plato himself speaks of God and the gods almost

[2] Campbell, *Religion in Greek Literature,* page 18.

[3] This statement needs an unexpected qualification. We shall return to it again.

[4] Campbell, *Religion in Greek Literature,* page 351.

in the same breath. The most, apparently, he would do for the popular religion is to have its literature thoroughly expurgated.

"For if, my Sweet Adimantus, our youth seriously listen to such unworthy representation of the gods, instead of laughing at them as they ought, hardly will any of them deem that he himself, being but a man, can be dishonored by similar actions; neither will he rebuke any inclination which may arise in his mind to say and do the like. And instead of having any shame or self-control, he will be always whining and lamenting on slight occasions." His "Sweet Adimantus" agreed with him and the philosopher proposed for his ideal state a censorship which would protect the mind of the Athenian youth—which has a familiar sound.

THE THREE LEVELS OF GREEK RELIGION

There were actually three levels of Greek religion—a very old religion of Earth and Hades, fear shadowed and rooted in a dim antiquity; the bright and heroic religion of the Olympians; and finally the ripened religion of noble and penetrating minds for whom God is "the one divine soul or spirit and who manifests himself in and to them."[5] But these three phases never lie in cleancut strata. They are buckled and broken like the earth strata so that one finds the first and the last strangely near in the official cults of the city states, and the minds of philosophers and dramatists.[6]

Racially Greece was a deposit from <u>successive migrations</u> which came in from the north. Michelet compares the land to a trap with three compartments, and easier to get in than get out of. Once a group got down into one of these sea-faced pockets, their wanderings were over, particularly if other and following groups were pocketed behind them. They were pleasant traps to be caught in, sun-washed, kind to vines and dusty, gray olive trees, with valleys for corn, clear rivers for nymphs to bathe in and reeds for Pan to hide in while he

[5] Edward Caird, *The Evolution of Theology in the Greek Philosophers,* Vol. I, page 220.

[6] L. R. Farnell organizes Greek Religion into four periods: The Prehistoric Period from (say) 1500 B.C. to 900 B.C., dimly known; the second period, 900 to 500 B.C., adequately documented; the third period, 500 to 338 B.C., richly documented and splendid with art; the final period in which the Greek spirit followed his phalanxes to Egypt and across Western Asia and, though much changed by so considerable an adventure, had still force enough to leaven everything it touched. (Outline History of Greek Religion.)

watched them, little mountains to shut a foe out and higher mountains for the High Gods to use, marble everywhere, copper enough and a little gold and silver in the islands and more across the Ægean and always the sea with its

> . . . sprinkled isles,
> Lily on lily, that o'erlace the sea.

But still it was a trap. Those whom it caught had no choice but to root down in the soil and across slow centuries create their states, their civilization and their soul until they had forgotten that there were ever nomads and called their distant kinsfolk barbarians. The land was not empty when the Achæans came into it. (There never seems to have been an empty land.) Remnants enough of very ancient civilizations are being discovered to indicate an old, old perfection in art, attendant wealth and luxury. It is named as the historian pleases, Pelasgic, Minoan, Mycenæan or some combination of them. What really matters is that this old Mediterranean stock combined with the Aryan to make the Greek and very substantially to affect his religion.[7]

Conservative scholars believe that the Aryan brought with him from the grassy plain only Zeus—old Dyaus the "bright one"—and Hestia, Zeus of the Sky and Hestia of the hearth. The Bright-One for praise and the goddess of the hearthstone for the daily sacrifice of the father-priest and the consecration of home life. Other scholars are inclined to allow for a more generous importation of divinities.

[7] The history-dawn folk in Greece seem to have been the Pelasgians (or Ægeans), short, dark and straight-haired. They probably came by the sea and from the south and east and like the "dark people" in India just stayed on, peasants and serfs, with a power to outlast any invader through their perfect adaptations to their environment. The Minoans next came up from Crete where they had labyrinthian palaces with bathtubs and plumbing, 1500 B.C., clothes which gave their women a mid-Victorian silhouette, a rich commerce and a finished art. They imposed their rule upon the Pelasgians and continued their culture supremacy beyond the Achæan invasion. Mycenæan art was their creation. The blond from the north came next. He celebrated his conquest of Crete after a general blond fashion by destroying the great palaces, but was more conservative on the mainland. He occupied the palaces which were much better than anything he could build himself and encouraged the art. Thucydides paints a vivid picture of the restless character of these early invaders, which does not altogether sustain Michelet. He attributes the happy state of Attica to the fact that its soil was too poor to encourage invasion and that the less fortunate seeking an asylum there were hospitably received. Huntington concludes that this long mixing of the adventurous and capable explains Athens specifically and Greece generally.

The religion native to the soil, they say, generally supplied the goddess cults, the invaders brought the gods with them.

The festivals which were intended to promote and conserve the fertility of fields and flocks belonged to this oldest and lowest stratum of Greek religion. It needs long living in a land to create festivals which reflect its seasons, its crops and the instructed ways of the husbandman's craft. Some of these rituals—the Athenian "ox murder" for example, in which the priest who slew the sacrificial victim after it had eaten barley or wheat immediately fled and only the ax was finally brought to judgment, belong to a very ancient level of faith and need half Frazer's *Golden Bough* for explanation—though the burlesque issue of the trial sounds a rather modern note.

There were always two shadows across the perfect beauty and what Ruskin has called the "everlasting calm" of Greek faith and life. The darker shadow was cast by fate, the "necessity" of the tragedians who used a name for it which sounds like a shaken chain. This, too, I think, was brought from the "Grassy Plain," though Homer does not consistently personify destiny as a supreme deity. Temperamentally it is an aspect of that brooding melancholy which northern races have never quite escaped, the "black spot" in their blood. It is some inheritance also from the Vedic "Rita," the power behind all power, the law above all law. The Olympians are subject to it just as the Hindu gods who could not burn a straw without the permission of Brahma.

Plutarch fought the second shadow in a certain essay on the fear of the supernatural by which he meant superstition. Saul of Tarsus, who certainly knew his Greek world, did not miss the mark when he saluted the men of Athens as "too superstitious."[8] Plutarch had no use for a religion of fear, but what he was condemning was "the *real* religion of the main bulk of the people." That was a placation—a "please-go-away" religion. Its worship took forms common to primitive religion the world around. The devout gave malicious spirits benignant names to flatter and get them to go away. "The beings worshiped were not rational, human, law-abiding gods, but vague, irrational, mainly malevolent . . . spirit things, ghosts and

---

[8] Jane Ellen Harrison (*Prolegomena to the Study of Greek Religion,* page 241) offers an ingenious explanation of the altar to the "Unknown God." It was one of many altars set up at the purification of Athens. They were built wherever the sacrificial sheep happened to lie down in the Areopagus and dedicated to the "Nameless Ones" of the Underworld. She has Diogenes' word for the existence of such altars.

bogeys . . ."[9] Harrison maintains that the rites of the lower stratum are characterized by a deep and constant sense of evil to be removed and of the need of purification for its removal. She calls them rites of Aversion since they were generally intended to avert evil. She supports her contention by an examination of Greek festivals as fascinating as it is impossible here to reproduce. But many of the rites can be paralleled in the folk ways of all Europe.

Since the first edition of this book appeared a most commanding contribution to the study of Greek religion has been published.[10] It would be impossible to make full use of their material without rewriting the chapter entirely and with no real profit. But summary of their general position is useful, mostly for its clear, strong organization of the whole development of Greek religion through twenty eventful and never entirely disconnected centuries.

They date the beginnings of Cretan civilization toward 3000 B.C. The Cretan-Mycenaean religion was well provided with divinities, a majority of them feminine (this agrees with Harrison). It was associated with country sanctuaries and was thus a religion of peasant farming folk; it is associated with a palace and on this side was the religion of the royal household. This civilization reflected the influence of the Eastern Mediterranean basin; many of its sources are to be sought in Asia. Elements of it returned to Asia with Greek colonization and there flowered anew and richly. And it persisted after the Nordic invasions of the Greek Peninsula and never thereafter disappeared. The Ægean element in Greek religion is not to be lost sight of—ever.

There is, therefore, a strange persistence of type in Hellenic religion. Athena with her owl and her serpent was worshiped in a Cretan palace, a Mycenaean Megeron, and set in marble and ivory loveliness before the Parthenon. She grew more austerely beautiful and wise with the centuries, but she was always Athena. Rural cults with their festivals of little fields and vineyards, reflecting seed-time, harvest and vintage, are the oldest recoverable forms of Greek religion. Nothing united these but the old, old way of nature and men. There was, before the classic period, a revival of emotional religion—

---

[9] Jane Ellen Harrison, *Prolegomena to the Study of Greek Religion,* Cambridge University Press, page 7.

[10] *Le Génie Grec Dans La Religion, Par Louis Gernet et André Boulanger*—94 Rue D'Alisia, Paris, 1932.

the Dionysian—which took place in a period of social crises and created new religious values and forms.

The unity of Greek religion dates from the entrance of the city upon the scene and the creation of a common consciousness which is more truly described as religious and cultural than national. Literature and art developed, enriched and fixed the final forms of religious Hellenism. Philosophy began its own inquiries and took the inherited religious conceptions for one of its fields. The inquiring Greek mind was thus set free from both myth and cult; insight and reason took their empty seats and a new epoch was dated. Greek political life, Gernet and Boulanger maintain, always functioned in the "cadre de la cite"—in the frame of the city. As the political power of the cities dissolved, individualism increased.

The effect of this on Hellenic religion was far-reaching. Skepticism grew, schools of philosophy which combined a practical wisdom about life with a system of ethics and speculations as to the nature of the universe formed and fixed themselves, the mystery religions supplanted the old cults with new and fascinating symbols, rituals and disciplines. Like the flood waters which this morning's papers report (March 12, 1936), mind and spirit escaped their ancient channels and spread questingly abroad. The tendency toward Universalism was accentuated by the conquests of Alexander. Hellenism felt and acknowledged the influence of that East we have already studied and the East was in its turn affected. From Mesopotamia to the Adriatic and the Delta of the Nile religion became syncretistic, without form but never void. This was the world into which Christianity came—and the Greek spirit was waiting.

In the most general way this is the thesis of these distinguished authorities, filled in with a wealth and precision of documenting impossible even to indicate. They are, of course, strongly under the influence of the social theory of the origin and development of religion but we do not see that their conclusions invalidate this chapter nor challenge its facts. They do supply a frame and organization which any group studying Greek religion today needs to take into account.

THE "DARK RELIGION"

In Greece the divinities first worshiped are underworld divinities. (The technical name for this religion of fear and shadow is Chthonic as opposed to the bright Olympian religion.) The altars to the Olympians were high and splendid and the heads of white cattle sacrificed there—their necks garlanded and their horns gilded—were lifted toward the sky as the priest also with upturned faced drew his knife across their throats. The altars of the divinities of the nether world were low and the victim's head was bent over it that the blood might soak into the earth. The High Gods were served with burnt offerings, fat-wrapped thigh pieces, whose odor was grateful to them; the nether gods were given blood to drink to appease their wrath.

The terrors of fear-haunted simple folks are formless, being mostly an affair with their own imaginations and their imaginations are limited. It needs the poet, the artist and occasionally the theologian to give form and substance to the spectral world after which, since its power to endure at all is in its mystery and formlessness, it is doomed. When a ghost begins to sit for its photograph, its phantom course is finished. The very old ghosts and "haunts" and mischief-doing spirits of Greece ran very much the same course.

They are as old as death in Greece, though it would be a too sweeping generalization to say that all of them are the souls of the dead. They are the spirits of mischance, the elusively malign. They are the part of the machinery of a primitive philosophy dealing with the unknown. But the whole order of them *is* locked up with the spirits of the dead. The Kēres are as old as any. Some of them are harmless, some baneful. A very old vase painting represents them fluttering like butterflies out of a burial jar (so the dead in the sculptured representations of the last judgment over the portals of Notre Dâme or Bourges push up their coffin lids). Another painting represents Herakles beating a very impish Kēre with his club and taking the little winged figure very seriously indeed.

An orphic hymn to the club-Brandisher which the painting seems to illustrate prays him to "bring allayments of all diseases."[11] This makes the Kēres near kin to the dust and wind spirits which brought pestilence to Babylon. The Kēres caused blindness and madness. They take many and deceitful shapes, get inside one's mouth when one's mouth is open and create evil diseases. They make the wine drinker thirsty and then drunk, they plague animals and plants, they become the bearers of old age and death and finally death itself, or else they begin to make frightful faces and become Gorgons or put on a deceitful loveliness and become sirens.

[11] Harrison, *op. cit.*, page 167.

Sirens belong to windless seas and magic islands, "singing women of the sea" with the bones of those they have wooed to death rotting around them. But the winged forms under which they are generally represented show them plainly enough to have once been departed spirits. Later Greek writers made their music an allure—the forgetfulness of mortal things and the homesickness of the soul for some land of pure delight—which shows what a poet can do with a ghost. The Sphinx belongs to the same family beginning as a "tomb-haunting bogey" and ending as a riddle-asking prophetess. Finally the Erinyes come strongly out of these backgrounds to become the avengers of blood unjustly spilt. The Hellenic dramatists use the Erinyes and the furies very much as Shakespeare used conscience. They pursue Orestes and take their course through literature and legend until, as Mrs. Harrison says, "they go to people a Christian Hell."

These ghosts and bogeys were nearer the common folk than the Olympians. The Homeric hymns and epics sung around their camp fires were meant for chiefs and little kings, to glorify their descent from the gods and celebrate their prowess. (The old Vedic hymns are much like that.) Meanwhile the common soldiers were very likely doing business with the Kēres or some other earth divinities since they, the common soldiers, were very near to the earth at the best and likely soon to return to it. The Greek form of this old and quite universal spirit-haunted religion also happily supplies an art to illustrate it.

The vase paintings and the like have one curious feature in common; there is nearly always a snake or so in the composition. Medusa —one of the Gorgons—even uses them for a coiffure. This means terror suggestion but it means more, the snake is the link between the underworld and the earth-surface world, a most natural form for the dead to return with or a netherworld spirit to take. The very early hero cults picture the hero with a snake behind him—the snake often bearded, which is the first step in changing it to a man. Every suggestion, then, of the first level Greek religion locks up on a cult of the dead and the worship, for purposes of propitiation, of underworld spirits.

THE RELIGION OF MOTHER EARTH

All this is most likely to have been the contribution of the Mediterranean stock which the Argives found in possession of the land.

But the light and beauty-loving Hellenic spirit sought other material of which to make a religion. The artist touched even the faces of the furies with a certain sad, stern beauty, the dramatists made them serve ethical ends and the racial genius carried the racial faith up toward bright Olympus. There is nevertheless a considerable region between a snake infested tomb and the home of the High Gods. The Greek dedicated this, the region of vineyards and barley fields and olive groves, to the Earth-Mother and her retinue. Earth-Mother has belonged to every land and religion and has, in Greek mythology, a very distinguished though not always entirely respectable line of descent. She emerges first as the "Lady of the Wild Things," attended by lions and deer. She is not yet the divinity of cultivated fields; she is the mother of all life quickened in her womb and destined to return to her dust.

She is humanized as the Child-Rearer, a symbol of general motherhood, taking changing names and forms, but she is best known under the form a primitive agricultural people gave her and lives in mythology as Demeter, the grain-mother. In this form she is related to Frazer's Vegetable Spirit, and remotely, to all fertility divinities. She has her place in the tangled web the "tale-tellers" have woven to account for barren winter fields and vernal resurrection. The flutes of Tammuz in the streets of Babylon echo her sorrow, Astarte in the dark and dust of the underworld is one with Kore, her daughter.

Now this aspect of Greek religion is entirely a woman's affair. Field work was generally the business of primitive women everywhere since primitive man was busy with hunting and fighting. Primitive Greece was no exception; "First of all," said Hesiod, "get a home, and a woman and an ox for the plough," though he advises a man to send a slave woman and not his wife to the field with the oxen. Beside the culture of any growing thing was an aspect of the mystery of the reproduction of life with which women were most vitally concerned. Proper rites and ceremonials were needed to insure the fertility of fields and flocks and primitive farming was in addition a sweaty, back-breaking business. The Achæan warrior was quite content to leave it all to his women and, since they paid for it with pain and weariness, they had the right to make goddesses of the deities involved.

Demeter is the oldest of those shining ones who were sometimes matron and sometimes maid and sometimes like Aphrodite (not altogether a woman's divinity) neither. Walter Pater tells her piteous story and follows her changing fortunes in an essay which repeats in English prose the cadences of Hellenic poetry.[12] It is too beautiful to paraphrase and too long to quote. It is in substance how Persephone the daughter of Demeter was carried away to the underworld and how her mother sought her sorrowing and in her anger sent a year of famine upon the earth in which the human race was like to perish. Whereupon Zeus commanded the king of the nether world to return Persephone whom he had greatly desired. Hermes whose horses ran willing on such an errand brought her back. But Zeus decreed that she should thereafter spend one third the year with Aidoneus and Demeter consenting "suffered the earth to yield its fruits once more, and the land was suddenly laden with flowers and waving corn." In such a way as this a Greek poet explains the flowerless fields of a brief Greek winter[13] and their vernal transformation. There are echoes in the cry Persephone sent back when the dark of the underworld closed down upon her and the desolation of primitive humanity when winter fell.

But how much more there is here than just that. Pater himself, after following Demeter through poetry and art, says that this myth "illustrated the power of the Greek religion as a religion of pure ideas—of conceptions which having no link in historical fact, yet, because they arose naturally out of the spirit of man, and embodied, in adequate symbols, his deepest thoughts concerning the conditions of his physical and spiritual life, maintained their hold through many changes . . ." That statement begs a good many debated questions, Demeter and Persephone were by no means just "pure ideas" to Greek women. But they did grow into vivid and personal forms through the bright action of Greek imagination and always with something added which made it possible for Pater to say, that Greek religion is a religion of "pure ideas." "Pure ideas," he adds, "which having no link on historical fact . . . yet arose naturally out of the spirit of man, and embodied in adequate symbols, his deeper thoughts concerning the conditions of his physical and spiritual life."

[12] *Greek Studies,* page 81 et seq.
[13] A Greek winter is not to be trifled with. Hesiod advises a soft coat and a woolen tunic, felt lined, oxhide boots and a cap of felt to "keep your ears from getting wet. . . . Finish your work before dark clouds from heaven wrap round you . . . and soak your clothes. . . . For this is the hardest month, hard for sheep and hard for men."

GREEK RELIGION BEGINS WITH CHAOS, NOT CREATION

There are no creation "tales" in Greek mythology, nor a creator. The Greek accepted the universe, something of its substance had always been there. Homer believed water or ocean to have been the source of men and gods alike. Hesiod spanned the immeasurable distance between chaos and the world with a comma. "Verily at the first chaos came to be, but next wide-bosomed earth, the ever sure foundation of all the deathless ones . . ." What follows is the creation of an imagination which endows abstractions, "pure ideas" if one please, with the power to love, beget and bring to birth.

Day and the bright spaces of the sky are the children of night and the shadow-world. Wide-bosomed earth "bore starry heaven, equal to herself, to cover her on every side and to be an ever sure abiding place for the blessed gods." She brought forth also long hills and the fruitless deep (at a poet's touch geological æons become a song). She mated with Heaven and produced, among other more or less desirable offspring, Kronos and Rhea. Kronos (Time) hated his father with a proper Freudian complex. Father Heaven also hated his own progeny, "presumptuous children" and hid them away in the dark. Kronos, upon his mother's complaint and taking advantage of a favorable occasion, did his father a dreadful injury.[14]

This first and not wholly compatible marriage between Heaven and Earth people the earth with giants among whom the Titans stand out strongly. They endure as elements of anarchy whom Zeus finally conquered. Hesiod's recital takes fascinating turns. Many of his passages have the same quality as Bunyan's "Pilgrim's Progress." The children of Strife are Battles, Murders, Manslaughters and other indictable offenses against the Greek criminal code. He traces the descent of all shadowed things: Sleep and Dreams, Blame and Woe, Doom and the Fates. He half deifies lovely aspects of the natural world, as though the sun-flecked ripples and quiet pools of little Grecian rivers should become living spirits and the sea should have a separate sprite for every glancing wave.

His fancy creates Winged Pegasus whose early service it was to bring to Zeus the thunder and lightning and the Muses, daughters

[14] This myth accounts for the separation of Heaven and Earth and is paralleled in Egyptian mythology.

of Zeus, who celebrate in song "the reverend race of the gods." Since poets have always needed a winged horse to ride they later claimed Pegasus and found him useful. He populated the "coasts of Illusion" with creatures of wonder and mystery. He tells how Ocean fathered the Nile and the silver eddies of Hellenic streams and how also, and properly, Tethys the mother of the rivers bore "a holy company of daughters who with the Lord Apollo and the Rivers have youths in their keeping." These are the nymphs whose very names are music, daughters not of the ocean but of an imagination which saw the gleam of rosy bathers in every stream and their elusive whiteness in the olive groves. The genius which once made the world alive with forms of light and beauty had, like the daughters of Ocean, youth in its keeping. When this was lost, something was gone which has left the waters shadowed and the groves lonely.

When Hesiod comes actually to the genesis of the Olympians he takes a fresh start and marries Kronos, who seems to have recovered miraculously from his injury, to Rhea his sister (daughter of Heaven and Earth). Rhea bore him splendid children; Hestia (hearth-goddess), Demeter the grain-mother, Hera and Hades. Kronos' disposition was as unlovely as his father's and he swallowed his own offspring. Rhea saved Zeus by a trick, Prometheus brought men the priceless gift of fire and Zeus, beside punishing Prometheus cruelly, made "an evil thing for men as the price of fire," the ancestress "of the deadly race and tribe of women" of whom, generally, Hesiod speaks in such terms as to lead one to believe that his experience with them had been unhappy.[15]

The battle with the Titans follows in due time and with their defeat the world became very much as Hesiod knew it—"a disk surrounded by the river Oceanus and floating upon a waste of waters" with Hades somewhere at the heart of it. Victorious Zeus established himself and his family upon Olympus, Hera was his wife and sister, Athena was born from his head, the Demi-gods were the result of his numerous and often very discreditable amours. Other deities, Aphrodite, Ares, Hephaestus "the limping one," were added to the immortals. In this fashion a Greek of Homer's time conceived his gods and the past.

[15] Symonds makes Hesiod's Pandora and his general references to women a text for a suggestive paragraph on the general status of "Women in Greek literature and life," "the greatest social blot upon their brilliant but imperfect civilization." *The Greek Poets,* Vol. I, page 183.

GENESIS OF THE GREEK GODS

Now that Olympus is empty and the mystery gone from the groves and the streams we have nothing left but to ask questions—Who were these gods and where did they come from, and how are they related to the divinities of other lands and races? No scholar of repute now accepts the early and misleadingly simple theory that they are all personified nature forces. The opinion of Harrison that the women goddesses of the Greek Pantheon are modifications of Earth-Mother conception seems strongly supported. These goddesses, she thinks, symbolize the two stages of a woman's life, as maiden and mother. They are, therefore, in one form or another the personification of woman force in life and society. The masculine deities on the other hand are the general contribution of the northern element in the Greek racial stock. There are nature personifications among them but there is something else and something new.

All religions have personified their gods but the Greeks did more; they humanized their gods, projected their own virtues and passions against the sky line of Olympus. Someone has said that in other religions the human is deified, in the Greek religion the divine is humanized.[16] Where the Greek genius has had its perfect way in dealing with his divinities they have become not only extraordinarily vivid personalities but the symbols and incarnation of some aspect of life or society. One must not press this too far but it is true enough. Ares is the god of war, Hermes in time becomes the god of Trade, Athena is the goddess of wisdom and Aphrodite the goddess of love.

Zeus is always, somewhere in the background, what he began to be in the Vedic hymns; he is "the Bright One," the sky god, the general celestial expanse with what is therein contained. But Zeus is also the general force and wisdom of a society both masterful in its dealing with others and self indulgent. Poseidon is always certainly a personification of the ocean and Apollo easily becomes the sun god though it is doubtful if he were that to begin with, being, when we find him first, the god of wild things and coming down

---

[16] The myth began this. The rite or cult comes first, then the myth, which is a kind of theological commentary on the rite or cult, explains and supports it. Then (in Greece) the poet clad the myth with music and more imagination, the dramatist brought insight, then the sculptor turned marble into Zeus or Apollo—and there is your god—vividly alive.

from the north by the forest pathways. But Poseidon and Apollo end as clean-cut personalities human-motived.

One may be very sure that the forces which have shaped all polytheistic religion gave creative form to the Greek religion. It had already outgrown primitive animism in the earliest discoverable forms of it, though it still continued the fear of the dead and a dread of the underworld. But directly the real genius of the race came into action these gods and goddesses whose genesis is so obscure became so tremendously alive that they are more to us now after two thousand years than some of the people who live in the next street.

Many things have combined to this end. Europe had no foundation literature for 1500 years save the Greek classics. Rome went to school to them and sent her sons to Greece to finish their education when she was the mistress of the world. They furnished textbooks of all the schools. The Christian Church strongly and naturally protested this use of them but failed sadly in creating a secular literature to take their place. The leaders of the early church were matured in their culture. They ruled the mind of the world from the Nile to the Roman camps in Britain until, in the general ruin of the ancient world, they passed into an eclipse whose shadow lay long and dark across Europe.

If the eclipse were never quite total, it was because the classics had in them a gift of light which could never quite be darkened. When literature was reborn with Dante, Virgil was his guide. After the West had rediscovered the classic world Homer and Virgil furnished school boys their textbooks again, poets tuned their lyres to classic themes—and the gods found a secure abode. A classroom is a poor place alongside Olympus but it confers a more tenacious sovereignty.

THE CREATIVE GREEK GENIUS

And yet one doubts if even classic literature could have kept the Greek gods so long alive if the Greek genius had not made them so vital. The Homeric hymns to the divinities are more than a distillation of "tales" told a thousand times and never twice quite the same, they are more than the perfect creation of a poet's devotion, his joy in the happy use of his art; they are character sketches of the most definite sort. The Greek genius for the right adjective does it as nearly as any other single thing, along with a pictorial imagination in which every detail tells and nothing is too much—and always the poet gets inside the god. So Pan with his goats' feet and his two horns and his love of merry noise, wanders with dancing nymphs through wooded glades, divinely irresponsible with his pipes of reed to play him home at nightfall. One would think the poet had been spending a care-free afternoon with him.

The Pythian Apollo speeds from earth to the home of Zeus, and there the muses sing to his lyre the unending gifts of the gods and the sufferings men endure at the hands of the gods. Doubtless the thought of all this added an enjoyable melancholy to an Olympian soirée, the felicities of the celestials needing just that background for contrast. Since there is nothing to be done about it, the goddesses join hands and dance while wise Zeus and gold-tressed Leto "rejoice in their great hearts as they watch their dear son playing among the undying gods." The Greek thought none the less of the Olympians for their serene detachment from a shadowed world. He would have climbed Olympus and danced with them if he could, and since he could not he rejoiced that there were such as they— bright, unsaddened and immortal.

If the poet could get to Olympus only in imagination, the gods could easily enough come down. Apollo came to build a temple and an oracle to which men might come even from the wave-washed isles. Aphrodite came down to offer her loveliness to Anchises. Zeus came down for amorous adventures. Athena, Hera and Aphrodite came down to ask Paris' decision in a classic beauty contest, a difficult affair which ended in the Trojan war to which they all came down. In a general and loose way the gods control human destiny. There is always among them a deposit of mystic power. When Zeus nods the issue is determined though he is not eager to come into action and for all his wisdom, may be tricked. They have very human weaknesses; Hermes grows tired on a long journey, Hera perfumes her body before she goes to her lover Zeus, the Olympians may be wounded or even beaten in a fight but they have immortal ichor in their veins and no wound is fatal.

They have like passions with men and the poet does not hesitate to make them ridiculous. On the whole they have a divine sympathy for the human estate. Olympus, itself, is not wholly unlike a

Tennysonian Camelot with its head above the clouds. Zeus' palace is the finest, being floored with gold—perhaps there is in this some remnant of a faith for which the Bright-One was the Sky-God, and the level golden clouds of dawn and sunset his thresholds— but it is more likely to be a poet's ideal of how a king should be housed. His associates have their own houses, their own thrones and their own retinue, the city is walled and its gates are guarded by the hours. Hephæstus still keeps his workshop and there is even a court physician. Their divine force is sustained by nectar and ambrosia and Hebe their cup-bearer is kept busy. The Greeks did their gods well.

Prayer and the Olympians

Theologically, the gods know everything; actually they do not always know their own business. Odysseus gets a long way out to sea before Poseidon knows that he has set sail, Poseidon comes up to help the Greeks while Zeus is looking the other way. They can be entreated through prayer, though Homeric prayers are generally brief—half-wish and half-petition. The heroes do not trouble the gods unnecessarily; the suppliant is commonly in dire need or a tight place. But prayers were said as a part of the day's worship and wide-wandering Odysseus said a prayer before going to his wide-wanderer's bed. The liturgic prayers were more formal. The Greeks believed that "all men need the gods" and that prayer was answered. The Greek was really devout. He began any new enterprise with prayer, greeted the dawn with a petition, had grace at meals, prayed before he entered the athletic games, or went hunting. The exhibitions at the theater were opened with prayer as well as the meetings of the political assemblies.

Pericles never spoke without a prayer that he might "utter no unfitting word." Such prayers as survive ask for the human things which bind the millenniums together, that the city may have good fortune, the state be prosperous, the crops good and women may bear children—or that the weapons of war may be no more needed. Socrates simply prayed the gods to send good things, holding that they knew better than he did what was good for him and that any man ran a risk in asking for wealth or power; they might turn out to be an evil. The petitioner urged his case because his request was reasonable, or because he had been a worshiper of the god addressed, or simply because the god was kind.[17] Greek prayer was always a venture, a man's sin might prevent an answer or else the matter, being fixed by divine decree, might be beyond even the power of Zeus to change. A man must, moreover, help the god to answer his own prayer. Herakles would not help a carter out of the mud till he had urged his oxen against the yoke and put his shoulder to the wheel.

Since there were so many gods to be prayed to, the choice of the proper divinity was a nice matter. Even the oracles were consulted about it. The instructed prayed to one god in the country (Socrates favored Pan), another in public assembly, another in the home. Women prayed to Demeter and Persephone—the old goddesses of field working women, or brought their affairs of the heart to Aphrodite, who was sure to be sympathetic. One naturally prayed to the god who specialized in the interest involved. The personal devotion of the suppliant might also give weight to his prayer and make a favorable answer more probable. Since the Olympians were in a measure competitors for the devotion of Hellas any high-god liked to see his temple full of worshipers and would remember his own. There was a good deal of *do ut des*—I give that thou mayest give—in Greek devotion—though the Greek had no monopoly of that—but a few prayers remain which express a spirit of selfless devotion; very likely there were more of which we have no record.

A man might pray as Odysseus prayed when the sea was near engulfing him, or as the heroes prayed on the battlefield, or by his own hearthstone or in the temple before the image of the god, but though he bared his head he stood upon his feet and looked his divinity in the face. The contradictions of the Hellenic conceptions of the gods are irreconcilable; the gods are both careless of mankind and careful for them, they are capricious and just, fate is absolute yet men are morally responsible. In the final development of his religion, the Greek disassociated power from the gods; it became an abstraction, "the divine," "the godlike," but it was not incarnate in Zeus and his associates. The sense of the inevitable, awesome and impersonal, always shadowed the Hellenic approach to life and when

---

[17] See Arthur Fairbanks' *Greek Religion*, pages 61 and 62. The citation references at the bottom of those pages show how inclusive a scholar's investigation has to be to write two paragraphs.

God finally emerged through the insight of the great thinkers he was a Platonic idea of perfection rather than an Hebraic embodiment of power.

Of course, the Olympians are assembled and standardized. The Homeric cycle—and blind Homer himself—recast and unified a wealth of material drawn certainly from remote and misty sources. One may forgive Kipling the irreverence of his verse for the clarity of his insight:

> When 'Omer smote 'is bloomin' lyre,
> He'd 'eard men sing by land an' sea;
> An' what he thought 'e might require,
> 'E went and took—the same as me.

"The chief religious achievement of Homer and his fellows was to intensify the anthropomorphic trend in Greek religion, to sharpen and individualize the concepts of divinity, and to diffuse throughout the Hellenic world a certain uniformity of religious imagination,"[18] which is another tribute to literature. All the Olympians had backgrounds and histories of their own. Something of this shows even through the Iliad. Zeus really lives at Mount Ida, Poseidon in the wine-dark sea, Ares comes from Thrace, Aphrodite from Cyprus, Pallas-Athena watches above Athens. These were all group, "department" or region deities at first assembled by a poet's imagination. Their Olmpian city which no wind can shake nor any rain wet was built, like Camelot, by music and will last as long as dreams and music last, while,

> . . . the utter cloudless lift is spread o'er all, and white splendor runs
>   through it everywhere;
> And therein the Gods, the Happy, all days in gladness wear.[19]

If one adds (following Lewis Campbell) that the legends on which the Iliad and Odyssey are based, were carried from the Greek mainland to the seaboard of Asia Minor and there adorned and recast, one has said enough about the Olympians.

This section leaves out or condenses too much. What it leaves out has minor value for the general reader, but the student should know what is omitted or too much generalized and correct it by some

[18] L. R. Farnell, *Outline—History of Greek Religion.*
[19] Morris' translation of the Odyssey, quoted by James Adam, *The Religious Teachers of Greece,* page 31.

study of his own. The little local cults, the peasant festivals, seasonal and near to earth, did not leave their mark upon matured Greek religion as they did on Roman religion but they were always there. Hesiod, not Homer, is their poet. His book is a kind of cross between the *Farmers' Almanac*, a treatise on small farming and the home-life of the gods and goddesses. The religion of the Homeric cycle is aristocratic and urbane.

The primitive cults did not surrender without protest. "There was," says Gernet (*Le Genie Grec dans la Religion, loc. cit.*), "in the old popular religions a rich vitality and reserve that if the need arise produces revolutions." He considers the invasion or upthrust, of the Dionysian cult such a revolution. Here was the beginning of the long procession, remote and often nocturnal, of the mystery religions. It was heralded by the Bacchantes, wild-eyed with wind-blown hair, crying "Evoe" to the faint, far music of the flute, doing unseemly things, religiously drunk and sacredly mad.

Their madness dissolved the barriers of "me," rebaptized the individual in nature, made him a communicant with vegetable and animal life. The individual both lost and found himself in such religious expressions. They broke down social barriers and emotionalized commerce with divinity. "They express the idea of deliverance and liberty, evoke social and religious aspirations." The cult of Dionysius, says Gernet, is the only cult in the historic period which still testified to a primitive rhythm of religious observance. It was a wild resurgence of the peasant religion and conserved states of spirit and emotions which the religion of the city-state was beginning to supplant.

The cities fashioned their own proper cults. The cults gave new character to old divinities who never quite lost their primitive character. There were enough minor divinities, heroes and demons—though Greece was never demon-haunted. The distinction between the hero and a minor god is unfixed: Herakles is now a hero, again a god. The high-gods are the creation of a long period, the survivals of many competitors for Olympus. They are made by history and their histories are made. They are given personal precision not so much by their names as by the adjectives which qualify the names. They are rarely without their adjective; they come trailing some wind-blown garment of their primitive function.

Therefore, each one of them has his or her long history. It is the task of the specialist to trace these histories through. The student or general reader should at least recognize that the final, vivid personification of any one of them was the accomplishment of centuries; that the whole affair was not so simple as this section would seem to suggest.

THE PRIESTHOOD

Hellenic worship naturally took many forms. The priests were not "ordained"; they claimed no mystic gift separating them from the secular world; unusual qualifications in morals and piety were not even demanded nor a special or secret knowledge. Physical beauty was required. Also there were no priests at large; a priest was always connected with a particular shrine without organic connections with the priests of other shrines. The conditions of appointment varied. Priestesses usually served the shrines of goddesses though the situation might be reversed. The office might be held for a year, during good behavior, or for life. It was sometimes a kind of family "living," the family having given the money to build the temple or honored the god of it in some unusual way. The priesthood then passed to the eldest son of the former hierophant or else it passed by will or was filled by casting lots. In the little monarchies the king might appoint the priest, in the little democracies the people chose him. Occasionally the office was sold to the highest bidder, though the buyer must conform to the requirements of the office. In Athens the fortunate were chosen by lot from approved candidates.

The office was often worth bidding for, often not. There was much the same sacred inequality in salary as prevails in the contemporaneous Christian ministry. The prices paid for the honors and emoluments in a certain city varied from ten to four thousand six hundred drachmas. The returns came from sacrifice fees, a percentage on the administration of the temple endowments (some of them were considerable), grazing rights on temple lands, "the use of the manse," exemption from taxes and military service and other rather familiar sources. There was also "kudos"—the glory. The priests of the great shrines were held in high honor, given front seats at the theatres and the games, and, in distinguished instances, a gold crown or even a statue at the end of their term. It was all an official civic affair and the clear-headed Hellene made no pretense of investing it with sentiment.

The hierophant wore, while officiating, a robe of purple or purple broidered white. "The garments of purple dye point to a ritual placation and the service of the underworld. . . . Crimson-purple is blood color, hence it is ordained for the service of the dead."[20] The ungirt priests of Athens and Eleusis are ghostly memories but the purple still shows proudly in the vestments of ecclesiastics. The priest bore a staff, the priestess a key (the crook and the key may still be seen), sometimes they wore a crown or the fillet of the gods. They might be asked to remain celibate during their term of office and were now and then subject to the restraint of some forgotten "taboo"; cheese was forbidden one priestess, fish another, beans and goat's flesh to still some others.

The priest was the appointed agent of deity at his shrine and had a wide range of duties. He knew the ritual and was necessary to the proper performance of the sacrifice. He dealt with the fugitives who sought asylum at the shrine, bought, in the name of his god, the slave whom his master brought for emancipation, indicted the impious and acted against them in the courts in the name of the god. He was in general the mediator between the human and divine. His office, therefore, was holy but he was sacred only while he served his shrine and his god.[21]

The religion of classic Greece was an aspect of the conduct of the state. The city was the center of it since a Greek city had a value which no city now possesses. The citizens were blood kin, the heroes were their ancestors, the soil was sacred because the dust of the great dead consecrated it. The antique city has lately been subjected to a most careful examination, particularly by French historians.[22] It grew up around a clan aristocracy and a cult religion. The common folk were given the protection of the powerful—a protection which had its price. After a long period of struggle the citizenry asserted their power and the cities became little democratic states—built on an economic basis of slavery, turbulent, freedom loving, capricious and glorious in art and literature. The state did not take the administra-

[20] Harrison, *op. cit.*, page 249.

[21] This account of the priesthood is condensed from Arthur Fairbanks, *op. cit.*, page 76, et seq.

[22] See *La Cité Grecque*, G. Glotz, Paris, 1928.

tion of religion away from the families whose birthright it was without a struggle—sometimes, as we have seen, the priestly office was retained by a great family.

RITUAL, LITURGY AND ORACLES

Time, pride, wealth and devotion created a rich ceremonial of worship. No human practice is so rooted always and everywhere in an immemorial past as worship or carries with it, sometimes in a word or a posture or the color of a priest's vestments, such survivals of old faiths and old ways. Greek worship was no exception, human faith was already old even in Greece when the processions made their imposing way to high and sculptured altars and temples of pillared beauty.

Divination was an important element in all Hellenic official religion. The will of the gods could be known from the flight of birds or even a sneeze. The liver and gall bladder omens of a later period sound suspiciously like a Chaldean importation, having much the same character. Dreams were highly regarded. They came, so Homer believed, through gates of horn or gates of ivory. The dreams which steal through the ivory gates are lying dreams but those that use the gates of horn are true. Unfortunately it needed experimental experience to tell which gate had been used. Also there were soothsayers and such other dealers in "futures" as still persist among us, a craft which has always been practiced by those who have had doubtful success with their own pasts. In late classic times the cities were full of them—adventurers from the Orestes and the Euphrates.

The Greeks honored most highly the two oracles of Dodona and Delphi. At Dodona the priest heard the will of deity in the whispering leaves of the sacred oak. At Delphi Apollo spoke through the divine madness of his priestess. It all began with sheep grazing —so the legend says—on the slopes of Parnassus, a mountain later claimed as particularly their own by poets since they too are inspired. The sheep, affected by a vapor issuing from the mountainside, did strange things, the curious shepherds breathed the same fumes and began to prophesy. A temple to Apollo was built over the spot which in time grew into a splendor of temples, terraces, treasuries and a theatre.

The gray rock of a mountain still looks down upon a stretch of ruins which testify to the extent and magnificence of the shrine. A lovely ritual governed the deliverance of the priestess; she bathed in the waters of Castalia, drank from the spring Cassotes and chewed the bitter leaves of the laurel of Apollo before she mounted the tripod. The modern suspects auto-hypnotism—perhaps it was volcanic gas. The incoherent answers were written into verse by attendant priests, sealed and given the questioner. They were often engagingly ambiguous. Croesus was told that if he made a war a great kingdom would be destroyed, which turned out to be his own. The advice of the Athenians to take to their wooden walls in the Persian War was more to the purpose as Salamis proved. The oracle influenced and unified Greek policies through a long period. Fairbanks calls it "the Vatican of antiquity."

Hellenic worship grew into standardized forms which but expressed and controlled the national genius. There was always an outstanding custom of <u>votive offerings</u>. These were partly propitiatory, partly in gratitude for past favors, partly in expectation of further kindnesses and partly a friendly commerce with the very human gods. The gift bringer does not hesitate to suggest what he wants in return nor remind the divinity of past benefactions. Signal mercies evoked signal gifts—the first fruits of a generous harvest, a temple built in gratitude for deliverance from some plague; some splendid thing to commemorate a victory. Napoleon cast captured cannon into pillars whose bas-reliefs review a proud campaign; the Greek hung up the captured shields of beaten warriors in his temple of a god, or dedicated to the high-gods the prows of captured galleys.

A nameless sculptor once made a marble replica of one of these votive galley prows at the command of Demetrius Poleorcetes and set Niké herself on it with wings spread to the sea winds and wind-blown drapery, tried in the very poise of her, brave adventure in the face we shall never see, and a power, even in her broken loveliness, to make the stairs which the Kings of France once used a road to Samothrace and Salamis. One could almost reconstruct the daily lives, deliverances and signal deeds of the citizenry of Hellas from the individual offerings often rich in naïve imagination. A thirsty soldier gives a frog to show that he found water, a shepherd a little lion to show from what he saved his sheep and himself, a maiden leaves her dolls with Artemis because she is a woman now and soon to be married, the athlete leaves the wreath he won and the official his civic crown.

The walls of the temple of Æsculapius (the doctor-god) were hung with models of eyes to which he had restored sight, or limbs to which he had given action. There is a kind of humane friendliness in it all as though the god—or goddess—was never far away and really cared and helped.[23]

THE TEMPLES

Centuries of votive gifts from the individual and the state are bound to enrich any shrine and the accumulated wealth flowered into art and architecture. Greek art was not the hand-maiden of religion, it was a corporeal aspect of it. The artist was dear to the gods, his genius was their inspiration—were they not fellow crafts-men? The great artists worked both for the state and the deity; the social quality of Greek religion made the two services one. Wealth, devotion and genius crowned the hills beneath whose de-fenses cities had grown up, with temples whose perfection of pro-portion and detail was one of the few final human accomplish-ments. Temples also blossomed into marble around old shrines facing the wine-dark sea, or in little valleys among the olive groves. They sheltered Zeus and Apollo, Athena or Aphrodite in marbles and bronzes; the simulacra of what a god might be if he were incarnate and what men and women might be if they were divine.

No smoke of burnt offerings ever darkened the interior of the temples, but the serene figures—who always faced the east—could watch the sacrifices on the altar before his temple. These altars smoked with burnt fat, the pavements were crimson with shed blood (if the priests' vestments were blood splashed, their crimson-purple hid the spot). The priest directed the ritual, the music of flutes brightened the ceremony, the victims were hung with garlands, the participants wore white garments and wreaths of flowers. The vase paintings which represent such ceremonies have a dignity and beauty to conceal the fact that the white sheep upon the altar is soon to be killed and the white altar made incarnadine. A feast followed the sacrifice and the devout ate what the gods had left. The sacrifice

---

[23] The custom persists; the walls of St. Etienne du Mont in Paris are lined with tablets thanking St. Genevieve for timely help in examinations as though she had been one of the coaches for the students of the University of Paris.

thus ended as a communion meal shared by men and gods. Later when religious conceptions not native to the "bright" worship of the Hellenes began to change the older feast with the gods, the divinity would be believed to furnish the table with his own flesh, the Sacraments of the Mysteries appear and a wilder music stirred the votaries.

The sacrifices were of various sorts and offered for many reasons. They were offered to propitiate the gods, obtain purification from actual or ritual sin, to further an enterprise as a pure act of worship or, later, as a sacramental ceremony. But whatever they were and for whatever purpose, the grave and beauty-loving spirit of the Greek gave them quality which lifted them above the grossly material. They were always going on, in the great festival times, in the happy conduct of life, in seasons of unusual danger or significance, in great pillared temples, before some little shrine, always the piety of a people going out in a procession which time has arrested only to make timeless.

> What little town by river or sea shore,
> Or mountain-built with peaceful citadel,
> Is emptied of its folk, this pious morn?
> And, little town, thy streets forevermore
> Will silent be; and not a soul, to tell
> Why thou art desolate, can e'er return.

The Games

No study of Greek religion is complete without some mention of the games, for these also were an aspect of religion. One can only guess how it all began. Certainly in the Greek belief that every aspect of life is an affair with the gods, possibly there is a naïve persuasion that if a man had only his speed in race or his skill in wrestling to offer the gods, they would accept it. Farnell[24] thinks the intertribal athletic contests would be held at some shrine. The sanctity of the shrine would guarantee a kind of "truce of god" and the guests, being gentlemen, would join in the local worship since there were no high ecclesiastics to forbid it. The games themselves would thus take on a religious character. I think myself the reasons go deeper; they were an aspect of the happy religiosity of Hellenic

[24] *The Higher Aspects of Greek Religion*, page 96. It might have directed its moral passion toward some things less worthy to endure.

life and love of beautiful action. It is our curious secularization of life in the name of religion which makes it all strange to us.

At any rate, the great Panhellenic festivals gave the Hellene a needed sense of unity which nothing else quite supplied. The Olympian games were held every four years. Months before heralds went about Greece to proclaim a sacred peace for their observance. All the states sent participants; the merchant came with his wares, and the poet with his ode already sketched for the unknown victor. The games began with a sacrifice to Zeus before whom judges and contestants took their oath to "play the game." Only the fit and the right were allowed to contend ("unless he have contended lawfully"). The victor gained nothing but a wreath of wild olive and might lose his life. The games created their own settings of stadium and temple, the chosen youth of Greece contended in a noble, light-washed nudity which taught Phidias the symmetry of perfectly muscled bodies. The athletes devoted their strength and skill to Zeus, Pindar sang their praises, grateful cities received their victors, the crowns were hung in the temples and though their leaves withered the recollection of the triumphant was always green. All this for a thousand years— no war interrupting and no civil strife dishonoring the truce. Christianity put an end to it.

Family religion and domestic morality naturally centered about the hearth. Time and change swept always widening circles around it to include the tribe, the city and finally the state, but the centrality of the hearthstone was never quite lost. The ancestors of the Greek had brought Hestia in to Greece with them, the hearthstone was her altar and the centuries kept her fires alight. The city maintained a perpetual fire in the town hall. The common meal of the household shared by the living, the discarnate and the gods became "the communion meal" of all the devout and finally the sacrament of the Mysteries. It takes many things to light and keep alive a household fire, kinship, love, memory-shared experience, the unbroken continuity of the generations and the favor of the divine. All these shone through the flame of the Hellenic hearth. Farnell and other scholars much under the influence of the social theory of religion trace the entire development of the "bright" Hellenic religion from the hearthstone and the cult of the family.

Naturally then, one vivid aspect of Greek religion locks up on individual and home worship. There the father is priest—the priesthood of the father is the oldest of holy offices—and no detail of daily life unconsecrated. Journeys were begun and ended in family worship; the bride crossed her new threshold seeking the blessing and protection of the family divinities to whom she came; birth and death were hallowed with a wealth of religious ceremonial. Some little cupboard shrine was the part of the furnishing of every proper house; from these the little gods of property and good fortune, trade and marriage listened to prayer, accepted the diurnal sacrifice, and guarded their own.

THE FINAL PHASE

The last and greatest phase of Greek religion belongs to another region. The religion of the state was the affair of the priest and the archons, the hearthstone religion was the affair of the household but the ultimate nature of God and the meaning of individual life for the divine was the affair of the dramatists and philosophers and took its own enormously creative line. The high-gods and their altars belong to poetry, mythology and art; the reality of them has vanished with the cities whose ruins we explore and the temples whose fragments we treasure. But the contribution of the free Hellenic mind endures. The Greek was always a theologian—never content until he had found a luminous intellectual form for God-words and God-wisdom, but he had no professional theologians.

For the first and perhaps the only time in the general history of religion, a succession of minds of absolutely the first class dealt with religion without any exterior control and without dissociating it from the general interest and free play of the intellectual life.[25]

[25] The Greek was not so tolerant as he is here pictured. Anaxagoras was called before the Athenian court for describing the sun as an "incandescent stone and the moon as just earth." Protagoras was banished for early agnosticism. Athens put a price on Diagoras' head because he lampooned the mysteries. Socrates was put to death for ruining the faith of youth in the gods of Athens and exalting strange gods. Aristotle fled before the Athenian inquisition. Other philosophers were banished. This is not tolerance. Impiety was then an offense against the Greek law. The trouble is to define piety and impiety as the Greek conceived them. He is not consistent.

In spite of Anaxagoras' experience there was no conflict of science and religion in Greece. The detachment of the gods from the universe as a going concern is the key. Nature—φύσις (physics)—was one thing, the Olympian order another. We owe our conception of "nature" to the Greek. He laid the foundations of science—the first real science—because he looked at nature with a free, inquiring mind, directly, and not through temple windows and with no priests to forbid.

The past supplied them only a plastic material, no organic science challenged or corrected them. The general interest of Hellenic thinkers was speculative rather than practical. They accepted the world as it was and asked questions only of themselves. Plato, whose regnant influence has reached so far saw in the natural world at best only the shadow of a brighter order. Why should one be much concerned about it? As the creative force of Platonism began to be spent it became increasingly mystic and unreal and his great light passed into eclipse for a thousand years. Religion has always protested against the rival authority of science, but it has always taken to the clouds without it.

The forms through which these restless speculations ranged are as various as the thought was free. Sometimes they are a lyric poem, sometimes an ode. They supply the dramatist a motif and the philosopher a theme. The choruses echo them as the tragedy of a doomed house unfolds. Socrates entangled overconfident Athenian youth in the web of them on a street corner, they were discussed in the market place or the grateful shadows of pillared porches. But always something of which poet, philosopher, dramatist or market-place orator was only the vehicle gave form and beauty to the current of their thought. Civic pride built the dramatist a theater as it built the god a temple and Athena looked down upon it all from her high station above the city, while, with only the sky for a roof, the Athenian citizen heard Aeschylus and Sophocles and Euripides deal in classic form with timeless questions.

They dealt with life and death, good and evil, the state of the immortal dead and how the gods dealt with men—and what there was beyond the gods. The most lofty minded of them never really escaped the older faith. Socrates who died saying, "The hour of departure has arrived, and we go our ways—I to die and you to live, which is better only God knows," could pray to Pan of a summer day in the country. Plato felt acutely the immoral character of the old mythologies but he never sought to dethrone the popular deities. Perhaps he felt them necessary to a popular religion and the security of the state. He was anxious, however, to educate his countrymen in true understandings of the divine nature.

The dramatists, like Kipling's Homer, took what they might require from Olympus, hero tales or mythology. They always subdue their material to artistic ends and usually to moral and theological—

using "theological" very freely—ends. They tend to spiritualize old legends and force mythology to symbolic meanings—a device the more professional theologian of a later time often found useful. Hellenic religion is sublimated—I do not know a better word—beneath the touch of Aeschylus. "The dark traditions of the past, which it is his cue to dramatize, are transfigured with a light from heaven calculated to lead mankind into a more excellent way."[26] He lifts Zeus high above Olympus and crowns him with ascriptions of wisdom and power which the purest devotion might use. He resolves the dark mystery between the will of the gods and fate by making all destiny the will of Zeus—and just, though darkly seen.

> Though the deep will of Zeus be hard to track,
>   Yet doth it flame and glance
> A beacon in the dark, mid clouds of chance that wrap mankind.
>
> .   .   .   .   .   .
>
> God from His holy seat in calm of unarmed power,
>   Brings forth the deed at its appointed hour.[27]

All the centuries since have found no nobler voicing of the will and way of the divine with our humanity entangled in the dark than that.

A stanza from the first chorus of Agamemnon could, with the change of a single word, be put into any modern hymn book and sung to the edification of the congregations—if they could find a tune for it.

> Zeus,—by what name so e'er[28]
> He glories being addressed,
> Even by that holiest name
> I name the Highest and best.
> On him I cast my troublous care
> My only refuge from despair;
> Weighing all else, in him alone I find
> Relief from this vain burden of the mind.

The "bright" religion of Greece is not greatly concerned about sin in the abstract—if there ever has been any such thing. The dark religion does reflect a fearsome sense of the anger of unfriendly

---

[26] Campbell, *Religion in Greek Literature*, page 272.
[27] *The Suppliants*, Morsheads' translation quoted by James Adam, *The Religious Teachers of Greece*, page 143.
[28] Campbell, *op. cit.*, page 274.

powers which need to be propitiated; but this is because men are subject to their general empire rather than any haunting consciousness of having offended them. There is also some persistence of the very primitive belief that an imponderable evil may attach to the body through the violation of mores and taboo, but the sense of a natural moral wrongness and alienation from the gods is missing. The Greek was one of William James' "once born" men. Until something else which was partly the contribution of the East and partly a deepening sense of frustration attendant upon the general decay of his civilization and his force came into action, he had no desire to be born again. The sense of social sin, violation of the right of hospitality and the simple rights of one's fellowmen is older than the sense of personal sin.

THE SHADOWED SIDE OF LIFE

The sins of the flesh never troubled the early Hellene, they did not exist for him. He strongly maintained the integrity of marriage—on the wife's side, but took no shame for his body nor what it asked or gave. He disciplined the strength of it, loved the beauty of it—there is an account of an enemy given honored burial because of his beauty—and used the senses of it for a harp to play upon. He long maintained the serene unconsciousness of the Garden of Eden before the serpent came in—he did not know that he was naked. His stronger feeling was for masculine beauty and there is, from a more sensitively moralized point of view, a very dark and perverted side to all this. Hesiod's opinion of women "a necessary deduction from the happiness of life" pervaded the whole of Greek literature and found its most sinister expression in the opinion of Plato "that to be a woman-lover as compared with a boy-lover was sensual and vile."[29] It was only when Greece was very old and the East had contributed something alien to the Greek spirit that Plotinus blushed because he had a body.[30]

But Greece did grow conscious of all the shadowed side of life, a consciousness which always leads to moral reflection. It needs time

[29] J. A. Symonds, *The Greek Poets*, Vol. I, page 183.
[30] See in general Symonds' chapter on Aristophanes, Vol. II, for a brilliant discussion of this subject. On the other hand—that baffling—and sometimes perverted—love of the Athenian for beautiful youth had its higher side. Plato dealt with it searchingly in the Phaedrus.

and much wearing experience before an individual or a race begins to enquire deeply into the causes of sorrow, misfortune, evil disposition, and how the Divine balances its scales. The final outcome of such brooding inquiry is moral insight, and the quality of the moral insight it engenders is perhaps the final test of any religion. The moral insight of the Greek had its blind spots, but it had also a noble veracity.

The Greek dramatist finally laid hold of this theme strongly since it is always the office of the dramatist to deal with moral consequence in situations clearly drawn and moving swiftly to some always inevitable conclusion. The Homeric poets laid the blame for both disaster and sin at the door of the gods. They deified bewilderment and infatuation in Ate, daughter of Zeus, and made her the villainess of the piece—or else Zeus himself. The Trojan War was the result of the "envy of the gods," and other sad things as well. The great Ones do not want men too great; happiness is always held tremulously on the edge of their disfavor.

This is an old belief which has never been quite outgrown—the divine nature is jealous. "The God," said Herodotus, "will not suffer any but himself to think high thoughts." Later, Hellenic reflection modified this but retained the dark, human side of it. The supreme impiety for the Greek moralist is an arrogant pride which drives men to their doom. Infatuation follows pride and thereafter the end is sure; pride is man's own contribution, the bewildered doom-struck blindness is the divine penalty. Aeschylus would have agreed with Paul that "when sin is mature it brings forth death."

The suffering of the humble is another matter. The Greek early sensed that inequality in human estate which greatly perplexed Job. "How then, son of Kronos, dost thou think fit to deal the same measure to sinful and just, careless whether their hearts are turned to moderation or to insolence?" The thoughtful maintained the justice of God though his ways were blind—a man most likely suffered for his sin or else for his father's fault. Sophocles took a kinder view. His Antigone—in whom the august quality of conscience obeying the "higher law" begins to emerge, suffered greatly and was innocent. Some hope of justice in another world begins dimly to emerge, also suffering begins to be seen as a discipline of the soul and finally a road to knowledge—"We learn by suffering." There is also in Sophocles a clear sense of the complexities in which humanity is entangled with issues beyond our human vision, if we could see it all, it would be too right. "Courage, my child," said the Chorus to Electra, "courage; great Zeus still reigns in heaven, who sees and governs all."

ENTER THE DOUBTING MIND

But Euripides was not so sure. By his time the old religious foundations had been broken up, not through any long passage of years (Aeschylus gained his first prize in 484 B.C., Euripides his in 441), but through a growing sophistication of Athenian life, the exaltation of reason, the clever subtleties which went with it and a softening of morals—Athens was cultivating an intelligentsia. Naturally the gods suffered at their hands—Euripides may not have played to the gallery, but he was sure of the applause of the boxes. What his predecessors spiritualized he denied. There is something of the Book of Ecclesiastes in him; his Hippolytus dies saying:

> Lo, how am I thrust into Hades, to hide
> My life in the dust!
> All vainly I reverenced God, and in vain unto man was I just.

He shows the deeds of the High Gods in all their unlovely wrongness and asks why anyone should pray to them. Adam (to whom with Campbell and Symonds I am greatly in debt for these sections), quotes a passage of his coming to us through Justin Martyr which disposes of all the gods,

> Doth any say there are gods in heaven?
> Nay, there are none.

And yet his doubt resolved itself into the star dust of a vaster faith, pantheistic it is true, yet not without a mystic beauty and a strangely modern note.

> Seest thou the boundless ether there on high
> That folds the earth around with dewy arms?
> This deem thou Zeus, this reckon one with God.

The skepticism of Euripides was a sign the Olympians should have heeded. Their temples grew mellow with that golden brown old marble takes, their altars were daily ensanguined with a spurt of sacrificial blood till the stone might have taken the red to the heart of it, but their day was done though its twilight would not fall for five hundred years. They had met the doubting mind; the first time, I think, we too have met it in all this study of the ascent of faith.

The doubting mind became an interrogation point in Socrates. He had, a little, the face of Pan to whom he loved to pray and a genius for asking questions. He believed that he was god-inspired— though his critics sometimes thought he had only an unusual flow of words—to examine every accepted position and challenge every false persuasion. Adam says that the union of prophet and rationalist is so rare that we do not know what to do with it. One is not so sure of that. The Hebrew prophet was a good deal of a rationalist himself, having a gritty way of dealing with the religious superficialities of his time. At any rate, Socrates had, like Joan of Arc, his voices and they brought him to about the same issue, though he died an easier death—condemned, so his judges said, for misleading the youth of Athens and denying the gods—he who prayed to Pan.

The undercurrent of his teaching was more positive than his telling Socratic dialogue. He left his disciples eager for the truth, he warned them against the unexamined life, he urged a courageous moral insight which would not allow itself to be cheated by appearance or beguiled by love of intellectual ease. He was the first of the "seekers" in quest of the true, the beautiful and the good. The quest was the thing; even if one reached the goal there was nothing to do but set out again. He broke up old fixations, he was the ploughshare for a new order. He was never afraid to stand alone. "Though all the world agree with you, I one man, do not agree." He was at heart deeply reverent as he was humane and forgiving. He prayed to another than Pan asking only what was best and leaving his case with God. He died as though death were a great adventure into a land where a man might find the sons of God for judges and converse with heroes and poets, persuaded that "no evil can happen to a good man, either in life or after death."

The Platonic Ideal

Plato sowed where Socrates ploughed and his harvest is never done ripening. He is moreover one of the two or three highest of heights from which—or whom—streams of ruling ideas and faiths have flowed down and on until, without them, we should have to rewrite the history of the inner life of western civilization and would not know how to do it. He is besides so massive a fact that no two quite agree in their approach—and to dispose of him in a paragraph or two is what the Hellenic called the great sin—presumptuous pride.

But one may say (following Edward Caird just now) that he took over Socrates' unfinished task, the quest for the best, which should be the end of all action. That question-asker appears to have believed that happiness was the goal, though happiness is a poor equivalent for Socrates' key word. It was literally "well-daemonized" —but that does not make sense either, save as we remember that he believed that the urge and guidance of his life came from God, "for men of Athens, I honor and love you, but I shall obey God rather than you." He believed, I should think, that to be well-led, rightly inspired, was happiness, that happiness was the wage for following the gleam or, more truly, that happiness was the proof that the gleam was well followed—only the gleam must be true.

Plato followed the gleam and found the source of it in the soul. It was, he said, the memory of another and more ideal state of which we had once been citizens, bringing with us at birth some dim remembrance of its "heavenly delights and visions of unconceivable beauty." Truly in our descent we have been compelled to cross the plain of Forgetfulness and drink from the river of Unmindfulness but, unless a man drank too intemperately, some recollection was left and if he dug deep enough into himself he would find it there. Also if he should follow very questingly the gleam of the ideal so discovered it would lead him to the Good.

The Good then—and the whole of the long and noble movement of Plato's mind is here packed into a poor, bare sentence—The Good is the unity of all power and beauty and rightness in a real and unseen order which exists over against and beyond this little fleeting world of sense and time. The ideal is the only real, the luminous and timeless actual. The Good is the ultimate cause of Knowledge and Being. It needs then only to take one letter out of Good—The Good is God, God is the Good. Of course, it is not so simple as that— religion is not a game with words. Plato needed a "First-mover," a Divine intelligence, a Being and a bond in which to unite his Kingdom of Spirits, the many-rayed realities of the soul—one "Master light of all our seeing." That was God.

Those who study him now trace in slow laborious ways the steps by which he seemed to climb. But what if he never climbed at all, having first found his God through the winged intuitions of the poet and the need of his own spirit, and then came back to build the stairs for others to climb by? As long as men are men the Good can never be left impersonal. At any rate, the ascent of Greek faith reached its peak in him. The slow urgence of the Greek genius, reason guided and free to take uncounted turnings, came home at last to a way of thinking about God which has ever since controlled all free and reasonable approaches to the Divine. It is not unrelated to the Hindu quest for the real and undergirding. It has supplied the idealist his guide posts for more than twenty centuries. The modern scientist does not forbid us to find behind his drift of cosmic force a supporting reality which we know best, as Plato knew it, through ourselves. Beyond this summit there are only the stars.

THE AFTER LIFE

The immortality of the soul is both departure point and goal for Plato. The Greek always believed it, at first as all primitive people do—the soul simply leaves the body at death to haunt its death spot if it be not piously buried—the shadow of a shadow. By Homer's time the discarnate were housed in Hades, good and bad alike. Hades was dull and sunless and the Hellene, loving both action and sunlight, always went down to it most protestingly. There are hints of it as located in the west, hints also of some Island of the Blessed reserved for the favored. The main thing in the development of the belief is a certain "thickening" of the shades. They cease to be "phantoms of men outworn" and take on a force of personality—no great blessing since the resources of Hades were so sadly limited. The Mysteries did much to create the lovely hope of a really blessed immortality though they made it conditional upon initiation.

Aeschylus treated death much as all poets have done, sometimes it is the greatly desired friend of the troubled, the "sole cure of woes incurable" and sometimes only the gate to Hades. He recognizes a future judgment and proper penalties for the impious, Hades the divinity of the nether sphere being the judge, but the Greek never rehearsed the drama of the last judgment as the Egyptian did. Sophocles sounds a brighter note; poor Antigone cherishes the hope that she will meet her father and mother and the brother for whose peace she died. In certain passages, much debated over, Euripides says that after death the body returns to the earth and the reason is merged in the deathless aether which may mean the general celestial space, or God.

Socrates seems to have maintained a reverent agnosticism but the general atmosphere of his teaching has the feel of a faith that believes the way to Hades "a pilgrimage worth making." "What would a man not give if he might converse with Orpheus and Hesiod and Homer? Nay, if this be true, let me die again and again." But there was always the "if." It is universally agreed that Plato believed in immortality,[31] his whole philosophy demands it. The soul has its own existence beyond the reach of time and change. As far as he follows the fortune of it beyond death, he seems to believe that the soul came from God and there returns after its wanderings are done and its purification accomplished.

In perhaps his most vivid and magnificent passage Plato represents the chariot of the soul as drawn by two horses, "one of them is noble and of noble origin, the other is ignoble and of ignoble origin." The figure is too splendid to be clear but the immortal steed will bear the soul to beauty and light, the other drags it down. It is only as all low desires are curbed and love purged of the impulses of the flesh and the immortal steed given free rein that the soul accomplishes its destiny. "For those who have once begun the heavenward pilgrimage may not go down again to darkness and the journey beneath the earth, but they live in light always."

A passage in plainer prose confesses the finest reach of Greek faith and the end of all Hellenic purpose as most nobly entertained —"But he who has been earnest in the love of knowledge and true wisdom, and has been trained to think that these are the immortal and divine things of a man, if he attain truth, must of necessity, as far as human nature is capable of attaining immortality, be all immortal, as he is ever serving the divine power."[32]

This is the deathless bequest of Greece to religion—to approach it in the love of knowledge and true wisdom and to think that these are "the immortal and divine things of a man."

---

[31] Hardly immortality in our sense for the soul was pre-existent. Also he believed in transmigration.

[32] Timaeus, near the end.

CHAPTER X

The Gods Reach Rome

THE LAND AND ITS RACES

THE story of Rome," says Marion Crawford, "is the most splendid romance in all history"; and he proves his thesis in six hundred tapestried pages. As far as one can see across so long a time, Crawford has put the secret of Roman Empire in two sentences: "First, the profound faith of natural mankind, unquestioning, immovable, inseparable from every duty, thought and action; then fierce strength, and courage, and love of life and possession; last, obedience to the chosen leader, in clear liberty, when one should fail, to choose another. So the Romans began to win the world and won it in about six hundred years."[1] The actual disentangling of all the strands which made Rome and made her mistress of the world is not quite so simple. There was the land to begin with; what the map shows it, a boot-shaped peninsula with a backbone of mountains, an amplitude of sunlight, a volcanic soil growing anything from Indian corn to grapes for Lachrimæ Christi, walled off to the north by the Alps, and strategically central for the control of the entire Mediterranean littoral.

The race was as important as the land. It was mixed as all dominant races have been, though with probably more Mediterranean and less Nordic strains than the Greek; the historian fumbles a bit in appraising its elements. He is, at present, inclined to fill up his melting pot from various and unexpected sources. Excavations now going on beneath the palace of Augustus pass through at least six civilizations. The lowest strata were the folk who had lived in Italy ever since there had been an Italy at all, a nameless race—unless one calls them Western-Mediterranean—who kept near the soil and left their curious tombs and nothing else. These who followed and subdued them built, so Carter thinks,[2] their round huts on the hilltops and

[1] Marion Crawford, *Ave Roma Immortalis,* Vol. I, page 3.
[2] *The Religion of Ancient Rome,* page 8.

fortified them with palisades and, being much in need of salt, carried on some traffic with the inhabitants of the salt marshes at the mouth of the Tiber. They called the road they used "Salt Road," Via Salaria, oldest of Roman roads.

The Etruscans were the third stratum from the bottom up. They are known by their graves, their craftsmanship, their art which is both beautiful and unseemly, and tradition. They were also a mixed stock—a blending of the Italian people in North Italy with an invading race which came in from the east feeling their way in adventurous little galleys from island to island across the Ægean (and leaving traces of their passage there), and along the southern coast of Italy where the shadows of the mountains lie across deep valleys and a sapphire sea washes a sun-loved shore. They made their first landing on the Tuscan coast and there built their earth-walled cities—all this by 800 B.C.

From their Tuscan coasts the Etruscans eventually crossed the Apennines to build their cities in the valley of the Po. Of these, Bologna still remains and Mantua finds a during voice in Virgil. They moved also toward the south conquering and walling Falerii —having learned to wall a city with stone by this time, till they came down into the valley of the Tiber, using Salt Road, maybe, and then though they did not know it, their destiny was accomplished. For they seized Rome.

Seven Hills Which Made History

There twenty-five hundred years ago, was the center of Europe, the center of Italy, and a river road to the sea and all its coasts. The boundary lines between the territories of three or four Latin tribes then ran crookedly between some isolated hills a little below the junction of the Tiber and the Anio which stand nearer to one another than most of the other hills of Latium. The folk who held them, being too near to disregard one another and too wise to be always fighting, made a covenant between themselves and a wall around the hills and Rome began. The strategic nearness of these little hills, says Freeman, gave a new direction to the history of the world.

The hills presently took on proud names, how Rome got its own name is disputed. One wishes that the pious legend of Romulus and

Remus were true. It was certainly named after one of the clans. The older historians say the Ramnes, a Latin gens, furnished the name; others maintain it to be Etruscan. It is no great matter—what does matter is that the Romans named religion. It is strange enough that, until the word was found, all that commerce with the unseen which had housed itself in templed splendor or built its altar to Heaven under the open sky, assembled its armies of priests, winged its prayers with faith and darkened the air with the smoke of sacrifices, had existed in an awesome anonymity.

Whether the Etruscans named Rome or not they ruled it in a proud, hard way until the Latins overthrew them and set out to win the world. There are then three levels of native Roman religion as there were three levels of Greek religion: the old persistent near-to-the-earth faith of a primitive land-working and land-loving people; a religion intimately related to the national consciousness of the growing state; and the official form which both corrected and systematized; an immemorial inheritance. The adaptation of the Olympians and their legends is a side issue as well as the whole-hearted abandon with which Rome later gave herself to the eastern Mysteries.

THE PATTERN OF PRIMITIVE ITALIAN LIFE

We see the old, old Roman faith through little facts assembled by an almost inconceivable labor and pieced together according to the pattern which a scholar thinks he finds in their dusty fragments, or else a pattern upon which he has already determined and into which he fits them. It is all very much like the reconstruction of a Neanderthal man from some teeth and a bit of his skull; the result is an impressive tribute to the sculptor's resource but the subject might be justly surprised at the result. Only the Italian farmer living two millenniums and a half ago, in some cleared space beneath the shadow of his wooded hills—steadfast, laborious and practically devout in a world of much wonder and no little fear—could tell the scholars who resurrect his faith from its dust whether they are right or no and he would very likely have no words to tell them.

There was no nonsense about him; he was denied the gift—divine or fatal as one pleases—of imagination which the Hellene possessed, he had instead the power to conquer, organize and rule. He was the ideal conservative, he never let anything quite go, hoarding old customs when the reason for them was gone, building his inherited ways into the structure of his faith and his state. We owe what knowledge we have of his threshold religion to this habit and he never surrendered it. When the time came for him to make a Christian Church, he took his past into it and invested his new creation with the sanctity of the immemorial and imperial.

He wove the fabric of his almost prehistoric faith out of the things that must not be done, and an ordered way of doing the things that should be done and always with the sense of co-operation with powers—or a power—not himself. He was not far from a very primitive animism when he began, though animism will not quite do. His persuasion of a personal unseen about him was never clear till he went to school to the Greek. The oldest Roman rituals are mostly meant for purification; the evils from which they sought deliverance were real but they were formless. One does not discover that vivid sense of a nether world whose divinities needed to be placated, which wet the earth before low Hellenic altars with sacrificial blood. The Roman did have a very compelling sense of nameless evils which would follow any neglect of the duties and customs in which the security of his society was established.

A man lived in constant danger of infection from mysterious evil—very much as our grandfathers lived in danger from a malarial miasma. The evil might come from the holy—as well as the unholy. The sacred to begin with was not necessarily the morally excellent; it was simply a fenced-off region into which a man ventured at his own peril. He built the fence through some persuasion of the need of it which seemed entirely reasonable to him at the time. His successors forgot the reason but kept the fence. Social consideration consecrated it, the priest found it useful, since keeping it in repair and saving people from the consequences of trespassing into tabooed territory was his peculiar office, and so the system fastened itself tenaciously upon the primitive world.

Religio AND THE PERILS OF PRIMITIVE LIFE

A world in which one was always in danger of stepping over an unseen line into a forbidden region, of doing the "wrong thing," a world in which one was always, so to speak, playing a game with unknown and apparently capricious players, never quite knowing what the next move would be and finding out the rules only by the costly, blundering process of trial and error, was a trying world to live in. There was a feeling of anxiety, a sense of scruple, a constraint as though an unseen net were spread to catch the feet of the unwary. The Roman had a name for that sense and the actual outcome of it in the conduct of life. He called it Religio. No definition quite defines it since it is shot through with awesome wonder and arresting reverences; it is fear-touched and yet it is not all fear; it is constraint and yet there are emancipations in it. It did not in the earliest expression of it need a god to call it out. It is inherent in the mystery of life, an aspect of the human pilgrimage through an order to which man is not entirely native, the constraint of the alien in a strange land.[3]

The violation of any taboo makes the violator an unsafe person to associate with. He must be disinfected before he can mix with his fellowmen. Primitive disinfection began with the outside of him since mischief attached itself to the outside of him, being a real though imponderable thing which got on his skin and might therefore be washed off. But this was too crass even for the primitive mind; the sense of danger remained but the explanation of it was lost. Something of the whole subtle matter persisted in all ceremonial uncleanness and persists still in modern theologies, as if sin were something imponderably apart from a deed and its motivation. In its most mystic and sacrificial forms purification began to reach for the soul.

Religion included the disinfection as well as the constraint which should have kept the unhappy out of trouble and, since there was always the danger of unwitting violation, it was wise from time to time to hold some general ceremony of purification to atone for the past and insure the future. These are the sources out of which Roman religion issued. Every dangerous—or unusual thing—thus had a penumbra of religious ceremony. The new born were taboo and needed lustration within eight or nine days. They were given their names at the same time because a name had a mystic and defensive value (that custom also persists, though much sublimated).

[3] The substance of this is Ward Fowler's contribution in his *Religious Experience of the Roman People*.

There was, of course, a fearsome contagion in death, a cypress bough over the door warned visitors out; those who followed the corpse to the tomb or the pyre were sprinkled with water and compelled to step over fire. Strangers were particularly dangerous. They were not allowed to share the local sacrifices—an early form of close-communion—and would be expelled from a city in seasons of general purification. The actual reason for this might be the priest's fear of some infection for which he had no proper remedy. At the same time both the Greek and the Roman made hospitality near the most sacred of duties; the right of the stranger guest was inviolable as long as he remained under the host's roof-tree. Doubtless self-protection lay at the root of this also. Since the stranger was dangerous his good-will should be secured at once through a sacrament of food and drink. After that both the host and guest would be put upon their best behavior, the rites of hospitality were hallowed by custom and became a richly humanizing influence in classic civilization.

Examples of Taboo

The primitive criminal was always a taboo breaker and therefore a social outcast. He was put in chains but permitted to wander about; the chains seem to have been a brand—the mark of Cain for all the world to see and hear—rather than a restraint. Also iron itself was taboo and the fettered one was thus twice isolated. The list of taboo things is long and puzzling though, as Fowler notes, blood is not among them. That, he thinks, was because primitive Roman society had reached a level upon which life itself had become sacred. There is no trace of human sacrifice in Roman ritual. The most august religious office in Rome was the very ancient priesthood of Jupiter—The Flamen Dialis. These are names to linger over since Dialis is the old Aryan Dyaus changed but recognizable and Flamen is as certainly Flame-dealer or Fire-keeper. The Flamen Dialis kept the sacrificial fires alight on the oldest altar of his race.

But he paid for his high station. The divinity that doth hedge about a king was nothing alongside the prohibitions which hedged his pontifical person. "He was forbidden to touch a goat, a dog, raw meat, beans, ivy, wheat, leavened bread; he might not walk under a vine, and his hair and his nails might not be cut with an iron knife." He belonged, beyond doubt, to the dim dawn of Latin history, the last of a dynasty of Magician Kings who needed them-selves to be guarded from the menace of a magic filled world if they were to work their own successfully.[4] But his magic power had been lost through time, the creator and undoer of all magic—and only the hedge remained to witness what Rome feared before all the world was afraid of Rome.

Places also were taboo, most of them later became sacred—made over, that is, to the gods, but in this dawn time they were fenced off only by religio-awesome constraint. All burial places were thus religious, so were the spots in which a thunderbolt might have buried itself. This antique feeling "that there were places a man must shrink from entering" has continued, being itself transformed, to make altars holy and churches sacrosanct and invest the very soil on which man has suffered greatly or greatly dared with some mystic quality to save it from profanation. If one adds to this that time itself has been invested with a like constraining awe and certain days and seasons become religio (religiosi), we have the key to that conse-cration of time which began by making the Roman calendar and ended by making the Christian year.

Any superstition is a kind of Peter Pan reason—reason which has never grown up but is always able to account for its processes and conclusions if one can get its point of view. A day would get tabooed because it was the anniversary of a misfortune or defeat and once it got a bad name it was lost. Presently its reputation would not only be beyond repair but it would contaminate the days which immediately followed it. There would thus be a period in any month when justice could not be done in the courts, marriages would turn out unhappily, sacrifices be of no avail and battles be lost. The state would next recognize all this in its laws and customs; certain parts of the month would then be "nefasti" days on which no public business could be done, whose very light was darkened by some sense of divine displeasure. Now all this was Roman "religio." It was awesome anxiety, a sense of constant dealing with an unseen power strong both to ban and to bless which made every step into the unknown a peril.

[4] Frazer begins those studies which, in *The Golden Bough*, go so far with an account of the priest of Diana at Nemi who had nothing left of a once great office but its peril.

Religio A SAFEGUARD

Something must be done with such states of mind. A man can not keep on being always afraid and get his work done. Still less could fear-haunted soldiers conquer the world. The practical Latin mind took this whole matter of fear banishment in hand, working instinctively through a long line of social development and always with a deep natural sagacity. The result would be a system, of course, in which a priesthood would take over the commerce of the human with the divine, mature its own technique of propitiation and purification and assure the anxious that, because the proper and healing things had been done, the hearthstone, the state and the soul were secure.

Faith—the confidence which accepts and acts upon these assurances—is always the link between the perturbed soul and the peace bringer. Then the system is complete; it is no longer "religio," the anxiety of the fear-haunted in face of the mystery and risk of life, it is religion, the established power and peace-giving relationship between men and the Power which manifests itself to them. Strange transformations attend the progress of a system like that. Fear is transmuted into trust, strain into confidence, wonder into reverence, questioning into adoration. The Power itself becomes personal and considerate, chance and happening resolve themselves into the will of God.

> Well roars the storm to those that hear
> A deeper voice across the storm.

As far as the Western world is concerned, religion has become just this more nearly than any other single thing, though countless confusing lights and shades play through it. It is the security of the human spirit in the infinite mystery. Such a security as John Henry Newman found the august echo of in the words which turned him to Rome. Securus judicat orbis terrarum.

There are two roads out of the nervous fear of ignorance. Magic is one, being a way of avoiding consequences and securing results in which there is no connection between the end and the means save the capricious resource of the magician. Even magic had a deposit of reason in it which Frazer has examined illuminatingly, but magic is always anti-social; it puts too much power in the hands of the magician. Even hats lose their reasonable use if some one is always getting rabbits out of them and an agricultural community with an irresponsible weather maker at large would never know what to plan on. Both the Church and the State have always put the magician outside the pale. Rome took a strong line against magic though there are evidences enough of its shadowy survival from primitive times.

FARMSTEAD AND HEARTHSTONE RELIGION

The other road is the social development of religion and here the family is the point of departure. It is the most conservative of human institutions; immemorial ways lurk in the shadows of the hearthfire. The Hearthstone religion of Rome is as fascinating as the fire about which it centered and the flickering lights of it play across old fields and old ways. Rome has supplied us the word for religion; it has also supplied us the word for family. The clan (gens) was the primitive basis of Latin social organization and so continued, even when imperial roads led from the golden milestone to the last frontier of civilization.

But the religious and economic unit of the clan was the household and the folk in it, free and slave, with their gear and their livestock all shut up within the farmstead walls. The older European states have never outgrown this. The French peasant lives under the same roof with his horses and his cows, the time-mellowed flint walls of Northern England maintain an assuring separateness of the household against the world. The ancient religion of the family is bound to reflect the elemental human experiences, hallowed by the continuity of the generations. The Roman homestead stood by itself in the pagus—the clan holding—(township will do—incidentally it gave us the word pagan) with the family holding immediately around it. The familia would have certain very simple but imperative concerns: the boundaries of the family fields, the burying ground of the family dead, water for man and beast—and the hearthfire.[5]

The religion of the homestead was fashioned then out of toil and peril and the near friendliness and constant ways of earth and sky. It was seed time and harvest and the winter's food and next spring's

[5] All this is Fowler's suggestion.

seed stored behind the central fireplace (focus, "bright place," how right the word is). Custom fixed and hallowed what convenience began. The seasons furnished the first calendar and timed the ways of men to shortening and lengthening days and cosmic masteries. A countryside shares the general conduct and experiences of all its folk. Things a city never knows become their festivals, festivals which always reflect the ways of nature, a harvest ripened and brought in, the turn of the sun at the winter solstice and the like. The Augustan poets, who had the love for the simple life a sophisticated society usually develops vicariously, and a poet's love for the country and its customs, as well as a magic way with words to tell it, have left in their songs many allusions to these festivals—though they can hardly have been so idyllic as the poets make them. Something must be allowed for Horace's fancy as he dreams of quiet upland pastures of an early December morning in Rome.

This near and steadfast family life needed near and steadfast powers to maintain it. These powers are not gods yet, hardly the little household gods whose names a school boy remembers. The Roman was slow to personalize his divinities, he was quick to organize the "powers" he worked with in practical ways. We have seen how Hestia came down into Greece with the Aryan Hellenes. She came into Italy as well, changing an initial H to V and not otherwise changed. The hearth was the seat and altar of Vesta, the table was before the hearth and the granary behind it. The family-father sat at the head of the table, his folk about him above the salt-box, the slaves at the foot of the table and Vesta watched it all. She had baked the cake and earned her share; at the end of the meal a broken piece of it was thrown into the fire from the patella (the church still has its paten) during a reverent silence. Vesta represented —as near as may be—the spirit of the home but the granary needed looking after and Latin devotion furnished the granary-keepers— the Penates.

THE HOUSEHOLD DIVINITIES

These, Vesta and the Penates, were always under the roof-tree, but the family demanded a specialized "power" to assure its continuity. Devotion supplied that also in a word which has suffered many changing fortunes. The Genius of the family of which, in a way, the family-father (pater familias) was always the incarnation, presided over its destinies. The Genius was not quite the same as the shadowy double of the individual we have found in so many religions; it had more force. Its particular service was to continue the life of the family as the embodiment of the procreative power. Carter[6] is inclined to stress strongly the conceptions of physical reproduction which show dimly through ancient Roman religious life; the man had his Genius, the power to beget, the woman her Juno, the power to conceive. Fowler touches this side of early Latin religion lightly. The Genius conception was, at any rate, too suggestive to be thus limited. The Genius becomes the guardian spirit of the family and also that native and individual force by which a man is lifted to personal levels which make his family worth continuing.

The nearest approach to the Semitic Baal in early Roman religion is the Lar. Lar—an Etruscan word—also means Lord and, if the Etruscans came from Babylon as Carter thinks, there might be something in the parallel. The Lares seem to have been the guardian spirits of a locality (the Baalim were usually associated with fields and springs) with an especial predilection for cross-roads. The household holdings met at the cross-roads which thus furnished a strategic center for the general supervision of neighborhood property and a convenient meeting place for the Lares of the countryside (pagus). These were doubtless sociable spirits not liking to be alone of a long winter evening and the practical Roman, feeling much the same way himself, built a chapel for them at the cross-roads with a niche in it facing each family allotment of land and fixed therein an altar for the family Lares of the neighborhood.

The household slaves, lonely and landless, had no place nor share in the family worship though they were doubtless the descendants of those most primitive folk who once owned all the land. A shadow of their ancient estate persisted in their right to worship the crossroad spirits, as though they had nothing to revere save what haunted the land they had lost. Some humane stirring moved the family to give them permission to worship their "Lords" as they sat below the salt in the family hall. Vesta and the intimacies of the hearth were not for them—but they need not go out into the cold to say grace after meals. It might besides have been a waste of their time; they had also a certain responsibility when the family-father had gone to

[6] *The Religious Life of Ancient Rome*, pages 11, 25, 26 et passim.

war. So the Lares came into the house by way of the foot of the table, and thereafter the Lares and Penates—the spirits of the field and the granary—were always present in household devotion.

RELIGION AND DAILY LIFE

This devotion controlled the general conduct of farm life. We house at present the divinities which look after line fences in the office of the registry of deeds—though there is an old Anglo-Saxon custom of pacing the line—but the anxiety (religio) of the Latin fathers about their landmarks in a time when it was easy to move them created an effective device. They held a festival of terminals each year. The boundary stone was garlanded, a little earth altar built and the fire for it brought from the house-hearth by the house-mother. A small boy held a basket of grain and grapes, a small girl— they were all clothed in white—dropped them into the fire and added a honey cake (an echo of the Vedas here). The stone was sprinkled with lamb and pig blood and the festival ended with a feast and praise to Terminus. It was a lovely sunlit grouping with dark-skinned and dark-eyed children making a sacrament of old and necessary things. Nor in after times one may be sure would they forget where their ancestral land began.

The bride was brought from her own home and introduced to Vesta and the Penates with solemnity and tact. Her crossing the new threshold was an especially critical moment—who could tell what unfriendly spirits would cross it with her? She was actually carried across and after that her husband received her into the communion of fire and water. Her new born child was also a source of solicitude (religio again) in more senses than one. The ceremonial defense of the child against mischievous spirits was never relaxed. Finally the dead must be so buried that they would find peace in the low house of the grave, take their proper course to shadeland and forbear to haunt the living. The excessively complicated ceremony of entomb-ment was all directed toward this end. (Even if the body were burnt, at least a bone had to be buried.) For fear that something might have been left undone, there was an annual ghost-laying festival with a curious use of black beans which were supposed to be the food shades fed on—perhaps this explains why they were taboo to the priest of Jupiter.

DIVISION-OF-LABOR GODS

The primitive Latin did not name nor too clearly personalize the powers by which he was encompassed. They make a brave showing, now that they are capitalized with sonorous Latin names, they were for him only the spirits of the farm and the household named from their functions—a practical specialization of the general power, the numen which controlled his little world. A numen is literally a head-nodder but since a nod of the head means assent, it is the symbol of will in action. (The nod of Zeus ruled men and gods.) Whether the Roman left to himself would ever have got much beyond the idea of a general divine power taking specific forms to forward practical ends, is a hard question to answer. He had to begin with no images of the gods, only their altars low and turf built. When stone altars came into use it was still the custom to place a sod on top it. Since the Vedic worshipers used an altar of fresh grass the sod on the altar has a long ancestry.

The Romans had an excess of department gods, superintendents, so to speak, of pretty much every aspect of the general machinery of life. There never was such a division of divine labor. It took twelve gods to get a field ploughed, planted, harvested and the grain marketed, forty-three to bring up a child properly, three to open a door[7]—the cupboard shelves must have been full of them. Tertullian and Augustine, to whom we owe a considerable knowledge of them, offer them as deplorable examples of pagan superstition, Usener as happy examples of Sondergötter (division of labor gods) and the authorities generally as half-way divinities between animism and theism. A careful use of a Latin lexicon strips them of a good deal of their god-hood. Their names are coined from simple things and deified by a capital letter (a useful device not confined to early Rome).

Cunina, brooding goddess of the cradled child, turns out to be a personification of the cradle. Imporcitor, the furrow god, becomes "qui porca in agro facit arando" (the "numen" who makes the furrows in ploughing a field). The rest of the agricultural and domestic pantheon are much the same. They are actions and processes invested with a mystic significance. The sense of a dim and

[7] Soper, *The Religions of Mankind*, page 122; also Fowler, *op. cit.*

nameless power is behind them but one may gravely doubt with Fowler whether they were ever the creation of a primitive folk faith. A sweating peasant never invented a dozen impressively named divinities to further the detail of his summer's work. He was too busy getting his crop in. These are the contributions of early Roman theologians who loved to exercise their inventive minds. Something also must be allowed for the zeal of Tertullian and the Bishop of Hippo to make a strong case against paganism. The Christian fathers are not uncolored media through which to see the dying faith of Roma Immortalis.

Meanwhile the Latin power began to center in a city-state. While the religion of the hearthstone and the ploughed field ripened into richer meanings for the steadfast conduct of life and a laborious and frugal folk were sowing the seed of an empire in their furrowed fields, Rome grew also under her Etruscan kings. They had set an inviolable wall around it which linked the city with the furrowed field: "With a bull and a cow yoked together they drew a furrow in a circle, turning the soil toward the center of the circle . . . and the place from which they ploughed the dirt they called the trench, and the clods the wall." This was the pomerium, the spiritual wall of the city and all within it was sacred to the old gods of Rome. The lengthening walls of stone outgrew the mystic boundaries of the old city, but there was long at the heart of Rome a region into which no strange god might enter. The next development of Roman religion took place inside the pomerium.

A Roman Year

The consecration of time was organized into the calendar year with a plentiful allowance of the ancient equivalent of Saints Days. A modern churchman would find the calendar of Numa very intriguing—its capital letters, abbreviations, cryptic references being not unlike the general scheme of his own. A generous allotment of time, about one-third of the year, was given to the divine. All but two of the one hundred and nine days devoted to the gods and their festivals are odd number days. Three months in the aggregate would seem a considerable time to subtract from the working year of a community which had the world to conquer. The general current of the annual enterprise of Rome may be followed through the festivals, while the scholar finds some light upon vanished divinities and ways of worship even in the most cryptic signs.

The festivals themselves are a fascinating interweaving of agriculture and war. Rome measured her year from March to March, March being Mars month and the proper time to begin the two ancient crafts of Rome, fighting and farming. Fighting came first. How the past comes to life through these ancient rituals! The days are already bright and warm, Mars' priests are shouting and singing old hymns which have a power to kindle a fire in a man's spirit, through the streets. They know their business, these "holy jumpers" (Salii), inspired by a passion older than any god, using words so old they did not understand them themselves. No matter; the rattle of spear on sword with which they punctuate their chants translates them into a universal language.

> Strike for your altars and your fires
> Strike for the green graves of your sires.

And Rome makes ready to strike. The arms which she takes down and brightens have gathered more than rust during the winter. Some unseen evil may have fastened upon them to turn their fighting edge. The recruits bear them proudly to the field of Mars and fall in, armed, each in his appointed place, soldiers of destiny. Today they will only march across some blue hills toward the south, tomorrow (as time goes in Rome) they will take transport to Carthage, the day after to Britain or the Nile. The spring sunlight plays from shield to short thrusting sword, the spears are like a sapling forest, the ranks are very still.

Then the march of the priests begins. (Some priest's march will still thread the city streets when the legions are only a memory.) Their procession circles the soldiers three times and between each circuit they sacrifice to Mars and pray that the shield-bearers may come home victorious and their enemies be confounded. The old men look on and remark upon the general falling off in the quality of the recruits since their day; the women smile through a quick mist of Italian tears. Four days later the trumpets are lustrated, that they may give forth no uncertain sound. Four days later still the horses are brought out and the ceremony repeated for them. Some horse-racing to see if the ritual has been effective naturally follows. The army is ready now and marches away of an April morning, through crowded, shouting streets. Women march by their men till they are through the gates and turn back silently. There is no shouting now, only the faint echo of the bronze trumpet comes back.

But armies must be fed and the granary gods given a store to guard. Latium turns to farming; there is still plenty of time:

. . . though Winter be over in March by rights,
'Tis May perhaps ere the snow shall have withered well off the heights.

April is a busy month. Everything is done gravely and with due regard to the proper duties. The white oxen sweat under the yoke and the furrow-god is invoked. The grain is planted and unborn calves are sacrificed to Earth-Mother. The snow melts off the high pastures of the Apennines above hills "over-smoked by the faint gray olive trees." The sheep and cattle are lustrated, as the army was, to fit them for the chances of the mountains. The vines show green and the vineyards need divine protection, the grain shows signs of heading, the green of it brightened by the red bell of the wild tulip and Robigus, the red mildew, is propitiated. The harvest ripens, the granaries are opened and cleaned. The grain is gathered and stored with the same sense of divine co-operation, the autumnal festivals common to all lands and times are happily carried through.

The soldiers come home in October. Some new territory has been added, always at the price of dead youth and a slowly diminishing agrarian population—a process which eventually left Rome so economically impoverished that she lived only by plunder, turned little holdings into great slave-tilled estates and her armies into training schools for the races which were to conquer her. But all this is still beyond undreamt of horizons of time when the bronze trumpets are heard outside the city gates and the troops march in. Nor is it any concern of the priests of Mars who are out on the streets again, if only their lord has been well served. But since the army has brought back the taint of bloodshed with it and the contagion of alien lands it must be purified again, man and horse, shields and bronze trumpets. The autumnal lustrations are finished with a horse race and the sacrifice of the winning horse to Mars, who has now had enough fighting for the season and can, as Rubens afterwards loved to picture, turn his attention to Venus. The soldiers who are come home may help a little about the late harvest—as one used to see a soldier en permission in France helping a woman or two

and an old man build a wheat rick, his helmet and tunic on the
stubble, and overhead a low-flying plane coming back from the line.

A little later, and soldiers and civilians give themselves whole-
heartedly to the Saturnalia, a season of unseemly license associated
with the turn of the sun at the Winter solstice and fertility rites so
old that the young men who ran about the streets striking women
with leather thongs did not know why they did it.[8] The wise Christian Church will presently change the Saturnalia into Christmas,
finding sufficient evidence, as it believed, for the birth of Jesus at
that date and so directing an old enthusiasm toward a more devout
and blameless end. February, being a dull month on the farm, is
given over to the cult of the dead and a Roman year—say 500 B.C.—
is ended. Life was not lacking in color even then.

The Roman Gives Order and Authority to Religion

Now such rites and ways as these were the essential elements native
to the race and the soil in Roman religion. They reveal a land-
holding, land-loving, land-tilling people whose avocation was war,
they reveal Roman discipline and organization. The festivals are
routine hardening into custom. The rites of purification are taken
away from the magician and given to a priesthood who are themselves the religious aspect of a state to which the centuries brought
an always more massive solidity. The cultures we have so far studied
have each made their contribution to the procession of the gods.
Egypt invested the little enterprise of life with the august and ethical
significance of immortal issues, Chaldea set her gods on thrones of
administration with a power over human destiny, yet not too high
to hear a penitent's confession.

Gautama freed the soul in its pilgrimages from the seductive web
of this present world, taught his followers to consider every consequence of their thoughts and deeds and touched with tenderness the
shadowed ways of life. The Brahman seeking ultimate reality found
the soul of the Universe and the soul of the Sage a seamless robe—
and all else an illusion. Confucius and the Chinese Sages taught men
to take instruction from the ways of heaven and repeat the order
and rightness of it in their own lives. The Greek made his gods

---

[8] For a fascinating account of a contact of Christianity with the Saturnalia, see
Frazer's *The Golden Bough*, abridged edition, pages 583-85.

bright and human, illumined religion with poetry, art and imagination and in his moments of supreme insight found the road to God through his own vision of an eternal excellence.

Rome did none of these things. She borrowed most of her gods, and the mythology which went with them. She tenaciously continued and transmuted old customs. But she made a ritual of her worship and her faith, and invested the affairs of the soul with order and authority. She relieved the individual of "religio," the stress and strain of the spirit in its dealings with the mystery and venture of life and assumed it herself in her august and assuring administration of religion. And she has continued all this without a break for twenty-five hundred years.

Many things happen in such a line of religious development and they began to happen soon. Once the festivals were standardized, they lost their significant contacts with reality. Harvest festivals once came at harvest time and linked the garnered field directly to Ceres or Demeter. Now the harvest festivals became standardized dates on a religious calendar and something was gone—something which is always going out of religion as soon as it becomes a deposit and a program. Field ways were carried into the city with nothing to make them real save dim recollection and a poet's song—very much as though a man should make harvest-home out of a successful deal in wheat. On the other hand, new meanings were taken on by old ceremonies; the continuity was unbroken but changing experience supplied a new material, and Rome illustrates it all. It becomes in the end material for Fowler and Frazer and Wissowa to puzzle over, vistas through which to see priest-king, magician-king, dark-eyed folk sweating for their bread and thanking the gods for it, labor touched with holy meanings—and the legions marching away to war.

THE INFLUENCE OF GREECE

The Latins were slow to personalize their gods, being content to do no more than name the powers they worked with after the thing done, granary-god, furrow-god, cradle-goddess, numina near and neighborly. The old names are adjectives in action, they are the ways the numen—a numen is a being with a will—works. Now any kind of religion—even the most nebular—issues in some kind of worship and worship is a personal relationship needing a personalized deity with a name—the nameless never possess individuality. A poet caught in some web of Victorian doubt may sing——

> That which we dare invoke to bless;
> Our dearest faith: our ghastliest doubt;
> He, they, One, All: within, without;
> The Power in darkness whom we guess.

But the devout petitioner for divine favor wants a better address.

The early Romans found themselves in very much the same position as Tennyson—without the doubt. Fragments of old ritual imply as much, the priest gave Jupiter his own choice of titles, "Jupiter, greatest and best, or by whatever other name you wish yourself to be called." The very ancient belief that a god's name should not be pronounced lest in naming him a power is given to others to entice him away, may have inspired this caution; it is more likely a reminiscence of a time when the gods had no names.

An official priesthood with its own particular shrine and daily or seasonal ritual would be a direct influence in individualizing the numen worshiped. He can not long continue an unknown god under such circumstances; his priests are there to prevent just that. A lively imagination will, of course, be a great help, also poets who will supply him a lovely garmenture of legend. The Roman somewhat lacked imagination and poets can not be had to order, but there was always Greece just across the Adriatic with a wealth of just these things and a happy willingness to share them with the world. Early Roman religion passes over into the polytheism with which we are so familiar through the influence of Greek literature which captured the Roman mind when the still vague divinities of Latin faith were ripe for transformation.

DIVINITIES NATIVE TO LATINS

Later Roman theology distinguished between indigenous gods (Dii Indigites) and imported gods (Dii Novensiles). The indigenous ones were such as we have already considered, with additions enough to bring their number up to about thirty. They were mostly on the same general level, sharing between them the general supervision of Latin life. There were a few native soil divinities of a more general power and authority; the greatest of these was Jupiter. Like Zeus among the Hellenes he came in with the migrants from the grassy plain, the sky-god of all Aryan folk, thunder armed. The specialists do not agree as to how he found his regnant way to the Capitoline Hill. Fowler believes he came in with the Latins and was worshiped by them wherever they happened to be, from any hilltop open to the sky with the oaks he loved on the slopes below. He had thus long reigned from the Alban Mount before the Etruscans built him a temple there.

Carter thinks his cult to have been Etruscan from the first. No matter who brought him to Rome, he became more than anyone the incarnation of the power and majesty of the state. His worship fostered a growing sense of nationality and created among his worshipers a puissant consciousness of unity. "He was supreme god, a Power, if not actually a Person, who presided over the league of Latin cities and held them together by the strong moral bond of good faith, and the religious bond of a sacramental meal."[9] The taboos surrounding his ancient priest show how precious that personage was since he needed to be so carefully looked after. An oath taken before him was the most sacred obligation into which a Roman could enter. Was he not the all-seeing sky from whom nothing could be hidden? Fowler notes, with great insight, how this strong sense of the binding power of an oath sanctioned by the Heaven-God held the Roman to his pledged word and furnished a foundation of integrity for the structure of his empire—Cicero knew long before Tennyson that:

> Man's word is God in man.

Janus has long been a puzzle to scholars. Fowler thinks him to have been the ancient guardian of the city gates, an important duty. No one knows where he got his two faces, though a gatekeeper could easily use them both. He became the keeper also of entrance days and lives on in the entrance month to the year. He was also called the Opener (Patulcius) because his temple was open in war time and the Closer (Clusius) because it was shut in peace time. A really lovely title makes him guardian of the gates of the dawn. He was addressed first of all the Roman deities in any prayer, Vesta was invoked at the end of all petitions and her temple associated with

[9] Ward Fowler, *Roman Ideas of Deity,* page 37.

her eternal fire in the Forum—the heart of Rome. When the Olympians came across the Adriatic Mars naturally inherited the general mythological holdings of Ares, but he had a status of his own in Italy from early times. He became in the end a more imposing figure than Ares had ever been, that one being a good deal of a blusterer and not highly regarded by the Greeks. Rome really taught Mars his business, gave him fighting enough to satisfy any war-god and set him upon a more than Olympian throne.

For all that something of the wolf and the wild clung to him tenaciously. An old name for him—favored by the poets—was Mavors, which seems to mean the cutter. He was also called Mamers or Marmor, which the Latin lexicon thinks comes from an old Sanskrit root meaning to shine; Mars is therefore the bright one. His wolf and his general early character seem to make him an incarnation of the menacing spirit of the new rough country through which the Latins pushed down as they came into Italy. He threatened sheep and cattle in the upland pastures, he hid in the edges of the clearings.

The oldest land protection rites ask him to be merciful to the cattle and placate him with the sacrifice of an ox, a sheep and a pig. He was best kept at a distance, he had a field of his own, the campus Martius, outside the walls of early Rome—no temple inside till the time of Augustus. As Fowler suggests some trace of his primitive wild-country nature surely persists through all this. He seems actually to have come into the city through his very natural association with weapons since the spears and shields of the Salii were sacred to him. The ways in which he became the war-god belong to the slow curious processes of the human spirit working through association and suggestion with a logic all their own.

Juno was another outstanding old Latin divinity. She eventually became the daughter of Saturn and wife and sister of Jove—a statuesque and ample figure of a woman much worshiped by women, with an especial concern for prospective mothers, a sort of divine Queen Guinevere. What she was gives scholars a joyous occasion for debate. Carter (as we have seen) makes her the feminine opposite of the masculine Genius—a woman's power to conceive and continue the race—the eternally feminine.[10] She was at least vague and hos-

---

[10] Fowler is inclined to agree with him, but adds that Dr. Carter told him he (Carter) had changed his mind about that explanation.

pitable enough to take on the general characteristics of Hera when that much tried goddess came to Rome and what she thereafter grew into was due to the ingenuity of the priest, the imagination of the poet and the sculptor's conception of full bosomed matronly beauty. Minerva was the third of the Etruscan three who were templed on the Capitoline. She was the goddess of handicraft and working men, which would indicate that she was the contribution of town living, hand working folk—a new element in Roman society.

Vesta was always there. She has been the inseparable comrade of the northern races, food-cooker, warmth-giver, making a little bright space walled by the dark into which love and life were gathered. The high-gods have come and gone but the mystic friendship of a whispering flame on the hearthstone endures. She has been the home-maker for humanity and, as her assuring nearness begins to be lost in the mechanism of our own complex world, something is gone which we do not yet know how to recapture.

The Greek cities built her an altar-hearth in the town-hall and kept it perpetually alight—a glowing symbol of communal life. Rome built her a little circular temple at the heart of Rome and consecrated six virgin priestesses to guard her fire there. They rekindled it on each first day of March by rubbing wood against wood, as though fire also must be reborn of its first parents and the sophisticated mistress of the world be taught how civilization began. The virgins themselves were to begin with only the unmarried daughters of the old Latin familia. They became in time an institution of state haunted by something older than any state—the hearth service of womanhood. There was never a statue of Vesta—who can carve a flame in stone?—but the broken statues of her priestesses still remain, voiceless witnesses to the one religion which has in it no constraint of fear—the bond of the hearthstone and the home.

WORSHIP AND RITUAL

What we have so far considered of Roman religion is rich in human ways, the general outcome of a devout and practical-minded people dealing with the potent and vague forces about them. The Greek brought such a system into a bright order by vividly human-izing his divinities. The Roman brought it into order by making an official ritual of worship out of it. That sentence would bear a deal of elaboration but it has the support of the specialist and is the key to the official Roman religious order. In view of the tenacious domination of Rome in the religion of the Western world, it is the key as well to great ranges of the development of Christianity. Rome recognized the right, law, obligation, relation (the august phrase jus divinum is almost impossible to translate) by which men and the gods are mutually bound. It was, on the legal side of it, a contract religion. Certain things must be done or left undone to keep the peace (pax) between the two parties—and they must be done according to rule. Fowler describes "the whole Roman religion of the city-state as a legal process going on continually."[11]

There was a kingly power in the priest and a priestly quality in the king. One does not find the jus divinum in any single code. It included every aspect of social religion. The deities must be placated and maintained in full force by sacrifice and prayer. All pledges made to the gods must be rigorously kept. City, land and people must be guarded against any kind of evil by the appointed rites of purification. The will of the gods—perhaps the most difficult task of all—must be discovered through such signs and omens as they were graciously minded to vouchsafe—and all this must be done at the "proper times and places by authorized persons skilled in the knowledge of the ritual." Now all this was a considerable and serious undertaking.

There was always an austere side to Roman religion. Their sacrifices were more somber than the Hellenic sacrifices, and the separate character of the priesthood much more in evidence. Nor is the sense of a common meal shared by the gods and their worshipers so strong in early Roman religion as it was in Greece or came afterwards to be in the Mysteries. Roman priests were chosen and set apart by ritual, personæ gratæ to the gods whom they served. There were gradations of rank among them with the Pontifex Maximus, high priest, at their head. Their vestments were in part or altogether red or purple—the symbolic color of blood sacrifice. (The vestals who sacrificed no animals wore white.) Their headdress was distinctive, they were the consecrated ones. The grave conduct of their sacrifices matched the sacredness of their office. The victims were chosen for their perfect fitness, they were led to the altar adorned with garlands

[11] *The Religious Experience of the Roman People*, page 170.

and ribbons, they must go willingly to the sacrifice and the omens must be right.

No word must break the solemn silence as the priests with veiled heads despatched the willing victim. The parts were disposed of according to ritual, enough going to the priests to provide food and some revenue. The sacrifices were always accompanied by prayer. A single phrase found in many ceremonies, "be glorified or strengthened" (macte esto) seems to indicate that the Romans shared the old Vedic belief that the prayers of men fostered the strength and glory of the gods. All very old faith attaches to prayer a magic power if only the right words be said—the Romans shared this. The metric structure of the earliest ritual prayers shows their recitation to have been accompanied by a dance. Upon its nobler levels Roman prayer was as prayer has always been, a simple and devout petition to the gods for their mercy and favor. But even that natural exercise of it is conditioned, the words used must be the approved words, the ritual be official.

VOTIVE DEDICATION

There are bound to be private priestless dealings with the gods in any religion. In Rome this took the form of vowing something to the proper divinity if only he do the right thing. Inscriptions on cups and vases show them to have been the grateful gifts of the devout and since cutting letters in stone is slow work, the formula which publicly witnessed that an honest-minded citizen had paid up willingly got reduced to the initial letters of the words—V. S. L. M. There is a moral value, Fowler holds, in such inscriptions cut in straggly Roman letters—they indicate a saving sense of gratitude.

The public vows were another matter, being a part of the covenant relation between the gods and the state. On stated occasions the consuls solemnly vowed the devotion of the state to Jupiter for another year "for the safety of the republic," and asked the divine favor in return. They were fair-minded about it; upon one occasion when the official form of words which besought the immortal gods to make the prosperity of the state "better and greater" was being repeated, the censor, Scipio Aemilianus, objected. The republic, he said, was already sufficiently prosperous and great. A similar modera-

tion might wisely characterize the official devotions of some other
republics. Of course, unusual situations were sure to call out all
sorts of votive promises. In the extremity of the Punic Wars the
people promised to devote to Mars or Jupiter all the new born—
including children—of a single spring. The undertaking has something of the quality of a legal document, with one or two shrewdly
drawn clauses, but it illustrates a quality of devotion, which for all
its bargaining, seeks the favor of a god through a great self-
renunciation.

Detail is tedious in this region, there is so much of it, though
there should be room for the really noble account of the General
who in the midst of battle, his army beginning to give way, prayed
the gods in words which majestically re-echo the power and faith
of Rome, to prosper their own and confound their enemies. He
vowed himself to the gods of the dead as the price therefor—and
rode alone into the enemy's ranks to pay his vow. So Regulus also
kept his faith to Rome and his pledged word to Carthage and went
back to death.

> As though some tedious business o'er
> Of clients' court, his journey lay
> Toward Venafrums' grassy floor
> Or Sparta-built Tarentus bay.

Making contracts with the gods is a delicate affair. The second
of the high-contracting parties is not always adequately represented
and the party of the first part is apt to write in both sides of the
agreement. After which, if things do not turn out well, the gods get
the blame. The Roman was usually respectful to his divinities even
when they disappointed him, but a long series of misfortunes tries
the faith even of the most devout; they will naturally turn to other
gods—if other gods are available—being persuaded that their own
are indifferent or do-nothing gods. The Greek had a happy saving
clause in his engagements with his divinities; he did not ask too
much of them, he knew that getting him a bigger and better Greece
was not their entire Olympian business. He was also a philosopher
with a saving sense of humor. There was no place for philosophy or
humor either in the Roman jus divinum, the very rigidity of it was
its strength and its danger.

New Gods Come to Rome

Roman religion was deficient in other ways. It lacked light and color, was emotionally arid, its divinities were always in danger of becoming abstractions, the relations of the human and divine were too largely official. "The Greek idea of men as the sons of gods, with all the intercourse and companionship which such a descent implies was . . . incomprehensible and terrible to the Roman mind."[12] If, then, a long period of misfortune should try Rome's faith in her old gods, one might confidently expect far-reaching changes in the austere faith of the republic. The changes came.

Careful students analyze the contributory causes with an attention to detail impossible here. The very structure of Roman society changed. The old order had been patrician—very much as if Rome were governed by the Latin equivalent of our own Society of Colonial Wars. The state priesthoods were limited to the patricians, the state was actually governed very much as eighteenth century England by great houses with their roots in the land. But a city set at the crossroads of the world can not maintain a patrician aloofness from the world.

There were Greek cities all along the southern coast of Italy; their clever traders and craftsmen began to move to Rome. The Roman himself began to be interested in trade and travel. A city growing in wealth and population needed things; the demand created the craftsmen and the craftsmen created the guild. The traveler came home to tell his neighbors about new gods, the alien citizens brought their gods with them. The republic still maintained the pomerium, the mystic line around the city no strange deity could cross. But how can you quite discover what forbidden merchandise a man brings through a city gate in his soul?

A never-ending procession of new gods began to come to Rome. Hercules came—a sun-god to begin with probably—a do-something deity, the god with the big-stick. They made him a shrine in the cattle market. Castor and Pollux came, cavalry gods of a dashing character agreeable to the soldiers of the Roman horse. Minerva came (Carter associates her with the Etruscan three), patroness of the craftsmen's guild. Fowler thinks her an old Italian divinity to

[12] Carter, *The Religious Life of Ancient Rome*, page 45.

whom the Etruscans added enough of Athena to make her in time
the Roman equivalent of that sage goddess. Diana came, chaste hunt-
ress and moon-slip of a woman. It was more a matter of changing
her name than her nature; she had long possessed, as a wood spirit
under another name, a place in the dim Roman pantheon. She was
thus quite ready to take over the richer personality of Hellenic
Artemis; Diana owed her position partly to the diplomacy through
which Rome was consolidating her power among the Latin tribes.

The new gods represented interests from which the Roman patrician kept apart and which the Latin farmer did not understand.
They belonged to the new Rome of trade, business and handicraft.
Something was needed to command the devotion of all the people
and set a splendid sign of national unity above the factions of the
narrow, crooked streets. Jupiter had been long in Rome, they now
rebuilt his temple on the Capitoline and built history into the rising
courses of its walls. Its foundations were Etruscan but the super-
structure was Rome—the Latin had at last asserted himself over the
Etruscan. They associated Juno and Minerva with Father Jupiter
but the goddesses became shadows there; Jupiter, the sky-god, universal and all seeing, reigned practically alone—not so much a new
god as the incarnation of a new force in the world.

THE INFLUENCE OF THE CARTHAGINIAN WARS UPON ROMAN RELIGION

The self-assertion of the Latin finished the first phase of Roman
history. The real genius of the race had freed and unified itself.
Now it was ready to challenge any competitor for the mastery of the
Mediterranean world—Carthage accepted the challenge. The issue
was long and desperately contended and more than once uncertain.
Such periods foster both doubt and superstition. It was like that in
Rome. Doubt turned the people against their own gods for whom
Hannibal seemed entirely too much. Superstition turned them with
an excess of belief toward new faiths.

It is as hard to account for the "Sibylline books" as for a modern
dream book. Such things grow out of formless superstitions, happy
coincidences and the misdirected ingenuity of the human mind. The
story is that the last Tarquin—who certainly did not profit by his
purchase—bought them from an old woman who wanted her price,
which would mean that some form of the Greek belief in inspired

oracles had got into Rome by the beginning of the fifth century B.C. We know that Apollo had had priestesses in Hellas by that time and the air was full of oracular sayings coming, in popular belief, from a mysterious woman in Asia Minor—the Mother Shipman of her time. Such sayings could easily get into a book,[13] the oracle could easily be located anywhere one pleased. She would as naturally suggest an inspired source of information to which the perplexed could turn. The World War years help us to understand that also. The Roman went to the medium instead of to church.

Now this would be like searching the mists for a shadow save for two pertinent facts. The whole notion of personal inspiration was alien to the established Roman order and, when admitted, it brought an entire alien order in with it. The habit of consulting the Sibylline books in any time of trouble grew. After an icebound winter, an unseasonably hot spring and a plague, the books were consulted by order of the Senate: result, something Rome never saw before—the images of six Greek divinities on couches before tables spread with food and drink. Apollo, Mercury and Neptune, the three who afterwards really counted, were rank outsiders about whom nobody but south Italy Greeks knew anything at all. Besides there were the images. This was making a show of religion and a direct appeal to that craving for a new sensation which eventually undid the austere simplicity of Roman life, drenched the sands of the arenas with blood and flowered poisonously in the decadence of the post-Augustan age. Emotion drenched rites and expiations began to take the place of the old jus divinum. The "peace of the gods" was broken, and never recovered.

The "Great Mother" Brought to Rome

Two hundred years B.C. the republic was again in great peril. Hannibal had been defeated but held his mountain fastnesses, there had been a ruinous hailstorm and the books were again consulted. This time they told the Senate that if the Great Mother of the gods were brought to Italy she would drive Hannibal out. Five men-of-war were sent to Asia Minor for the lady and came back with a shapeless stone—the Mother of the gods. She was received in state

[13] Fowler dates the permanent collections of the utterances into a book at 367 B.C. and makes Cumae the headquarters of the Italian cult.

at Ostia by Publius Scipio and a retinue of noble matrons who carried her in their arms through incense and crowded streets to the temple of victory. She was presented with gifts, the gods were given a banquet and there were games. Something more came to Rome than a shapeless stone in her following. The first of the oriental cults came with wild eunuch priests and brazen cymbals. The Orontes had begun to empty into the Tiber.

Rome became a world power and wealth came with empire. One discovers strange parallels to far more recent history. The Senators grew rich through the government of the provinces, the group below them through farming the taxes. Money demands an investment; there was nothing in which to invest save land and slaves. The small landholder was bought out, mortgaged out, crowded out. He went to Rome and joined the unemployed; social revolution followed, the demagogues corrupted the electorate, a professional soldiery was created and militarism entered history. The old priesthood lost its force, became the shadow of things ended. A political priesthood supplanted them, the temples fell into decay, deserted and vine covered monuments of the past. Private sacrifice was abandoned, the old religion of the hearthstone became only a memory. "Childless marriages became the rule and the sacrifices lapsed for lack of those who could carry them on."[14]

The extension of their power blinded the people to the decay of their ancient institutions while the necessities of "world politic" faced the Roman forces east. Macedonia had been an ally of Hannibal, Syria an ally of Macedonia. Greece was like over-ripe fruit ready to fall. The odds and ends of Alexander's Asian empire were at anybody's mercy and worth plundering—Rome and her politicians needed the plunder—and there was always Egypt. It was not easy however to move a war-weary people to new and remote wars of conquest. The Senate and the consuls found religion useful in this crisis, and began that way of using it for political and militant end which has since proved so successful. They handled the affair deftly. The gods were put on display and grain distributed at a quarter the cost. A season of prayer was ordered, the soothsayers reported that the prayers were heard and victory assured, the gravest

---

[14] Carter, *The Religious Life of Ancient Rome,* page 54. Ferrero's *History of Rome* is a fascinating study of the economic decay of Italy.

of the consuls assured the populace that war was the will of the immortal gods. The entire technique sounds a most familiar note.

The war prospered but religion suffered, not being meant, perhaps, to be used exactly so. The cynical held the opinion—also held later—that religion was extremely useful for controlling and directing a capricious electorate, but might be dispensed with if all men were really wise. A religion used to stir the popular emotions is bound to become increasingly emotional and credulous. Roman religion became just that. Rome conquered the East but the East followed the legions back and shared their triumphs. The passionate cults of Asia Minor, which sought communion with deity through intense emotional excitement, savage sacraments, and the questionable participation of women in their rituals were welcomed by a populace emotionally unstable and eager for any new sensation. There was a nobler and prophetic element in all this still to be considered, but for the time Rome had won the world and lost her soul.[15]

THE REFORMATION UNDER AUGUSTUS CAESAR: EMPEROR-WORSHIP

Then the clock of history struck a new hour. Augustus Caesar established his empire on the foundations Julius Caesar had laid. He knew the Roman mind shrewdly and, since everything was new, he took every care to honor the old. He began with the ruined, ivy grown temples. Rebuilt they would be shining signs for all the world to see that the ancient peace of the gods still held. A tenacious body of belief in the old gods, still alive, responded to his appeal. His revival was a real revival and secured the historic Roman religion three hundred years of life. The temples he built or rebuilt were Grecian in architecture—not the austere Doric but generally the flamboyant Corinthian, the gods they housed owed their characterization to Greek mythology. But no matter—the authority and administration were Roman.

Augustus did his work imperially. "I have rebuilt eighty-two temples," he tells us, being careful to add, "by the decree of the Senate." A lovely new temple for Apollo crowned the Palatine, the Forum became a pillared splendor, brick was everywhere changed to marble and Rome saw her glory incarnate and her future assured. The poets

---

[15] The association of games with the state religion dates from this period. But the Roman games had always a lower tone than the Greek games.

sang it as Shakespeare and his fellows sang of Elizabethan England and when, seven hundred and thirty-seven years after the founding of the city, a noble celebration was decreed to crown such high achievements and proclaim a new age for Rome and the world, Horatius Flaccus composed an ode which the school boys and girls sung,[16] and which school boys still translate. Meanwhile, a Jewish boy seventeen years old, in a distant Roman province had redated history in his birth—though neither Augustus nor Horace knew it.

After Augustus the entire Roman system locked up on emperor-worship. That was essentially non-Roman in spirit. It had come to Rome from the east before the Augustan age. It was an incarnation of the majesty, power and dominion of the empire in the person (first) of the dead emperors. The cult unified the empire spiritually and when one considers the elements which the state had to hold together—all the folk from north Britain to the Cataracts of the Nile—the need of some center of spiritual unity is plain. Jupiter, greatest and best, had been the religious keystone of the unity of the republic. Now Jupiter becomes only a name, being one god in Gaul and another in Egypt. But all the world knew Caesar. The ancient Latin conception of a man's genius was elastic enough to offer the conservative conscience a compromise.

One did not worship Caesar—only his Genius. If one worships the Genius of Caesar "dead and turned to clay" among the shades—surely a devout action—one can also worship the Genius of a very much alive Caesar. The whole affair belonged, to begin with, to the shadowy borderland between loyalty and worship. Augustus inaugurated it with the temple of god-Julius in the Forum where Julius Caesar's body had been buried. Thereafter it took its course. Now and then an emperor protested—"I confess that I am mortal, Conscript Fathers," said Tiberius, adding that he wanted no immortality save doing his duty. Later emperors were not so scrupulous. No phase of Roman religion made early Christianity more trouble; for the worship of the emperor was more than religion, it was the oath of allegiance to the state.[17]

---

[16] Forty years ago ancient inscriptions relating to these games were found and one may read "Carmen Composuit, Q. Horatius Flaccus."

[17] The "Emperor Cult" was a Hellenic contribution, the Orient collaborating. The idea of the god-man was congenial to the Greek mind and the heroic legend reinforced it. It took outstanding form in the dogma of the divinity of Alexander. Easy to move it all to Rome. See *Le Genie Grec, op. cit.,* pages 472 et seq.

STOICISM AND ITS PLACE IN ROMAN LIFE

There was also a religion of philosophy, the matured attitude of strong, independent minds toward life, its relationships and its issues. Rome ripened men of great intellectual force and high devotion to duty. Such men found little in the state religion to command their intellect, little in the Mysteries to command their moral support, and they had no intention of taking a shower bath of bull's blood in the caves of Mithras. They had only philosophy left and naturally looked to Greece for systems and sanctions. The Roman was not by nature a philosopher, he could only use other men's systems and not all of those.

In general Greek literature reached the citizens of Rome very much as French literature reaches New York, say, through the stage. (Mythology supplied the risqué equivalent of the novel.) The Roman comedian adapted Greek comedy to Roman audiences and the gods suffered in the process. But the cultured Roman of Cicero's time had the same feeling for Athens that we (in America) have for the literary and artistic shrines of Europe—some of Cicero's letters express that in a lovely way. Young men were sent to Greece to complete their education and the more thoughtful and sensitive were bound to be deeply influenced thereby.

But this is the story of religion and not of letters or philosophy and one may say in a word that the loftiest ranges of Greek speculation— the Platonic—escaped the Roman mind and temperament. Epicureanism on the whole did no more than supply a sanction for the pleasure-loving way into which the masters of the world had fallen, though Lucretius, its Latin poet, attacked the superstitions of his contemporaries in the name of Epicurus. He was the "humanist" of his time, eager to "burst the fast bars of nature's portals" and establish the supremacy of the free and instructed soul. Carter calls him one of the few Latin mystics.[18]

One line of Greek thought, however, not greatly fruitful in Hellenic soil, bore a really noble fruitage in Italy. It began, in Greece, with Diogenes in his tub—an acid excess of individuality and a quite complete return to nature. The cynic had soured on the general arti-

[18] *Religious Life of Ancient Rome,* page 60.

ficiality of his time. He was the classic debunker, but underneath[19] his mordant words and tempers he was feeling after reality. (The cynic often masks a sensitive and saddened spirit behind a mocking scorn—and takes his defeats to his tub.) Stoicism saw the inexorable limits of circumstance and the pity of illusion-led lives, but instead of running away from it all sought to transmute it "into the calm strength of a rational faith" and the brave conduct of life. It developed a supporting philosophy which has always needed only to be changed a little to become a noble religion.

The universe—said the Stoic—is one and reasonable, being shot through with a divine purpose. Man himself is the expression and instrument of this divine purpose, his task is to live bravely according to nature—which is right, and guided by his reason since the reason is the divine in man. A system like that slips easily over into pantheism, but if one puts God where the Stoic put "nature" he can say with St. Paul, "For we know, that to them, who love God all things work together for good," and nothing can undo us. The Roman genius laid hold strongly of the practical side of this system. The Stoic became the moralist of the empire.

There was no other source of moral teaching. "The priests of paganism were only, so to speak, the officers of the cult and limited themselves to their ceremonies. How could they have taught morals without denying Jupiter, Venus and all their gods?"[20] What conscience Rome had before Christianity was the creation of these teachers, the great names in Roman history illumine the Stoic gospel. They illumine also the shadowed periods of Roman history, having a force to maintain the citadels of their own spirits inviolate in the shock of civil war or the slow eclipse of the splendors of the empire. They sought in the noble words of Bossuet to detach themselves from the life of sense and pleasure and live "according to that divine and immortal part which is in us."

Seneca counseled his friends by the light of it, Epictetus found by that same light occasion to praise God though he was a poor, lame slave and Marcus Aurelius dealing with his own conscience on a lonely throne or the embattled outposts of the empire asserted his supremacy over circumstance. "But fortunate means that a man has

---

[19] Edward Caird, *The Evolution of Theology in Greek Philosophy*, Vol. II, lectures 16-20.
[20] Martha, *Les Moralistes Sous l'Empire Romain*, page 1.

assigned to himself a good fortune; and a good fortune is good disposition of the soul, good emotions, good actions." This assertion of
the supremacy of the soul is touched with sadness. All things grow
old, fall into decay and pass away—"smoke and ash and a tale, or
not even a tale." But why should a man complain? "Thou hast em-
barked, thou hast made the voyage, thou hast come to the shore;
get out."

> If my boat sinks 'tis to another sea.

A man should therefore bear himself as fit for immortality and
leave the issue to the eternal. "Depart then satisfied; for he also who
releases thee is satisfied." In his noblest moments of meditation
Marcus Aurelius was led—as Martha says—to the frontiers of Christianity. He lacked only a more sure sense of God and St. Paul's
mystic power to find the good will of God in all the changing circumstances of life. When the high light of what we call paganism
began to darken it died away, in the souls of the great Stoics, from a
very noble height.

THE PAX ROMANA

One must distinguish, of course, between the religion of Rome and
the empire. For three hundred religious years there was nothing but
the empire from Persia to Scotland. The Pax Romana created an
order in which frontiers ceased to exist. Roman toleration allowed
subject peoples to continue their ancestral worship, the Hebrew and
the Druid both sacrificed beneath the sovereignty of the Imperial
Eagles. An inevitable blending of cults and faiths followed. An
Egyptian could find his gods in Rome, a Roman his on the Nile. The
specialist calls this syncretism and any disentangling of its elements
is a subtle and endless task. One phase of it—the fusion of Hellenism
and Hebraism in Alexandria—has created a library of literature.

We have seen again and again in this study what universal elements any religion contains and how the gods change their names
rather than their natures. Put them all together for centuries under
one imperial order and they will weave a fabric of religion whose
crossed and recrossed lines can never be disentangled. The significance of all this for the history of religion is that, though there was

no religion in the changing classic world fit and formed to be a universal religion, the foundations for a universal religion were being laid.

The beginnings of the faith which was to inherit the empire were already in Rome by the middle of the first century A.D. and within less than a hundred years Rome felt the menace of it in strangely prescient ways. Thereafter, throughout the empire, one may write the story of the widening rise of Christianity if he is following one line, or the story of the slowly falling twilight of the Olympian gods if he is following another. Their bright beauty had long since felt the chill of their approaching eclipse.

The Mysteries supplanted them with those who sought some deliverance and communion with the Divine. Mithras took the army from Mars. The high-minded met circumstance with Stoic courage and sought a brotherhood, warmed a little with love, in human affairs; the forgotten folk of the empire found comradeship in guilds and fraternities which had a religious sanction. But the mighty fabric of the Roman state remained inviolate. The legionaries kept the frontiers, the official priesthood celebrated their sacrifices and kept their festivals. The temples, taking on the golden brown of old marble, stood open and unscarred, their worship supported by state revenues and guarded by the authority of the state. But those who used them were always fewer.

Then the state became nominally Christian. The final chapters of the end of paganism have the pathos of all great things doomed and reluctant to accept their doom. The last centuries of the empire witnessed a general improvement of morals, a flowering of high-mindedness with which the mind of the new religion, as revealed through its officials and doctrinal spokesmen, does not always favorably compare. It was as if Rome grown very old forgot the follies of her season of pleasure and power and, adding the grave wisdom of dearly bought experience to the dim prophecies of her youth, went out to meet her end like her Stoic emperor—master of her own soul—and unafraid. But Rome could not die.

The final conflict between Christianity and paganism took place around the altar and statue of Victory in the Roman Senate. State support had already been withdrawn from the official worship, the stipends of the priests and the Vestals had been allocated to the im-

perial postal service, the temple lands had been taken by the State.[21]
The temples were left open—just that and no more. Then the emperor Gratian undertook to remove the Statue of Victory from the
Senate Chamber. She had stood there since the time of Augustus,
inviolate, majestic, the incarnate genius of triumphs and battles. The
Senators had for centuries burned a grain of incense upon her altar
before they took their places, they had taken their oaths of allegiance
to successive emperors with their hands lifted toward the statue. She
was not marble, she was history and pride, all that made Rome
great—she was also a source of real embarrassment to a Christian
emperor.

Symmachus, a Senator, and Ambrose, Bishop of Milan, argued the
case. It was already prejudged but certain passages of the Senator's
speech have a noble and moving quality as though dipped in the
"tears of things." He was for the time the voice of the city from
whose walls Hannibal had been turned back, through whose gates
Caesar and Vespasian had come in. He was the voice also, though he
did not know it, of the carefree gods in the city of Olympus, the
nymphs in little rivers, Pan with his pipe on the hillsides, and all
the pagan sense of a world in which beauty is the gift of the gods
and the senses their harp-strings. For all these were in the shadows
behind Symmachus. They lost their case—great Pan was dead.

After that the events moved quickly. In 391 A.D. Valentinian forbade his pagan subjects to make their sacrifices, enter the temples,
worship the images. A little later the prohibitions were extended to
the ancient altars of Vesta and the Lares; not a garland could be
hung on the door posts, not a grain of incense be burned in the
hearthstone fire. After that nothing was left. The temples were
empty, their gildings gathered dust, the gods had only the owls for
company. In 410 A.D. Rome opened its gates to an enemy for the first
time in eight hundred years and the Alaric went in. Strangely
enough he used the Salt Road gate, the oldest road to Rome. Thirty
years later the Vandals plundered the desolate mistress of the world.
Meanwhile Augustine had written the "City of God." But what
Lucan sang of Pompey was true in a vaster sense of Rome, "His
spirit could not rest in the glowing embers, nor scanty ashes contain
that mighty shade."

[21] Boisser, *Le Fin Du Paganisme*, Tome I, pages 259 et seq. Gibbon's chapter on the
Final Destruction of Paganism tells the same story very nobly. Boisser's chapter and
Gibbon's supply also admirable studies in the contrast of French and English styles.

The Twilight of the Gods

THE procession of the gods westward from the grassy plain ended in the mist and deeply shadowed forests of the north. It was long in ending; the Sky-God ruled the Teuton for a thousand years after he had lost the classic world, Thor still hurled his hammer at the Frost Giants while the bells of Notre Dâme called Paris to Mass, but it ended. The general relation between levels of religious conceptions and culture levels is now a commonplace— the one conclusion of Tylor's school which has not since been questioned. A religious genius like Zoroaster—or the prophets generally —may break through the level of his time with a higher conception and lift religion with him; but he still leaves his world the painful task of growing up to him and a good deal of what he gives it is pulled down to that world's general level and sadly colored by it. His present stones him, the future builds his monument, what Mohammed calls "the steep" is slow and hard to climb.

Polytheism belongs not so much to a fairly low level of civilization and intelligence, for Polytheistic Greece was rich in culture and intelligence, as to its own level of what a coiner of golden phrases has called "imaginative dominion over experience." When religious imaginative insight began to unify the powers which manifest themselves in the universe and find in them the Power which so manifests itself, the "half gods" go. The Olympians were already taken with a mortal sickness before Christianity challenged them. Did not a voice from the island of Paxis command an Egyptian sea-farer to announce "the Great Pan is dead"? When Pan is dead no medicine can save Zeus.

The older conclusions about family trees of the north European races are just now much questioned and the earlier conclusions about their religion are equally questioned. But I think it is safe to say that idealized forms of nature worship did persist in Northern Europe until they gave way to Christianity and the old Aryan divinities of the sky and the storm found their last stronghold there. They suffered many changes in their long migration. The imagination peculiar to any race and time has always supplied the gods their garmenture. The Greeks peopled the olive groves with maidens of immortal youth, lovely to be desired and gave the deities on Olympus such diversions as the Greek himself loved.

The poets of the north made Valhalla the abode of heroes who fought gloriously and drank deep and woke to fight and drink again —which are possibly the diversions the Teuton loved, and yet the myths of the north have in them an art which the Greek myths never had. They are the twilight of religion and the dawn of literature, the prelude to the noble and many toned music of the poetry of the northern races. Northern paganism had a somber quality southern paganism never had. There the spirits of the dead are fearsome things, their Hel, older than any Valhalla—for the bards invented that—is dark and dismal. If the dead take boat and go west their destination is no sunbright land but an island lost in the mist, the tears of the living fall "bloody, dark, cold, chilly, fraught with sobs" upon their breasts.[1] Or else they ride across the sky with Odin and his Furious Host so that one may hear them crying in the winter winds.

Yet one discovers through and behind the artless art of the bard and the far more significant folk lore of the north the persistence of the dawn faiths—that all the workings of nature are caused by personal agents. There is little, if any, of primitive spiritism left in the fully developed northern mythology and it is all highly poetized. The engaging conceit that Hoder, the blind winter god, was tricked by Loki—god of fire possibly and mischief certainly—into slaying Balder the summer god, lacks the convincing simplicity which attends the old ritual.

Odin (there are many ways of spelling his name) was the head of the pantheon, but the conceptions of him have the inconstancy of the northern sky. "He is god of the wind, of agriculture, of war, of poetry,"[2] or he is the sky itself. He is lord of Valhalla, old and tall and one-eyed, he wears a broad brimmed hat, a cloak of many colors, he rides a dapple gray horse Sleipner of most curious breeding.[3] Two ravens perch upon his shoulder and report to him what men say and do. They are always flying out and coming back:

---

[1] De la Saussaye, *The Religion of the Teutons,* Boston, 1902, page 295.

[2] Saussaye, *op. cit.,* page 224.

[3] See R. B. Anderson, *Norse Mythology,* Chicago, 1898, page 225, for the detail.

Hugin and Munin
Fly each day
Over the spacious earth,
I fear for Hugin
That he come not back,
Yet more anxious am I for Munin.

Two wolves attend him, he wears a wonderful ring and carries a spear which never misses the mark. The somewhat sophisticated symbolism of all this is plain—the colored cloak is the blue-gray vault of the sky and his eye the sun, Odin was likely a wind god to begin with, his various attributes and furnishings being thus best explained. Thor comes next with the hammer which always comes back to his hand, the implacable enemy of the frost giants, protector of men and the lesser gods and always the thunder god. The poet loved him for his deeds and furnishings, the warrior loved him for his valor and common folk loved him because he ended northern winters and rode up with the rains. It is not always easy in the abundance of Thor lore to distinguish between the earth-born nature myths and the poets' embroidered contributions. Malory's endless winding tales of the heady exploits of Arthur's Knights are colorless alongside Thor's gorgeous fighting, and the bard's way of telling them—

Laughed then Thor's
Heart in his breast;
Severe in mind
He knew his hammer,
First slew he Thrym
The king of giants,
Crushed them all
That race of giants;

Slew the old
Sister of Thrym
She who asked
For a bridal gift;
Slap she got
For shining gold,
Hammer blows
For heaps of rings;

Thus came Odin's son
Again by the hammer.[4]

Tyr (or Tiu) is more likely to have been old Dyaus, the Aryan sky-god than any other in the Teutonic pantheon. He lives in the calendar—Tuesday is his day—but has no prominent character in the myths. This, I should think, is proof that he is far from home and the recollection of their ancestral skies grown dim for those who worshiped him. And yet in that strangest and most fearsome of myths—when the wolf Fenris shall at last break the chain which binds him—a chain forged out of the sound of the footfalls of cats, the beards of women, the roots of mountains, the sinews of bears, the breath of fish and the spittle of birds—and go out ravening to destroy men and the gods, it is Tyr who will kill him and himself be killed. Father Sky is the last defense, as he was the first source of the gods. When he is gone nothing is left.

There are groups of lesser gods, who represent confused and shifting phases of nature action, in the shadows behind the great celestial divinities. The nature cults of the north were always austere, the murky passion of the eastern fertility cults disappears before the breath of cold mist burdened winds, Ishtar and Astarte found few sanctuaries among the oak and pine. Freyr-worship has a trace of the deification of the procreative power. Frigg, the wife of Odin, is the wisest and most respectable of matrons, Freyja is less discreet and consequently more desired, but the allure of Aphrodite is gone with the temples of Paphos and the doves who loved to nestle in the roundure of her bosom. The women who haunt the northern pantheon are battle goddesses who ride down helmeted to the strife, protectors of heroes who bear the souls of the slain up to Valhalla riding the winds. There is also a flight of swan maidens through the old tales who, if they can be caught out of their swan-shift, make any man a most desirable bride—though hard to keep.

. . . . .

The Norns are the three fates of the north—they continue the haunting human instinct that a man's fate is woman made. They are variously named but they are always at the cradle side weaving

[4] Anderson, *op. cit.*, page 335. Anderson's philosophy of myths would not be accepted by the modern school, but his wealth of material and vivid narration are pure joy.

the destiny of the new born. They are capricious in their gifts, giving much to some and little to others, laughter or tears as they please.

> In the mansion it was night;
> The Norns came,
> Who should the prince's
> Life determine,
>
> .   .   .   .   .
>
> With all their might they spun
> The fatal threads.

There is no end to the vivid poetry, deeply moralized of the faith of the north. The world tree Ygdrasil grows through it, the last grandiose expression of a conception common to many religions. The tree of life was, Barton believes, the palm in Chaldea; it becomes an ash in the north, nations are its branches, humanity its leaves, it strikes its roots through all the world down into the serpent world. Mimir's fountain of wisdom is beneath one root of it. The serpent Nidhug gnaws another root—death is always gnawing at the root of life.

Loke (or Loki), is neither entirely the personification of some force in nature nor the sheer creation of a poet's invention. He is what the somber north has always felt of the mischief and mischance of life, the incalculable element too vast and vague to furnish a manageable thread to any Norn. He may have been fire to begin with, old Agni the comrade of Dyaus in millennial migrations but, if he is, it is curious that while Greece and Rome subdued fire to the human needs of the hearthstone, the north magnified the destructive caprices of it and made it the force which baffles and undoes. Loki is not the "spirit that denies" so much as the spirit which mocks, the element which mixed with any craft or enterprise robs it of complete perfection. There is no calculating his caprice. He thwarts the gods and then saves them from the situations he has created. His laughter is the vast sardonic laughter which has had long echoes in northern literature, the laughter which Heine heard on his mattress grave, the laughter of the trapper at the trapped. Only the Teuton or the Slav could ever have created Loki.

In the myth of Balder, one of the most richly poetic of them all, Loki is the villain. It is a rehearsal of the death and recovery of

life in the northern year. Behind it is the shadow of a colder dark
than a sunless Norwegian winter, the twilight of the gods themselves. Dark fate rimmed the bright Hellenic horizon, the doom
of the terrestrial and celestial order darkened the Teutonic sky. All
things are perishable, even the gods. In their conception of the final
issue the people of the north saw through their mists a vision the
south never caught—save perhaps in the Stoics' idea of the return
of the Age of Gold, they saw the triumph of some vaster force than
Thor and Odin in the regeneration of the world. They saw it as
Francis Thompson saw it:

> I dimly guess what Time in mist confounds,
> Yet ever and anon a trumpet sounds
> From the hid battlements of Eternity,
> The shaken mists a space unsettle then
> Round the half-glimpsèd turrets slowly wash again.

Their haunting sense of the imperfection of all created things is
half the key to this, their high-hearted persuasion that the vast
processes of their world could not issue in futile defeat is the other
half. They lived divided in their own souls in a world of endless
strife, they sought an end to life's disharmonies, they reached

> To where beyond these voices there is peace.

Their drama of last things takes on an unequaled grandeur. The
Fenris-wolf will break his mystic chains and the Midgard serpent
drive the sea across the land, the ship of the dead, made of the
nails of dead men and finished at last, will be the only craft afloat.
Ygdrasil trembles to the last hidden roots of it, the gods ride out to
their last great battle, fire breaks out from the caverns where it has
been shut up.

> The sun darkens,
> The earth sinks into the ocean;
> The lucid stars from heaven vanish;
> Fire and vapor
> Rage toward heaven;
> High flames involve the skies.

Wagner has made the tragic splendor of all this articulate in his
stormy music but no stage can supply the setting. The regeneration
of the world is less vividly conceived, they saw the battlements of

the Eternal only through the mists of time—yet they saw them touched with light.

> She sees arise
> The second time,
> From the sea, the earth
> Completely green;
>
> .   .   .   .   .
>
> The fields unsown
> Yield their growth;
> All ills cease;
> Balder comes.

The gods could ask no more splendid apotheosis than that.

Beyond the Roof of the World

W E CAN not understand history save as we see it in some relation to religion; we can not understand religion save as we see it in relation to migrant races and the rise and fall of cultures. Like the clouds across the sky and their shadows across the fields, the two go on together. Nor can their movements be so separated that one can say, this or that was first. Men have always said to their gods—as Ruth to Naomi—"Do not press me to leave you, to turn back from following you; for wherever you go, I will go; and wherever you lodge I will lodge," and so the gods for all their godhead might seem to say to men, while from the grave-yards of dead faiths and vanished races one may hear the faint and final confession of their indissoluble destiny: "Wherever you die, I will die, and there will I be buried."

The whole difficult matter of racial character and racial movement is therefore tied up in one bundle with any study of religion. This involves geography as geography involves the contours of the continents, rivers and their valleys, mountain barriers and the passes through them, sea-washed shores and the harbors which indent them, earth roads and water roads, and all that we mean by climate. Race again is shaped or changed by migration, migration is controlled by economic conditions, the fecundity of races and their native restlessness and capacity for adventure. Economic conditions change with changing climatic conditions. It all seems an endless chain, and religion—always—is enmeshed in the links of it.

. . . . . .

Something of this we have already seen. The valleys of the Nile and the Two Rivers nurtured the gods of Egypt and Babylon. The folk of the grassy plain setting out upon their long and fateful journeys won for their gods half of Asia and the whole of Europe. Save for their passage through the passes of the Himalayas they followed always the westering sun. The West was for them the call of destiny and they acknowledged no barriers of land or sea till by way of the West they had returned upon the East again. You may call it destiny if you will; the specialist has a more prosaic explanation. The open roads, he says, were always toward the West. They went west because the roof of the world shut them away from the East.

They have had the freedom of five of the seven seas—but the uplands of Asia and the littorals of the Pacific belonged to other races. And yet between the roof of the world in Asia and the shores and islands of the Pacific there was a seventh or eighth of the habitable globe and always folk enough to fill it, mostly too full. It would in the end turn out easier for the West to go east by sea and until they had ships and sailors to do it—the East for its own undoing furnishing them a mariner's compass—the Far East would be there alone, between the roof of the world, its own coastal seas and the long surges of the Pacific; alone while historic time grew old.

Its folk had been there alone so long before any history other than their own legendary history of themselves began, that no one can tell, nor they themselves save in legend, where they came from or how their ancestors entered and possessed the land. Some specialists in human origins solve that problem simply: the human race, they say, originated on the eastern slope of the roof of the world. That leaves the problem in reverse—how then did we get west? It's all a puzzle.

What made the races so different is also a puzzle, but the fact remains.[1] It is now held that a "pure race" is wishful thinking. We have all been cast and recast in the melting pot, but Huntington recognizes eight main types and two of these belong to the roof of the world and beyond. The significant thing is that, having been there alone so long and having a great native force, they would develop their own civilization. Their strength would be in their endurance to outlive famine and flood and make good their population losses with an immense fertility.

They inherited no great gift for speculation, they loved old, slow, solid ways, but they had an almost unbelievable capacity for toil, a deft and patient touch to make a great art of little things, every phase of which was stamped with their own genius, the genius of

[1] Ellsworth Huntington, *The Character of Races*, Charles Scribner's Sons, New York, 1924, is a fascinating attempt to solve the puzzle.

their race and their aloneness. Their religion, therefore, would be native to their soil as they were, matured with little change through millenniums as they were. They too would find the material of their religions in dealing with earth and sky, as all races, but when they had shaped its pattern, that would be different as their art was different. A Grecian urn and a Chinese vase may both be clay but each race has made of the clay something else—so of their religion.

· · · · ·

It is, of course, entirely untrue to say that there were no roads across the roof of the world. There were. The trader used them or else he made them. Some of the enviable fellowship whose motto is "for to admire an' for to see" must always have used them. They were not good for armies to move over and the conqueror stayed at home. He left them to the traders, to the missionary who will always follow a trail with souls at the end of it and the philosopher who, being used to very high roads, makes nothing of the roof of the world.

Chinese intellectuals went down into India to see what they could of that world and its faiths and brought back sound reports still useful. The Buddhist missionary followed them and in the end reached Japan. The ancient peoples received this new faith and set their own stamp upon it, as they have upon all importations. Europe did not know for centuries that this had happened—nor much else about the Far East. A Marco Polo made a brave narrative of high adventure; the Franciscan missionaries went and came home; the eastern gates stayed shut—and the roof of the world barred the west. So oriental religion, art and culture and steadfast races with skin, hair, color and language alien to the Aryan and all his inheritance took their immemorial way. And the people beyond the roof, having none other to ask about faith, questioned earth and sky, therefrom received their answers and of those answers and their own wisdom made their faiths.

CHAPTER XI

Confucianism: The Religion of Heaven

THERE are now in the Freer Museum in Washington two pieces of jade cut and polished when the world was very young. They are lovely in their cool, smooth green, worn smooth by much reverent handling, marred a little by time but not much. They are very simple; one is a disk, perhaps half an inch thick and four inches in diameter perforated at the center by a circle an inch in diameter, a little solid jade wheel. The other is two inches square, six inches long turned with square shoulders to cylindrical ends and bored through from end to end with a circle. It is also grooved on the sides perhaps to indicate strata. They are Heaven and Earth.

The little jade heaven is plain enough being the horizon encircled firmament with the sun at the center of it. The earth symbol is not so evident, though the Chinese believed the earth was square and the terminal cylinders might be the great altars of earth and heaven. These are among the oldest religious symbols in the world and they have the essential quality of the faith they symbolize, clean cut, cool to the touch, simple, weighty and touched with the awesome vastness of the unity of the universe. Since there has been any recorded history, China has worshiped Heaven and Earth and, though the altar of Heaven is just now desolate, it gathered about it in the memory of those still living the pride and devotion of an empire. Time, geography and race have combined to create that worship, and, very greatly, time.

THE ANTIQUITY OF CHINA

The Chinese claim for themselves a staggering antiquity. A conservative chronicle dates Confucius 2,267,000 years after creation; the more generous reckon the first man P'an-Ku to have finished his really gigantic task ninety-six million years ago. He was both creator and the stuff out of which the earth was formed. He sepa-

325

rated heaven and earth (there is an echo of Egyptian lore in this), cut away the masses of the firmament till the sun and moon and stars shone through, labored for eighteen thousand years and grew in stature and bulk as he toiled. He perfected his task by his death: "His head became mountains, his breath wind and clouds, his voice thunder . . . his flesh the fields, his beard was turned into stars, his bones into metals; his dropping sweat increased to rain, and lastly the insects which stuck to his body were transformed into people."[1] (The Babylonian epic of creation celebrates a parallel use of the body of the dragon Tiamat.)

The legendary histories follow the completion of P'an-Ku's work with the Three August Periods—The Reign of Heaven, during which the heavens were actually formed, the Reign of Earth during which the earth was shaped and ordered, and the Reign of Man during which it was properly populated. Ten periods of ascent follow the Reign of Man, wherein the growth of Chinese civilization from the caveman to the sage is dimly seen through a wealth of legend and exaggeration. Dependable tradition begins about 3000 years B.C. China is very old.

Dr. Ellsworth Huntington is quite content to begin Chinese history with the Ice Age. He makes an especial study of China in his brilliant interpretation of racial character and force in terms of climate and physical geography. The glacial epochs, Huntington maintains, created all the conditions favorable to a process of natural selection and mixed Europe, Asia and Africa in a human melting pot. But, since China was never glaciated, the ice sheets affected that celestial kingdom in reverse, so to speak. The conditions which buried Europe in ice through a period which years have little meaning to date, through an excess of rainfall, made the arid regions of Asia more habitable. Population naturally increased in these regions through both immigration and a high birth rate. At the close of the glacial epochs, the uplands of Central Asia became arid again, the surplus population was compelled to move out and, having nowhere elso to go, they followed the three great Chinese rivers seaward.

[1] S. Wells Williams, *The Middle Kingdom*, Vol. II, page 139, quoted in *An Outline History of China*, H. G. Gowen, page 21.

The Land Made Its History

The map of China is the key to this history. The Yellow River, the Willow River and the Pearl River drain the roof of the world. If one draws a line due northeast by north from Mount Everest to the top of Manchuria, a line 2600 miles long, substantially every tributary to the three rivers rises east or southeast of it. Behind it is a territory of at least 1,700,000 square miles which has belonged to the Chinese Empire in its peak periods of sovereignty. The few rivers of this vast region never reach any sea; they lie across a map like broken threads, they are lost in arid reaches, empty into salt lakes. Such regions are always the nursery of nomad races; archæologists, whose opinions carry weight, believe that the Desert of Gobi was the nursery of the human race.

These arid uplands bred populations of "black-haired people"—so the classic Chinese histories describe their race—which they were not able to support. Any continued unfavorable change in climate was sure to release a horde of them, hungry for land and bread, with that power for swift fierce conquest which the desert gives the nomad. They came down upon agricultural eastern China as the rivers come down in flood. Drouth, invasion, conquest, flood and famine have combined to reduce China periodically to an anarchy from which only a people with an enormous power of passive resistance and strong racial force could recover. The essential strength of the population has actually been renewed in these tragic baptisms, through the infused vigor of the conquerors—but the cost in human life and order has been enormous.

These cycles of Chinese history have given an unequaled quality of patient endurance to the Chinese character. China is an anvil which has worn out many hammers; the conquerors themselves have been subdued by what they won. It is hard to wear down 300,000,000 people who are so frugal that they will cultivate a piece of land a tablecloth would cover and who make a religion of parenthood. Professor Giles says, "if the Chinese people were to file one by one past a given point, the interesting procession would never come to an end. Before the last man of those living today had gone by, another and a new generation would have grown up, and so on forever and ever.[2]

Thus for almost fifty centuries of remembered or recorded history China has carried on between the roof of the world and the four seas. The names of her eighteen provinces have the spaciousness of the four quarters of the compass, East and West, North and South. Her rulers are remembered by dynasties. Her art has been so perfect that a few of its porcelains and jades enrich any museum. Her civilization was matured before the walls of Rome were built. Her mandarins wore jackets embroidered with gold while our ancestors painted themselves with woad. Her silks enriched the traders whose caravans followed roads, now blocked, from the Mediterranean to the Yellow Sea. Her ports lured the sailor folk of centuries whom she furnished a compass by which to find them. The loot of her palaces has enriched the barbarian of the North and the armies of the West. For millenniums her desert hinterlands, mountain-walled, shut her in upon herself and she maintained her culture and habits inviolate.

What of her faith and her soul? Something besides climate, geography and natural selection has shaped a race like that.

A RELIGION MODELED AFTER THE UNIVERSE

The difference between the religions of China and India is the difference between the uplands and the jungle and yet each is a religion of the universe. The universe, for the Indian sage, was woven, warp and woof, upon Brahma. The soul-self became the only reality, Brahma the World Soul, and individuals only bubbles of the sea of his being. All else was an illusion, the universe in all its reach and splendor only a dream. For the Chinese sage the universe was order. He was not concerned—though this is a bitterly contested point—with the mystery it both reveals and hides; he was concerned with its methods and its processes. There is a general agreement that this is the tap-root of Chinese religion, though religion is too loose a word for the whole system which is at once a faith, a philosophy and a discipline of life.

From seven hundred to four hundred B.C. three Chinese sages,[3] Lao-

---

[2] Quoted by Gowen, *op. cit.,* page 14. The paragraphs take on a new significance in the light of events in the Far East in 1934 and 1935.

[3] DeGroot, *Religion in China,* Putnam, 1912, page 6 et seq.

Tze, Chwang and Kwan[4] gave this system the classic form, in which, modified by Confucius, it still exists. A name was supplied for it in a writing which DeGroot calls "the canon of Tao and virtue." Virtue is plain enough, though Chinese virtue has its own distinctive qualities, but what is Tao? DeGroot defines it as the Road or Way— "The Road or Way in which the universe moves . . . the Order of the World, Nature or Natural Order. The universe has a "Way" then. It is no illusion but a vast and sovereign process, the procession of the seasons, growth and decay and all the mutations of life and things, set in the frame of time, the creator and the destroyer. India chose from all this such gods and goddesses as might be kind to any impulse of the worshipers and in worshiping them the devotee deified his own desire. China sought to subdue its own will and mind to the will and mind of the universe and made a virtue of obedience.

There is an arresting parallel between the philosophy of the Stoic —the high discipline in which Marcus Aurelius schooled himself on the throne of the Roman Empire—and the virtue in which the Chinese Sage sought to mature his soul. The Stoic spoke of the laws of nature, the Sage of the Tao of the universe. Both in the end meant the same thing. Neither had a sure sense of a controlling personality behind the natural order. The Stoic believed that "all things are implicated with one another and the bond is holy; . . . for there is one Universe made up of all things and one god who pervades all things," but this god was dimly seen and often doubted.

The universe whose "Way" the Chinese sage sought to discover and obey was an "animate universe which imposed its will (upon him) imperiously and irresistibly," but his sense of what animated the universe was dim. He might have said, as the stoic Emperor said, "Do not look around thee to discover other men's ruling principles but look straight to this, to what nature leads them, both the universal nature—and thine own nature . . . I go through the things which happen according to nature until I shall fall on the

---

[4] Full name Kwan-Tsze-Ching or-T-uw. Troublesome things these Chinese names. A specialist who ignores a sage under one name bows to him under another. This Kwan wrote a voluminous book probably in the seventh century B.C. which, DeGroot thinks, "would actually carry the existence of Taoism up to the dawn of the reliable history of East Asia." *Religion in China, op. cit.,* page 28. Actually the current of China's religion carries many very ancient elements. These were in the 6th century differentiated into the Confucian-Taoist streams.

rest—," with this one difference; the Emperor believed that reason was his only guide; the Sage, that virtue was living as "perfectly as possible in accordance with the Tao of the universe."

There remained only to find out what the "Way" of nature was and frame the laws through obedience to which the favor of nature is secured for the individual and the state. In the most inclusive way Chinese religion is the worship of Heaven and Earth and is always propitiatory. Religion is therefore only one aspect, though a very important aspect of the "system" by which the whole structure of Chinese society is veined; in fact, China has been the "system" in action for at least three thousand years. It needs patience to analyze it and more patience to follow through even its mass detail. But this chapter has no value without doing just that.

THE RELIGION OF HEAVEN AND EARTH: THE TWO SOULS

Heaven is more than the firmament. The religion of Heaven is neither pure sky-worship nor sun-worship. Heaven is the positive and fructifying force in the universe; it is warmth, light and the favor of Nature's way. It is also the male part of the universe, the beneficent cosmic soul, the Yang. The earth is the female part of the universe. (This belief in Mother Earth and Father Sky is an almost universal article in ancient creeds—only Egypt made Earth the father.) The Earth, the other cosmic soul, is cold and darkness, the Yin. These two are the Way and the Law of the universe, its Tao. All birth and death, all growth and decay, all winter cold and summer warmth, seasonal procession and terrestrial response are their combinations and mutations. The universe, said the Sage, is woven upon immutable order. Yang is the warp of it. Yin is the woof of it. Tao is the whole of it. Tao is to China what Brahma was to India and God to Judea, Islam and the Christian West. It is man's task to imitate the "Way" of Heaven and Earth; that is his way, Tao, to happiness.

He is native to it himself, being born of the union of Heaven and Earth, incorporating the essential nature of each. China thus explains that duality of human nature, its contradictions and embattled entanglements which have been the perplexity of the philosopher and the agony of the saint. China has one great psalm of perplexity but no literature of inner struggle. Since man is born of Heaven and Earth, he has two souls—an Earth-soul and a Heaven-soul. The Earth-soul is his Kwei, the Heaven-soul is his Shen. The sages do not explain how these two souls are fused in one consciousness, but they know that when a man dies his Earth-soul returns to Mother Earth through the slow decay of flesh and bone, while his Heaven-soul returns to that which gave it "to move on high as a shining light." This sense of the earth-born and the heaven-born in man taking their separate ways at death has supplied a motif for a sad music of mortality. "Then shall the dust return to the earth as it was; and the spirit shall return unto God who gave it." But the Chinese preacher had his own committal service; Shen to Yang and Kwei to Yin.

All the beings of the world have in them some particle of the Heaven-soul and the Earth-soul. These divide themselves into innumerable parts which together constitute an endless tide of being. They flow out in creation, they are reabsorbed in the dissolution of what they have, for a season, animated. They act of themselves, they need no law but their own "Way." The universe is crowded with them, they animate even inanimate objects. There is a residue of animism in this of course. DeGroot says, "The primeval form of the religion of the Chinese, and its very core to this day is Animism." "It is based," he says, "on an implicit belief in the animation of the Universe, and of every being or thing which exists in it." And yet it is Animism or Spiritism with a difference. It begins with the belief in an animated universe, the whole comes before the parts. There is no indication in most authorities that China ever began with little local spirits, thing spirits, water spirits, tree spirits —what one will—and built the steps of its particular—

> . . . great world's altar stairs,
> Which slope thro' darkness . . .

up to an animated universe—and, maybe, up to God out of them. China began at the top of the stairs and came down, or else the stairway was built so long ago that there is no memory of climbing it.[5]

[5] This needs qualification. Ancient Chinese religion, says F. E. A. Krause, was derived from observation of nature and man's dependence upon it and theories of the soul and beliefs respecting the dead. Hence, worship of nature and ancestor-worship. He thinks there was an ancient-worship of gods of the soul, heavenly bodies, mountains, rivers, trees, rock and the like. Taoism was all this universalized

DID OLD CHINA FIND ONE GOD?

But what did China find at the top? Was Chinese religion ever monotheistic? John Ross, Scotch missionary, thinks it was. (Unfortunately, the publishers omitted to date his book *The Original Religion of China*, but since he was "United Free Church" the book must be fairly contemporaneous.) The most ancient classics, he contends, use the Chinese words for "Heaven" and "Supreme Ruler" interchangeably throughout to denote the One God and only Supreme Ruler over heaven and earth. He documents this conclusion pretty solidly with quotations from the histories and the odes to prove that "Heaven" or the "Supreme Ruler" is recognized as seting up and dethroning kings, that its decrees are immutable and just, and that by It kings rule and rulers decree justice.

Dr. James Legge, sometime professor of Chinese language and literature at Oxford, is a recognized authority. His careful study of primitive Chinese characters supports Ross. Characters which mean "lordship" and "government" impersonally become personal and individual when "Supreme" is added and the personal and impersonal are used interchangeably. "Heaven was to the Chinese fathers, I believe, exactly what God was to our fathers. Whenever they took the great name upon their lips, . . . the two characters show us the religion of the ancient Chinese as a monotheism.[6] DeGroot does not support this conclusion. If the old China religion was monotheistic then it touched that land with a lonely splendor of faith; it was the first monotheism.

A primitive Chinese monotheism parallel to the faith of the Hebrew prophet and psalmist is improbable. The entire range of underlying speculation is against that conclusion. But the idea of an animated "Heaven" controlling human destiny is a noble idea, and plastic enough to take its meanings not from curious Chinese characters but from the mind and temper of those who use it. The meanings of religion must always be sought in the awesome emotions and suppliant needs which lift—

> . . . from out of dust
> A voice as unto him that hears.

but never personalized. Religion and philosophy are merged. Clemen, *Religions of the World*, Harcourt Brace, N. Y., 1931, Chapter III.

[6] James Legge, *The Religion of China*, Oxford, page 11.

They are strangely constant. By such tests all prayers become akin; any praise sounds the same note. Psalmist, prophet, and sage may appeal, in words carrying the same burden, to a supreme power, and yet it may be a far cry from the God of the devout Christian missionary to the Heaven of the Chinese classics.[7]

A SPIRIT-HAUNTED UNIVERSE

DeGroot's careful analysis bears this out. The universe is both automatic in its action and spirit-filled and spirit-controlled. These spirits ranging from the high-gods to the bean-curd god are not the servants of the Most High, "ministers of His that do His pleasure." They are emanations of the Yang and the Yin, heaven and earth, light and darkness, warmth and cold, the friendliness and hostility of the universe. The friendly spirits serve the needs of men; the spirits of darkness are mischief-makers; but between them they make the world what it is.

The Chinese actually found a moral use for the unfriendly spirits; they keep men straight through fear. Also they belong to the Tao— the Way of the Universe—very uncomfortable realities, but not to be affronted. The sense of a sovereign order so constituted captured the Chinese imagination. "How bountiful," said Confucius, "is the beatific work of the Kwei and the Shen! We look for them, but we do not see them; we listen for them, but we do not hear them; they incorporate themselves in every being and everything without exception. They cause all people under heaven to fast and purify themselves. . . . When they offer their sacrifices, they, like an ocean, seem to be over their heads and to their left and right."[8]

Since everything, animate or inanimate, being nothing else than a part of the animated universe, has its good spirit or evil, the Shen and Kwei are everywhere. The gods are the "good spirits" of anything one pleases, the celestial bodies, the sky pageantry, mountains and rivers, the furnishings of the Earth. The demons are equally

[7] There are very early folk-songs of thanksgiving for wheat and barley "which God appointed for our nourishment." Thanksgiving and petition are recognized in the canonical books. Hastings, *Religion and Ethics,* page 551. But these would not imply monotheism.

[8] Many of these quotations are taken as DeGroot cites them; others later, are directly from the writings of Confucius. For the reasons given in the introduction, I do not cite the documents.

the bad spirits of just these same things because the lower order shares everything impartially with the higher. Naturally the evil order, being nearer and more fearsome, asserted a dread sovereignty over the popular Chinese mind. No land is so demon-possessed as China. These evil spirits make the dark a terror. They besiege and capture the souls of the living. Their touch causes boils and tremors. The ghosts of the ill-buried dead, an old and universal superstition, haunt their former dwellings. They fill the sky with spectral armies, cause drought and famine, pull the swimmer under water, and trouble the embryo in the womb. Even the pigtails of the devout are not safe from their mischief.

They take animal form or change from beasts to men or maidens and seduce their victims. These spectral armies can be frightened away by noise in which the besieged have become adepts. The explosion of a boy's firecracker on the Fourth of July is the far echo, on a peaceful front, of a desperate warfare in which China has been engaged for ages. These evil spirits do not, however, according to the Chinese theologians, act without the authority, or at least the silent consent of Heaven. They are the instruments of justice and the fear of them puts the fear of Heaven in the hearts of men. "The purpose of the worship and propitiation of the gods is to induce them to defend Man against the World of Evil Spirits, or by descending and living among men to drive those spirits away by their overawing presence." The world of devils has thus a very practical religious value. Other religions have profited by much the same fear-begotten devotion.

Heaven is always just. If the demons ride through the night, it is because the gong beaters below deserve what they are getting. The friendly spirits help the devout, reinforce the armies of good kings and reward piety. They may even help the student in his examinations though, on the other hand, an evil spirit often contributes to his failure. (It would still be convenient to blame a malicious Kwei for a bad piece of writing.) In general, demonology has made the Chinese a fearsome but a religious people; when one's most secret deeds are watched by unseen avengers, one is likely to take care.

TAUGHT TO LIVE BY HEAVEN

But there is a brighter and a more positive side to Chinese faith and morality. Man as well as the universe has his Tao, his Way.

His character is—or ought to be—the reflection of the character of the universe. He should learn from Heaven how to live. Virtue is the result, the expression of the Heaven Way of living. Happiness is the harvest of virtue.

The sages are generally agreed that men are naturally good, though some acute observers maintained that human nature is a mixture of both good and evil, a man's character really depending upon his education. One pessimistic heretic held man to be innately depraved. Natural goodness seems, however, according to Chinese ethics, largely to consist in being natural, though nature, as the sages define it, carries a noble connotation. Everything according to Chinese philosophy, is right through being what it is according to the "will" and "way" of Heaven.

"The celestial law adjusts for each one the natural endowments which constitute his character." Therefore, they must be good though this natural goodness does admit of improvement. "Cultivation" is the classic word and cultivation and goodness are synonymous. "The Tao, acquired by comprehensive study consists in the manifestation of beneficent virtue, which is the fruit of enlightenment." The Western doctrine of a "new birth" has no place in Chinese thought. Socrates and the sages would have got on famously. They both agreed that ignorance is the root of wrong character and the instructed man is the saint—provided he lives up to his instruction. The whole Chinese ethic, then, is a system and standard of instruction. It seeks to make the Tao—the way of man—one with the Tao of Heaven. It is the Stoic's "live according to nature." One could almost call it "moral naturism."

The Chinese temperament is naturally the key to the Chinese ideal of life, though it would be as true to answer that the ideal has shaped the temperament. Centuries of give and take between the faith of China and the soul of China have subdued each to the color of the other. There is no trace of that weariness of life which lay like a shadow across India in Chinese wisdom literature. There is no more trace of the ardent eagerness for life which has characterized the West. The idea of transmigration by which India was hag-ridden was absent. Immortality becomes longevity. There is an eminently sensible hard-bitten character to the whole system. The metaphysics which finally entangled Hinduism, the distrust of desire, save the one desire to cease desiring which enervated

Buddhism, the excess of theology which burdens Christianity are all wanting in Taoism.

Its central concern is character: "What heaven has bestowed is the character; following the character is the Tao—the way and law—" This is the first sentence of the first chapter of the bible of Confucianism. The four cardinal virtues of Taoism are too general for daily use.[9] They have, therefore, been "stepped down" to perhaps the most finely drawn and balanced moral code in which any people have ever been disciplined. Primitive societies have been veined with customs and taboos, old Roman Society was penetrated by ritual, Chinese life and thought have been controlled by the good rules of human conduct. The names for character and the good rules of human conduct have a monosyllabic directness; character is "sing" and the laws of social life are "li." The li sustain the state; they "have their roots in heaven, their divisions on the earth, their branches even among the spectres and the gods; they extend accordingly to the worship of the dead and sacrifices of any kind, also to archery and chariot driving . . ., to marriage, to audiences and missions."

The literature in which all this is set forth are the sacred books of China. They are much like the Hebrew book of Proverbs, the wisdom of the sage and the experience of the poet tied in one bundle; they have a little preaching, not too much, in them; they include ethical education, political wisdom, a native shrewdness, unconscious humor, a ballast of banality and timeless insight. They are really, a "wisdom literature," sagaciously practical. There are no haunting echoes of humanity's psalms in them, nor any confession wrung out of sorrow and defeat. They are the serene uplands of contemplative morality touched by an austere light. They are invested with the authority of great names. They took their final forms before the Christian era. They have since then been much commented upon, but never changed.

They are without any claim to inspiration, these bibles of China.

[9] The Four Cardinal Virtues are the virtues of the celestial order. "Heaven has priority, it is all-pervading, beneficent and immutably correct." These, like the English common law according to Blackstone, "are deficient through their generality," and the Sages find it difficult to reduce them to definite instruction. "Priority," for example, seems to mean that the eminently virtuous man "becomes the first and principal among men." The others are interpreted in the same general and somewhat vague fashion. The Chinese classics are really a system of value-judgments.

They are the classics of Chinese literature (which has been outstandingly ethical and political). They supplied the subject matter for the scholar and the knowledge of them was for long the door to preferment in the state. The crisis of an ambitious young Chinese student's life was the day he was shut up in the old Chinese equivalent of an election booth with his brush, his ink cake, his memory and his good and evil spirits to pass his examination upon these books. If he succeeded, he was a made man; if he failed, the future was barred. Not even the alibi of malicious interference from the unseen world could save his face.

Any account of Chinese religion must begin, as Krause[10] says, with the general fund of thought in the oldest Chinese literature. But this most ancient literature is not specifically religious. It is ethical, social, accurately or inaccurately historical. In no literature other than philosophic Hinduism are the philosophical and religious so inextricably fused save perhaps in the now emerging philosophy of religion here in America. Nor does Chinese thought ever find complete expression in any one document. There was certainly a distinct development of Chinese thought before it took literary form, and the vastness of China would as certainly favor divergent philosophies and conflicting emphases. Then and there as here and now the orthodox is some final fixation of a fluid past—thereafter sacred.

The two systems which this chapter contrasts—on the whole too sharply though they become in their issue two separate systems—grew up out of the ancient soil of fundamental Chinese conceptions derived in substance from two sources: "Observation of nature and the sense of man's dependence upon it" and "theories of the soul and beliefs regarding the dead." (These have always been humanity's dominant concerns.)

There is, really, no good term by which to name the religion of China which antedated this literature. It is not Confucian for Confucius was yet to be born; it was not Taoism for Lao-tze had not yet appeared. One writer calls it Sinism [which is much like calling it Chinism]; another Sinaean religion. It is doubtless true that much of what came to be known as Taoism existed before the sixth century which produced China's two great sages, but with this century began the crystallization of Chinese religion into two comparatively divergent systems.

[10] *Religions of the World, op. cit.,* page 79.

TAOISM BECOMES QUIETISM: THE SECRET OF CHINESE PLACIDITY

Lao-tze was the earlier of the two sages. He was born in 604 B.C., is said to have borne a surname indicating some peculiarity of the ear, and to have been visited at one time by Confucius who, after an interview with him, compared him, because of the lofty vagueness of his philosophy, to a soaring dragon. He was likely in that interview in one of his more exalted moods for he was really a gentle soul and a mystic.[11] At any rate he and his disciples, especially Chuang-tze (or Chuango-tze) gave to Taoism a distinctly passive character.

Imitation of the "way" of Heaven is always the secret of correct terrestrial behavior. "A holy man copies his line of conduct from heaven" but, Chwang adds, "does not try to further its works or designs" which is one of the differences between the East and the West. Heaven is firm, therefore the highly virtuous are firm. It is impartial, just and unselfish. The virtuous are impartial, "the partial man brings confusion and anarchy into the world under heaven." Other heavenly virtues follow in impressive enumeration—order, compliance and non-compliance, self-effacement, disinterestedness, unselfishness and finally a certain emptying oneself of self which is the nearest approach to mysticism in the Chinese system. "Heaven is emptiness; Earth is quietude; they do not struggle together"; therefore, the man of Superior Virtue is placid and contented.

Just here the Chinese Sage reaches the threshold of a great matter. No religion ever escapes the question, "What shall a man do with himself?" First and last self is humanity's most troublesome possession. The answers are various enough: lose it, said Gautama, in the peace of Nirvana; lose it, said the Brahman, in the world soul; lose it, said Jesus, in loyalties to a supreme cause. Empty it, said the older Chinese classics, of desire and passions, only thus can divinity enter it. "Therefore, I say, if you remove knowledge and wisdom from you, what then can lead you to strive for anything? And if there be nothing within you, what plans will you ever make? And

---

[11] Iconoclastic modern criticism questions whether there ever was a Lao-tze and whether his classic, the Tao-Teh King is not a later compilation. They do not seem to make out their case.

if you strive for nothing and lay no plans, you will be without cares"—which is "emptiness" indeed.

All this is so akin to the teaching of Gautama as to make it plain enough why Buddhism found an open door in China. It is also an aspect of all mysticism. Saul of Tarsus had his own doctrine of the "emptied" life. So had Marcus Aurelius and Thomas à Kempis. But how can the sage "remove knowledge and wisdom" from him and cultivate them at the same time? There is a right name for this state of soul, though China did not coin it. France named it in the eighteenth century, it is "quietism" the withdrawal of the mind from worldly care and ambitions and the passive contemplation of God and his attributes.

Well, this is a fascinating road for those who have the temperament for it, but it has one danger—it may at a great cost to society entirely withdraw the contemplative from the rather demanding affairs of life. Old China was strongly in the way of finding its peace in the contemplation and imitation of the universe—a sufficiently difficult task for any quietist, and losing its practical force. Something of that has endured ever since, it has become in a paradoxical way the secret of China's strength. Restlessness, say the Sages, defeats its own ends; a masterly inaction is the secret of power. Practically, that means, I suppose, letting the things which harry the soul or the state wear themselves out. The wise made a more imposing philosophy of it.[12]

They also made a religion of it. The empty man is God's man or Heaven's chance. Whatever high and universal spirit there is enters unto him, he shares the qualities of the divine and "becomes a god among gods": "the man of the highest order is a god, . . . neither death nor life makes any change in him, and how much less should anything which causes good and evil be able so to do?" These god-men have generally been located in some distant province and been invested with supernatural powers. Their godhood, as far as they came under observation, was reconciled with the fact of their mortality by such accommodations as devotion has always been adept in. One saint was eaten by a tiger, but, says the sage who praises him, "the tiger merely devoured the outward man." Others confessed that the death of god-men was beyond their power to ex-

[12] The China of 1936 is caught between its inherited philosophy and Western militarism gone far east.

plain. In general all that discipline of the soul through detachment
from the world and the mortification of the body, which is one
aspect of all religion, has grown in China out of this philosophy of
quietism.

ENTER CONFUCIUS

Confucianism was a reaction against all this. It brought Chinese
thought and conduct back into the general current of a practical
virtue gained through education and stability.[13] The practical man

[13] This statement needs to be qualified or clarified or both. It is substantially supported by DeGroot, *op. cit.*, chapters 3 and 4, but it telescopes chronology. Confucianism was not a calculated reaction against Taoist quietism. It did become a
corrective. Confucius visited and honored Lao-tze in his retirement but, says DeGroot,
"The doctrine of the suppression of wisdom, which seems to have been a part of
the great Taoist principle of emptiness, was rejected by the school of the great sage."
"The greatest impulse to this dissent was given by the grandson of Confucius." He
taught "virtue by instruction" and to this "China owes its literary civilization." This
following estimate of Confucius by Mr. Lo-Shan Peng (now in 1936 an Auburn
student), a graduate of the University of Nanking, interpreter for Mott and Eddy,
unusual in mind and experience, will interest students.

"Confucius himself was an educator, a political teacher and social reformer. His
masterpiece, 'The Spring and Autumn,' was a political treatise. His reference to
prayer, worship and destiny was insignificant compared with his interest in and
sayings on social and political problems.

"When asked about death and the proper duties to the spirits and the gods, he
replied: 'Not know life, how know death? Not know how to serve men, how know
how to serve the spirits and the gods?'

"A historically minded man, Confucius did not openly repudiate the spirits and
the gods of the people. But he told one of his disciples: 'Revere the gods, but keep
aloof from them.' And in the Analects, this rule was laid down: 'Worship as if
something were present; worship a god as if he were present.' Commenting on this
point, Dr. Hu Shih has said somewhere that Confucius was like a fisherman who,
knowing that there was no fish in the pond, pretended to catch fish by casting his
net into it.

"However, Confucius hoped to bind society together without the benefit of the
gods by teaching benevolence in the rulers and submission in the ruled, kindliness in
the elders and respect for old age in the young, generosity in the older brother and
humility in the younger brother."

Mr. Peng then quotes extensively on filial piety which Confucius stressed, and
continues: "Three-quarters of a century ago, Mr. Tseng Kuo-fan, a great Chinese
scholar, lived in retirement at his home town after the sickness and then the
death of his mother. Then the Taiping Rebellion broke out and threatening the
Manchu dynasty it lasted fifteen years. The Taipings dared to challenge Confucianism
and therefore Tseng Kuo-fan emerged from his retirement to champion his religion.
And it was he who saved the alien government of the Manchus. In his declaration
against the rebels, he said with all sincerity, 'Confucius is weeping in his grave!
How can we, scholars, refuse to help him?' Even today many such scholars in China

has never had any use for quietism: this present world is too full of things to be done. The churchman has always seen in it a solvent of his authority; the statesman does not want to rule a nation of dreamers. Confucius, who gave his name and great force to that standardization of ethics which has been ever since the orthodox Chinese system, was not a churchman, though he had a sound feeling for authority. He was practical, socially minded and a lover of the full rounded life. He felt besides that Chinese quietism was leaving out one of the four cardinal virtues: that cultivation of the superior life which comes through wisdom. He founded a religion of Humanism.

Confucius did not agree with some earlier teachers that a man becomes wise through emptying himself of knowledge and wisdom. He believed in virtue by instruction combined with study and became himself the most illustrious example of his own gospel. His name and memory are held in lonely honor. "His fame overflows the Middle kingdom and reaches the barbarians of the North and South; wherever ships and wagons can go, or the strength of man penetrates; wherever there is heaven above and earth below; wherever the sun and moon shed their light, or frosts or dews fall—all who have blood and breath honor and love him. Therefore it may be said that he is the peer of God."[14]

This is a sufficiently generous appreciation but the measured verdict of a German scholar is also arresting—"After the lapse of more than two thousand years the moral, social and political life of about one-third of mankind continues to be under the full influence of his mind." Confucius was born in 551 B.C., at the heart of an epoch-making century. Three great religions, Zoroastrianism probably, Buddhism, Confucianism and the dawn of Greek philosophy are its gift to the world. It was a troubled time in China. The feudal provinces were in revolt against the "Middle Kingdom," famine and pestilence had followed war. Fields were left uncultivated because there was no labor to tend them. Instruction failed because there were no teachers. Under similar circumstances Israel produced the prophet. China produced the teacher.

Confucius' father belonged to the K'ung family, a man of un-

---

can still hear 'Confucius weeping in his grave' although they do not confess to be Confucianists."

[14] Quoted by H. H. Gowen, *An Outline of Chinese History*, Part I, page 68.

usual strength and courage. He once held up a gate alone until his comrades could escape from a city in which they had been caught. He found himself, when almost seventy years old, the father of nine daughters and one crippled son. His distinguished family being thus in danger of extinction, he set about to avoid that danger and was eminently successful. He sought a second wife from an honorable family, the older daughters wanted no bridegroom of three score and ten, but the youngest dutifully left the decision to her father: "You will go, my daughter," he said and she went. There is a tradition that she prayed for a son at Mount Ni; another that her son was born in a cave in the mountain while she was on a pilgrimage; another still that the baby's head was shaped like a mountain. So they called him K'ung K'in (Kiung of the Mountain) which imposing name has been latinized into Confucius. Another authority makes his family name Kung, his title Fu-tsu (philosopher?) Kung, Fu-tsu became Confucius.

His Early Life

Signs and wonder attended his birth. Two dragons guarded the house in which he lay; wise men came from afar to salute mother and child; the mother heard celestial music and a voice of benediction from the sky. The child was saluted as a throneless king. Behind this web of legend is the established fact that Confucius was well born, the son of a vigorous old man and a young woman. His father died and left his three-year-old son in the care of his mother who, though handicapped by poverty, trained him carefully. He afterwards remembered gratefully this discipline of poverty: "When I was young my condition was low, and therefore I acquired my ability in many things." He took the only road open to a youth in his condition and bent his mind to learning, having an especial regard for antiquity and a great disregard for the futile ceremonialism of the religion of his time. "The Golden Age of China, with its perfectly virtuous, semi-divine rulers, threw a lasting spell over his imagination and he sought to reestablish the troubled state about him in the perfect and saving wisdom of the ancient wise and great."

He married at the age of nineteen and may have later been divorced though that is uncertain. He had a son toward whom he maintained a distant and philosophic reserve. He became a public teacher in his twenty-second year, winning directly a strong following of those "who wished to increase their knowledge of the history and the doctrines of the past." A fee of dried fish was sufficient provided the bearer brought also a thirst for instruction. He sought to teach men to think for themselves. "I do not open the truth to one who is not eager to get knowledge, nor help out one who is not anxious to explain himself. When I have presented one corner of a subject to anyone, and he can not from it learn the other three, I do not repeat my lesson."

A GREAT TEACHER

His gift for teaching was the secret of his immediate success. Within a dozen years he was the outstanding teacher in China, advertised by the patronage of the nobility and honored by the confidence of the poor. The University of Confucius must have been much like the University of Paris in those great days when Abelard led the young men who came from every part of Europe to hear him lecture, a university which had nothing but youth—the timeless quest—and a great teacher.

It was a peripatetic—a walk-about-university, actually in session and location wherever Confucius happened to be. He was the entire faculty: "the pupils walk with him, and ask questions on all conceivable subjects: on literature, music, costume, court etiquette, war, taxation, statesmanship." One sees dimly through all this a master and disciple relationship in which affection is the only binding force and the shaping of outlooks and tempers more consequential than any concern about sheer facts. Most of the facts Confucius knew were wrong anyhow but he belonged to that elect fellowship who have had a power to reach and redirect the springs of action and assert a transforming sovereignty over the human spirit.

One may say, with careful restraint, that the sources of the most creative influences in the general stream of history are to be sought —and found—in just such relationships. Socrates and Plato in the bright streets of Athens, Gautama in the groves and by the streams of northwest India, Zoroaster in the uplands of Persia, Confucius in a low Chinese town, Jesus in Galilee, have made empire and world politics colorless through their lonely power to share with others their sense and vision of some range of truth or reality whose meaning for life is supreme and enduring.

Dr. H. C. Du Bose in a vivid account of Chinese religion, written out of a long residence in China and a wide knowledge of the Chinese classics[15] finds four causes for Confucius' influence; his books became the standard of religion, moral and political wisdom; he organized the literati into a host of well disciplined minds, he exercised great power over his personal disciples and was magnified through their enthusiastic admiration. Few men have been so greatly praised. "The talents and virtues of other men are as mounds and hillocks which may be stepped over; Confucius is the sun and moon which cannot possibly be stepped over." He was like Heaven itself, so high that there are no steps by which to reach him.

He was also honored officially, being made successively a revenue officer, supervisor of fields, herds and parks, governor of a Chinese city, and finally "Minister of Crime" in the Kingdom of Loo. Order and prosperity attended his administrations. The herds he supervised became famous, the city he governed safe, honest and quite proper; "men and women walked apart, a parcel might in safety be dropped along the road, honest prices were asked for goods." Even the dead were guarded against trickery. "Coffins were four inches thick." His honors undid him. The governor of a rival state fearing the prosperity of the Kingdom of Loo sent the King thereof a gift of horses and dancing girls. Confucius found himself unable to compete with their allure and reluctantly left a court which had lost interest in the virtues of the Superior Man. Philosophers have generally not been happy at Court—Seneca in the Golden Palace, Goethe at Weimar and Plato in Syracuse were all in a position to sympathize with the Sage of China.

HIS DIFFICULTIES AND DISCOURAGEMENTS

Confucius was thereafter for a term of years a wanderer like Dante climbing other men's stairs and eating other men's bread. "How savoreth of salt the bread of others, and how hard a road the going down and up another's stairs." He was always in quest

[15] *The Dragon, Image and Demon—or the Three Religions of China*, London, 1887.

of a king who would not only honor a philosopher but imitate him. The great received him gladly, for his fame had gone before him, "but no one was prepared to accept his principles and act them out." He was once offered the revenues of a town by a prince who rejected his advice. He replied that rice to eat, water to drink and the bent arm for a pillow were enough if wisdom and virtue were not lost. "Riches and honor acquired by unrighteousness are to me as a floating cloud." His declining years were darkened by a sense of futility. He had held hopes of some wise ruler who would, through his influence, transform the empire. These hopes were disappointed.

He did not see that his patient work with "the cotton clothed masses" among whom his power was lodged and with whom he lived and died, was to be the secret of his throneless administration. He felt also that such divine revelations as had been granted the ancient sages were denied him. The mountain-headed one was never caught up into the Seventh Heaven. Few great teachers have had less of the mystic in them than Confucius nor, save for the celestial music his mother heard and the dragons who guarded his natal roof, is there any intimation in legend or literature of supernatural intervention in his favor, or any display on his part of supernatural power. He lived and died in the austere light of reason and plain fact.

This lack of heavenly validation also disturbed him. "It is all over with me," he exclaimed in one of his more despondent moments. Again he said, "My doctrines make no way; I will get upon a raft and float about the sea." Matthew Arnold was once greatly delighted to find a flaw in Franklin's victorious common sense; Confucius is so eminently sensible that one rather welcomes some display of human nature in a sage who was reckoned the Companion of Heaven and the Peer of God.

The disciplines of his homeless years were certainly contributory to a character of rare force and power. He sums up the stages of his own career in an oft quoted passage—

At fifteen, my mind was bent in learning,
At thirty, I stood firm.
At forty, I had no doubts
At fifty, I knew the will of God

At sixty, I could trust my ears
At seventy, I could follow my heart's desire without transgression.

He was both credulous and superstitious in little harmless ways
and modest. He was, he admitted, the equal of any in learning,
but there were aspects of his own character which caused him
solicitude. His self-depreciation, one feels, is rather like a great artist's
dispassionate estimate of a picture he has done—a tribute to the
unattainable perfection of art itself, rather than an estimate which
he would wish others to accept. The Chinese now hold that Confucius was sinless, a dogma probably borrowed from Western missionary preaching and applied to the founder of Confucianism in
ways he would be the first to protest against.

Toward the end of his life Confucius is said to have made a
solemn ceremony of dedicating his writings to Heaven. He built
an altar, placed his books upon it, thanked Heaven for having been
able to finish them (a thanksgiving in which other authors would
gladly join), and prayed that they might be of lasting benefit to
his fellow countrymen. Like Gautama he foresaw his death. He
died feeling this his work had been in vain and quite alone. They
say that once in his travels he came to a river and sent his disciple
to ask a couple of men working in a field where the ford was. One
of the men asked in turn who the driver of the carriage was. "It is
Confucius," his disciple answered. "What! Confucius of the Loo
State?" "Yes," replied the disciple. "Ah," said the man, speaking
figuratively, "he knows the ford."[16] But he came to the last "ford"
with dim eyes.[17]

THE OUTCOME OF HIS LIFE WORK

As one sees the work of Confucius in contour he corrected the
excessive quietism (with a stoical cast) into which the teachers who
preceded him were leading China. He might have taken this counsel of Chwang as a text to teach against. "My pupils, take the attitude of doing nothing . . . Forget your relations with other people, set free your will and deliver your soul; be nobody or nothing

[16] Herbert A. Gilles, *Confucianism and Its Rivals*, London, page 69.

[17] His family continues. One of them, the fifty-fifth generation, was lately Minister
of Industry and Commerce in China.

and behave as if you had no soul.[18] Confucius opposed a positive attitude to this "be nobody or nothing" gospel. He taught his disciples to be constantly considerate of their relations with other people. He says little or nothing about the soul. I do not find that word in the index of Dawson's *The Ethics of Confucius*, an admirable digest of his system.

His ideal was the "Superior Man" living a life of inner harmony and harmoniously adjusted to every relationship. This was so near the Greek ideal of life that one asks instinctively why the outcome of it was so splendidly different there. Where is the "little more"[19] in Greece which made the difference between two civilizations which are worlds apart. There is a difference between the Chinese and the Greek to begin with. Also Greece added the thirst for richness of life to the thirst for harmony, moreover Greece added the quest for beauty to the quest for goodness and followed the gleam of a Supreme Excellence which touched her perfect poise with a divine discontent. The music Confucius heard was muted on the creative note. He is said to have been passionately devoted to music and the story of his life cut in stone on the walls of the Confucian temple in his native town shows him always playing upon his harp. He would forget food in his love for music.

He did more than play upon the harp; he sought to make a grave and noble music of life. He idealized the past of China, believed himself to be reestablishing and conserving the ancient virtues and the ancient truths. His critics say that this gave a static quality to his teaching which is reflected in the static quality of Chinese civilization. He "fixed" the past. That is doubtless true, though he really supplied a new point of departure for the ethical life of his nation and there is a general and inclusive quality in his ideals which might easily make them adaptable to changing conditions. They are actually a wine which could be poured into new bottles. Confucianism has made China tenacious; it should not of itself have made China static, save as it turned men too much toward self contained values which make the restless drive of wealth and empire of little account.

He never actually broke with Taoism. Heaven is still the music

[18] Quoted by DeGroot, *Religion in China*, page 128.
[19] Oh, the little more, and how much it is!
And the little less, and what worlds away!

and the law to which men must conform. But he did so recast the old system that Confucianism became a distinct thing. All scholars agree in recognizing three faiths and conduct systems in China: Taoism, Confucianism and Buddhism. There is actually no clear frontier between them; it is possible to be all three at once; a Buddhist can take what he pleases out of the ethics of Confucius and touch them with some flame of religious passion, or else maintain that he is carrying through to their consistent conclusion the old doctrine of holiness through emptying one's life of desire and living the ascetic life. "The fact is," says DeGroot,[20] "that the three religions are three branches growing from a common stem," and that stem the old religion of the universe. Confucianism became the state system and consequently hard and intolerant, especially in its early relations with Buddhism.

CONFUCIAN WRITINGS

The general system of Confucius is standardized in his own writings and the writings of his school. He probably wrote only one book himself, known as "Spring and Autumn." Since he wrote that in his seventy-second year, it is certainly autumnal. A collection of his conversations was made by his disciples after his death known now as "The Analects." He and his disciples edited some of the older classics. These are known in English as "The Book of Changes,"[21] "The Book of Filial Piety," "The Book of History," "The Book of Poetry" and "The Book of Ceremonies." There would naturally be commentaries and further developments of the doctrine, but the Chinese way of making the classics final has tended to limit Chinese theological literature.

The "Four Books" which contain the essence of Confucianism are "The Analects," "The Great Learning," "The Doctrine of the Mean" and "Mencius." The English translation (done by James Legge) of the four with proper introduction and comment make a quarto volume of only 200 pages. Five such volumes, says the trans-

---

[20] *Op. cit.,* page 2. Confucianism became the State-religion under the Han Dynasty (206 B.C.-221 A.D.). Its authority spread as that Dynasty consolidated the entire state. It suited the political purposes of the emperors.

[21] Confucius set great value on the "Book of Changes." He said at seventy that he would willingly spend the rest of his life reading it!—a difficult task our Chinese students say.

lator, would contain all the "Classics." The sacred literature of China is therefore far more manageable in bulk than the holy books of Buddhism and far more orderly in structure and plain in sense than the sacred books of India. There is nothing of the jungle in them. The Analects are a little like the Dialogues of Buddha in naïve charm and the Hebrew book of Proverbs in their practical and sententious wisdom.

Miles Mender Dawson, member of the Confucian Society of China, has done a distinct service to his society by organizing the general teaching under seven heads, supplying happy illustrative passages. Wu Ting Fang, late minister to the United States from China, has furnished, with laconic brevity and Confucian gravity, a foreword. "Confucius," he says, "strove to make the human being good—a good father, a good mother, a good son, a good daughter, a good citizen. Though his truths were unpalatable at the time of their enunciation, they have lived to bear good fruit" and "will surely help the struggler in the mire of perplexity to find his way out to the clean, substantial foothold of manliness and integrity."

THE "SUPERIOR MAN"

The West has never really recognized, I think, the enormous attention the Buddhistic and Confucian East have given to the problems of human conduct. There is a quality of ethical analysis in Confucianism which Western ethics can hardly equal. There is a subtle searching of the springs of action in Buddhism which the West can hardly match save as we are now approaching it in our new studies of human nature. One might hazard an epigram: The West has defined life in terms of religious destiny and defined religion in terms of doctrine. The Buddhist and Confucian East have defined life in terms of character destiny and made religion a ceremonialism. If the religious passion of the West at its best and the ethical passion of the East at its best could be fused the result might be a rebirth of the human spirit.

But this is Confucius.

The bare enumeration of the virtues of the Superior Man—superior to others, for Confucius saw no evil in that generous ambition—and superior always to the self he has been—is like an index of an examination of morals. He has purpose, poise, self-sufficiency, earnestness, thoroughness, sincerity, truthfulness, purity of thought and action, mutual hospitality, courage, firmness, ease, dignity, and a dozen other admirable virtues. It needs Confucius' touch to bring these dry bones to life. For example: "What the Superior Man seeks, is in himself; what the ordinary man seeks, is in others." "The Superior Man is catholic and not partisan; the ordinary man is partisan and not catholic." "The Superior Man thinks of virtue; the ordinary man thinks of comfort." "The Superior Man has dignified ease without pride; the ordinary man has pride without dignified ease." "To be able to judge others by what is in ourselves, this may be called the art of virtue."

"When one cultivates to the utmost the capabilities of his nature and exercises them on the principle of reciprocity, he is not far from the path. What you do not want done to yourself, do not do unto others." This is the Golden Rule of Confucianism. Open the Analects almost anywhere and one finds some arresting wisdom. "These are three things the Superior Man guards against. In youth, when the physical powers are not yet settled, he guards against lust. When he is strong, and the physical powers are full of vigor, he guards against quarrelsomeness. When he is old, and the animal powers are decayed, he guards against covetousness."

"There are three friendships which are advantageous, and three which are injurious; friendship with the upright, friendship with the sincere, and friendship with the man of much observation—these are advantageous. Friendship with the man of specious airs; friendship with the insinuatingly soft, and friendship with the glib tongued —these are injurious." "There are three things"—these reflections love threes and fives and nines—"of which the Superior Man stands in awe. He stands in awe of the ordinances of Heaven, he stands in awe of great men, he stands in awe of the words of sages."

CONFUCIAN DOMESTIC LIFE

These sentences are like jade but pages of them would grow jade heavy. The ethics of Confucianism are rich in detail as to domestic life: "A happy union with wife and children is like the music of lutes and harps." There was evidently some debate about the sanctity and even the necessity of marriage in the time of Confucius. This spirit is gravely rebuked: "He who thinks the old embankments useless and destroys them, is sure to suffer from the desolation caused by overflowing waters; and he who should consider the old rules of propriety useless and abolish them, would be sure to suffer from the calamities of disorder. Thus, if the ceremonies of marriage were discontinued, the path of husband and wife would be embittered and there would be many offenses of licentiousness and depravity." That judgment seems to stand.

Concubinage is recognized and divorce permitted. Failure to bear a son, too loose a tongue and jealousy of the husband are accepted pleas. But a man may not divorce his wife if she have no home to which to go, nor if she has mourned with him three years for his parents, or if he married her in poverty and has become rich and honorable. Parenthood has a religious sanction through ancestor worship, hard for the West to understand. This virtue has challenged and conquered the wasting consequences of war, pestilence and famine for two thousand years. The very dust of the land is its dead blown abroad by the wind, but the living are always there.

The filial virtues are much dwelt upon: "The Master said, 'A youth when at home should be filial, and, abroad, respectful to his elders. He should be earnest and truthful, he should overflow in love to all, and cultivate the friendship of the good. When he has time and opportunity after the performance of these things, he should employ them in polite studies!'" "The Master said, 'While a man's father is alive, look at the bent of his will; when his father is dead, look at his conduct. If for three years he does not alter from the way of his father, he may be called filial.'" Children in turn are to be treated with affection and respect. A disciple said once to the Master: "I should like, Sir, to hear your wishes." The Master said: "They are, in regard to the aged to give them rest; in regard to friends, to show them sincerity; in regard to the young, to treat them tenderly." Women are only shadows, very necessary indeed to the going concern of father and son, but without domestic or social status of their own.

There is a kind of grave music in all this teaching about the duty of a son to his father. Upon his father's death, every son should go into a period of three years' mourning which is really a spiritual retreat. Every anniversary of the death of parents must always be piously observed. A father's name must never be mentioned except upon the anniversary sacrifices and always with tears. The conduct of one's life is the greatest tribute one can pay to the dead. Dawson says with great insight[22] that "This devotion both to living and departed parents—the so-called 'ancestor worship' of the Chinese . . . is the chief incentive, other than the innate desire to grow and to become and be a superior human being, to which Confucius appeals." The West may judge this a narrow foundation, but it has borne the great structure of Chinese morality. "The Superior Man while his parents are alive, reverently sacrifices to them. His chief thought is how, to the end of his life, not to disgrace them." One of the odes says it all in two lines—

> When early dawn unseals my eyes
> Before my mind my parents rise.

The Superior Man and the State

The relation of the Superior Man to the state includes the whole Confucian theory of statecraft and government. The ideal state is governed by a Superior King whose benevolences bless his subjects and whose virtues challenge them to imitation. "The art of governing," said the Master, "is to keep its affairs before the mind without weariness and to practice them with an undeviating consistency." Tsze-Kung asked about government; the Master said, "The requisites of government are that there should be sufficiency of food, sufficiency of military equipment and the confidence of the people in their ruler." The Master also said that if of these requisites one had to be surrendered to save the other two, military equipment should go first and if two must be given up food should go next. For, he said, "From of old, death has been the lot of all men; but if the people have no faith in their rulers, there is no standing for the state."

The system further maintains that government exists for the sake of the governed, that order is essential, and that the state is established to secure for its citizens the five blessings: ample means, long life, health, virtuous character, and an agreeable personal appearance; and to defend them against the six calamities—early death, sickness, misery, poverty, a repulsive appearance and weakness.[23] The

---

[22] *The Ethics of Confucius, op. cit.*, page 170.
[23] *The Ethics of Confucius, op. cit.*, page 186.

ancient Chinese analyzed the social and economic conditions favorable to the "five blessings" with surprising insight. There is hardly a problem of the modern political economist which the classics do not discuss wisely nor any present concern of the socially minded they do not anticipate. Mencius taught the single tax twenty centuries before Henry George and free trade equally long before Richard Cobden. He also shared with Bryan the distrust of armaments and with Henry of Navarre the not-to-be-debated confidence that a contented people are the sure support of any throne.

Always excepting Plato's Republic, there is no such examination of the nature of the state, the duties of rulers and the conditions of social well-being to be found in any literature down to our own time. The counsels are usually shrewd and hard-bitten. Confucius was dealing with China as it was and not Greece as it might be; which is perhaps the most considerable difference between the Republic and Confucian politics. There is, however, some suggestion of the ideal state in the Confucian system, though eminent scholars are not agreed as to whether the Master is speaking of a Golden Age which existed when the world was new and human concord still supreme or a felicity to be realized when all men are superior and, like himself at seventy, can follow their hearts' desires without transgression. It all turns on a nice distinction in Chinese verb tenses.

At any rate the ideal is there whether past or future. It is called the Grand Course or The Great Similarity, a state whose citizens are ruled by a public and common spirit, whose rulers are virtuous and able, speech always sincere and relationship always harmonious. There are none poor or uncared for and none idle or without work. The lonely are cherished and the sick and maimed maintained. Each is for all and all for each. Doors can be left unlocked for there are no thieves, cities need neither moats nor walls for there are no enemies. Most commentators date all this in the dateless past and I should think Confucius' habit of mind and his idealization of the past support them. It is something that the Master, who did not often or long look away from things as they are, saw once a golden light along his gray horizons—setting or rising sun, it has its glory. He would perhaps not forbid us to hope that it is a rising sun.

Is Confucianism a Religion?

But is Confucianism a religion? So far as we have come evidently not. It is an austere but noble morality. It has had for twenty centuries the value for China religion has had for other lands. It has commanded reverence and obedience and been invested with sanctity. Confucius, as Dr. Du Bose says, was the Moses who wrote the moral law of China on the Mount of Conscience—but that Mount was lighted by no supernatural splendor.

Confucius did see men in relation to the Universe and here his system rises toward and sometimes reaches a purely religious level. It did not influence the popular faith and was unaffected by it. Confucianism was set in the old Chinese world like jade in an ancient temple. The inherited order carried on around it. The spectral armies still drove by. Heaven and Earth pursued their sovereign courses.

It would not be true to say that Confucius cared for none of these things. He believed in a supernatural world whose numberless spirits, unseen and unheard, are always brushing by the living and influencing their fasts and their sacrifices. He believed in the continued existence of the dead; "all who live," the Master said, "must die and dying, return to the earth. The bones and flesh molder below and, hidden away, become the earth of the fields. But the spirit issues forth and is displayed on high in a condition of glorious brightness." The most ancient religion of China, and Confucianism as well, are reticent as to the state of the discarnate. "The subjects on which the Master did not talk, were extraordinary things, feats of strength, disorder and spiritual beings." There are no lands beyond the sunset or fields of asphodel in the classics. The popular need for paradise, purgatory and hell was, however, abundantly met by Chinese Buddhism which supplied all three and with a satisfying fullness of detail which would have astonished Gautama.[24]

Confucius was scrupulous about sacrifices to ancestors. "He sacrificed to the dead as if they were present. He sacrificed to the spirits as if the spirits were present." And yet even in this about which he feels so deeply, Confucius is reported as half-agnostic and wholly

---

[24] Legge believes that Purgatory is a Buddhist contribution growing out of the doctrine of transmigration, but that an eternity of Hell for the individual Soul is a tenet peculiar to Taoism.

cautious. "If I were to say that the dead have consciousness, I am afraid that filial sons and dutiful grandsons would impair their substance in paying their last offices to the departed; and if I were to say that the dead have not consciousness, I am afraid that unfilial sons and undutiful grandsons would leave their parents unburied. If you wish to know whether the dead have consciousness or not, you will know it when you are dead. There is no need to speculate upon it now."[25] He is at least considerate of the discarnate since they doubtless have affairs of their own. The sacrifices should not be too often repeated. Spring and Autumn are the proper times. The Autumn sacrifices should be offered silently and sadly, the vernal sacrifice with hope and music. And he adds an injunction by which some in our own time might profit. "Do not take liberties with or weary spiritual beings."

Confucius' teaching about a man's relation to Heaven is much the same as the earlier Chinese faith. He is dependent upon Heaven for his being, though he is Earth-born as well. Heaven and Earth maintain life; he is subject to their authority; a man's ways are known to Heaven. "The Master said, 'Alas! there is no one that knows me.'" "Tsze-Kung said, 'What do you mean by this saying, that no one knows you?'" "The Master replied, 'I do not murmur against Heaven. I do not grumble against men. My studies lie low, and my penetration rises high. But there is Heaven; that knows me.'" This is not the faith of the Hebrew one hundred and thirty-ninth Psalm—but it is not alien to it.

Matthew Arnold defined religion as morality touched with emotion. It is this lack of the emotional element in the Master which makes the essentially religious part of his system so rarefied and restrained. Mencius, who lived two hundred years after Confucius, had a warmer nature and there is, naturally, a stronger religious strain in his teaching; "He who delights in Heaven will affect with his love and protection the whole empire. He who stands in awe of Heaven will affect with his love and protection his own kingdom . . . the accomplishment of the great result—that is with Heaven." How far he had in mind only the commanding order of the universe to which

[25] Quoted by Dawson, *The Ethics of Confucius, op. cit.,* page 275. Dawson doubts its authenticity. One does not find the word immortality or its equivalents in the indices of the Four Books.

all human endeavor must be subject and how far he felt behind those awesome ways a living will to revere and save, he alone could tell us.

Giles finds in Mencius a sustained faith in a God in whose image man is created, through whom right prevails and wrong is punished, whose gifts are love and peace—"Charity of heart is the noblest gift of God; it is a house, so to speak, in which a man may live in peace,"— and whose service is the chief end of man. "To waste no thoughts upon length of life, but to cultivate rectitude—that is to do the will of God."[26]

Confucius himself occasionally speaks in purely religious terms. "He who offends against Heaven has none to whom he can pray." In the Seventh book of the Analects and the thirty-fourth chapter there are a few sentences through which to see further into the jade walled spirit of the Master than any other thing he said, save that Heaven knew him. "The Master being very sick, Tsze-loo asked leave to pray for him. He said, 'May such a thing be done?' Tsze-loo replied, 'It may. In the prayers it is said, "Prayer has been made to the spirits of the upper and lower worlds."' The Master said, 'My praying has been for a long time.'" Certainly the idea of a just and controlling Providence shows with restraint through the teachings of Confucius and his disciples. Perhaps the very reticence of these ancient seekers touches the rare confessions of their faith with the more moving light.

THE POPULAR RELIGION OF CHINA

But all this is no more the whole religion of China than Chinese jades and bronzes are the whole of China. Whether pure Confucianism is a religion or not, China has made a religion out of it and twenty centuries have both fixed and changed it. DeGroot's Chinese religion whose substance is the worship of the universe, whose great branches are Taoism, Confucianism and Buddhism, is too simple. The faith of China like the faith of any other land has had ninety generations of hundreds of millions of human folk for a channel to flow through. It carries the saturation of everything from the atavistic superstition of the ignorant to the meditation of the sage. The tributaries which have fed it can no more be separated in their general

[26] *Confucianism and Its Rivals,* Hibbert Lectures, 1914, pages 91 et seq. This is the strongest argument for Confucian Theism I have found.

current than the tributaries which feed from their hinterlands the Yellow River itself.

Confucianism has maintained an official distinction through its status as a state religion. It apparently took form as a religion in reaction to the driving impact of Buddhism. By the time that Saul of Tarsus was preaching a new gospel in the streets of Greek cities the teachings of the Master had fallen into eclipse, the old religion had become either a philosophy for the elect, or a religion of wizards and greedy priests who would work miracles for a price. Nothing was sure save that for every living person in China there were a hundred disembodied spirits. The fearsome lived in a land populated with the dead; there was nothing else for popular faith upon which to fasten.

Then Buddhism found its way across the roof of the world. There is a legend of a dream which led an emperor to send a mission into the West to find the disciples of the golden man he had so seen with a halo around his head. The mission brought back two Buddhist priests and their sacred books. By the time that Constantine made Christianity a state religion Buddhist priests had a temple in the Imperial Palace of China. It met an actual need. The teeming population were not superior men, they sensed dumbly the weariness of life and longed for deliverance. The form of Buddhism which won China offered Buddha as a personal Savior to whom the burdened could pray. The living Universe was too distant and too august for the troubled to pray to.

By the beginning of the fifth century A.D. the majority of the people are said to have been Buddhist. In general Buddhism and old Taoism so fused as to form a new syncretistic religion. The bequest of Gautama was greatly changed, but it furnished China with temples and priests, a popular worship, paradise, purgatory and hell. It created also an asceticism not native to the land, and supplied an abundance of idols housed by the Buddhist temples. This, too, was alien to the old Chinese faith and a Confucian poet of the seventh century made a verse about it which sounds a little like one of Addison's hymns:

> Now, I have heard the faith by Buddha taught
> Lauded as pure and free from earthly taint;
> Why then these carved and graven idols, fraught
> With gold and silver, gems and jade, and paint

Fools that ye are! In this ignoble light
The true faith fades and passes out of sight.[27]

Chinese Buddhism took the monastic form it has generally taken everywhere and filled China with monasteries and shrines. The parallels with Christian monasticism are so striking as to force one to believe that more passed from one religion to the other than is on record. The monks and nuns are celibate, they fast, they meditate. They wear vestments, chant their liturgies, say midnight masses and prayers for the dead, adorn their altars with flowers. The mystery religions and later, in the West, the splendid and dramatic Catholic liturgies, witness how humanity responds to such a richly colored and incense-scented appeal.

CONFUCIUS JOINS THE PROCESSION

Confucianism really became a religious cult with an official status and Imperial sanction to check the strong tide of Buddhism. While Theodoric King of the Ostrogoths was making Italy his kingdom and the splendor of Rome had become a memory, the first Confucian temple was built and dedicated. An image of the sage was placed in the temple and sacrifices were offered before it, though sacrifices to the Master are older than the temple. Women had long been praying for children at the shrines of the man who inquired if it were permitted to pray. By the end of the sixth century there were temples to Confucius in every considerable city in China, the first Manchu emperors extended them to the market towns. The images of Confucius gradually disappeared and wooden tablets bearing the names of Chinese saints and sages covered their walls. The temples became China's Halls of Fame.

The tablets of Confucius are now always on the north wall. The great sages are to the right and left and then in order of proper precedence, the tablets of the ancestors of Confucius, the honored wise and the great Confucian scholars; altogether there are about one hundred and seventy tablets in a Confucian temple. The families of departed scholars are naturally eager to see their learned ancestors thus exalted but since the verdicts of the past are subject to review, an element of insecurity attends the honor. The minor sages are in

[27] Quoted by Giles, *op. cit.,* page 209.

much the position of a popular hero who has a Paris street named after him, or an artist who has a picture hung in the Luxembourg. The tablet may be removed to a less honorable position or else taken down altogether. And it may be put back. The tablet of Fan Nung was removed after nine hundred years of serene and honored prominence. Two hundred years later it was restored. Dr. Giles suggests that "some such system should be tentatively applied to the monuments in Westminster Abbey and to other injudiciously crowded shrines."

The Spring and Autumn sacrifices are celebrated in these temples with pomp and ceremony. The ranking civil authority is the chief celebrant, attended by magistrates and military officers, musicians and dancers. Candle-lighted altars are set before the tablet of Confucius. An ox, a sheep and a pig are offered in the center of the hall, with a roll of white silk. The silk is the symbol of purity, the ox of stability, the pig of determination, the sheep of food and clothing. All the while the dancers perform their sacred dances. The spirit of Confucius, the lover of music, descends and shares the ceremony when the music begins. He is welcomed with a hymn—

> Mighty art thou, O Confucius,
> Perceiver of the future, endowed with foreknowledge,
> Compeer of God our father and of earth our mother,
> Teacher of the myriad ages,
>
> .   .   .   .   .
>
> Thy voice has a music of metal and silk.
> By thy aid the sun and the moon run their courses
> And the stability of the universe is preserved.

All this has been continued for fourteen centuries or more for a man who said, "In a hamlet of ten families there may be found one as honorable and sincere as I am but not so fond of learning."

The state religion of China reached its most imposing ceremonial on the night of the winter solstice and in the sacrifice offered by the emperor—when there was an emperor—on the altar of Heaven in Peking. All the pride of the empire, all the fine restraint of Chinese art, all the wealth of the symbolism of the worship of the universe is built into that altar—open to the winter sky—and the marble terraces which lift it toward Heaven. No other altar in the world is like it, no other altar has continued so long a ritual so ancient.[28]

On the longest night in the year—and but yesterday as China measures time—the emperor and all his court, their rich garments shining with subdued splendor in the torch light, took their appointed places. The emperor offered incense, jade, silk, broth and rice-spirits before the tablets of Heaven and his ancestors, bowing his forehead against the marble pavement. The tablets of the celestial bodies, the clouds, the winds, and the rains were also honored. Music and dancing attended the slow and immemorial pageantry of the sacrifices; when that sacrifice ended something was lost from the world which time can never replace. Perhaps it is not gone. In 1913 the President of the Chinese Republic requested the prayers of the Christian world for the Republic and the request was enthusiastically received. Christendom has always been willing to give its prayers to China. Two years later the President performed the ceremonial worship on the old altar with a scarcely diminished splendor. An altar before which the devotion of the centuries has worshiped is, of all human creations, the most difficult to destroy.[29]

CRUMBLING ALTARS

The altar of Heaven lay open to the sky but China had and has countless other altars. Many of the lesser gods are deified sages and servants of human well-being. Others are the personification of nature forces dim or clearly seen. Others still are gods of walls and moats, gods of mountains, gods of palace doors. The three hundred and sixty Chinese trades have their three hundred and sixty gods, each with his legend and his cult. The number of these little gods is always changing. Like the tablets on the walls of the temples they disappear and others take their places—or else the places stay empty. Even a Christian medical missionary may join the Chinese pantheon. Arthur Jackson lost his life fighting the plague in Manchuria; at the memorial service held in his honor the viceroy prayed—

[28] Nature worship, Krause says, was the religion of the governing classes. The cultus of sacrifice and prayer was originally in nature's temples. The worship of Confucius needed houses. The conduct of worship was the duty of the head of the family, the monarch and state officials. The state religion had no specialized priesthood.

[29] No subsequent president has attempted to restore the ceremony. It is not without significance perhaps that the new Emperor of Manchukuo has built an altar of Heaven near his capital.

O Spirit of Dr. Jackson we pray you intercede for the twenty million people of Manchuria, and ask the Lord of the Sky to take away this pestilence, so that we may once more lay our heads in peace upon our pillows.

In life you were brave, now you are an exalted spirit. Noble spirit who sacrificed your life for us, help us still and look down in kindness upon us all.

In such ways as this Western Christendom made its saints. There is no difference, I think, save that instinct and not authority canonized Dr. Jackson. It still remains to be seen what the soul of China will do to Western religion.

There is, of course, a wealth of daily ceremonialism through every aspect of Chinese life as far as that has not been changed by the general impact of Western education. The burial services particularly are rich in symbolism. Selecting a site for the grave demands the nicest consideration. One is not buried easily in China. And always the Unseen World, whose population is always increasing, is so near that the garments of the living brush the spirits of the dead. No study of Chinese religion begins to indicate how the entire structure of Chinese society has for thousands of years looked upon ancestor worship particularly and generally upon the organization of the family, of which ancestor worship is the sign and support. Chinese ancestor worship continues elements old as primitive spiritism. dateless hospitalities to the lonely and roofless departed. It carries also the really noble conception of a "corporate union with the disembodied and unseen" which has made time a shadow for China and surrounded the living with the innumerable fellowship of the dead.

A series of lectures which I heard a brilliant young Chinese give some time ago was such a study of the far-reaching consequences of the dissolution of these old loyalties and older sanctities as to lead one to consider, with a strange pity, what follows when a fabric woven upon the loom of the ages begins to ravel and be undone. The desert and the mountain barriers have been pierced to the west and north. The sealed ports are open to the east, the altar of Heaven begins to be forgotten. The dead begin to be only dust.

· · · · · ·

Seven years later— And China stands the Niobe of nations "between two worlds, one dead, the other powerless to be born."

CHAPTER XII

"The Land of the Gods": The Religions of Japan

AMY LOWELL wrote a poem once and called it: "Guns as Keys; and the Great Gate Swings." It is as one pleases, very free verse or very colorful prose, or else a half-enchanted third dimension which is neither verse nor prose, but it is insight and art and history. It contrasts in antiphonic phrases the spirit and action of the West setting out high-handedly and high-heartedly to violate the sanctuaries of the East forbidden to the alien and the spirit of old Japan behind closed gates whose forcing was to have consequences neither Daniel Webster nor President Fillmore nor Commodore Perry could have foreseen.

> A Yankee ship sails down the river,
> Blow, boys, blow—

And while a proud lady of a ship, all a flutter with red, white and blue ribbons curtsied to the shores of Chesapeake Bay, three men in Japan, says Miss Lowell, tried to join hands around an old pine tree whose girth they could not between them span, while Fujiyama, "majestical, inevitable" watched them; or a silk merchant laughed as plum blossoms fell on the breast of a woman in her robes of silk; or a procession of sword- and spear-bearers followed some car of the gods through honey-gold streets to the music of flutes and singing; or the ladies "Wisteria Blossom," "Cloth of Silk" and "Deep Snow" watched the peonies in the temple garden at Asakusa. "The East is East and the West is West—And never the twain shall meet." But they did.

The Japan whose representatives unwillingly received President Fillmore's letter to the Emperor (enclosed in a golden box, value $1,000) was so late as the middle of the last century, a land of which the West knew strangely little. Marco Polo had once brought back alluring rumors of it centuries after the Portuguese had discovered it. Jesuit missionaries seeking to convert had stained with their blood the hinges of the Gates out of which they were thrust. And the

Great Gate stayed shut. New England sea captains out for whales released the forces which finally opened them. "The whale and the whaler," said Michelet, "have revealed the ocean, traced its liquid highways and discovered the secrets of the globe."[1] The whalers wanted ports in which to refit; steam navigation (just beginning) wanted places to recoal; merchants wanted trade, industry, a market; Christian missionaries wanted converts. The West was strong and the East, apparently, quite helpless.

> A Yankee ship sails down the river,
> Blow, boys, blow—

THE ISLANDS AND THEIR INHABITANTS

Geographically Japan is a long, crooked chain of islands which, if one begin with Formosa and end with the Kuril Islands, reach from 20° to near 60° north. Geologically it is one of the newest of lands born of the travail of volcanoes and tragically subject to earthquakes. For the critical historian it is one of the most recent of nations since its documented history dates only from the end of the fifth or the beginning of the sixth century A.D. Racially the aborigines were probably migrants from the Asian mainland, with Malayan elements in the south, Koreans in the center and other strains in the far north. Griffis[2] thinks one conquering tribe, probably from the mainland, began to be paramount as early as the second century A.D. and sees dimly "historic events and personages so early as the fourth century." Islam had crossed the Pyrenees to meet Charles the Hammer and be halted at Tours before Chinese culture, reaching Japan first through Korea, made written records possible. The proud tradition of a line of rulers, children of the sun and "unbroken for ages eternal" does not stand examination.

We are dependent upon the accounts of Chinese travelers for what knowledge we have of the penetration of the archipelago by Chinese culture and some pride of race may also color these accounts. In 545 A.D. and again in 552 King Semiei of Kudora sent a letter to the Emperor of Japan (very much like President Fillmore though there is no mention of a golden box), urging both the excellence and the

---

[1] All, as far as the whalers were concerned, for a better light than candles, stays for corsets and supports for hoop skirts.

[2] *The Religions of Japan*, Chas. Scribner's Sons, New York, 1895.

evident destiny of Buddhism. Buddhist missionaries followed the letter and Chinese institutions and culture crossed the narrow seas with a full and history-making force.[3] How history does repeat itself. It is interesting also to note that the Japanese Emperor so solicited was cautious in his request for Buddhist missionaries but eager to be supplied with doctors, druggists, soothsayers, almanac-makers and artisans.

JAPANESE RELIGION AN AMALGAM

It is impossible, therefore, clearly to separate the early secular history of Japan from its religious history. Japanese religion has been—and is—what Griffis calls an amalgam, whose three elements are Shinto, Buddhism and Confucianism. They can not in their actual fusion be clearly distinguished, being blended in the life and worship of the people very much as Taoism, Confucianism and Buddhism are blended in China. A devout Japanese may be all three at once though scholars who are impatient of amalgams and love clean-cut distinctions assign to each of the three elements its proper functions: Shinto, says Griffis, furnishes theology; Confucianism ethics and the rules of social life, and Buddhism a way of salvation. These distinctions are in general followed by most authorities.[4]

SHINTO (THE WAY OF THE GODS)

Shintoism is the only one of the three native to Japan, the old near-to-the-earth religion upon which the others were superimposed. It has rehearsed in its long growth all the phases of religious growth. Those bench-levels of faith and cult which may be traced through all culture levels around the world were there once on the remote shores washed by the Sea of Japan. Something of all this witnesses to some communication—lost in the morning twilight of unrecorded history

[3] Arthur Lloyd, *The Creed of Half Japan*, E. P. Dutton & Co., New York, 1912. Chapter XVII.

[4] The best organized study of Japanese religion, past and present, not too long or technical is *The Faith of Japan*, Tasuka Harada, The Macmillan Co., New York, 1913. A little more technical but still highly readable, *The Development of Religion in Japan*, G. W. Knox, G. P. Putnam's Sons, New York, 1907. Exhaustive, rather technical and factual well documented, *Shinto (The Way of the Gods)*, W. G. Aston, Longmans, Green & Co., New York, 1905. Longer still, *The Religions of Japan*, 2 vols., W. E. Griffis, Charles Scribner's Sons, New York, 1895.

—between widely separated regions, as though the same currents which carried fauna and flora and men themselves in unsought adventure carried faith also and the dim vision of dim gods. Something of it is certainly indigenous; given the same culture levels and the same forms of religion appear. They were *there* in man's approach to the mystery of his life and his world.

Specialists trace, analyze, refer and speculate. Sun-worship has been a feature of Tartar religion but sun-worship in Japan may be only a coincidence, though it so developed that the sun, as a goddess, became the head of the Shinto pantheon, her worship persistent and universal and the Emperor hailed as her son. The North has always worshiped the sun.[5] There are traces of Korean elements in Shinto, some suggesting similarities of names and cults.[6] But the primitive levels of Shinto are the Animism and Spiritism of all religion and did not need to be imported. Shinto, Aston holds, to be essentially a religion of gratitude and love. "The Great Gods—the Sun-goddess and the Deity of Food—are beneficent beings." They are to be worshiped with laughter. "Every living man may feast his eyes with tokens of their love."

The deities themselves are either nature forces personified or else heroes deified, and the name Kami covers them all. It is a convenient word since it carries the general meaning of superiority either in station or quality. The sources of a river, the hair of the head, "The Lord High Executioner," the Mikado, the mistress of the household and the High Gods are all Kami. In its most inclusive religious sense it is arrestingly akin to the *Mana* of the Polynesian and the *Wakanda* of the Algonquin. Whatever possesses preëminent power is Kami, the evil as well as the good. Whatever is strange, to be wondered at, adored or feared through some virtue (or essence?) of it is Kami. It would correspond also to the old Latin numina; it includes things, animals, the unseen supernatural, the wise and the valorous, the Divine and of late the Christian God.

Clearly, therefore, the gates of Kami open in and out, or down or up. The Supreme Kami may be reached, as in the general evolution of religion, by an ascent from level to level of those sovereign powers by which life is encompassed, to which it is subject, or else men

---

[5] The too short emergence of an unclouded sun this April morning, 1936, after sunless months in these regions makes that quite understandable.

[6] For sources for the study of Shintoism, see Aston, *op. cit.,* Chapter I.

themselves of some high distinction may be endowed with Kami and thereafter take their seats among the gods. These two sources of religious thought merge their streams and color each the other in Shinto. As upon Jacob's ladder, which also reached from earth to heaven, there is an ascending and descending traffic; there gods and men meet and pass. A deity may come down from his high estate, like Weland in Kipling's "Puck of Pook's Hill," who began as a most demanding deity and ended as blacksmith. (Kipling's light touch has in it there a profound philosophy of religion: a god who asks too much of his worshipers is very likely to fall out of the procession.) A mortal man, like Michizane, may climb up and become the god of learning.

The stages common to religion: Animism, Spiritism, etc., are evident in Shinto though confused. When and so far as classification is possible, Aston finds six classes of gods, three nature-gods and three man-gods. The nature-gods may be individuals as the sun, classes as trees, and properties as the god of growth. (The vegetable spirit of so many aliases.) Man-gods are individuals, classes or quite abstract qualities as though masculine strength should be deified. Whether one begins with Tylor for whom some projection of personality into winds and waters and all the movement of the mystery and power of primitive man's circumambient world was fundamental, or with Durkheim who assumes only a sense of a general power to begin with, later to be particularized and personalized, the personification of nature-gods or any god is inevitable. Shinto did this.

The natural difference between men and gods, said a Japanese scholar so late as one hundred and fifty years ago, is that the gods are high and men are low. The Shinto deities, he thought, are about ten feet high. The grammatical structure of the Japanese language does not compel one to say he or she. The Shinto deities may, therefore, be sexless or else their sex is indicated by the myth or the addition of designating terminations. Japanese art takes slight account of sex distinctions.[7]

JAPANESE MYTHOLOGY

Directly the gods or goddesses either are personified they must be supplied with a family tree and given a proper and not always edi-

[7] Aston, *op. cit.*, pages 15-20.

fying biography. Imagination takes them in hand, art and poetry serve them. Devotion magnifies them, the blameless desire to win them converts and extend their empire gives a kind of propaganda quality to the literature which grows up about them. Enter the myth.[8] Most mythologies have a creation cycle and most creation myths begin with a period of anarchy or chaos which is ended by a deity who subdues the Titans or the Dragon, or gives form and order to what was without form and void. Japanese mythology begins with dim, morning-time deities whose many-syllabled names reflect the awe and perplexity with which man first saw his world.

One of them, "Heaven-august-center-master-deity," the ingenious think, was the Pole-star. At any rate they represent early attempts at deity-making and are useful mainly to provide proper ancestors for Izanagi and Izanami, the creator deities of Shinto. These, in a legend out of which a Japanese artist might have made a picture, stood on the floating bridge of Heaven and thrust down the "jewel spear of Heaven" to find if they could find what lay in the depths beneath them. They found the ocean and the brine which dripped from their jeweled spear coagulating formed an island to which they came down. They there married, set up housekeeping and their children were the islands of Japan. The floating bridge of heaven was, the commentators think, the rainbow.

The myth grew with many elaborations and some naïve touches of unseemly humor in which scholars find references to the ancient marriage rites of Japan. A woman in travail with islands is subject to many perils. The procreation of deities is even more hazardous and Izanami in giving birth to the god of fire sickened and died. Thereafter Izanagi sought her sorrowing and followed her to the land of Yomi[9] the land of darkness. Izanagi thus joined the sad procession of questing and bereaved love which moves through so many religions: Isis seeking Osiris, Ishtar following Tammuz, Demeter following Persephone and Orpheus wooing Eurydice back to the music of his harp.

Since after her death Izanami was worshiped by offerings of flowers and flutes and singing this is certainly a Japanese variant of the almost dateless myth of winter-death but she did not return to the

---

[8] Some contemporary Christian theologians are stressing the religious value of the myth in rather unexpected ways.

[9] There can be no possible connection but the Vedic god of the dead was Yama.

upper world. "My lord and husband, why is thy coming so late? I have eaten already of the cooking-furnace of Yomi. . . . Do not thou look on me." Izanagi disobeyed her and saw only corruption. "Now," she said, "I am put to shame." So he speedily ran away and Izanami sent the ugly females of Yomi to pursue and slay him. He escaped them, reached after many mischances the upper world and blocked the gate to the abode of the dead with a great stone. Thereafter he built himself a house of gloom in a lonely island and dwelt alone in silence. Something of the same motif appears in the myths of the sun-goddess and her mischief-making brother, Susa-no-wo, a rain-storm god, of many and valiant adventures. There is in the story of Susa saving a maiden from a dragon, a touch of Hercules and Perseus. The myths change with time and become obscure enough to perplex even specialists. Between them they trace the genealogy of the Mikados to the sun-goddess, and finally lose themselves in the epic of Jimnu with whom perhaps, as with Rama, mythology is merged in dim and legendary history.

There is in the Shinto pantheon thus assembled little order and less limit; the deities are plastic as the caprice and imagination of generations of myth-makers shape and reshape them. Some sense of primeval struggle, of deeply opposed hostilities colors the older myths. The protagonists change their names but not essentially their natures. The sky is not deified, celestial phenomena are, cults of star-gods seem to have been introduced from China, earth-worship is native to Shinto and naturally earthquake gods since the noise of an earthquake might be made by the gods who were building another island. Mountains and rivers and the sea have their divinities though the river-gods have no individual names. Fire, water and wind are sure to furnish deities to a pantheon of nature gods. There were also function gods, like the god of growth; these, Aston calls, the personification of abstractions. Hachiman, the war-god, is one of the later deities. Temmangu, the god of learning and writing, is highly honored. He would be, of course, the patron-god of authors and professors but he accepts the worship of whoever loves learning. "Children who are learning to read and write and their teachers all without exception enjoy his blessings."

He is, says Aston, undoubtedly a deified human being (the gods of pure celestial descent seem to have had other than purely literary interests). He is furnished with a legendary history in which he established a system of national education, was known as the Father of Letters, became prime minister (in the year in which, half across the world, King Alfred who also lived learnedly, died) and, suffering the usual fate of the scholar in politics, was driven by a jealous rival into exile where his piteous prayers reached the gods. But there is no end to all this. Even so capable a scholar as Knox finds Shintoism hard to systematize. Its logical development—if there is any logic in it—was deflected by both Confucianism and Buddhism. It has run a fluctuating course for almost twelve hundred years. What would be true of it at one period would not be true in another.

WORSHIP

Naturally Shinto created shrines, rituals and a priesthood. Shinto worship was and is much like all worship on the same culture levels. The shrines, for the most part hardly more than glorified huts, are themselves offerings. They are not necessarily dedicated to only one deity. They vary in importance and the custody of them belongs to a department of the government. Shinto prayers are ceremonial rather than personal. There are no prayers of confession and self-dedication; moral and spiritual blessings are not sought and there is (Aston) no reference to a future life. Buddhism seems to have met the need of those who sought release and redemption. Such petitions as one finds in modern Shinto prayer ask for no more than prosperity, domestic happiness and the like: "Peace to the country, safety to the family and plentiful crops."

There are traces of primitive human sacrifice though these are as much associated with ancient burial customs which provided the dead with attendants and service proper to their station as with ceremonials of worship. At some early period (though not so early as the legendary dating) a humane emperor recognized that "the practice of following the dead is not good" and asked his cabinet to advise him. One of his ministers submitted an admirable expedient. He summoned the guild of clay-workers and directed them "to take clay and form therewith shapes of men and horses and various objects." "Henceforth," he said, "let it be the law to substitute things of clay for living men." "The expedient," said the emperor, "hath greatly pleased our heart. . . . Henceforth let not men be buried." The shrewd Egyptians did much the same thing.

Shinto can not be said to have a sacerdotal priesthood. The priestly office is as much a function of government as religion. The Mikado is chief priest though he delegates his function for the most part. There are hereditary corporations who prepare the offerings and administer the rites. The Kannushi (Deity-Masters) are appointed by the state. They are not exempt from military service, need not be celibates, may return to the laity and wear a costume which is really "one of the official dresses of the Mikado's court."[10]

There were in 1932 15,375 Shinto priests and more than 50,000 national, prefectural and village shrines. There are some 61,500 private shrines. The domestic rites of Shinto are simple: a god-shelf in the corner of a room, strips of paper with the names of the gods favored by the household, a shrine for them to live in, perhaps an image, two jars for rice whiskey, vases for flowers and a little lamp to be lighted every evening. That and some light of devotion which, though it burn before strange shrines, we have never heretofore found wholly extinguished. Shintoism always carried a popular margin of magic and divination and created elaborate ceremonials and festivals but "its later history was one of neglect and decay." What vitality it had was due mostly to Buddhist ideas.

A succession of Japanese scholars beginning in the seventeenth century sought to revive pure Shintoism.[11] It was a nationalistic

[10] Shinto as a religion of loyalty and patriotism naturally makes the emperor the central figure. His person by constitutional enactment is inviolable. A modern Shinto writer in an article evidently meant for Western readers says of him, "he represents in his person the divine ancestors and at the same time the unbroken line of the Imperial Family to be perpetuated for all ages. He is the source of power which gives eternal life to his subjects and has himself eternal life. . . . The Japanese Constitution does not derive its power from the physical forces of coercion as is often the case with those of other nations. It derives its authority from the voluntary efforts of the people to uphold the way of the gods and make it the way of the nation. And as the Supreme Ruler of the land and its people, stands the Tenno who is divine and inviolable—the object of national adoration and reverence. The Tenno is the central figure of Shinto as he is the Supreme Ruler of the country. . . .

"At the same time the Tenno is the object of worship at these ceremonial occasions as a personification of the deities. He, it must be remembered, represents in person everything the nation has been and will be— He it is in whom Amaterasu-o-mikami dwells. Thus are polity and religion identified in Shinto, and it is this identification perhaps more than any other influence which explains the unique solidity of the Japanese nation." Katsuiko Kakehi, *An Outline of Shinto,* "Contemporary Japan," Volume 1, pages 589-596, passim, March, 1933.

[11] Shinto conceived as a national religion of loyalty or patriotism must, to be effective, of course, have the following of the entire Japanese people. The government sensed this and made certain of its practices compulsory upon all her citizens. This

movement and a reaction against the dominance of Chinese ideas and customs. Their enthusiasm, says Moore,[12] for Japanese culture, literature and religion, their insistence upon the divine genesis and right of the Mikado, "contributed not a little to the movement which resulted in the political restoration of 1868." It is no accident then that there has been of late in Japan a strong official support of Shinto-ism. Shinto is an aspect of Japan. Kami is so inclusive and catholic a turn as to include the land itself, its customs and its cults, its memories, its pride and its ambition. It exalts the emperor, makes a religion of patriotism and continues memories. It is rooted "in the affections of the people, their trust in the national powers and destiny. . . . It is the spirit of old Japan, Yamato Damashii."[13]

JAPANESE CONFUCIANISM AND BUDDHISM

It is impossible here to follow through and disentangle the strands of Confucianism and Buddhism in Japanese religion. The Japanese "Way" of life owes much of its ethical and social content to Confucius, not a little of its cosmic philosophy to Taoism. The Buddhism which entered Japan by way of Korea was the Buddhism of the north, the Great Vehicle which had already added Gautama to the procession of the gods, become excessively speculative and made of Gautama not only Buddha the enlightened, but Buddha the Savior. It met a need neither Shintoism nor Confucianism could fill. It was easy to find a place for Buddha in the wide hospitable Shinto frame.

at once, however, brought a reaction from both Buddhist and Christian Japanese who held that such an order contravened the principle of religious liberty which Japan, as a modern state, had accorded to her people. The values in state ceremonials seemed too great to be sacrificed. A means was therefore found which enabled her to continue with these ceremonials and at the same time to avoid the charge of the other religionists. By imperial decree Shinto was divided into two classes which are now known as state or shrine Shinto and sectarian Shinto. State Shinto was declared not to be a religion at all. The government placed the direction of the State Shrines under the Bureau of Shinto Shrines while sectarian Shinto is considered as on the same plane with Buddhism and Christianity, and is administered under the Bureau of Religions in the Department of Education. There are some thirteen well-recognized Shinto sects, some of which are very active, and in the more recent decades have adopted many of the methods employed by Christianity in propagating themselves. For a discussion of this question, see D. C. Holtom, *Modern Japan and Shinto Nationalism*, U. of Chicago Press, rev. ed., 1947.

[12] *History of Religions,* Charles Scribner's Sons, New York, 1913.

[13] Knox, *op. cit.,* page 77.

He was himself an incarnation and revelation of the hidden reality of the universe. He could, therefore, easily become the incarnation and revelation of Kami, and Buddhism was in this form of it a religion with an appeal both to need and devotion. Buddhism became and continues the religion of the great bulk of the Japanese people. Harada[14] quotes the confession of faith of an old woman which explains the power of Buddhism. She was, she said, old and a woman, not expected to be wise, weak and sinful with no hope in herself but in Amida Buddha. He became, she believed, incarnate and came to earth to deliver man; her hope and the world's hope are in his suffering love. "I am not in a hurry to die but I am ready and I trust that through the gracious love of Amida Buddha I shall enter into the future life . . . and be free from sorrow." There may have been in this confession transmuted elements of Christianity. No matter. A religion which nourishes such a faith has deep, deep roots.

Buddhism has nowhere been more vigorously modernized institutionally than in Japan. There is a Buddhist Salvation Army, a Y. M. B. A. and a Y. W. B. A. They follow the technique of Western Christianity in the Japanese universities. High Buddhist churchmen use aeroplanes, the Shin sect have over two thousand preaching stations. There is a voluminous Buddhist press, enthusiastic missionary societies. (There were a half-dozen years ago twenty-six Buddhist priests in the United States with one hundred thirty-six preaching halls and over seven thousand followers.) The more advanced are even working for Buddhist Church—or more accurately—sect-union.[15]

BUSHIDO: THE SPIRIT OF LOYALTY

The actual motivations which have made and now sustain Japan are not the creation of its religions. They are the expression of something else which, if a religion is to be known by its fruits, is really a religion—the religion of loyalty. One may call it a creation of Japanese feudalism, the ascending scale of loyalties to always higher liege-lords which were the binding ties of feudalism. It is in part a product of Buddhism, perhaps the strangest issue of that faith which has found so many strange issues and as remote from Gau-

[14] *Op. cit.,* page 103.
[15] For a full development of the last paragraph, see Pratt, *The Pilgrimage of Buddha, op. cit.,* Chapter XXV et seq.

tama beneath his Bo-tree as a plumed knight from Jesus of Nazareth. It was a soldier's creed as though Mithra had come to Japan. Many things combined to create it—and something besides in the very soul of Japan.

There is an old martial chant—the admonition, they say, of an imperial guardsman to his descendants in which its spirit sings:

> If on the sea he served,
>   To the waves his corpse,
> If on shore he served,
>   To the moor his bones
> Would he gladly fling
>   For the Sovereign's sake.[16]

Kipling caught and re-echoes this strain eleven hundred years later:

> "There's never a flood goes shoreward now
>   But lifts a ship we manned;
> There's never an ebb goes seaward now
>   But drops our dead on the sand."

The Samurai were during the feudal period the high-born in each clan. After the Restoration in 1868 the Samurai class disbanded but the Samurai spirit lived on. Gratitude, honor, justice and self-sacrifice are associated with loyalty. In these children are trained and soldiers disciplined, together they contribute that imponderable thing called honor for which a Japanese lives, in the loss of which he dies. "All sins, great and small, may be forgiven on repentance and no scar remain, except two; the flight of a Samurai from the post where he should die, and theft. These leave a life-long wound which never heals." This also is Yamato Damashii, the soul of Japan. Death, therefore, is only an incident in the high conduct of life. "Man ought to die; or he ought not to die." The main thing is that he should die to some purpose. He may make of self-inflicted death an apology or an expiation. His highest object of desire should be to die for the sake of his sovereign, or to serve a great occasion, his generation or the long future.

THE IDEA OF FUTURE LIFE

This naturally colors the Japanese conception of life beyond death. Under certain conditions the Japanese would reverse Tennyson's

[16] Harada, *op. cit.,* page 115.

song—" 'Tis Death Not Life for Which We Pant." Death not immortality, becomes the consummation of noble living. This chapter has already said, following recognized authority, that the doctrine of a future life has no place in Shinto. But the old myth of Izanagi and Izanami includes Izanami's departure for Yomi, the land of darkness. It is a hideous and polluted land but the dead there are conscious. Ancient Japanese literature recognized the soul, Tama, which could have an existence apart from the body and without the body power to act.

Ancestor worship which was certainly developed and confirmed by Chinese influences, if they did not create it, implies life after death, but supplies no details. Buddhism supplied abundant detail. Harada (to whom the last sections of this chapter are deeply in debt) notes that Japan rejected Karma and reincarnation. The "Pure-Land" sect, which had its origin in China, "taught definitely . . . the existence of individual souls, salvation through faith in Amida and the life everlasting in Paradise." How far Christianity, of which there had been remnant influences in Japan since Francis Xavier (1550) contributed to this modification of orthodox Buddhism is beyond our power to trace. The Pure-Land (Jodo) faith developed a very real hell and a very bright heaven, edifying accounts of peaceful, happy deaths, the communion of saints and its own literature. It was and is the faith of common folk, whose lives are so bare as to make them meaningless without the hope of immortality. "The more thoughtful and educated are neither agnostic nor pantheistic. The immemorial center of Japanese faith is not in the life to come."

When Commodore Perry opened the Great Gates two forces followed him; the secular culture of the West, armed, inventive, scientific, industrial—and Christianity. These two have never been reconciled in the West, they have not been in the East. Their action, reaction and interaction in the islands born of Izanami's travail are as yet an unfinished chapter in history. Recently[17] I heard Kagawa. He is what Christianity dreams to make of all lands and all men. The militant power of the Empire is what the West has made of Japan. Some of his staccato sentences suggested what Christianity has done. It has leavened what it has not converted. The disciples of Gautama keep Christmas, Kami has become also incarnate in Christ,

[17] April 16, 1936.

Japanese religion is becoming syncretistic. There were intimations in his address of what Christianity might have become had it gone East instead of West. The timeless struggle between the gentleness of Jesus and Gautama and the militant powers of this present world is continued beneath the shadow of Fujiyama.

WHAT WORLD WAR II DID TO SHINTO

The final defeat and occupation of Japan in 1945 has had profound effects upon Japan's religious life. State Shinto has disappeared completely as a state cult, by the direct order of the occupying forces. The shrines remain, the rituals and ceremonies may still be carried on as before, but they are no longer supported by the state. They must depend, as all other forms of religion in Japan—all of which are by constitutional direction on a plane of exact equality—upon voluntary contributions of the people if they are to continue. No one can be forced to support them nor worship at them. Nor may any official, national or local, participate in the ceremonies in representative capacity. The basis of the belief in the divinity of the Emperor was removed at a stroke when Emperor Hirohito announced over the radio to all the people on New Year's Day, 1946, that the Emperor was not a living god and that emperor worship was based on a false conception. He further declared it to be untrue that the Japanese people were superior to other races and destined to rule the world.

Though deprived of special status before government, there is a long history behind what was formerly State Shinto; a great prestige, extensive properties, a priesthood, a literature and doubtless many sincere and devoted followers. What place it may take in Japanese religious life in the future is too early to say. Dr. Holtom's conclusions concerning the matter on the basis of a long and intimate acquaintance with it and a careful examination of its values, is that: ". . . in Shinto survives the oldest institutional life of the Japanese people—older even than the emperor system. In spite of all the changes of fortune that have come to it Shinto lives on. . . . The Japanese people are possessed of a powerful determination to keep Shinto alive and significant. Its will to live is as strong as is the will to live on the part of the nation itself. It may change, it will not die."[18]

[18] D. C. Holtom, *Modern Japan and Shinto Nationalism*, rev. ed., p. 212. Used by permission.

The Children of the Black Tents

THE Semite remains his proud, tenacious, disparate self upon the Assyrian tablets and the plateaus of Arabia, in the hair tent and the skyscraper. Historically we know him as the swarthy son of sundrenched lands, sometime possessor of the Fertile Crescent from the Nile to the Persian Gulf, still possessor of the desert between. He has always been the comrade of the camel and the date palm and— a little—of the dusty-gray olive, at heart a nomad even in walled cities and bringing the prophet's passion out of the desert to declare a deathless truth or ravage a ripened civilization. Arabia is more likely to have been the real nursery of his soul and his ways than any other land.[1] There he pitched his black tent and from there his restless sons set out for kinder lands, Babylonia, Syria, Palestine, Abyssinia, the Pillars of Hercules and, in their most far-flung adventure, to meet the Frank upon the field of Tours.

The religion of the Semite has always been an inseparable aspect of his mind, his morals and the conduct of his society. It is by no means the only expression of his genius but it has been the enduring expression. His empires have dissolved like the sun-dried brick of the hanging gardens of Babylon and left only a formless débris. Only his proud gods on carved tablets are left of his palaces, the call to prayer is the only echo of his Saracenic splendor—but the Hebrew psalms are said around the world and Hebrew prophecies still shape the policies of regnant states.

His gods have always been lords of dominion, rulers of places, little places, a field, a city or a countryside to begin with, Lord of Heaven and Earth to end with. They have always been vigorously concerned with administration. The Greek personalized his divinities under the aspect of beauty and desire and set them on stormless Olympus half careless of mankind. The Semite conceived his divini-

[1] See Geo. A. Barton, *A Sketch of Semitic Origins,* New York, 1902, Chap. I: P. M. J. LaGrange, *Etudes Sur Les Religions Semitiques,* Paris, 1905, page 41 et seq.

ties under the aspect of power and saw Jahveh on Mount Sinai dictating the moral law through the lightning.

The misty north anticipated the twilight of the gods, the Semite in his loftiest insight conceived God sub specie aeternitatis—as the eternal. The great gods of the imperial Semite races have been fire and sword-served, kind to their faithful followers, but keeping judgment for the alien and the disobedient. It was the genius of the Semite to personalize the spiritual and conceive the divine in ways before which pale abstractions disappear. His vivid imagination contributed to this and the quality of his language as well. He thought in images, his words are symbol and poetry.

And yet there is always something of the desert in his faith and his psalms—strange alternations of tenderness and imprecation, like the tender wonder of the desert at sunset and the hot hardness of it at noon. He has given us the splendor of the Cherubim and Seraphim and the evil ones who come up with the wind and dance in the dust. The lesser spirits of Greece are shy and beautiful, fauns and nymphs, glimpsed through olive groves, and Pan in the reeds by some friendly little river. The lesser spirits of Northern Europe love mischief but they love the hearthstone also and are not above doing a man or a maid some kindness or homely service. The jinns of Arabia may be the slaves of the lamp or the ring, but their freedom is fearsome.

．　．　．　．　．

One controlling conception pervades all Semitic religion with far-reaching consequences—the distinction between the sacred and the impure—or else in another form between what can be touched and eaten and what carries with it a pollution needing ceremonial correction. The Semite had no monopoly of this. But the great Semitic religions built these distinctions of the permitted and forbidden into tenacious systems of ritual law which time has not dissolved.

Ceremonies of consecration grow out of these ideas and create a sacred furnishing of temples and a sacred garmenture of holy ministrants. That, too, has outlived ancient temples. Sacred places asserted their sovereignty over Semitic devotion. They may not have belonged to the god to begin with[2]—only a spot like an oasis or a wooded height richer than others in its suggestion of some supernatural life. If the spirits who lived there were strange to the tribe

[2] La Grange, *op. cit.,* page 180.

it was to be shunned; if the presiding deity was their friend they made it a shrine for their worship. At first these sacred places were open to the sky, marked, perhaps, by boundary stones. In time they were temple-walled, with some last hidden sanctuary where the priest adventured into the very presence of the god. The Cult of Sacred Stones—about the origin of which students are much divided—is associated with the cult of sacred places. Hills and mountains were invested with an unusual sanctity. If one adds to this the ideas of consecrated persons and consecrated times—all rooted in the same general conceptions—one has in substance the elements which entered into Semitic religion—all but one.

These details would be of little value save to those insatiably curious were it not for the destiny which has attended Semitic religion. It was caught by a vaster current than its own. And it brought with it incredibly old beliefs, dim vistas of the desert life, controlling conceptions of ritual and consecration, folk lore, the forms of a primitive oath, idealized memories of patriarchs and seekers after God, old battle songs and chants of deliverance. For the Semite has always had a reverence for the written word which invested what has once been enshrined in his sacred books with an inviolable sanctity and authority. Thereafter whether a scripture had come down nameless from a dateless past, or—like the Koran—had been created in his own lifetime, it ceased to be man's word and became God's word—the source of his faith and the law of his life.

For the Semite believed as no other race has believed that a man may be so God-inspired that his message is the absolute articulation of the divine, the interpretation of the present and the unveiling of the future. The prophet thus became the supreme expression of his religious genius—the voice of religious certainty charged with ethical passion. His nature fitted him for this commanding form of expression. Some element of strange brooding lay at the heart of it, some rare sensitiveness which objectified the strongly felt, some courage to say "thus saith the Lord," some unique bequest, a consuming passion for righteousness. And he had a gift of noble eloquence and a power to make a song of a vision. So he moved the world.

The centuries have become his disciples, monotheism his gift to religion.

CHAPTER XIII

The Hebrew Prophet Challenges the Gods

THE short twilight had begun to fall across a royal city in Northern Palestine and the narrow streets were deep in shadow. The fires in the squares where the caravans halted for a night and herdsmen from upland pastures guarded the wool or the sheep they would sell in the morning, cast a fugitive light upon tired men and beasts. Some sound of song and lutes could be heard from behind closed courtyard doors. The folk of Bethel were sufficiently religious; in the morning they would burn their dough as a thank-offering, but the night was for pleasure. The prosperous were rich enough for ivory divans, dainty food, ashlared houses, perfumes and wine, but they had no thought for the bleeding wounds of the nation or the estate of the poor. And the poor were very poor, being always in debt to money lenders with nothing to pledge but themselves; they would sell themselves for a pair of sandals.

Then a voice was heard above the crooning music and the confusion of the caravanserai:

Listen to this word of mine against you, house of Israel, listen to this
    dirge:
'Fallen, fallen, never to rise, is maiden Israel;
low on her own land she lies, with none to raise her.'

    .   .   .   .   .

You who make justice a bitter thing,
trampling on the law,

    .   .   .   .   .

Houses of ashlar you may build,
but you shall never dwell in them;
vineyards you may plant,
but you shall drink no wine from them.

    .   .   .   .   .

The Eternal declares. [1]

[1] *Amos* 5. This and subsequent quotations from James Moffatt, *The Bible: A New Translation.* Revised Edition (1935). Harper & Brothers, Publishers.

Amos, the herdsman of Tekoah, had begun to speak and a new epoch was dated in the history of religion.

The history of the Hebrew people is so much a part of their religion that no study of that religion is possible which does not follow the contours, at least, of the forces and the centuries which brought Amos to Bethel. He is the first of the great prophetic group, but what he said is only a faint though noble music unless it be backed with the long past out of which it was made articulate. It is now the commonplace of any study of the Hebrew religion that the prophet is the key to Israel's supreme contribution to religion and the history of Israel supplied the background for the prophet. Amos may wait and the fires go out while we turn to the past.

THE STRATEGIC POSITION OF PALESTINE

Michelet says that the geography of France is the history of France and that is so true of Israel that geography comes first. The land to which Amos spoke is a limestone shoulder of a country thrust up two thousand feet above sea level for perhaps a hundred miles between the Lebanon Mountains and the northern frontiers of the Arabian peninsula. It falls away on one side to the narrow coastal plain of the eastern Mediterranean, on the other side to the Jordan valley. The significant history of it is west of the Jordan River; all its tremendous drama was confined to a region little larger than the pleasant hill and meadow counties west of the Connecticut River in Massachusetts.

The geographical position of Palestine has kept it in the movements of history ever since Amen Hotep of Egypt set the solar disk in the standards of the Pharaohs and carried on a diplomatic correspondence with clay tablets for stationery. The genius of the race who held it, always in hazard, for almost fifteen hundred years made it the homeland of two great religions and the foster-mother of a third. Christianity carried substantially the whole deposit of Hebrew history and religion into the current of western faith and civilization and that mighty stream has carried them around the world. The mountains of Palestine, its blue, hill-sheltered lake, its one river and its bitter sea are household names. There might still be children, doubtful of the rulers and presidents of their own countries, who could name the kings of the Hebrew people.

One may see from the hills above Nazareth the Mediterranean, the Jordan valley and the strategic plain through which, since history began, the caravan trade of the Fertile Crescent has passed between Egypt and Mesopotamia. The merchants of Thebes and Memphis, the adventurers of Ur and Nippur, the proud traders of Tyre and Sidon, Damascus, Babylon and Nineveh, have all used the Valley of Esdraelon for a high road. The kings of remembered empires and forgotten little states have used it for their armies and their battles. And yet Palestine was always a little apart, guarded by her hills and the stubborn aloofness of Israel. The whole of the relation of the Jew to epochal centuries, to Egypt, Babylonia, Syria, Persia, Greece, Rome and the world since, is typified in that location, washed by every passing tide, involved in every change in the balance of world power and yet maintaining a spiritual and racial integrity unconquered and undissolved.

Racially the whole region has always belonged to the Semite, save for some vague period of Hittite occupation, though generally subject to the overlordship of either Egypt or Mesopotamia. The little Hebrew Kingdoms were never independent of some control from either the Nile Valley or the valley of the Two-Rivers, save in periods when the balance of power was shifting between Babylon and Nineveh or a Pharaoh had troubles enough at home to keep his armies within the Delta. Israel occupied generally the unhappy position of a buffer state and its domestic politics reflected that situation often acutely. Whatever passed for a Hebrew King's Cabinet would be nationalistic, pro-Egyptian or pro-Assyrian in a way to perplex a weak sovereign, raise factions in the streets of Jerusalem—so long accustomed to faction—and give prophet Isaiah subject matter for a message to be read twenty-five hundred years later in a Christian church.

In general Palestine suffered most from the northern powers. Egypt was most likely to make trouble by seducing a Judean King from his allegiance to Assyria with the offer of military help which usually turned out a broken reed and brought swift chastisement from the long arm of Nineveh. The cultural and religious influences of Babylonia left the deeper mark upon the Hebrew mind; with the exception of a few arresting parallels between the Hebrew Psalms and the devotional literature of Egypt, Hebraism was far more deeply in debt to Chaldea than to Egypt. But the memory of some sojourn in Egypt dominated the Hebrew's recital of his history, as the flight from Egypt furnished Dante a music to which the Mount of Purgatory trembles as its pilgrims move from terrace to terrace in their steep ascent.[2]

Palestine was never, since the history of the Fertile Crescent began, an empty land nor without cultural and political contacts with the controlling forces of Western Asia, though the Abraham of the Book of Genesis moves through it with none to forbid him, chasing the little kings of Elam and Shinar with a handful of men. The Hebrew loved his land with a passion time has not undone. He wove the fields and hill slopes and little brooks of it, its vineyards and olive orchards into his Scriptures until they take the color and contour of it, the "feel" of it, the very quality of its light. Even now the pages of the Old Testament come to life as one motors north from Jerusalem. Though nothing under cover seems more than a legend or a memory, there is an assuring veracity in the worn contours of the land itself and the immemorial ways of its folk. Also the Hebrew claimed the title-deeds of it from Jehovah and invested his possession of it with an epic splendor.

The Epic of the Exodus

The materials for his narration of his occupation of it were drawn from many sources and so combined and edited that three generations of scholars have spent more labor upon them than has been spent upon any other documents, and still find themselves at odds about details. The accounts themselves are too familiar to need retelling. They begin with the story of Creation and the entry of death and sin into the world and two exiles from a watered garden fenced out by the flashing swords of cherubim, with Abraham the seeker led by a gleam, to whom God speaks under the oaks of Shechem and Mamre. In due time his son and grandson go famine driven to Egypt where Joseph becomes Pharaoh's prime minister. Other Pharaohs forget Joseph and the descendants of Abraham become bond slaves to build treasure cities for their master. Moses is brought up in the King's palace, finds the Eternal in the desert, humbles the pride of

[2] In exitu Israel.

Egypt and leads his people through the parted arm of the sea, while
the delivered bondsmen sing:

> Thou didst blow thy blast, and the sea covered them,
> like lead they sank into the mighty deep!
> O Eternal, what god is there like Thee,
> . . . gloriously supreme.[3]

The Eternal writes His laws on tablets of stone from fire crowned
Sinai, guides the hosts with a pillar of cloud by day and fire by
night, gives them water from smitten rocks, feeds them with manna,
scourges them for their apostasy, turns them back into the wilderness, grants Moses a vision of the land he may not enter and buries
him there.

> But no man saw that sepulcher,
> And no man saw it e'er;
> For the Angels of God upturned the sod
> And laid the dead man there.

Jordan in flood parts to let the invaders through, the walls of Jericho
fall at the sound of their trumpets and fire-led and cloud-guarded
Israel came into Canaan.

> O happy Israel! No folk like you,
> Victorious through the Eternal!
> He is your shield of succor,
> The sword of your success.

This epic of deliverance has had a long repercussion. It has inspired the noble music of the Hebrew Psalms, furnished Christianity
an analogy for the wilderness wanderings of life, supplied a basis for
the faith of three great religions, a code of morals which the English
common law accepts and enforces, the accredited account, until
within seventy-five years, of the beginning of all history and the
world—and the negro slave a motif for his spirituals of hope and
despair. But it has left the student a perplexing problem.

THE PROBLEM OF RECONSTRUCTING EARLY HEBREW HISTORY

One accomplishes nothing by saying that all this is embroidered
tradition. One must still ask why it was believed and upon what

[3] *Exodus* 15: 10-11, Moffatt's translation.

basis of fact. This is the task to which the scholarship of the last three generations has addressed itself and always in a disturbing atmosphere. For these recitals became, in the belief of both Jews and Christians, the inspired and inerrant word of God; they have furnished a hallowed support for confidences by which men have lived and for which they have died. The analysis of them has thus become more than a problem in the reconstruction of history which would, under any circumstances, be difficult enough. It has involved the very bases of authority in Western religion and has thus assumed an importance out of all proportion to the secular significance of the facts. No devout Jew or Christian cares whether Abraham built the Kaaba at Mecca or not, being quite sure that he did not; but his conversation with the Eternal under the Mamre oaks is another matter.

The conclusions of the specialists reflect this situation. They have yielded inherited positions slowly and only under the compulsion of the slow accumulation of a critical knowledge. The conservative save as much as they can, the most critical let almost everything go; the most fair-minded can only feel their way back into a region which is buried beneath the dust of millenniums, obscured by the habit of the Hebrew historian and guarded by the militant faith of Christianity as the Tree of Life by the swords of cherubim.

The Hebrew historian had the conviction—a conviction for which as we shall see he was probably in debt to his prophets—that all his racial past had been an affair with the Eternal, he focused the entire splendor and sovereignty of God upon Israel. He combined the naïveté of a child with a grave majesty of spiritual understanding; beneath his touch history was the recitative of a Divine adjudication which left no fault unpunished, no loyalty unblessed. He had no dates but the past. He had for his "sources" an older book or two— like the book of Jasher, creation legends common to his world and his time, old songs (actually of great evidential value), dim tribal memories so often recast in the telling of them that the art of telling is perfect, recollections of signal deliverances, Deborah under the palm trees and blind Samson getting a great price for his two eyes.

Two interwoven documents tell such things as these. They are no older in the actual writing of them than the ninth century B.C. One of them was written by a nameless historian in the little Kingdom of Judah, the other by a nameless historian of the Northern Kingdom.

After the destruction of the Northern Kingdom, they were combined in a single narration with little or no attempt to adjust their very considerable differences. The modern critic calls them "J" and "E" and does what he can to disentangle their interwoven strands.[4]

As though this were not enough, the reformers of a later period re-edited and strongly moralized the whole cycle of early traditions to conform them to their own rituals and religious ideals and published them as chapters of Moses' autobiography. This is substantially the material—although it suffered still further additions and recensions—which inquiring scholarship must sift and interpret. The Egyptian taskmaster, so we are told, gave the children of Israel no straw for their tale of sun-baked brick. The Hebrew historian was under no such handicap. His narratives are threaded with the survival of old customs, the frayed remnants of old faiths, idealized survivals haunted by what he did not understand himself. The most significant light which shines upon the past from these pages of his, hallowed by the devotion of generations, is cast by what he has artlessly incorporated; strange and seemingly inconsequential facts which have the gleam of veracity in them. His straw is not straw at all; it is the ore of fact in the plastic clay of his credulity, his poetic imagination—and his epoch-making faith.

The Relation of the Hebrew to Egypt and Chaldea

Egypt and Chaldea furnished Israel his far horizons. His history is always somewhere between them just as the entire movement of the civilization he shared is always somewhere between them. The Semite established himself early and solidly in the valleys of the Nile and the Two Rivers and suffered such changes as the admixture of blood and long residence in established centers bring to the nomad. The conquering Semites took on the habits of empire and wealth, they kept the gods they found in their new homes and touched them with something of their own spirit. Then, religiously, their creative force hardened down and, though they built temples of wonder, their temples housed do-nothing gods in Egypt and an hierarchy of gods in Babylon and Nineveh. There was always, as

---

[4] The introduction to Moffatt's translation gives the accredited conclusions of scholars, the translation with its brackets and different types follows the different documents plainly.

there is still, a restless drift of the true nomad between the two regions, sons of the desert who preserved some sense of kinship between their tribal groups—though kinship did not always mean friendship. The most convenient symbol of this kinship was a common ancestor whose memory time enhanced, whose deeds pride magnified.

This scheme of racial history is paralleled by the traditions of many primitive peoples and gains a certain support from what we know of the rise of the Greek city state. It is by no means impossible that an early society should be organized around the persistence of certain dominant families or that, in tribal society, there should be a basis of fact in traditions which go back to the clan. It is difficult to go much further than this in dealing with the patriarch stories of the Hebrews. Most authorities do not go so far; for them Isaac and Jacob and Jacob's sons are tribal personifications and their deeds and fortunes are only what the tribes believed about their own adventurous and corporate past. The "song of the tribes" seems to bear this out. Its vivid characterizations have a deal of time packed between the lines as though the tribes had long shown of what stuff they were before some patriotic and sharp tongued bard reviewed the past, as Michelet calls the roll of the provinces of France with a thousand years of history behind him to lend weight to each splendid characterization—

> A lion's whelp is Judah!
> My son, you take cover, sated with prey!
> He crouches, couches like a lion,
>   like an old lion—who dare rouse him?
> The sceptre never passes from Judah,
>   nor ever the staff of sway,
> till he comes into his own,
>   and makes the clans obey.[5]

The more iconoclastic make a clean sweep of all the patriarchs. Loisy thinks them to have been the primitive gods of the shrines with which their legends are associated,[6] a conclusion difficult to support. If a man has ever been a god he should come down through legend trailing some clouds of his celestial glory; there is not a time-whipped shred of divine about the Hebrew patriarchs. They have

[5] *Genesis* 49: 9-10. Moffatt's translation.
[6] Alfred Loisy, *The Religion of Israel*, New York, 1910, page 26.

an excess of purely human characteristics. These fascinating stories do indicate some early association of the Hebrew nomad with Palestine—an association not impossible in a region of free movement, across which tides of sovereign control ebbed and flowed during periods in which any measure of events is lost and centuries foreshorten in the

> dark backward and abysm of time.

Oriental frontiers have always been fluid, and nomadic society was equally fluid. The attempt to run boundary lines through Genesis and Exodus is about as futile as setting up landmarks in water. The thirteenth and twelfth centuries B.C. were particularly a time of restless folk movement[7] from the Aegean to the Euphrates. It would be easy to carry along desert tribes, always haunting the frontiers of well-watered lands, in the backwash of movements so vast. It is no long distance from the borders of Palestine to the northeastern borders of Egypt. The Hebrew nomad ranged the desert between and watched both gates.

He remembered later—and very vividly—that he found the gate of Egypt open, and having entered it, was trapped there. The Egyptian recollections are less precise since Egypt had more to remember. Some mention is made of the Chabiri, a warlike people who were adding to the troubles of the realm. If these were Hebrews, they had invaded Canaan as early as fourteen hundred B.C. The more conservative assume some connection between the settlement of desert tribes in Egypt and the Shepherd Kings who, having been once nomads themselves, would be hospitable to them. In due time the Shepherd dynasty was overthrown and the rulers who took their empty thrones had no use for the Bedouin and the Bedouin, having no use for the forced labor to which the new Pharaohs subjected them, took the first opportunity to escape.

Sayce[8] believes that an invasion from the east afforded a cover under which the Hebrew tribes who had been building the treasure cities of Goshen made their escape. The Hebrew historian makes a vaster issue of it all. They were delivered by their God who sent Moses to the King of Egypt with such a command as no King had heard before: "Go to the King of Egypt and tell him that 'the

[7] John Runnett Peters, *The Religion of the Hebrews*, Boston, 1914, page 51.
[8] *Early Israel and the Surrounding Nations*, New York, 1899, page 49.

Eternal the God of the Hebrews has met us. Pray let us travel for
three days in the desert, then, that we may sacrifice to the Eternal
our God.'" The fact that according to the context "the Eternal their
God" did not contemplate their return is a detail. The call of Jahweh
came to Israel from the desert. Primitive Hebraism is a desert-
nurtured religion.

Primitive Hebrew Religion

It is easy to make poetry of all this, as Renan does, and call the
Semitic shepherd a native monotheist, awed by the stars and the
wind-swept loneliness of the desert into the sense of the brooding
presence of God and thereafter more sure of him than anything in
the world. There is just enough truth in this to make it misleading.
Monotheism was the religious contribution of the Semite to the world
but there is no evidence that he began as a monotheist. The light in
which the prophets found their one true God was slow in rising
and it is only by reflecting it backward that the glory of it touches
Israel in the wilderness. Israel was long in learning monotheism but
Israel did come into Palestine believing that Jahweh[9] was his God
and he was Jahweh's chosen. Edom and Moab might have what
dealings they pleased with what gods they pleased, there was only
one God for him.

No name exactly describes this faith. It admitted the existence of
other gods but it was not a polytheism. It affirmed the sovereignty
of Jahweh over other deities but it was not henotheism, it demanded
the entire devotion and obedience of the Hebrew but it was not
monotheism. If one might coin a creaking name for it, it was focal-
theism, the centering of the devotion of a religiously minded race
upon one deity with an intensity which cast all other worship into
the shadow and in time made shadows of all other gods. It is the
marvel of the story of religion that historically the long Procession
of the Gods was halted not before Brahma the world soul but Jahweh
the tribal deity of desert nomads.

This pregnant faith was served by circumstances. The very iso-
lation of the wilderness served it, not because it left the nomad
nothing but God, but because it left him alone and long alone with

[9] It is quite necessary to use "Jahweh" and "Jahwism" in studying the development
of the Hebrew religion. They have now a precise and generally accepted meaning for
which there are no useful synonyms.

the only God he had. Egypt and Babylon, Athens and Rome accumulated deities, conquered them, imported them, presently made a pantheon of them in which they watched one another gravely, with an altar outside for the unknown god to cover contingencies. Monotheism has never grown out of a system like that.[10] (Greek monotheism was the creation of philosophers who crossed a dream with an argument and begot the conception of Eternal Excellence; but Eternal Excellence never had a temple or an altar.) The best that can come out of such a system is a major god—Ashshur in Nineveh or Zeus in bright walled Olympus. Very likely the worshiper of many gods always carried on the main business of his devotion with some one divinity who best served his need, just as Socrates prayed to Pan when he was abroad in the olive grove; just as the devout of a faith which dares to have saints choose their own saints, or Pompilia chose

> . . . the poor virgin that I used to know
> At our street corner in a lonely niche,—
> She, not the gay ones, always got my rose.

But the desert left the Hebrew no choice and Jahweh left him no choice either—"For I, the Lord, thy God, am a jealous God." This jealousy of Jahweh was no academic attribute. It was a passion which left his followers no option of sharing their offerings and their prayers with any rival deity. Call it all the investment of a conception of deity with the strange particular intensity of the Hebrew temper and it makes no difference in the outcome. The jealousy of Jahweh walled Israel from the world and made him "a peculiar people" dedicated to the service of Jahweh, serving other gods at the peril of his state and his soul, keeping the blood stream of his race uncorrupted by alien strains. This, I say, made possible the final emergence of a monotheistic faith which the currents of religious history have caught and carried around the world. The intolerance of Hebrew religion finally assured the essential triumph of its conception of God.

A jealous God is neither an easy nor kind deity to serve. He is capricious by any human test, flamingly revengeful of any affront to his sovereignty, always on the watch for any slip, and urging the devotees to the annihilation of his enemies. Any religious war catches

---

[10] Dr. Braden challenges the implication that only in a small isolated state is the development of monotheism possible.

something of this temper and becomes the cruelest of fighting; the religious wars of the Hebrews still dye the pages of the Hebrew sacred books with red. Was not the Lord their God a jealous God? But there was destiny at the heart of it all. The time has come when Moffatt can veil the naïve religious idealisms of Jahweh worship with the gracious phrase: "The Eternal thy God," and his translation be nobly right. But Hebrew faith came a long road before the Twenty-third Psalm set to timeless music the understandings of God that translation voices.

Jahweh-worship

Jahweh-worship as a corporate force in the life of the Hebrew people began with Moses—that statement seems reasonably secure—but what is the reality behind the wonders and theophanies with which the accounts of the Exodus are invested? We do not find among the representative authorities any who entirely deny the historicity of Moses. The more critical makes him the medium through which Jahweh-worship reached and in a measure unified the Hebrew tribes, and not the creator of it; but his place is secure. He is too deeply embedded in the whole body of Hebrew recollection to displace. Zoroaster has a far less solid claim for critical recognition. Unless we are to reduce religion to an impersonal evolution—and it is certainly not that—Moses must be numbered among the makers of religion.

The grandiose garmenture with which he has been furnished is another matter. He was nurtured in Egypt but he did not find Jahweh in Egypt, he found his duty, his destiny and his God beneath the shadow of the mountains of the Sinaitic peninsula. The old accounts make it all an awesome dealing between Jahweh and Moses, and veiled in mystery—any meeting of the human and the divine must be veiled with symbols. The imagination which has given the splendid symbol of the burning bush to literature was of a noble order, but the significance of these accounts is not in their margin of wonder splendid or naïve.

Jahweh lived in the wilderness. "For you have seen for yourselves," he said, when the fugitives are safe under Sinai, "what I did to the Egyptians and how I bore you safe on eagles' wings and brought you hither to myself."[11] Moses' fear that the Eternal will not go on with him from Sinai must be taken very literally. The old poems embedded in the narratives like fragments of archaic rock in conglomerate are most significant:

> From Sinai came the Eternal
> From Seir he dawned on us,
> From Paran's range he rayed out,
> Blazing in fire from the south.

There is a tradition that Moses married into a priestly family of this general region and so became a member of the tribe by adoption and blood ritual.[12] Jahweh faith was then in all probability the local and ancestral faith of those tribes of the loose Hebrew Confederation which lived in the southern Sinaitic territory.[13] Moses accepted it, though the influence of his wife and its priests and the symbolic fire kindled a flamelike passion to deliver the oppressed in Egypt and, in the name of the Eternal, to make a nation of them and win for them a land of their own. The old memories of some earlier occupation of Canaan turned his face and his faith to the north. The rest is history made sacred by the devotion of a race who invested all their past with the splendor of Divine purpose and the irresistible élan of Divine power.

One must feel one's way with many conjectures, through the accounts of it written centuries later, but the issue is plain—Israel came into Palestine and brought Jahweh with him. Mohammed and Mohammedanism illustrate, in an undisputed field, what religion personally mediated can do to fuse Semitic society and release Semitic forces. In each instance religion gave a new quality to social morality, though there was a potential wealth of moral development in the Mosaic system, which Islam never attained. Beyond any debate the pious Hebrew historian wrote back into the wilderness code the

---

[11] *Exodus* 19: 4.

[12] What is perhaps the most curious passage in the Hebrew Sacred Books (*Exodus* 4: 24-26) bears directly on this point. Moses was a stranger in Jahweh's territory without the proper cult sign and so in mortal peril. His wife marked him with ritual blood and "the Eternal" let him alone.

[13] An outstanding group of scholars believe the Kenites to have been the original Jahwists. See Barton, *A Sketch of Semitic Origins*, pages 275 et seq., for a full discussion of this point. R. W. Rogers, *The Religion of Babylonia and Assyria*, believes the name of Jahweh can be found in Babylonian records 2000 B.C. It is hardly likely that the name began with the Old Testament records.

moral development of later centuries and invested new codes and rituals with the august authority of Moses' name, but through all the tangled web one may trace an unbroken development of moral insight and moral passion. Moses did at least three momentous things: he united Israel in the worship of Jahweh, he established religion in moral obedience and he disciplined a stiff-necked people through the personal ascendancy of a man who spake face to face with God. The judgment of time which assigns him a place among the great lawgivers of history is just.

EARLY CONCEPTION OF JAHWEH

But all this is to anticipate an outcome of which there would have been little evidence in the twelfth century B.C. Religion is always an unescapable association of supreme insights and confidences with the limitations of those who entertain them. Saul of Tarsus once remarked apropos of this whole great matter that, "We have this treasure of earthen vessels." The vessels of primitive Israel were quite earthen and the treasure they held was curiously compounded. They invested Jahweh with attributes from which the humane passion of all the Hebrew prophets and the powerful solvent of the understanding faith which a son of Israel finally gave the world have not been able to free him. There are passages in the old songs of the Hebrew people which put upon the lips of deity the passion of desert tribes whose victorious swords are still red from religious wars.

> I will whet my flashing blade,
>   gripping justice by the hilt,
>
>   .   .   .   .
>
> I drench my arrows in their blood,
>   my blade devours their bodies—
> blood of the slain and prisoners,
>   of braves with flowing locks.[14]

The translators of the King James Version have supplied the ode from which the foregoing lines are taken: they call it "Moses' song which sets forth the perfection of God."

Jahweh was a war-god—the time and the race could do with no less; he was, maybe, a fire-god in the most primitive understanding

[14] Deuteronomy 32: 41-42, Moffatt's translation.

of him, but he was never a nature god.[15] Israel did not take over the demoralizing conception of fertility deities which dominated Babylonia and of which there are traces in Arabia so late as the time of Mohammed. The people, quite literally, fell for these engaging divinities when they found them in Canaan but the spokesman of Jahweh never for a moment permitted any identification of him with them; on the contrary they fought the whole system to an ensanguined end in the name of Jahweh.

Jahweh always moves, and freely, above natural phenomena. He controls them, gives and withholds rain, furnishes his armory with hailstone; he can even stop the sun, but he is never the rain cloud, the sun or the storm. The persuasion of Jahweh's absolute dominion over any force or event seams Hebrew devotion. Anything becomes possible for him and his servants; iron may float, rivers be parted, a drenched altar so kindled that the very stones are burnt. Given a people who have no scientific sense of natural law, a world in which there is no law at all but Jahweh's will and such things are, for the narrator, as natural as anything else. This is the key to the wonder narratives of early Hebrew history, but it is also the key to something vaster. This confidence sometimes naïvely, sometimes splendidly expressed, kept Jahweh from being dissolved into pantheism or worshiped with shameless rites. If the sun is a god, then, with the growth of scientific knowledge the godhead of the sun gets lost, but if the Eternal has a dominion beyond the pageantry of the seasons and slow drift of constellations, then—

> Grass withers and flowers fade,
>> because the breath of the Eternal blows upon them;
>
> . . . . . .
>
> but our God's promise stands for evermore.
>
> . . . . . .
>
>> Lift high your eyes, look up;
>> who made these stars?
>> he who marshals them in order,
>> summoning each one by name.[16]

[15] For an ingenious attempt to relate Jahweh, before he became the God of the Hebrews, to the primitive fertility goddess of the Semitic, see Barton, *op. cit.*, page 280 et seq. The author also discusses circumcision in the same connection. But Barton seems strongly under the influence of one idea—the significance of the date palm in Semitic religion.

[16] *Isaiah* 40, passim, Moffatt's translation.

These are the persuasions which have kept monotheism alive for thirty centuries. The dark earthiness out of which it grew ought not to blind the student of religion to the light-touched heights to which it finally lifted itself.

Jahweh was from the first vividly personified. The Greeks humanized the gods, the Semite personalized them, the Hebrew made Jahweh amazingly real. He did this by virtue of a creative imagination, an unquestioning faith and a strange audacity. Jahweh came down and walked in a garden in the cool of the day, a shameful couple could hide from him, and yet he had Cherubim at his bidding. He talked with Abraham under the Mamre-oak and must visit Sodom personally to see if the reports of its wickedness are well grounded, and yet he is master of human destiny. It is all childish, capricious, anthropomorphic and yet this conception of a deity rich in all the attributes of personality was capable of an indefinite extension in the direction of holiness and love.

JAHWEH A MORAL GOVERNOR

Jahweh, even from the first, was a God who made for righteousness. Primitive Israel clothed him with a strangely woven garment of moral administration, though their conceptions of him have the moral contradictions of the race and the time. He was not above instructing Moses to deceive Pharaoh—he was relentless against his enemies, merciless with his own unrepentant followers, asking an eye for an eye and a tooth for a tooth—and yet "It is the Eternal, the Eternal a God pitiful and kind, slow to be angry, rich in love and loyalty." Even in the old songs justice is the hilt of his sword.

Some dim feeling for justice, some shadowed sense that the Divine must be right and right his supreme concern colors the oldest narratives—"Shall not the judge of all the earth do right?" The Hebrew idea of Jahweh had a power at the heart of it to be recast and take new insights and understanding to itself. It contained from the first the pregnant conception of a Divine power above nature and yet directing it, personal in action and reaction and the moral governor of the world. These are the elements which have hitherto given monotheism its religious values and sustained the devout of three great religions. If these confidences should be lost, the idea of God as a meaningful force for humanity will disappear in the vast impersonal drive of the cosmic order.

Jahweh worship was entangled from its beginning in inheritances older still. The ways of the race and the time set their marks upon it and these marks persisted. That is an inadequate phrase. These ancient inheritances are woven through the very structure of the Hebrew sacred literature, warp of its web. Little by little that past is being recovered. It is the characteristic past of all religions with clear traces of animism, fetishism, stone-worship, reverence for sacred waters, sacred spots and sacred mountains, magic, witchcraft, divination and astrology.[17] The folk-lore of the desert, folk and festival ways, cast and recast, are all continued far into the Kingdom period. They are all in the record; sometimes in an obscure allusion, sometimes in a song or hero tale, sometimes in a law or a ritual and always the more convincing because they are so unconsciously told.

There is little evidence in the Hebrew Scriptures of the primitive Semitic belief that the divinities were kinsmen of the clans—a name or two perhaps like Abram—but generally the sense of contract relation has supplanted any vivid belief in blood relation. A man could choose his divinity and make a bargain with him—as Jacob did at the Bethel—"If God will be with me and guard me on this journey, giving me food to eat and clothes to wear, so that I return to my father's house safe and sound . . . then I will give thee faithfully a tenth of all thou givest me." Or else the Divinity could take the initiative which is the general tenor of the Hebrew Scriptures— Israel is the chosen of the Eternal. This sense of covenant relation to the Eternal is the cornerstone of the Hebrew religion.

JAHWEH-WORSHIP A "CONTRACTUAL" RELIGION

Israel was under bond to worship Jahweh and him only, obey his commands, sacrifice to him and bring him offering. Jahweh was under bond by the sanctity of his word to protect his own, give them a land to live in, guard its frontiers, bless its fields with rain and happy harvests, and the devout with children, length of years and prosperity. The nomad could think of nothing more to ask of the Eternal than that—save mercy for his weak humanity and

[17] For a clear, well-documented proof of this, see Laura H. Wilde, *The Evolution of the Hebrew People*, New York, 1917, Chapter XII.

pardon for his sins. In time the vision of the prophet lifted the nomad's dream of felicity to noble heights and lighted it with the splendor of Messianic expectation but the essential terms of the covenant endured; if Israel worshiped and obeyed the Eternal would guard and give. His word stood sure and since poor Israel first and last suffered many things, sharing the general misfortunes of humanity and particular misfortunes of their own, the Hebrew moralist conceived all the shadowed side of life, whether for the individual or the state, as the penalty of sin and disobedience.[18]

It is not always easy to trace the connection, but it was there— it had to be. So Job's friends indicted him for the sins he knew he had never committed as he sat amidst the ashes and sweat in his soul to find an issue from his tragedy which fitted both the facts and the justice of God. So the prophets scourged a little state caught in the drive of imperial politics for the sins which sacked Samaria and besieged Jerusalem. (And there were always sins enough to support the prophets' indictment.) So when the last of the prophets saw with clear, sad eyes that broken Israel had no power of itself to set up again the throne of David, they built their hopes of deliverance upon celestial armies led by a Heaven-sent deliverer—God had promised and He would not fail.

Christianity took over the general religious understandings of the Hebrew and rewrote them in its theologies. Thus the persuasion that all loss and pain and sorrow are God's punishment for sin has endured to perplex the suffering devout and add, sometimes, a darker shadow to lives already shadowed enough. One must add that other religions than Hebraism have believed this but its deep rooting in western faith is a direct bequest of the old Hebrew doctrine of a covenant relation between the Eternal and Israel.[19]

The story of Abraham and Isaac would indicate some habit of human sacrifice not too far behind Hebrew beginnings, but even in the oldest covenants the blood of animals may be substituted, in the rituals of redemption, for the blood of human beings. Primitive Hebraism shared with all primitive religion a system of taboos on places, animals and days. There was also circumcision. That cere-

[18] For example: Deuteronomy 29:22-29. This so late as the seventh century B.C. Recent translations change "covenant" to contract, a helpful translation.

[19] For a careful study of the primitive religion of the Hebrews see John Punnett Peters, *The Religion of the Hebrews,* Boston, 1914, Chapter III.

mony, being both widely observed and obscure, has supplied the curious great opportunity for conjecture.

It is justified as a hygienic measure but that is not likely to have been the Hebrew notion. Its association with puberty rites is reasonably clear, given the primitive mind—but the Hebrew circumcised babies. It is likely, among other things, some remnant of sacrifice to fertility divinities; it may well have been the last vestige of human sacrifice. The Arabs "stepped down" human sacrifice to the offering of some part of the body whose loss would occasion little inconvenience; which seems to be the explanation of Arabic circumcision. The Hebrew made it an outward and evident sign of the Jahweh covenant, the circumcised being Jahweh's people, and a rite of admission into the nation. They eventually denied the uncircumcised any expectation of a favorable estate at the end of the world.

It is generally agreed then that the Hebrew took into Canaan considerable elements of the old Semitic religion, the new worship of Jahweh, a commandment-code, some ritual of festival and sacrifice and that these last reflect the leadership of Moses. The character of the Commandment codes which date from the wilderness is much debated. What seems the earliest of them is very simple and the conclusion of it has a legal touch as though it were the duty of the party of the second part in a contract between Israel and Jahweh. It is also, if it *is* the earliest code, the first draft of the Ten Commandments.

Never carve yourselves any metal gods. Hold the festival of unleavened cakes. . . . All the first-born belong to me. . . . Any first-born boy you may buy back. . . . For six days you shall labour, but on the seventh day you shall desist from work. . . . You must hold the festival of Weeks. . . . and the festival of ingathering. . . . You must never present the blood of any sacrifice with leavened cakes, and no part of the sacrifice at the passover festival must be left over all night. . . . You must not boil a kid in its mother's milk. . . . Write these words down, for these are the terms of the compact I have made with you and Israel.[20]

They carried with them also the ark of the covenant which was the visible symbol of the Divine Presence.[21]

[20] *Exodus* 34: 18-28, Moffatt's translation. For a well-supported argument that the "Ten Commandments" are earlier than this code, see Peters, *op. cit.,* page 97.

[21] The "ark" seems really to belong to a very early stratum of Hebrew religion and to reflect Egyptian influence. The Egyptians carried their gods about in boats or else shut them up in shrines in their temples. The actual contents of the portable

The Influence of the Cults of Canaan Upon Hebrew Religious Development

Israel found distant relations in Canaan and a religion far less austere and demanding rooted in the soil. The Hebrew ceased to be a nomad, settled down to the agricultural life and the next period in his religious development reflects the change. Life became more easy, society more complex. There was property for one thing—the nomad has so little—and there were the god and goddesses of a pleasant little land, givers of corn, wine and oil, asking in return to be worshiped by old and alluringly easy rites or else by very cruel rites. The next period—and it was a long period—of Hebrew religious development reflects the influence of Canaan nature-worship upon the religion of Jahweh.

The moral strength of Jahwehism was its complete divorce from the fertility-worship which had laid its spell upon Babylon and made Astarte under changing but always alluring forms the goddess of life and desire. The religious strength of Jahwehism was its conception of a God who set the sun and the stars in their places but was never sun-god or moon-god. The Baals and the Baalets of Canaan challenged the worship of the Eternal at just these strategic points. They were the "lords" of the fields and waters, local and anonymous save as they took their names from the cities they ruled or the shrines at which they worshiped.

The universal symbolism of seasonal life and death colored their worship. Their followers mourned their death in the brief desolation of Palestinian winter fields with self-mutilation, sought to stay their wrath with the sacrifice of children. They celebrated the vernal resurrection with shameless festivals, they offered to their goddesses the virginity of their women and the honor of their men. There was a touch of sun-worship in it all and the ardent forces of their divinities were symbolized in the animal forms under which they were worshiped, or else in symbols still more stark and primitive. A worship like that creates its priesthood, its rituals and its shrines,

---

shrine are much debated. There seems no logical stopping place between the accepted account that it carried the tables of the decalogue written by divine dictation and the belief of the more iconoclastic that it carried a sacred or symbolic stone, for which Semitic religion furnishes many parallels.

and there was kinship enough between Canaan and Israel—their languages were very similar—to make the fusion of their religions easy. Besides the festivals grew out of the soil itself and were there to subdue to their immemorial ways any who used the soil. All this was waiting for Israel—and it made religious history.

The Hebrew narratives sharpen antagonisms which were sharp enough. They tell a story of conquest, but they note also—and with pious regret—that conquest was not carried through to extermination. That was asking too much of the soldiers of Jahweh, at least it was asking too much of masculine human nature. If invaders do not depopulate a land they are pretty sure to marry its women and adopt its most persistent habits, which is probably what happened on the uplands of Palestine three thousand years ago. Some conformation of Hebrew ways to the very genius of the land was unescapable.

Their new status as peasant farmers with land holdings and a little personal property demanded new laws. Personal security and property rights were invested with a divine sanction. The Eternal promised in return idyllic conditions for the farmer: "I will give you the rains in due season, the land shall bear its crops, . . . your threshing shall last till the time for vintage, and your vintage shall last all the time for sowing. . . . I will grant you peace in your lands."[22] Israel did not keep his side of the covenant. The easy morals of Canaan seduced the sons of the Hebrew religious leaders, serpent-worship and bull-worship invaded the temple itself, the sanctuaries of Baalim and Ashtoreth found willing worshipers. "In part the Canaanite elements were permanently incorporated in the religion of Israel modifying both its forms and its conceptions, in part they were sloughed off after a fierce battle which left its marks in a certain puritan and exclusive tendency of that religion."[23]

The Rise and Office of the Prophet

Jahweh-worship might easily have dissolved into the nature-worship of the time and Jahweh himself become one of the many Baals of the land. Dawning monotheism was saved by the passion of the prophet for Jahweh and the prophet's ethical insight. The hawk and

[22] *Leviticus* 26; passim, Moffatt's translation. But this book is probably late.
[23] Peters, *op. cit.,* page 123.

dog-headed ones of Egypt had temples to make Solomon's temple
a poor affair, endowments richer than the whole of Palestine and
retinues of priests, Ashshur and Marduk went out with their armies
and came back with their spoil, but Jahweh had his prophets and
these through their spiritual genius secured for the Eternal the
dominion of the future.

Hebrew prophecy was a development. The prophet was, to begin
with, a soothsayer using such tools and tricks as these confidants of
the gods have always used. The not too remote ancestors of the
prophets operated in the "no man's land" between the normal and
the mysterious which has always been the perplexity of the ignorant
and the opportunity of the adroit or the inspired. Saul, for example,
who went out to find his father's asses and found a kingdom instead,
fell in with a "band of dervishes coming down from the height with
lutes, drums, flutes and lyres." Whereupon the spirit of the Eternal
inspired him and he became "a different man." The event passed
into a proverb but the comment of a bystander that the enthusiasts
were "men of no family"[24] is priceless. The prejudice of the eminently
respectable against the prophet is evidently of long standing. But
there was a potency in Hebrew prophecy to make it the most significant force in the history of religion and the prophets themselves
voices of the Eternal.

They emerged in the great crises of national life—the drives of
Philistia, Syria, Assyria, Babylonia, they sounded a various note,
sometimes of courage, sometimes of judgment, sometimes of hope
and sometimes of such pathos as touches certain passages of Jeremiah
with the tears of things. They invested their utterances with the
most august of sanctions—"thus sayeth the Lord." They came to
kings' palaces and the temple courts as from a direct commerce with
the Eternal, they brought the mystic awesomeness of the Divine to
the affairs of troubled little states and lifted the concerns of Judah
and Ephraim to the high level of the counsels of God.

Their persuasion of their Divine commission made them proudly
disregardful of the dignity of kings. They rebuked King Ahab for
Naboth's vineyard and King David for Uriah's wife. They went
further than that. When King Ahab married a daughter of Phoenicia,
and "turned to serve Baal and made him an image of Astarte" so

---

[24] 1 *Samuel* 10: 5 et seq. The prophets are generally patriots and nationalists but
they do not like kings. This is reflected in the Samuel narratives.

doing more "to vex the Eternal the God of Israel than all the kings before him,"[25] Prophet Elijah not only mocked and slew the priests of Baal but raised the kingdom against Ahab, changed the royal succession and directed Jezebel to a most unroyal death. The prophets of the ninth century B.C. defended the sovereignty of Jahweh against the gods of the region. They gave Israel a strong sense of his destiny and religious duty, made the nation Jahweh conscious. The narratives which have had such a far-reaching effect upon three great religions and the mind of western civilization were written under the commanding influence of the religious spirit which the prophets both intensified and released.

The prophets used religious conceptions whose development antedated their messages. But they did exalt what was best in the old, purge it of its more unworthy elements and behind the veils of old names and forms, shape a conception of God which was to rule the future. The prophet's passion for Jahweh, his flamelike certainty that Israel was Jahweh's chosen, slowly shaped the spirit of the nation. It began to create a literature. It inspired nameless historians to touch old memories with the splendor of Jahweh's purpose and made the deliverance of the bond folk of Egypt the revelation of his power. Those who thus invested the affairs of an inconsiderable people with Divine concern and illumined their progress from bondage to freedom with the light of Jahweh's pillar of fire builded better than they knew. Faith never has and never can operate in a vacuum. It wants bright threads of proof through the somber fabric of life and history so that men can say, "Here and here was God and this and this he did." These books in which God is always so near that a bush burns with his fire or a mountain smokes with his presence and the weak prevail through his might and no wrong against him prospers, have done more than any argument to keep monotheistic faith aglow in Western civilization.

There was always a rising and falling of little kingdoms in the Asian hinterlands of the eastern Mediterranean. They flourished through some favorable combination of kind circumstance and capable kings. They fell into eclipse when the ascendant powers of Egypt or Mesopotamia, or the weakness of their kings or both together undid them. The Hebrew state shared their general fortune. It had its brief glory under David and Solomon; then, following old lines

[25] *1 Kings* 16:20-23.

of tribal change, it fell apart. A united Hebrew kingdom would have found its situation difficult, the divided kingdoms wasted their force in sordid wars between petty kings and became the spoil of the northern powers. Assyria has written something of how all this turned out upon her stone-cut records; the Chronicles of Israel tell more, but how the prophet dealt with it all has made religion.

The Prophet Brings His World to Judgment

The prophet never forgot that Jerusalem was once the unthreatened capital of a prosperous state, that a Hebrew king once ruled from the River to the Great Sea. This supplied a background—whose brightness time and memory magnified—against which to see the later low estate of Israel and an ideal of future felicity. The Hebrew believed that his God would not permit the glory of Israel to remain in perpetual eclipse, and that a King would reign again and gloriously from the throne of David. This prophetic hope has had an influence upon both Hebrew and Christian faith impossible to overestimate. The Psalmist sang: "For the Eternal has chosen Sion as the seat that he desires. . . . There will I make David's dynasty flourish, and my chosen king shine prosperously."[26] The Christian sings

> Hail to the Lord's Anointed,
> Great David's greater son

and both have the prophets for their authority.

The situation the prophet actually faced was disillusioning. Their kings did almost everything but "shine prosperously." The fugitive greatness of his past had planted proud imperishable dreams in the spirit of Israel, the contrast between that past and his persistently unhappy fortune was beyond debate, the reconciliation of it all with the sovereign purpose of God became the motif of the prophet's music. These unhappy and quarrelsome little states could not be the final issue of Jahweh's purpose. It was not for this that seas had been parted and Sinai haloed with flame and the word of the Eternal pledged to Moses. The prophet doubted his king and his people, his priests and sometimes himself, but he never doubted his God.

[26] Psalm 132. Moffatt's translation.

The constancy of the Eternal was always his background and his confidence.

> Come now! Do you not understand,
>   have you not heard,
> That the Eternal is an everlasting God,
>
>   .   .   .   .
>
> He never faints, never is weary,
>   his insight is unsearchable.[26a]

Why then had the enterprise of the Eternal been so halted? What could Israel do to restore his broken fortunes? What was the meaning of a discipline so bitter? What had the future to offer of recompense and redemption? The prophet of Israel wrestled with these questions for three hundred years. Their messages were conditioned by changing circumstances and cover a wide front, for the prophet was a many-sided man. He was the popular preacher of his time with a strong sense of the dramatic and a gift for what would now be called sensationalism. He was the first of the satirists, a keen observer of the detail of social habit. There is a touch of Juvenal in Isaiah and the prophetic literature is as valuable source material for social conditions in the east during the prophetic period as the Latin satirists for social conditions in Rome. One hears with Amos the crooning music of Bethel and sees the money-lenders taking sandals in pawn. Isaiah etches in acid lines drunken priests vomiting on the altars, one can hear the anklets of the "haughty daughters of Sion" jingling and see the jeweled trifles on their toilet tables.

The prophet had an eye for his world and his time and a way to bring dead civilization to life in phrases like "winged fleets, where the great Nile flows through" or Tyre the "crowned queen whose merchants were very princes." Ezekiel who lived in Babylon and should know describes how walled towns were taken and the menace of Nebuchadnezzar's army.

> So many are his horses that their dust covers you;
> All your streets he tramples with his horses' hoofs.

The same Ezekiel has a priceless catalogue of the merchandise low galleys carried, unshipping their oars at night-fall in the ports of the Red Sea and the Levant, or the caravans carried across the Arabian desert—no catalogue at all but a bright beauty of romance and

[26a] Isaiah 40:28. Moffatt's translation.

craftsmanship, an index to the wealth and luxury of a vanished world.

> Quinquireme of Nineveh from distant Ophir
> Rowing home to haven in sunny Palestine
> With a cargo of ivory,
> And apes and peacocks,
> Sandalwood, cedarwood, and sweet white wine.

The prophet had also a keener sense than anyone else of the forces in action in his time. Isaiah was a shrewd appraiser of Assyria and Egypt and the drift and doom of their imperialism. The prophet saw all this in terms of its moral values, conceived all moral values in terms of the will of God. His anticipation of the future—shot through with gloom and glory—of the states and forces in action about him was always the projection of moral consequences against the horizons of the unrealized. He evaluated his world in terms of its moral, social and religious conditions—no one had done anything like that before.

The prophet was a poet who made literature, a force which made history, a voice through which religion was reborn, the high source from which ethical monotheism has sprung, and he did all this with the sins and sorrows of Israel as his point of departure—those and the just constancy of the Eternal. If the Hebrew state had been a prosperous and going concern it might have had a comfortable and commonplace history, but never an Amos, Micah or Isaiah. Instead there was little Israel did not suffer. The outcome was epochal in the history of religion. The outcome was a religion.

"Israel's religion," as has been said, "was like the pearl which grows by the pain and death of the oyster. The decline and the fall of the state and the sufferings of the people only stimulated the prophets to new insights, leading them to enunciate these great spiritual truths that have become the permanent possession of mankind. It is literally true that the enduring elements in the Old Testament religion were built upon the ruins of the state."[27] They were built upon more than that, they were built upon the travail of the questing human spirit sure of God and little else, they were built upon disappointment and hope deferred and tears and the whole

[27] Albert C. Knudson, *The Religious Teaching of the Old Testament*, Boston, 1918, page 39.

shadowed fortune of humanity out of which religion issues and of which Israel was the historic incarnation. In due time Israel disappeared as a state but the timeless assurance of its prophets wrung from such a winepress endured.[28]

THE APPARENT FAILURE AND THE ENDURING CONTRIBUTION OF THE PROPHET

It is difficult to reduce the vivid passionate messages of these makers of religion to an ordered system. How shall we make a theology of Amos' anger at heartless greed, or Micah's insight, or Hosea's broken heart or Isaiah's vision of God, or Jeremiah's tragic acceptance of accomplished fact, or the music of the prophet of the Exile, or Ezekiel's celestial chariot, or Daniel's image with its feet of clay? Also certain by-products of the prophetic spirit are confusing. It was easy for them to promise too much, the detail of their religious theory was too rigid. The relation between national apostasy and drouth or grasshoppers is vague to any but the prophetic mind. It does not always follow that a religious reformation will halt an invading army. It has required, first and last, a good deal of adroit apologetic to square the event with their prediction.

The prophet left a tradition of expecting too much too soon, a heady way of overlooking the massive entrainment of facts and forces, which has issued in a good deal of puzzled disillusionment. (One of the trying tasks of the minor prophet has often been to explain why the glowing visions of the major prophet have been so slow of realization; something of this still persists in the too impatient religious idealism of the West.) They did not always see with Bishop Butler that "things are what they are and the consequences of them will be what they will be," though Jeremiah did see that and got small thanks for saying so.

This perhaps is the secret of the relatively futile issue of their mission as far as the political aspects of Hebrew history are concerned. They did not save the northern kingdom from Assyria nor the southern kingdom from Chaldea. The priest and his ritual

[28] The fact, Knudson argues, that monotheism originated among a small people on the road to political ruin is so contrary to the normal operation of the human mind as to be a proof of "a special manifestation of the Spirit of God." One ventures to suggest that these are the only conditions under which the rise of real monotheism is possible.

eventually had their way with the religion of the nation, the prophet could not even save the Hebrew from himself, he could not even save himself—"O Jerusalem, Jerusalem, thou that stonest the prophets." But he did something greater than any of these things. He began with Jahweh and the limitations of archaic Hebrew faith, he ended with a conception of God which has commanded the consent of the centuries. He began with a religion ethically inadequate, he ended with a religion shot through with moral splendor. He began with a religion that dealt with men in the mass, he ended by affirming the spiritual responsibility and destiny of the individual, and though his own sun set dark and sadly he left the world its supreme hope.

He began with the constancy and justice of God, he believed with Carlyle that "The great soul of this world is just, with a voice soft as the harmony of the spheres, yet stronger, sterner, than all the thunders; this message does now and then reach us through the hollow jargon of things, this great fact we live in and were made by." Since God was just, sin cast the shadow which fell so darkly and so long across his people. Four sins mainly he believed. Idolatry to begin with, the shameful idolatry of Baal and Astarte. First and last, then, from Amos who saw "father and son go in to the same girl, a profanation of my sacred shrine" to the prophet of the exile who shriveled idolatry in the fire of his sarcasm—"A metal image!—that the workman casts and the goldsmith gilds, the solderer plating his work and fastening it tight with nails!"—they proclaimed the futility, the wickedness, the sheer stupidity of idolatry till they mocked and scorned and laughed the long procession of the gods out of history.

Second, the sterility of mere ritual. They all moved freely in the region of a direct approach to God. (Incidentally the very freedom with which they treat sacrifices, Sabbaths, and the like is a certain proof that these things had not in their time become a sacrosanct system hallowed by the name of Moses.) Religion, they believed, was a matter of temper and strangely simple—

> How shall I enter the Eternal's presence,
> and bow before the God of Heaven?
> Shall I come to Him with sacrifices,
> with yearling calves to offer?

.   .   .   .   .   .

O man, he has told you what is good;
what does the Eternal ask from you
but to be just and kind
and live in quiet fellowship with your God?[29]

So Micah reached the supreme insight of all religion. They were all alike in this, from Micah on fire against mere ritual to Jeremiah warning against mere temple trust till their day was done.

THE PROPHET AND SOCIAL JUSTICE

They were the first to root religion in social justice. Amos who came into Bethel with his poor merchandise saw that. He saw the shadow—or the flame—of Jahweh's justice along all the horizons of his world from Ashdod and Tyre to the palaces of Assyria, and doom for Israel. And when he sought in Israel the sin that cast so long a shadow he found it not only in the shrine but in the market place.

Listen to this, you men who crush the humble and oppress the poor,
Muttering, "When will the new moon be over, that we may sell our
    grain?
When will the Sabbath be done that our corn may be on sale?"
And all to buy up innocent folk, to buy the needy for a pair of shoes

.   .   .   .   .

Your sacred festivals? I hate them—
Your sacrifices? I will not smell their smoke

.   .   .   .   .

No more of your hymns for me!
No, let justice well up like fresh water,
Let honesty roll in full tide.

Nothing like this had ever been heard before. There in Bethel where the quick twilight fell and little fires illumined tired faces and crooning music sounded faintly, Amos brought religion down from the skies and out of the temples and away from smoking altars and made it one with social justice. His sonorous music has found a long reverberation. It is heard in later prophets, and the parables of Jesus, it has supplied a religious motive for social regeneration, it has given

[29] *Micah* 6: 6-8. Moffatt's translation.

a humane reality to religion which has kept it from being smothered in theologies or undone in entirely emotional mysticisms.

The fourth sin the prophet indicated was less dramatic and more insidious. Isaiah is the representative prophet here. It was the secularization of national life or more accurately a misleading confidence in political adroitness and calculating diplomacy. The prophet did not always allow due force to the massive entrainment of facts and situations but they were never easy optimists and the great prophets did see the forces in action along all the horizons of Israel very clearly. Their inherited faith that the nation was Jahweh's charge and that he would keep his word if the people kept theirs, colored all their prophecies but they went further than that.

They saw that Judea could not play the game with Assyria and Egypt by using their pieces. Politics and diplomacy were not the Hebrew province. Religion was their mandate and if they administered the provinces of faith and goodness and loyalty to God with simple-minded courage and devotion they could leave the rest to Sennacherib and Pharaoh-Necho—and leave them to the Eternal, "whose hearth is in Sion, whose home fires are within Jerusalem." It was the business of Israel to keep these home fires burning.

> O self-willed sons, says the Eternal, bent on no plan of mine,
> Weaving a treaty that I never sanctioned,
>
> . . . . .
>
> To shelter beside the Pharaoh and get Egypt to protect them
>
> . . . . .
>
> and never consulting the Eternal
>
> . . . . .
>
> Egyptians are but men, not God,
>
> . . . . .
>
> In returning and rest shall ye be saved,
> In quietness and confidence shall be your strength.[30]

The true strength of a nation, the prophet taught, is its devotion to human well-being, loyalty to spiritual values, the conservation of its own genius. "World-politic" is a misleading interest leading only to tragic issues. A nation is not a hammer to break another nation with or a pawn in a crafty game. It is an aspect of a vaster purpose, the guardian of some great human value. Blindness to that is the costliest of national blunders. The demonstrations of history would seem to be on Isaiah's side. Jeremiah, who lived through one of the many

[30] *Isaiah* 30, passim.

sieges of Jerusalem to see the proud taken into exile, went even further. He saw that an excessive and militant patriotism may contribute to the destruction of a state, becoming a vice instead of a virtue. He died in Egypt, a broken, defeated man, but if they had set up a monument for him they might have carved on it twenty-four hundred years before Edith Cavell—

Patriotism is not enough.

JAHWEH BECOMES THE ETERNAL

These then are the general indictments the Hebrew prophets brought against their people and, in reverse, the ideals they urged upon them. They affronted the respectable, angered the patriot, irritated kings and priests, but they slowly purified and spiritualized Hebrew religion. They let a light into the Jerusalem temple which showed it the shelter of poor gods and worse rites and now and again the temple got cleaned out. The zeal of reforming kings broke up Baal and Ashtoreth local shrines and by the beginning of the seventh century their general influence brought about a marked advance. The priest registered that advance in his codes and rituals, the moralist retold Hebrew history in pious documents whose noble moral insight must not be obscured by the device they used to invest their reformation with the sanction of Moses' authority—most effective evolution has been done in the name of the past.

What they did for Israel is part of the history of that peculiar people, what they did for God—more exactly the conception of God —is a creative part of the history of religion. In their long brooding upon their own experience and the experience of their race, in their interpretation of facts and forces in terms of the Divine Will, in their affirmation of what the Eternal would do, they were driven up or back upon an always finer—the word is totally inadequate—sense of what He ought to be. They discovered and rediscovered God in the three sources in which humanity has from the first apprehended the reality "of a power not themselves," nature, history and the lonely questing of the human spirit. The prophet used the witness of nature in unequal ways—a good vintage was the wage of loyalty, locusts were a providential chastisement, or else the skies are the tent of the Eternal and he marshals the stars in order, calling Aldebaran and Rigel and Sirius by name while they answer "here."

The sense of the majesty of God in nature, being the concern of the poet rather than the prophet, finds its noblest Hebrew expression in the Psalms and Job. History, made and in the making, supplied the prophet his outstanding material to be recast as the way of Jahweh with the nation. The steps are clear but the conclusion is stupendous. Hebrew religion began with the sense of a local God, Sinai first, Canaan afterwards, but always within frontiers. Naaman the Syrian could not worship Jahweh outside Palestine unless he took two mule loads of the sacred earth home to build an altar on. But since, for Amos and Isaiah the Eternal was using Syria or Assyria to scourge apostate Israel, he was moving outside Canaan and had a sovereignty in alien capitals. The frontiers of divine administration rolled back, the prophet saw nothing anywhere which was not an aspect of providence, the Eternal became for them God of the Nations.

There had always been in Hebrew religion the sense of a general creative and controlling power, not Jahweh the tribal, but Elohim the Universal. The specialists think that conception to have lacked the vivid personal quality Jahweh possessed. Beneath the prophets' touch the two conceptions fused, Jahweh became universal, the vaster power became richly personal and Jahwism ceased to be what the scholars labor over and became what faith has confessed and Moffatt translates; the Eternal who cares and governs, disciplines and blesses. Once this conception emerged—the unseen goal toward which all the procession of the gods had been moving—the spiritual enrichment of monotheism followed augustly. Attribute after attribute was discovered in the Eternal and left as a bequest to faith.

Hosea was taught that justice was not enough through his violated hearthstone and his own great nature. The way of the Eternal, he said, was more than the way of justice, it was also the way of Love, the blackest sin was the sin against love, the surest force was a love to wear down all ingratitude and win through its own power to suffer and endure.

> I loved Israel when he was young,
> Ever since Egypt I called him my son,
>
> . . . . .
>
> Ephraim, how can I give you up?
> Israel, how can I let you go?[31]

[31] *Hosea* II, passim.

With this key the prophets approached the problem of suffering and searched the hidden root of it, sought to reconcile it with the love and goodness of God, discovered that suffering is redemptive as well as punitive, saw at last that love must suffer—if it is to save, felt their way into the nature of forgiveness and atonement, reached the enduring realities of the moral process, and charged their conceptions of God with the splendor, the tenderness, the reality of it all until love became the Eternal and the Eternal love.[32]

The prophet began, as noted, with the belief that Jahweh was concerned only with the corporate life of the nation, that the folk of it were blessed or banned in the mass, innocent and guilty lumped together, children's children paying out the debt, their teeth on edge with the paternal sour grapes. As the nation broke down this conception broke down. It could not break down completely for there is the truth that folk are all tied up in one bundle in it, but the later prophets corrected it. The Eternal deals also with the individuals, his accounts are kept with "one and one and never with two and two," his mercy stands between son and father, the new heart of the individual is a new departure in the covenant of the Eternal.

Finally, the prophet left Israel a quenchless hope. No discipline could be final, no ruin of the state irrevocable. As long as there was a nation he prophesied that the Eternal would return, and heal it. When its affairs seemed hopeless, he prophesied that a remnant would be saved, when the land was desolate and its people in exile he prophesied that the "redeemed of the Eternal shall return and come singing into Zion," the caravans come again to Jerusalem whose walls foreigners shall rebuild, whose wealth will make silver as common as iron. Time could not dim nor misfortune eclipse this splendid vision. As the fortunes of the little Jewish state grew more hopeless and the shadow of an alien imperialism fell darkly across the land, the expectations of a supernatural delivery took on an always more assured form.

It built itself into a wealth of Messianic expectation, associated itself with a grandiose imagination of the end of the world order whether that order was a Grecian dynasty ruling Syria or imperial Rome. It kept a passion of expectation alive among dispersed Jews and supplied the Hebrew soil out of which Christianity issued to

[32] Knudson, *op. cit.*, treats this development with distinction and documented solidity.

hold in trust also the conception of the unity, the love, the moral perfection and the expectation of the universal empire of God, which was the bequest of the Hebrew prophet to religion.

THE HEBREW SACRED LITERATURE

The long and devout history of Israel created a literature the sifted remnants of which, canonized, constitute the "Old Testament." This literature has been within the last fifty years subject to a most searching examination, the general outcome of which has been to root it directly in the history and experience of the Hebrew people and illumine its proper historic backgrounds. It has gained thus in real meaning and value. It reflects, naturally, developing religious insights, always heightened moral standards and a continually enriched sense of the mystery and travail of the human enterprise. The processes of religious development, particularly, are now more clearly revealed in the Hebrew sacred books than in the literature of any other religion, which in itself gives these books a unique value for the student of religion.

But many other things have combined to invest these books with a unique value for the devout. The Hebrew language was essentially poetic, its words were glowingly imaginative and concrete and lent themselves to the vivid representation of religious conceptions in very concrete ways. The Hebrew temperament was an aspect of Hebrew speech—it spoke in figures and the figures came. One has only to compare the Psalms with the more devotional passages of the Upanishads to see how real Jahweh was as compared with the dreaming Brahma and in what intimacy of fellowship the Hebrew lived with his God. The faith, the language and the spirit of Israel combined to make religion like light and fire and song and daily bread, no shadowy abstraction but the detail of life's daily commerce with the Eternal and the demonstration of the reality of God's power and love and mercy.

History for the Hebrew had no meaning save the unfolding revelation of the will and way of his God. He had no secular history, his history as he conceived and told it was religion. It became a drama of action and suffering, triumph and defeat offering literal fact, moral teaching and allegorical or spiritual significance. The basis of the Old Testament is history thus moralized and charged with a religious content, and the books of the prophets. But there is a vast deal besides. The Hebrew sacred books subdue to the religious passion of Israel and for the glory of Israel's God the old Chaldean creation poems, the legends of the flood, the immemorial memories of the region and the time. There are hero tales and idylls of little Bethlehemic harvest fields where Ruth gleams among the alien corn and reports of how Jewish boys won favor in the courts of Persian kings, or else how a Jewish girl defeated a palace plot with her beauty and bent Xerxes to her will.

The Greek period left its traces in the book of Ecclesiastes. An ardent oriental love song got embedded in the canon to supply Bernard with themes for many mystic sermons and interpretations the poet author would have thought strange indeed. There is the gnomic wisdom the East loved so well, the sententious redaction of long experience and the meditation of the sage. There is the noble music of Job, first of the great dramas of doubt grappling with the timeless question, given suffering to find God. There are the psalms-lyric expression of a devotion for which the thunder was the voice of God, the pageantry of the seasons his glory trailing the earth, the temple at Jerusalem his sanctuary, the sins of the repentant his sorrow and the suffering of the righteous his concern.

And everything thus remembered, believed, borrowed or dreamed suffered a noble change beneath the touch of the makers of this literature, mostly anonymous and doing their slow creative work for five hundred years. The unmoral creation process of Chaldea became the drama of the power of the Eternal and human fault and frailty, the hero tales carry some moral to instruct successive ages, the wisdom literature is veined with gold, and the psalms have become a treasury of devotion to voice every aspect of human experience and modulate the liturgies of Christianity with their grave music.

The psalms have probably had more influence in enriching the religious consciousness than any other part of the Hebrew scriptures. They are its redaction through time and insight, passion and persuasion, of the very spirit of religion. They have been repeated by the generations in every experience and extremity. They have supplied hallowed forms for confession, praise and prayer, they have created the very atmosphere in which religion lives. Their lovely cadences have become a part of great literatures. The twenty-third psalm is enshrined in the heart of the believing world, its assurance

"The Lord is my Shepherd" fulfills the quest with which religion began. In time all this was invested with the august authority of an infallible revelation and, being carried over into the main current of European Christianity, had an influence in the making of the Western mind difficult to overestimate.[33]

The Hebrew Scriptures were generally translated into the major European languages at a time when these tongues were not yet entirely subdued to standardized literary forms and so capable of being plastically influenced by their poetry and rich imagery. The stately King James version of the Bible has richly colored English literature and ennobled English speech. Luther's vigorous translation was a landmark in the history of the German language and the missionary passion of Christianity has carried the literature of Israel with it around the world. What Amos chanted in Bethel while the crooning music of an order whose dust has been blown down the winds of time was faintly heard, and the little fires of the caravanserai cast their last shadows and went out, is still said or read in almost every living tongue.

CONCLUSION

The more direct influence of the Hebrew faith is a fascinating chapter in the general history of religion. The priest centered his national religion in Jerusalem and developed a ritual which demanded a retinued temple for the performance of it. That aspect of the religion was centralized and greatly dependent upon circumstance. It had little influence outside of Palestine save as the Jews came home to Jerusalem, for the great feasts; it did keep the consciousness of the "home fires in Zion" alive and sustained the race consciousness of a scattered people. Toward the end of the pre-Christian era the Jew organized a local worship of a more simple character and borrowed a name for it from the Greek. The synagogue furnished the center for his worship outside Jerusalem, it was altarless and priestless but the sacred roll was treasured there, read on the Sabbath in ordered fashion and commented upon. There was also a proper order of prayer. There had never been anything like this in religion anywhere.

[33] R. E. Prothero, *The Psalms in Human Life,* E. P. Dutton, New York, 1908, illustrates the uses and associations of the Psalms through history in a fascinating way.

After the exile the Jews became a far-flung people. They followed Alexander to Alexandria and their children learned Greek, they were thereafter free of the Hellenic world. When Rome stretched her long arm eastward, the Jew took to the Roman roads, traded and settled in all the cities of the empire. He interpenetrated pagan civilization, he took the synagogue with him and his monotheistic faith. The procession of the pagan gods had already become dim and fretted by time. There were seekers everywhere who found in the Eternal of Israel the end of their quest. These proselytes were an appreciable element in the population of the Empire and eventually furnished Christianity an open door to the classic world. Judaism made its most significant contacts with the Hellenic spirit in Alexandria. There Plato met the prophets.

His philosophy had already lost its noble clarity and the prophets were far from home but Philo undertook to establish a going concern between them. Neither Plato nor the prophets would have recognized the result, which belongs to the borderland between philosophy and theology rather than to any history of religion which would not be lost in the clouds. It was all an aspect of that meeting of religions, dreams and brave conjectures which followed the creation of an Empire in which there were no longer any national frontiers and all races and gods were equally at home. But the influence of this attempted reconciliation of Hellas and Palestine had a far-reaching effect upon early Christianity and one may find traces of it in Mohammedan Persia a thousand years after the Jew who dreamed of baptizing the spirit of Greece into the faith of Israel.

The first destruction of Jerusalem left the Jew without a temple, the second left him without a land and presently Islam took it all. But Judaism persisted. It organized itself around teachers and schools of interpretation, being particularly strong in Babylonia. The faithful kept the law, the Rabbi wove a tissue of comment about it, legends multiplied; but wherever there were Jews enough the trumpet sounded thrice from the roof of the synagogue at sunset on the sixth day of the week.

To holy convocations the silver trumpet calls.

Through over 1800 years the Jew, sometimes wanderer, more often an alien confined in the Ghetto, persecuted often, despised by his Christian neighbors, has kept alive his faith, and a definite sense of his Jewishness. His religion has never, unlike his sister faiths, hardened into a creed. The nearest Judaism comes to a creed is the thirteen-point statement of the great Jewish philosopher, Maimonides, in the twelfth century. The great mass of commentary, legend and Rabbinic interpretation of the Torah was finally collected to form the Talmud, which has been the outstanding source of Jewish teaching and practice since the sixth century A.D. A code setting forth the fundamental requirements of ritual and use known as *Shulhan 'Arukh* has served since the sixteenth century as the basis of Jewish religious ceremonialism.

But the Jew has been after all a part of the world and it was natural that the changes of the nineteenth and twentieth centuries should affect his faith as it has all other faiths. As a result of these influences Judaism today is divided into three camps, one the liberal or reformed which has set aside a great part of the traditional ceremonial as no longer of value. Its stress is dominantly a prophetic one. Reacting strongly against this is Jewish orthodoxy which refuses to yield anything in their past. In between are to be found those who will not go all the way with orthodoxy, but are opposed to the extreme liberalism of the reform group. They are known as the "conservative" group.

But common to all three groups are a firm faith in the oneness of God and His ethical character, and in one form or another a living conviction of the Jew's mission as a peculiar people in the world. Nor has the ancient hope of a "restored Israel" by any means disappeared. Modern "Zionism," though variously regarded by different groups, is the current form of the age-old hope of the prophets, that a "remnant shall return." Already it has begun to rebuild Palestine and secure for the homeless and persecuted some measure of peace in the land of their fathers.

In the modern world Jewish childhood is subjected to strong influences that tend to carry them away from the synagogue. Jewish parents, not unlike Christian fathers and mothers, and Jewish rabbis like Christian preachers, are disturbed concerning the religious life of their children and young folk. But the devout still assemble to hear the law and the prophets, keep their ancient feasts, repeat the prayers which so many sorrows had charged with haunting meanings, dream of their promised future and confess their timeless faith:

Hear, O Israel, the Lord our God, the Lord is One, and thou shalt love the Lord thy God with all thy heart, and with all thy soul, and with all thy might.[34]

The history and the race which made that confession articulate have supplied a faith to pregnant centuries and sovereign civilizations.[35]

[34] For any question about Judaism as the final phase of the Hebrew religion, see George Foot Moore's monumental volumes, *Judaism,* Harvard University Press, 1927.

[35] This chapter needs to be supplemented in important particulars which involve a far more particularized consideration of the development of the Messianic hope. Nearly every religion has some hope of a golden age to come. It is an almost inevitable disposal of hope deferred, of glowing expectations quenched by the realistic issues of history. All Messianic hope involves a Messiah, a God-sent deliverer who will finally defeat the forces of evil and assert the Divine Power over a rebellious world. It involves a drama of last things, an eschatology in which the ripening of time for the Messiah, his advent and his battles are set forth in a wealth of imagination, and it involves his established kingdom of unbelievable peace and prosperity reserved for the long suffering devout and loyal.

Hebraism in its last phase was thus characterized beyond any other religion. This includes the Messianic expectation and the character of the Messiah; the time and circumstance of his coming; the supernatural recasting of the very framework of earth and sky; the perfect felicity of the new order. All this created the literature of what one may call "the drama of last things," the most grandiose drama ever conceived by faith and imagination. There are intimations of this in the Old Testament but its full development is to be found in a literature which was in full flower just before the beginnings of the Christian era, but the examination of it hardly belongs to a study like this.

One can not, however, understand the beginnings of Christianity without some knowledge of it. It was taken over into Christianity and influenced its whole development and it persists among us still. There are passages in the Gospels and especially the Book of Revelation which are vividly influenced by Hebrew eschatology if they are not in fact fragments of its literature embedded in Christian documents.

CHAPTER XIV

Mohammed: Prophet of Allah[1]

AT THE dawn of the seventh century of the Christian Era, in the streets of Mecca might often be seen a quiet, thoughtful man, past the meridian of life, his Arab mantle thrown across his shoulders, his head scarf drawn low over his face; sometimes gently sauntering, sometimes hurrying along, heedless of the passerby, heedless of the gay scenes around him, deeply absorbed in his own thoughts—yet withal never forgetful to return the salutation of the lowliest, or to speak a kind word to the children who loved to throng about him."[2] He had been suckled by a Bedouin foster-mother, and spoke in the lordly language of the black tents. "Verily," he said, "I am the most perfect Arab among you; my descent is from the Coreish, and my tongue is the tongue of the Beni Sad." And now that tongue had begun to kindle a fire.

In the name of the merciful and compassionate God.

By the afternoon! verily, man is in loss! save those who believe and do right, and bid each other be true, and bid each other be patient.[3]

"Verily, man is to his Lord ungrateful."[4] Mohammed was bringing Mecca to judgment—and Mecca had begun to protest. Historians amuse themselves with the futile "ifs" of things that never were. "If," says Gibbon, "a Christian power had been maintained in Arabia, Mohammed must have been crushed in his cradle and Abyssinia would have prevented a revolution, which had changed the civil and

---

[1] Wherever one places Mohammedanism in the history of religion, he is almost sure to be wrong. Chronologically it is the last of the great religions. It needs both Hebraism and Christianity for a background—and yet to put it last is by another sort of logic to make it the ultimate issue of the procession—which it is not. Putting it here is Dr. Braden's gracious accommodation to Dr. Atkins' insistence. The chronological reader can read it last if he pleases. The teacher will use his own judgment.

[2] Ameer Ali, *The Spirit of Islam*, London, 1922.

[3] Sura CIII, translated by E. H. Palmer, *Sacred Books of the East*, New York, 1900.

[4] Sura C.

religious state of the world." The "ifs" are phantoms. Mohammed, his face half veiled, called Mecca to repentance or judgment. The rest is history.

BIRTH AND BOYHOOD OF MOHAMMED

He was born in Mecca of a widowed mother in August 570 A.D. John III being Pope at Rome, Justin II Emperor of the East and Chosroes King of Persia. His family had long been the most important in Mecca, having shared between them for one hundred and fifty years the princely privilege of entertaining the pilgrims who came to worship the Black Stone, but Mohammed's uncles were reduced both in station and possessions and the Coreish were divided by inherited feuds. In the time of Mohammed's great-grandfather Hashim, there had been a great passage of competitive boasting[5] between Hashim and his nephew Omeyya, in which Omeyya was both aggressor and loser. It was trivial enough at the time, but the consequences of it eventually convulsed the Islamic Empire.

Mohammed's grandfather discovered and restored the ancient well Zemzem. Having long been childless, he asked of Providence ten sons and vowed that if they were granted, he would sacrifice one of them to Deity. In due time he was blessed with the ten and embarrassed by his vow. He cast lots to see which son he should offer and the lot fell upon Abdallah whom he greatly loved. Now a life might be ransomed in Arabic law for ten camels and Abd al Muttalib cast lots again between his son and ten camels; Deity chose the son. The father added ten other camels and cast the lots, Abdallah against twenty; he lost. At the tenth throw—Abdallah against a hundred camels—Providence accepted the camels and Abdallah lived to become the father of Mohammed, though he did not live to see his son. He died on a journey and left Aminah and her unborn child, five poor camels, some goats and a slave girl.

When the child was born, his grandfather took him in his arms to the Holy House, thanked God and called him Mohammed which means "the praised."[6] When his foster mother had weaned and re-

---

[5] Actually a trial of superiority, a curious Arabic ceremony in which each contestant valiantly recites his own virtues and leaves the decision to an umpire.

[6] The account of all this part of Mohammed's life is generally taken without specific citation from Sir William Muir, *The Life of Mahomet*, 1894.

turned him to his mother she sent him back to the black tents, "take him with thee back again to the desert; for I fear the unhealthy air of Mecca." Some sort of sickness (epilepsy is the usual explanation) overtook him when he was four years old and so troubled Halima that, after an anxious year, she finally restored him to his mother. He always remembered his foster mother with the greatest affection and when he had prospered through marriage gave her a camel and forty sheep, and spread his mantle for her to sit upon. He also gratefully remembered the tribe in whose tents he had lived and was kind to them when the fortunes of war made them his captives.

Mohammed's mother died when he was seven, his grandfather two years later. The sorrow of his boyhood estate probably cast a long shadow over his life and certainly ripened him in some sense of dependence upon an unseen guardianship which he afterwards gratefully acknowledged. "Did He not find thee an orphan and give thee shelter?"[7]

After the death of his grandfather the care of the boy fell upon his uncle. The principal event of his boyhood was a caravan trip with his uncle so far as North Syria through time-worn regions whose cities were only splendid memories. This expedition brought him into some brief contacts with Eastern Christianity. A twelve-year-old boy is an eager and observant traveler and Mohammed long afterwards remembered the lights in lonely monastic cells. Life in Mecca was anything but colorless in 580 A.D. Pilgrims were always coming or going, there was an annual fair three days' journey away where all the wares of the East were on sale and all the poets of Arabia could be heard, and youth could find other and more doubtful merchandise than rugs and spices. The poets influenced Mohammed more markedly than the merchandise or the dancing girls and perhaps, as Muir suggests, the hopeless religious estate of embattled Arabs, Jews and Christians impressed him more deeply still. It was a weltering world.

In the name of the merciful and compassionate God,

.   .   .   .   .

We have surely created man in trouble.
Does he think that none can do aught against him?

[7] Sura XCIII.

He says: "I have wasted wealth in plenty"; does he think that no one
sees him?
Have we not made for him two eyes and a tongue? and two lips? and
guided him in the two highways? but he will not attempt the steep![8]

HIS YOUNG MANHOOD AND MARRIAGE

It was just as well that he was sent to the hills with the sheep and
goats. He, too, he said, like Moses and David, had been a shepherd—
"Verily, there hath been no prophet raised up, who performed not
the work of a shepherd." The silence and the stars, the swift dawns
and the quick fall of night became for him the revelation of a Power
before whom the clamor of contending religions fell away into silence; "God, there is no god but he, the living, the self-subsistent.
Slumber takes him not, nor sleep. His is what is in the heavens and
what is in the earth. . . . His throne extends over the heavens and
the earth, and it tires him not to guard them both, for he is high
and grand."[9]

Twice, he tells us, he set out to share the shameless pleasures of
the town and twice he was prevented. After that, he sought them
no more. He grew into grave young manhood and his uncle took
him from following flocks and made him a trader. It was now that
they began to call him "the trusty." He led a caravan into Syria for
a Meccan woman of affairs and again came into contact with Christianity, this time with a ripened and inquiring mind. He found good
folk among them as he after testified, but from the system as he saw
it he returned with destiny-making finality.

Khadijah, for whom he was traveling, was another matter. She
was a widow, fair, forty, wise, well-to-do, much sought after in marriage. She had refused the chief men of the city but this engaging
young man won her heart. The lady took the initiative through the
mediation of a discreet servant. The go-between inquired into the
reason of Mohammed's unmarried estate. "I have nothing," he said,
"in my hands wherewithal I might marry." "But if haply that difficulty were removed and thou wert invited to espouse a beautiful and
wealthy lady of noble birth, who would place thee in affluence,
wouldst thou not desire to have her?" Mohammed prudently asked
the lady's name, and answered, "I am ready."

[8] Sura XC.
[9] Sura II, 255-260. This is the famous "verse of the throne," often inscribed in
mosques.

Khadijah secured her father's consent by a device afterwards made difficult by the prophet's prohibition of wine. When he came out of his cups he was surprised both to find himself in a wedding garment and to learn that he had performed the ceremony. Khadijah bore Mohammed two sons and four daughters; both the sons died early, a misfortune which influenced the prophet's later matrimonial relations and, very greatly, the later leadership of Islam. She was his first convert, always his wise adviser, faithful and understanding. It is no easy thing to be the wife of a prophet or receive behind the curtain a man who has come directly from an interview with the Angel Gabriel.

The man she married was in the early prime of Arabian manhood, spare in figure, above middle size, well boned and broad chested. His head was unusually large, his forehead broad and commanding. He had large black, searching eyes under arched and meeting eyebrows, an aquiline nose, good teeth well apart. "His expression was pensive and contemplative," his beard—"by the beard of a prophet"—was thick and black. He walked quickly and as though he were going down hill.[10] He was of winning manners, generally silent in company, but when he spoke it was to the point. He held his passions in leash, loved his friends and hated his foes as an Arab should. He awed the stranger but, upon acquaintance, awe changed to affection.

For fifteen years, things turned out as they might. The Eastern empire and Persia wore themselves out in fighting, so preparing a strategic opening for any third power as yet unwasted. Gregory the Great became Pope. Saint Augustine set out from Rome for Canterbury. Saint Columba died in Iona. Chosroes II of Persia captured Jerusalem and took away the True Cross. Heraclius became Emperor of the East, Khadijah's caravans came and went prosperously and they rebuilt the Kaaba—the Holy House—in Mecca. Mohammed found a way of satisfying the various competitors for the honor of putting the sacred Black Stone in its place and ended by actually pushing it into the wall himself. It has been worn smooth by the kisses of the faithful for twelve hundred years now.

The Turning Point in His Life

What was happening in Mohammed's spirit was more important than any of these things. He was now forty years old, a brooding

[10] Muir, *op. cit.,* pages 24 and 25.

man in a shaken world. The dissolution of the old Imperial order
reached its climax in five hundred and forty-seven A.D. Rome had
been totally deserted for six weeks. Europe was for whomsoever
could take it. The shifting, rising, always dissolving little kingdoms of
Goth and Frank, Burgundian and Lombard made Western history
like the turns of kaleidoscope mostly in red. The beginnings of nations and cultures were in those pregnant impermanences—but there
was no pattern yet. The Eastern empire was being driven in under
the shelter of the walls of Constantinople—strong walls still, and
destined to stand inviolate for nine centuries. Northern Africa had
become a channel for successive and ensanguined tides of conquest
and plunder.

The religious world which Mohammed knew at all, or any remote
report of which reached him, was equally anarchical. Jerusalem had
been twice destroyed and the Jews generally driven out of Palestine.
Judaism had, however, reorganized itself in new centers under the
authority of noted teachers and was still a leavening power in the
East; its teachings and traditions were known in the streets of Mecca,
and wherever the caravans of Khadijah went for trade. Were not
the Arabs themselves sons of Abraham and had not the sweet waters
of their Holy Well Zemzem broken out miraculously in the desert
to save Hagar and Ishmael? There was nothing to prevent an Arab
from accepting the Jewish faith save the age-old enmity between the
Arab and the Jew.

Eastern Christianity was in a piteous estate. This is so much a commonplace in any study of the life of Mohammed and the rise of
Islam as to make development unnecessary. Ameer Ali[11] says that
the shapes assumed by Christianity in the centuries which preceded
the advent of Islam "were fantastic." His adjective is not ill chosen.
(Incidentally, an examination of doctrinal Christianity by a keen
minded and scholarly Mohammedan is interesting reading. His
sources are too limited, but the play of his mind is absorbing.) Greek
Christianity had been for three hundred years surrendered to excessive and embittered doctrinal controversies. Words had ceased to
have meaning and seamed the church with factions. The saintly
wasted their sanctity in desert solitudes, the fiercely devout did cruel
things in the streets of the old cities, the ignorant in their worship of
Icons were not far above idolatry.

[11] *Op. cit.,* page XIV.

Christianity had made some appeal to Arabia—Coss, Bishop of Najran, is remembered as both eloquent and earnest—but the peninsula, though rimmed by Christianity, was, as a whole, uninfluenced. Muir lays the blame on the Arabs whose "vagrant habits eluded the importunity of missionary endeavor; while their haughty temper and vindictive code equally resented the peaceful and forgiving precept of the Gospel." It is only just to the Arab thus indicted to say that, while turning the other cheek was alien to his nature, he had seen no convincing evidence of the "peaceful and forgiving precepts of the Gospel" in the corporate life of the Eastern bishoprics and had a lively memory of a Christian Abyssinian King who was kept only by accident from sacking Mecca in the year of the prophet's birth. Actually the matter goes deeper; into as yet irreconcilable qualities of mind and temper.

There was also the unhappy state of his own city and country. Mecca had been for long the principal station on one of the two great caravan routes between the Indian ocean and the Mediterranean. It was also the "Cathedral City" of Arabia, though its cathedral was wholly roofed by cloth and half walled by curtains. (The Arab believed that Abraham had built it.) Religion and trade were thus the immemorial interests of Mecca. The great Meccan families used their wealth to entertain the pilgrims, sought the control of the Kaaba to further their prestige and profited in return by the whole situation. For centuries the devout had made the seven circuits of the Holy House, kissed the Black Stone, drunk from the sacred well. Long before Mohammed, trade had begun to fall off through the use of the sea routes and religion was more important than ever. What would happen if all that should be ended?

THE MAKING OF A PROPHET

For one man had begun to see with doubtful eyes the great god Hobal and the three hundred and sixty-five little gods which the Kaaba housed. The pride, wealth and jealousy of the great seemed evil things supported by a lie. The time was ripe for judgment—and for God.

No prophet has ever shared with the world the last secret of his commerce with the Eternal. He can only bring back the burden and the vision of it. The psychologist being less reticent is quite ready to explain the prophet to the world. He is a man whose subconscious mind receives and stores deeply impressions which other men dismiss lightly. He is given to reverie which takes a moral and religious direction and his meditations leave a tenacious deposit in his subconscious self. He has the mystic's power to objectify what he deeply feels and is abnormally suggestible. He has a neurotic temperament which creates an increasing sense of strain with his environment. In time he reaches the breaking point and then the whole content of his subconscious mind, given form by suggestion to which he himself has unconsciously contributed, breaks through and subdues him entirely to the passion and authority of it; his mystic temperament makes voices and visions of it and he sees the Lord high and lifted up, or else entertains the Angel Gabriel.

There is a large element of truth in this analysis but the mystery still remains. Suggestion may be only the psychologist's name for some openness of human personality to a range of influences whose authority is in no wise diminished by the fact that they are as viewless as the wind. There may still be, to use that great figure, a blowing of some wind which is what the prophet has always believed it to be—the inspiration of the Eternal. There is still the power of commanding personalities to take lesser, broken, unfinished things and, passing them through the alembic of their own souls, release them unified, transformed and regnant. The poet and musician possess this power in the domain of art, the prophet possesses it in the field of religion. He comes in burdened with destiny from his vigils under the stars and, lo, God has become real to a nation and history never afterwards is the same. Mohammed belonged to this elect fellowship.

Such conditions as we have noted fed into his reflective and powerful mind. He must have been dissatisfied with his native religion and haunted by the sense of something more true and fine. He was doubtless in debt for this, without being clearly conscious of the debt, to both Judaism and Christianity. He was doubtlessly also in debt to some infiltration of the idea of a Supreme God from the general faith of his race. Arabia was too closely related to Israel to have been entirely uninfluenced by the Hebraic faith. The idea of one God may have always illumined the black tents with a faint but never quite extinguished light. There is a tradition of certain Hanifs, who were associates of Mohammed's, a cousin of his wife among them.

These were seceders from the accepted faith of the time, seekers[12] for something beyond it. (Mohammed calls Abraham a Hanif—which falls in with the Hebrew tradition.) Such as these were vague figures in the long procession of the pilgrims of faith. Mohammed himself was for a time a Hanif in spirit.

He withdrew himself from the world "among the solitary valleys and rocks near Mecca. His favorite spot was a cave in the declivities at the foot of Mount Hira, a lofty conical hill two or three miles north of Mecca. Thither he would retire for days at a time; and his faithful wife sometimes accompanied him."[13] The austere loneliness of the scene suited the austere spirit of the man and the travail of his spirit began to find words. He came down from his vigils to chant in the streets of Mecca:

In the name of the merciful and compassionate God,
The Smiting!
What is the smiting?
And what shall make thee know what the smiting is?
The day when men shall be like scattered moths; and the mountains
   shall be like flocks of carded wool.[14]

The only dependable key to the movement of his mind during this—or any other period—is the Koran, which is in hopeless disorder. It is strongly held that he began with a belief in the imminent end of the world and sought unselfishly to warn his own people; that the refusal of the world to end compelled him, as it has so many others before and since, to recast his message; with the turn of the tide after his flight to Medina, he began to seek his own honor and advantage. Bell believes that he began with an appeal to his own people in Mecca "to recognize and worship the true God and to show thankfulness for his bounties."[15] Also "that from the first the religious form at which he aimed included moral and social reform," and that, finally, finding his fellow townsmen both worldly and hostile he began to threaten them with the wrath to come. Bell supports his argument solidly with citations from the Koran. This is a matter

[12] Richard .Bell, *The Origin of Islam in Its Christian Environment,* London, 1926, page 57.
[13] Muir, *op. cit.,* page 35.
[14] Sura, CI.
[15] *Op. cit.,* Lecture III.

for specialists, and since they do not agree, the rest of us are quite helpless.[16]

His First Proclamation

If the Hebrew prophets furnish any parallel, some sense of doom is more likely than anything else to be the first reaction of the prophet's spirit, since he sees the fugitive and the wrong as already under judgment,[17] but whether Mohammed began with mountains to be carded like wool or with a gentler note is immaterial. The epoch-making aspect of his message is in the first line of all the chapters of Koran and most of all in the one hundred and twelfth Sura:

> In the name of the merciful and compassionate God.
> Say, "He is God alone!
> God the Eternal!
> He begets not and is not begotten!
> Nor is there like unto Him any one!"

There was originality in this. For twelve hundred years the Hebrew had been binding, "Hear, O Israel; The Lord our God is one Lord" upon the frontlets between his eyes and writing it upon the posts of his house. Mohammed knew that and yet his belief in the unity and greatness of God comes molten as though it were wholly new. He is never done with the wonder of it: The splendor and passion of his conception of God are his own contribution.

Your God is one God; there is no God but he, the merciful, the compassionate,
Verily, in the creation of the heavens and the earth, and the alternation of night and day, and the ship that runneth in the sea with that which profits man, and in what water God sends down from heaven and quickens therewith the earth after its death, and spreads abroad therein all kinds of cattle, and in the shifting of the winds, and in the clouds that are pressed into service between heaven and earth, are signs to people who can understand.[18]

Ameer Ali has woven[19] a bright web of the sayings of the Koran

---

[16] Ameer Ali confines himself to general statements about the "call."
[17] For parallel utterances in the Hebrew prophets, see Amos 1:2 and Micah 1: 3 & 4; one would almost think Mohammed had been reading this in his cave.
[18] Sura II, 158-160.
[19] *Op. cit.*, pages 143 et seq.

about God. It is poetry and ascription and praise and the sense of God in dawn and dark and rain, the stars, the pageantry of the seasons. He is Lord of the Seas and the Ships, of the East and the West, Creator and Judge, and yet "He is merciful and forgiving."

O our God, punish us not if we forget and fall into sin: blot out our sins and forgive us.

They said of Spinoza that he was "God intoxicated." One could say the same thing of Mohammed. It is true the theologians call him a deist and not a theist. He would have sung with Joseph Addison:

> The spacious firmament on high,
> With all the blue ethereal sky,
> And spangled heavens, a shining frame,
> Their great Original proclaim.

rather than with George Croly—

> I ask no dreams, no prophets' ecstasies,
> No sudden rending of the veil of clay,
> No angel visitant, no opening skies;
> But take the dimness of my soul away.

It is, however, asking a good deal to expect the worshipers of the Black Stone to distinguish between theism and deism. Nor was there much in the Christian Icon-worship of Mohammed's time to suggest the difference.

He Claims to Be the Voice of God

It is generally agreed that Mohammed claimed no inspired authority to begin with: he threatened Mecca with smiting "on his own." Then something happens: the word "we" comes in—

> In the name of the merciful and compassionate God,
> By the fig!
> And by the olive!
> And by Mount Sinai!
> And by this safe land!
> We have indeed created man in the best of symmetry.
> Then we will send him back to the lowest of the low;
> Save those who believe and act aright;
> For theirs is a life that is not grudged.[20]

[20] Sura XCV.

It is no longer Mohammed who is speaking, it is Deity. There is doubtless a psychological road here also for which the experience of many a mystic supplies a fascinating chart, but the road is obscure. It is, I suppose, the increasing objectification (an awkward word) of inner experience, a deepening commitment of self to mysterious tides of authority. It is attended with grave dangers—pride and self-assertion and the possibility of mistaking the voice. Mohammed himself shared these doubts, was not unconscious of the dangers. The traditions which represent him as contemplating suicide because he feared the spirit which haunted him to be the spirit of the evil and the mortal danger of speaking falsely in the name of God, are so true to the general experience of the mystic, who always has his black night of the soul, that they may be accepted. According to the same general body of tradition, he found great comfort in Khadijah during this disturbed period.[21]

Tradition, of course, could not allow earth and sky to remain indifferent to events so momentous. Celestial regions were shaken by the tumult in the prophet's soul, the jinns who had long haunted the outskirts of the heavens were driven from the skies by balls of fire; nightly the heavens were bright with such portentous lights though they seemed to the uninstructed to be falling stars. Finally the sense of a Divine Commission objectified itself in a vision of the Angel Gabriel who brought him a direct command:

> In the name of the merciful and compassionate God.
> Read,[22] in the name of thy Lord!
> Who created man from congealed blood!
> Read, for thy Lord is most generous!
>
> .   .   .   .   .
>
> Taught man what he did not know![23]

Students are agreed that this is the first "revealed" chapter of the Koran and that, thereafter, Mohammed spoke "literally *in the name of the Lord.*" The command to "arise and preach" naturally fol-

[21] The embroidery of the legend is less dependable and naturally Mohammed devotion has made them multi-colored as a rug. For example, when Mohammed was once much in doubt as to the character of the spirits he was entertaining, Khadijah made him test them by changing positions. The apparitions persisted. She then removed her veil and they modestly withdrew. She concluded that they were of a proper angelic deportment. Muir, *op. cit.,* page 50 et seq.

[22] Muir translates this "recite."

[23] Sura XCVI.

lowed. Islam had begun. The opposition he encountered may gradually have driven Mohammed to this final entrenchment in Divine
authority—"thus, saith the Lord" is an end to any argument, save
possible argument as to the fact. Mohammed evidently encountered
such doubts and later reasserted his vision with Gabriel with enriched details:

By the star when it falls, your comrade errs not,
Nor is he deluded! nor speaks he out of lust!
It is but an inspiration inspired! One mighty in power taught him, and
  appeared, he being in the loftiest tract.
Then drew he near and hovered o'er! until he was two bows' length
  off or nigher still!
Then he inspired his servant what he inspired him;
The heart belies not what he saw! What, will ye dispute with him what
  he saw?[24]

CONVERTS AND OPPOSITION

Mohammed's first converts were among those who knew him
best: Khadijah, Ali his cousin and adopted son, Abu Bekr, a rich
merchant who spent the greater part of his fortune in redeeming
slaves persecuted for their fidelity to the new faith and became the
first Caliph. There were perhaps forty converts at the end of three
or four years, family and tribal interests determining both acceptance
and opposition. Those who had vested interests in the old Kaaba
worship furnished the nucleus of a long and bitter opposition, the
people who had mocked him as a dreamer and let him pass took to
weapons when he began to assert the damnation of their ancestors.
Some believers returning from a season of prayer were attacked and
their leader struck an opponent with a camel goad. (This was the
first blood shed in Islam.)

The prophet's appeal during this period was ethical and rational.
He had as yet no force to offer as alternatives to the Koran, the
sword or tribute and no mind to do it but the growing opposition
put Mohammed and his followers in a dangerous position. Those
who had strong family connections were reasonably safe but the
slaves and poor folk kept the faith at the risk of their lives. Mohammed advised the unprotected to leave Mecca, and even Arabia. Ameer

[24] Sura LIII: 1-15.

Ali maintains that the prophet's much debated lapse from the faith, which now occurred, was to secure some toleration for his followers. The lapse is mainly significant as showing a survival of Semitic fertility-worship in Mohammed's Mecca. His fellow townsmen had three goddesses who seem to have been reincarnations of that ubiquitous lady of many aliases, Ishtar of Babylon.[25] Conservative Mecca does not seem to have been greatly concerned about god Hobal, but their goddesses were another matter and they made them a test case.

Mohammed bowed to the storm of protest and in one recital of the fifty-third chapter of the Koran added that the intercession of the three Meccan goddesses might be useful with Allah, "these are the exalted females whose intercession verily is to be sought after." His townsmen were quite willing to "adore God" with this quali-fication and worshiped as they were bidden. The report of a recon-ciliation reached the exiles in Abyssinia but it brought no peace to the prophet's soul. When the night fell and Mohammed, as was his custom, recited the chapter to Gabriel, that one reproached him: "Thou has repeated before the people words I never gave unto thee."[26] Whereupon the next day, the prophet gave the Sura as it now stands: "They are but names which ye have named, ye and your fathers; God has sent down no authority for them! They do but follow . . . what their souls lust after!"[27]

The position of the Moslems was worse after the event than before. They were outlawed by public proclamation and lost their means of livelihood. Mohammed's uncle, who had so far been his protector, advised flight or silence. "O my uncle," the prophet replied, "if they place the sun on my right hand and the moon on my left, to force me to renounce my work, verily I would not desist therefrom until God made manifest His cause, or I perished in the attempt." During this period, Hamza, "the lion of God," and Omar became his follow-ers. Omar brought the Saracenic Empire in his sword hand.

Mohammed's faction lay shut up in a defile among the neighbor-ing hills for two years and then a reconciliation, providentially fur-thered by the fact that white ants ate up the decree of exile, was

[25] For a scholarly discussion of the whole subject, see Barton, *op. cit.,* pages 234 et seq.

[26] See Muir, page 79.

[27] Sura LIII: 20.

effected but Mecca had become impossible. A savage passage of invective between the prophet and his remaining uncle, which Mohammed at Gabriel's direction incorporated in the Koran, shows how the factions hated one another.

> In the name of the merciful and compassionate God.
> Abu Laheb's two hands shall perish! and he shall perish!
> His wealth shall not avail him, nor what he has earned!
> He shall broil in a fire that flames, and his wife carrying
> Faggots—on her neck a cord fiber.[28]

His fellow townsmen pelted Mohammed with dirt; the fate of Islam was in the balance. Also Khadijah died. She had been a really noble influence in the prophet's life and he never forgot her. "I was never," said Ayesha, "jealous of any of his wives save that toothless old woman."

THE FIRST AND SECOND PLEDGE OF ACABA

And now history turned upon the smallest of hinges. The pilgrimage season brought crowds to Mecca to whom, as they would hear him, Mohammed appealed. He fell in one day with a little group from Medina who belonged to a tribe closely associated with the Jews; their idolatry sat lightly upon them, and they knew the doctrine of the one God. He asked them if they would receive, protect and follow him at Medina. They approved, they told him, his teaching but the city was so weakened by feuds that they could protect no one—hardly themselves. But they would, they continued, carry his proposal home with them, seek the response of their neighbors and report next pilgrimage time. It was now 620 A.D.

At last his teachings had found a congenial soil. Judaism, with no mind to do it, had done a groundwork in and about Medina without which his whole work might have failed. The next year Mohammed met twelve men from Medina in a lonely place outside of Mecca and the twelve took the "First Pledge of Acaba": "We will not worship any but one God; we will not steal, neither will we commit adultery, nor kill our children; we will not slander in anywise nor will we disobey the prophet in anything that is right." And Mohammed answered: "If ye fulfill the pledge, Paradise shall

[28] Sura CXI.

be your reward. He that shall fail in any part thereof, to God belongeth his concern either to punish or forgive." Upon this pledge and the second pledge of Acaba made later, which included fealty to Mohammed, the empire of Islam was built.

The twelve went back to Medina, missionaries of the new faith, and there it spread like fire. Visions of something vaster than he had so far dreamed of stirred Mohammed at Mecca. Gabriel carried him on a winged steed between dark and dawn to the temple of Jerusalem where the ancient prophets received him as one of them. He was thereafter borne from heaven to heaven till he came face to face with God—Zoroaster had a similar experience—from whose Presence he brought the command that his followers were to pray five times a day. One may still see upon the rock, beneath the dome of the Mosque of Omar in Jerusalem, the print of the prophet's foot made when he dismounted from his winged horse. The Koran notes the experience in "the Chapter of the Night Journey":

> Celebrated be the praise of Him who took His
> Servant of a journey by night from the sacred
> Mosque to the Remote Mosque . . . to show him of our signs.

The vision is a priceless psychological document. Mohammed was beginning to have a sense of world mission. A year later seventy-five came back from Medina with reports of a great growth in his following. He met them again in secret at Acaba. An artist should paint the scene and call it the birth of a Religion—Burnoose-clad men, two veiled women, the prophet against the dark and destiny in the shadowed faces. The spokesman of the group pledged their lives to the prophet's cause and defense—(the women pledged no more than their faith)—"Stretch out thy hand, O Mohammed" and he stretched it out, Bara "struck his hand thereon, as the manner was in taking the oath of fealty. The seventy came forward one by one and did the same."[29] And they went home through the dark. The man to whom they pledged themselves was now ripe for the last phase of his life.

The chapters of the Koran which may be dated from this period reflect his confidence, a terrible intensity of conviction:

[29] Muir, page 126.

Verily, it is the speech of a noble apostle; and it is not the speech of a
poet;—little it is that ye believe!
And it is not the speech of a soothsayer—little it is that ye mind; [it is]
—a revelation from the Lord of the worlds.
Why if he had invented against us any sayings,
We would have seized him by the right hand,
Then we would have cut his jugular vein; nor could any of you have
kept us off from him.

. . . . . .

Verily, it is certain truth!
Therefore celebrate the name of the mighty Lord![30]

When a man who believes that has found a race with fire in their
veins to strike hands with him in the dark, anything is possible.

THE HEGIRA

Many of the Moslems had already left Mecca but the prophet
waited for a sign. It came in a plot against him; "—but God plotted
otherwise, and God is the best of plotters." Two swift camels had
been kept waiting, a guide who knew secret routes was ready,
Mohammed and Abu Bekr fled. They lay hid in a cave until the
pursuit slackened. The legends tell how Allah took care of his own
—a spider spun its web across the cave mouth, a tree grew up to
hide it, wild pigeons perched in the tree. Abu Bekr felt their lonely
peril but the prophet was assured. "We are but two," he said, "but
God is in the midst, a third."[31] It was now June 20, 622 A.D., and
the fifty-third year of the prophet's life. Islam dates its history from
the Hegira.

Twelve days after leaving Mecca, Mohammed and Abu Bekr,
clothed in white Syrian garments, attended by the chief men of the
town in bright armor and welcomed by shouting crowds, rode
through gardens and orchards of palm trees into Medina. The
prophet left the choice of his residence to his camel. He purchased
the courtyard in which she lay down from two orphan boys for
ten pieces of gold, and began to build a mosque for Allah and
two houses for himself. Islam was at home in Medina.

[30] Sura LXIX, 40.
[31] Muir, page 135.

What followed becomes one of the great dramas of history. The curtain rises through the gardens and palm trees of Medina to show a mosque and two houses and a man whose hitherto swordless hands held an imponderable dominion. There is no time in the swift action ever to reset the stage. It widens as one watches it— a series of dissolving views sweeping toward an always vaster horizon. The lights fall across the lava-seamed uplands of Arabia, Syrian pasture lands, the alluvial valley of the Two Rivers, the arid plateau of Persia, the Delta of the Nile, the long bright littoral of the Southern Mediterranean and the orange groves of Spain, losing themselves in equatorial Africa and the islands of the Malayan Archipelago, illumining, on the banks of the Indus, Allah's share of the immemorial splendor of India.

Across a stage so set and lighted the Saracenic hosts go out to battle with a forest of lances and a thousand wind-whipped banners. They meet the armies of Persia and Byzantium. They adventure beyond the Pillars of Hercules and the Pyrenees and are halted by Charles Martel on the plain of Tours. The echo of Roland's horn comes back from Roncevaux; Greek fire falls from the beleaguered walls of Constantinople. The complaint of a Christian hermit releases the passion of Christian Europe and the lights fall upon the shields and breast-plates of the long procession of crusaders. They gild the domes of Bagdad and brighten streets in which Haroun-Al-Raschid sought adventure and the tales of Arabian nights were told and loved. They fall across the high mosques of Cairo and rest a little upon scholars and poets who touch their foreheads to the tessellated pavements while the call to prayer sounds from minaret to minaret.

They illumine the city of Constantine captured at last by nomads who ruin the Empire of Islam and accept the faith of Mohammed. They touch with splendor brave fighting under the walls of Vienna and Don Juan of Austria going down to his ships. They shift again to fall upon Lawrence rousing tribes whose ancestors had followed the prophet, to turn the flank of a battle line reaching from the North Sea to the Persian Gulf. They are quick enough, perhaps, to reflect the ricochet of shells in Palestinian passes where David and Jonathan fought with the Philistines. Was there ever a drama like that?

LEADER AND LAW-GIVER

Mohammed came to Medina much as John Calvin came to Geneva and, allowing for any number of differences, the parallels are arresting. For a little an idyllic peace (if one may follow Ameer Ali) prevailed amidst the gardens and date palms. The town changed its name. It had been Yathrib, now it was Medina, the city of the prophet. The mosque was roofed with palm leaves and had no pulpit. Mohammed preached much on charity—alms, he said, overcome all things. "A man's true wealth hereafter is the good he does in this world to his fellowmen." "Oh, Prophet," said one of his disciples, "my mother is dead; what is the best alms I can give away for the good of her soul?" "Dig a well for her and give water to the thirsty." Islamic worship took the form it still retains. Because it wearied Mohammed to stand, a pulpit was built toward the southern wall. He faced Mecca[32] in prayer and commanded the people to do as he did. The prophet gave the salutation of peace from the pulpit; the call to prayer was sounded; he came down to prostrate himself, remounted the pulpit to preach. (The longer chapters of the Koran have much the character of rather wandering sermons.) The people worshiped unafraid and nothing troubled them save that their women bore no children, which was attributed to some sorcery of the Jews.

Mohammed began by dealing generously with the Jews (he seems to have had some hope of winning them over). But the gulf between the Arab and the Jew was too wide to be bridged. Mohammed had very soon to reckon upon Jewish opposition, and he dealt sternly with the seditious. Meanwhile, affairs went badly between Mecca and Medina. Who began the fighting is no great matter. Given the situation, the temper of the race and the time, it was inevitable; the Holy Wars had begun. In the end, the prophet took Mecca and broke the image of Hobal and the lesser gods. "Truth has come and falsehood has vanished; verily, falsehood is transient." Bilal sounded the call for prayer from the top of Kaaba, and it has never since ceased. Islam was supreme in Arabia; Mohammed was supreme in Islam.

This event-driven development of a purely religious mission into

[32] He is said to have begun by facing toward Jerusalem, afterwards toward Mecca.

a political autocracy left a deep mark upon the prophet and his religion. His gospel of mercy got entangled in endless fighting, his disinterestedness was tried by power and pride and there was always the essential contradiction, which other faiths than Islam have had to face, between the true nature of religion and the business of fighting. Mohammed comes through it all as well as one could expect. He was generous to the vanquished, loyal to his own followers and unexpectedly tolerant in an intolerant time toward the believing religions, though his hatred of idolatry was a consuming fire. He knew the folk with whom he had to deal and laid no burden upon them beyond their natural power to bear;—"God desires for you what is easy, and desires not for you what is difficult." This general principle of accommodation is the key to perplexing aspects of Islam and one of the secrets of its power.[33]

The fundamental habits of Arabia were not disturbed—save the use of wine, gambling and burying female children alive. In general, using old times and old ways for a background, there was a substantial amendment of morals. Polygamy is standardized to four wives, though concubines are permitted. "He restrained the power of divorce possessed by the husbands; he gave to the woman the right of obtaining a separation on reasonable grounds; and toward the end of his life he went so far as practically to forbid its exercise by the men without the intervention of arbiters or a judge." Slavery, of course, he left untouched, though he urged the redemption of Moslem slaves from unbelieving masters and the humane treatment of all slaves.[34]

[33] Doughty has a mordant sentence or two about this: "The old Semite currencies in religion were uttered anew under . . . the stamp of the (expedite, factious and liberal) Arabian spirit and digested to an easy, sober rule of human life. *Wanderings in Arabia,* page 25, abridged edition.

[34] Ameer Ali, *op. cit.,* page 244. The status of women in Islam is a strategic point for non-Moslem criticism. For a strongly drawn indictment of the moral standards of Islam in this region and the prophet's own inconsistencies, see *Islam,* Zwemer, Student Volunteer Press, New York, page 42 et seq. For an equally strong drawn defense, see Ameer Ali, *op. cit.,* chapter 5 generally. Ameer Ali supplies backgrounds which are certainly needed for an intelligent judgment. Doughty is useful for a vivid picture of the levels of Bedouin life today. In general the Eastern mind and its inheritance must certainly be taken into consideration. Doughty says that the manner and morals of the Arabian Nights belong to the cities and not the hair tents. But the imagination which produced them with all its "complexes" must certainly be taken into consideration in any appraisal of Eastern morals. There is something older than Islam.

See that ye feed them with such food as ye eat yourselves; and clothe them with the stuff ye wear. And if they commit a fault which ye are not inclined to forgive them sell them, for they are the servants of the Lord, and are not to be tormented.[35]

He always freed his own slaves.

The Koran also reflects Mohammed's matrimonial experiences. He considered these important enough to be matters of celestial concern and in one instance Gabriel intervened to bring peace to a quarreling harem. Mohammed could laugh "till he showed his back teeth" but in his inspired capacity his sense of humor sometimes failed him. His marriages afford all his biographers opportunity for characteristic excursions. He limited his followers to four wives; he seems himself at one time to have had ten.[36] Since he was about fifty years old when this phase of his temperament first asserted itself, the psychologist and doctor between them may find another explanation. The facts stand. Confucius said: "At seventy, I could follow what my heart desired, without transgressing what was right." Mohammed died at sixty-three.

MOHAMMED'S LAST YEARS

Toward the end of the prophet's life all Arabia sent in its allegiance and there was little fighting. Being free to make the annual pilgrimage to Mecca he put on the pilgrim's garb and set out with a hundred camels marked for sacrifice, and all his wives. He performed all the appointed rites and preached a farewell sermon. He ended by saying: "Oh, Lord! I have delivered my message and discharged my ministry." The people answered: "Yes, verily, thou hast." He fell ill of a fever upon his return to Medina. He had been given poisoned meat some four years before, and now laid his illness to the delayed effects of the poison. He had lived an abstemious life—in food and the like—but he had suffered many things, borne many cares, and his seasons of mystic absorption had drained his vitality. He anticipated his death and said his Nunc Dimittis—

[35] Sura CX, Muir's translation.

[36] Ameer Ali explains some of these as marriages of policy, others of consideration for homeless women, a desire for a son may have been a factor. Any standardized biography will give the details.

When the help of God shall come and the victory, and thou shalt see
   men entering the religion of God in troops,
Then celebrate the praises of thy Lord, and ask pardon of him for he
   is merciful.[37]

There are rich and tender traditions of last days and words. When
he could no longer conduct prayers he gave that office, which seemed
to carry with it the future headship of Islam, to Abu Bekr. He died
in the arms of Ayesha, whispering: "Lord grant me pardon; and
join me to the companionship on high eternally in paradise: Pardon!
The blessed companionship on high." He left seven gardens be-
queathed to him, according to tradition, by a Jew. These grew dates
of unusual sweetness and "were afterwards dedicated perpetually
to pious uses." He left also three other properties: two of these were
devoted to the uses of the faith, one the prophet assigned for the
support of his own family. He would not take so much as a basket
of dates for his own use from the tithes.

Moslem devotion has clothed him with glistening raiment of virtue and the most searching criticism still leaves him rich in admirable qualities. He had pregnant silences and seasons of kindling
speech. He mended his clothes, cobbled his shoes, helped his wives
in their household tasks and lived humbly when his word was law.
He ate with his fingers and licked them clean, he relished dates
dressed with milk and butter and bread cooked with meat, ate
sparingly and often had not food enough. Ayesha said, "The prophet
loved three things—women, scents and food; he had his heart's desire of the two first, but not of the last." He wore white chiefly
and hated silk. "Such stuff it does not become the pious to wear."
He was easy of access, given to hospitality, a friend to the poor
and sad, gentle with children. He was, for the time, just and restrained in the exercise of power and generally clement to the conquered. He was constant in prayer and kept vigils of devotion. Two
phases of his character shadow the picture; his extreme uxoriousness
and many bitter incidents in the religious wars.

He left also a book, a religion and the militant and missionary
passion of Islam.

[37] Sura CX, Muir's translation.

The Assembling of the Koran

The Koran is the creation of the genius of a race and a tongue, the traditions and mores of Arabia, the diffused and popular understandings of Judaism and Christianity common to the religion and the time, the movement and circumstances of Mohammed's career, and that brooding insight for which the prophet had no explanation save that God gave it to him and the voice of it was the voice of God. The genius of his language invested his message with poetic majesty. There is a necessary rhythm in the very structure of it which echoes alike from mosque and synagogue and cathedral. "The Koran is written in the rhetorical style and, as Arabic literature, has never been equalled."[38] It consists exclusively of the revelations or commands which Mohammed professed from time to time to receive through Gabriel, as a message direct from God . . . these divine messages continued throughout the three and twenty years of his prophetical life."[39]

Since it is doubtful if he could read or write, these messages were written down by others as they were delivered and upon any material at hand, or else preserved in the tenacious Eastern memory. During the prophet's life no attempt was made to assemble the widely scattered fragments; after his death their preservation became a vital concern. Omar took the matter in hand and commanded Zaid, who had been Mohammed's secretary, to get the text together and arrange it. He did this, gathering what he sought "from palm-leaves, skins, blade bones and the hearts of men."

He presented the finished work to Omar but there was still the enormous difficulty of variant readings. Othman determined to save Islam from a peril which he was shrewd enough to see had divided the Jews and Christians into argumentative sects. He had an authorized version made and commanded all other editions to be burned. Since then the Koran has been textually unchanged. Its chapters are curiously named through incident and association, the transitions are broken, the style direct as an arrow flight or wearyingly discursive. It is everything Mohammed knew and believed Arabia to need. It touches every aspect of life from the intimacies of

[38] Palmer, *op. cit.,* page LV.
[39] Muir, *op. cit.,* pages XV, et seq.

the marriage chamber to the prayers of the devout. Palmer uses twelve pages of double column fine print to index it and thirty-eight pages to abstract its contents.

Its Sources and Vitality

The Koran is a stream fed by tributaries from many sources. It has singing rapids of noble eloquence, pools of star-lit meditation, strong currents of practical injunction and cloudy and confused reaches, but it has carried Moslem faith and practice for almost fifteen hundred years. Tisdall[40] has traced outstanding elements in the Koran to five sources: Ancient Arabian beliefs and Practices, Sabean and Jewish Ideas and Practices, Christianity and Christian Apocryphal books, and Zoroastrian Contributions. It reflects the temper of those who, having endless time to hear, asked of a narration only that it should go on and on, loving it all the better because they had heard it before. There is no logic in the Koran then, nor any order save the order of a discursive intellect, following "association paths" whose only key is Mohammed's mind. The chapters of the Heifer, the Ants, and the Spider, the Kneeling, the Angels, and the 109 others have long assumed for the Moslem that awesome and mystic character with which any religion invests its sacred books. Reverence has hallowed, ritual consecrated, authority validated and faith sublimated the Suras until they have become for Islam the voice of God.[41]

[40] W. St. Clair Tisdall, *The Original Source of the Quran*, New York, 1905.

[41] The reverence of the Semite for the written word took hold of it and fixed it and the very awesome finality of it involved Islam in those difficulties in which any religion ruled by a book is involved. One may doubt whether Mohammed himself anticipated the absolute authority the Koran has asserted over Islam. He certainly made no attempt to assemble its widely scattered fragments. He did insist on the truth of his own revelations and their authority over his followers, but he may well have had in mind his own living, continuous message and not the deposits of it on leather, bones and palm leaves. He believed in the saving authority of the Jewish and Christian Scriptures.

"Say,—I believe in the book which God has sent down; and I am bidden to judge justly between you. God is our Lord and your Lord; we have our works and ye have your works; there is no argument between us and you. God will assemble us together and unto Him the journey is." (XLII: 14.)

Mohammed began by making the Old Testament for the Jew, the New Testament for the Christian and the Koran for the Moslem of equal authority. Each religion had its book, each religion its prophet. In the outcome he asserts the supremacy of the Koran over other scriptures, but he never questioned the authority of the other Scriptures. (Muir, *op. cit.*, page 148.)

For the Moslem of the eighth century the Koran was alive. It repeated what he had heard in the black tents or the crooked streets of the old towns, or by his campfire while the desert wind blew cold and Aldebaran and Rigel ruled a wondrous sky of stars. He had no other book nor wanted one, for the songs of his poets were colorless beside this which was drama, poetry and destiny told in words he knew and a music to which his spirit was tuned, and the best guide he had in the world which he too felt was nothing "but a play and a sport." Those who read it to him remembered the prophet or remembered those who knew the prophet; also it was the voice of God no less divine because God talked about things he knew. For the Western reader the Koran is haunted by echoes of the Hebrew and Christian sacred writings. Something of this is due to a language common to both the Koran and the Old Testament, more is due to the confused and indirect way in which the substance of the older religious books reached the prophet.

The controversialist offers these facts to prove that the Koran is not infallibly inspired, the specialist to discover the sources of an epochal book. They are quite as useful to indicate the confused religious mind of western Asia in the seventh century A.D. Mohammed's own faith and ruling religious ideas do subdue the otherwise vast confusion of the Koran to their own ends. There is hardly a page of the book without its obscure allusions, its murky passions—and gleams of the splendor of God. The Koran is a book of law as well as of religion. Its broken sentences, its seemingly inconsequential exhortations have become the last authority for believing races and lands. But at heart it is the book of Mohammed's certainty of God. There is the flame which never quite leaves any page dark or cold and sometimes rises to an incandescent glory. The burden of the Koran is the call which has sounded from minaret to minaret across centuries and continents: "God is great. I bear witness that there is no God but God. I bear witness that Mohammed is the Apostle of God; Come hither to prayers!" And if it be the morning call— "Prayer is better than sleep."

ISLAM

The whole of Islam as a religion is in that haunting cry. The word Islam means resignation, the root of it being Salam which means "the peace due to duty done or obligation discharged." It is the Salem of the Hebrew Scriptures and the Christian hymns. Non-Moslem commentators stress its passive aspect, Ameer Ali gives it a more positive character, "striving after righteousness." The Koran defines this righteousness: "Righteousness is not that ye turn your faces toward the east or the west, but righteousness is, one who believes in God, and the last day and the Angels, and the Book, and the prophets, and who gives wealth for his love to kindred, and orphans, and the poor, and the son of the road, and beggars, and those in captivity; and who is steadfast in prayer, and gives alms; and those who are sure of their covenant; and the patient in poverty, and distress, and in time of violence; these are they who are true, and these are those who fear."[42]

Islam then is a religion of faith, devotion and good works. There is really but one principal article in its creed. Belief in God—and in Mohammed, his prophet. No faith could be stripped more bare of metaphysic, no religion would seem to offer less opportunity for a highly developed theology. Its monotheistic faith has something of the quality of high noon in the desert, the sun is everything, there are no shadows, no mist-softened horizons. I suppose any devout spirit supplies some mystery to veil its approach to the divine but there are no Cherubim in the Koran who veil their faces with their wings before the Divine Glory.

The theologian says that the faith means "a belief in the unity, immortality, power, mercy and the supreme love of the Creator." The wealth of names under which God is invoked by the Moslems is a better testimony to the conception of the Divine Nature into which the faith has ripened than theology. These names—there are ninety-nine of them—are personified attributes beginning with Ar-Ra'hman—the Merciful and ending with Az-Zabur, the Patient. They are reverent and understanding names; only a rich devotion could have coined them. They are for the most part objective, setting forth the glory, goodness and power of God—being such attributes as the wise would ask of an ideal sovereign. One name only has a mystic quality,—Al-Batin, the Innermost.

There is also an hierachy of angels in whom a Moslem must believe, "pure, sexless, fire-created who neither eat nor drink, but do the will of God." They "celebrate the praises of their Lord, and ask forgiveness for those who are on earth." Some of them are

[42] Sura II, 170. Compare *Micah* 3: 8.

called by majestical names which with little change live still in
poetry and art, Mikail, Azrail the angel of death, and Israfil, who
will sound the trumpet to wake the dead. The angel "good-will"
presides over heaven, Malik "the ruler" over hell.

Two angels attend every human being to set down his every action and, as if this were not enough, two others visit him in his tomb
directly he has been buried and examine him in the faith. If his
answers are assuring he is left in peace, if not he is terribly beaten[43]
—and there is still hell. There are also clouds of good and evil spirits,
the genii and Ifrits of the Arabian Nights, who need only
Scheherazade to be imprisoned in a bottle or become slaves of lamp
and ring. But these are marginal beliefs; faith in God is central. He
is the Creator, though the Koran has no book of Genesis. The Koran
does remember that man was made of clay. It knows also that he
begins as an embryo and is mostly content with that, being more
concerned about his future than his past.

The "steep" way of Islam is not too steep; it takes men as they
are and undertakes considerably to elevate them, with due regard
to the amount of elevation the kind of human nature it deals with
will stand. "And what shall make thee know what the steep is? It
is freeing captives, or feeding on the day of famine, an orphan
who is akin, or a poor man who lies in the dust; and again to be
of those who believe and encourage each other to patience, and encourage each other to mercy—these are the fellows of the right!"[44]
Kindness is urged toward kindred and servants, parents are to be
honored, justice sought, the passions subdued, usury is forbidden
and any complaint about one's state. Everything is done in the sight
of God, which is a ground for rejoicing rather than fear for "God
will not burden any soul beyond its power" and since any man is
likely to go wrong, "Seek pardon of your Lord and be turned to
him; verily, My Lord is merciful, loving."[45]

A Moslem's dealings with God are direct. Prayer is the supreme
medium. If a man pray in a mosque he will have company and
holy association, but prayer can be offered anywhere; the devout
spirit makes any spot a temple. The only Koranic command beyond
the command to be constant in prayer is that the believer shall face

---

[43] Palmer, *op. cit.,* page LXIX.
[44] XC: 15.
[45] Sura XI, 90. Ameer Ali's translation.

toward Mecca, but since it is impossible that the simplest religion should not take on some ritual form, the actual practice of Moslem prayer has become more formal than that. The official prayers have been continued in Arabic but a movement is now on foot to change that.

The prayer known as the Prayer of David would sound no alien note in any Treasury of Prayers. "O Lord, grant to me the love of thee; grant that I may love those that love thee; grant that I may do the deed that may win thy love; make thy love to be dearer to me than self, family or than wealth." The conclusion of the prayer of Ali[46] is no less noble: "Thou, my Lord, art my Refuge; Thou art the Forgiver, I am the Sinner; I am groping in the dark; I seek thy knowledge and love and mercy; forgive my sins, O my Lord and let me approach thee, My Lord."[47]

I have noted already the stress of Islam upon alms giving.[48] Mohammed meant also to fasten Mecca in Moslem devotion; the believer prays toward it and the devout are commanded to visit it once. There is a proper ritual to be gone through at the shrine and there a camel, sheep or goat is to be sacrificed, apparently the only remnant of the sacrificial system in Islam. The pilgrims must abstain from quarrels and "commerce with women" and provide as they can for the journey, "but the best provision is piety." To have accom-

[46] Ameer Ali, *op. cit.*, pages 163 et seq.

Note.—I remember most vividly an afternoon in Saint Sophia when hundreds of men bowed themselves again and again beneath its great spaces, empty of everything except rugs and lamps, the soft afternoon light, the memories of fateful centuries—and men like Ali reaching through their shadows toward God. Observers of western evangelical Christianity report a great falling off in assemblage entirely for purpose of prayer. It would be a curious thing if the prayers of the faithful should continue to wash the walls of a Moslem mosque with sonorous music when the tides of prayer have ebbed from Christian churches. [Atkins.]

[47] For an appreciative discussion of the place of prayer in Islam see Arnold, *op. cit.*, page 147 et seq.

[48] Fasting and pilgrimages are also religious duties. Fasting is the general bequest of the East to religion—an aspect of the general ascetic discipline of sense life. It is a hard matter to trace its hidden roots; they are in some general sense the persuasion that the body is evil or mischievous and needs for the sake of the soul to be kept strongly in hand. The Fast of Ramadan demands entire abstinence from food and water from the time "a white thread can be distinguished from a black one at dawn" until night. Eating and drinking are permitted after nightfall; but the discipline of a waterless day in Arabian mid-summer is demanding, though exemptions are granted to the sick, the traveler, the student, ailing women, and the "soldier doing God's battle against the assailants of the faith."

plished the pilgrimage confers a distinction on any Moslem; he wears the sign of it in the color of his headdress as a decoration.

THE CENTRALITY OF GOD IN ISLAM

"The persuasion of the reality of God is the secret of the religious power of Islam. God is. His sovereignty is supreme. He is the ultimate will acting through all the chaos and confusion of the world and men have only one duty—obedience to that will in every positive deed and the acceptance of it in every condition."[49] The fate, the "necessity" of the Greek tragedian, the "Rita" of the old Aryan have for the Moslem become incarnate in the will of God. One can trace the development of this doctrine through the Koran. It was not theology to begin with; it was a battle-cry and emblazoned on the Moslem banners. One finds a parallel between Mohammed in Medina and John Calvin in Geneva—each a militant faith defenseless in a hostile and embattled world. What was there then for the Reformer or the Prophet to fall back upon save the embattled will of God?

When it comes to actual fighting the confidence that the issue is in the hand of God is a force to break every opposing line. Mohammed sent his followers out to battle with the assurance that life and death were already determined for them—if death it were best met on the battlefield with a garden of peace and running water beyond the red burning sand. Predestination is a paradoxical doctrine. As long as it is the molten conviction of the hard beset who believe themselves on God's side, it is a tremendous reinforcement. When it hardens down into fatalism, it weakens initiative and creates an entirely passive attitude which may become the resignation of the saints or an excuse for a slothful spirit and a stagnant society. The shadow of Kismet has lain deep across Moslem lands.

The final issues of life for Islam are Heaven and Hell—such a Heaven as an Arabian would love, and a "pukka" Hell. This was a faith common to the region and the time drawn from many sources. The non-Moslem dwells upon the sensuous character of the Moslem paradise. The Moslem apologist says that this is really to be taken in a symbolic sense, since Mohammed had to accommodate spiritual things to the understanding of the nomad. The only thing a Moslem needs to believe, says Ameer Ali, in substance, is that each

[49] Abridged from Bishop Lefroy; quoted in Arnold, *op. cit.*, page 415.

man shall render to God an account for deeds done in the flesh, "and that the happiness or misery of the individuals will depend upon the manner in which they have performed the behests of the Creator." Islam in time developed a school of mystics who reduced, as other mystics have done for other religions, the material of Mohammed's paradise to the Beatific Vision.

For the most part, Mohammed's paradise is a kind of a celestial oasis, "a garden beneath which rivers flow." There is the sound of the running of sweet waters through the pages of the Koran as through the Hebrew Sacred Books. The garden and the river are however subject to considerable embroidery; "and the reward for their patience shall be Paradise and silk! reclining thereon upon couches, they shall neither see therein sun nor piercing cold.[50] And close down upon them shall be its shadows; and lowered over them shall be fruits to cull . . . flagons of silver shall they mete out; . . . and there shall go round about them eternal boys! when thou seest them thou wilt think them scattered pearls; and when thou seest them thou shalt see pleasure and a great estate!"[51]

There are also "girls with swelling breasts of the same age as themselves" and a cup of flowing wine; "no headache shall they feel therefrom, nor shall their sight be dimmed." It is of course possible to allegorize all this though soldiers of Abu Bekr and Omar are quite unlikely to have done it; they were not fighting for allegorical plunder or dying for an allegorical bliss. There are names for heaven: The Abode of Rest, the Abode of Peace, the Garden of Eternity, the Garden of the Most High, the Garden of Pleasure. There are also various and suggestive names for Hell: The Abyss, The Raging Fire That Splits Everything to Pieces, The Fierce Fire, Gehenna and the like. The Moslem Hell is fire. Its hot blasts, boiling water, and pitchy smoke make it an ill couch. Mohammed's vivid imagination would have gained little in detail by an acquaintance with Dante's Inferno. Mohammedans borrowed the "Bridge of the Separator" from Zoroastrianism and made much the same use of it.

Islam is then a religion of an intense belief in God, made manifest in confession, prayer, obedience, charity and devotion—a faith of vivid contrasts, unsoftened by mystery, native to the spirit of the

[50] An echo of the Book of Revelation.
[51] Sura LXXVI, 15-20.

Arab, native also to the light-flooded plateaus from which he came down to teach it, preach it, live for it and die for it. No faith has commanded a more devoted following or afforded a more tenacious resistance to the appeals of other religions. One may only conclude then there is in it that deep unity of temper, history, habit, institution and faith which makes of any historic religion a supreme expression of the whole force of the human spirit. Mohammed created and released one of the greatest forces of history.

The heat of Islamic monotheism would be consuming save for one thing: God is merciful. Mohammed never reached and searched the hidden places of the human spirit. He has a feeling for the poor and the sad but there are no beatitudes in the Koran, dealing at their source with those desires and imaginations of which deeds are only the ripened fruit. The old laws of an eye for an eye and a tooth for a tooth are not repealed; they are re-enacted. Nor is there any injunction to turn the other cheek and go the added mile. The finality of the Koran has given a static quality to Islam and tended to fix the social institutions and moral standards of seventh-century Arabia and continue them into a world to which they no longer belong.

THE CONQUESTS OF ISLAM

Before Mohammed died, awakened and unified Arabia had challenged the Byzantine and Persian Empires along frontiers which had always been drawn in the sand. Within twelve years after his death the Persian King was an exile, Jerusalem, Antioch and Alexandria were subject cities of Islam. The countries Islam took were weakened by endless fighting. The Saracen was like a flame. It was bloody fighting. After the battle of Allis so many of the captured were beheaded on the banks of a canal that for three days "the corn for the army was ground by the reddened flood."[52] The Moslems who died found their silken couches in Paradise, the living found their Paradise in loot. Religion ceased to be a motive, the freebooters of the desert were raiding the hoarded wealth of Persia, Syria and Egypt. A fifth went to the cause, the rest to the army.

They say that Omar wept while dividing the spoil of Jalola. "I foresee," he said, "that the riches which the Lord bestoweth on us

[52] Muir, *The Caliphate*, page 55.

will be a spring of worldliness and envy, and in the end a calamity to my people." The first Caliphs kept their hands clean. Abu Bekr had a pittance a day with maintenance for a camel and a slave. Omar dined on barley water and made any passerby his guest. The leadership of Islam fell into less devout hands but its drive went on. For a hundred years "the representatives of Mohammed ruled over a vaster continuous empire than the world has beheld before or since—the same will was absolute on the banks of the Indus and on the banks of Douro, the same sovereign was prayed for in the temples of Narbonne and the temples of Samarcand."[53] The ruler himself possessed a power no sovereign ever claimed. He was head of Islam, the religion, vice-gerent of the prophet and absolute head of Islam the state. He wore the crown and the mitre.

This could not last and Islam broke apart partly because the governmental organization of it was not equal to the impossible and very greatly through quarrels over the succession. The old tribal feuds of Mecca, the old jealousies of Mohammed's sonless harem, came to life to plague Islam. The "trial of superiority" between Hashim and Omeyya found its event in the division of the Caliphate. Thereafter there were two and sometimes three rival Caliphs excommunicating one another and fighting among themselves. It is a subject for the specialists. The divisions ran curiously parallel to the schism in western Christianity. The Eastern Caliphate ruled from Bagdad city of the Arabian Nights, romance and allure, the capital and Vatican of Islam. Cordova was the seat of Western administration.

After the destruction of Bagdad, Cairo was for two hundred and fifty years the religious capital of Islam. The sultan of the Seljukian Turks inherited the holy office with the conquest of Egypt and Constantinople and ruled the Moslem world from the city of Constantine the Great. Now the Republic of Turkey has abolished the Caliphate, enacted civil and criminal codes to displace the Koranic law, translated the prayers into Turkish and gravely informs dark-eyed Turkish children that "if Mohammed had lived in our day he would have commended Boy Scouting and modern games like football, tennis and hiking"—also that he would have worn a hat.[54]

---

[53] Freeman, *History of Conquest of the Saracens*, London, 1876, page 61.
[54] Kirby Page, "Nationalism Interprets Islam," *The Christian Century*, Jan. 22, 1930.

ISLAM AND CHRISTIANITY

The relation of Islam to Christianity is a study in itself.[55] Mohammed knew the substance of the New Testament narrative only through different reports, the life of Jesus mostly through the apocryphal gospels (and those not first hand), Christianity itself only in debased, sectarian forms. There are a score of references to Jesus in the Koran including the Annunciation. "When the angel said, 'O Mary! Verily God gives thee the glad tidings of a word from him: his name shall be the Messiah Jesus the Son of Mary, regarded in this world and the next and of those whose place is nigh to God.' . . . She said, 'Lord! how can I have a son when man has not yet touched me?' He said, 'Thus God creates what he pleases. When he decrees a matter he only says BE and it is.' "[56] This does not mean, however, that Mohammed accepted Jesus as Divine. The key to the intensity of his monotheistic teaching is his reaction against the doctrine of the Trinity.

It is probable that in his most high-minded period, the prophet dreamed of a simple and universal God-centered religion in which Arab, Jew and Christian could unite—a noble and moving vision. As forces older and stronger than any prophet began to come into action that dream faded and the irreconcilable apartness of the three religions asserted itself. Also a natural conviction that his was the only true religion displaced his earlier and more inclusive attitudes. In 627 A.D. Heraclius, who had beaten the Persians in the battle of Nineveh and restored the true cross to the Church of the Holy Sepulchre, received a message sealed with the seal of "Mohammed the Apostle of God." It bade him cease his idolatrous worship of Jesus and his mother, acknowledge the mission of the prophet and return to the worship of the one true God. Heraclius forbade his ministers to take any account of the missive.

Chosroes, King of Persia, received a similar summons, which he treated as Jehoiakim did a communication from Jeremiah.[57] When this was told Mohammed he prayed "Even thus, O Lord, rend thou

---

[55] Bell, *The Origin of Islam in its Christian Environment,* London, 1926, is a scholarly and just-minded study of this.

[56] Sura III, 40.

[57] *Jeremiah,* 36: 22-23.

his kingdom from him." Kings have commonly found the correspondence of prophets irritating, but how could these kings have foreseen the imperial force which lay behind that rude, silver seal? These letters were the message of a fanatic, a religious imperialist or a prophet as one wishes to interpret them; they were certainly a presage of the missionary passion of Islam. An inevitable conflict was shaping itself, and the outcome has made history.

The impartial student must recognize that the early Moslem treatment of subject Christian regions compares favorably with the general habit of the time. Heraclius made a bloody massacre of Jews after his capture of the city. When Omar the Moslem took Jerusalem from Heraclius, he received the Patriarch courteously and confirmed the Christians in the possession of their shrines and churches. He forebore to pray in the church of the Resurrection and did his devotions under the sky.[58] When the crusaders took Jerusalem from Islam, Raymond d'Agiles, an eyewitness, says that "in the temple and porch of Solomon the horses waded in blood up to their knees."[59] When Saladin took the city from the Crusaders, he allowed the clergy to take away their sacred vessels and treasure, "rewarded with gifts the virtue and piety of his enemies" and left the Holy Sepulchre to the Christians.[60]

In general, the People of the Book were not forced to change their religion; they were required to pay tribute in return for which they were entitled to protection. The articles of capitulation for one old Mesopotamian town are representative: "In the name of God the merciful and compassionate. . . . He (the Moslem General) grants them security for themselves, their gods and their churches, which will not be destroyed or occupied if they pay the tribute which is due from them, and do not make any treacherous uprising; on condition also that they do not build any new church or place of worship, and do not use publicly any bell or Easter celebration or cross. God is witness and in him is sufficiency as witness."[61]

The antagonism created by centuries of fighting, the harsh tempers of new Moslem races, the pride of conquering Caliphs naturally

---

[58] *The Caliphate, Its Rise, Decline and Fall,* Muir, London, 1892, pages 144, 145. Ameer Ali, *op. cit.,* page 221.

[59] Michaud, *History of the Crusades,* Vol. I, page 224. He adds "up to the bridles" but up to the knees would seem enough.

[60] Michaud, *op. cit.,* page 430 et seq.

[61] Bell. *op. cit.,* page 172. See revised edition for stronger statements.

affected the relation between Moslem and Christian and have left a
dark record on both sides. But the Christians of Syria preferred
Moslem to Greek rule; the Nestorians, though excommunicated by
the Great Church as heretics, have survived for centuries under
Moslem rule; the decay of Coptic Christianity in Egypt was as much
due to its own factional corruption as the intolerance of the Caliphs;
the Christians under Islam in Spain were allowed generous freedom.
Things were harder in the Balkans and Greece under the Ottoman
Turk but something must be charged to the general characteristics
of that race. The Eastern Saracenic Empire was overthrown by mi-
grating hordes from North Central Asia. These adopted Islam, but
the racial genius which built Bagdad and Cairo and flowered into
art, literature and the beginnings of science perished at their hands,
and Islamic civilization never had thereafter the high distinction of
its golden age. Beyond debate, the Christian subjects of Islam were
under constant pressure to conform, and Christian populations were
largely absorbed and there were Christian captives and galley-slaves
enough to move the pity of Europe (though John Knox was for a
while the galley-slave of his Most Christian Majesty, King Henry of
France). In a sentence, through the general inhumanities of a thousand years the Moslem compares favorably with the Christian in his
treatment of the alien in race and religion.[62]

SECTS AND SCHOOLS

Islam had been seamed by controversies over the holy succession.
It had been equally seamed by purely religious controversies. One
would think so simple a creed could not father any sect or heresy
save the denial of God. But Islam has had so many divisions and
doctrinal controversies as to lead one to believe that the roots of
sectarianism are in human nature and not in creeds. The Moslem
Doctors of Divinity, far from regretting their embattled sects, see in
them a sign of the purity of their faith and offer their multiplicity as
a sign of their superiority over Christianity.[63] If Islam has, by that
test, done better than Christianity, it is a superior religion indeed.

Its fundamental controversies are about Free-Will and Predestina-

[62] Arnold, *op. cit.,* discusses in great detail the relation of Islam to Christianity.
He concludes that Mohammedanism has not depended on force for its existence.

[63] Freeman, *op. cit.,* page 103.

tion and the right of Reason against Authority. The looseness of the Koran supplied endless material for comment and contention. The religions of conquered lands and races have reacted upon the faith. Its development reflects the changing philosophies and speculation of a thousand years, the subtleties of the Eastern mind and the habit of folk who love to talk in cool arcades of old towns and the black tent. Islam had created the Epicurean fatalism of Omar Khayyam:

> The Ball no question makes of Ayes and Noes,
> But Here or There as strikes the Player goes;
> And He that toss'd you down into the Field,
> HE knows about it all—HE knows—HE knows.

> There was the door to which I found no key;
> There was the veil through which I might not see;
> Some little talk awhile of *Me* and *Thee*
> There was—and then no more of *Thee* and *Me*.

It has evolved a mysticism which parallels the general experiences of all mystics. These Moslem mystics call themselves "the followers of the Road" and are known as Sufis in opposition to the Sunnas and other schools. The waymarks of their road are the familiar guide posts of the Mystic Way: Repentance, Abstinence, Renunciation, Poverty, Trust in God, Satisfaction. There is endless detail in their discipline but the end of the path is the loss of self in God:

> The true mosque in a pure and holy heart is builded;
> There let all men worship God;
> For there he dwells, not in a mosque of stone.[64]

The love of God becomes the only motive: "O God! if I worship thee in fear of Hell, burn me in Hell, and if I worship thee in hope of Paradise exclude me from Paradise; but if I worship thee for thy own sake, withhold not thine everlasting beauty!"[65] Oriental poetry and literature reflect this phase of Islam. The poetry touches those erotic borderlands we find in much mystic poetry and there are strange anticipations of the sayings of the European mystics:

> When my Beloved appears
> With what eye do I see him?
> With his eye, not with mine,
> For none sees him except himself.[66]

[64] R. A. Nicholson, *The Mystics of Islam*, London, 1914, page 61.
[65] *Idem*, page 115.
[66] *Idem*, page 167.

"The eye," said Eckart, "with which I see God is the same eye with which he sees me." Afifuddin and the father of German mysticism meet at the end of the road.

The bitter controversies over the succession left Islam permanently separated into two major divisions. The Sunnites are numerically vastly in the majority and are generally considered the Orthodox Moslems. The Shiahs or the followers of Ali have always maintained that the spiritual headship of Islam should descend by divine appointment in the line of the prophet's family. The head of the church must also be distinguished for the purity of his character (a test many Caliphs would have found difficult). They therefore withdrew into a church within a church and since the Caliphate was essentially a theocracy—a state God-ruled and a church politically administered in the person of one man, this made them rebels as well as schismatics; the result was a succession of civil wars. Persian Mohammedans believe that the last true successor of the prophet disappeared in the tenth century and still lives, attended by the faithful, in a mysterious city from which he will some day ride out to save the world. Modern Bahaism has grown out of this belief to build its Temple of Unity on the shores of Lake Michigan.

CONCLUSION

Moslem civilization and culture are studies in themselves, the creation of race, religion, regions, the genius of rulers and scholars and the current of time. The Moslem naturally loves the high lights, the non-Moslem will not let us forget the shadows. There are lights and shadows enough for both. Bagdad, Cairo and Cordova were the efflorescence of a distinctive genius. While Europe felt its way through the dark ages and the church authorities were fearful of the free play of the human mind and sometimes darkly repressive, such science and philosophy as were then possible did find a sanctuary under the Star and Crescent. Islam taught Europe Aristotle, medicine and some beginnings of science. Literatures were created, cities spread themselves under azure skies, domed and gilded and slender-spired. Scholars sought universities whose gowned faculties adorned their chairs. The Crusaders and then the Mongol invasion destroyed Saracenic culture, but we who think too often that little counts besides Greece and Rome and Medieval and Modern Europe have no case to dispute the splendor of it or the eager or creative play of its spirit. It lingered longest in Spain. There the splendor and the tragedy of Saracenic civilization found their last expressions in orange groves and gardens whose romance never grows old and palaces whose beauty captures the imagination. The Moor had not long left Granada when Columbus sailed west.

The call to prayer is no longer heard from the minarets of Cordova but it is still heard in Europe, Africa, Asia and the Pacific Islands. There are thirteen million Moslems in Russia alone. One in five of India's vast population is a Moslem, the largest single group of the prophet's followers in the world. Java alone has twenty-three million and under the American flag the Moros of the Philippines daily say their prayers in the language of the prophet. Nor has the missionary spirit of Islam failed. No longer do Mohammedan armies march and countermarch across the world, but peaceful missionaries of the faith are scattered widely through Asia, Africa and Europe. Even America has become for them a foreign mission field and has a few small groups who look toward Mecca when they pray. What Western civilization and the forces with which all religions have now to reckon will do with it is beyond calculation. When one has read the authorities for whom Islam is a false religion and those for whom it is the only true religion and the juster student who sees its lights and shadows, he will find no kinder judgment touched with insight than in some sentences of Duncan McDonald, who is speaking not of the Koran but the Arabian Nights—apropos of magic and enchanters and the strange excursions of the untutored mind—"But the world of the Arabian Nights is God's World. There is sun and air and the sense of an ultimate justice. Joy comes in in the morning there, and so for all his belief in magic and his sense of the power of enchanters the Moslem is a man. He stands on God's earth, beneath his sky, and at any time can enter the Presence and carries his wrongs to the highest court. Between him and Allah there stands nothing and he is absolutely sure of Allah."

PROLOGUE

A Questing World

THE North saw the gods ride out to their last great battle in the West while their seats were as yet unshaken, their reality as yet unquestioned. Under what compulsion the North did this is beyond our power now to discover. They may not have known themselves. They saw dimly but felt keenly the vast unfolding of a drama in which even the gods were only actors, whose curtain falls to rise again. They saw the last act sadly through their mists and though Loki's laughter is never unheard, the gods are not mocked as they die.

In Rome the older order was deeply wounded, the Jus Divinum violated when the Great Mother and a retinue of foreign gods came to the Eternal City and thereafter Roman religion is always in flux. "Religio," the ordered administration of mores and social health by a compact with the gods and the proper dealings with them through a priesthood which represented both the gods and the state, was challenged by "Superstitio" which was, as much as anything else, the individual setting out on his own particular pilgrim's progress, choosing his own guides—many of them quite strange and new—and making a scandal of his quest for salvation. At least the Roman conservative was scandalized. Cicero was one of the first to draw a distinction between religio and superstition. Epicurus had already in Greece sought to deliver men from current superstition (whose chief support seems to have been fear) by throwing the baby out with the bath. The gods, he said, are do-nothing gods. Reason should be a man's master for nature is reasonable. Beyond the flaming walls of the world there is nothing but the dark.

Nevertheless Superstitio was religiosity of a warmer sort than the State religion, an upthrust of the questing spirit and thereafter there were elements in Roman religion both new and pregnant. In Greece Euripides doubted and Aristophanes mocked the gods. In both Greece and Rome changes incident to the always widening structure of the empire recast society and profoundly affected religion. The old

order stood as the Acropolis brooded above Athens or the temple of
Jupiter guarded the hearts of Rome, but the currents of life which
washed their marble columns carried a confusion of elements.

THE INFLUENCE OF ALEXANDER'S CONQUESTS UPON RELIGION

Alexander's conquests furnished not only an epochal date in
universal history but a most significant date in the history of religion.
What followed his phalanges, what broke against their lance-heads
is a commonplace—dissolution and rebirth. Whatever frontiers of
empire, mores, culture, language, race and religion had maintained
the integrity of Greece against old Syria, and the Persia of Cyrus
and his successors and the separateness of Western Asia generally
against European Hellenism, disappeared. Thereafter influences
flowed both ways and it is not easy to say which region gained or
lost most. Alexander had all the genius of an empire maker—save
the power to govern himself. He was tolerant of all religions in his
patchwork creation. They might worship how and what they pleased
and, in addition, he accepted benignly their worship of himself.
Religion was universalized in the sense, at least, of being no longer
localized. Stubborn Palestine was the only exception. It lifted its
limestone shoulders militantly above the meeting, merging faiths and
cults; "Thou shalt have no other gods before me."

Rome took all this over in the centuries after Alexander. When
Augustus Caesar was done consolidating and organizing, the Mediterranean basin had become the Graeco-Roman world. Caesar might
and did rebuild the temples of the Graeco-Roman gods but they
could no longer house the worship nor monopolize the adoration of
the empire. Dates, one said, help in such generalizations of more
than three centuries of history but they confuse as well. The new and
the old, especially in religion, are always in action and their com-
pounds, precipitates and fermenting reactions become almost the
despair of the student of religion. In a fairly dependable kind of
way we may set out three aspects of what Augus,[1] in a study invaluable to the student of religion, calls "that now vanished world"
and yet even in Western Christendom not vanished at all. These

[1] *The Religious Quests of the Graeco-Roman World,* Charles Scribner's Sons, New
York, 1929.

three are: The Mystery Cults, Gnostic Speculation, and Syncretism (Melting-Pot Religion).

The Mystery Cults

Reference has already been made in this study to these cults, something in the first chapter, something in Egypt and Babylon, more in Greece and Rome, which means that they are very old and in one form or another attend the procession of all the gods. They have for a long generation now been exhaustively studied, especially in their bearing upon Christianity. What is actually known about them is arrestingly less than what has been written about them.

We have already noted in the study of Roman religion the general character of Mithraism; how it appealed to the Army and followed the legions to Dalmatia or Hadrian's wall, and how, more than any other of the mysteries, it might have had some chance of winning the empire. For only a religion of mystery quality, content and method, could have won the empire of the future into which the empire dissolved. The classic gods and goddesses could not do that. They were crowned and sculptured ghosts. No national or racial religion could do it. The nations were dead—or still to be born. Racial religions were everywhere and nowhere.

The mystery cults were both universal and, as we would now say, unilateral. They were also fluid, adaptable, tenacious. They were rooted in ancient human ways with earth and sky and rooted deeper still in the needs and experiences of life. They acknowledged the rhythm of life and death and rebirth, the aeonian, cosmic pulse which beats through the farthest star to the systole and diastole of the human soul. They made a religion out of universal and constant elements of experience. Their seat was not on the Parthenon or the Capitoline Hill but in the fears and hopes, the dreams, the sufferings and the quenchless glow of our human pilgrimage. Religion thus rooted has in it a power of perpetual resurgence.

They agreed in believing that there is in man an immortal element alien to this present world, needing to be released to return to its heavenly source; that there is a ritual of release; that the soul may be purged of sin; that there was a saving grace in sacramental meals through which the faithful shared or even repeated the experiences of deity; that those thus cleansed and supported were sure of immortality. Also that the future offered no hope to the uninitiated. This is the bare framework, upon which the drama of deliverance was built. The mysteries were associated with the memories and experiences of beloved deities.

They came almost without exception from the East—even the Greek mysteries have some Asian contribution behind them. They found hidden meanings in old myths, they carried into new regions the rites associated with seasonal vegetable death and resurrection, they mourned the death and celebrated the resurrection of their gods. The vivid symbolism, the fascinating drama of their initiations led the initiates through alternations of fear and hope, darkness and light, until, clothed in white, they come through an ecstasy of spiritual rebirth into redeemed oneness with their divinities and by rebirth a citizen of the Eternal order.

They rescued the lonely and forgotten from the numbing anonymity of the empire, made them friends of those who had shared with them the secrets of Eleusis or the sanguine baptism of the Taurobolium. They were warm with emotion; love came into religion.

They repeated in their ceremonies of initiation the three stages of deliverance and changed life which because we find them in every age and region, are phases of an unescapable law, inevitable stages in our pilgrim's progress if it do issue in darkness. These three stages are: Purgation, Illumination and Union. They are elastic enough to permit many variations, but beneath all variety is their three-fold constancy. The mystic called it the "Mystic Way"; St. Paul said, "Put off, be renewed, put on."[2] Jesus said: "If any man will come after me, let him deny himself and take up his cross and follow me." Out of these three movements the mysteries made their disciplines and their liturgies. They had vows of secrecy, confession, a period of probation, baptism or other forms of lustration, sacrifices, fastings, scourgings, prayer.

When the initiate was thus purged, he was solemnly and secretly received, certainly with words and forms and symbolisms which made the experience transforming and unforgettable. The initiate was thereafter reborn. He could say of his divinity: "I am thou and thou art I." He no longer feared death, it was then for him only the gate of life. He had found release from the sense of sin which in

[2] *Ephesians* 4: 24.

forms different from any so far studied lay like a shadow across the empire about which so many shadows had begun to gather.

Naturally there were temples and worship. Isis had matins and vespers, white-robed and tonsured priests. At the appointed hour the veil of her shrine was drawn aside and there she was waiting, richly robed for adoration. There has always been the sound of chanting in every temple and the hymns and chants in the temple of Isis have carried far. Even the most cautious scholars recognize the influence of the mysteries upon the Graeco-Roman world. Their relation to Christianity has been for thirty years now a subject for warm debate. Their value for those who have followed the procession of the gods is that here and at last religion has become an aspect of experience; disciplined, directed, purposefully created.

GNOSTICISM

Religion became something else; it became a saving knowledge of which there are as many characterizations as there are specialists in the study of it. It is too complex to be safely generalized, too vast in murky detail to be considered here at any length. It drew its sources from almost the entire hinterland of ancient cult, religion and speculation. Babylonian mythology, Persian dualism, the Orphic quest for redemption, Jewish theology, Greek philosophy, Symbolism, Analogies, Oriental theosophy and the boundless capacity of the human mind to build grandiose structures of speculation all combined to create and confuse it.

The Gnosticism which plagued Christianity for almost two hundred years is not the Gnosticism—the formless, frontierless mélange of speculation which followed the twilight of the gods. It was itself a kind of twilight, a tension of light and darkness, but its elements of light, which sometimes seem to do little more than make the vast confusion of the religious mind of the period discernible, were the light of a rising, not a setting sun. The important thing for us here is not what Gnosticism was nor the vague, questing, formless content of its speculations. The important thing is that in the Graeco-Roman world from Alexander to the Antonines the "fountains of the great deep were all broken open and the windows of heaven were opened." That is: the pagan religions were breaking up, frontiers disappeared, cultures met and merged, Persian dualism, Hebrew

monotheism, the salvation quests of the mystery religions, the sublimation of immemorial myths, a decadent Greek philosphy and a
sense of all the shadowed, evil side of life, all combined to create
systems hung on "sky hooks" whose only control was the strange
power of the human mind to build its grandiose creations.[3]

In such a system the sky is the limit. You may have a most
demanding asceticism—the soul must assert itself against the body,
or you may have corporeal license—since the body has no relation to
the soul what it does can not affect the soul. There will be gradations
of powers by which, in a later development, the Absolute Good
which can have no contact with our evil order is stepped down to a
Creator who could and would make a planet like ours. There was
an unbelievable multiplication of dusty-named sects, there must have
been teachers, preachers, system makers, consultants and "life-adjust-
ers" whose names are hopelessly—and happily—lost. One would not
dare to say that religion had ceased to be a discipline. It had certainly
become what passed for an intellectual vocation.

In a sense, of course, Gnosticism itself is a product of Syncretism,
the result in speculation and frontierless confusion of the fusing of
the multiple streams of religion and thought that flowed through the
Mediterranean basin. We are concerned with it because it was an
anticipation of a new-world religion. The hospitalities of mind which
made it possible would offer open doors to such a religion if and
when it appeared. There would naturally be in so fluid an order subtle
interchange of influence. Religious currents can no more run side by
side without some mixing of their streams than any other movements
of human culture.

The relation of nascent Christianity to the religious movements
of the Graeco-Roman world has therefore become a vital and vexing
question. The reader will have seen already how much there is in
Christianity arrestingly similar to the Mystery Cults, what echoes of
Gnosticism there are in the letters of St. Paul, what aspects of
Syncretism there are in the faith which won the Western world, and
how much of a diluted, unconfessed Christianity there might be in
the temples of Serapis and the chapels of Mithra. There is a widespread difference between the extreme "right" which holds that

[3] One must not forget that it was a period of unusual intellectual force with little
scientific sense and no scientific knowledge as we understand that term. The human
mind does not work well save on a basis of observed and verified fact.

Christianity owes nothing but a religiously bankrupt environment to the Graeco-Roman world and the extreme "left" which finds in Christianity only the potent mystery-religion which finally displaced all the rest.

There was no need to borrow or to lend too much. This study of the historic development of religion has missed the mark if it has not shown out of what compulsions religion issued and how its channels and forms were waiting for it through deep necessities of life. Something older than either Christianity or the mystery religions was beneath them both: the need of deliverance and the laws of life by which deliverance is achieved. If the oldest mysteries found in the death and resurrection of the Vegetable Spirit—or some incarnation of it—the mystae found also in the sequences of their inner and outer lives something of which Attis and Osiris could and would become the symbols, and not misrepresent the drama of the soul, Christianity could not escape nor did it seek to escape the necessities of the drama of redemption. It only organized it around its own center and invested it with its own authority.

THE OPPORTUNITY FOR A NEW RELIGION

Actually the Graeco-Roman world offered an unparalleled opportunity for a new religion. Its hospitality to new religions was an open door, its frontierless unity made an opportunity as ample as civilization, its spiritual hunger opened hidden doors into the lives of the questing, the varieties of its quest made approach possible along a wide front. Its passion for salvation offered the strategic point of approach. Its wealth of form and inheritance would supply a ready garmenture for any religion which came unfurnished with such necessary things. The new religion would need, if it were to assert itself universally, to be strongest just where competitive religions were weakest, and especially strong in some element of universal appeal. It would certainly need a passionate persuasion of its own truth and commanding destiny, and it would need at the same time a power of plastic accommodation to circumstance, a way of taking and using and becoming what it needed from the order into which it came—and then forgetting that it had ever done it.

It must always be becoming something else and always remain itself, which means that it must have something at the heart of it in irreconcilable opposition to the world it would both win and transcend. Sometime about the middle of the first century a much-traveled Jew, driven by an urge he could not escape, crossed from Troas to Macedonia in a galley freighted with destiny and brought that religion with him.

CHAPTER XV

Christianity

THE relation of Jesus to the religious inheritances and situation of his time is the proper point of departure in any study of Christianity. His position was amazingly, unexpectedly strategic. Geographically, it was nearer than Rome to the center of world civilization. Asia Minor had been for centuries a melting pot in which all kinds of religions were fused and recast. Egypt and Chaldea were within easy reach; imperial commerce and travel used the eastern coasts of the Mediterranean and the old caravan routes of Syria. Palestine was on the Greek side of the classic world. No religious movement beginning in Jerusalem could reach Rome without passing through the sphere of Hellenic influence and no interest of the human mind or spirit ever escaped that influence unchanged. The creative play of the Greek mind upon Christianity during the first three centuries made its creeds and, save for Augustine, its theologies. Guignebert thinks it made Christianity.[1] From the hills above Nazareth, Jesus could see the blue water which washed all these coasts of destiny.

It happens now and then that the ruling ideas of an age pass through a personality great enough to receive and transform and redirect their entire movement; thereafter they are never the same. If Einstein's theories should stand the test of time he will have accomplished that transformation for the physics of space and time. Plato did it for philosophy, Copernicus for astronomy, Dante for the medieval mind. Jesus stood in point of time and inheritance just at the one spot which made it possible for him to do this for religion. Judea was a small country and Jesus' fellow-countrymen were a sorely tried and difficult people, but they held the mandate of monotheism for the world. The Hebrew religion was the one religion of the ancient world which had any pure spiritual content, any commanding moral content, and any adequate conception of God. It was ritualized almost to death, tied up with race pride,

[1] Charles Guignebert, *Christianity*, New York, 1927, pages 87-91, page 89 especially.

fenced off—though the door of the synagogue was open at a price—but it possessed the noblest of sacred literatures, the vision and passion of the Hebrew prophet, the devout and timeless music of the Psalms—and God.

No religion but a monotheistic religion could have carried across the last twenty centuries with force enough to serve the religious needs of the Western world. The only possible alternative was a Platonic idealism. But Plato's God was a divinity for the intellectually elect. It is difficult to imagine Clovis wielding his battle-axe for an ideal of eternal excellence, or the Emperor Henry standing barefoot in the snow begging Pope Gregory to readmit him to the communion of the beautiful, the true and the good. Also it is doubtful if Pope Gregory had the keys of that imponderable kingdom. The great races in whose devotion historic Christianity was established needed a vividly personalized God to believe in; a God for whom their lives had meaning and with whom they could carry on a mystic personal commerce. Jesus of Nazareth gave that kind of faith in God to the world.

He did it so simply that the wonder of it almost escapes us. God was his strength, his guide, his Father, his unseen friend. He spoke to and of him as if he were always within call. He saw everything in the light of God's concern. God winged the sparrows' flight, clothed the flowers with beauty, was opulent and unfailing in his gifts, knew the needs of his children before they voiced them in a prayer. Jesus withdrew from the demanding crowds to lonely hours of communion with his Father; he spoke to him from the agony and gray desolation of the cross as a man speaks to a friend. And he left the record of all this not as an argument but as unquestioned and unreasoned experience, the very light and atmosphere of faith. Christianity has made much of lesser miracles, been served or puzzled by them, but I would restrainedly say at the end of this study of what religion has been from the dim dawn of it, that the unique fact in religion is this: that the religious experience—for it was nothing else—of a Galilean carpenter gave final content to a faith in God in which ever since the devout of western civilization have found their peace. He left the world but two alternatives: the impersonal drive of cosmic force or loving kindness as the Ultimate Reality.

Jesus' second ruling idea was the Judaic expectation of the Kingdom of God. The key to his own sense of mission and message must be sought in his Kingdom teaching, but there are great differences of opinion about his conception of the Kingdom and its program.[2] The religious authorities of Jesus' time were not agreed about the Kingdom program. The Hebrew prophets covered a wide front. There is a line in their writings which anticipated the regeneration of their sorely tried state through suffering and the unfailing providence of God. A later line anticipated a divinely commissioned deliverer. There was, besides, the popular mind of Jesus' time of which we have little knowledge save as it must have been reflected in the curious writings of the first century A.D.

What line did Jesus really take? It is a critically difficult question. He certainly opposed the impulse to force the issue by armed revolt against Rome.[3] His non-resistance teaching is best understood from this approach. Christian orthodoxy believes that he proclaimed himself the suffering Messiah and Son of God sent to save the world. A small but influential group of scholars believe he accepted the whole program, offered himself as the agent of it, was disappointed by the event, and sought the cross, expecting to return in conquering power after his death.[4]

But the value of the religion of Jesus is not in this sharply controverted region. Every religious leader combines the temporal and the enduring, belongs to his own time and transcends it. Jesus' Kingdom teaching may be—is, as reported—shot through with ideas and expectations peculiar to his time, but he added something of his own which has endured—his ideal of the realm of God of which the righteous are citizens, whose laws are love and mercy, whose values are the values of character and which in its human splendor

---

[2] Every fully developed religion has had some belief about the fate of the world and humanity. These beliefs would make a book in themselves. They were always concerned about the fortunes of the dead; they did not always speculate about the future of the world. Judaism developed the expectation of the sudden interruption of the going human concern, with far-reaching consequences and for its own particular profit. The makers of wise names call these speculations eschatology. A rather small but very competent group of scholars believes Jesus' teaching to have been in substance eschatological.

[3] See Vladimir Simkhovitch, *Toward the Understanding of Jesus,* New York, 1921, a book as illuminating as it is short—a key book.

[4] Shirley Jackson Case, for example, holds that he did not even offer himself as the Messiah but rather as a prophet of preparation for the Kingdom, believing that God "would himself both judge and redeem the people of his choice." *Jesus, A New Biography,* Chicago, 1927, Chapers V and VI. This also is Guignebert's position.

and the regnancy of the will of God in and through it, is the pre-destined issue of the human enterprise.

THE BEGINNINGS OF CHRISTIAN FAITH

Jesus' teaching can be put in a dozen printed pages but it was pregnant with religious destiny. He took the old law, the old ethic, the old understandings of God and recharged them with reality; he made righteousness a creative spirit; he sought the control of the motives of life and conduct; he followed conduct to its hidden sources in thought and desire. He made glowing good-will the law of life, and said that whatsoever a man would have done to himself he should do to others. He did all this as a wandering teacher, finding texts and occasions as they offered, freely sowing, as he said, broadcast, telling an unforgettable story to illustrate the grace of compassion, the love of God, or the tests by which man would stand or fall in the Day of Judgment. And he touched all he said with a poet's insight, a prophet's passion, and the mystic's certainty of God.

It may be possible to trace elements of his teaching to older sources; aspects of it as reported are difficult to reconcile and the literal application of many of his injunctions to a hard driven self-assertive society is more difficult still. Something is lost beyond recovery. Much has been changed by the media through which his teaching has been both transmitted and refracted, but his creative force is the tap-root of Christianity.

No wonder then that those who knew him best found in what he was something greater than anything he said or did. Their devotion has made the recovery of the historic Jesus perplexingly difficult but it has also made Christianity what it has been. The oldest of the Gospels (Mark) veins his ministry with works of supernatural power and ends with the assurance of his resurrection from the dead. Later Gospels add the annunciation and virgin birth and enrich the detail of the resurrection. The prologue to the last of the four (according to St. John) affirms his pre-existence from all eternity and offers him as the agent of creation.

He moves thereafter through divinely august events as "the Christ, the Son of God who was to come into the world."[5] Christian doctrine organized itself around this belief and Christian devotion translated

[5] *John* 11:27, Moffatt's translation.

it into awe and worship. Any consideration of the reported elements of the miraculous in the life and ministry of Jesus belong to a critical study of his life. They are just now receiving searching examination with no considerable agreement in the conclusions reached. The documentary evidence for unusual power in dealing with sickness and disturbed personality is as strong as any other concerning him. The critical student has found some key to it all in the mind of the time which reported Jesus. Perhaps Rufus Jones is as near to the fact as any when he says that those who knew Jesus could not report their impressions of him without using such a medium.[6] It is the form in which they reported his personality to the world.

His immediate followers certainly expected the speedy fulfillment of the Jewish Messianic program. Their own assurance of his resurrection reassembled them in Jerusalem after his crucifixion, confident and electric with a missionary passion. Faith in the resurrection made Christianity. Jesus does not seem to have been concerned about organization. His supreme interest was in religion. The *religion* of Jesus was his way of life, his trust in God, his high detachment from the transient concerns of life, his entire confidence in the conquering power of sacrificial love, of which the cross might be taken as a symbol, his conception of a human society established in complete devotion to the ethical and religious ideals of which he was the voice and incarnation. If in his presentation of this society the temporal and timeless aspects of it so meet and merge that the disentanglement of them is now impossible, it was because he saw all life *sub specie aeternitatis*, in the form of the eternal.

Christianity was for a while essentially that. It had not even a name, save a gleaming window kind of a name which is once or twice mentioned almost incidentally in the book of The Acts; it was called a way and its adherents were followers of "the way." They lived a communal life sharing their possessions, which was easy because they had no expectation of needing them long. Otherwise they were observed for their mutual affection and devotion. They were blameless watchers for a millennial dawn, not as yet disengaged from the Jewish church. Christianity might have continued essentially that, a Jewish sect living in Jesus' way and reconciling as best they could the issue of events with their belief that he was the Messiah—which would have been possible. They had only to keep

[6] In a lecture recently heard by the author.

postponing his return until there was no longer any Jewish state for him to return to. There was in fact such a sect, the Nazarene,[7] which gradually faded out of the picture.

Among the non-Jewish folk who had no consuming desire for the end of the world Christianity might also have become a way of religious life, commending itself by the grace and goodness of it, simple, open to any seeker, a daily commerce with God, richly humane. Such a religion would have created no imperial church, built no cathedrals nor left any record of disputes and persecutions. But it might also have proved what Jesus actually hoped for, and, in the end, demonstrated the power he said his way possessed. But it would not have won the world in three hundred years. Saul of Tarsus, as nearly as one can reconstruct the situation from the New Testament, set it upon that conquering road.

Concerning Saul of Tarsus

Saul was born in Asia Minor about the beginning of the Christian era. He boasted both his Hebrew descent and his birthright, Roman citizenship. He always acknowledged the spell of the empire and conceived Christianity in imperial terms. He grew up in his native town, Tarsus, the seat of an important university strongly under Stoic influence. Tarsus itself was an old Greek town thoroughly cosmopolitan and rich in an actual and legendary history, which reflected the movement of race and empire in western Asia for centuries. There was no better city anywhere to school a sensitive youth in the religious complexities of the classic world, or better acquaint him with its unsettled state.

Saul was both sensitive and reflective. Religion was the supreme interest of his life. He developed an unusual catholicity of spirit, ripened in sympathy with humanity. He was educated in the doctrine and intellectual method of his own people, sharing to the full their memories and hopes. His complete ease in the Graeco-Roman world and his Hebrew inheritance made him a unique liaison officer between the two fundamentally contrasted orders. The key to many difficult regions in his thought is just there. He had a gift for far-ranging speculation, he thought in universal terms, and yet he

[7] See George Foot Moore, *Judaism,* Harvard University Press, 1927, Vol. I, pages 90 et seq.

never escaped the forms of thought in which the Jewish schools trained him. No maker of the Christian mind ever took more nobly audacious flights or wrote with a more inspired and lyric beauty, and yet he lived and died a Hebrew of the Hebrews, being taken finally from a riot in the temple at Jerusalem to prison and martyrdom in Rome.

He brought to Christianity five things without which it is impossible to calculate what it would have become: a creative mind of the first rank highly trained by the standards of his age, the temper of the mystic, the experience of the "twice born," a world-wide vision of the possibilities of the faith into which he was reborn, and, greatest of all, the fateful gift to see just where and how Christianity might make its appeal to the Graeco-Roman world. He began as the bitterest opponent of the way, he ended as its passionate supporter and tireless, fearless missionary. Between his conversion and his death he set a mark upon it it has never lost.

There is no record that Paul (one would better use the name by which he is best known) ever saw Jesus, though it is possible he did. He quotes him only once, though the ideals of character and conduct he afterwards urged upon his churches are thoroughly in the spirit of the Sermon on the Mount. He seems to have come under the spell of the serene and selfless courage of the folk he harried, to have seen a victorious light in the face of stoned Stephen and to have felt that these had a secret eminently to be desired. He records a soul-searching struggle in one vivid phrase, "it is hard to kick against the goad."

His struggle ended in a blazing experience in the Damascene desert. He was struck down by the Power he had set out to break. He rose blinded, the bond-servant, as he was proud to call himself, of Jesus Christ. All the other leaders of apostolic Christianity had ripened through association with Jesus of Nazareth; Paul came in through the resolution of an inner struggle.[8] Call it a drama of the soul projected against the sky by Paul's mystic temperament; the epochal thing is that Paul's reborn life centered in the Jesus of his faith and vision. The historic Jesus of Galilean fields and Jerusalem streets became the Christ of faith and experience. The Christ took precedence over Jesus and so became independent of circumstance

[8] There are three accounts of his conversion: *Acts* 9: 1-9, *Acts* 23: 1-10, *Acts* 26: 10-17.

and time to support the devotion of the future, create mystic comradeships, and issue in the massive development of Christian doctrine. Soon the followers of "the way" began to be called Christians.

Paul invested the Christ with the offices of the Jewish Messiah; his earlier writings make that plain enough.[9] But as the tide of destiny carried him into the Graeco-Roman world he shaped his message to meet the need of that world. Paul found his open door to the classic world in the men and women, mostly Greek, who had become converts to Judaism. These were free-minded enough to accept a more satisfying faith. Their search was not for a new world order but for deliverance. As Paul's mission carried him more deeply into the old pagan world a changed approach became inevitable. The Greek loved his world too well to want it destroyed, the Roman was too proud of the Empire to pray for the wreck of it to advantage the Jews. The record of the life-and-death struggle involved in disengaging new Christianity from old Judaism is written through all Paul's letters. Single-handed he saved it from a Judaic provincialism. His deliverance gospel carried Christianity into the full current of the quest for salvation which ran so strongly through the lands across which he came and went for twenty years.

CHRISTIANITY ARMS ITSELF FOR ITS WARS

Christianity organized itself for its mandate. It created an authoritative literature, sacred books telling and retelling the life of Jesus,[10] the letters of Paul and other leaders combining teaching, exhortation and a new ethic, and one marvelous book, written for the assurance of martyrs and the comfort of the church, whose grandiose lights fuse an ancient splendor of apocalyptic drama with the light cast by the fires of persecution. These books reflect the developing faith and need of the church. Elements in them are drawn from sources beyond our power to trace but they invested the life of Jesus and teaching of Jesus with a supreme authority. They doubtless read back to its earliest beginnings a content Chris-

[9] It is begging a crucial point to say that Paul alone did this. It involves Jesus' own conception of his mission. Also the apostles and the Jerusalem church accepted Jesus as the Messiah. But we are concerned just now with Paul.

[10] Burnett Hillman Streeter, *The Four Gospels,* New York, 1925, is one exhaustive study by a great scholar of the sources and formation of the gospels. There is an enormous literature on the New Testament.

tianity had already acquired in its adjustments to the spirit and need of the world it had set out to win. At any rate they had in them all that the future was destined to develop. Christianity was fixed.

Thereafter its history is the account of conflicts within and without. It records an always crescent mastery of an always changing world, a vast and many-sided growth which absorbed elements from every religion it displaced and from every culture over which it asserted itself. Naturally, its own nature was changed, but its power to subdue alien elements to its own spirit and uses preserved its character and continuity; everything Christianity touched became Christian. The accidents of history—or the drive of destiny—carried it west and not east. What would have happened to a Christianity consistently developed in the Orient is beyond conjecture.

It began in the meeting place of the East and the West, and maintained for four hundred years a struggle on two fronts. On the west it faced the massive order of classic paganism, which it defeated and supplanted at immense cost. It was challenged by the allurements of sense, the Roman state religion, and the dramatic appeal of the mystery religion. It conquered paganism because paganism was already sense-weary and ready for a change from Mars and Mercury and Venus to the disciplines of asceticism and the assertion of the inner life over the cheating sovereignty of this world. The excess of this reaction carried it far from the attitude of its founder and introduced elements which have plagued it ever since. But there were actually in the religion of Jesus world-denying elements which are of the essence of the Christian faith and through which, by that paradox, Jesus announced, it is to conquer the world.

It conquered the Roman state religion because that was fretted and undone. The shadowy gods of Mount Olympus and the Seven Hills had no power to stand against the vigorous monotheism touched with an infinite tenderness which was the supreme religious bequest of Jesus. It won the society of the empire by beginning with the slaves and the socially disinherited, lonely and hopeless folk with nothing to lose and everything to gain, lost in the vast impersonality of the empire. To such as these Christianity brought a sense of personal worth which gave their lives new meaning, a brotherhood in which race and station ceased to count. The Christian slave and his master shared the same sacramental meal. It lighted the somber horizons of life with the gleam of an assured hope in immortality. The confidence Christians carved on the headstones of their dead or upon the walls of the catacombs, where they hid in the dark while death in frightful forms waited for them in the light above.

Christianity displaced the mystery religions because it met the need which had called them into being more directly and upon a nobler level. Angus,[11] in a fascinating chapter, cites many explanations of the victory of Christianity in a strongly contested field and adds his own. Christianity, he says, won the Graeco-Roman world through its intolerance, its catholicity of spirit ("the religion of Humanity"), the tenacity of its faith, the authority of its sacred books to which it added the authority of the Hebrew sacred books in their Greek translation, the satisfaction it brought to the widespread sorrow of the ancient world and the vital fact that it centered not on an idea nor a ritual act but upon a personality to whom the gospels gave historic reality. Attis and Osiris were myths and their worshipers knew it;[12] Mithras was an idealization of sun-worship; but Jesus was a person whose story any might read, and there was always the noble monotheistic content of Christianity. It won because it was essentially a better religion than any of its competitors. Also it won in no little degree by taking from them what was most effective in their appeal and richly dramatic elements from their ritual.

Christianity saved itself by the force of its organization from the dissolving allure of philosophic speculation with which the East tempted and almost undid it. It had a genius for effective organization which no other religion parallels, the authority of its scriptures and the regnancy of its creeds. It was in debt to Rome for the final perfection of its organization and to the Greek mind for the articulation of its creeds. When they were finally formed after centuries of embittered controversy, they established Jesus Christ as the incarnate Son of God—"very God of very God and very man of very man"—and left a future of which they knew nothing to explain, defend, and adjust it all as best it could. But they did incorporate a conception of the relation of God to man which has had an incalculable value for faith and devotion. And the creeds were always

[11] *The Mystery Religions and Christianity,* New York, 1925, Chapter Seven.
[12] That statement begs too many questions.

there, recited, ritualized, awesomely mysterious, to mold the mind of generations while the ancient order dissolved and a new world shaped itself through endless travail.

SCHISM AND CONQUEST

So vast a process involved its schisms and its shadows. Christianity fell apart on the old line of cleavage between the Greek and the Latin worlds. It inherited in the west the last imperishable form of Roman authority and assumed the tutelage of the fierce and vigorous races who stood awestruck in the midst of what they had ruined. Augustine of Carthage and Hippo, having learned in his own soul how helpless the will is before the drive of passion, formulated a theology of the human estate which left men no resource but the saving grace of God, and which bowed fearsome generations in the appeal for a salvation that must be given and not earned. Mother Church was there to give it.

She invested her authority with a supernatural sanction, her priesthood with the power to confess and absolve and change bread and wine into the broken body and shed blood of Jesus Christ. She repeated in the Mass the pale and solemn scene on the Mount of Crucifixion. She incorporated all this in stately liturgies and built (presently) great churches rich in symbolism to house the incessant processes of her worship. She asked nothing less than the souls of men and men gave them gladly, being assured of salvation through their devotion and obedience.

Christian missionaries won the kings of little Saxon states in England for whom life was like the flight of a bird through their audience chambers—a swift going from the dark to the dark. They met the twilight of the gods in Teutonic forests with the dawn of the faith they preached and smote lustily at Thor's oak, which fell without dire consequence. An imperial church consolidated all these gains and tirelessly extended her imponderable frontiers. There was nothing from the Danube to the Atlantic which did not belong to the Church.

She asked for the minds of men as well as their souls and men gave them also. Subtle thinkers formulated philosophies to support her dogmas and liturgies. If there were here and there a recalcitrant thinker he was corrected—or otherwise dealt with. The victory was always at a price. The high gods were long since gone, but the elusive spirits, creatures of something older and more tenacious than the gods themselves which always attended their processional, were not so easy to dispose of. They came back through folk-habit and immemorial rites. If they found themselves outwardly changed and in strange company, they kept their surprise to themselves, having already suffered many changes and being too old to care.

The Christian year continued seasonal festivals old as winter death and vernal resurrection. They were renamed, charged with new association and very greatly improved (one of them at least) in manners and morals, but they remained to witness to the molds in which devotion was first cast and the revelation of the "Power not ourselves" in earth and sky which first taught men to believe and to hope.

The Church, being very wise in her understanding of human nature, allowed generous limits in many directions to her communicants but delimited them inexorably by faith and obedience. She demanded creedal faith from the priesthood, but did not encourage the laity to concern themselves too much about matters which were too high for them. They must believe in Mother Church and her mystic power to adjudicate the spiritual destiny of her children. This faith became, in the issue, one aspect—and the most considerable—of the general mind of society.

The Church claimed the mandate of the keys of heaven and hell from Jesus Christ through St. Peter. She added purgatory to serve the very human weakness of those she shepherded and so became the warden of three gates. The calendar of the Church was the measure of time. The liturgies of the Church were the occupation of the cleric, the sacraments of the Church the power by which she laid hold of life at its peak points of experience. The parish priest was near as birth and death, with bishops, cardinals and popes in some more remote and sovereign state; God was somewhere above them all; but the body and blood of Jesus Christ were on every altar and the saints were always kind. The Church dealt with these mysteries. A man had only to deal with the Church.

THE OLD ORDER CHANGES

Varieties of temperament asserted themselves in time. Religion has always been impatient of channeled ways. No church can be quite catholic enough for everybody. The devout began to find a more direct and less costly way to God than the somewhat complicated church way. The mystic sought the assurance of the Divine presence through the travail and discipline of his own spirit and was so sure of what he found that nothing else mattered. The common folk of North Europe developed a simple piety, largely independent of sacraments and the church technique, and fashioned on the way of Jesus. It began to recapture the primitive spirit of the Gospels which had been long overlain, and to manifest itself in charities and the humane concern for poverty and suffering. Those who fell into this way asked only to be known as the Friends of God or by some similar name. These were forces of disintegration but they possessed great religious promise.

Christianity during its imperial period had never entirely lost the humanitarian impulse which lies so deeply imbedded in the teaching of Jesus. It recast private morals, especially in the region of sex relationship. It made marriage a sacrament and gave a new quality to family life. It ended gladiatorial shows; it helped humanize the later legislation of the Roman empire; it threw its force against slavery, although the Church was slow in freeing its own serfs. It discouraged the endless petty fighting of the middle ages. The Church controlled individual morality through the case system of the confessional. A great deal can be said for that system, wisely administered. The moral guardianship of the state which is now the habit of society is a doubtful substitute for it.

In general, however, the primary concern of the Church was in the administration of the enormous sacerdotal system she had developed. The stress and inevitable abuse of an authority like that began to fret a world in which new forces were in action. The issue was the Protestant Reformation, which was, in the whole of it, the recasting and realignment of northern European society. The Reformation did not at once greatly change the content of the Christian mind. It did strategically shift the center of authority. It admitted, under cover, the right of private judgment though it was slow to allow the exercise of the right which it claimed as its Magna Charta.

It enthroned the authority of the Old and New Testaments and invested that authority with an infallible completeness which has not borne examination. The Reformation was both destructive and constructive. It dissolved a noble ideal which was perhaps impossible and had certainly fallen into an unideal state. It released forces which have issued in self-governing states and churches and made Christianity an adventure in liberty. The older church profited by it, in its turn, being moved thereby to a too long postponed housecleaning and taking on a new vitality through having to meet an alert competitor. In general, there was a recovery of the essential religion of Jesus.

The sectarian development of Protestant Christianity was inevitable; Protestantism became a many-branched growth whose root is free inquiry dealing with the mystery of religion and the Bible. The manifold Protestant communions reflect varieties of religious temperament, very human prejudices and the entirely material desire, even of the pious, to have something of their own more divinely right than anybody else's. A detailed examination of the forms Protestantism has taken is beyond the scope of this book. In general, they fall into three groups: communions like the Anglican and Lutheran which took over, with many changes, the corporate religious life of pre-reformation England and North Germany and the Scandinavian countries, and continued their worship in old churches and cathedrals, with elements of the old liturgies and modifications of old authorities; the communions, generally Calvinistic, which entirely supplanted the corporate Latin Catholic order with creeds and administrations which sought to reproduce primitive Christianity; and the communions of a more independent church government which began the great adventure of democracy in the ordination of pastors and the conduct of their own religious affairs by the laity.

But these outstanding types have been crossed and re-crossed in their development until the disentangling of their unities and divergencies is a study in itself. They have been costly in the finer qualities of the spirit they claim to incarnate and in a needless duplication of organization, but they have made religion more interesting to their communicants and saved its freer development. Since every great religion has made a similar many-branched growth this variety of development would seem to be of the inevitable nature of religion. The passion for conformity is strangely unteachable.

The spirit of inquiry which the Renaissance released accepted no frontiers and took Christianity itself as one of its provinces. The forces which are now in action to question and possibly recast religion itself are most vigorous in the civilization with which the Christian mind has been most intimately associated. It has taken therefore the first shock of the drive. Its present estate reflects the profounder confusions of the modern mind and yet it is meeting an unparalleled situation with great resource and that sense of universal mission which has been for two thousand years its driving force.

The Making of the Christian Mind

An impartial estimate of Christianity by one nurtured in the faith is almost as difficult as crossing Zoroaster's "Bridge of the Separator." Criticism is almost sure either to be veined by subtle apology or edged with reaction. Any analysis is sure to be colored by temperament. And yet the just-minded student must subject his own religion to the same detached appraisal to which he has subjected the others.

Christianity has had from the first an almost unparalleled self-consciousness. Its intolerance was one secret of its force. The lonely separatedness of its beginnings, the sifting persecution to which it was long subject, and its life-and-death conflict with paganism left an indelible emphasis upon the Christian mind. It gave Christianity a militant spirit alien to the gentleness of the Gospels. It developed a line of attack which recognized no virtue in the enemy and admitted no fault on its own side. The long struggle, equally bitter, inside the Church which ended in the creeds and a rigid definition of orthodoxy intensified this militant self-consciousness. The outcome of four hundred embattled years which left a religion, which had begun so sheerly helpless, the one victorious and upstanding force in an anarchical world, fixed Christianity's persuasion of its God-given mandate. It has never since lost it.

Christianity has always been haunted by the conviction of its initial completeness. It has been strangely slow to admit the principle of development. Its theologies claim to have been resident in its sacred books. Its most imperial organization reads back an authority which makes the power of the Cæsars ridiculous into the fellowship of Jesus and his disciples on the hills of Galilee. The competitive communions have generally been ready to recognize alien elements in their rivals but never in themselves. Until almost our own time early Christianity has been approached as though it began in a world empty of anything save shadow gods and dead faiths. (The influence of the speculative Greek mind and the genius of Rome for organization have been recognized, but the old ways of the human spirit to continue its inheritances with new names and new authorities have not been adequately recognized.)

The learned have wrestled with the letters of Paul as though the key to his elusive passages were in a Greek lexicon and not in living folk and street-corner arguments in old cities, where the pregnant quest for God and peace illumined the dust of a dissolving religious order with both a pathetic and a prophetic light. This persuasion of its initial completeness has been a saving element in Christianity for it has called it back again and again to its fountain head, reshaped it in the spirit and mind of Jesus and so given it a power of self-renewal no other religion has seemed to possess. But it has emptied its accepted histories of that recognition of growth fed by many elements, without which any account of Christianity is only a pious pattern.

Christianity has always been what it was becoming, the religious mind—if the word "mind" be made inclusive of all that has grown out of it—of western civilization. It has taken content and color from every element that civilization inherited and all the contributory streams which have fed into it. It was carried immediately into a milieu opposed at almost every point to the mind and spirit of its founder. The Greek could let nothing go till he built it into a structure of speculation, while the luminous simplicities of the beatitudes and the Sermon on the Mount are as free from speculation as the bright atmosphere of mountain uplands are from dust. Rome could let nothing go without organizing it—and how can love and the sense of God's brooding presence be organized?

CHRISTIANITY AND THE WESTERN WORLD

The militant individuality, the élan vital, of the North found nothing native to itself in the gentleness and renunciations of Jesus. It honored them with a gesture and retired them into the shadows, fit perhaps for a monk at his vigils but meaning nothing to an insurgent race or a predatory baron. One may honestly wonder how far Western civilization has really cared for Christianity as a religion and how far it has found in it one more opportunity for the exercise of its fateful "will to power," carrying it to supremacy by a force not its own and alien to its very spirit. Certainly no religion has been more entangled in ecclesiasticism or been so excessively institutionalized, when all the while its founder seemed to believe that it needed only to be left alone with the troubled spirit of man.

It has been as excessively indoctrinated. That process began before the last gospel was written and initiated a structure of creeds and theologies which have been its preoccupation for centuries. The religion of Jesus has seemed sometimes only an errant ghost within the vast ramifications of that structure, wandering homeless from corridor to corridor with no alternative save to seek a shelter in sacraments and liturgies and sacerdotal authorities and finding them all piteously strange.

Finally, Christianity has been carried down into the current of an industrialism which glorifies the wealth its gospels proclaim a deadly hindrance to citizenship in the realm of God, and into the massed self-assertions of a nationalism which refuses citizenship to an alien who claims Christian liberty of conscience in the event of war. It has had to adjust itself as best it could to all such things and also to a scientific spirit which recognizes no interruption in the close-linked sequence of cosmic law and force, while Christianity traces its genesis to a series of supernatural events. And all this while, until yesterday, China followed unchanged the wisdom of Confucius, the disciples of Gautama sat in placid meditation, and India dreamed with Brahma that all existence is a dream.

And yet Christianity has kept on being Christianity. Its power to subdue to its own spirit so many alien elements and slough off its own abuses and corruptions proves some incalculable force in it. What is that force?

For one thing Christianity has always been a religion of hope. It inherited the Jewish Messianic hope and has not always known what to do with it. The remnants of that curious program of falling stars and parted skies which it has carried over into its literature and theologies belong to a dead cosmogony. The first Christians looked up at every dawn to see the Heavens opened and the Son of Man descend with his angelic retinue. The heavens have opened but only to reveal depth beyond depth of lonely cosmic space. Yet the hope has remained, being too vital to be lost.

The horizons across which it views the future have always been touched by some assuring light. It has held, in many changing forms, to an issue of the human enterprise worthy of the cost. Existence, Christianity holds, is not Brahma's dream to be dissolved into less than nothing when he awakes. It is the valiant enterprise of God. It is not Gautama's wheel, dipped in tears as it turns. It is a progress directed toward an ethical and spiritual victory guaranteed by the Divine purpose. Christianity is not a defeatist religion. Say what one will of such a hope, there is no denying its practical force in the conduct of life. It has here fallen in with the temper of the West; a religion of meditative inaction could never have held vigorous races in northern climates.

The optimism of Christianity is by no means unqualified.

> The very source and fount of day
> Is dash'd with wandering isles of night.

It has always taken a far more despairing view of human nature than its founder. Something of this is due to ascetic elements which came in from the East, a good deal to Paul who saw little in his world to assure him and who remembered his own past with bitter regret. Quite as much is due to Augustine who made, for the glory of God, a dogma of human depravity and a drama of man's natural moral impotence. He doubtless had facts enough, including his own experience, to give him a good case, but one may reasonably doubt whether God is so glorified. The rigid theologies which Augustine fathered have had an immense driving force but they have been a clouded medium through which justly to see our rather complicated human nature.

Christianity built up its explanation of the problem of evil on a penalty basis. Its spacious theories turned society away from the actual study of the complexities of human nature and the tangled rooting of human problems. We are only just now beginning to correct that costly error. Original sin has been a covering phrase for

> . . . pangs of nature, sins of will,
> Defects of doubt, and taints of blood,

along with many other things the poet does not catalogue. I should think few of its assumptions have led Christianity so deep into uncharitable ways, so far from the spirit of its founder. It has been the source of dark fears and hard ways of man with man. It has been too easy. For much the same reason Christian thought has not concerned itself enough with tracing moral consequences back to their causes or following through, in the individual and society, the creative projection of motive, desire and deed.

Christianity has balanced the accounts of life too starkly in terms of heaven and hell which is final enough—but there is another system of accounting. And yet Christianity is and has been a religion of courage and hope. Its courage is rooted in a finer motivation than the fatalism of Islam; its hope is a luminous aspect of its faith in a sovereign God of infinite good-will.

THE ETHICAL INHERITANCE OF CHRISTIANITY

The ethic of Christianity is drawn from three sources. It inherited the Ten Commandments, the noble social passion of the Hebrew prophets and Israel's conviction that morality is the will of God for humanity. Jesus reissued the Hebrew law. The goodness he commanded was a righteousness of purpose, desire and even imagination motivated by love. It is possible that he looked upon the world as too near its term greatly to engage or fret the citizens of the Realm of God. If a Roman soldier sweating under the sun of Palestine hailed a craftsman from his shop to carry his pack a thousand paces, why, go two thousand with him—there was a road ahead the legions would not be using.

But even if one allow that the way of Jesus was a pro-tempore way, a fashion of life to be followed bravely for a little while until a happier fashion should come with a regenerate world, then this astounding conclusion follows: the way one should live in this world if it is to end tomorrow turns out to be the right way to live in it if it is to go on till the sun is dead. Jesus taught a detachment from sense and time which is the only secret of any mastery over them. Only Gautama discovered this secret in any degree corresponding to the insight of Jesus. But Jesus' insight is far richer in positive life: "I am come," he said, "that they might have life and have it above measure."[13]

[13] This is from the fourth Gospel. It may be "doctrinized" but it is true to Jesus' spirit.

Wealth, he taught, was a net to snare men. He taught the higher resistance, the power of love and patience to wear down antagonisms. Life was a thing man lost by holding fast to it. Lose it for something greater and it would be found again. He was content with no perfection less than the God-like. He said to tax-gatherers and fishermen, "Be ye therefore perfect as your Father in Heaven is perfect," and left humanity its supreme summons. He saw that a cross might become a throne to rule from and a sword by which to conquer. He made his own cross just that.

Christianity is, as Lake says, essentially a world-denying religion. It has been, historically, associated with anything but a world-denying civilization. The result has been a strain for which hitherto no resolution has been found. The more critical hold that Christianity has never succeeded in creating a Christian civilization; the more despairing maintain it never can. The mind of Jesus has certainly never entirely penetrated and subdued the Western world. China has been more consistently Confucian than Europe or America has been Christian, largely, I suspect, because Confucius was native to China, his wisdom and his ways were one with the culture and temperament of his people. In the West almost every phase of the economic, industrial and international situation has been a sector in the long battle line between Christian idealism and the conduct of society.

And yet for all this, the ethic of Christianity is commandingly adequate. It is the survival and enrichment of the best-tested experience of our race. It is many-sided enough for general human need. It has been fruitful in a long succession of folk whose grace and goodness are a revelation of the possibilities of human nature. It is particularly rich in a humaneness which has slowly and at great cost subdued naturally fierce races to a creative consideration for the suffering. It has given Christian civilization a clearly recognizable character. Those who are just now proposing substitutes for it are by no means agreed. Many of their experiments seem doubtful and very often they end, like Mr. Walter Lippmann, by letting in through the window, slightly disguised and with another calling card, the Christian virtues which they have shown the door.

Christianity has had a power of self-criticism and self-correction which must always be taken into account. Something of this is doubtless due to the vigor of the civilization with which it has been associated and the influence of the scientific and philosophic temper of the West. It has shared the pregnant processional of the centuries which have cast and recast European civilization through the unspent force of the latest "lords of time." If they have been at issue with its spirit they have more than once rebaptized it in some new release of their own passion for a better human estate. When civilization has left the socially disinherited nothing else, they have found in this faith a shelter and comfort. So the Friends of God turned from the inhumanities of their time to the "life of the spirit," and the weavers in old Flemish cities, with no other hope, took refuge in the praise of God. On the other hand Western Christianity has hitherto shared the social, political, and economic advances of Western society and has contributed to the realization of them.

But the force of self-correction in Christianity has owed much to the authority of its sacred books. They have always been there with their arresting revelation of what Christianity has missed and their luminous revelation of what it ought to be. The haunting urge of this religion to be always returning to its sources has, more than any other thing, kept it growing. It has refused to be lost in an alien order or to haul down its flag. It has maintained its proud aloofness from a world which has as constantly entangled it. It has always been insurgent, an anvil to wear out many hammers, with a way of becoming again and again a hammer itself. If it had done Western civilization no other service than to keep alive, for protest and correction, an ideal so opposed at crucial points to the temper of that civilization I think its most exacting critic could not deny its usefulness. When one surveys the embattled character of Western history since the fall of the Roman Empire, he may be pardoned for maintaining that its saving lights are gleams through the murk, the pity and the splendor of it, of what has been most essentially Christian.

THE SOVEREIGN CHRISTIAN DOCTRINES

But all this leaves the most significant things unsaid. Christian doctrine has locked up on two centers. The effort to find an adequate form for its doctrines has kept Christianity excessively occupied, but the religious content of these doctrines is that the Divine became humanly real in Jesus Christ and that this revelation is redemptive. The creeds themselves are but glass through which to see darkly the controversies of their respective times. But they do witness the Christian confidence that God is not remote, but immanent. There is no impassable gulf between the Divine and the human,

> And so the Word had breath, and wrought
> With human hands the creed of creeds
> In loveliness of perfect deeds,
> More strong than all poetic thought.

What grew out of this belief is by no means so simple as these four lines which bridge the depths with a song, but there is a religious approach in the Christian doctrine of the incarnation capable of adjusting itself to new insights with assuring power. Whatever the theologians have tried to say, general Christian faith has found in God the qualities of which Jesus was the expression, and this, never in some cold reasoned way, but in a mystic warmth of adoration. There is a parallel here between the development of Buddhism and Christianity. The Buddhist came in time—and no long time, either—to believe that Gautama was a revelation of a supreme reality out of which he came and to which he returned. The naïve forms that faith assumed ought not to blind us to the significance of it.

Ultimate reality is an empty thing to worship. The philosopher, trained to rarefied atmosphere, may make a debate but not a religion of it. There is no key to ultimate reality save nature and man. Christianity affirmed Jesus Christ to be of the nature of God and left experience to make a religion of its affirmation. Experience left theology to rationalize it, which theology has never been able to do, and made a worship of it—liturgies and hymns and a splendid symbolism which art both used and adorned. Perplexed reason turned to worship in the doctrine of the Trinity for example—Christianity's most cherished doctrine. Authority affirmed it; orthodoxy defended it; heresies grew out of it; theology wrestled with it and surrounded it with clouds of words. But devotion does not want crystal clear horizons. It wants encompassing mystery, mists which open to reveal mystic immensities and then close in again to leave the vision and the wonder. Then a poet makes a hymn of it:

> Holy, holy, holy, Lord God Almighty!
> All thy works shall praise thy name, in earth, and sky, and sea.

Holy, holy, holy, merciful and mighty!
God in Three Persons, blesséd Trinity.

And reverent repetition invests words with something no words can say.

Christianity has hitherto found a great part of the secret of its power in those very elements which make it, as a religion, the most complex of the three monotheistic religions. It has never been a pure monotheism as one finds monotheism in the Hebrew Psalms or the Koran. It has put a strain on faith, sometimes even on credulity, that Judaism and Islam have not exerted, but in its historic development this has served its mastery over the Western mind. Christianity has been so strong because it has been so much. Its mysteries have nurtured devotion. Its apparent irrationalities have challenged faith. Its tough-fibered doctrines have exercised the mind. Its assurances have sustained the hard beset. Its absolutions have healed the conscience-sick and the appeal of its Cross has humbled pride to the dust.

Its complexities have added to its power. They are no accident. They are the slow creation of its Hebrew genesis, the Mediterranean civilization in which it took doctrinal and administrative form, the need of untutored races with a boundless capacity for faith, who must be taught by symbols and who only asked of the symbols that they should tell more than they could say, and the religious mysticism of the northern races. These have given it a many-faceted play so that there has been a light in some turning of it for every variety of temper. And now if it should be left alone with the Orient long enough it would become something else still, and not cease to be itself.

CHRISTIANITY A DELIVERANCE RELIGION

It has been, above everything else, a deliverance religion. It won its first response in what it offered to an age whose ancient social and natural bonds were breaking up and which was groping blindly toward some "deeper emotional satisfaction for the emotional needs of mankind." Its success in this field certainly led it to strengthen this line of its appeal, but something more than the discovery of an effective propaganda carried it into this channel. The entire outcome of the religious development of the past was shaping toward the quest for redemption. To this issue the procession of the gods had come. It was not enough for faith to issue into a really noble monotheism vocal with noble praise. The essential alienation of the human spirit from its time and sense setting, its sense of estrangement from the Divine, demanded also a way of redemption and reconciliation. All religion is deliverance. Christianity has made deliverance central.

It took over altars older than its own altar and sacraments whose immemorial beginnings we are just beginning to discover. It seized upon the law and truth of life toward which men were feeling their way through many confusions: the law that there is no way of deliverance save as the innocent suffer with and for the wrong, and strength spends itself for weakness. It reached the supreme insight of faith; God must suffer and share with men, or his ways with them are not just. It carried this insight to its last luminous height: Love is the only deliverance and love must suffer to save. "God is love and they that abide in love abide in God." Christianity offered the world the Cross.

Out of these elements Christianity created its Drama of Deliverance. It invested the death of Jesus with redemptive power and added the doctrine of the Atonement to the Incarnation. Then the Christian scheme of Redemption set out to win the world. In its fully developed form it included creation from verge to verge and time from the dawn of time till eternity. It made every man who believed the focus of an infinite concern. It bowed humanity to the dust to exalt the mercy of God, while the sense of being so sought and saved lifted man from the dust and gave an immeasurable value to his soul. The Church fixed it in its creeds; theologians made the acceptance of it the test of faith; worship set it to music in the Te Deum; art emblazoned it upon pictured windows. It was repeated in the drama of the mass and made efficacious in the mystery of the sacraments. Dante and Milton made epics of it; it formed the mind of Christianity. It has been for almost twenty centuries Christianity.

The inner life of the believer reflected the procession of his faith. There is a profound difference between Catholic[14] and Protestant devotion but for both, the interests of the soul takes precedence

[14] I use the word in its popular sense.

over all earthly things. This mortal life became a prelude to eternal felicity—or eternal woe. The uncertainties which attended the outcome made everything colorless (at least they should do that but the devout have generally shown a lively interest in what Paul called "this present world," which should make one careful about too general statements). Confessional literature reveals the forms this drama of the soul can take. John Bunyan knew himself a prize for which God and the devil were contending. None of Cromwell's battles had the action which took place in Bunyan's soul nor were so attended by destiny. John Wesley's "class meetings" were the scenes of thrilling recitals; the gray dusty world of colliers and weavers was only a shadow for folk whose souls were lit with the splendors of salvation. Which is exactly what had happened to the men and women whom Paul gathered out of the streets of Rome and Corinth, to tell them that they were the sons and daughters of God for whom creation had been waiting, and that they were already risen with Christ.

Its Hymns the True Voice of Christianity

The hymns of the Christian churches are a finer medium through which to see all this than their theologies. They represent the faithful in a hostile world besieged without and within, with no safeguard but the power of God and nothing wherein to trust but the cross. They voice the peace the believer has found, assure him of safety and comfort, exhort him to trust and confidence, and kindle him with ardor and valor.[15] They celebrate the glory and happiness of eternal life in cadences which are twice music—once in the Latin hymns of Bernard of Cluny, singing the glory of the New Jerusalem, from which the noblest of them are translated; once in the English into which Neale has translated them:

> Thine ageless walls are bonded
> With amethyst unpriced;
> The saints build up its fabric
> The corner-stone is Christ;
> The cross is all thy splendor,
> The crucified thy praise;

[15] These phrases are taken from the arrangement headings of a very good and representative Protestant hymn book.

> His laud and benediction
> Thy ransomed people raise.

And there is, besides, Dante's vision of the Sempiternal Rose whose radiance is the light of God, whose petals the innumerable redeemed.

These hymns voice also a great assurance of comfort for the bereaved—no loss love suffers is final. Death is robbed of its sting, the grave of its bitterness; heavenly mansions will assuage the homesickness of the soul.

> There, from the music round about me stealing,
> I fain would hear the new and holy song,
> And find, at last, beneath thy trees of healing,
> The life for which I long.

In this fashion Christianity established the whole of life as an awesome processional for which time is only a setting and this world the petty stage. It is bounded, as Carlyle has said, by two eternities, but the light which plays upon it rises from beyond the hills of time and need know only a little twilight and no final dark.

Christianity has been the projection of all this into the conduct of Western life for twenty centuries. It has been a religion of redemption saving the faithful from sin and offering the assurance of an endless life, the revelation of God's will in obedience to which a man is secure, a philosophy of the universe, and the whole truth about God and man. It has been the mystics' "overflowing fullness of inner life," Thomas à Kempis' Imitation of Christ and St. Francis' espousal of Lady Poverty. It has been a mysticism which has found its peace in the complete loss of life in Christ and testified thereto in noble hymns.

> I fare with Christ, my Lord,
> This path, the path I choose;
> They joy who suffer most with him,
> They win who with him lose.

It has been an imperial ecclesiastical organization setting its foot on the neck of kings, and the world-renouncing life of the eremite or the monk. It has been the Protestant adventure in spiritual freedom and the Quaker's spirit-led life. It has been a force to color civilizations, the zeal of the missionary, the devotion which has sent the selfless to live with the leper, and a humanitarian passion for social justice. It has been every one of these things and it is still most of them.[16]

Its courage and sacrificial passion have enriched the annals of humanity. It has shadowed its bright picture with arresting divergences from the spirit of its founder. If it were taken out of European history, that history would have to be rewritten, and no one would know how.

Christianity is just now mobilizing upon a third front. It is reaching for social motivation and the recasting of the massed habits of society into forms essential to the full realization of its essential spirit. It may be that this is as crucial and difficult as any enterprise it has ever undertaken. The literature, worship, and practical program of all the churches reflect strongly this comparatively recent expression of the Christian mind. It is certainly becoming less theological, less other-worldly, and more humanitarian. There is the possible danger in this, the latest of its enterprises, that it may suffer, as it has heretofore sometimes suffered in its passion to win the world, through its impatience and its aptness to use weapons which are no part of its true arsenal. Jesus himself indicated in one of his enigmatic sayings that the Kingdom of God can not be taken by violence. Corporate Christianity has sometimes thought it knew better.

Time may wear away what time has built but the Christian student who has inquired of all religions their secret and sought, as honestly as he knows how, to hear their confessions and honor their confidences, if only whispered from their dust, may express his own personal conviction that time will not wear away Jesus' way and truth and life. They belong to the enduring and have proved themselves not only an assuring shelter in the mystery of the universe but an aspect of that law and order in which the only secure conduct of the enterprise of life is to be found.

Christianity is strangely like the Gothic cathedrals which have sheltered its rich and mystic worship. They were built out of the resolution of many conflicting strains, their audacity was their danger, their carven recitatives were subject to the wearing years, their fretted

---

[16] For a brilliant resumé of the historic element in Christianity, see a quotation from the published address of Dr. Arthur C. McGiffert in the author's *Making of the Christian Mind*, New York, 1928, page 322.

adornment took the strength from stone, they offered too much to all those forces before which even

ancient and holy things fade like a dream.

But they have so far stood to make a home beneath their arches for something in the souls of men without which it would be homeless, and to offer a floor for the devout to kneel on, from which they rise persuaded that the suppliant gesture toward the unknown with which religion began has found there its supreme answer.

CHAPTER XVI

Religions of Ancient America

THE AZTEC FAITH

I T IS usual," says Lewis Spence in his fascinating account of the *Myths of Mexico and Peru*,[1] "to speak of America as a continent without a history. The folly of such a statement is extreme. For centuries prior to European occupation Central America was the seat of a civilization boasting a history and a semi-historical mythology second to none in richness and interest." This history has only begun to be exposed within the last seventy-five years and the task is still incomplete. The archaeological difficulties have been enormous. The devastations of war and plunder have leveled ancient temples of fabulous wealth and cities of a strange and vanished splendor. Political disorders and sequences of revolution have hindered the investigators of what remains of cultures whose high accomplishments have become only discredited traditions. Tropical growths have swallowed up palaces and temples, and made the living barriers which surround them inpenetrable. The paths of the air still supply the only approaches to many regions once thickly populated. The curiously inscribed monuments of these vanished cultures furnish no key to their deciphering. Egypt had her Rosetta stone and Chaldea had the inscriptions at Persepolis, but the Maya have left only their jungle-incumbered ruins.

The Conquistadores of Spain had no concern for what they destroyed; only their lust for gold and jewels. The record of their conquest should be written in red. They carried an unbelievable wealth to Spain, or lost it when their ships were sunk or captured. One would think that the sea floor itself of the Spanish Main would be bright with what the Montezumas and Incas had treasured. The Catholic missionaries, who followed the conquerors, had naturally more interest in the social customs and religious beliefs and practices

[1] Dingwall-Rock Limited, New York, n.d., p. vii.

of the natives. But they felt bound to destroy temples and idols and shrines as well as most of the hieroglyphic writings in the process of converting the natives. To one of these missionaries, however, Bernardino de Sahagun, the historian of Mexican religion, owes a debt difficult to evaluate.[2]

Save perhaps the Mormons, no one has yet claimed that the Americas were the cradle of the human race, but the origins of American man have otherwise been most variously explained. He must have come from somewhere, either by land or sea, and long ago. So long ago that there may have been plains, now submerged, which linked the American continent with Asia. This supposititious equivalent of the "grassy plain" might well have supplied a route of migration for prehistoric adventurers. The Asiatic origin of the various American aborigines is now generally admitted, some dating it as far back as the tertiary era. Most ethnologists have looked to Behring Strait for a practical sea or land bridge for migration. Geologists suggest a land bridge, due to the once higher level of the North American Continent.

There is also the possibility of sailors carried by wind or sea currents across the Pacific. There are reports of ships long ago seen off the Pacific coast, decorated with gold and silver, laden with the merchandise of far Cathay, but for this there is no dependable proof. In general, a study of Mexican and Central American religion does not involve an examination of all such theories, but the evolution of their cultures, certainly, demands centuries of time and a ratio of genius of a very high order. One may assume, therefore, successive waves of migration, the folk of the earlier migrations probably being much more gifted than those who followed them. Certainly the migrants of a later date who pushed the Mexican down the western coast had far more power to destroy than to create. There is a curious parallel here with the migratory movements of the Aryan across his "grassy plain" into Europe. The civilization builders went first and they were followed by the civilization destroyers. All this is reflected in Mexican mythology which remembers Quetzalcoatl coming from the land of sunrise to teach the Mexicans the arts of life and civilization. When

[2] Fra Bernardino de Sahagun, *A History of Ancient Mexico*, translated by Fanny R. Bandelier, The Fisk University Press, Nashville, 1932. Written before 1577, the manuscript was not published until 1829. The story of its varied fortunes is a most interesting one, as told in the short biography of the author contained in the volume, pp. 3-20.

his mission was accomplished he was lost in the dawn as mysteriously as he arrived.

In the old paintings he is clothed with a black gown "trimmed with white crosses." It is likely, therefore, that in long retelling legends have been colored by the teachings of Catholic missionaries. His return was naturally expected. The natives believed that Cortez was the hero god coming back. They were, in time, most tragically disillusioned, but the widespread expectation amongst the natives of the appearance of some superman, or supermen, aided the Spaniards in their conquest. All this, myth and memory and prophecy combined, does at least indicate that the Americans the Spaniards found and conquered did have some dim sense of other peoples in other lands beyond the seas, a very, very old ancestral memory.

The dominant race the Spaniards found here called themselves "those who live by rule" (Nahua), to distinguish themselves from lawless people. They came, they thought, from the "Place of Reeds" (Aztlan) anywhere between Behring Strait and Mexico. In their wanderings, as they remember them, they had been in the "country of bright colors" and "the Place of the Seven Caves." These are Spence's translations of names, for us unpronounceable, which suggest New Mexico or Arizona.

They came in successive and more or less aimless waves, either led by a restless desire or pressed on by other people from behind. The Toltecs came first. They were a race of builders and skilled craftsmen and what, in their account of themselves, is legend and what is history are beyond disentangling. The legends tell of cities with jeweled walls—like the New Jerusalem, of temples with panelings of gold and a sheen of jewels. In time a wicked king incurred the wrath of the gods who would not be placated. There were plagues like those of Egypt. The weakened state was invaded by rude peoples. Their cities were destroyed and their Empire ended. Historians accept all this cautiously.

The variety of Nahua tribes does not here concern us. They say that the historic conquest of the Spaniards in Mexico was over the Aztecs, a superior tribe nicknamed "Aztec" (Crane people) because they originally lived in the marshes. According to their own traditions, they built Mexico City about 1325 A.D. on an island in the marshes—much as Benice got built. At the time of the conquest it contained 60,000 houses and a population of 300,000, with intersecting avenues true to the points of the compass, crossed by canals and with a chain of causeway bridges crossing the lake.

Their temples and palaces were solidly built and imposingly extensive. The greatest of these, the temple of the war god, Huitzilo-pochtli, situated in a vast walled enclosure 4800 feet in circumference, covered an area larger than an average city block, rising in six plat-forms, each smaller than the lower one. Three hundred and forty steps led around the terraces to the top where were located huge towers which contained the images of the tutelary deities, and the sacrificial altars. When the victorious Spaniards entered these towers they were bespattered with human blood, remnants of the futile sacrifices which the priests had offered the war god to move him to save the city. A sacred fire burned perpetually in the temples as a symbol of the never-to-go-out Nahua power. There were six hundred of these fires in Mexico City alone. The temples, not the palaces, were the real centers of national life. Only the emperor was more power-ful than the head of the priestly hierarchy.

In many ways Mexican and Central American religions deserve more consideration than the limits of this chapter make possible. All religion, as we have seen following Ward Fowler, is an attempt to find first a working and then a thought system in right relation with the power manifesting itself in the universe. Naturally, the smaller the worshiper's universe the simpler his religion. As his universe expands his religion must accommodate itself, though always with a lag. It is generally held that religions on the same cultural levels have funda-mental similarities, however separate in time and space. In the reli-gions so far studied there are geographical and historical relations and continuities. We have, for example, followed the Sky Gods across the grassy plain, or studied what has happened to an old nature wor-ship through the speculative action of the East Indian mind, or traced the confidences and insights of the Hebrew prophet through Chris-tianity and Mohammedanism.

But there in Mexico and Central America was a religion which seems almost completely indigenous to the races, the soil and the climate of the Americas. Whatever was once, if ever, brought across the Pacific is lost beyond recovery. We have only the mind and spirit of the Nahua and the Maya dealing with the mysteries of existence.

Fundamentally, their religion was a system of nature worship and a way of securing the favor of the gods. To that their temples, their priesthoods and their litanies of worship were dedicated.

The Mexican pantheon as Sahagun describes it, about 1560, was overcrowded. There were gods for everything, everybody and everywhere. They might, in a very loose way, be classified as war and power gods, nature gods and human relation gods, as the gods of the traders, for example. Their functions, however, are so entangled that it is very difficult to be specific about their offices. Their names are descriptive, as near as may be, either of their natures or of their offices. It is possible that some of them—like Quetzalcoatl—which means "Feathered Staff" or "Feathered Serpent," might have been heroes made into gods. Legends portray him as nurtured in the arts of civilization and finally exiled through the devices of a wicked magician. He is persistent under one conception or another in Mayan and Peruvian religion. He might be, as near as may be, god of the sky vault, the sun and wind, Lord of all celestial phenomena.

He (Quetzalcoatl) was one of three gods who stood out above the rest at the time of the Conquest, at least in the official worship, though probably the humbler deities of weather and corn were most worshiped by the common people. Tezcatlipoca was regarded as the highest of all. Indeed he was on the way to becoming almost a monotheistic object of worship by a few of the more advanced leaders of the day. But Huitzilopochtli, the war god, the special patron of the Aztecs, was worshiped more elaborately than any. His was the greatest of the temples, described above, and to him were the greatest number of human lives sacrificed. This was quite natural since the Aztecs were an exceedingly warlike people, still in the process of expanding their rule when the European conquerors came to Mexico.

There were goddesses, though not so many as the male divinities. One of the principal goddesses was Civacoatl—snake woman. She was the lady of sorrows and her gifts were poverty, pain and tears. They also called her Tonantzin, "our mother." This combination of names Sahagun thought proved that the Mexicans knew what happened between our mother Eve and the snake who deceived her. The food divinity was naturally a goddess. The goddess of medicine and medicinal herbs was called "our grandmother." She had a retinue of worshipers, physicians, surgeons, mid-wives and fortune tellers. They did everything they could to please her. Among other things they bought a woman captive to impersonate her. This understudy they fed delicately and entertained with dances to keep her spirits up. She certainly needed all the diversions they could contrive, for on the feast day of the divinity whom she represented they killed and flayed her. Women who died in giving birth to their first child became malignant spirits. They traveled together through the air and being sad themselves brought sorrow to living mothers by afflicting their children. When they were abroad children were best at home, and fearsome mothers sought to placate these malignant spirits by offering them food.

The goddess of water was sister of the god of rain who had power over the seas and rivers. Tempests and whirlwinds were his servants and all who made their living on the little or the great waters were his devotees. No one name was enough for the divinity which Sahagun calls "carnal matters." His specific translations reflect the temper of the ascetic Christian monk, but his objective descriptions are significant. For, as near as may be, here are the Nahua parallels of the age-old fertility cults, though strangely bare of light, color, beauty, romance or any such suggestion of winter death and vernal resurrection as are dramatized in the Grecian myths. Aphrodite does not rise from the sea. Ishtar does not mourn for Tammuz, nor is there any music of Orpheus' harp wooing back Eurydice from the nether world.

There was on the whole no place for illegal or romantic sexual relations in Mexican religion. On the contrary, a very stern morality. But the goddesses had the power to provoke desire, and they had also the power to pardon its transgressions at a price.

There is a ritual of confession and penance which Sahagun describes in full detail. The confession made to a priest of authority must omit nothing out of shame or cowardice, always under oath. The penitences and atonements were exacting; fasting and thorn-pierced tongues through which twigs, hundreds of them, would be passed if the sins were mortal. Consequently, sinners often put off confessing the very great sins till they were old men, since once having done penance and being absolved they must thereafter sin no more. They did this also to escape inexorable civic penalties, because adultery was punished by death. The Christian fathers therefore were led to suspect those who sought in some ways the easier discipline of the Christian confession. Sahagun concludes that the Mexicans went to confession at least once a year before they had any knowledge of the Christian faith. It is possible, however, that he read Christian conceptions into Mexican customs which really were not there.

There is little sign of adoration in the Nahua cults, their divinities bring anything but adorable. "Yellow Face," however, the fire god, was loved for his comforting and domestic services as well as feared for his destructive qualities. The rituals of his worship were red only with the blood of quails and were of the domestic character which the children shared. Every four years the great of the land gave Yellow Face (Yxcocauhqui) a special feast. Everybody danced and drank and parents selected godfathers and godmothers for their children. But one needs to remember that Fra Sahagun's use of his own church terms are probably misleading. For example, "confession, penance, communion, godfather, godmother" add overtones of suggestion the Aztec might not have understood.

There was another fire god who was worshiped by fasting and abstinence between the sexes. Violators were punished by what are now called "social diseases." (But were such "social diseases" native to America?) He was worshiped also by bleeding ears and pierced tongues which were evidently substitutes for mortal sacrifice, human sacrifice, that is, stepped down (of which there are examples in other religions), and votive offerings of foods in symbolic shapes. There was a minor god, Omecatl, the divinity of feasts and hospitalities, who meted out proper punishment to the inhospitable. It was desirable to have an image of this god in the house when one entertained one's relatives; since his priests carried the image to the household which sought the honor of entertaining him they, the priests, very likely profited by the honors shown their divinity.

This feast involved a sharing of food and drink which Sahagun calls "communion." We have noted already the divinity of rivers and waters, but there was a minor divinity who invented fishing nets and fish spears and oars to row with. Sahagun's long account of Yiacatecutli, the god of the merchants, is more interesting for its description of Aztec merchants and peddlers than for the originality of their worship. They were shrewd, adventurous, with a gift of "boring" into alien or hostile regions. They were often away from home a long time and on their return boastful of their exploits. They made a show of their gains and in gratitude for wealth or deliverance from peril sacrificed a slave or so when they got home. These could be purchased at slave markets and the more skillful were often kept for domestic service.

In general, every guild had its patron divinity, and it is quite possible to get a definite picture of the social and economic life of the land and of the people from their religious cults. They certainly had a far from primitive culture, so intimately tied up with their religion as to make any disentangling of the secular and religious impossible. We have already seen in this general study how early Roman society, for example, was in constant commerce with its divinities. But the Central American cultures seemed to have been the most outstanding example in the long history of religion of the saturation of a secular culture with religious cults.

The focus of Aztec religion was what passed for an altar, and their altars were always red with the blood of human sacrifice, drenched with it. The principal purpose of their wars seems to have been captives enough for sacrifice. All sacrifice was, to begin with, meant to meet some need of the divinity to whom the offerings were made; burnt offerings to delight or nourish him by their odor, blood offerings to renew or sustain his strength. So in the "dark" religions the blood meant for underworld divinities was poured upon the ground. In other religions here studied human sacrifice has faded out of the picture, or else been replaced by symbolic or substitutional sacrifice.

There was substitution in Aztec worship—blood drawn from the tongue or ear was smeared upon the image of the idol, especially when the priests were the celebrants. They—the priests—naturally disliked being killed and flayed themselves. But there were always war captives who had no choice in the matter and here pages of narrative may be condensed into paragraphs. The captives were sometimes allowed to make a show of defending themselves with four pine clubs and a sword which they were given, but since their swords were wood and they were tied to something very like a millstone with a hole in it, that defense generally came to nothing, though occasionally the most courageous were freed. In the end the great majority of them were bent back over the stone, their breasts opened with sharp flints, their hearts torn out and held up before the god image. After that, in some of the festivals, the remains were eaten.

The basis for all this seems to have been the belief or fear that without such donations of blood the gods themselves would grow old or lose their strength. The sacrifices, therefore, were meant to keep them young and strong. Sometimes in domestic sacrifices the priest acted for the god and offerings were made to him vicariously. Or else the celebrants would go about wearing the skins of the victims sacrificed and so apparently appropriate for themselves some of the advantages of the sacrifice without its pains and penalties. Cannibalism had probably the same general purpose to thus absorb the strength of the victims and to share their sacrifices.

There were eighteen months of twenty days each in the Mexican calendar. Each month had its specific ritual of worship and sacrifice to specific deities. This eighteen-month calendar of worship and sacrifice, ritualistically patterned, constituted the Aztec religious year, under some general seasonal control. To all this there are many parallels in other religions whose observances are in some way attuned to the progress of the seasons. February was dedicated to the rain god, Tlaloc. One should say, parenthetically, that most of the major Mexican divinities had names which are not given in the body of the text because they are long, hard to spell, harder to pronounce and hardest of all to remember. Moreover, the authorities do not agree as to either their respective ranks or their half-a-line-long spelling.[3] They are in a loose way descriptive.

Children were sacrificed to the rain god from the tops of mountains up to which they were carried in highly decorated litters, attended by singing and dancing processions. If the children, whose hearts were to be torn out, shed many tears those who offered them were glad of it. These tears, they thought, promised an abundance of rain. All this is a particularly pathetic form of sympathetic magic; the Roman matrons who prayed for rain did no more than loosen their hair to the winds. March, vernal equinox time, was dedicated to the worship of the sun, the great chief. He was honored by the sacrifice of slaves and captives in most barbarous ways, scalping and cannibalism. These sacrifices were probably symbolic. The captives represented lesser divinities who were slaughtered to sustain the sun. For this festival the image of Totec, the sun god, was adorned with solar symbols.

The third month, April, was dedicated to a flower goddess. No one dared smell a flower before the first blossoms were offered to her. But this festival was by no means idyllic; children were offered to the rain god and there were purification rites of which there was certainly

[3] A list of the principal deities will be found in a footnote on p. 505.

great and literal need, holding over from the sacrifice to the sun god. The fourth month belonged to the god and goddess of maize. The rich decorated their homes, girls carried ears of corn on their backs for next year's seed. Also, with a cruel logic they began to buy children for the next season's sacrifice to the rain god.

The June festivals were dedicated to Titlacoa. This divinity also and more commonly known as Tezcatlipoca, was the Nahua god of gods. He was lord of the night winds, life-giver and life-destroyer, and like the winds on high places his boisterous vigor was always undiminished. He was also judge of all mankind and carried the mirror shield of inexorable justice. Like all the deities who head the Pantheon of a conquering race he appropriated the qualities of subject deities. He occupies a supreme position in Mexican mythology. The inventor and guardian of the usages of civilization, if civilization was to endure he must be ceaselessly worshiped and placated.

His festival was distinguished by ritual which is the best known of them all, a ritual which has greatly interested all students of religion and with which Frazer deals at length in *The Golden Bough*. At this festival a youth was sacrificed who had been dedicated, so to speak, to the sacrifice a year before. He must be a youth without blemish, the best of all the war captives, and of a manly beauty. He was then given a name and garmented with the vestures of the gods. He thus became for one year a god himself, awesome and venerated. He went abroad only at night, attended by a proper retinue. He had only to ask for what he wanted and it was his. The greatest in the land were proud to entertain him. A month before his predetermined death he was married to four of the most beautiful maidens in the realm.

Then on the fateful day he kissed them good-by with tears, he broke his flutes one by one upon the stone step by which he climbed to death; the high priest dismissed him to the comradeship of the gods; opened his breast with a flint knife and held up his heart to divinity. There should be some relationship of all this to the summer solstice but it is not apparent. Sahagun says it was the Aztec equivalent of Easter. There is, as we have seen, a ritual identification of man and God running through old Mexican worship as though there might be an interchange not only in strength but in dignity. But there seems nothing in any religion quite parallel to the sacrifice of this youth, both fortunate and unfortunate.

July, the sixth month, was sacred to the rain gods (again). During this feast priests who had committed some fault in the observance of their almost impossibly complicated rituals were terribly punished. The rites of the seventh month were dedicated to the goddess of salt, a woman's festival in which they danced and sang. The ninth month belonged to the war god; the tenth month to the fire god; the twelfth month was dedicated to gods who had wandered away and come back again into their temples and shrines, and so on and on.

In the detailed narration of the rites and rituals of these eighteen months there is a vast deal of repetition, for after all worshipers can only do about so much for their divinities. In a general, though accurate, way the economic, social and political life of the people were reflected in their beliefs and worship, deeply and constantly. The account of their monthly festivals does no more than confirm this at wearisome length. The Nahua could have had time for little else. They painted and dressed their images grotesquely but symbolically.[4] They worshiped them in their temples or carried them abroad. They had torch-light processions; they seemed to have been always dancing; the sound of flutes and conch shells was heard unceasingly and, always and everywhere, here was a religion drenched with the blood of sacrifice and, in certain festivals, barbarous cruelty toward captives. Their temples must have smelled like slaughter houses, and since the worshipers wore the skins of flayed human sacrifices for days their ceremonial baths were far more than a religious duty.

Their creation myths began with a time before time when the sky was darkness and the earth was ooze and slime. The creative divinities were the masculine sky god and mother earth. Out of his giving and her receiving earth life began. In one myth the gods, after some hesitation, created four men out of cornmeal, but they feared their own handiwork, another example of the old jealousy of the gods. In order that these men might not become like gods themselves they limited their vision, put them to sleep and created four women. By these eight the earth was populated. The fire god gave them fire, they were taught to offer human sacrifice and died. There were flood myths and a Mexican Noah, Neta, and his wife, Nema, who outrode the flood in a hollow log. The Aztec theologians divided eternity into

[4] The "Sublimation" of this in modern Mexican art might be worth speculating upon.

epochs or suns, usually four. Each period ended with some great disaster. For our centuries of one hundred years they substituted a "sheaf" of fifty-two years and always grew fearful of some disaster toward the end of a fifty-two year cycle.

Their dead went west, or else the soul, freed from the body, faced a perilous journey through the gloom of the other world. Naked and under a wooden yoke it received sentence and thereafter with only a dog for company the soul faced every peril imagination could conjure up. It was all arrestingly similar to the journey of the soul through the darkness of the underworld in the Egyptian *Book of the Dead*. If the spirit wins through it does reverence to the god of the underworld and meets the friends already there. Also, as in other religions, particularly the Egyptian, there was an earthly paradise, well watered and fertile, where a chosen few lived in felicity.

Common people, who died in ordinary ways, went to the dark abode of the Lord of Death. The Nahua got scant comfort from his religion in life and little hope from it in the article and event of death. Few religions, if any, are so deeply shadowed. Sahagun notes three abodes of the discarnate. For all those who died of ordinary diseases a most sombre place was waiting with neither light nor windows, much like the Chaldean underworld. For them there is no return, and they are all soon forgotten. A terrestrial paradise awaited those who deserved it because of some particularly loathsome disease or death by lightning. There they would live cool and comfortable with no lack of food nor of flowers, since it was always summertime. The great warriors went to heaven—comrades of the sun—where there were trees of many sorts, and the blessed received the gifts the living offered them. After four years of such felicities these fortunate souls became birds of iridescent plumage and flew about to drink honey from all the flowers.

The priesthood was graded as to rank and highly specialized. The various gods had their own priestly retinues with various and extremely demanding rituals. It needs five pages in Sahagun even to outline the divisions of priestly duties. It would seem to have been one of the most complicated orders of temple worship in the history of any religion. The priests were dedicated to the services of the temples and the gods by their parents, and rigorously trained in the House called "Calmecac," which seems to have been a kind of monastic

seminary. The one eventually most perfect was elected high priest
by the king and the foremost men of Mexico. He bore thereafter the
name of the supreme deity. Even those of lowly birth were eligible
to the highest priestly orders.

The disciplines under which the priests were trained were most
severe, and the penalty for any lapse might be a slow and tortured
death. Candidates for the priesthood were taught music, manners,
how to read the stars, interpret dreams, and count the years. They
must eat sparingly, were vowed to celibacy, not to tell lies, and to
live devoutly in fear of God. Sahagun's short chapter about the election of the high priest is strangely objective, the tribute of one priest
to another. The high priests—there were two according to Sahagun—
took the names of two of the high gods.[5] They were chosen for wisdom and sanctity. They must be "virtuous, humble, peace-loving,
compassionate, tender-hearted and live in the fear of god." And yet
thereafter their hands could never have been entirely clean of human
blood. The long history of religion records nothing more seamed with
contradictions. The priests lived austere and laborious lives, sparing
neither the people nor themselves. Their influence was omnipresent,
their power almost without limits. Yet they do not seem to have been
greedy for position.

It is extremely difficult, either to generalize or systematize Mexican
religion. It seems to have been a crossed and re-crossed system of
nature worship shaped by lost inheritances, racial and tribal movements, elaborated by the priesthood, and attended by a cloud of
myths. It reflected or expressed the peculiar genius of a highly capable
and highly religious people. It was beyond debate almost completely
indigenous. The Mexican gods had no procession save the winds and
the thunder and the waves and mother earth. Sahagun's narrative
leaves the impression of a culture whose main concern was religion.
Its crowded calendars of worship and sacrifice seemed to have left
time for little else. There is always the sound of music, the rhythm
of dancing, the rites of fasting and feasting. They must, for all the
grim shadows, have enjoyed it. The festivals and the rituals of the
functional divinities indicate a background of varied secular occupa-
tions. The Spaniards found a relatively high civilization with great

[5] One was called Quetzalcoatl or Teotectlamacazqui, the other Tlaloctlamacazqui
after the rain god Tlaloc, according to Sahagun.

wealth and the panoply of power so interwoven of religious faith and rites that without the religion civilization would have fallen apart.

It is reported that the lady Papan, or Papantzin, sister of Montezuma II, died and was buried with proper pomp in a vault which seemed secure. Next morning her small niece saw the princess in the palace gardens. The lady Papan had considerable difficulty in getting anybody to believe that she was still alive and so tell the emperor. Finally, given audience, she reported that she had been led through vast spaces by celestial messengers toward waters covered by ships, manned by a host who called themselves "Children of the Sun." These, her guide said, were to bring the true faith to her people and deliver them from the valley of dry bones in which they were lost. This report greatly troubled the king but his sister, so the questionable legend goes, was the first of the royal family of Mexico to become a Christian. Now of their ancestral faith only the dry bones are left.

Some of the more important gods and goddesses of the Aztecs:
Centeotl, Cinteutl—maize god
Chalchihuitlicue—goddess of water
Chicomecoatl—goddess of food
Civacoatl—woman of the snake, also called Tonantzin—our mother
Coatlycue—goddess of flowers
Huitzilopochtli, Vitzilopuchtli—war god
Mictlantecutli—god of the dead or underworld
Mictecacioatl—goddess of the dead, the consort of Mictlantecutli
Mixcoatl—god of the chase, husband of Coatlycue
Omeciuatl—mother goddess of human species
Ometecutli—father god of human species
Ometochtli—one of many gods of *pulque*, the intoxicant
Paynal—a lesser divinity of war, especially of sudden attack
Quetzalcoatl—"feathered serpent," god of wind, culture hero, etc., "the returning god"
Tezcatlipoca—"smoking mirror," highest of the Aztec gods, mythological adversary of Quetzalcoatl
Titlacaoan—Tezcatlipoca
Tlalculteutl—goddess of "carnal matters"—Aztec Venus
Tlaloc—Tlalocantecutli—Aztec rain god
Tonantzin—our mother—Civacoatl
Totec—sun god

Tonatiuh—sun god
Xiuhtecutli—god of fire
Yxacatecutli—god of merchants
Yxcocauhqui—"Yellow face," fire god

MAYA RELIGION

The Mayan culture was long the enigma of historians, and the Mayan ruins the despair of the archaeologist. The once Mayan territory is now the heel of Mexico, Chiapas, Guatemala and the Peninsula of Yucatan. Chiapas seems to have been their cultural center. There tropical jungles possess astounding ruins of palaces and temples. Their builders, Spence thinks, were the supreme intellectual race of America. They owed nothing to other cultures. Their arts and industries were their own creations. Maya is still a living language in Chiapas, and the many dialects of Guatemala have affinities which seem to indicate a mother tongue for them all. Their entrance into these regions is a mystery, but their civilization was old, very old, when the historian began to be curious about it. It was in process of decay when the Spaniards discovered it. What is now left are the ruins of the temples and the palaces. The cities they once adorned are gone. Morley does attempt a reconstruction of their history, a story of forced migration and forgotten wars between rival groups and the rise and fall of rulers. Considering the paucity of records he seems almost to know too much and his history to be in part supposition.[6]

The Maya's left their own records, manuscripts and inscriptions, but very little of all this can be deciphered. In addition, the Spaniards took no care to preserve this literature or else destroyed it. There are three manuscripts extant, one of them in Paris and one in Madrid. They would seem to be about Maya mythology, though the Mayans themselves would not have so named them. But since they can be read only in gaps and guesses they are not very informative. Maya writing was symbol or picture writing and since a column of it looks like a wall of very small, rather square or rounded characters, it has been called "Calculiform" or pebble-shaped.

The story of the attempt to read these riddles recalls the deciphering of Chaldean tablets, with no parallel success. Scholars think they

[6] Sylvanus Morley, *The Ancient Maya*, Stanford Univ. Press, 1946.

know the signs for the four points of the compass, for the sun, for day, for morning, for months, for beginning and end, for lapse of time. They think they know also their numeral system. But the scholars are not agreed as to whether the characters are merely pictures, represent ideas, or like an alphabet stand for a sound. It is all very much like the jungle which hides the ruins. Some of the figures of men and gods on the "Tablet of the Cross" have the quality of Egyptian drawing. Mayan and Nahuan mythology seemed to Spence to have had a remote and common source, and were thereafter varied and distinguished by all the historic processes which tend to modify the structure of worship and belief.

That divinity of many aliases, Quetzalcoatl, wind god in Mexico, for example, becomes Kululcan, a thunder god for the Mayan,[7] probably due to climatic changes. The Mayan divinities are vividly pictured in the manuscripts, but their names are so uncertain as to lead one authority to suggest that they be indicated by letters of the alphabet, fifteen of them from "A" to "P," and so for the Mayan, the Procession of the Gods ends in a filing cabinet. We have seen how much the names of cherished divinities have meant to their votaries, as used in prayer or praise. The Psalmist says, "Let us praise the Name of Jehovah" but no Mayan psalmist ever said, "Let us praise the name of 'A' for his name alone is excellent, his glory is above the earth and the heaven."

A dualism old as Zoroaster seems to characterize Mayan mythology; light against darkness; the joy of life against death and fear. When the Europeans found the Maya the gods of gloom and foreboding were in the ascendent, and no wonder. They seemed to presage disaster, and disaster came. But there were gleams of hope through the darkness, light and peace would come again. God "A" in the codices, identified by Morley as Ah Puch, is a fearsome figure. He is garmented with the symbols of death and corruption, lord of death and hell, ruler of the home of the dead in the west. God "B," or Chac, the rain god, is also the deity of the elements and culture. He is pictured planting maize and carrying tools, the Mayan equivalent, apparently, of Quetzalcoatl.

[7] So Spence, *Myths of Mexico and Peru*, p. 83. This is to identify him with Chac the rain god, which Morley agrees is possible. He is also, however, identified by some as god "K," or the wind god, from his identification with Quetzalcoatl. (Morley, *op. cit.*, pp. 229-30. Spence thinks that he was also a sun god.)

Nothing definite is known about god "C." He is possibly a god of the Pole star. "D" is identified by Morley as Itzamna, Lord of the heavens, who stood at the head of the Maya pantheon. He was son of Hunab Ku, the creator. "E" was maize god and looks very much like a stalk of corn. The character of "F" is not clearly indicated, but he seems to be associated with war and human sacrifice. "G" is surely the sun god and needing to sustain him offerings of human blood. "H" is unidentified. "I" is a water goddess, also goddess of childbirth and weaving. Her hair-do is a snake. She is represented as carrying an earthern pot from which water flows. The dominant thing about "K" is his nose, but no one knows why he is thus caricatured. Then there is "the old black god" earth deity, perhaps, dwelling in the dark and very likely one of the oldest deities in the collection. Travelers could claim god "M" for he has a pack on his back like a deified peddler, but he was also a war god, called by Morley Ek Chuah, or else the deity of the unfortunate, "the poisoner of the days." "O" sits spinning, the goddess of homemaking, worshiped by married women. "P" looks like a frog, surely a water god, kind to farmers in their plowing and sowing.

There was, as among the Aztecs, an elaborate religious year with varied festivals to the appropriate deities. There was a patron divinity for each of the twenty days of the month. Sacrifices of many kinds were offered to the gods, among them human sacrifice, which seems to have been introduced from the Aztecs. It was not practiced to the same extent among the Mayas as among the Mexicans. Perhaps most spectacular of such offerings was at Chichen Itza where victims were thrown alive into a deep well of sacrifice where they drowned. Recently the principal well has been dredged and yielded enormous quantities of human bones as well as gold and jewels which seem also to have been sacrificed thus by worshipers.

The official religion of the state and the more advantaged classes, was carried out with great pomp and ceremony, centering about the greater gods of the pantheon, but the popular worship of the people, dominantly agricultural, had to do chiefly with the gods of rain and of corn, as well as other figures known as "chacs" who presided over various phases of the agricultural process upon which they depended most for their livelihood, and numerous lesser deities concerned with the simple necessities of daily living.

The Spanish friars who first sought to convert the Mayas to Christianity were amazed to find among them ceremonies somewhat similar to baptism, communion, and confession, also monasteries and convents not unlike their own. These could only have been the work of the devil, they thought.

Life was believed to go on after death. The wicked among the dead went to Mitnal, a rather dark and dismal underworld abode, lowest of nine underworld regions, ruled over by Ah Puch, god of death, or Hun Ahau, a cold rather than a hot hell. There were twelve heavens presided over by twelve gods of the upper world.[8] One was a place of rich vegetation to which for some reason suicides went. Another resembles somewhat the Christian heaven, and thither went those who had lived good lives. It is entirely probable that this ethical consideration derived from Christian influence. But there also went, apart from any ethical requirement, warriors and priests, those sacrificed to the gods and women who died in giving birth to children.

Their temples were built upon mounds, terraced, four-square in design and of an enthralling mystery. Palenque in Chiapas is perhaps the most famous. When discovered in 1774 there were the ruins of eighteen palaces, twenty great buildings and one hundred and sixty houses. The dates of the buildings cannot be definitely determined, but the palaces and temples are as old as the thirteenth century. There is no room here for detail, and only photographs could make them real; in magnitude and detail they are beyond description. The architect wonders how stones could be set as these stones are set without mortar and with no tools but other stones and sand. The temples housed the priesthood, contained their royal suite, and must have been crowded. There were underground chambers for human sacrifice and burial. Mayan mythology is best known through a collection of written leaves composed by a Christianized native of Guatemala in the seventeenth century, copied and translated by a Spanish monk, lost for a long time, like the temples, much sought for, and finally found in 1854.

Some critics think the collection too much colored by Biblical knowledge to be dependable. Spence defends its originality. The myths are curiously fanciful, naïve, and wander on and on. There is always a sense of conflict and something unfinished. They begin

[8] There were thirteen gods of the upperworld, but the lowest of the upperworld regions was the earth itself. Morley, *op. cit.,* p. 216.

with the universe wrapped in gloom, the wind god commanded the earth to appear, and it did. Then the gods in council debated what to do next. They first created animals and then made little men. But these puppets misbehaved and the angered gods decided to destroy them. There was a flood, great birds tore at them, their very tools turned against them, they were ground by their own millstones, bitten by their own dogs and burned by their own cups and platters. Finally, all that was left of them were little monkeys.

There are memories also of giants whose overthrow the gods willed and carried through in the long succession of hero tales in which the heavenly twins Hun-apu and Xbalanque met many dangers from which, however, they always escaped. Death had no power over them and they passed triumphantly through the dark houses of the underworld bringing immortality to life, after which they were fixed in the skies.

Finally, the gods once more determined to create man, though for fear that men should become as gods they clouded his vision. There were four men to begin with and four wives for them, created while they slept (this is also a Mexican belief). Those eight were ancestors of all humanity, but there was yet no light in the skies. The newly-created prayed for light and peace and found neither. They sadly needed fire in their sunless world and the fire god obliged them, but the rains were always putting their fires out. Then after many journeys they first saw the sun from a mountaintop and went wild with delight. Then they grew old and died, one by one, and they were not. A poet put into one singing line the mysteries of life and death with which these myths deal:

From the great deep to the great deep he goes.

The interpreters tried to get history out of all this, but the results seemed questionable. At any rate, they were old tales, like all folklore, worn both smooth and endlessly elaborated through much retelling, to be interpreted as much by the fancy of the interpreter as by any other rule for their interpretation. They were as in most primitive religions what passed for wisdom when the Maya world was young. Much of the reconstruction of their religion sounds like conjecture, also passing for wisdom, now that the world has grown old.

PERU

Lewis Spence, *The Myths of Mexico and Peru*, chapters 5 and 6, thinks the ancient Peruvian civilization to have had a lower standard of general culture than the Aztec and the Maya. His examination of that culture, however, makes a better case for it than this general statement indicates. The Quechua-Aymara race had no method of written communication nor any adequate system of reckoning time. But the ruins of their buildings which survive are of a surprising and grandiose character, mute records of incredible toil. Without any tools, save bare hands and other stones, these vanished builders rivaled the monoliths of Baalbec. They suited their ways to the configuration of their country, high, lonely, vast, mountain walled, mountain divided, and insufficiently watered. Cereals cannot ripen and animals are rare. As far as the inhabitants of these heights and valleys knew there was no other world nor people anywhere. And yet out of such dreariness and desolation the Incas made an empire three thousand miles long and four hundred miles broad.

The historian knows little or nothing for certain of the prehistoric nations of the Andes. The remnants of their buildings awe the archaeologists' amazement. Who were they who built out of stones, whose transportation would tax the modern engineer, fitted together as by master masons, such high walls and terraced fortresses upon strategic cliffs? And why did they build them? To defend some vanished people against now vanished foes? Myths and legends of real beauty and dramatic quality may contain some racial recollections of that Cyclopean time. At any rate, the Peruvian people, when the Spaniards discovered them, were a fusion of many races. A civilizing and a dominant race seems to have come from the south, possibly the highlands of Bolivia, which they named "World's End."

They settled along the shores of Lake Titicaca and developed the arts of irrigation and terrace building. Two groups are indicated with different but related languages. One group, the Aymara, spread through the high Andes ranges. The other group, the Quechua, settled in warmer valleys. In time the power of the Incas was consolidated, and evolved a really remarkable civilization. These people terraced mountains, bridged rivers and built roads to match our own roads. They adorned their temples and palaces with gold and silver, had hot and cold water to bathe in, all of which made contemporary Europe in the fourteenth and fifteenth centuries seem crude.

And all this for the Spaniards to loot! The walls of the Temple of the Sun in the "Town of Gold" were plated with gold. Behind the great altar was a golden plate encrusted with gems—the symbol of the Sun God, and around were seated many of the mummified Inca kings, each on his own throne with his sceptre in his hand. There were lesser temples in the sacred city dedicated to the lesser heavenly bodies. The moon, the mother of the Inca race, was symbolized by a silver plate, around which sat the mummies of the Inca queens. In the rainbow temples there was a kind of planetarium. The temple furnishings were gold and silver, the various water pipes were silver. The gold is gone but the walls of the House of Gold still stand and the Temple of the Sun is a Christian church.

The Inca state was totally totalitarian. Its economy was not entirely communistic but it was state-controlled. The lower classes possessed no property, farmed the allotment assigned them which was changed yearly. The Peruvian calendar was crude. Its fixed points were the four sun festivals, the two equinoxes and the two solstices. There were twelve lunar months, poetically named to register the sequence of the seasons for an agricultural people and because all this was south of the equator everything was in reverse from a North American viewpoint. Their winter solstice is our June, and in our December their sunlit days are longest. Their religion was thus sun and moon controlled, fundamentally a nature-worship and state-controlled to the last detail. Since the Peruvian state and people were a fusion of many earlier cultures the state religion had long lost its primitive character. To begin with, there was a multiplicity of local gods whose images were not far removed from fetishism: trees, mountains, stones and the like. Their animal worship suggests totemism. All this is the familiar pattern of primitive culture religion around the world. Their myths reflect the belief that their ancestors came out of the earth; therefore, certain spots were reverenced by primitive folk as places from which their ancestors had quite literally come to life. Stone worship was, of course, a phase of this belief. Stones are the entrails of the earth; also, they may have been men.

These objects of popular worship are designated by the name

huaca, a Quechua word which has various meanings. One derivation of the word is from the root *huacan* meaning to howl, since native worship was usually accompanied by a dirgelike wailing or howling. *Huaca* then might mean a place of howling.[9] Means says that the most usual meaning is simply a holy thing, animate or inanimate.[10] Generally the *huacas* were objects of tribal or provincial worship, often very simple and without benefit of any official priesthood. Then there were *conopas,* very much like *huacas* but rather objects of personal or household worship, similar to the old Roman *Lares* and *Penates.* Vegetable growth spirits were called mothers. Each plant had its own specific mother; the Saramama mother, or maize mother, was most important. There would be a cornstalk image of the lady and she would be put in their worship and consulted about next year's crop. All these lowly, near-to-earth deities were for the common people. The great ones had their own great gods, ancestors of the tribe, and there were oracles supposedly wise about everything, including affairs of the heart.

Rain and thunder were worshiped under various names. The Incas incorporated such local strong gods into one officially approved thunderer with a temple and revenues of his own. His sister, the Rain Goddess, carried water jars and when he broke them it rained, about all of which there is a little poem and a web of myths. There were two other Peruvian gods of the first rank: the earth and "the creative agency." These, with the thunderer, were the Peruvian trinity. The earth spirit was Dual. Pachacamac, the male principle, is neither the earth nor what is therein contained, but the spirit which animates all things which come out of the earth. His nearest parallel is the Wauconda of the North American Indian, or the Mana of the Polynesian, a creative force taking protean forms. Or else Wordsworth's sense:

> Of something far more deeply interfused
> Whose dwelling is the light of setting suns
> And the round oceans and the living air
> And rolls through all things.

[9] H. G. Wells made a highly satiric use of this habit in one of his fantastic tales "Rampole Island" in which he compares phases of our press and legislative procedure to these old howling places.

[10] Philip Means, *Ancient Civilizations of the Andes,* Charles Scribner's Sons, New York, 1931, p. 418.

It was no long step from this conception to the conception of a creator whose word was omnipotent. An extant Peruvian prayer preserves his creative commands; "Let earth and heaven be," "Let a man be," Let a woman be," "Let there be a day," "Let there be night," "Let the light shine."

This god they called Viracocha. Inti, or Ynti the sun god, was the principal object of official Inca worship, the head of the pantheon, and a most elaborate set of rites and ceremonials was carried out in his honor. But on one occasion the great Inca Pachacutec, who had entirely rebuilt the Coracancha, or Temple of the Sun, and had assembled all the priests of the country to celebrate its completion, suddenly asked them if after all there might not be some power greater than the sun, who, for all his greatness, seemed nevertheless to be limited. Could he shine by night? he asked. Clouds covered his face at times and he could not penetrate them. Might there not be a power greater than he who had brought him into being? He then expounded to them his idea of a Creator God, Viracocha, or Pachacamac, as the Maker of the World and the Foundation of all that is Excellent. The priests accepted his teaching and so Viracocha came to be regarded as the Supreme God. But his worship was never popularized. It was only for the ruling classes. The Chronicler,[11] who tells this story, ends by saying that thereafter the Inca spoke to the sun as a friend or kinsman, but to Viracocha he prayed with the greatest humility. One wonders a little if there may not be echoes of half-forgotten Christian missionary teachings here.

A complicated mythology indicates different stages in the evolution of Peruvian religion, which it is very difficult to simplify, for there is "mother sea" beside mother earth, "Pachacamama." But curiously, mother earth is mountains, rocks and plains. Means thinks that this creator god was much older than the Incas, belonging clearly to what he designates as the Tiahuanaco II culture period, dated about 600-900 A.D., which culture was found both in the highlands and the coastlands. He was more commonly known as Viracocha in the higher regions and as Pachacamac on the coast. Irma was a variant coastal name.[12] The worship was apparently on a very much nobler level, aesthetically and morally in the highlands than on the coast.

The cult of the sun, Inti, as observed above, was distinctly the Inca

11 Father Cabello as told in Means, *op. cit.,* page 428.
12 Means, *op. cit.,* pp. 424-25.

court cult. Eventually, as one could expect, he became the ancestor of the Incas. He had possessions in every village; lands were cultivated for his temple services, his great festival was celebrated during our winter solstice, a ceremony of dramatic splendor recalling the ceremonies at the vanished Chinese altar of Heaven.

Another festival was held in June when south of the equator the days began to lengthen. A new fire was kindled, sun-kindled in the golden temple by means of a concave mirror. There was human sacrifice in Peruvian worship, but far less than in Mexico. In the creation myths man was literally earth-born, or else the creator made images of clay and divided the images into nations, each with its own language and customs. Upon these images the Creator Spirit breathed the breath of life, and then commanded them to enter the earth, whence they eventually came upward, each nation in its proper place. And there is a legend of a flood which almost drowned the sun itself, with a proper provision for selected survivors.

There thus appear to have been really three levels of religion. At the folk level there was the worship of the *huacas*, the *huaca* cult. At the highest level there was a relatively subtle and sophisticated quasi-philosophical Viracocha worship limited to the Inca caste. In between these was the official sun worship of Inti, which Means considers to have been a sort of compromise reaching down, on the one hand, to embrace some of the local *huaca* cults, and upward, on the other hand, toward the more subtle worship of the invisible powers of the universe. In this very elasticity and the fact of its being supported and controlled by the state, he suggests that this Inca Sun-worship was startlingly, and in some ways, comically, like the Church of England.[13]

The Peruvian deathbed was surrounded with inquiring and, more or less, mourning friends and relatives, asking "Where then goest thou? Why dost thou leave us?" They told the warriors how brave they, the warriors, had been, and then hastened their deaths by suffocation, after which they made the deathroom dark so that the soul could not find its way back. The Peruvian conception of a future life seems to have been rather dim and formless, though evidently they believed the soul survived. The discovery in their tombs of many objects used in the common life is mute testimony to this belief. They carefully mummified their dead. The Incas, as

[13] *Op cit.*, p. 431.

befitted children of the Sun, were transported at death to their father, the Sun, and continued to live together as a family. Those of less noble rank lived in an underworld under the sway of the god of the dead.

The wealth of Peruvian myths cannot even be indicated here. They suggest imagination, poetry, a sense of romance and adventure. And, since they were indigenous, they testify to the vigor of the Peruvian mind. The Spaniards in their hatred of idolatry destroyed much which would now be of great service to the historian. What is recoverable, as Spence says, are windows through which we see the gleam and glitter of a civilization more remote than India or China. The ghost "of peoples and beliefs not the least solemn and splendid in the roll of dead nations and vanished faiths."

Appendix A

AIDS TO THE STUDENT

The following pages include Questions and Exercises, Topics for Report and Discussion, and Suggested Readings for each chapter. The titles with publisher and date of most of the books listed here will be found in the general bibliography in Appendix C, along with a considerable number of additional books in which no specific assignment is made. (See note on page 571.)

CHAPTER I: FAITHS OF THE DARK AND THE DAWN

Questions and Exercises

1. How has the study of religion changed in recent decades?
2. What is the method of the scientific study of religion?
3. Criticize the statement "Religion is an instinct." See further T. H. Hughes, *The New Psychology and Religious Experience.* p. 130, ff.
4. How does Freudian psychology color theory with reference to the origin of religion?
5. Criticize Whitehead's definition of religion. p. 7.
6. Criticize the dream theory of the origin of religion advanced by Tylor.
7. What is the justification, if any, of Durkheim's theory of the social origin of religion?
8. What is the meaning of totemism? Is it religious?
9. How may magic and religion be distinguished?
10. Which is earlier, magic or religion?
11. What is fetishism? How are fetishes made?
12. What is animism?
13. How does primitive man conceive of the soul? How many souls are there?
14. Where does the soul go at death according to primitive belief?
15. How does ancestor-worship rise? How widely is it practiced?
16. How does nature-worship rise? What nature powers are most commonly worshiped? Why?
17. How widespread is sun-worship? Are any vestiges of it to be found in Christianity or Judaism? What? See further *Encyclopedia of Religion and Ethics.* Volume 12, p. 48, ff. *Art. Sun, Moon, and Stars.*

Topics for Report and Discussion

1. Is there a "science of religion"?
2. Survivals of magic in modern religion and life. Make a written list of examples most frequently found.
3. The definition of religion.
4. Taboos, their origin and importance.
5. The universality of some form of religion.
6. On a world map indicate the regions where "primitive" religions are chiefly found.

A Project

In any study of the history of religion comparison of religions with one another is inevitable. A valuable method to use in comparing the deities is to make a dictionary or catalogue of the gods. This will be found helpful in a review of the course as well.

The dictionary might be made in any of several forms.

1. An alphabetical list.
2. A classified list.
3. A list by religions (alphabetically arranged within the religion). It can be most easily and effectively made on cards or thin sheets of paper and arranged in a vertical file. On each card or sheet should appear the following:

1. The name or names of the god.
2. The religion in which it appears.
3. Where found (country or region).
4. When—the period of the development of that particular religion. This will have no meaning in some religions where the gods are relatively constant.
5. The functions of the god.
6. Page reference in text or other source.
7. Any other facts the student may care to note.

An example:

1. Indra.
2. Hinduism.
3. India.
4. Vedic Period.
5. Storm-fertility-war.
6. Atkins. p. 152-156. H. D. Griswold, *Religion of the Rig-Veda.* Chapter 7, etc.

Supposing the classified list is to be made, each card should have in the upper left-hand corner the class name and in the upper right-hand corner, the name of the deity. Filing within the class should be alphabetical.

The same god will sometimes fit into more than one class. A card making a cross reference to where the cards containing the above information can be found will make it unnecessary to write the material more than once. Some of the general classes and subdivisions would be:

1. Nature
     sky
     sun
     rain
     moon, etc.
     trees
     animals
       elephant
       snake, etc.

2. Functional
     war
     hunt
     music, etc.

3. Abstract

4. Deified men

5. Cosmogonic deities.

Expand it as you go by putting those which do not fit the general classes into a miscellaneous group. Other general classes may thus emerge.

Suggested Readings

1. Read at least concerning one primitive religion. Choose one of the following:
     Robert H. Lowie. *Primitive Religion.* Chapters 1, 2, 3 or 4.
     Robert H. Lowie. *The Crow Indians.* Chapters 11 and following.
     Encyclopedia of Religion and Ethics. Articles, Ainu, Andaman Islanders, Polynesians, or Todas, etc.
2. On the theories as to the origin of religion.
     E. W. Hopkins. *The Origin and Evolution of Religion.* Yale University Press, 1923. Chapter 1.
     W. Schmidt. *The Origin and Growth of Religion.* Dial Press, New York, 1931.
     Robert H. Lowie. *Primitive Religion.* Part 2. Boni & Liveright, New York, 1924.
     Emile Durkheim. *Elementary Form of the Religious Life.*
3. On the definition of religion.
     "The Definition of Religion, A Symposium." *Journal of Religion.* Volume 7, pp. 113-35; 284-314.
     "Trends in the Re-definition of Religion." *Journal of Religion.* Volume 8, p. 434-53.

4. On Totemism.
   Encyclopedia of Religion and Ethics. Art, Totemism. Volume 12, p. 393-407.
   Sir James G. Frazer. *Totemism.*
   Emile Durkheim. *Elementary Forms of the Religious Life.*
   W. Schmidt. *Origin and Growth of Religion.* Chapter IX.
5. On Fetishism.
   George Foot Moore. *Birth and Growth of Religion.* Charles Scribner's Sons, New York, 1926. Chapter 2.
   W. Schmidt. *Origin and Growth of Religion.* Chapter V.
   Encyclopedia of Religion and Ethics. Volume 5, p. 894, ff.
6. On Primitive Monotheism.
   W. Schmidt. *Origin and Growth of Religion.* Part 5, Primitive Belief in High Gods.
   Le Roy, A. *The Religion of the Primitives.*

CHAPTER II: THE SPHINX-GUARDED GODS OF THE NILE

Questions and Exercises

1. In what way does the geographical situation of Egypt affect its early religious development?
2. How does it happen that so many records of the ancient Egyptian civilization remain?
3. What is the significance of the Sphinx?
4. What was probably the earliest form of religion in Egypt?
5. What relics of animal-worship remain in Egyptian religion?
6. How many Egyptian gods were there?
7. What is the key to the complexity of Egyptian religion? Explain your answer.
8. Why was religious unity never thoroughly achieved in Egypt?
9. What was the effect of Egyptian conservatism upon the development of religion?
10. Is Egypt more or less consistent in its religious ideas than other faiths?
11. How is the creation of the world accounted for?
12. What significance, if any, is there in the fact that to the Egyptian the earth divinity was male and the sky divinity female?
13. To what was due the attempt to systematize Egyptian religion?
14. What were the more important triads?
15. What was the place of the sun in Egyptian religion?
16. Contrast the earlier and later religious architecture of Egypt.

17. How were the temples built and maintained?
18. What was the function and importance of the priesthood?
19. What is the Ka?
20. What was the importance of embalming?
21. What was the Book of the Dead?
22. Who was Turn-Face?
23. How do you account for the enmity between Set and Osiris?
24. How were the dead judged?
25. Trace the rise of Amon-Ra.
26. Account for the reform of Akhnaton.
27. What reasons underlie the apparent return to animal-worship?
28. What features of Egyptian religion went beyond Egypt into the Graeco-Roman world?

Topics for Report and Discussion

1. The relation between religion and the political development of Egypt.
2. Pyramids, their meaning and importance.
3. The importance of preserving the body—the embalming process.
4. The reforms of Ikhnaton. Was his a genuine monotheism?
5. The discovery of King Tutenkhamon's tomb.
6. The Osiris-Isis stories.

Suggested Readings

1. Grace Turnbull. *Tongues of Fire.* pp. 13-27; 57-73.
2. E. A. Budge. *Book of the Dead.* Chapter 125, The Negative Confession.
3. E. A. Budge. *The Literature of the Ancient Egyptians.*
4. Sir Arthur Weigall. *Life and Times of Ikhnaton.*
5. James H. Breasted. *The Development of Religion and Thought in Ancient Egypt.*
6. James H. Breasted. *Dawn of Conscience.*

CHAPTER III: THE GODS AND FAITHS OF BABYLON AND NINEVEH

Questions and Exercises

1. Compare the geographical situation of Babylonia and Assyria with that of Egypt.
2. Which civilization was probably older? Why do you think as you do?

3. How extensive were Babylonia and Assyria proper?

4. Compare the early political organization of Babylonia with that of Egypt.

5. Are the same relationships between politics and religion discernible in Babylonia as in Egypt? If different, how account for the difference?

6. What was the racial character of the Babylonians? What was the Zi? Compare this with the Egyptian Ka.

7. What was the nature of the earlier religion of the Babylonian region?

8. Does the Hebrew religion betray any traces of the influence of this early faith? What?

9. What light does this early religion throw upon belief in angels?

10. Who were the Semitic peoples? What are their characteristics? What especial capacity did they have for religion?

11. Define henotheism. Does this definition agree with what you find in the dictionary?

12. What was the nature of the great divinities of Babylon?

13. How do Babylonian triads differ from those in Egypt?

14. Did climate have any marked influence upon Babylonian religion? What?

15. Characterize each of the members of the great Babylonian triad. What was the origin of each?

16. Distinguish between Enlil, Ninib, and Nergal as sun-gods. Why were there so many sun-gods?

17. What especial function was performed by Shamash?

18. Compare the moon gods of Babylon and Egypt. Why should the moon have been worshiped so universally?

19. What place did the female divinities hold in Babylonian religion generally?

20. How do you account for the importance of Ishtar?

21. Trace the rise of Marduk to supremacy among the gods of Babylonia.

22. Compare the creation story of Babylonia with that in Genesis.

23. How does Ashshur differ from Marduk?

24. What were the main features of the Babylonian temples?

25. How was the priesthood organized? How important was it in the life of the people?

26. Compare the Babylonian Deluge story with the Hebrew.

27. Who was the Babylonian Noah?

28. Why did Adapa lose immortality? Is there anything in the Bible corresponding to this?

29. What were the means of divination employed in Babylonia? Do any of these still persist? Has divination any religious basis?

30. What was the relation of Babylonia's religion and ethics?

31. How did the Babylonian think of the after life? Contrast this with Egypt.

32. How was Ishtar related to the underworld? How is this interpreted naturally?

Topics for Report and Discussion

1. What are angels? What place do they hold in present-day religion?
2. Are Semitic peoples endowed with a special "genius for religion"?
3. Why were there so many gods of overlapping function in Babylonia? e.g., sun-gods.
4. Did the Hebrews borrow anything from the Babylonian stories of the beginnings of the world? (See Morris Jastrow. *Hebrew and Babylonian Traditions.*)
5. How do you explain the rise of the various types of divination? Does divination have a religious basis? (Special reports on Astrology, Hepatoscopy.)
6. Compare present-day fortune telling with ancient Babylonian practices.
7. What seem to have been the major contributions of Babylonia to the ongoing stream of religious development?
8. Compare Babylonian business ethics with current practices?
9. Why did Babylonia not reach a monotheistic faith?

Suggested Readings

On Divination.

The Heyday of the Fortune Tellers. Harper's Magazine. Volume 164; 236-46.

Superstition in Cellophane. Christian Century. Volume 49; 222-24.

Profiteering Prophets. American Magazine. Volume 113; 34-35.

See magazine indices for recent articles on astrology, numerology, fortune telling, etc.

For greater detail regarding the individual gods, see

Morris Jastrow. *Aspects of Religious Belief in Babylonia and Assyria.* Chapter 2.

R. W. Rogers. *Religion of Babylonia and Assyria.* Chapter 2.

The romance of the rediscovery of Babylonia and Assyria.

R. W. Rogers. *Religion of Babylonia and Assyria.* Chapter 1. Recovery of a Lost Religion.

Interesting Babylonian literature.

R. W. Rogers. *Cuneiform Parallels to the Old Testament.* The Creation Story. The Deluge. The Descent to Hades. Ethical Incantations and Wisdom Literature.

Also see Sacred Books and Literature of the East. Volume 1.

R. F. Harper. The Code of Hammurabi.

CHAPTER IV: ZOROASTRIANISM: THE RELIGION OF EMBATTLED
LIGHT AND DARKNESS

Questions and Exercises

1. In what way is Zoroastrianism related to the religion of India? To the European religions?

2. What is the "Bible" of Zoroastrianism? What is its general character?

3. Was Zoroaster an historic figure? When and where did he live?

4. Do we have other than legendary stories of his life?

5. How do you account for the demoniac opposition to him found in the legends?

6. What are the characteristics of a prophet?

7. How did he arrive at the conviction of his call to be a prophet?

8. What did Herodotus report concerning the religion of Zoroaster?

9. Who was his first important convert and what effect did his conversion have upon the fortunes of the new faith?

10. How much of this is legendary and how much is fact?

11. What was the manner of the prophet's death?

12. What was the essential nature of Zoroaster's reform?

13. How did he think of God?

14. Contrast the explanation of evil in Buddhism, Hinduism, Hebrew, and Zoroastrian religion.

15. What place did Ahriman hold in his system?

16. Was Zoroaster a monotheist?

17. What were the Amesha Spentas?

18. How did Zoroaster conceive of the life after death?

19. How were the good and bad separated in the after-life? Compare with the Egyptian judgment.

20. What was to be the outcome of the struggle between Ahura-Mazda and Ahriman?

21. What influence did Greek thought have on Zoroastrianism?

22. How did Zoroastrianism influence the religion of the western world?

23. How was Zoroastrianism changed in later times?

24. What effect did Zoroastrianism have on Judaism and Christianity?

25. Who was Mithra? Trace his fortunes in Persian religion.

26. What was the nature of Mithraism? What influence did it have upon the religion of the Roman empire?

27. Who are the Parsees? What is the character of their faith? How does it differ from early Zoroastrianism?

28. What are the Towers of Silence?

29. What is the importance of fire in their cult? Was this a part of original Zoroastrianism?

30. What of the Zoroastrians in Persia?

Suggested Readings

How a present-day Zoroastrian interprets his faith.

M. N. Dhalla. *Zoroastrian Theology.*

Ethics as taught by a modern Zoroastrian.

M. N. Dhalla. *Our Perfecting World.* Especially Chapter 1. Zoroastrianism and other ways of Life.

On Mithraism.

Franz Cumont. *Oriental Cults in Roman Paganism.*

Harold R. Willoughby. *Pagan Regeneration.* Chapter 6.

On the Ethical Teachings.

M. M. Dawson. *The Ethical Religion of Zoroaster.* Macmillan, N. Y., 1931.

M. Buch. *Zoroastrian Ethics.*

On the Gabars or Zoroastrians in Persia.

Encyclopedia of Religion and Ethics. Art. Gabars. Volume 6. p. 147-156.

On the final judgment and after life.

E. H. Sneath. *Religion and the Future Life.* Chapter 5, by A. V. Williams Jackson.

On the Expected Messiah.

E. H. Sneath. *Id.* Chapter 5.

Topics for Report and Discussion

1. Purification rites in Zoroastrianism.
2. The origin of the fire cult.
3. The modern Parsee community in India.
4. The Gabars—or the Zoroastrians in Persia.
5. Are there any Zoroastrians in the United States?
6. To what extent is astrology bound up with historic Zoroastrianism?
7. The "three wise men," legend or fact?
8. The Towers of Silence.
9. In what ways may Zoroastrianism have influenced Christianity?
10. Will Zoroastrianism survive as a *living* religion?

CHAPTER V: THE FAITH OF OLD ARYAN INDIA

Questions and Exercises

1. What is Hinduism?
2. Who were the Dravidians?
3. Who were the Aryans?
4. What is the Rig-Veda? How important is it in the study of ancient India?
5. What seem to have been the needs which Vedic religion was invoked to satisfy?
6. What vestiges of still older religion remain?
7. How do you explain the many sun-gods?
8. Characterize Indra.
9. What was the nature and function of Agni?
10. What was the nature and function of Soma?
11. What was the meaning of "Rita"?
12. What were the function and importance of Varuna?
13. How did the Vedic people think of creation?
14. Who are the ancestors of the human race?
15. What was the nature of their after-life beliefs?
16. What brought about the decay of Vedic religion?
17. How did popular religion differ from that found in the Rig-Veda?
18. What was the Atharva-Veda?
19. Compare the magic here found with that among the other primitive peoples.
20. What part did environment play in the passing of Vedic religion?

Topics for Report and Discussion

1. The Aryans, who were they and whence did they come? How is India's culture linked with that of Europe?
2. The pre-Aryan population of ancient India. How did it influence the subsequent development of religion?
3. The correlation of Vedic religion with the economic life of the people.
4. The ethics of the Rig-Veda.
5. The rise of Caste in India.

Suggested Readings

On the Aryans.
Cambridge History of India. Volume 1. Chapter 3. The Aryans.
H. D. Griswold. *Religion of the Rig-Veda.* Chapter 1.
R. B. Dixon. *The Racial History of Man.* (N. Y. 1923) p. 243-44.
On pre-Aryan India.
Cambridge History of India. Volume 1. Chapter 1.
On the Rig-Vedic age.
Cambridge History of India. Volume 1. Chapter 4.
Maurice Bloomfield. *The Religion of the Rig-Veda.*
H. D. Griswold. *Religion of the Rig-Veda.*
Ethics of the Rig-Veda.
E. W. Hopkins. *Ethics of India.* Chapters 1 and 2.
John McKenzie. *Hindu Ethics.* Chapters 1 and 2.
Readings in Vedic Literature.
Sacred Books and Literature of the East. Volume 9.
A. A. McDonnell. *Hymns of the Rig-Veda.* (A representative selection.)
Hymns of the Rig-Veda. Wisdom of the East Series.
Grace Turnbull. *Tongues of Fire.*
The Mythology of India.
Mythology of All Races. Volume 6.

CHAPTER VI: BUDDHISM: GAUTAMA SITS UNDER THE BO-TREE
CHAPTER VII: BUDDHA JOINS THE PROCESSION

Questions and Exercises

1. What are the facts concerning the birth of Gautama—When? Where? His family?
2. What does "Buddha" mean? What was the family name?
3. Why did he renounce his home and family?
4. What is an ascetic? Was Gautama still a good Hindu when he became one?
5. What was the "enlightenment"? Can it be explained psychologically?
6. Why did he become a missionary?
7. How long and extended was his ministry?
8. What led to the founding of "the Order"?
9. What was the manner of his death?
10. How far did Buddhism spread?

11. How has the Buddha himself come to be regarded by his followers?
12. How account for the mass of legend that grew up about him?
13. How was his birth foretold?
14. What were the surroundings of his youth?
15. How extensive is the literature of Buddhism?
16. What are the keys to the Buddhist System?
17. How did he relate himself to his religious heritage? Was he ever consciously other than Hindu?
18. What was his attitude to the gods?
19. How did he regard the caste system?
20. What was his method of teaching?
21. How explain the "pessimism" of Gautama?
22. What were the "Four Noble Truths?"
23. Is Buddhism a religion?
24. How did he understand Karma?
25. What was his conception of Transmigration?
26. Out of what is the moral order of Buddhism woven?
27. How does liberation come?
28. What is the chain of causation?
29. What is the eightfold path?
30. Compare Jesus and Buddha in respect to their ideal and its achievement.
31. What is the foundation of the Buddhist ethical system?
32. In what respect are Gautama, Plato and Aquinas akin?

Topics for Report and Discussion

1. Fact and legend in Buddhism.
2. The birth stories of the Buddha.
3. Was Gautama an atheist?
4. The psychology of the experience of enlightenment.
5. Was primitive Buddhism really a religion?
6. The nature of Buddhist scripture.
7. Gautama as a teacher.
8. How good a Hindu was Gautama?
9. How reconcile the doctrine of no-soul and the Buddhist belief in transmigration?
10. Buddhism in America.
11. The meaning of Nirvana.
12. Buddhist heavens and hells.
13. Did Buddhism influence Jesus?
14. Buddhism and women.

15. Buddhism and war.
16. The modern Buddhist revival.
17. The rise of Mahayana.
18. Buddhist sects in China and Japan.
19. Asoka, the first Buddhist king.
20. The reason for the decline of Buddhism in India.

Suggested Readings

1. On Buddhist Literature.
   Paul Carus. *The Gospel of Buddha,* or
   F. H. Woodward. *Some Sayings of the Buddha,* or
   Sacred Books and Literature of the Early East. Vol. 10.
2. On Gautama, the Founder.
   Rhys Davids. *Buddhism.*
   Ed. J. Thomas. *The Life of Buddha as History and Legend.*
   Mrs. C. A. F. Davids. *Gautama the Man.*
3. On Gautama in legend and story.
   Sir Edwin Arnold. *The Light of Asia.*
   A. F. Herold. *The Life of Buddha.*
4. On the spread of Buddhism.
   A. Hackmann. *Buddhism as a Religion.*
   J. B. Pratt. *The Pilgrimage of Buddhism.*
5. On Hinayana or Southern Buddhism.
   J. B. Pratt. *The Pilgrimage of Buddhism.* Chapters 7, 8, 9, 10.
   Kenneth J. Saunders. *Buddhists in Southern Asia.*
6. On Mahayana or Northern Buddhism.
   J. B. Pratt. *The Pilgrimage of Buddhism.*
   In general—Chapters 11, 12 and 13.
   In China—Chapters 14-20.
   In Japan—Chapters 23-31.

   See also on Chinese Buddhism.
   R. F. Johnston. *Buddhist China.*
   Karl Reichelt. *Truth and Tradition in Chinese Buddhism.*
   On Japanese Buddhism see also:
   A. J. Reischauer. *Studies in Japanese Buddhism.*
   On Thibetan Buddhism.
   Sir Charles Bell. *The Religion of Tibet.*
7. On Buddhist Ethics.
   Encyclopedia of Religion and Ethics. Art. Vol. V, pp. 447-55.
   S. Tachibana. *Buddhist Ethics.*
   J. B. Pratt. *Op. cit.* Chapters 2 and 3.

8. On Buddhism in The Modern World.

Charles S. Braden. *Modern Tendencies in World Religions*. pp. 122-127, and 152-168.

J. B. Pratt. *Op. cit.* Chapters 32 and 33.

9. Buddhism and Christianity.

B. H. Streeter. *Buddhism and Christianity*.

J. B. Pratt. *Op. cit.* Chapter 34.

CHAPTER VIII: HINDUISM REGAINS MOTHER INDIA

Questions and Exercises

1. Why did Buddhism disappear from India?
2. Trace the rise of the idea of Brahma.
3. Differentiate between East and West as to their approach to the world.
4. Can East and West understand each other?
5. What was the "way of knowledge"?
6. What was the salvation ideal of the philosophers?
7. What are the Upanishads?
8. How did Indian speculation account for the creation?
9. What is meant by "the ultimate world ground"?
10. What is meant by reincarnation? How is it described in the Upanishads?
11. What does the author mean by the statement: "The soul is the key to Indian thought"?
12. What is the Atman?
13. Trace the process which ended in the identification of the self with the ultimate reality, Brahma.
14. What were some of the consequences of these religio-philosophic views?
15. How is sin regarded in the Upanishads?
16. What is the "knowledge" by which salvation is attained?
17. What is the meaning of Maya?
18. What is the ultimate destiny of the soul?
19. Is this annihilation?
20. What is meant by Yoga?
21. How would you characterize the system of thought as a whole? Or is it a system?
22. What are the "keys" to this system?
23. What was the measure of Greek influence on Indian thought?
24. How do you explain the rise of the great personal gods?
25. What is the Hindu "trinity"?

26. Trace the history of the rise of Vishnu.
27. What is the meaning of incarnation?
28. How many incarnations had Vishnu?
29. What is the character and importance of Rama?
30. What is the character and importance of Krishna? Trace the rise of his worship.
31. What were the origin, nature, and function of Shiva?
32. How is he worshiped?
33. What is the nature of the symbolism of this faith?
34. How are ethics and religion related in this period of Hinduism?
35. What are the Laws of Manu?
36. What importance attaches to the four stages of life?
37. What is the meaning of Bhakti?
38. What is the Bhagavad-Gita? How important is it in India's religious life?
39. Who are the Jains?
40. What are the distinguishing characteristics of Jainism?
41. What are the three Jewels?

Topics for Report and Discussion

1. Caste in India.
2. Untouchability in India.
3. The religion of Gandhi.
4. The religion of Tagore.
5. The place of the holy man in Indian society.
6. Sectarianism in Hinduism.
7. Recent social and religious reform in India.
8. The effect of recent nationalistic feeling on religion.
9. The indirect contribution of Christianity to Hinduism.
10. The Brahma-Samaj.
11. The Ramakrishna Mission.
12. Yoga practice in India.
13. The Arya-Samaj.
14. Indian attitudes toward Christian missions.
15. Non-injury, its meaning and importance in recent Indian political activity.

Suggested Readings

In the Literature of India.
    The Bhagavad-Gita—various translations. Preferably, The *Song Celestial* by Edwin Arnold.

Sacred Books and Literature of the East. Volume 9, a good selection.

Temple Bells. Edited by A. P. Appasamy. Selections from the devotional literature of India.

On India and Indian life in general.

Gertrude Emerson. *Voiceless India.* A first-hand study of an Indian village.

Yeats-Brown. *Lives of a Bengal Lancer.*

Margaret Noble. *The Web of Indian Life.*

S. Radhakrishnan. *The Hindu View of Life.*

Rabindranath Tagore. *The Religion of Man.*

M. Gandhi. *Story of My Experiments with Truth.*

C. F. Andrews. *Mahatma Gandhi's Ideas.*

An Indian view of Hinduism.

C. R. Das. *Hinduism.*

D. S. Sarma. *A Primer of Hinduism.*

S. N. Das Gupta. *Hindu Mysticism.* Open Court Pub. Co., Chicago, 1927.

On Hinduism in the Modern World.

Charles S. Braden. *Modern Tendencies in World Religions.* Macmillan, N. Y., 1933. Chapter 2.

H. D. Griswold. *Insights into Modern Hinduism.* Henry Holt, N. Y., 1934.

L. S. O'Malley. *Popular Hinduism.*

Paul Brunton. *A Search in Secret India.* E. P. Dutton, N. Y., 1935.

Nicol McNicol. *Living Religions of India.* London, 1935.

D. S. Sarma. *Hindu Renaissance.*

CHAPTER IX: THE GODS COME TO MOUNT OLYMPUS

Questions and Exercises

1. How did Greece differ from India in its outlook on life?
2. What were the various levels of Greek religion?
3. What were the origins of Greek religion?
4. What is meant by Chthonic religion?
5. What function did the Keres perform? Compare them with the "spirits" of primitive religions.
6. How important was the Earth Mother, Demeter? Compare her story with that of Ishtar.
7. Whence came the Olympic gods according to Hesiod?
8. What is meant by the statement: "The Greeks humanized their gods"?
9. What has kept the Greek gods so long alive in the world?
10. What were the general characteristics of the Olympian gods?

11. How were they worshiped? On what occasions?

12. What was the function of the priests? How did they differ from priests of other faiths? Compare Japan today.

13. Compare divination in Greece with that in Babylonia.

14. What part did the great oracles play in Greek life?

15. Of what sort were the sacrifices and offerings and what purposes did they serve?

16. How do art and religion relate to each other in Greece?

17. In what sense were the Olympic games religious? Are they so in modern times?

18. How did religion manifest itself in the family?

19. What was the attitude of the Greeks toward the physical body?

20. How were religion and ethics related in Greece?

21. What contribution, if any, did the poets and dramatists make to religion?

22. What was the attitude of Socrates to the Olympian faith?

23. How did Plato conceive of God?

24. What was the Greek belief in the after-life?

Topics for Report and Discussion

1. Oracles—their origin and significance in Greek Life
2. The temples of Greece.
3. The Greek drama and religion.
4. Was there any Hindu influence upon Greek thought?
5. What influence did Greek religion have upon Christianity?
6. What can be discovered about Greek religion in the New Testament?
7. What vestiges of ancient Greek religion may be found within Christianity? (See Hyde, W. W. *Greek Religion and its Survivals*. Boston, 1923.)
8. The religious ideas of Socrates.
9. The place of religion in Plato's thought.

Suggested Readings

On the "Personal" religions.

Harold C. Willoughby. *Pagan Regeneration*. Chapter 2, The Greater Mysteries at Eleusis. Chapter 3, Dionysian Excesses. Chapter 4, Orphic Reform.

On the Philosophers.

Clifford H. Moore. *Religious Thought of the Greeks*. Chapters 5 and 6.

George Foot Moore. *History of Religion.* p. 492-539.

Plato's Dialogues—*The Phaedo.* Jowett's translation.

On the poets and dramatists.

Clifford H. Moore. *Religious Thought of the Greeks.* Chapter 3.

George Foot Moore. *History of Religion.* p. 477-492.

The student should familiarize himself with the major Olympian figures.
Any standard book of classical mythology may be read. Most libraries
will contain several such books. The following are widely used:

H. A. Guerber. *Myths of Greece and Rome.*

Howe & Harrer. *A Handbook of Classical Mythology.*

Louis H. Gray. *Mythology of All Races.* Volume I.

Charles M. Gayley. *The Classic Myths in English Literature and Art.*

CHAPTER X: THE GODS REACH ROME

Questions and Exercises

1. What was the racial composition of the Roman people?

2. Who were the Etruscans and what did they contribute to the culture of Rome?

3. Did climate and geography play an important rôle in the development of Roman religion?

4. What was the character of the primitive Roman faith? How does it compare with the religion of early Greece?

5. What was the meaning of "religio" to the Roman?

6. Compare the taboos of early Roman religion with those of other primitive peoples.

7. What taboos surrounded the priesthood?

8. What was the nature of the religion of the family?

9. What was the function of Vesta in early religion? In later times?

10. What was the Genius? Compare this with the Egyptian "Ka" and the Babylonian "Zi."

11. What were the origin and function of the Lares? Penates?

12. What was the general character of the early Roman Divinities? Or were they really divinities?

13. How important were religious festivals in the life of the Roman people?

14. Does the importance of Mars reveal anything as to the character and habits of the Romans?

15. What was the Saturnalia? What connection has it with Christmas?

16. How did Roman religious development differ from that of other great ethnic faiths?

17. What changes did religion undergo as Rome became a city-state? Why?

18. What was the probable origin of Jupiter? Was he of Aryan origin?

19. What were the origin and functions of Juno? Minerva?

20. What is meant by the statement, Roman religion was "a contract religion"? Is this true of any other religion? *Cf.* Hebrew covenants.

21. What was the nature and organization of the priesthood in later Roman religion? Compare this with the priesthood in Greece.

22. What was the nature of prayer as practiced by the Romans?

23. Is the author right in his judgment as to the deficiencies in Roman religion?

24. How may the radical changes in Roman religion in later times be accounted for?

25. What new elements came into Roman religion from abroad?

26. How did the new gods differ from the old and how relate themselves to the old?

27. What were the Sibylline books? What part did they play in changing Roman religion?

28. What is a Sibyl?

29. Was there any relation between the political and economic changes in Rome and the changes in her religion?

30. How do you account for the rise of emperor-worship? Is it found in any other religions?

31. What was Stoicism and what influence did it have upon Roman life? Who were the great stoic philosophers of Rome?

32. What was the Roman policy toward the religion of conquered peoples? Did this have any effect on Roman religion?

33. What was the essential opposition of Roman religion to Christianity?

34. What brought about the final dissolution of Roman religion?

Topics for Report and Discussion

1. The old Aryan elements in Roman religion.
2. List the Olympian Gods—Greek and Roman in parallel.
3. The penetration of Greek culture into Rome.
4. The rise of emperor-worship. Compare it with manifestations of emperor-worship in other cultures.
5. The nature, content and influence of the Sibylline books.
6. What did Roman religion contribute to the developing Christian faith?
7. The ethical teachings of Marcus Aurelius.

8. The effect of imperialism on Roman religion.
9. The Isis cult in Rome.
10. The cult of the Great Mother in Rome.

Suggested Readings

On survivals of Roman religion.
   Gordon Laing. *Roman Religion.*
The writings of the great Stoics.
   Selections from Marcus Aurelius, Epictetus and Seneca. Grace Turnbull,
      Tongues of Fire. pp. 335-390.
On the Oriental cults in the Empire.
   Franz Cumont. *Oriental Cults in Roman Paganism.*
   Harold R. Willoughby. *Pagan Regeneration.* Chapters 5, 6, and 7.
   S. Angus. *The Mystery Religions and Christianity.*
   S. Angus. *Religious Quests in the Graeco-Roman World.*

CHAPTER XI: CONFUCIANISM: THE RELIGION OF HEAVEN

Questions and Exercises

1. How old is Chinese civilization?
2. What are the main features of Chinese geography?
3. What was the origin of the Chinese peoples?
4. What is the probable population of China?
5. What were China's contributions to early European culture?
6. Contrast the religion of India with that of China.
7. Compare the Stoic and the Sage.
8. What was the "Way"?
9. What is the meaning and importance of Yang and Yin?
10. What are the Shen and the Kwei?
11. Was early Chinese religion a monotheism?
12. In what sense is Chinese religion dualistic?
13. Explain "the explosion of a boy's firecracker on the Fourth of July is the far echo on a peaceful front of a desperate warfare in which China has been engaged for ages."
14. What was the Chinese view of human nature?
15. What is the key to the Chinese ideal of life?
16. Does China have a Bible?
17. Compare the Chinese and the Buddhist conception of the self.
18. What is quietism?

19. Against what in the older Chinese religion was Confucianism a reaction?

20. When and where was Confucius born?

21. What other founders of religion belong to his century?

22. What were the facts with respect to his family, birth and early life?

23. What was his method of teaching?

24. What experience had he as an office holder?

25. What caused his disappointment in his later years?

26. What were the outstanding personal characteristics of the man?

27. How did he die?

28. Compare the Confucian superior man idea with the Greek ideal of life.

29. How do the three religions of China relate each to the other?

30. What are the Confucian books?

31. What are the characteristics of the superior man?

32. Compare the Confucian ideal of reciprocity and the golden rule.

33. What was the Confucian teaching with reference to the family relationships?

34. What is the importance of "filial piety"?

35. What was Confucius' view of the state?

36. Compare the Platonic and Confucian view of the state.

37. Is Confucianism a religion?

38. What did Confucius teach about the future life?

39. What is the importance of ancestor worship in China?

40. Who was Mencius and how did his work relate to that of Confucius?

41. What was Confucius' idea and practice of prayer?

42. In what sense was Confucianism the state religion?

43. Trace the entrance and development of Buddhism in China.

44. Is Confucius a god?

45. What is the altar of Heaven?

46. Why has its use been discontinued?

47. What lesser gods are worshiped in China?

48. How is the modern world affecting Confucianism?

Topics for Report and Discussion

1. What has been the effect of the revolution upon religion in China?

2. To what extent have Christian missions influenced Chinese religion?

3. The cult of Sun Yat-Sen.

4. The Buddhist revival in China.

5. The origin of Shang Ti and Tien.

6. The effect of Communism on Chinese religion.
7. The breakdown of the family in China and its effect upon religion.
8. The Chinese Renaissance.
9. The Youth Movement in China.
10. Ancestor Worship.

Suggested Readings

1. In Chinese literature.
    The Analects or *Sayings of Confucius.*
    The Canon of Reason and Virtue, in Sacred Books and Literature of the East.
    Lin Yu Tang, *The Wisdom of China and India.*
2. On Confucius.
    Ricard Wilhelm. *Confucius and Confucianism.* N. Y., 1931.
    James Legge. *Life and Teachings of Confucius.* London, 1875.
    Carl Crow. *Master Kung.*
3. On Confucianism.
    H. H. Giles. *Confucianism and Its Rivals.*
    W. E. Soothill. *The Three Religions of China.*
    Francis Wei. *The Spirit of Chinese Culture.*
4. On Modern Tendencies in Chinese Religion.
    Charles S. Braden. *Modern Tendencies in World Religion,* N. Y., 1933, chapter 3.
    Hu Shih. *The Chinese Renaissance,* Chicago University Press, 1934.
    R. F. Johnston. *Confucianism in the Modern World,* N. Y., 1935.
5. On Buddhism in China.
    Chas. S. Braden. *Op. cit.* p. 122-127.
    J. B. Pratt. *Op. cit.* Chapters 16-20.
    Karl Reichelt. *Truth and Tradition in Chinese Buddhism.*
6. On the State Cult of Confucius.
    John Shryock. *The Rise and Development of the State Cult of Confucius.*
7. On Chinese Life in General.
    Lin Yu Tang. *My Country and My People.*

CHAPTER XII: "THE LAND OF THE GODS"—THE RELIGIONS OF JAPAN

Questions and Exercises

1. When and how was Japan opened to Western influence?
2. What was the origin of the Japanese people?

3. What has been the influence of China upon Japanese culture?

4. Of what is Japanese religion an amalgam?

5. What was the general nature of early Shinto?

6. What is the meaning of "Kami"?

7. How does Aston classify the Gods?

8. How does Japanese mythology account for the Japanese islands, Japanese gods, and the rulers?

9. What part do Izanagi and Izanami play in the story of Japanese beginnings?

10. What is the place and importance of Amaterasu, the Sun-goddess in Shinto?

11. How do you account for Temmangu, god of learning?

12. How do Shintoists worship?

13. What are the nature and function of the priesthood?

14. Do the Japanese practice emperor-worship?

15. What was the "revival of pure Shintoism"?

16. Distinguish between State Shinto and Sectarian Shinto.

17. What part does Buddhism play in Japanese life?

18. What influence has Confucianism in Japan?

19. What is Bushido?

20. What is the Japanese view of the future life?

21. What is the "Pure-Land" faith?

22. How is the conflict of cultures in Japan influencing religion?

Topics for Report and Discussion

1. How do you account for the persistence of nature worship in modern Japan?

2. Bushido, the way of the warrior.

3. Japanese Emperor-worship.

4. Is State Shinto a religion?

5. The rapid development of the various Shinto sects, as Tenrykyo, Konkokyo, Omotokyo, etc.

6. Is there any correlation between Shinto and the twentieth century imperial outthrust of Japan?

Suggested Readings

On the mythology of Japan.

Mythology of All Races. vol. 8.

The Kojiki. The early chapters.

Sacred Books and Early Literature of the East. Volume 13.

On State Shinto.
  D. C. Holtom. *The National Faith of Japan.*
  Id. *The Political Philosophy of Modern Shinto.*

On Shinto by Japanese Writers.
  Genchi Kato. *Shinto, the Religion of the Japanese Nation.* Tokyo. 1926.
  M. Anesaki. *History of Japanese Religion.*
  Y. Hibino. *Nippon Shindo Ron, or The National Ideals of the Japanese People.* Cambridge, 1928.
  Kakehi Katsuhiko. "An Outline of Shinto." *Contemporary Japan.* Volume 1, pp. 584-597, March, 1933.

On the Gods.
  W. G. Aston. *Shinto, The Way of the Gods.*

On Shinto in the Modern World.
  Charles S. Braden. *Modern Tendencies in World Religions.* Macmillan, New York, 1933. Chapter 4.
  D. C. Holtom. *Modern Japan and Shinto Nationalism.* Rev. Ed., 1947.
  Robert O. Ballou. *Shinto, the Unconquered Enemy.*

CHAPTER XIII: THE HEBREW PROPHET CHALLENGES THE GODS

Questions and Exercises

1. Who was Amos?
2. How did the geographical situation of Palestine influence religion?
3. Trace the tradition of Israel from the beginning to the conquest of Canaan.
4. How did the Hebrew historian think of his people and their relation to God?
5. What were "J" and "E"?
6. Is there an historical basis for the Hebrew tradition of the patriarchs and the sojourn in Egypt?
7. What was the early Hebrew idea of God?
8. What in their surroundings and history led to a monotheistic conception?
9. When did Jahweh worship begin?
10. Was Moses an historical figure?

11. What was the origin of the Jahweh faith?
12. What was the work of Moses?
13. Was Jahweh a war-god?
14. What power was exercised by Jahweh?
15. Are there special religious values in monotheism?
16. What was felt to be the relationship between God and Israel?
17. Are there indications of human sacrifice in early Hebrew religion?
18. What was the nature of the earlier codes?
19. What influence did the Canaanite religion have upon Israel's faith?
20. How did the changing economic conditions of Israel affect their religious development?
21. What was the function of a prophet in Israel?
22. What was the origin of the Hebrew Messianic hope?
23. How were the ill fortunes of Israel explained?
24. How did the prophets perform their work?
25. Name and characterize the more important prophets of Israel.
26. What was the contribution of Amos?
27. Against what sins did the prophets struggle?
28. What, in general, was the influence of the prophets?
29. What hope did the prophets hold out to Israel?
30. What varied types of literature does the Old Testament contain?
31. What has been the influence of the Psalms?
32. What were the origin and function of the Synagogue?
33. What caused the spread of Judaism over the world?
34. What is Neo-Platonism?
35. What is the present-day status of Judaism?

Topics for Report and Discussion

1. The formation of the Old Testament.
2. A detailed study of the life and contribution of such important figures as Amos, Isaiah, Ezekiel, Jeremiah, David, etc.
3. Make an outline of the historical development of Israel.
4. The religion of the Canaanites.
5. The development of the Messianic hope.
6. The changing views of the after life in the Old Testament.
7. The Apocalyptic element in late Judaism.
8. The place of the temple in Hebrew religion.
9. The Hebrew solution of the problem of evil.
10. The origin of the major Hebrew taboos.
11. Zionism today.

12. The Reform Movement in Judaism.
13. Judaism—civilization or religion?

Suggested Readings

In the literature of the Jewish faith.
  Assigned sections in the Old Testament.
  Selections from the Talmud in *Sacred Books and Literature of the East;
    Everyman's Talmud.*
On the History of the Hebrew People.
  Brooke Peters Church. *The Israel Saga.*
  Charles F. Kent. *History of the Hebrew People.*
  Herbert L. Willett. *The Jew Through the Centuries.*
  Lewis Browne. *Stranger than Fiction.*
  A. L. Sachar. *History of the Jews.*
On the development of the religion of Israel.
  H. T. Fowler. *The Origin and Growth of Hebrew Religion.*
  George Foot Moore. *History of Religion, Volume 2, Judaism.*
On the development of the idea of God.
  Shailer Mathews. *The Growth of the Idea of God.*
  Chas. N. Pace. *Ideas of God in Israel.*
  Hastings Bible Dictionary, Art. God.
  Encyclopedia of Religion and Ethics, Art. God, Hebrew.
  Harry Emerson Fosdick. *A Guide to Understanding the Bible.* Chapter 1.
On Prophets and Prophecy.
  Cornill. *The Prophets of Israel.*
  F. C. Eiselin. *Prophets and Prophecy in Israel.*
  J. M. P. Smith. *The Prophets and Their Times.*
  Elmer Leslie. *The Prophets Tell Their Own Story.*
  Phillip Hyat. *Prophetic Religion.*
On the Old Testament.
  Julius H. Bewer. *Introduction to the Study of Old Testament Literature.*
  Chas. F. Kent. *Origin and Permanent Value of the Old Testament.*
  Laura H. Wild. *Literary Guide to the Bible.*
  Harry Emerson Fosdick. *The Modern Use of the Bible.*
On Judaism in the Modern World.
  Charles S. Braden. *Modern Tendencies in World Religions.* Chapter 7.
  Charles S. Braden. *Varieties of American Religion.* Chapters 15, 16, 17.
  David Phillipson. *The Reform Movement in Judaism.*
  F. W. Isserman. *This is Judaism.*
  Louis Finkelstein, *et al. Religions of Democracy.*

CHAPTER XIV: MOHAMMED, PROPHET OF ALLAH

Questions and Exercises

1. When and where was Mohammed born?
2. What is known concerning his family and his childhood?
3. What contacts with other religions did his caravan journeys afford him?
4. Whom did he marry, and what influence did this have upon his career?
5. What was happening in Europe and Asia Minor about this time?
6. What were the religious forces in Arabia during the early manhood of Mohammed?
7. What was the state of Christianity in Arabia?
8. What was the religious importance of Mecca?
9. How may the experience of the prophet be explained psychologically?
10. Is this the whole explanation?
11. Who were the Hanifs and what relation did Mohammed bear to them?
12. Under what conditions did Mohammed get his earlier revelations?
13. Where did he get his idea of the Unity of God?
14. Distinguish between a Deist and a Theist.
15. Was Mohammed a typical mystic?
16. How were his first converts won?
17. How account for the strong opposition that met him?
18. How did the opposition affect him?
19. How did Mohammed happen to leave Mecca for Medina?
20. What was the "night journey"?
21. What was the importance of the Hegira? Date it.
22. Who was Abu Bekr?
23. What effect did Mohammed's change to Medina have upon him?
24. What was his attitude toward the Jews?
25. What gave rise to the Holy Wars?
26. How did Islam change the habits of Arabia?
27. What was Mohammed's teaching and practice with regard to marriage?
28. What was the manner of his death?
29. What were the outstanding personal traits of the prophet?
30. How did the Koran come into being?
31. What were its major sources?

32. What was Mohammed's attitude toward the Jewish and Christian scriptures?

33. What is the place and importance of the Koran in Islam?

34. What is the meaning of *Islam*?

35. What is the Creed of Islam?

36. What is their belief with reference to Angels?

37. What is the Moslem practice of prayer?

38. What is the "secret of the religious power of Islam"?

39. Are Moslems fatalists?

40. What is the Moslem conception of Heaven?

41. What is their idea of Hell?

42. Trace the spread of Islam.

43. What was the Caliphate? When and why did it disappear?

44. What has been the relationship of Islam and Christianity?

45. Compare the Arabian Moslem attitudes toward Christianity with those of the Turkish Moslems.

46. What divisions have arisen in Islam?

47. Who are the Sufis?

48. What has been the Moslem contribution to science and philosophy?

49. How is the modern world affecting Islam?

50. Is modern Islam still a missionary faith?

Topics for Report and Discussion

1. Was Mohammedanism spread chiefly by the sword?

2. Islam in Europe and America.

3. Islam in India.

4. Islam in China.

5. The Moslem attitude toward women.

6. Islam and slavery.

7. Modern apologists' views of Mohammed.

8. Pan-Islam, a political threat.

9. The Hindu-Moslem conflict in India.

10. Education in Islam.

Suggested Readings

1. In Moslem Literature.

> *The Koran*——May be found in *Everyman's* edition, and the Modern Library. Selections are included in Grace Turnbull, *Tongues of Fire; The Bible of the World, The Bible of Mankind, The World's Great Scriptures.*

Harvard Classics, Volume 45 and *Sacred Books and Literature of the East*—Volume VII.

Stanley Lane-Pool. *Speeches and Table Talk of Mohammed.*

2. Concerning the Prophet.

    a. By Moslem writers.

        M. R. Bengalee. *Life of Mohammed.*

        Ameer Ali. *The Spirit of Islam.*

        Maulvi Mohammed Ali. *Mohammed.*

        Iqbal Ali Shah. *Mohammed the Prophet.*

    b. By non-Moslem writers.

        1. Literary or popular treatment.

            Thomas Carlyle. *Heroes and Hero Worship*—Mahomet.

            Washington Irving. *Life of Mahomet.*

            R. F. Dibble. *Mohammed*—a biography in the modern manner.

        2. Scholarly treatment:

            Sir Wm. Muir. *The Life of Mahomet.*

            Emile Dermenghem. *The Life of Mohammed.*

            D. S. Margoliuth. *Mohammed.*

3. Concerning the spread of Islam.

    Samuel Zwemer. *Across the World of Islam.*

    W. Wilson Cash. *The Expansion of Islam.*

    Sir Thomas Arnold. *The Preaching of Islam.*

    Murray Titus. *Indian Islam.*

4. Islam in the Modern World.

    Charles S. Braden. *Modern Tendencies in World Religions.* Chapter V.

    Henry E. Allen. *Turkish Transformation:* A study of religious and social development.

    H. A. R. Gibb. *Wither Islam?*

    H. A. R. Gibb. *Modern Trends in Islam.*

    Smith. *Indian Islam.*

    Ruth Woodsmall. *Moslem Women Enter a New World.*

5. On Islamic Culture.

    Sir Thomas Arnold. *The Legacy of Islam.* See also the magazine *Islamic Culture.*

6. On Islam in the West.

    See Braden. *Op. cit.* Chapter V.

    Cash. *Op. cit.*

    See magazine *The Moslem Sunrise,* published in Chicago, Ill.

    Also *The Review of Religions*—London.

CHAPTER XV: CHRISTIANITY

Questions and Exercises

1. What was the religious inheritance of Jesus?
2. What did he add to the current conception of God?
3. What was his conception of the kingdom of God?
4. How was the Kingdom of God to come?
5. How did the early Church come to think of Jesus?
6. What was the religion of Jesus?
7. What was the nature of the religion of the early Christians?
8. Who was Saul and what did he bring to Christianity?
9. What did he do to Christianity?
10. Was he influenced by the mystery religions?
11. How was the New Testament formed?
12. How account for the rapid spread of Christianity and its conquest of paganism?
13. In what way was it superior to the mystery religions?
14. What did the Church owe to Rome?
15. How did Christianity spread through Europe?
16. What was the origin of the major Christian festivals?
17. What was the influence of the Church on Medieval Europe?
18. What led to the Reformation?
19. What gave rise to the denominations within Protestantism?
20. Why was Christianity intolerant? Was this necessary?
21. Is there a difference between Christianity and the Church?
22. Does Christianity fit into a modern industrialized world?
23. Is Christianity always optimistic?
24. How had the Church regarded human nature?
25. What is the meaning of "Original Sin"?
26. What are the sources of the ethics of Jesus?
27. Is Christianity a world-denying religion?
28. What is the importance of the power of self-criticism?
29. To what extent does this rest back upon its sacred books?
30. What are the two centers of Christian doctrine?
31. Is Christianity a pure monotheism?
32. Contrast the idea of deliverance in Christianity and Buddhism.
33. What do the Christian hymns reveal concerning Christianity?
34. What is the social gospel?
35. Is Christianity an enduring way of life?

Topics for Report and Discussion

1. What is the difference between a Trinitarian Christian and a Unitarian Christian?
2. The Christianity of Abyssinia.
3. The Nestorian Christians.
4. The making of the New Testament.
5. The difference between the Eastern Orthodox Church and the Roman Catholic Church.
6. The difference between Protestant and Roman Catholic belief.
7. The recent movements toward Church union.
8. The elements in common between the major Protestant denominations.
9. The distinctive features of the student's own denomination. How it relates to the main stream of Christian development.
10. The Salvation Army.
11. What Jews and Christians have in common.
12. Christianity's adjustment to the new world of science.
13. What would it mean to Christianize a country?
14. The motives and methods of modern Christian Missions.
15. The Social Creed of the Churches.

Suggested Readings

1. Concerning Jesus. The list here is so extensive that an arbitrary choice of a few books representing different approaches to Jesus must be made.

    S. J. Case. *Jesus—a New Biography*.

    Walter B. Denny. *The Career and Significance of Jesus*.

    E. I. Bosworth. *Life and Teachings of Jesus*.

    B. Harvie Branscombe. *The Teachings of Jesus*.

    Thomas Walker. *The Teaching of Jesus and the Jewish Teaching of His Age*.

    Walter E. Bundy. *The Religion of Jesus*.

    E. F. Scott. *The Ethics of Jesus*.

    John Baillie. *The Place of Jesus Christ in Modern Christianity*.

    Ernest C. Colwell. *An Approach to the Teachings of Jesus*.

2. On Paul and his work.

    Percy Gardner. *The Religious Experience of St. Paul*.

    Adolf Deissman. *Paul, A Study in Social and Religious History*.

    Sir. Wm. Ramsay. *St. Paul the Traveler and Roman Citizen*.

    B. W. Robinson. *Life and Letters of Paul*.

C. C. Quimby. *Paul for Everyone.*
Harrison F. Rall. *According to Paul.*

3. Christianity and the Mystery Religions.
   S. Angus. *Christianity and the Mystery Religions.*
   Christianity and Modern Knowledge, Chapter V.

4. The History of the Church.
   Edward Bevan. *Christianity.*
   H. K. Rowe. *The History of the Christian People.*
   C. H. Moehlman. *The Story of Christianity in Outline.*
   Roland C. Bainton. *The Church of Our Fathers.*

5. The New Testament.
   Edgar J. Goodspeed. *The Story of the New Testament.*

6. Christianity in the Modern Age.
   Gaius G. Atkins. *Religion in Our Times.*
   Charles S. Braden. *Varieties of American Religion.*

7. On Catholicism.
   Roman—Cardinal Gibbons. *Faith of Our Fathers.*
   Eastern Orthodox—Bulgakov, S. N. *The Orthodox Church.* Translated by Elizabeth S. Crane (London, 1935).

8. On Protestantism and its divisions.
   H. Richard Niebuhr. *The Social Sources of Denominationalism.*
   Stanley I. Stuber. *How We Got Our Denominations.*
   James H. Nichols. *Primer for Protestants* (Assn. Press, N. Y., 1947).
   Elmer T. Clark. *Small Sects of America.*
   Marcus Bach. *They Have Found a Faith* (Bobbs Merrill, Indianapolis, 1946).

9. Christianity and the Social Order.
   Harry F. Ward. *Our Economic Morality and the Ethic of Jesus.*
   Walter Rauschenbusch. *Christianity and the Social Crisis.* (Somewhat out of date now, but historically its appearance marks a new epoch in the history of modern Christianity.)
   W. W. Van Kirk. *Religion Renounces War.*
   F. Ernest Johnson. *The Church and Society* (Abingdon Press, N. Y., 1935).
   Kirby Page. *Jesus or Christianity.*
   E. Stanley Jones. *The Choice Before Us.*
   D. C. Macintosh. *Social Religion.*
   John Bennett. *Social Salvation.*

10. On Church Unity.
    Henry Pitney Van Dusen. *World Christianity.*
    O. Frederick Nolde. *Toward World-Wide Christianity.*
    William Adams Brown. *Toward a United Church.*

CHAPTER XVI: THE RELIGIONS OF ANCIENT AMERICA

Questions and Exercises

I

1. Is America a continent without a history?
2. What was the attitude of the Spanish conquerors toward the religion and general culture of the Indians?
3. What is the generally accepted origin of the American Indians?
4. How could Asiatics have reached America?
5. What was the Aztec belief concerning the god who was to return?
6. What influence did this belief have upon the conquest of Mexico?
7. Who were the Nahuas? The Toltecs?
8. Describe the great temple of the war god Huitzilopochtli?
9. What was the fundamental nature of the Aztec religion?
10. What was the nature and function of Quetzalcoatl? Tezcatlipoca? Huitzilopochtli?
11. Describe the principal goddesses.
12. What parallels between Christian and the Aztec institutions and ceremonies were found?
13. What was the place of human sacrifice in Aztec religion? Describe the various types of such sacrifices.
14. What was the nature of the "church year" in Aztec religion? Describe the typical monthly feasts.
15. What did the Aztecs believe about the creation of the world and man?
16. Did they believe in an after-life? Discuss.
17. Discuss the priesthood, its organization, function and practices.
18. Describe the monastic system of the Aztecs.

II

1. Where did the Maya civilization develop?
2. What are our sources for the knowledge we have of it?
3. Describe Maya writing. What do we have left of it today?
4. Who was Kukulcan?
5. How are the gods usually indicated in the literature concerning the Maya religion?
6. What gods can be definitely identified?
7. Was human sacrifice practiced by the Mayas? Where? An example.
8. Distinguish the different levels of Mayan religion.

9. What did they believe about the after-life?
10. Discuss their ideas of the creation of the world and man.

III

1. Where did the Incas live? What was the nature of the country they inhabited?
2. What was the nature of their culture at the time of the Conquest?
3. Describe the Temple of the Sun in Cuzco.
4. What were the chief objects of worship in the official cult?
5. What were *huacas? canopas?*
6. Who was Ynti or Inti?
7. What was the nature of Viracocha?
8. Was there a "church year" among the Incas?
9. What were the three levels of religion?
10. What was their belief concerning the after-life?

Topics for Report and Discussion

1. How do these religions compare with those already studied? On a vertical scale, where would you place them?
2. Is anything left of these ancient religions today? Where is it found?
3. What, if anything, in these three faiths seems to be common? Is there any borrowing of one from another?
4. Compare the general archaeological work done in the Americas with that in the old world.
5. The influence of Christianity upon some of the reported religious ideas and institutions, e.g., Quetzalcoatl, the cross, baptism, etc.

Suggested Readings

1. On the mythology of the various religions.
   Lewis Spence. *Myths of Mexico and Peru* (Dingwall-Rock, Ltd., New York, n.d.).
2. On the Literature.
   Daniel G. Brinton. *Rig-Veda Americana*, Sacred Songs of the Ancient Mexicans.
   Id. *The Maya Chronicles.*
3. On the general cultural background and religion.
   (a) Aztec:
   J. Eric Thompson. *Mexico Before Cortez* (Charles Scribner's Sons, New York, 1933).

(b) Maya:

> Sylvanus G. Morley. *The Ancient Maya* (Stanford University Press, 1946).

> J. Eric Thompson. *The Civilization of the Mayas* (Field Museum of Natural History, Chicago, 1922).

(c) Inca:

> Phillip A. Means. *The Ancient Civilization of the Andes* (Charles Scribner's Sons, New York, 1931).

4. On the similarities between Aztec and Mayan Religions and Christianity.

> Charles S. Braden. *The Religious Aspects of the Conquests of America* (Duke University Press, Durham, N. C., 1930).

Appendix B

TERM PAPER TOPICS

Most of these have actually been written upon. In addition to this list many of the topics suggested for each chapter could easily be made the basis of a paper. The list is only suggestive. It could be expanded endlessly.

1. The dance in religion.
2. The relation of magic and religion.
3. Taboos, ancient and modern.
4. Music in religion.
5. Art and religion.
6. Buddhist art.
7. The intoxicant gods in various religions.
8. The origin and history of the Devil.
9. The place of women in various religions.
10. The trail of the serpent in the world's religions.
11. Divination.
12. The fertility cult in various faiths.
13. The rise and development of the student's own particular denomination.
14. The political philosophy of Confucius.
15. The political philosophy of modern Shinto.
16. The spread of Islam, where and how?
17. Oracles.
18. The Sun Yat-Sen cult in China.
19. The moral and religious training of children in Islam—or any of the religions.
20. The life and times of Ikhnaton.
21. Asoka, the first Buddhist emperor.
22. Thibetan Buddhism.
23. Christian and Buddhist parallels.
24. Hebrew and Babylonian parallels.
25. Zionism.
26. The rise of the reform movement in Judaism.
27. The definition of religion.
28. The rise of religious humanism.

29. The drama in Indian religion—or any other religion.
30. Religion and healing.
31. An intensive study of the life of any one of the founders of the religions.
32. A study of the life and contribution of any of the great constructive leaders in any of the religions, e.g., Paul, Mencius, Isaiah, St. Francis, etc.
33. Monasticism in various religions.

Appendix C

BIBLIOGRAPHY

The following bibliography makes no pretense of being exhaustive. It is rather suggestive. In addition to most of the books in which specific assignments have been indicated in Appendix A, it consists of books which will be found useful in penetrating further into the study of the various faiths than is provided for there. It forms a fairly adequate working library for the not too technical scholar.

HISTORIES OF RELIGION IN GENERAL

Addison, J. T. *Life Beyond Death in the Belief of Mankind*. Houghton Mifflin, New York, 1932.

Archer, John Clark. *Faiths Men Live By*. Thomas Nelson & Sons, New York, 1934.

Braden, Charles S. *Man's Quest for Salvation*. Willett, Clark & Co., Chicago, 1941.

Friess, H. L. and Schneider, H. W. *Religion in Various Cultures*. Henry Holt, New York, 1932.

Haydon, A. E., *The Biography of the Gods*. The Macmillan Co., New York, 1941.

Hume, Robert E. *World's Living Religions*. Charles Scribner's Sons, New York, rev. ed., 1926.

Jurji, Edward J. *The Great Religions of the Modern World*. Princeton University Press, 1946.

Moore, George Foot. *History of Religion*. 2 vol. Charles Scribner's Sons, New York, 1913, 1919.

Religions of the World. Edited by Carl Clemen. Harcourt, Brace & Co., New York, 1931.

Sneath, E. H., Editor. *Religion and the Future Life*. Fleming H. Revell, New York, 1922.

Sneath, E. H., Editor. *The Evolution of Ethics*. Yale University Press, New Haven, 1927.

Soper, Edmund D. *The Religions of Mankind*. Abingdon-Cokesbury Press, New York, rev. ed., 1938.

Concerning the modern aspects of the various religions three books appeared prior to the publication of the 2nd edition of this book. They were Charles S. Braden, *Modern Tendencies in World Religions*, The Macmillan Co., New York, 1933; Albert C. Widgery, *Living Religions and Modern Thought,* Round Table Press, New York, 1934; and A. E. Haydon, *Modern Trends in World Religions,* University of Chicago Press, 1933. Only the last named is any longer in print, the others being available only in second-hand bookstores, though both are found generally in college and university libraries. These books are all in some respects out of date, for time and World War II have wrought significant changes both in thought and practice in these religions. They may still be used helpfully, however, as indicating what was happening earlier in the present century if it be pointed out that from about 1933 on some changes have taken place. Unfortunately no more recently written books covering the whole field are available, though Prof. H. A. R. Gibb has written concerning the more recent trends in Islam.

GENERAL REFERENCE WORKS

Encyclopedia of Religion and Ethics. 12 vols. and index. Charles Scribner's Sons, New York, 1908-1927.
Dictionary of Religion and Ethics. Edited by Shailer Mathews and Gerald B. Smith. The Macmillan Co., New York, 1921.
Encyclopedia of Religion. Edited by Vergilius Ferm, Philosophical Library, Inc., New York, 1945.
Mythology of All Races. 13 vols. Marshall Jones Co., Boston, 1916-1932.

THE SACRED LITERATURES OF THE RELIGIONS

Ballou, Robert O. *The Bible of the World.* Viking Press, New York, 1939.
Browne, Lewis, *The World's Greatest Scriptures.* The Macmillan Co., New York, 1946.
Harvard Classics. Volumes 44 and 45. P. F. Collier & Son, New York, 1910.
Sacred Books of the East. 50 vols. Edited by Max Muller. Oxford University Press, London, 1879-1894.
Sacred Books and Early Literature of the East. Edited by Charles F. Horne. 14 vols. Parke, Austin and Lipscomb, Inc. New York, 1917. An excellent and varied selection from all the religions. Few critical notes attached.
Sohrab, Mirza Ahmad, *The Bible of Mankind.* Universal Publishing Co., New York, 1939.
Tongues of Fire. Edited by Grace Turnbull. Macmillan Co., New York, 1929. A very good one-volume anthology.
Treasure House of the World's Living Religions. Edited by Robert E.

Hume. Charles Scribner's Sons, New York, 1932. A topical anthology. Thoroughly documented throughout.

On the Literatures—General

Holliday, Carl. *The Dawn of Literature.* T. Y. Crowell Co., New York, 1931.

Martin, A. W. *Seven Great Bibles.* World Unity Library, New York, 1930. On particular literatures see under various religions.

Chapter I

Durkheim, Emile. *Elementary Forms of the Religious Life.* G. Allen and Unwin, London, 1915.

Frazer, Sir James G. *The Golden Bough.* 12 vols. The Macmillan Co., London, 1911-1915.

Hopkins, E. W. *The Origin and Evolution of Religion.* Yale University Press, New Haven, 1923.

LeRoy, A. *The Religion of the Primitives.* The Macmillan Co., New York, 1922.

Lowie, Robert H. *Primitive Religion.* Boni & Liveright, New York, 1924.

Moore, George Foot. *The Birth and Growth of Religion.* Charles Scribner's Sons, New York, 1923.

Radin, Paul. *Primitive Religion.* Viking Press, New York, 1937.

Schmidt, W. *The Origin and Growth of Religion.* Translated by H. J. Rose. The Dial Press, New York, 1931.

Tylor, E. B. *Primitive Culture.* London, 1913.

In addition to these general books, consult *The Encyclopedia of Religion and Ethics,* and the numerous monographs describing the religion of particular peoples, as the Polynesians, Melanesians, Bantu, Ashanti, American Indians, Eskimos, etc.

Chapter II

Breasted, James H. *A History of the Ancient Egyptians.* Charles Scribner's Sons, New York, 1920.

Breasted, James H. *The Development of Religion and Thought in Ancient Egypt.* Charles Scribner's Sons, New York, 1912.

Id. The Dawn of Conscience. Charles Scribner's Sons, New York, 1933.

Budge, E. Wallis. *The Gods of the Egyptians.* 2 vols. Open Court, Chicago, 1904.

Budge, E. Wallis. *The Literature of the Ancient Egyptians.* J. M. Dent & Sons, London, 1914.

Erman, Adolph. *A Handbook of Egyptian Religion.* Constable & Co., London, 1907.

Naville, Edouard Henri. *The Old Egyptian Faith.* G. P. Putnam's Sons, New York, 1909.

Petrie, W. M. Flinders. *Religious Life in Ancient Egypt.* Constable & Co., 2nd ed., London, 1932.

Weigall, Arthur. *Life and Times of Ikhnaton.* T. Butterworth. London, rev. ed., 1923.

Chapter III

Chiera, Edward. *They Wrote on Clay,* Edited by George Cameron. University of Chicago Press, 1938.

Harper, Robert F. *The Code of Hammurabi.* University of Chicago Press, 1904.

Jastrow, Morris. *The Religion of Babylonia and Assyria.* Ginn & Co., Boston, 1898.

Id. The Civilization of Babylonia and Assyria. J. B. Lippincott Co., London, 1915.

Id. Aspects of Religious Belief and Practice in Babylonia and Assyria. G. P. Putnam's Sons, New York, 1911.

Id. Hebrew and Babylonian Traditions. Charles Scribner's Sons, New York, 1914.

Olmstead, A. T. *History of Assyria.* Charles Scribner's Sons, New York, 1923.

Rogers, Robert W. *The Religion of Babylonia and Assyria.* Eaton and Mains, New York, 1908.

Id. Cuneiform Parallels to the Old Testament. Abingdon Press, Cincinnati, 1912.

Sayce, A. H. *The Religion of Ancient Egypt and Babylonia.* T. and T. Clark, Edinburgh, 1902.

Woolley, C. Leonard. *The Sumerians.* Oxford University Press, London, 1929.

Chapter IV

Buch, M. A. *Zoroastrian Ethics.* Baroda, 1914.

Cumont, Franz. *The Oriental Religions in Roman Paganism.* Open Court Publishing Co., Chicago, 1911.

Dawson, M. M. *The Ethical Religion of Zoroaster.* The Macmillan Co., New York, 1931.

Dhalla, M. N. *History of Zoroastrianism*. Oxford University Press, London, 1938.

Dhalla, M. N. *Our Perfecting World*. Oxford University Press, New York, 1930.

Dhalla, M. N. *Zoroastrian Theology*. New York, 1914.

Zoroastrian Civilization from Earliest Times to 651 A.D. Oxford University Press, New York, 1922.

Hearn, W. E. *The Aryan Household*. Longmans, Green and Co., London, 1891.

Jackson, A. V. Williams. *Persia Past and Present*. The Macmillan Co., New York, 1906.

Jackson, A. V. Williams. *Zoroaster, the Prophet of Ancient Iran*. The Macmillan Co., New York, 1901.

Moulton, James Hope. *Early Zoroastrianism*. Williams and Morgate, London, 1913.

Moulton, James Hope. *The Treasure of the Magi*. Milford, London, 1917.

Rogers, R. W. *History of Ancient Persia*. Charles Scribner's Sons, New York, 1929.

Chapters V and VIII

Archer, John Clark. *The Sikhs*. Princeton University Press, 1946.

Bloomfield, Maurice. *The Religion of the Veda*. G. P. Putnam's Sons, New York, 1908.

Cambridge History of India. Volume I. Cambridge University Press, 1922.

Das, C. R. *Hinduism*. G. A. Natesan & Co., Madras, 1924.

Dasgupta, S. *Hindu Mysticism*. Open Court, Chicago, 1927.

Id. History of Indian Philosophy. 3 vols. Cambridge University Press, 1922.

Deussen, Paul. *Philosophy of the Upanishads*. Charles Scribner's Sons, New York, 1908.

Eliot, Sir Charles. *Hinduism and Buddhism*. Longmans, Green and Co., London, 1921.

Farquhar, J. N. *An Outline of the Religious Literature of India*. Oxford University Press, 1920. An almost complete listing of the sacred writings of Hinduism, Jainism, Sikhism and Buddhism and the chief translations of each. The bibliography is invaluable.

Geden, A. S. *Studies in the Religions of the East*. C. H. Kelly, London, 1913.

Gowen, H. H. *A History of Indian Literature*. D. Appleton & Co., New York, 1931.

Griffith, R. T. H. *Hymns of the Rig-Veda*. 2 vols. E. J. Lazarus Co., 3rd ed., Bevares, 1920.

Griswold, H. D. *The Religion of the Rig-Veda.* Oxford University Press, London, 1923.

Hopkins, E. W. *The Ethics of India.* Yale University Press, New Haven, 1924.

Hume, Robert E. Translation of *The Thirteen Principal Upanishads.* Oxford University Press, London, 2nd. ed., 1931.

Keith, A. B. *The Religion and Philosophy of the Veda and the Upanishads.* Harvard University Press, Cambridge, 1925.

MacAuliffe, M. S. *The Sikh Religion.* 6 vols. Oxford University Press, 1915.

McDonnell, A. A. *Hymns of the Rig-Veda.* Oxford University Press, London, 1922.

McKenzie, John. *Hindu Ethics.* Oxford University Press, London, 1922.

McNicol, Nicol. *Living Religions of India.* Student Christian Movement Press, London, 1934.

Marshall, Sir John Hubert. *Mohenjo-daro and the Indus Civilization.* 3 vols. A. Probsthain, London, 1931.

Masson-Oursel, Paul. *Ancient India and Indian Civilization.* Kegan Paul, Trench, Trubner & Co., London, 1934.

Noble, Margaret. *The Web of Indian Life.* Longmans, Green and Co., Bombay, 1918.

Pratt, J. B. *India and Its Faiths.* Houghton Mifflin Co., Boston, 1915.

Radhakrishnan, S. *Indian Philosophy.* 2 vols. The Macmillan Co., New York, 1923.

Id. The Hindu View of Life. George Allen & Unwin, London, 1927.

Sarma, D. S. *The Hindu Renaissance.* Madras, 1946.

Id. What is Hinduism? G. A. Press, Madras, 1939.

Id. Primer of Hinduism. The Macmillan Co., London, 1929.

Schweitzer, Albert. *Indian Thought and Its Development.* Henry Holt, New York, 1936.

Stevenson, S. *The Rites of the Twice-born.* Oxford University Press, London, 1920.

Id. The Heart of Jainism. Oxford University Press, London, 1915.

Tagore, Rabindranath. *The Religion of Man.* The Macmillan Co., New York, 1931.

Wheeler, J. T. *Short History of India.* The Macmillan Co., London, 1899.

Whitehead, H. *Village Gods of Southern India.* Oxford University Press, London, 1916.

CHAPTERS VI AND VII

Aiken, Charles F. *The Dhamma of Gotama the Buddha and the Gospel of Jesus the Christ.* Marlier and Co., Boston. 1900. A critical inquiry into the alleged relations of Buddhism with primitive Christianity.

Arnold, Sir Edwin. *The Light of Asia.* 1879. Has appeared in numberless editions and is included in many anthologies.

Anesaki, M. *History of Japanese Religions.* Kegan Paul, Trench, Trubner & Co., London, 1930.

Bell, Sir Charles Alfred. *The Religions of Tibet.* The Clarendon Press, Oxford, 1931.

Bigandet, Mgr. *Vie on Légende de Gaudama.* Paris, 1878.

Carus, Paul. *The Gospel of Buddha.* Open Court Publishing Co., Chicago, 1894.

Coomaraswamy, A. K. *Buddhism and the Gospel of Buddha.* G. P. Putnam's Sons, New York, 1916.

Coomaraswamy, A. K. *Hinduism and Buddhism.* Philosophical Library, New York, 1943.

Copleston, R. S. *Buddhism Primitive and Present in Magadha and in Ceylon.* Longmans, Green and Co., New York, 1892.

Davids, Mr. and Mrs. T. W. Rhys. *Sacred Books of the Buddhist*; a translation. Oxford University Press, London, 1910.

Davids, T. W. Rhys. *The Hibbert Lectures.* Williams & Norgate, London, 1881.

Davids, Mrs. C. A. F. *Gautama the Man.* Luzac & Co., London, 1928.

Davids, T. W. Rhys. *Buddhism: Its History and Literature.* G. P. Putnam's Sons, New York, 1907.

Davids, T. W. Rhys. *Buddhist India.* G. P. Putnam's Sons, New York, 1903.

Eliot, Sir Charles. *Japanese Buddhism.* Longmans, Green and Co., New York, 1933.

Eliot, Sir Charles. *Hinduism and Buddhism.* Longmans, Green and Co., London, 1921.

Geden, Alfred S. *Studies in the Religions of the East.* C. H. Kelly, London, 1913.

Hackman, A. *Buddhism as a Religion.* W. C. Probsthain & Co., 2nd ed., London, 1910.

Hamilton, Clarence H. *Buddhism in India, Ceylon, China, and Japan; a Reading Guide.* University of Chicago Press, 1931.

Herold, A. F. *The Life of Buddha.* A. & C. Boni, New York, 1927.

Holmes, Edmond. *The Creed of Buddha.* John Lane Co., London, 1919.

Johnston, R. G. *Buddhist China.* J. Murray, London, 1913.

McGovern, William. *An Introduction to Mahayana Buddhism.* Kegan Paul, Trench, Trubner & Co., London, 1922.

Pratt, J. B. *The Pilgrimage of Buddhism.* The Macmillan Co., New York, 1928.

Reischauer, A. J. *Studies in Japanese Buddhism.* The Macmillan Co., New York, 1917.

Reichelt, Karl. *Truth and Tradition in Chinese Buddhism.* Commercial Press, Shanghai, 1927.

Saunders, Kenneth J. *Buddhists in Southern Asia.* The Macmillan Co., New York, 1923.

Smith, Vincent A. *The Early History of India—Including Alexander's Campaign.* The Clarendon Press, Oxford, 1908.

Steinilber-Oberlin, E. *The Buddhist Sects of Japan.* George Allen & Unwin, London, 1938.

Streeter, B. H. *The Buddha and the Christ.* The Macmillan Co., London, 1932.

Tachibana, S. *The Ethics of Buddhism.* Oxford University Press, London, 1926.

Thomas, Edward J. *The Development of Buddhist Thought.* Kegan Paul, Trench, Trubner & Co., London, 1927.

Thomas, Edward J. *The Life of Buddha as Legend and History.* Kegan Paul, Trench, Trubner & Co., London, 1927.

Wheeler, J. T. *A Short History of India.* The Macmillan Co., London, 1899.

Woodward, F. L. *Some Sayings of the Buddha.* Oxford University Press, London, 1925.

CHAPTER IX

Adam, James. *The Religious Teachers of Greece.* T. & T. Clark, Edinburgh, 1908.

Butcher, S. H. *Harvard Lectures on Greek Subjects.* The Macmillan Co., New York, 1911.

Caird, Edward. *The Evolution of Theology in the Greek Philosophers.* MacLehose & Sons, Glasgow, 1904.

Durant, William. *The Life of Greece.* Simon & Schuster, New York, 1939.

Fairbanks, Arthur. *A Handbook of Greek Religion.* American Book Co., New York, 1910.

Farnell, L. R. *Outline History of Greek Religion.* Duckworth & Co., London, 1921.

Farnell, L. R. *The Higher Aspects of Greek Religion.* Williams & Norgate, London, 1912.

Gernet, Louis & Boulanger, Andre. *Le Genie Grec Dans la Religion.* Paris, 1932.

Harrison, Jane Ellen. *Prolegomena to the Study of Greek Religion.* Harvard University Press, Cambridge, 1916.

Hyde, Walter W. *Greek Religion and Its Survivals.* Marshall Jones, Boston, 1923.

Jowett, Benjamin. *Dialogues of Plato.* 4 vols. Charles Scribner's Sons, New York, 1907.

Macchioro, V. D. *From Orpheus to Paul.* Henry Holt, New York, 1930.

Moore, C. H. *The Religious Thought of the Greeks.* Harvard University Press, Cambridge, 1916.

Murray, Gilbert. *Five Stages of Greek Religion.* Columbia University Press, New York, 1930.

Nilsson, Martin P. *A History of Greek Religion.* Translation by F. J. Fielden. Clarendon Press, Oxford, 1925.

Nilsson, Martin P. *Greek Popular Religion.* Columbia University Press, New York, 1940.

Symonds, John Addington. *Studies in the Greek Poets.* Harper & Brothers, New York, 3rd ed., 1920.

The Legacy of Greece. Edited by R. W. Livingstone. Clarendon Press, Oxford, 1922.

Tucker, T. G. *Life in Ancient Athens.* The Macmillan Co., New York, 1906.

Willoughby, Harold C. *Pagan Regeneration.* University of Chicago Press, 1924.

Chapter X

Angus, S. *The Religious Quests of the Graeco-Roman World.* Charles Scribner's Sons, New York, 1929.

Bailey, Cyril. *Phases in the Religion of Ancient Rome.* University of California Press, Berkeley, 1932.

Carter, Jesse. *Religious Life in Ancient Rome.* Houghton Mifflin Co., Boston, 1911.

Cumont, Franz. *Oriental Religions in Roman Paganism.* Open Court, Chicago, 1911.

Fowler, William Warde. *The Roman Festivals.* The Macmillan Co., New York, 1899.

Id. The Religious Experience of the Roman People. The Macmillan Co., London, 1911.

Id. Roman Ideas of Deity. The Macmillan Co., London, 1914.

Granger, Frank. *The Worship of the Romans.* Methuen, London, 1895.

Laing, Gordon. *The Survivals of Roman Religion.* Longmans, Green and Co., New York, 1931.

Epilogue—The Twilight of the Gods

Anderson, Rasmus B. *Norse Mythology.* Scott, Foresman & Co., Chicago, 1898.

De La Saussaye, P. D. Chantepie. *The Religion of the Teutons.* Ginn & Co., Boston, 1902.

McBain, A. *Celtic Mythology and Religion.* E. P. Dutton, New York, 1917.

McCulloch, J. A. *The Religion of the Ancient Celts.* T. & T. Clark, Edinburgh, 1911.

Wagner, Wilhelm. *Asgard and the Gods.* E. P. Dutton, New York, 1917.

CHAPTER XI

Creel, H. G. *The Birth of China.* Reynal & Hitchcock, New York, 1937.

Creel, H. G. *Sinism. A Study of the Evolution of the Chinese World View.* Open Court, Chicago, 1929.

Crow, Carl. *Master Kung.* Harper & Brothers, New York, 1938.

Dawson, Miles Menander. *The Ethics of Confucius.* G. P. Putnam's Sons, New York, 1915.

Day, C. B. *Chinese Peasant Cults.* Kelly and Walsh, Shanghai, 1940.

DeGroot, J. J. M. *Religion in China.* G. P. Putnam's Sons, New York, 1912.

Dore, Henri. *Researches into Chinese Superstitions.* 10 vols. T'Usewei Press, Shanghai, 1914-33.

DuBose, H. C. *The Dragon, Image and Demon.* Armstrong, New York, 1887.

Feng Yu-lan. *History of Chinese Philosophy.* Vol. I. Translated by Derk Bode. H. Vetch, Peiping, 1937.

Giles, Herbert A. *Confucianism and Its Rivals.* Williams & Norgate, London, 1915.

Goodrich, L. C. *A Short History of the Chinese People.* Harper & Brothers, New York, 1943.

Hu Shih. *The Chinese Renaissance.* University of Chicago Press, Chicago, 1934.

Johnston, Sir R. F. *Confucianism and Modern China.* Victor Gollancz, Ltd., London, 1934.

Legge, James. *The Religions of China.* Charles Scribner's Sons, New York, 1881.

Lin Yu-t'ang. *My Country and My People.* Reynal & Hitchcock, New York, 1935.

Lin Yu-t'ang. *The Importance of Living.* Reynal & Hitchcock, New York, 1938.

Lin Yu-t'ang. *The Wisdom of China and India.* Random House, New York, 1942.

Ross, John. *The Original Religion of China.* Eaton & Mains, New York, 1909.

Shryock, John. *The Origin and Development of the State Cult of Confucius*. Century Co., New York, 1932.

Soothill, W. E. *The Three Religious of China*. Oxford University Press, 3rd ed., London, 1929.

Waley, Arthur. *The Way and Its Power*. G. Allen & Unwin, London, 1934.

Wei, Francis M. *The Spirit of Chinese Culture*. Charles Scribner's Sons, New York, 1947.

Wilhelm, Richard. *Confucius and Confucianism*. Harcourt, Brace & Co., New York, 1931.

Yang, Y. C. *China's Religious Heritage*. Abingdon-Cokesbury Press, New York, 1943.

DeGroot, J. J. M. *Religion in China*. G. P. Putnam's Sons, New York, 1912.

Chapter XII

Anesaki, Masaharu. *The History of Japanese Religion*. Kegan Paul, Trench, Trubner & Co., 1931.

Aston, W. G. *Shinto, The Way of the Gods*. Longmans, Green and Co., London, 1905.

Ballou, Robert O. *Shinto, the Unconquered Enemy*. Viking Press, New York, 1945.

Benedict, Ruth. *The Chrysanthemum and the Sword*. Houghton Mifflin Co., Boston, 1946.

Griffis, William Eliot. *The Religions of Japan*. Charles Scribner's Sons, New York, 1895.

Harada, Tasuku. *The Faith of Japan*. The Macmillan Co., New York, 1914.

Hibino, Y. *Nippon Shindo Ron, or the National Ideals of the Japanese People*. University Press, Cambridge, 1928.

Holtom, D. C. *The Political Philosophy of Modern Shinto*. University of Chicago Press, 1922.

Holtom, D. C. *The National Faith of Japan*. E. P. Dutton, New York, 1938.

Holtom, D. C. *Modern Japan and Shinto Nationalism*. University of Chicago Press, rev. ed., 1947.

Kato, Genchi. *Shinto, the Religion of the Japanese Nation*. Tokyo, 1926.

Knox, G. W. *The Development of Religion in Japan*. G. P. Putnam's Sons, New York, 1907.

Nitobe, Inazo. *Bushido, The Soul of Japan*. G. P. Putnam's Sons, New York, 1905.

Bewer, Julius H. *Introduction to the Study of Old Testament Literature.* Columbia University Press, New York, 1928.

Cornill, Carl H. *The Prophets of Israel.* Open Court, Chicago, 1901.

Finkelstein, Louis, *et al. Religions of Democracy.* Devin-Adair Co., New York, 1941.

Fowler, Henry T. *The Origin and Growth of the Hebrew Religion.* University of Chicago Press, 1916.

Hyatt, James Philip. *Prophetic Religion.* Abingdon-Cokesbury Press, New York, 1947.

Isserman, Frederick W. *This Is Judaism.* Willet Clark & Co., Chicago, 1943.

Kaplan, M. *Judaism as a Civilization.* The Macmillan Co., New York, 1935.

Kent, Charles F. *Origin and Permanent Value of the Old Testament.* Charles Scribner's Sons, New York, 1914.

Kohler, Kauffmann, *Jewish Theology.* The Macmillan Co., New York, 1935.

Leslie, Elmer. *The Prophets Tell Their Own Story.* Abingdon-Cokesbury Press, New York, 1939.

Loisy, Alfred, *The Religion of Israel.* C. P. Putnam's Sons, New York, 1910.

Moffatt, James. *The Bible: A New Translation.* Rev. ed. Harper & Brothers, New York, 1935.

Moore, George Foot. *Judaism.* 2 vols. Harvard University Press, Cambridge, 1927.

Oesterly, W. O., and Robinson, T. N. *Hebrew Religion, Its Origin and Development.* The Macmillan Co., 1930.

Olmstead, A. T. *History of Palestine and Syria.* Charles Scribner's Sons, New York, 1931.

Peters, John P. *The Religion of the Hebrews.* Ginn & Co., Boston, 1914.

Robinson, H. W. *The Religious Ideas of the Old Testament.* Charles Scribner's Sons, New York, 1931.

Smith, H. P. *Old Testament History.* Charles Scribner's Sons, New York, 1903.

Smith, J. M. P. *et. al. The Bible.* An American translation. University of Chicago Press, 1931.

Smith, J. M. P. *The Moral Life of the Hebrews.* University of Chicago Press, 1923.

Smith, J. M. P. *The Prophets and Their Times.* University of Chicago Press. Rev. ed., 1941.

The Universal Jewish Encyclopedia. 10 vols. Universal Jewish Encyclopedia, Inc., New York, 1939-43.

Wild, Laura. *The Evolution of the Hebrew People*. Charles Scribner's Sons, New York, 1917.

Wright, George Ernest, and Fillson, Floyd V. *The Westminster Historical Atlas to the Bible*. Westminster Press, Philadelphia, 1945.

Sachar, A. L. *A History of the Jews*. Alfred A. Knopf, New York, 1918.

CHAPTER XIV

Ameer Ali, Syed. *The Spirit of Islam*. Christopher's, London, 1922.

Andrae, Tor. *Mohammed the Man and His Faith*. Charles Scribner's Sons, New York, 1936.

Arnold, T. W. *The Preaching of Islam*. Constable, London, 1913.

Arnold, Sir Thomas. *The Legacy of Islam*. Clarendon Press, Oxford, 1931.

Bell, R. *The Origin of Islam in Its Christian Environment*. The Macmillan Co., London, 1926.

Bengalee, M. R. *Life of Mohammed*. Moslem Sunrise Press, Chicago, 1941.

Cash, W. Wilson. *Christendom and Islam*. Harper & Brothers, New York, 1937.

Dermenghem, Emile. *The Life of Mahomet*. Geo. Routledge and Sons, London, 1930.

Dibble, R. F. *Mohammed*. The Viking Press, New York, 1926.

Donaldson, Dwight M. *The Shi'ite Religion*. Luzac and Co., London, 1933.

Encyclopedia of Islam. 4 vols. Luzac and Co., London, 1913-34.

Faris, N. A. *The Arab Heritage*. Princeton University Press, 1944.

Gibb, H. A. R. *Modern Trends in Islam*. University of Chicago Press, 1947.

Gibb, H. A. R. *Whither Islam?* A survey of Modern Movements in the Moslem World. Gollancz, London, 1932.

Hitti, Philip K. *History of the Arabs*. 3rd rev. ed. The Macmillan Co., London, 1946.

Ikbal, Mohammed. *Reconstruction of Religious Thought in Islam*. Oxford University Press, London, 1934.

Islamic Culture. A quarterly magazine. Published at Hyderabad-Deccan, India.

The Koran—various translations, Sell, Rodwell, Palmer (Sacred Books of the East, Vol. VI), M. Pickthall, *The Meaning of the Glorious Koran*.

Levy, Ruben. *The Sociology of Islam*. 2 vols. Williams & Norgate, Ltd., London, 1930-33.

MacDonald, Duncan. *The Religious Attitude and Life in Islam*. University of Chicago Press, Chicago, 1909.

Moslem World. A quarterly review of current events, literature and thought among the Mohammedans. Hartford Seminary Foundation, Hartford, Conn.

Muhammad Ali. *The Religion of Islam.* The Ahmadiyya Movement, Lahore, India, 1936.

Muir, Sir William. *The Caliphate; Its Rise, Decline and Fall.* The Religious Tract Society, London, 1892.

Nicholson, Reynold A. *The Mystics of Islam.* Bell, London, 1914.

Wensinck, A. J. *The Muslin Creed.* Harvard University Press, Cambridge 1932.

Zwemer, Samuel M. *Across the World of Islam.* The Macmillan Co., London, 1926.

CHAPTER XV

The Backgrounds of Christianity

Angus, S. *The Mystery Religions and Christianity.* Charles Scribner's Sons, New York, 1925.

Angus, S. *The Religious Quests of the Graeco-Roman World.* Charles Scribner's Sons, New York, 1929.

Glover, T. R. *The Conflict of Religions in the Early Roman Empire.* Methuen & Co., London, 1909.

Willoughby, Harold. *Pagan Regeneration.* University of Chicago Press, Chicago, 1929.

Concerning Jesus

Bacon, Benjamin W. *Jesus, the Son of God.* Henry Holt & Co., New York, 1930.

Baillie, John. *The Place of Jesus Christ in Modern Christianity.* Charles Scribner's Sons, New York, 1929.

Bosworth, Edward I. *The Life and Teachings of Jesus.* The Macmillan Co., New York, 1924.

Branscomb, Bennett Harvie. *The Teachings of Jesus.* Abingdon-Cokesbury Press, Nashville, 1931.

Bundy, Walter E. *The Religion of Jesus.* Bobbs-Merrill Co., Indianapolis, 1928.

Case, S. J. *Jesus, a New Biography.* University of Chicago Press, 1933.

Case, S. J. *Jesus Through the Centuries.* University of Chicago Press, 1932.

Case, S. J. *The Historicity of Jesus.* University of Chicago Press, 1915.

Grant, Frederick C. *The Gospel and the Kingdom.* The Macmillan Co., New York, 1940.

Goguel, Maurice. *The Life of Jesus*. The Macmillan Co., New York, 1933.

Guignebert, Charles A. *Jesus*. Kegan Paul, Trench, Trubner & Co., London, 1935.

Knox, John. *Christ the Lord*. Willett, Clark & Co., Chicago, 1945.

Klausner, Joseph. *Jesus of Nazareth*. The Macmillan Co., New York, 1929.

McCown, Chester. *The Genesis of the Social Gospel*. A. A. Knopf, New York, 1929.

Schweitzer, Albert. *The Quest of the Historical Jesus*. A. & C. Black, London, 1922.

Scott, E. F. *The Ethical Teaching of Jesus*. The Macmillan Co., New York, 1924.

Walker, Thomas. *The Teaching of Jesus and the Jewish Teaching of His Age*. George H. Doran, New York, 1923.

The History of the Church and Christian Thought

Angus, S. *The Mystery Religions and Christianity*. J. Murray, London, 1925.

Atkins, Gaius Glenn. *Modern Religious Cults and Movements*. Fleming H. Revell, New York, 1923.

Atkins, Gaius Glenn. *Religion in Our Times*. The Round Table Press, New York, 1932.

Atkins, Gailus Glenn. *The Making of the Christian Mind*. Harper & Brothers, New York, 1931.

Bach, Marcus. *They Have Found a Faith*. Bobbs-Merrill Co., Indianapolis, 1946.

Bainton, Roland H. *The Church of Our Fathers*. Charles Scribner's Sons, New York, 1941.

Bartlett, J. V., and Carlyle, A. J. *Christianity in History*. The Macmillan Co., London, 1917.

Bennett, John C. *Social Salvation*. Charles Scribner's Sons, New York, 1935.

Bevan, Edwyn Robert. *Christianity*. T. Butterworth, London, 1933.

Braden, Charles S. *Varieties of American Religion*. Willett, Clark & Co., Chicago, 1936.

Brown, William Adams. *Toward a United Church*. Charles Scribner's Sons, New York, 1946.

Browne, Lewis. *Since Calvary*, an interpretation of Christian history. The Macmillan Co., New York, 1931. (An interesting interpretation by a Jewish writer.)

Bulgakov, S. N. *The Orthodox Church*. Translated by Elizabeth S. Crane. London, 1935.

Christianity in the Light of Modern Knowledge. Blackie, London, 1929.

Gibbons, Cardinal James. *Faith of Our Fathers.* 91st ed. John Murphy Co., New York, 1917.

Goodspeed, Edgar J. *The Story of the New Testament.* University of Chicago Press, 1934.

Guignebert, C. *Christianity.* The Macmillan Co., New York, 1927.

Jones, E. Stanley. *The Choice before Us.* Abingdon-Cokesbury Press, New York, 1937.

Latourette, Kenneth S. *A History of the Expansion of Christianity.* 7 vols. Harper & Brothers, New York, 1937-45.

Lindsay, T. *History of the Reformation.* Charles Scribner's Sons, New York, 1906-7.

McGiffert, Arthur Cushman. *A History of Christian Thought.* 2 vols. Charles Scribner's Sons, New York, 1932-33.

McGiffert, A. C. *Protestant Thought before Kant.* Charles Scribner's Sons, New York, 1911.

Macintosh, Douglas C. *Social Religion.* Charles Scribner's Sons, New York, 1939.

Moeller, Wilhelm Ernst. *History of the Christian Church.* 3 vols. The Macmillan Co., New York, 1900.

Nagler, Arthur W. *The Church in History.* Abingdon-Cokesbury Press, New York, 1929.

Nichols, James Hastings. *A Primer for Protestants.* Association Press, New York, 1947.

Niebuhr, H. Richard. *The Social Sources of Denominationalism.* Henry Holt & Co., New York, 1929.

Nolde, Otto F. *Toward World-Wide Christianity.* Harper & Brothers, New York, 1946.

Page, Kirby. *Jesus or Christianity.* Doubleday Doran, Garden City, New York, 1929.

Quimby, Chester W. *Paul for Everyone.* The Macmillan Co., Toronto, 1944.

Rall, Harris Franklin. *According to Paul.* Charles Scribner's Sons, New York, 1944.

Rall, Harris Franklin. *Christianity.* Charles Scribner's Sons, New York, 1940.

Rauschenbusch, Walter. *Christianity and the Social Crisis.* The Macmillan Co., New York, 1907.

Robinson, B. W. *Life of Paul.* University of Chicago Press, rev. ed., 1928.

Rowe, Henry K. *History of the Christian People.* The Macmillan Co., New York, 1931.

Soper, Edmund D. *The Philosophy of the Christian Mission.* Abingdon-Cokesbury Press, New York, 1943.

Stuber, Stanley I. *How We Got Our Denominations*. Association Press, New York, 1927.

Sweet, W. W. *The Story of Religions in America*. Harper & Brothers, New York, 1930.

Van Dusen, Henry Pitney. *World Christianity*. Abingdon-Cokesbury Press, New York, 1947.

Van Kirk, W. W. *Religion Renounces War*. Willett, Clark & Co., Chicago, 1934.

Ward, Harry F. *Our Economic Morality and the Ethic of Jesus*. The Macmillan Co., New York, 1929.

Workman, H. *The Evolution of the Monastic Ideal*. C. H. Kelly, London, 1913.

Id. Christian Thought to the Reformation. Charles Scribner's Sons, 1911.

Richards, G. W. *Christian Ways of Salvation*. The Macmillan Co., New York, 1923.

CHAPTER XVI

Religions of Ancient America

Braden, Charles S. *Religious Aspects of the Conquest of Mexico*. Duke University Press, Durham, N. C., 1930.

Brinton, Daniel G. *Rig-Veda Americana, Sacred Songs of the Ancient Mexicans*. Philadelphia, 1890.

Id. The Maya Chronicles. Philadelphia, 1882.

Caso, Alfonso. *La Religión de los Aztecas*. Imprenta Mundial, Mexico, 1936.

Gann, Thomas, and Thompson, J. Eric. *The History of the Maya from the Earliest Times to the Present Day*. Charles Scribner's Sons, New York, 1931.

Means, Philip A. *The Ancient Civilization of the Andes*. Charles Scribner's Sons, New York, 1931.

Morley, Sylvanus G. *The Ancient Mayas*. Stanford University Press, 1946.

Palacios, Enrique Juan. *Arqueología de Mexico*. Imprenta Mundial, Mexico, 1937.

Reville, Albert J. *The Native Religions of Mexico and Peru*. Charles Scribner's Sons, New York, 1894.

Sahagún, Bernardino de. *History of Ancient Mexico*. Translated by Fanny R. Bandelier. Fisk University Press, Nashville, 1932.

Spence, Lewis. *Myths of Mexico and Peru*. Dingwall-Rock, New York, n.d.

Id., The Magic and Mystery of Mexico. David McKay Co., Philadelphia, 1930.

Spinden, Herbert J. *Ancient Civilization of Mexico and Central America.* American Museum of History Handbook, Series III, 1917.

Thompson, J. Eric. *Mexico before Cortez.* Charles Scribner's Sons, New York, 1933.

NOTE: These lists might have been expanded indefinitely, and new books are appearing every year. For background reading current novels and popular books of travel or biography are often available. In general specific titles of this class of book have not been suggested, but the alert instructor will be able to enrich the course greatly by calling attention to them. For example, the popular books of Pearl S. Buck and Lin Yutang on China, or of Hilda Werhner on India enable one to get the "feel" of the life of those countries as he does not get it usually in formal treatises. There is also a constant stream of articles in current magazines, sometimes beautifully illustrated, which can be used to great advantage to enhance interest in the various religions as they seek to adjust themselves to the modern world. *The National Geographic Magazine* and the former *Asia,* now *United Nations World,* are especially valuable, but occasionally also *Life* and the other pictorial periodicals contain interesting popular material.

Index